FUNDAMENTALS OF
BUSINESS
INFORMATION
SYSTEMS

Ralph Stair, George Reynolds and Thomas Chesney

Australia • Brazil • Japan • Korea • Mexico • Singapore • Spain • United Kingdom • United States

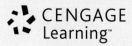

**Fundamentals of Business
Information Systems
Second edition**
Ralph Stair, George Reynolds and
Thomas Chesney

Publishing Director: Linden Harris

Publisher: Andrew Ashwin

Development Editor: Charlotte Green

Project Editor: Lucy Arthy

Production Controller: Eyvett Davis

Marketing Manager: Sally Green

Typesetter: MPS Limited, a Macmillan
     Company

Cover design: Adam Renvoize

For product information and technology assistance,
contact **emea.info@cengage.com**.

For permission to use material from this text or product,
and for permission queries,
email **emea.permissions@cengage.com**.

British Library Cataloguing-in-Publication Data
A catalogue record for this book is available from the British Library.

ISBN: 978-1-4080-4421-6

Cengage Learning EMEA
Cheriton House, North Way, Andover, Hampshire, SP10 5BE
United Kingdom

Cengage Learning products are represented in Canada by
Nelson Education Ltd.

For your lifelong learning solutions, visit **www.cengage.co.uk**

Purchase your next print book, e-book or e-chapter at
www.cengagebrain.com

Printed in China by RR Donnelley
1 2 3 4 5 6 7 8 9 10 – 14 13 12

For Tahseena

For Tahseena

Brief Contents

Contents

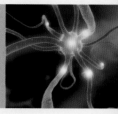

1 Overview

2 Technology

3 Business Information Systems

4 Systems Development

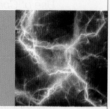

5 Information Systems in Business and Society

Preface

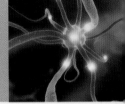

The second edition of *Fundamentals of Business Information Systems* continues the tradition and approach of the original United States editions of the text but introduces new content and examples that meet the requirements of students studying in the United Kingdom, Europe, Middle East and South Africa.

As with the original United States editions, this text covers the fundamentals of any introductory Management/Business Information Systems (MIS/BIS) course in nine chapters and brings the latest thinking and technologies from the field to the student. The text provides a comprehensive survey of the core concepts that make up modern information systems courses. *Fundamentals of Business Information Systems* deals with the role that information systems play in an organisation and the key principles a manager needs to grasp to be successful. These principles of information systems are distilled and presented in a way that is both understandable and relevant. In addition, this book offers an overview of the entire IS discipline, while giving students a solid foundation for further study in advanced IS courses, such as programming, systems analysis and design, project management, database management, data communications, website and systems development, electronic commerce applications, and decision support. As such, it serves the needs of both general business students and those who will become IS professionals.

Changes to this Edition

Fundamentals of Business Information Systems is based on the popular US textbook *Principles of Information Systems*. With a more international outlook, this book is suitable for students in the UK, Europe and South Africa on introductory BIS or MIS courses. The new title reflects the fact that this book has boosted its business emphasis but retained its technology focus.

Continuing to present IS concepts with a managerial emphasis, this edition retains the overall vision, framework and pedagogy that made the previous editions so popular. It is packed with up-to-date, real world examples and business cases and highlights ethical issues throughout. The cases are international in flavour and have a broader sector spread, reflecting a wider variety of business types (including SMEs). In addition, the book is completely up to date in terms of innovations in IT and has expanded sections on data modeling, data warehousing and data mining with examples, along with a new simpler, cleaner design.

Structure of the Text

Fundamentals of Business Information Systems is organised into nine chapters giving an overview of information systems, an introduction to information technology concepts, an examination of different classes of business information systems, a study of systems development and a focus on information systems in business and the wider society. Each of these sections is colour coded and new chapter level contents pages make the book even easier to navigate.

The content of each chapter is as follows:

Section 1: Overview

Chapter 1: An Introduction to Information Systems in Organisations

Chapter 1 creates a framework for the entire book. Major sections in this chapter become entire chapters in the text. This chapter defines information system then introduces major classes of business information systems. It offers an overview of systems development and outlines some major challenges that IS professionals face. It also gives an overview of business organisations and presents a foundation for the effective and efficient use of IS in a business environment. We have stressed that the traditional mission of IS is to deliver the right information to the right person at the right time.

Section 2: Technology

Chapter 2: Hardware and Software

This chapter first concentrates on the hardware component of a computer-based information system (CBIS) and reflects the latest equipment and computer capabilities – computer memory is explained and a variety of hardware platforms are discussed, including mobile technology. This chapter then examines a wide range of software and related issues, including operating systems and application software, open source and proprietary software, software for mobile devices and copyrights and licences.

Chapter 3: Organising Data and Information

Databases are the heart of almost all IS. A huge amount of data is entered into computer systems every day. Chapter 3 examines database management systems and how they can help businesses. The chapter includes a brief overview of how to organise data in a database, looks at database administration and discusses how data can used competitively by studying both data mining and business intelligence.

Chapter 4: Telecommunications, the Internet, Intranets and Extranets

The power of information technology greatly increases when devices are linked, or networked, which is the subject of this chapter. Today's decision makers need to access data wherever it resides. They must be able to establish fast, reliable connections to exchange messages, upload and download data and software, route business transactions to processors, connect to databases and network services, and send output to printers. This chapter examines the hardware involved and the world's biggest computer network, the internet.

Section 3: Business Information Systems
Chapter 5: Operational Systems

Operation systems, such as transaction processing systems, allow firms to buy and sell. Without systems to perform these functions, the firm could not operate. Organisations today are moving from a collection of nonintegrated transaction processing systems to highly integrated enterprise resource planning systems to perform routine business processes and maintain records about them. These systems support a wide range of business activities associated with supply chain management and customer relationship management. This chapter examines transaction processing systems and enterprise resource planning systems.

Chapter 6: Management Information and Decision Support Systems

This chapter begins with a discussion of decision making and examines the decision-making process. Both management information systems and decision support systems are examined in detail. Their ability to help managers make better decisions is emphasised.

Chapter 7: Knowledge Management and Specialised Information Systems

A discussion of knowledge management leads into a discussion of some of the special-purpose systems discussed in the chapter, including expert systems and knowledge bases. Other topics the chapter discusses include robotics, vision systems, expert systems, virtual reality, and a variety of other special-purpose systems. We discuss embedded artificial intelligence, where artificial intelligence capabilities and applications are placed inside of products and services.

Section 4: Systems Development
Chapter 8: Systems Development and Social Issues

This chapter examines where information systems come from. Systems investigation and systems analysis are discussed. This chapter provides specific examples of how new or modified systems are initiated and analyzed in a number of industries. This chapter emphasises how a project can be planned, aligned with corporate goals and rapidly developed. The chapter looks at developing a new system but also examines solving a problem by buying an existing IS that has already been developed.

Section 5: Information Systems in Business and Society
Chapter 9: Security, Privacy and Ethical Issues in Information Systems

This last chapter looks at security, privacy and ethical issues, something that is in the background throughout the text. A wide range of non-technical issues associated with the use of information systems provide both opportunities and threats to modern organisations. The issues span the full spectrum – from preventing computer waste and mistakes, to avoiding violations of privacy, to complying with laws on collecting data about customers, to monitoring employees.

About the Authors

Ralph Stair received a BS in Chemical Engineering from Purdue University, an MBA from Tulane University, and a PhD from the University of Oregon. He has taught information systems at many Universities. He has published numerous articles and books, including *Succeeding With Technology, Programming in BASIC,* and many more. Dr. Stair is a member of several academic organisations, including Decision Sciences Institute.

George Reynolds is an assistant professor in the Information Systems department of the College of Business at the University of Cincinnati. He received a BS in Aerospace Engineering from the University of Cincinnati and an MS in Systems Engineering from West Coast University. He taught part-time at Xavier University, the University of Cincinnati, Miami University and the College of Mount Saint Joseph, while working full-time in the information systems industry, including positions at the Manned Spacecraft Center in Houston, Texas; the Jet Propulsion Lab in Pasadena, California; and Procter and Gamble in Cincinnati, Ohio.

Thomas Chesney teaches and researches information systems at Nottingham University Business School. He has a PhD in Information Systems from Brunel University an MSc in Informatics from Edinburgh University and a BSc in Information Management from the Queen's University of Belfast. He has a Diploma in Learning and Teaching in Higher Education and is a fellow of the Higher Education Academy and a member of the Association for Information Systems.

Digital Learning Resources

The second edition of *Fundamentals of Business Information Systems* is accompanied by a range of exciting digital support resources, designed to support teaching and enhance the learning experience. Each resource is carefully tailored to the book and the needs of the reader.

■ A password protected lecturer site for instructors with resources such as an ExamView Testbank, PowerPoint Slides and an Instructor's Manual.

■ A fully tailored CourseMate site for students brings course concepts to life with a range of interactive learning and study tools that support the printed textbook. Additionally, the Engagement Tracker allows lecturers to assess students' preparation and engagement.

Student Resources

CourseMate

The more you study, the better the results. Make the most of your study time by accessing everything you need to succeed in one place. Read your textbook, take notes, review flashcards, and take practice quizzes – online with CourseMate. Resources include:

Interactive Learning Tools
CourseMate offers a range of interactive learning tools tailored to the second edition of *Fundamentals of Business Information Systems,* including:

■ Quizzes
■ Flashcards
■ Videos
■ PowerPoint presentations
■ Games
■ Links to useful websites
■ And much more . . .

Interactive eBook
An interactive eBook with highlighting, note taking, and interactive glossary.

To purchase access to CourseMate and these interactive tools visit www.cengagebrain.co.uk and search for the second edition of *Fundamentals of Business Information Systems.*

SAM (Skills Assessment Manager)

SAM (Skills Assessment Manager) is the premier proficiency-based assessment and training environment for Microsoft® Office. This program offers a real-world approach to applying Microsoft® Office skills. SAM includes Assessment, Training and Projects in Excel, Access and MIS concepts. The Assessment portion of this powerful and easy to use software is designed to help assess students' proficiency of the latest Microsoft Office software applications. The Training portion allows students to learn in the way that works best for them by reading, watching, or receiving guided help. The Projects portion allows students to work live-in-the-application on project-based assignments. For the latest news about SAM and details on how to purchase this program, please contact your local Cengage representative.

Lecturer Resources

CourseMate

Cengage Learning's *Fundamentals of Business Information Systems* CourseMate brings course concepts to life with interactive learning, study, and exam preparation tools that support the printed textbook. Watch student comprehension soar as your class works with the printed textbook and the textbook specific website. CourseMate goes beyond the book to deliver what you need!

Engagement Tracker

How do you assess your students' engagement in your course? How do you know your students have read the material or viewed the resources you've assigned? How can you tell if your students are struggling with a concept? With CourseMate, you can use the integrated Engagement Tracker to assess your students' preparation and engagement. Use the tracking tool to see progress for the class as a whole or for individual students. Identify students at risk early in the course. Uncover which concepts are most difficult for your class. Monitor time on task. Keep your students engaged.

Interactive Teaching and Learning Tools

CourseMate includes a range of interactive teaching and learning tools that enable students to revise for tests, prepare for class, and address the needs of students' varied learning styles. Tools include:

- Quizzes
- Flashcards
- Videos
- PowerPoint presentations
- Games
- Links to useful websites
- And much more . . .

Interactive eBook

In addition to interactive learning tools, CourseMate also includes an interactive eBook. You can take notes, highlight, search and interact with embedded media specific to your book. Use it as a supplement to the printed text, or as a substitute – the choice is up to you with CourseMate.

For more information about accessing CourseMate please contact your local Cengage Learning representative. A demo is available at: www.cengage.com/coursemate

Dedicated Instructor Website

To discover the dedicated digital support resources accompanying this textbook please contact your local Cengage Learning representative for login details.

Instructors Manual

An all new Instructor's Manual provides valuable chapter overviews; highlights key principles and critical concepts; offers learning objectives, suggested team activities and topics for discussion; and features possible essay topics, further reading and cases.

Sample Syllabus

A sample syllabus with course outlines is provided to make planning your course easier.

Solutions

Solutions to all end of chapter material are provided in a separate document.

Power Point Slides

A set of Power Point slides is available for each chapter to serve as a teaching aid for lecture presentations and help students focus on the main topics of each chapter.

Figure Files

Electronic copies of all the figures used in the edition are available for lecturers to create their own presentations.

Classic Cases

A set of over 85 cases from earlier editions of the textbook are included here, spanning a broad range of companies and industries.

ExamView® Test Bank

ExamView® is a powerful objective-based test generator that enables instructors to create paper, LAN- or Web-based tests from testbanks designed specifically for this textbook.

Walk-through Tour

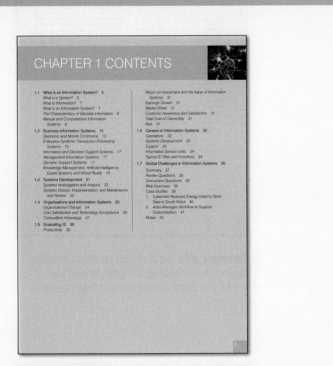

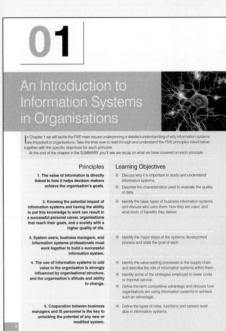

Table of Contents at the start of each chapter facilitates faster navigation through the text.

Principles and Learning Objectives are listed at the start of each chapter and reflect what you should be able to accomplish after completing each chapter.

Why Learn About sets the stage by briefly describing the significance of the chapter's content.

Information Systems at Work is an extra case in each chapter that relates how information systems are used in a variety of business career areas.

Ethical and Societal Issues is another case study, concentrating on ethical challenges and societal impact of information systems from the real world.

Summary at the end of chapter provides a thorough recap of the issues in each chapter, helping you to assess your understanding and revise key content.

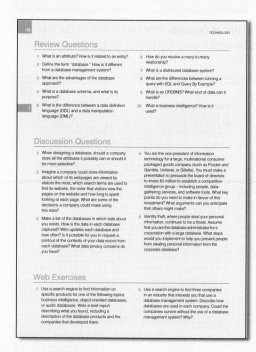

Key Terms are explained in the margin and explained in full in a Glossary at the end of the book, enabling you to find explanations of key terms quickly.

Review Questions help reinforce and test your knowledge and understanding and provide a basis for group discussions and activities.

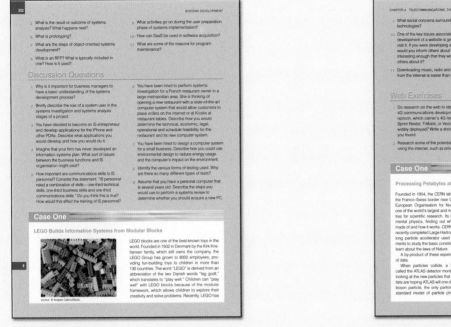

Discussion Questions ask more challenging, in-depth questions, suitable for more advanced learning and postgraduate students.

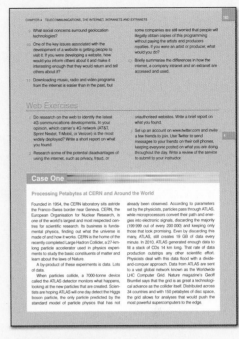

Web Exercises encourage you to apply your knowledge to the internet.

Case Studies at the end of each chapter provide a wealth of practical information. Each case explores a chapter concept or problem that a real-world company or organisation has faced.

Glossary provides definitions for key terms used throughout the book.

CHAPTER 1 CONTENTS

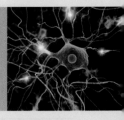

01

An Introduction to Information Systems in Organisations

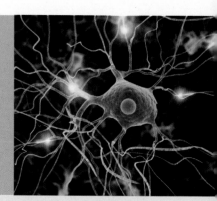

In Chapter 1 we will tackle the FIVE main issues underpinning a detailed understanding of why information systems are important in organisations. Take the time now to read through and understand the FIVE principles listed below, together with the specific objectives for each principle.

At the end of the chapter in the SUMMARY you'll see we recap on what we have covered on each principle.

Principles	Learning Objectives
1. The value of information is directly linked to how it helps decision makers achieve the organisation's goals.	▢ Discuss why it is important to study and understand information systems. ▢ Describe the characteristics used to evaluate the quality of data.
2. Knowing the potential impact of information systems and having the ability to put this knowledge to work can result in a successful personal career, organisations that reach their goals, and a society with a higher quality of life.	▢ Identify the basic types of business information systems and discuss who uses them, how they are used, and what kinds of benefits they deliver.
3. System users, business managers, and information systems professionals must work together to build a successful information system.	▢ Identify the major steps of the systems development process and state the goal of each.
4. The use of information systems to add value to the organisation is strongly influenced by organisational structure, and the organisation's attitude and ability to change.	▢ Identify the value-adding processes in the supply chain and describe the role of information systems within them. ▢ Identify some of the strategies employed to lower costs or improve service. ▢ Define the term competitive advantage and discuss how organisations are using information systems to achieve such an advantage.
5. Cooperation between business managers and IS personnel is the key to unlocking the potential of any new or modified system.	▢ Define the types of roles, functions and careers available in information systems.

Why Learn About Information Systems in Organisations?

Information systems are used in almost every profession imaginable. Sales representatives use information systems to advertise products, communicate with customers, and analyse sales trends. Managers use them to make major decisions, such as whether to build a manufacturing plant or research a cancer drug. From a small music store to huge multinational companies, businesses of all sizes could not survive without information systems to perform accounting and finance operations. Regardless of your chosen career, information systems you will use information systems to help you achieve goals.

This chapter presents an overview of information systems. The sections on hardware, software, databases, telecommunications, types of business information system, systems development, and ethical and societal issues are expanded to full chapters in the rest of the book. We will start by exploring the basics of information systems.

1.1 What is an Information System?

People and organisations use information every day. Many retail chains, for example, collect data from their shops to help them stock what customers want and to reduce costs. Businesses use information systems to increase revenues and reduce costs. We use automated teller machines outside banks and access information over the internet. Information systems usually involve computers, and together, they are constantly changing the way organisations conduct business. Information itself has value, and commerce often involves the exchange of information rather than tangible goods. Systems based on computers are increasingly being used to create, store, and transfer information. Using information systems, investors make multimillion-euro decisions, financial institutions transfer billions of euros around the world electronically, and manufacturers order supplies and distribute goods faster than ever before. Computers and information systems will continue to change businesses and the way we live. To define an information system, we will start by examining what a system is.

What is a System?

A central concept of this book is that of a **system**. A system is a set of elements or components that interact to accomplish goals. The elements themselves and the relationships among them determine how the system works. Systems have inputs, processing mechanisms, outputs, and feedback (see Figure 1.1). A system processes the input to create the output. For example, consider an automatic car wash. Tangible inputs for the process are a dirty car, water, and various cleaning ingredients. Time, energy, skill, and knowledge also serve as inputs to the system because they are needed to operate it.

system A set of elements or components that interact to accomplish goals.

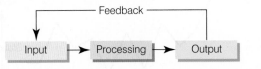

Figure 1.1 Components of a System *A system's four components consist of input, processing, output, and feedback.*

The processing mechanisms consist of first selecting which cleaning option you want (wash only, wash with wax, wash with wax and hand dry, etc.) and communicating that to the operator of the car wash. A feedback mechanism is your assessment of how clean the car is. Liquid sprayers shoot clear water, liquid soap, or car wax depending on where your car is in the process and which options you selected. The output is a clean car. As in all systems, independent elements or components (the liquid sprayer, foaming brush, and air dryer) interact to create a clean car.

efficiency A measure of what is produced divided by what is consumed.

System performance can be measured in various ways. **Efficiency** is a measure of what is produced divided by what is consumed. For example, the efficiency of a motor is the energy produced (in terms of work done) divided by the energy consumed (in terms of electricity or fuel). Some motors have an efficiency of 50 per cent or less because of the energy lost to friction and heat generation.

effectiveness A measure of the extent to which a system achieves its goals; it can be computed by dividing the goals actually achieved by the total of the stated goals.

Effectiveness is a measure of the extent to which a system achieves its goals. It can be computed by dividing the goals actually achieved by the total of the stated goals. For example, a company might want to achieve a net profit of €100 million for the year with a new information system. Actual profits, however, might only be €85 million for the year. In this case, the effectiveness is 85 per cent (85/100 = 85%).

system performance standard A specific objective of the system.

Evaluating system performance also calls for using performance standards. A **system performance standard** is a specific objective of the system. For example, a system performance standard for a marketing campaign might be to have each sales representative sell €100 000 of a certain type of product each year (see Figure 1.2a). A system performance standard for a manufacturing process might be to provide no more than 1 per cent defective parts (see Figure 1.2b). After standards are established, system performance is measured and compared with the standard. Variances from the standard are determinants of system performance.

Figure 1.2 System Performance Standards
(a) *Sales broken down by sales person*
(b) *Percentage of defective parts*

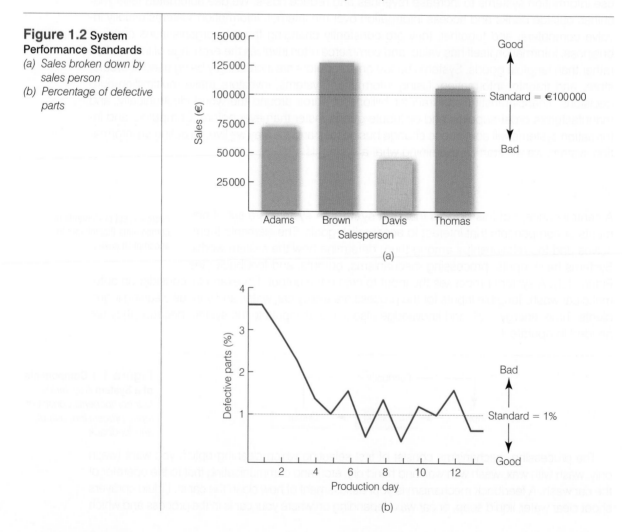

What is Information?

Information is one of those concepts that we all seem intuitively able to grasp, but find it tricky to define. In the 1940s, mathematician Claude Shannon suggested that "information is that which reduces uncertainty." Shannon was working on the technical problems involved in sending information over networks and this is actually quite different from what we in business information systems mean by information. Nevertheless, we can use his definition as a starting point. Imagine you wake up one morning unsure of the weather. When you open the curtains you see the sun shining so you know a bit more about what's it's going to be like today. Your uncertainty about the weather has just been reduced: therefore, looking out of the window gave you information. When you turn on your radio and hear the weather report, your uncertainty has been reduced further. When you look at the temperature gauge in your car, your uncertainty has gone down again. According to Shannon's definition, each of these events has, therefore, given you information.

However, we need a better definition than Shannon's when we come to think about information in a "management report" sense. Therefore, we will use a more general definition and say that information is a collection of facts. These facts can take many forms. The temperature gauge in the car gives information in the form of a number. The radio gives audio information. Looking out of the window gives visual information. Other forms include text, images, and video clips. Another term closely related to information is data. A philosopher might define data as variation.[1] A blank page contains no data, but as soon as there is a mark on the page – in other words as soon as there is a variation in the blankness – then data exist. The traditional information systems view is that as soon as we assign meaning to the mark on the page, the data has turned into information. Unfortunately, however, we still need a better definition to help us think about the meaning of data and information in a management report. Therefore, we will use the terms information and data interchangeably.

What is an Information System?

Now that we have defined the terms system, and information, we can define an information system: an **information system (IS)** is a set of interrelated components that collect, manipulate, store, and disseminate information and provide a feedback mechanism to meet an objective. It is the feedback mechanism that helps organisations achieve their goals, such as increasing profits or improving customer service.

In information systems, **input** is the activity of gathering and capturing data. In producing pay cheques, for example, the number of hours every employee works must be collected before the cheques can be calculated or printed. In a university grading system, instructors must submit student grades before a summary of grades for the semester can be compiled and sent to the students.

Processing means converting or transforming this input into useful outputs. Processing can involve making calculations, comparing data and taking alternative actions, and storing data for future use. In a payroll application, the number of hours each employee worked must be converted into net, or take-home, pay. Other inputs often include employee ID number and department. The required processing can first involve multiplying the number of hours worked by the employee's hourly pay rate to get gross pay. If weekly hours worked exceed 40 hours, overtime pay might also be included. Then tax must be deducted along with contributions to health and life insurance or savings plans to get net pay.

After these calculations and comparisons are performed, the results are typically stored. Storage involves keeping data and information available for future use, including output.

Output involves producing useful information, usually in the form of documents and reports. Outputs can include pay cheques for employees, reports for managers, and information supplied to stockholders, banks, government

information system (IS) A set of interrelated components that collect, manipulate, store, and disseminate information and provide a feedback mechanism to meet an objective.

input The activity of gathering and capturing data.

processing Converting or transforming input into useful outputs.

output Production of useful information, often in the form of documents and reports.

agencies, and other groups. As we have already said, output from one system can become input for another. For example, output from a system that processes sales orders can be used as input to a customer billing system. Computers typically produce output on printers and display screens. Output can also be handwritten or manually produced reports and documents.

feedback Output that is used to make changes to input or processing activities.

Lastly, **feedback** is information from the system that is used to make changes to input or processing activities. For example, errors or problems might make it necessary to correct input data or change a process. Consider a payroll example. Perhaps the number of hours an employee worked was entered as 400 instead of 40 hours. Fortunately, most information systems check to make sure that data falls within certain ranges. For number of hours worked, the range might be from 0 to 100 hours because it is unlikely that an employee would work more than 100 hours in a week. The information system would determine that 400 hours is out of range and provide feedback. The feedback is used to check and correct the input on the number of hours worked to 40.

Feedback is also important for managers and decision makers. For example, a furniture maker could use a computerised feedback system to link its suppliers and plants. The output from an information system might indicate that inventory levels for mahogany and oak are getting low – a potential problem. A manager could use this feedback to decide to order more wood from a supplier. These new inventory orders then become input to the system. In addition to this reactive

forecasting Predicting future events.

approach, a computer system can also be proactive – predicting future events to avoid problems. This concept, often called **forecasting**, can be used to estimate future sales and order more inventory before a shortage occurs. Forecasting is also used to predict the strength of hurricanes and possible landing sites, future stock-market values, and who will win a political election.

The Characteristics of Valuable Information

To be valuable to managers and decision makers, information should have some and possibly all of the characteristics described in Table 1.1. Many shipping companies, for example, can determine the exact location of inventory items and packages in their systems, and this information

Table 1.1 Characteristics of Valuable Information

Characteristics	Definitions
Accessible	Information should be easily accessible by authorised users so they can obtain it in the right format and at the right time to meet their needs.
Accurate	Accurate information is error free. In some cases, inaccurate information is generated because inaccurate data is fed into the transformation process.
Complete	Complete information contains all the important facts, but not more facts than are necessary (see the simple characteristic on page 9).
Economical	Information should also be relatively economical to produce. Decision makers must always balance the value of information with the cost of producing it.
Flexible	Flexible information can be used for a variety of purposes. For example, information on how much inventory is on hand for a particular part can be used by a sales representative in closing a sale, by a production manager to determine whether more inventory is needed, and by a financial executive to determine the total value the company has invested in inventory.
Relevant	Relevant information is important to the decision maker.

Table 1.1 *Continued*

Characteristics	Definitions
Reliable	Reliable information can be depended on. In many cases, the reliability of the information depends on the reliability of the data-collection method. In other instances, reliability depends on the source of the information. A rumor from an unknown source that oil prices might go up might not be reliable (even though it might be useful).
Secure	Information should be secure from access by unauthorised users.
Simple	Information should be simple, not overly complex. Sophisticated and detailed information might not be needed. In fact, too much information can cause information overload, whereby a decision maker has too much information and is unable to determine what is really important.
Timely	Timely information is delivered when it is needed. Knowing last week's weather conditions will not help when trying to decide what coat to wear today.
Verifiable	Information should be verifiable. This means that you can check it to make sure it is correct, perhaps by checking many sources for the same information.

makes them responsive to their customers. In contrast, if an organisation's information is not accurate or complete, people can make poor decisions, costing thousands, or even millions of euros. Many claim, for example, that the collapse and bankruptcy of some companies, such as drug companies and energy-trading firms, was a result of inaccurate accounting and reporting information, which led investors and employees alike to misjudge the actual state of the company's finances and suffer huge personal losses. As another example, if an inaccurate forecast of future demand indicates that sales will be very high when the opposite is true, an organisation can invest millions of euros in a new plant that is not needed. Furthermore, if information is not relevant, not delivered to decision makers in a timely fashion, or too complex to understand, it can be of little value to the organisation.

The value of information is directly linked to how it helps decision makers achieve their organisation's goals. For example, the value of information might be measured in the time required to make a decision or in increased profits to the company. Consider a market forecast that predicts a high demand for a new product. If you use this information to develop the new product and your company makes an additional profit of €10 000, the value of this information to the company is €10 000 minus the cost of the information.

Manual and Computerised Information Systems

An information system can be manual or computerised. For example, some investment analysts manually draw charts and trend lines to assist them in making investment decisions. Tracking data on stock prices (input) over the last few months or years, these analysts develop patterns on graph paper (processing) that help them determine what stock prices are likely to do in the next few days or weeks (output). Some investors have made millions of euros using manual stock analysis information systems. Of course, today many excellent computerised information systems follow stock indexes and markets and suggest when large blocks of stocks should be purchased or sold to take advantage of market discrepancies.

A **computer-based information system (CBIS)** is a single set of hardware, software, databases, telecommunications, people, and procedures that

computer-based information system (CBIS) A single set of hardware, software, databases, telecommunications, people, and procedures that are configured to collect, manipulate, store, and process data into information.

are configured to collect, manipulate, store, and process data into information. For example, a company's payroll, order entry, or inventory-control system is an example of a CBIS. CBISs can also be embedded into products. Some new cars and home appliances include computer hardware, software, databases, and even telecommunications to control their operations and make them more useful. This is often called embedded, pervasive, or ubiquitous computing. CBISs have evolved into sophisticated analysis tools.

technology infrastructure All the hardware, software, databases, telecommunications, people, and procedures that are configured to collect, manipulate, store, and process data into information.

The components of a CBIS are illustrated in Figure 1.3. Information technology (IT) refers to hardware, software, databases, and telecommunications. A business's **technology infrastructure** includes all the hardware, software, databases, telecommunications, people, and procedures that are configured to collect, manipulate, store, and process data into information. The technology infrastructure is a set of shared IS resources that form the foundation of each computer-based information system.

Figure 1.3 The Components of a Computer-Based Information System

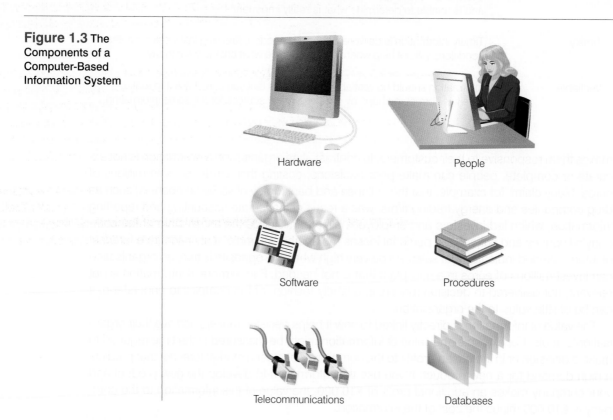

Hardware

People

Software

Procedures

Telecommunications

Databases

Hardware

Hardware consists of the physical components of a computer that perform the input, processing, storage, and output activities of the computer. Input devices include keyboards, mice, and other pointing devices; automatic scanning devices; and equipment that can read magnetic ink characters. Processing devices include computer chips that contain the central processing unit and main memory. Advances in chip design allow faster speeds, less power consumption, and larger storage capacity. Some specialised computer chips will be able to monitor power consumption for companies and homeowners[2] SanDisk and other companies make small, portable chips that are used to conveniently store programs, data files, and more. Processor speed is also important. Today's more advanced processor chips have the power of 1990s-era supercomputers that occupied a room measuring 10 feet by 40 feet. The most powerful computer in the world is currently China's Tianhe-1A supercomputer, which has a peak speed of 2.57 petaflops (which

hardware Any machinery (most of which uses digital circuits) that assists in the input, processing, storage, and output activities of an information system.

is roughly a two followed by fifteen zeros, processes per second). Located at China's National Supercomputer Centre in Tianjin much of the machine's processing power comes from chips more typically found in graphics cards. It is expected to be doing simulations to help Chinese weather forecasts and to help with work to locate undersea oil fields.[3]

Small, inexpensive computers and handheld devices are also popular. Inexpensive netbooks are small, inexpensive laptop computers that can cost less than €500 and be used primarily to connect to the internet.[4] In addition, the iPhone by Apple Computer can perform many functions that can be done on a desktop or laptop computer.[5] The One Laptop Per Child (Figure 1.4) computer costs less than €200.[6] It is intended for regions of the world that can't afford traditional personal computers. The country of Peru, for example, has purchased about 350 000 laptops loaded with about 100 books for children, who also teach their parents how to use the inexpensive computers.[7]

The many types of output devices include printers and computer screens. Some touch-sensitive computer screens, for example, can be used to execute functions or complete programs, such as connecting to the internet or running a new computer game or word processing program.[8] Many special-purpose hardware devices have also been developed. Computerised event data recorders (EDRs) are now being placed into vehicles. Like an airplane's black box, EDRs record vehicle speed, possible engine problems, driver performance, and more. The technology is being used to document and monitor vehicle operation, determine the cause of accidents, and investigate whether truck drivers are taking required breaks.

Figure 1.4 The One Laptop Per Child *This computer costs less than €200 and is designed for regions of the world that can't afford traditional personal computers.*

© Morten Svenningsen/Alamy.

Software

Software consists of the computer programs that govern the operation of the computer. These programs allow a computer to process payroll, send bills to customers, and provide managers with information to increase profits, reduce costs, and provide better customer service. The two types of software are system software, such as Mac OS X and Windows 7, which controls basic computer operations, including start-up and printing, and applications software, such as iLife and Microsoft Office, which allows you to accomplish specific tasks, including word processing or tabulating numbers. Software is needed for computers of all sizes, from small handheld computers to large supercomputers. The Android operating system by Google is an operating system for mobile phones and small portable devices.[9] Although most software can be installed from CDs, many of today's software

software The computer programs that govern the operation of the computer.

packages can be downloaded through the internet. Sophisticated application software, such as Adobe Creative Suite 4, can be used to design, develop, print, and place professional-quality advertising, brochures, posters, prints, and videos on the internet.[10] Nvidia's GeForce 3D is software that can display images on a computer screen that appear three-dimensional (3D) when viewed using special glasses.[11]

Databases

A **database** is an organised collection of facts and information, typically consisting of two or more related data files. An organisation's database can contain information on customers, employees, inventory, competitors' sales, online purchases, and much more. Most managers and executives consider a database to be one of the most valuable parts of a computer-based information system. Increasingly, organisations are placing important databases on the internet, which makes them accessible to many, including unauthorised users.

database An organised collection of information.

Telecommunications, Networks, and the Internet

Telecommunication is the electronic transmission of signals for communications, which enables organisations to carry out their processes and tasks through computer networks. Large restaurant chains, for example, can use telecommunications systems and satellites to link hundreds of restaurants to plants and headquarters to speed credit card authorisation and report sales and payroll data. **Networks** connect computers and equipment in a building, around the country, or around the world to enable electronic communication. Investment firms can use wireless networks to connect thousands of investors with brokers or traders. Many hotels use wireless telecommunications to allow guests to connect to the internet, retrieve voice messages, and exchange email without plugging their computers or mobile devices into a phone jack. With telecommunications, people can work at home or while traveling. This approach to work, often called telecommuting, allows a telecommuter living in England to send his or her work to the United States, China, or any location with telecommunications capabilities.

telecommunications The electronic transmission of signals for communications; enables organisations to carry out their processes and tasks through effective computer networks.

network Computers and equipment that are connected in a building, around the country, or around the world to enable electronic communications.

The **internet** is the world's largest computer network, consisting of thousands of interconnected networks, all freely exchanging information. Research firms, colleges, universities, high schools, hospitals, and businesses are just a few examples of organisations using the internet. Increasingly, businesses and people are using the internet to run and deliver important applications, such as accessing vast databases, performing sophisticated business analysis, and getting a variety of reports. This concept, called cloud computing, allows people to get the information they need from the internet (the cloud) instead of from desktop or corporate computers.[12]

internet The world's largest computer network, actually consisting of thousands of interconnected networks, all freely exchanging information.

The World Wide Web (WWW), or web, is a network of links on the internet to documents containing text, graphics, video, and sound. Information about the documents and access to them are controlled and provided by tens of thousands of special computers called web servers. The web is one of many services available over the internet and provides access to many hundreds of millions of documents.

The technology used to create the internet is also being applied within companies and organisations to create **intranets**, which allow people within an organisation to exchange information and work on projects. In South Africa, Intoweb has created intranets for Tau Mining, Affician Sky and Palace Group to manage human resources and analyse sales data.[13]

intranet An internal company network built using internet and World Wide Web standards and products that allows people within an organisation to exchange information and work on projects.

An **extranet** is a network based on web technologies that allows selected outsiders, such as business partners and customers, to access authorised resources of a company's intranet. Companies can move all or most of their business activities to an extranet site for corporate customers. Many people use extranets every day without realising it – to track shipped goods, order

extranet A network based on web technologies that allows selected outsiders, such as business partners, suppliers, or customers, to access authorised resources of a company's intranet.

products from their suppliers, or access customer assistance from other companies. If you log on to the FedEx site (www.fedex.com) to check the status of a package, for example, you are using an extranet.

People

People are the most important element in most computer-based information systems. The people involved include users of the system and information systems personnel, including all the people who manage, run, program, and maintain the system.

Procedures

Procedures include the strategies, policies, methods, and rules for using the CBIS, including the operation, maintenance, and security of the computer. For example, some procedures describe when each program should be run. Others describe who can access facts in the database, or what to do if a disaster, such as a fire, earthquake, or hurricane, renders the CBIS unusable. Good procedures can help companies take advantage of new opportunities and avoid potential disasters. Poorly developed and inadequately implemented procedures, however, can cause people to waste their time on useless rules or result in inadequate responses to disasters, such as hurricanes or tornadoes.

procedures The strategies, policies, methods, and rules for using a CBIS.

Now that we have looked at computer-based information systems in general, we will briefly examine the most common types used in business today. These IS types are covered in greater detail in Part 3.

1.2 Business Information Systems

Ideally an organisation should have one information system that does all of the jobs about to be discussed. However, this is very difficult to achieve. When an organisation does manage to create one system that does some or all of the jobs about to be described, it is called an Enterprise Resource Planning (ERP) system. An **enterprise resource planning (ERP) system** is a set of integrated programs that manages the vital business operations for an entire multi-site, global organisation. An ERP system can replace many applications with one unified set of programs, making the system easier to use and more effective. For an organisation that has an ERP, the systems about to be described can be considered to be sub-systems of the ERP. For organisations that have not managed to create an ERP, the systems about to be described can be considered to be systems in their own right. So even though these systems are discussed in separate sections in this chapter and explained in more detail later, they are often integrated in one product and delivered by the same software package (see Figure 1.5).

enterprise resource planning (ERP) system A set of integrated programs capable of managing a company's vital business operations for an entire multi-site, global organisation.

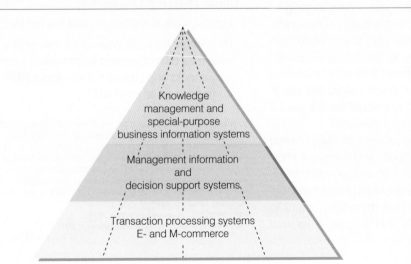

Figure 1.5 Business Information Systems
Business information systems are often integrated in one product and can be delivered by the same software package.

1

Information Systems at Work

SwiftRiver Helps Users Manage Data

Late in 2009, the leader of a large ethnic group in Uganda planned to visit the country's capital, Kampala. Leaders of another ethnic group opposed the visit. The protests that followed extended into several days of unrest, and several people were killed during clashes between police and rioters. The CEO of AppAfrica, Jonathan Gosier, tried to stay on top of the story but found it difficult to keep up with the deluge of information being published online. People on the ground were reporting on events using social networking sites, blogs, text messages and emails. "I just thought there has to be a better way of doing this. I had 20 windows open because you don't know how big this could be," Mr Gosier said.

One year later, with the non-profit organisation Ushahidi, Mr Gosier released SwiftRiver, a software product designed to mesh together thousands of pieces of information and ouput a single, unified and useful news feed. SwiftRiver is a free and open source platform that helps people make sense of a lot of information in a short amount of time. It was born out of the need to understand and act upon a wave of massive amounts of crisis data that tends to be generated in the first 24 hours of a disaster. To do this, it first gathers as many possible streams of data about a particular crisis event as possible. Then the stream of data is filtered through both computer algorithms and human judgement to better understand the veracity and level of importance of any piece of information. One filter rates the trustworthiness of a source, using algorithms to assign a score to a source based on the quality of their information over time. Another filter uses natural language processing tools to extract relevant keywords. For example, a tweet that said "there has been a flood in Bombay" might extract the words "flood" and "Bombay". These would then be used a search terms to find related messages.

The human part of the process involves filtering out inaccuracies, falsehoods, and irrelevant information. As a user reads a stream of information, they interact with the system highlighting parts that they think are false. Over time, the system begins to learn what information a user is looking for and begins to filter it more intelligently. "I think that humans are a very important part of the system, but you want to maximise their time," said Mr Gosier. Other filters remove duplicate messages. This is particularly important for finding information on Twitter, where the original source of a message can become blurred as people repeat and retweet the message around the web.

The same technology is now being used for commercial purposes. Companies are using it to create streams that search for mentions of their brand or products to read what people are saying about them. This information could be used to manage a customer relations problem before it got out of hand, by contacting disgruntled clients and dealing with their complaints before their negative message spreads.

Discussion Questions

1 Should news agencies ever rely on information from social network sites, blogs, texts and emails? Under what circumstances would this be acceptable, and under what circumstances would it be unacceptable practice?

2 Governments are often accused of creating propaganda to influence how people react to their behaviour. Do social network sites and blogs protect citizens from propaganda? Could such sites be manipulated by governments?

Critical Thinking Questions

1 How else could a company use this technology?

2 Do companies need policies for their staff who write their own blogs and tweets about what they should and should not say about their company and its products?

SOURCES: BBC, "Making sense of the web during a crisis," July 20, 2010. Available from: http://www.bbc.co.uk/news/technology-10685669. Accessed June 2, 2011.
Human Rights Watch, "Uganda: Investigate 2009 Kampala Riot Killings." Available from: http://www.hrw.org/en/news/2010/09/10/uganda-investigate-2009-kampala-riot-killings. Accessed January 6, 2011.
http://blog.ushahidi.com/index.php/2009/04/09/explaining-swift-river/. Accessed January 6, 2011.
http://swiftly.org/. Accessed January 6, 2011.
http://swift.ushahidi.com/. Accessed January 6, 2011.

The big advantage of using one ERP is that the information will be stored in a consistent and controlled manner, whereas with separate systems, there is the possibility of inconsistencies creeping in. For example, if information about one customer is stored in two systems, there is the possibility of one of them becoming out of date, which leaves the company with inconsistent data.

The most common types of information systems (or sub-systems) used in business organisations are those designed for electronic and mobile commerce, transaction processing, management information, and decision support. In addition, some organisations employ special-purpose systems, such as virtual reality, that not every organisation uses. Together, these systems help employees in organisations accomplish routine and special tasks – from recording sales, processing payrolls, and supporting decisions in various departments, to examining alternatives for large-scale projects and opportunities.

Electronic and Mobile Commerce

E-commerce involves any business transaction executed electronically between companies (business-to-business, B2B), companies and consumers (business-to-consumer, B2C), consumers and other consumers (consumer-to-consumer, C2C), business and the public sector, and consumers and the public sector. You might assume that e-commerce is reserved mainly for consumers visiting websites for online shopping, but web shopping is only a small part of the e-commerce picture; the major volume of e-commerce – and its fastest-growing segment – is business-to-business (B2B) transactions that make purchasing easier for corporations. This growth is being stimulated by increased internet access, growing user confidence, better payment systems, and rapidly improving internet and web security. E-commerce also offers opportunities for small businesses to market and sell at a low cost worldwide, allowing them to enter the global market. **Mobile commerce (m-commerce)** refers to transactions conducted anywhere, anytime. M-commerce relies on wireless communications that managers and corporations use to place orders and conduct business with handheld computers, portable phones, laptop computers connected to a network, and other mobile devices.

e-commerce Any business transaction executed electronically between companies (business-to-business), companies and consumers (business-to-consumer), consumers and other consumers (consumer-to-consumer), business and the public sector, and consumers and the public sector.

mobile commerce (m-commerce) Conducting business transactions electronically using mobile devices such as smartphones.

E-commerce offers many advantages for streamlining work activities. Figure 1.6 provides a brief example of how e-commerce can simplify the process of purchasing new office furniture from an office-supply company. In the manual system, a corporate office worker must get approval for a purchase that exceeds a certain amount. That request goes to the purchasing department, which generates a formal purchase order to procure the goods from the approved vendor. Business-to-business e-commerce automates the entire process. Employees go directly to the supplier's website, find the item in a catalogue, and order what they need at a price set by their company. If approval is required, the approver is notified automatically. As the use of e-commerce systems grows, companies are phasing out their traditional systems. The resulting growth of e-commerce is creating many new business opportunities.

E-commerce can enhance a company's stock prices and market value. Today, several e-commerce firms have teamed up with more traditional brick-and-mortar businesses to draw from each other's strengths. For example, e-commerce customers can order products on a website and pick them up at a nearby shop.

In addition to e-commerce, business information systems use telecommunications and the internet to perform many related tasks. Electronic procurement (e-procurement), for example, involves using information systems and the internet to acquire parts and supplies. **Electronic business (e-business)** goes beyond e-commerce and e-procurement by using information systems and the internet to perform all business-related tasks and functions, such as accounting, finance, marketing, manufacturing, and human resource activities. E-business also includes

electronic business (e-business) Using information systems and the internet to perform all business-related tasks and functions.

Figure 1.6 E-Commerce
Greatly Simplifies
Purchasing

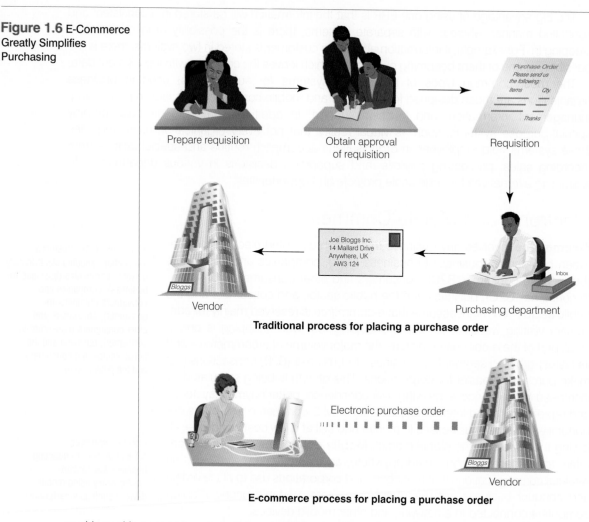

Prepare requisition

Obtain approval
of requisition

Requisition

Joe Bloggs Inc.
14 Mallard Drive
Anywhere, UK
AW3 124

Vendor

Purchasing department

Traditional process for placing a purchase order

Electronic purchase order

Vendor

E-commerce process for placing a purchase order

working with customers, suppliers, strategic partners, and stakeholders. Compared to traditional business strategy, e-business strategy is flexible and adaptable. An e-commerce system incorporates a transaction processing system.

Enterprise Systems: Transaction Processing Systems

Since the 1950s, computers have been used to perform common business applications. Many of these early systems were designed to reduce costs by automating routine, labour-intensive business transactions. A **transaction** is any business-related exchange such as payments to employees, sales to customers, or payments to suppliers. Thus, processing business transactions was the first computer application developed for most organisations. A **transaction processing system (TPS)** is an organised collection of people, procedures, software, databases, and devices used to record completed business transactions. If you understand a transaction processing system, you understand basic business operations and functions.

Operational systems help organisations perform and integrate important tasks, such as paying employees and suppliers, controlling inventory, sending out invoices, and ordering supplies. In the past, companies accomplished these tasks using traditional transaction processing systems. Today, they are increasingly being performed by enterprise resource planning systems. One of the first business systems to be computerised was the payroll system. The primary inputs for a payroll TPS are the number of employee

transaction Any business-related exchange, such as payments to employees, sales to customers, and payments to suppliers.

transaction processing system (TPS) An organised collection of people, procedures, software, databases, and devices used to record completed business transactions.

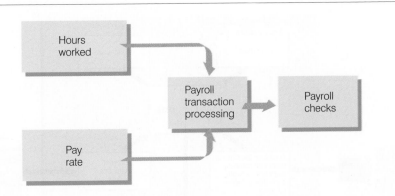

Figure 1.7 A Payroll Transaction Processing System *In a payroll TPS, the inputs (numbers of employee hours worked and pay rates) go through a transformation process to produce outputs (paychecks).*

hours worked during the week and the pay rate (Figure 1.7). The primary output consists of pay cheques. Early payroll systems produced employee pay cheques and related reports required tax authorities. Other routine applications include sales ordering, customer billing and customer relationship management, and inventory control. Some car companies, for example, use their TPSs to buy billions of euros of needed parts each year through websites. Because these systems handle and process daily business exchanges, or transactions, they are all classified as TPSs.

Information and Decision Support Systems

The benefits provided by an effective TPS are tangible and justify their associated costs in computing equipment, computer programs, and specialised personnel and supplies. A TPS can speed business activities and reduce clerical costs. Although early accounting and financial TPSs were already valuable, companies soon realised that they could use the data stored in these systems to help managers make better decisions, whether in human resource management, marketing, or administration. Satisfying the needs of managers and decision makers continues to be a major factor in developing information systems.

Management Information Systems

A **management information system (MIS)** is an organised collection of people, procedures, software, databases, and devices that provides routine information to managers and decision makers. An MIS focuses on operational efficiency. Marketing, production, finance, and other functional areas are supported by MISs and linked through a common database. MISs typically provide standard reports generated with data and information from the TPS, meaning the output of a TPS is the input to a MIS. Producing a report that describes inventory that should be ordered is an example of an MIS.

management information system (MIS) An organised collection of people, procedures, software, databases, and devices that provides routine information to managers and decision makers.

MISs were first developed in the 1960s and typically use information systems to produce managerial reports. In many cases, these early reports were produced periodically – daily, weekly, monthly, or yearly. Because of their value to managers, MISs have proliferated throughout the management ranks. For instance, the total payroll summary report produced initially for an accounting manager might also be useful to a production manager to help monitor and control labour and job costs.

Decision Support Systems

By the 1980s, dramatic improvements in technology resulted in information systems that were less expensive but more powerful than earlier systems. People at all levels of organisations began using personal computers to do a variety of tasks; they were no longer solely dependent on the IS department for all their information needs. People quickly recognised that computer

Figure 1.8 Essential
DSS Elements

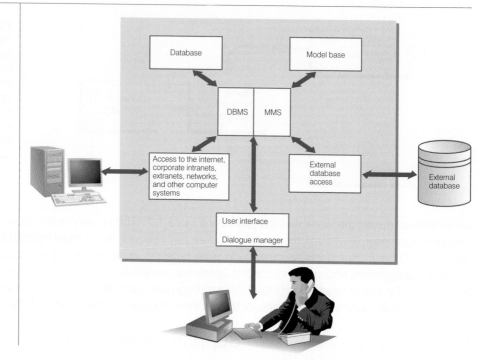

decision support system (DSS)
An organised collection of people,
procedures, software, databases,
and devices used to support
problem-specific decision making.

systems could support additional decision-making activities. A **decision support system (DSS)** is an organised collection of people, procedures, software, databases, and devices that support problem-specific decision making (see Figure 1.8). The focus of a DSS is on making effective decisions. Whereas an MIS helps an organisation "do things right," a DSS helps a manager "do the right thing".

In addition to assisting in all aspects of problem-specific decision making, a DSS can support customers by rapidly responding to their phone and email inquiries. A DSS goes beyond a traditional MIS by providing immediate assistance in solving problems. Many of these problems are unique and complex, and information is often difficult to obtain. For instance, a car manufacturer might try to determine the layout for its new manufacturing facility. Traditional MISs are seldom used to solve these types of problems; a DSS can help by suggesting alternatives and assisting in final decision making.

Decision support systems are used when the problem is complex and the information needed to make the best decision is difficult to obtain and use. So, a DSS also involves managerial judgment and perspective. Managers often play an active role in developing and implementing the DSS. A DSS recognises that different managerial styles and decision types require different systems. For example, two production managers in the same position trying to solve the same problem might require different information and support. The overall emphasis is to support, rather than replace, managerial decision making.

The essential elements of a DSS include a collection of models used to support a decision maker or user (model base), a collection of facts and information to assist in decision making (database), and systems and procedures (dialogue manager or user interface) that help decision makers and other users interact with the DSS. Software is often used to manage the database – the database management system (DBMS) – and the model base – the model management system (MMS) (see Figure 1.8).

In addition to DSSs for managers, other systems use the same approach to support groups and executives. A group support system includes the DSS elements just described as well as software, called groupware, to help groups make effective decisions. Kraft, for example, used iPhones and other mobile devices to help managers and workers stay connected and work together on important projects.[14] An executive support system, also called an executive information system, helps top-level managers, including a firm's president, vice presidents, and members of the board of directors, make better decisions. An executive support system can assist with strategic planning, top-level organising and staffing, strategic control, and crisis management.

Knowledge Management, Artificial Intelligence, Expert Systems and Virtual Reality

In addition to TPSs, MISs, and DSSs, organisations often rely on specialised systems. Many use knowledge management systems (KMS), an organised collection of people, procedures, software, databases, and devices to create, store, share, and use the organisation's knowledge and experience. In addition to knowledge management, companies use other types of specialised systems. The Nissan Motor Company, for example, has developed a specialised system for their vehicles called "Lane Departure Prevention" that nudges a car back into the correct lane if it veers off course.[15] The system uses cameras and computers to adjust braking to get the vehicle back on course. The system switches off when the driver uses turn signals to change lanes. Other specialised systems are based on the notion of **artificial intelligence (AI)**, in which the computer system takes on the characteristics of human intelligence. The field of artificial intelligence includes several subfields (see Figure 1.9).

artificial intelligence (AI) The ability of computer systems to mimic or duplicate the functions or characteristics of the human brain or intelligence.

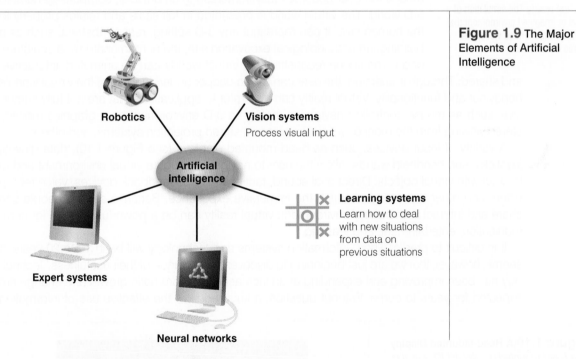

Figure 1.9 The Major Elements of Artificial Intelligence

Robotics

Vision systems
Process visual input

Artificial intelligence

Learning systems
Learn how to deal with new situations from data on previous situations

Expert systems

Neural networks

Artificial Intelligence

Robotics is an area of artificial intelligence in which machines take over complex, dangerous, routine, or boring tasks, such as welding car frames or assembling computer systems and components. Honda Motor has spent millions of dollars on advanced robotics that allows a person to give orders to a computer using only his or her thoughts. The new system uses a special helmet that can measure and transmit brain activity to a computer.[16]

Vision systems allow robots and other devices to "see," store, and process visual images. Natural language processing involves computers understanding and acting on verbal or written commands in English, Spanish, or other human languages. Learning systems allow computers to learn from past mistakes or experiences, such as playing games or making business decisions. Neural networks is a branch of artificial intelligence that allows computers to recognise and act on patterns or trends.[17] Some successful stock, options, and futures traders use neural networks to spot trends and improve the profitability of their investments.

Expert Systems

Expert systems give the computer the ability to make suggestions and act like an expert in a particular field. It can help the novice user perform at the level of an expert. The unique value of expert systems is that they allow organisations to capture and use the wisdom of experts and specialists.

expert system A system that gives a computer the ability to make suggestions and act like an expert in a particular field.

knowledge base A component of an expert system that stores all relevant information, data, rules, cases, and relationships used by the expert system.

Therefore, years of experience and specific skills are not completely lost when a human expert dies, retires, or leaves for another job. Expert systems can be applied to almost any field or discipline. They have been used to monitor nuclear reactors, perform medical diagnoses, locate possible repair problems, design and configure IS components, perform credit evaluations, and develop marketing plans for a new product or new investment strategy. The collection of data, rules, procedures, and relationships that must be followed to achieve value or the proper outcome is contained in the expert system's **knowledge base**.

Virtual Reality

Virtual reality is the simulation of a real or imagined environment that can be experienced visually in three dimensions. Originally, virtual reality referred to immersive virtual reality, which means the user becomes fully immersed in an artificial, computer-generated 3-D world. The virtual world is presented in full scale and relates properly to the human size. It can represent any 3-D setting, real or abstract, such as a building, an archaeological excavation site, the human anatomy, a sculpture, or a crime scene reconstruction. Virtual worlds can be animated, interactive, and shared. Through immersion, the user can gain a deeper understanding of the virtual world's behaviour and functionality. Virtual reality can also refer to applications that are not fully immersive, such as mouse-controlled navigation through a 3-D environment on a graphics monitor, stereo viewing from the monitor via stereo glasses, stereo projection systems, and others.

virtual reality The simulation of a real or imagined environment that can be experienced visually in three dimensions.

A variety of input devices, such as head-mounted displays (see Figure 1.10), data gloves, joysticks, and handheld wands, allow the user to navigate through a virtual environment and to interact with virtual objects. Directional sound, tactile and force feedback devices, voice recognition, and other technologies enrich the immersive experience. Because several people can share and interact in the same environment, virtual reality can be a powerful medium for communication, entertainment, and learning.

It is difficult to predict where information systems and technology will be in 10 to 20 years. It seems, however, that we are just beginning to discover the full range of their usefulness. Technology has been improving and expanding at an increasing rate; dramatic growth and change are expected for years to come. Without question, a knowledge of the effective use of information

Figure 1.10 A Head-Mounted Display
The head-mounted display (HMD) was the first device to provide the wearer with an immersive experience. A typical HMD houses two miniature display screens and an optical system that channels the images from the screens to the eyes, thereby presenting a stereo view of a virtual world. A motion tracker continuously measures the position and orientation of the user's head and allows the image-generating computer to adjust the scene representation to the current view. As a result, the viewer can look around and walk through the surrounding virtual environment.

Source: Courtesy of 5DT, Inc. www.5dt.com.

systems will be critical for managers both now and in the long term. But how are these information systems created?

1.3 Systems Development

Systems development is the activity of creating or modifying business systems. Systems development projects can range from small to very large in fields as diverse as stock analysis and video game development.

systems development The activity of creating or modifying existing business systems.

Individuals from around the world are using the steps of systems development to create unique applications for the iPhone. Apple has special tools for iPhone application developers, including GPS capabilities and audio streaming, to make it easier for people to craft unique applications. Apple is also allowing these systems developers to charge users in a variety of ways, including fixed prices and subscription fees.

People inside a company can develop systems, or companies can use outsourcing, hiring an outside company to perform some or all of a systems development project. Outsourcing allows a company to focus on what it does best and delegate other functions to companies with expertise in systems development. Outsourcing, however, is not the best alternative for all companies.

Developing information systems to meet business needs is highly complex and difficult – so much so that it is common for IS projects to overrun budgets and exceed scheduled completion dates. Her Majesty's Revenue & Customs (HMRC), which collects taxes in the UK, settled out of court with an outsourcing company to recover funds lost due to a tax-related mistake caused by a failed systems development project.[19] The failed project overpaid about €2.5 billion to some families with children or taxpayers in a low-income tax bracket. One strategy for improving the results of a systems development project is to divide it into several steps, each with a well-defined goal and set of tasks to accomplish (see Figure 1.11). These steps are summarised next.

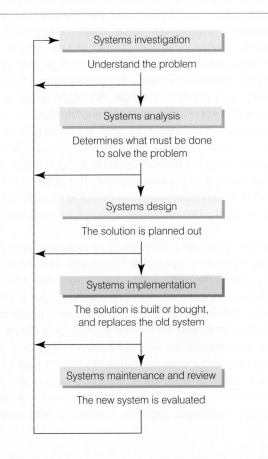

Figure 1.11 An Overview of Systems Development

Systems Investigation and Analysis

The first two steps of systems development are systems investigation and analysis. The goal of the systems investigation is to gain a clear understanding of the problem to be solved or opportunity to be addressed. A cruise line company, for example, might launch a systems investigation to determine whether a development project is feasible to automate purchasing at ports around the world. After an organisation understands the problem, the next question is, "Is the problem worth solving?" Given that organisations have limited resources – people and money – this question deserves careful consideration. If the decision is to continue with the solution, the next step, systems analysis, defines the problems and opportunities of the existing system. During systems investigation and analysis, as well as design maintenance and review, discussed next, the project must have the complete support of top-level managers and focus on developing systems that achieve business goals.

Systems Design, Implementation, and Maintenance and Review

Systems design determines how the new system will work to meet the business needs defined during systems analysis. Systems implementation involves creating or acquiring the various system components (hardware, software, databases, etc.) defined in the design step, assembling them, and putting the new system into operation. The purpose of systems maintenance and review is to check and modify the system so that it continues to meet changing business needs.

1.4 Organisations and Information Systems

organisation A formal collection of people and other resources established to accomplish a set of goals.

An **organisation** is a formal collection of people and other resources established to accomplish a set of goals. The primary goal of a for-profit organisation is to maximise shareholder value, often measured by the price of the company stock. Nonprofit organisations include social groups, religious groups, universities, and other organisations that do not have profit as their goal. As discussed in this chapter, the ability of an organisation to achieve its goals is often a function of the organisation's overall structure, culture, and ability to change. An organisation is a system, which means that it has inputs, processing mechanisms, outputs, and feedback. An organisation constantly uses money, people, materials, machines and other equipment, data, information, and decisions. As shown in Figure 1.12, resources, such as materials, people, and money, serve as inputs to the organisational system from the environment, go through a transformation mechanism, and then are produced as outputs to the environment. The outputs from the transformation mechanism are usually goods or services, which are of higher relative value than the inputs alone. Through adding value or worth, organisations attempt to increase performance and achieve their goals.

Information systems support and work within all parts of an organisational process. Although not shown in this simple model, input to the process subsystem can come from internal and external sources. Just prior to entering the subsystem, data is external. After it enters the subsystem, it becomes internal. Likewise, goods and services can be output to either internal or external systems. Providing value to a stakeholder – customer, supplier, manager, shareholder, or employee – is the primary goal of any organisation. The

value chain A series (chain) of activities that includes inbound logistics, warehouse and storage, production, finished product storage, outbound logistics, marketing and sales, and customer service.

value chain, popularised by Michael Porter in his book, *Competitive Strategy*,[20] reveals how organisations can add value to their products and services. The value chain is a series (chain) of activities that includes inbound logistics, warehouse and storage, production and manufacturing, finished product storage, outbound logistics, marketing and sales, and customer

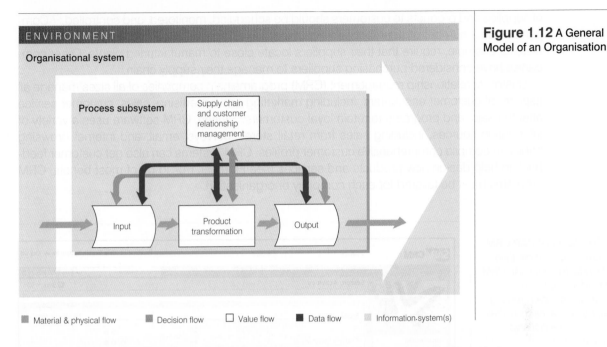

Figure 1.12 A General Model of an Organisation

■ Material & physical flow   ■ Decision flow   ☐ Value flow   ■ Data flow   ▨ Information-system(s)

service (see Figure 1.13). You investigate each activity in the chain to determine how to increase the value perceived by a customer. Depending on the customer, value might mean lower price, better service, higher quality, or uniqueness of product. The value comes from the skill, knowledge, time, and energy that the company invests in the product or activity. The value chain is just as important to companies that don't manufacture products, such as tax preparers, retail stores, legal firms, and other service providers. By adding a significant amount of value to their products and services, companies ensure success.

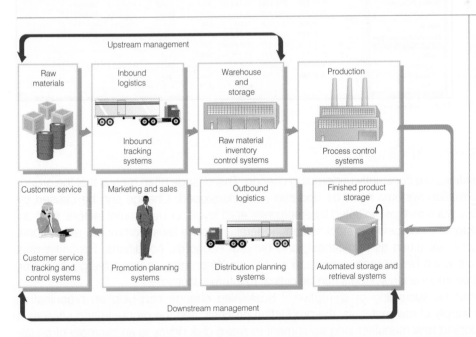

Figure 1.13 The Value Chain of a Manufacturing Company
Managing raw materials, inbound logistics, and warehouse and storage facilities is called upstream management. *Managing finished product storage, outbound logistics, marketing and sales, and customer service is called* downstream management.

Managing the supply chain and customer relationships are two key elements of managing the value chain. Supply chain management (SCM) helps determine what supplies are required for the value chain, what quantities are needed to meet customer demand, how the supplies should be processed (manufactured) into finished goods and services, and how the shipment of supplies and products to customers should be scheduled, monitored, and controlled.[21] Companies use a number of approaches to manage their supply chain. Some automotive companies, for example, require that their suppliers locate close to manufacturing plants. Other companies have considered purchasing suppliers to manage their supply chain.

Customer relationship management (CRM) programs help companies of all sizes manage all aspects of customer encounters, including marketing and advertising, sales, customer service after the sale, and programs to retain loyal customers.[22] Often, CRM software uses a variety of information sources, including sales from retail stores, surveys, email, and internet browsing habits, to compile comprehensive customer profiles. CRM systems can also get customer feedback to help design new products and services (see Figure 1.14). To be of most benefit, CRM programs must be tailored for each company or organisation.

Figure 1.14 SAP CRM

Companies in more than 25 industries use SAP CRM to reduce cost and increase decision-making ability in all aspects of their customer relationship management.

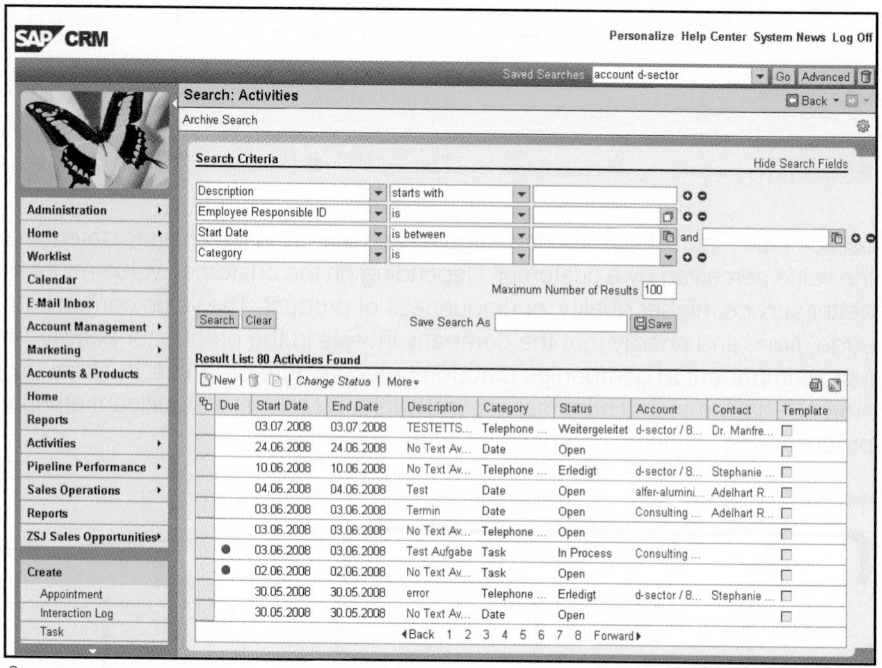

SOURCE: www.sap.com.

Organisational Change

Most organisations are constantly undergoing change. This change often means that the organisation's information systems must be updated or re-developed. Change can be caused by internal factors, such as those initiated by employees at all levels, or by external factors, such as activities wrought by competitors, stockholders, federal and state laws, community regulations, natural occurrences (such as hurricanes), and general economic conditions. Organisational change occurs when two or more organisations merge. When organisations merge, however, integrating their information systems can be critical to future success.

Change can be sustaining or disruptive.[23] Sustaining change can help an organisation improve the supply of raw materials, the production process, and the products and services it offers. Developing new manufacturing equipment to make disk drives is an example of a sustaining change for a computer manufacturer. The new equipment might reduce the costs of producing the disk drives and improve overall performance. Disruptive change, on the other hand, can completely transform an industry or create new ones, which can harm an organisation's performance or even put it out of business. In general, disruptive technologies might not originally have good performance, low cost, or even strong demand. Over time, however, they often re-place existing technologies. They can cause profitable, stable companies to fail when they don't change or adopt the new technology. On a positive note, disruptive change often results in new, successful companies and offers consumers the potential of new products and services at reduced costs and superior performance.

Ethical and Societal Issues

Who Is Interested in Your Social Network Updates?

More than two-thirds of the world's online population use social networks, such as Facebook, MySpace, and Twitter, to stay in touch with friends. In 2008, so-cial networks became more popular than email, with 66.8 per cent of internet users accessing member communities. Most members of social networks use a posting feature that allows them to share their day-to-day thoughts and activities with their circle of friends. Facebook calls these postings "updates," whereas Twitter calls them "tweets." Most users do not realise the value of their comments, updates, or tweets to people outside their circle but businesses are flocking to social networks to harvest consumer sentiment for use in guiding product development. They are also watching social networks to confront negative publicity. The broad scale use of social net-works and the careful analysis of billions of mes-sages have made it possible to collect public senti-ment and build customer relations in a manner never done before. But sifting through the babble to discover comments of interest is challenging.

A number of companies have sprung up to pro-vide products designed to monitor social media. Companies, such as Alterian, Radian6, Attensity, Visible Technologies, Conversion, and Nielsen On-line, provide social media monitoring systems for businesses and organisations. As a young technol-ogy, there is no standard approach to social media monitoring. Similar to a search engine, the systems typically traverse the continuous streams of com-ments in social networks, looking for key terms re-lated to specified products. Artificial intelligence (AI) techniques that automate the interpretation of user comments make it possible to quickly identify com-ments of particular interest.

Ultimately, they generate analytic and perform-ance reports for the human expert to evaluate. Systems that monitor social media enable useful information to be drawn from billions of seemingly mundane and unrelated messages. Monitoring social media can focus on brand reputation man-agement, public relations, or even market re-search. Companies, such as Comcast, a major communications company, hire full-time social media experts who interact with customers online to address problems and complaints. For example, if you complain about the Comcast service on Twitter, you might be contacted by a Comcast employee offering to help you. The social network service owners are well aware of the value of the information that flows over their networks. Most of them intend to build their business through the comments and attention of their members. Whether through targeted ads or selling access to user data, social networks can become very lucra-tive businesses. Why else would Twitter, a service with apparently no business model, be worth over a billion US dollars? Twitter's goal is to grow to one billion members and provide interested parties with the "pulse of the planet."

How do users feel about their "personal" com-ments being harvested to make billions for internet companies? With social network growth rates in 2009 ranging from 228 per cent for Facebook to 1,382 per cent for Twitter, users are either unaware or unconcerned. Regardless of what users think, it is likely that businesses will increasingly analyze the continuous flow of data over social networks to generate insights they can use.

(continued)

User Satisfaction and Technology Acceptance

To be effective, information systems must have satisfied users and be accepted and used throughout the organisation. User satisfaction with a computer system and the information it generates often depend on the quality of the system and the value of the information it delivers to users.[24] A quality information system is usually flexible, efficient, accessible, and timely. Recall that quality information is accurate, reliable, current, complete, and delivered in the proper format.[25] Studies have shown that user satisfaction and technology acceptance are critical in health care.[26] Doctors and other healthcare professionals need training and time to accept and use medical records technology and databases to reduce medical errors and save lives.

technology diffusion A measure of how widely technology is spread throughout the organisation.

technology infusion The extent to which technology is deeply integrated into an area or department.

You can determine the actual usage of an information system by the amount of technology diffusion and infusion.[27] **Technology diffusion** is a measure of how widely technology is spread throughout an organisation. An organisation in which computers and information systems are located in most departments and areas has a high level of technology diffusion. Some online merchants, such as Amazon, have a high diffusion and use computer systems to perform most of their business functions, including marketing, purchasing and billing. **Technology infusion**, on the other hand, is the extent to which technology permeates an area or department. In other words, it is a measure of how deeply embedded technology is in an area of the organisation. Some architectural firms, for example, use computers in all aspects of designing a building from drafting to final blueprints (see Figure 1.15).

Figure 1.15 *Some architectural firms use computers in all aspects of designing a building from drafting to final blueprints.*

© Petrea Alexandru/iStock.

The design area, thus, has a high level of infusion. Of course, a firm can have a high level of infusion in one part of its operations and a low level of diffusion overall. The architectural firm might use computers in all aspects of design (high infusion in the design area), but not to perform other business functions, including billing, purchasing, and marketing (low diffusion).

Although an organisation might have a high level of diffusion and infusion, with computers throughout the organisation, this does not necessarily mean that information systems are being used to their full potential. In fact, the assimilation and use of expensive computer technology throughout organisations varies greatly.[28] Providing support and help to employees usually increases the use of a new information system.[29] Companies also hope that a high level of diffusion, infusion, satisfaction, and acceptance will lead to greater performance and profitability.[30] How appropriate and useful the information system is to the tasks or activities being performed, often called Task-Technology Fit (TTF), can also lead to greater performance and profitability.[31]

Competitive Advantage

A **competitive advantage** is a significant and (ideally) long-term benefit to a company over its competition and can result in higher-quality products, better customer service, and lower costs. An organisation often uses its information system to help achieve a competitive advantage. A large Canadian furniture manufacturing company, for example, achieved a competitive advantage by reducing total operating costs by more than 20 per cent using its information system to streamline its supply chain and reduce the cost of wood and other raw materials.[32]

> **competitive advantage** The ability of a firm to outperform its industry, that is, to earn a higher rate of profit than the industry norm.

A number of factors can lead to attaining a competitive advantage. Michael Porter, a prominent management theorist, suggested a now widely accepted competitive forces model, also called the **five-forces model**. The five forces include (1) the rivalry among existing competitors, (2) the threat of new entrants, (3) the threat of substitute products and services, (4) the bargaining power of buyers, and (5) the bargaining power of suppliers. The more these forces combine in any instance, the more likely firms will seek competitive advantage and the more dramatic the results of such an advantage will be.

> **five-forces model** A widely accepted model that identifies five key factors that can lead to attainment of competitive advantage, including (1) the rivalry among existing competitors, (2) the threat of new entrants, (3) the threat of substitute products and services, (4) the bargaining power of buyers, and (5) the bargaining power of suppliers.

Rivalry Among Existing Competitors

Typically, highly competitive industries are characterised by high fixed costs of entering or leaving the industry, low degrees of product differentiation, and many competitors. Although all firms are rivals with their competitors, industries with stronger rivalries tend to have more firms seeking competitive advantage. To gain an advantage over competitors, companies constantly analyze how they use their resources and assets. This resource-based view is an approach to acquiring and controlling assets or resources that can help the company achieve a competitive advantage. For example, a transportation company might decide to invest in radio-frequency technology to tag and trace products as they move from one location to another.

Threat of New Entrants

A threat appears when entry and exit costs to an industry are low and the technology needed to start and maintain a business is commonly available. For example, a small restaurant is threatened by new competitors. Owners of small restaurants do not require millions of dollars to start the business, food costs do not decline substantially for large volumes, and food processing and preparation equipment is easily available. When the threat of new market entrants is high, the desire to seek and maintain competitive advantage to dissuade new entrants is also usually high.

Threat of Substitute Products and Services

Companies that offer one type of goods or services are threatened by other companies that offer similar goods or services. The more consumers can obtain similar products and services that satisfy their needs, the more likely firms are to try to establish competitive advantage. For example, consider the photographic industry. When digital cameras became popular, traditional film companies had to respond to stay competitive and profitable. Traditional film companies, such as Kodak, started to offer additional products and enhanced services, including digital cameras, the ability to produce digital images from traditional film cameras, and websites that could be used to store and view pictures (see Figure 1.16).

Figure 1.16 *The final roll of Kodachrome film, a widely-lauded quality colour film, was developed in January 2011, a fact lamented by many photographers.*[33]

© Shawshots Kodak archive/Alamy.

Bargaining Power of Buyers and Suppliers

Large customers tend to influence a firm, and this influence can increase significantly if the customers can threaten to switch to rival companies. When customers have a lot of bargaining power, companies increase their competitive advantage to retain their customers. Similarly, when the bargaining power of suppliers is strong, companies need to improve their competitive advantage to maintain their bargaining position. Suppliers can also help an organisation gain a competitive advantage. Some suppliers enter into strategic alliances with firms and eventually act as a part of the company. Suppliers and companies can use telecommunications to link their computers and personnel to react quickly and provide parts or supplies as necessary to satisfy customers.

Given the five market forces previously mentioned, Porter and others have proposed a number of strategies to attain competitive advantage, including cost leadership, differentiation, niche strategy, altering the industry structure, creating new products and services, and improving existing product lines and services. In some cases, one of these strategies becomes dominant. For example, with a cost leadership strategy, cost can be the key consideration, at the expense of other factors if need be.

Cost Leadership

Deliver the lowest possible products and services. In the UK, supermarket Asda has used this strategy for years. Cost leadership is often achieved by reducing the costs of raw materials through aggressive negotiations with suppliers, becoming more efficient with production and manufacturing processes, and reducing warehousing and shipping costs. Some companies use outsourcing to cut costs when making products or completing services.

Differentiation

Deliver different products and services. This strategy can involve producing a variety of products, giving customers more choices, or delivering higher-quality products and services. Many car companies make different models that use the same basic parts and components, giving customers more options. Other car companies attempt to increase perceived quality and safety to differentiate their products. Some consumers are willing to pay higher prices for these vehicles that differentiate on higher quality or better safety.

Niche Strategy

Deliver to only a small, niche market. Porsche, for example, doesn't produce inexpensive station wagons or large sedans. It makes high-performance sports cars and SUVs. Rolex only makes high-quality, expensive watches. It doesn't make inexpensive, plastic watches that can be purchased for €20 or less.

Altering the Industry Structure

Change the industry to become more favourable to the company or organisation. The introduction of low-fare airline carriers, such as EasyJet, has forever changed the airline industry, making it difficult for traditional airlines to make high profit margins. To fight back, airlines, such as British Airways, cut their flight prices and started to emphasise their strengths over low cost airlines in their advertising. These include landing in central airports rather than airports many miles out of the city they supposedly serve and that they have extra staff and resources to cope if there is a fault with an aircraft or adverse weather grounds all planes. Creating strategic alliances can also alter the industry structure. A **strategic alliance**, also called a strategic partnership, is an agreement between two or more companies that involves the joint production and distribution of goods and services.

> **strategic alliance** An agreement between two or more companies that involves the joint production and distribution of goods and services.

Creating New Products and Services

Introduce new products and services periodically or frequently. This strategy can help a firm gain a competitive advantage, especially in the computer industry and other high-tech businesses. If an organisation does not introduce new products and services every few months, the company can quickly stagnate, lose market share, and decline. Companies that stay on top are constantly developing new products and services.

Improving Existing Product Lines and Service

Make real or perceived improvements to existing product lines and services. Manufacturers of household products are always advertising new and improved products. In some cases, the improvements are more perceived than real refinements; usually, only minor changes are made to the existing product, such as to reduce the amount of sugar in a breakfast cereal. Some mail order companies are improving their service by using Radio Frequency Identification (RFID) tags to identify and track the location of their products as they are shipped from one location to another. Customers and managers can instantly locate products as they are shipped from suppliers to the company, to warehouses, and finally to customers.

Other potentially successful strategies include being the first to market, offering customised products and services, and hiring talented. The assumption is that the best people will determine the best products and services to deliver to the market and the best approach to deliver these products and services. Companies can also combine one or more of these strategies.

1.5 Evaluating IS

Once an information system has been implemented, management will want to assess how successful it has been in achieving its goals (see Figure 1.17). Often this is a difficult thing to do, and many businesses do not attempt to take anything more than an informal approach to evaluation.[34] Business can use measurements of productivity, return on investment (ROI), net present value, and other measures of performance to evaluate the contributions their information systems make to their businesses.

Figure 1.17 *South African legislation requires public information systems, including those used in hospitals, to be evaluated involving as many stakeholders as possible.*

© Daniel Laflor/iStock.

Productivity

Developing information systems that measure and control productivity is a key element for most organisations. **Productivity** is a measure of the output achieved divided by the input required.

productivity A measure of the output achieved divided by the input required. Productivity = (Output / Input) × 100%.

A higher level of output for a given level of input means greater productivity; a lower level of output for a given level of input means lower productivity. The numbers assigned to productivity levels are not always based on labour hours – productivity can be based on factors, such as the amount of raw materials used, resulting quality, or time to produce the goods or service. The value of the productivity number is not as significant as how it compares with other time periods, settings, and organisations.

After a basic level of productivity is measured, an information system can monitor and compare it over time to see whether productivity is increasing. Then, a company can take corrective action if productivity drops below certain levels. In addition to measuring productivity, an information system can be used within a process to significantly increase productivity. Thus, improved productivity can result in faster customer response, lower costs, and increased customer satisfaction.

In the late 1980s and early 1990s, overall productivity did not seem to improve as a company increased its investments in information systems. Often called the productivity paradox, this situation troubled many economists who were expecting to see dramatic productivity gains. In the early 2000s, however, productivity again seemed on the rise.

Return on Investment and the Value of Information Systems

One measure of IS value is **return on investment (ROI)**. This measure investigates the additional profits or benefits that are generated as a percentage of the investment in IS technology. A small business that generates an additional profit of €20 000 for the year as a result of an investment of €100 000 for additional computer equipment and software would have a return on investment of 20 per cent (€20 000/€100 000). In many cases, however, it can be difficult to accurately measure ROI.[35]

return on investment (ROI)
One measure of IS value that investigates the additional profits or benefits that are generated as a percentage of the investment in IS technology.

Earnings Growth

Another measure of IS value is the increase in profit, or earnings growth, it brings. For instance, a mail-order company might install an order-processing system that generates a 7 per cent earnings growth compared with the previous year.

Market Share

Market share is the percentage of sales that a product or service has in relation to the total market. If installing a new online catalogue increases sales, it might help a company increase its market share by 20 per cent.

Customer Awareness and Satisfaction

Although customer satisfaction can be difficult to quantify, about half of today's best global companies measure the performance of their information systems based on feedback from internal and external users. Some companies use surveys and questionnaires to determine whether the IS investment has increased customer awareness and satisfaction.

Total Cost of Ownership

Another way to measure the value of information systems was developed by the Gartner Group and is called the **total cost of ownership (TCO)**. This approach breaks total costs into areas, such as the cost to acquire the technology, technical support, administrative costs, and end-user operations. Other costs in TCO include retooling and training costs. TCO can help to develop a more accurate estimate of the total costs for systems that range from small PCs to large mainframe systems. Market research groups often use TCO to compare products and services.

total cost of ownership (TCO)
The measurement of the total cost of owning computer equipment, including desktop computers, networks, and large computers.

Return on investment, earnings growth, market share, customer satisfaction, and TCO are only a few measures that companies use to plan for and maximise the value of their IS investments. Regardless of the difficulties, organisations must attempt to evaluate the contributions that information systems make to assess their progress and plan for the future. Information technology and personnel are too important to leave to chance.

Risk

In addition to the return-on-investment measures of a new or modified information system, managers should also consider the risks of designing, developing, and implementing these systems. Information systems can sometimes be costly failures. Some companies, for example, have attempted to implement ERP systems and failed, costing them millions of euros. In other cases, e-commerce applications have been implemented with little success. The costs of development and implementation can be greater than the returns from the new system.

1.6 Careers in Information Systems

Realising the benefits of any information system requires competent and motivated IS person-nel, and many companies offer excellent job opportunities. Professionals with careers in infor-mation systems typically work in an IS department as web developers, computer programmers, systems analysts, database developers and administrators, computer operators, technical sup-port or other positions. In addition to technical skills, they need skills in written and verbal com-munication, an understanding of organisations and the way they operate, and the ability to work with people and in groups. Today, many good information, business, and computer science schools require these business and communications skills of their graduates. In general, IS pro-fessionals are charged with maintaining the broadest perspective on organisational goals. Most medium to large organisations manage information resources through an IS department. In smaller businesses, one or more people might manage information resources, with support from outsourced services. As shown in Figure 1.18, the IS department has three primary respon-sibilities: operations, systems development, and support.

Figure 1.18 The IS Department

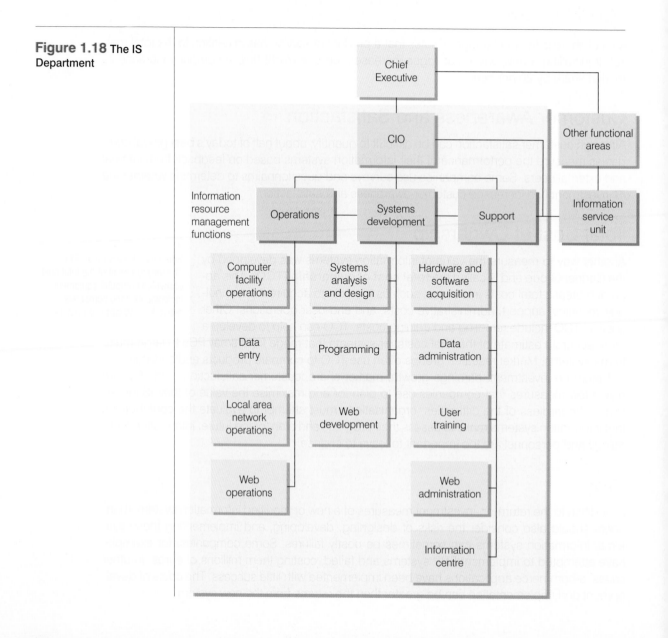

Operations

People in the operations component of a typical IS department work with information systems in corporate or business unit computer facilities. They tend to focus more on the efficiency of IS functions rather than their effectiveness.

System operators primarily run and maintain IS equipment and are typically trained at technical schools or through on-the-job experience. They are responsible for starting, stopping, and correctly operating mainframe systems, networks, tape drives, disk devices, printers, and so on. Other operations include scheduling, hardware maintenance, and preparing input and output. Data-entry operators convert data into a form the computer system can use. They can use terminals or other devices to enter business transactions, such as sales orders and payroll data. Increasingly, data entry is being automated – captured at the source of the transaction rather than entered later. In addition, companies might have local area network and web operators who run the local network and any websites the company has.

Systems Development

The systems development component of a typical IS department focuses on specific development projects and ongoing maintenance and review. Systems analysts and programmers, for example, address these concerns to achieve and maintain IS effectiveness. The role of a systems analyst is multifaceted. Systems analysts help users determine what outputs they need from the system and construct plans for developing the necessary programs that produce these outputs. Systems analysts then work with one or more programmers to make sure that the appropriate programs are purchased, modified from existing programs, or developed. A computer programmer uses the plans the systems analyst created to develop or adapt one or more computer programs that produce the desired outputs.

With the dramatic increase in the use of the internet, intranets, and extranets, many companies have web or internet developers who create effective and attractive websites for customers, internal personnel, suppliers, stockholders, and others who have a business relationship with the company.

Support

The support component of a typical IS department provides user assistance in hardware and software acquisition and use, data administration, user training and assistance, and web administration. In many cases, support is delivered through an information centre.

Because IS hardware and software are costly, a specialised support group often manages computer hardware and software acquisitions. This group sets guidelines and standards for the rest of the organisation to follow in making purchases. They must gain and maintain an understanding of available technology and develop good relationships with vendors.

A database administrator focuses on planning, policies, and procedures regarding the use of corporate data and information. For example, database administrators develop and disseminate information about the organisation's databases for developers of IS applications. In addition, the database administrator monitors and controls database use.

User training is a key to get the most from any information system, and the support area ensures that appropriate training is available. Training can be provided by internal staff or from external sources. For example, internal support staff can train managers and employees in the best way to enter sales orders, to receive computerised inventory reports, and to submit expense reports electronically. Companies also hire outside firms to help train users in other areas, including the use of word processing, spreadsheets, and database programs.

Web administration is another key area for support staff. With the increased use of the internet, web administrators are sometimes asked to regulate and monitor internet use by employees and managers to make sure that it is authorised and appropriate. Web administrators also maintain the organisation's website to keep it accurate and current, which can require substantial resources.

The support component typically operates the helpdesk. A helpdesk provides users with assistance, training, application development, documentation, equipment selection and setup, standards, technical assistance, and troubleshooting.

Information Service Units

An information service unit is basically a miniature IS department attached and directly reporting to a functional area in a large organisation. Notice the information service unit shown in Figure 1.18. Even though this unit is usually staffed by IS professionals, the project assignments and the resources necessary to accomplish these projects are provided by the functional area to which it reports. Depending on the policies of the organisation, the salaries of IS professionals staffing the information service unit might be budgeted to either the IS department or the functional area.

Typical IS Titles and Functions

The organisational chart shown in Figure 1.18 is a simplified model of an IS department in a typical medium or large organisation. Many organisations have even larger departments, with increasingly specialised positions such as librarian or quality assurance manager. Smaller firms often combine the roles shown in Figure 1.18 into fewer formal positions.

The Chief Information Officer

The role of the chief information officer (CIO) is to employ an IS department's equipment and personnel to help the organisation attain its goals. The CIO is a senior manager concerned with the overall needs of the organisation, who sets organisation-wide policies and plans, manages, and acquires information systems. Some of the CIO's top concerns include integrating IS operations with business strategies, keeping up with the rapid pace of technology, and defining and assessing the value of systems development projects. The high level of the CIO position reflects that information is one of the organisation's most important resources. A CIO works with other high-level officers of an organisation, including the chief financial officer (CFO) and the chief executive officer (CEO), in managing and controlling total corporate resources. CIOs must also work closely with advisory committees, stressing effectiveness and teamwork and viewing information systems as an integral part of the organisation's business processes – not an adjunct to the organisation. Thus, CIOs need both technical and business skills.

Administrators

local area network (LAN) A computer network that connects computer systems and devices within a small area, such as an office, home, or several floors in a building.

Local area network (LAN) administrators set up and manage the network hardware, software, and security processes. They manage the addition of new users, software, and devices to the network. They also isolate and fix operations problems. LAN administrators are in high demand and often solve both technical and nontechnical problems.

Internet Careers

These careers are in the areas of web operations, web development, and web administration. As with other areas in IS, many top-level administrative jobs are related to the internet. These career opportunities are found in both traditional companies and those that specialise in the internet.

Internet jobs within a traditional company include internet strategists and administrators, internet systems developers, internet programmers, and internet or website operators.

Systems Developers

Systems developers design and write software. Typically developers will be graduates with degrees in technical subjects, such as computer science, mathematics or engineering. However, many big employers have graduate recruitment schemes where degree subject is less important that an ability to learn. On such schemes, graduates are taught the skills they need. The skills needed by developers include the ability to design solutions to problems and communicate these solutions to other developers and to users and the technical skill to create these solutions. Software development can be can be extremely challenging and exciting.

Often, systems developers are employed to create software to support business goals, such as develop the organisation's transaction processing system. Alternatively, systems developers may work in a software house, where the software they write is the product the organisation sells. One of the fastest growing areas of software development is the games industry with many universities now offering degrees in games development.

Other IS Careers

Other IS career opportunities include technical writing (creating technical manuals and user guides) and user interface design.

Often, the people filling IS roles have completed some form of certification. **Certification** is a process for testing skills and knowledge resulting in an endorsement by the certifying authority that an individual is capable of performing a particular job. Certification frequently involves specific, vendor-provided or vendor-endorsed coursework. Popular certification programs include Microsoft Certified Systems Engineer, Certified Information Systems Security Professional (CISSP), Oracle Certified Professional, and many others.

> **certification** A process for testing skills and knowledge, which results in a statement by the certifying authority that confirms an individual is capable of performing a particular kind of job.

1.7 Global Challenges in Information Systems

Changes in society as a result of increased international trade and cultural exchange, often called globalisation, have always had a big impact on organisations and their information systems. In his book, The World Is Flat, Thomas Friedman describes three eras of globalisation[36] (see Table 1.2). According to Friedman, we have progressed from the globalisation of countries to the globalisation of multinational corporations and individuals. Today, people in remote areas can use the internet to compete with and contribute to other people, the largest corporations, and entire countries. These workers are empowered by high-speed internet access, making the world flatter. In the Globalisation 3 era, designing a new airplane or computer can be separated into smaller subtasks and then completed by a person or small group that can do the best job. These

Table 1.2 Eras of Globalisation

Era	Dates	Characterised by
Globalisation 1	Late 1400–1800	Countries with the power to explore and influence the world
Globalisation 2	1800–2000	Multinational corporations that have plants, warehouses, and offices around the world
Globalisation 3	2000–today	Individuals from around the world who can compete and influence other people, corporations, and countries by using the internet and powerful technology tools

workers can be located in India, China, Russia, Europe, and other areas of the world. The sub-tasks can then be combined or reassembled into the complete design. This approach can be used to prepare tax returns, diagnose a patient's medical condition, fix a broken computer, and many other tasks.

Today's information systems have led to greater globalisation. High-speed internet access and networks that can connect individuals and organisations around the world create more international opportunities. Global markets have expanded. People and companies can get products and services from around the world, instead of around the corner or across town. These opportunities, however, introduce numerous obstacles and issues, including challenges involving culture, language, and many others.

- ■ *Cultural challenges.* Countries and regional areas have their own cultures and customs that can significantly affect individuals and organisations involved in global trade.

- ■ *Language challenges.* Language differences can make it difficult to translate exact meanings from one language to another.

- ■ *Time and distance challenges.* Time and distance issues can be difficult to overcome for individuals and organisations involved with global trade in remote locations. Large time differences make it difficult to talk to people on the other side of the world. With long distance, it can take days to get a product, a critical part, or a piece of equipment from one location to another location.

- ■ *Infrastructure challenges.* High-quality electricity and water might not be available in certain parts of the world. Telephone services, internet connections, and skilled employees might be expensive or not readily available.

- ■ *Currency challenges.* The value of different currencies can vary significantly over time, making international trade more difficult and complex.

- ■ *Product and service challenges.* Traditional products that are physical or tangible, such as a car or bicycle, can be difficult to deliver to the global market. However, electronic products (e-products) and electronic services (e-services) can be delivered to customers electronically, over the phone, networks, through the internet, or other electronic means. Software, music, books, manuals, and help and advice can all be delivered over the internet.

- ■ *Technology transfer issues.* Most governments don't allow certain military-related equipment and systems to be sold to some countries. Even so, some believe that foreign companies are stealing the intellectual property, trade secrets, and copyrighted materials and counterfeiting products and services.[37]

- ■ *National laws.* Every country has a set of laws that must be obeyed by citizens and organisations operating in the country. These laws can deal with a variety of issues, including trade secrets, patents, copyrights, protection of personal or financial data, privacy, and much more. Laws restricting how data enters or exits a country are often called trans-border data-flow laws. Keeping track of these laws and incorporating them into the procedures and computer systems of multinational and trans-national organisations can be very difficult and time consuming, requiring expert legal advice.

- ■ *Trade agreements.* Countries often enter into trade agreements with each other. The EU has trade agreements among its members.[38] The North American Free Trade Agreement (NAFTA) and the Central American Free Trade Agreement (CAFTA) are other examples.[39] Others include the Australia-United States Free Trade Agreement and agreements between Bolivia and Mexico, Canada and Costa Rica, Canada and Israel, Chile and Korea, Mexico and Japan, the United States and Jordan, and many others.[40]

Summary

At the start of this chapter we set out the FIVE main principles within the area of information systems in organisations, together with the key learning objectives for each. It's now time to summarise the chapter by recapping on those FIVE principles: Can you recall what is important and why about each one?

1 **The value of information is directly linked to how it helps decision makers achieve the organisation's goals.** Information systems are used in almost every imaginable career area. Regardless of your chosen career, you will find that information systems are indispensable tools to help you achieve your goals. Learning about information systems can help you get your first job, earn promotions, and advance your career.

Information is a collection of facts. To be valuable, information must have several characteristics: It should be accurate, complete, economical to produce, flexible, reliable, relevant, simple to understand, timely, verifiable, accessible, and secure. The value of information is directly linked to how it helps people achieve their organisation's goals.

2 **Knowing the potential impact of information systems and having the ability to put this knowledge to work can result in a successful personal career, organisations that reach their goals, and a society with a higher quality of life.** Information systems are sets of interrelated elements that collect (input), manipulate and store (process), and disseminate (output) data and information. Input is the activity of capturing and gathering new data, processing involves converting or transforming data into useful outputs, and output involves producing useful information. Feedback is the output that is used to make adjustments or changes to input or processing activities.

The components of a computer-based information system (CBIS) include hardware, software, databases, telecommunications and the internet, people, and procedures. An enterprise resource planning (ERP) system is a set of integrated programs that can manage the vital business operations for an entire multi-site, global organisation. Information systems (or sub-systems of an ERP) can be classified into four basic groups: (1) e-commerce and m-commerce, (2) TPS, (3) MIS and DSS, and (4) specialised business information systems. The key to understanding these types of systems begins with learning their fundamentals.

E-commerce involves any business transaction executed electronically between parties, such as companies (business to business), companies and consumers (business to consumer), business and the public sector, and consumers and the public sector. The major volume of e-commerce and its fastest-growing segment is business-to-business transactions that make purchasing easier for big corporations. E-commerce also offers opportunities for small businesses to market and sell at a low cost worldwide, thus allowing them to enter the global market right from start-up. M-commerce involves anytime, anywhere computing that relies on wireless networks and systems.

The most fundamental system is the transaction processing system (TPS). A transaction is any business-related exchange. The TPS handles the large volume of business transactions that occur daily within an organisation. A management information system (MIS) uses the information from a TPS to generate information useful for management decision making.

A decision support system (DSS) is an organised collection of people, procedures, databases, and devices that help make problem-specific decisions. A DSS differs from an MIS in the support given to users, the emphasis on decisions, the development and approach, and the system components, speed, and output.

Specialised business information systems include knowledge management, artificial intelligence, expert, and virtual reality systems. Knowledge management systems are organised collections of people, procedures, software, databases, and devices used to create, store, share, and use the organisation's knowledge and experience. Artificial intelligence (AI) includes a wide range of systems in which the computer takes on the characteristics of human intelligence. Robotics is an area of artificial intelligence in which machines perform complex, dangerous, routine, or boring tasks, such as welding car frames or assembling computer systems and components. Vision systems allow robots and other devices to have "sight" and to store and process visual images. Natural language processing involves computers interpreting and acting on verbal or written commands in English, Spanish, or other human languages. Learning systems let computers learn from past mistakes or experiences, such as playing games or making business decisions, whereas neural networks is a branch of artificial intelligence that allows computers to recognise and act on patterns or trends. An expert system (ES) is designed to act as an expert consultant to a user who is seeking advice about a specific situation. Originally, the term virtual reality referred to immersive virtual reality in which the user becomes fully immersed in an artificial, computer-generated 3-D world. Virtual reality can also refer to applications that are not fully immersive, such as mouse-controlled navigation through a 3-D environment on a graphics monitor, stereo viewing from the monitor via stereo glasses, stereo projection systems, and others.

3 System users, business managers, and information systems professionals must work together to build a successful information system. Systems development involves creating or modifying existing business systems. The major steps of this process and their goals include systems investigation (gain a clear understanding of what the problem is), systems analysis (define what the system must do to solve the problem), systems design (determine exactly how the system will work to meet the business needs), systems implementation (create or acquire the various system components defined in the design step), and systems maintenance and review (maintain and then modify the system so that it continues to meet changing business needs).

4 The use of information systems to add value to the organisation is strongly influenced by organisational structure, and the organisation's attitude and ability to change. An organisation is a formal collection of people and other resources established to accomplish a set of goals. The primary goal of a for-profit organisation is to maximise shareholder value. Non-profit organisations include social groups, religious groups, universities, and other organisations that do not have profit as the primary goal.

Organisations are systems with inputs, transformation mechanisms, and outputs. Value-added processes increase the relative worth of the combined inputs on their way to becoming final outputs of the organisation. The value chain is a series (chain) of activities that includes (1) inbound logistics, (2) warehouse and storage, (3) production, (4) finished product storage, (5) outbound logistics, (6) marketing and sales, and (7) customer service.

Change can be caused by internal or external factors. According to the concept of organisational learning, organisations adapt to new conditions or alter practices over time.

5 Cooperation between business managers and IS personnel is the key to unlocking the potential of any new or modified system. Information systems personnel typically work in an IS department. The chief information officer (CIO) employs an IS department's equipment and personnel to help the organisation attain its goals. Systems analysts help users determine what outputs they need from the system and construct the plans needed to develop the necessary programs that produce these outputs. Systems analysts then work with one or more system developers to make sure that the appropriate programs are purchased, modified from existing programs, or developed. The major responsibility of a computer programmer is to use the plans developed by the systems analyst to build or adapt one or more computer programs that produce the desired outputs.

Computer operators are responsible for starting, stopping, and correctly operating mainframe systems, networks, tape drives, disk devices, printers, and so on. LAN administrators set up and manage the network hardware, software, and security processes. Trained personnel are also needed to set up and manage a company's internet site, including internet strategists, internet systems developers, internet programmers, and website operators. Information systems personnel can also support other functional departments or areas.

In addition to technical skills, IS personnel need skills in written and verbal communication, an understanding of organisations and the way they operate, and the ability to work with people (users). In general, IS personnel are charged with maintaining the broadest enterprise-wide perspective.

Review Questions

1 Explain some of the ways in which information systems are changing our lives.

2 Define the term system. Give several examples of a system.

3 What are the components of any information system?

4 What is feedback? What are possible consequences of inadequate feedback?

5 What is a computer-based information system? What are its components?

6 Identify three functions of a transaction processing system.

7 What is the difference between an intranet and an extranet?

8 What is the difference between an ERP and a TPS system?

9 Identify three elements of artificial intelligence. How could they be used in an organisation?

10 Identify the steps in the systems development process and state the goal of each.

Discussion Questions

1 Two definitions of information were given in this chapter: information is that which reduces uncertainty, and information is a collection of facts. Imagine closing your eyes and reaching into your bag. Maybe you can feel a book, a pencil or a calculator. Has this experience given you information? Why or why not?

2 Describe how information systems are used in your college or university. Can you think of any areas for improvement?

3 Can you think of any ways in which a DSS could be used in your life?

4 Discuss the potential use of virtual reality to enhance the learning experience for new automobile drivers. How might such a system operate? What are the benefits and potential disadvantages of such a system?

5 Discuss how information systems are linked to the business objectives of an organisation.

Web Exercises

1 Using an internet search engine, such as www.google.co.uk, search for information about someone you know. Summarise what you were able to find in a report.

2 Go to an internet search engine and search for information about knowledge management. Write a brief report that summarises what you

found and the companies that provide knowledge management products.

3 Using the internet, search for information on the use of information systems in a company or organisation that interests you. How does the organisation use technology to help it accomplish its goals?

Case One

Cybernest Reduces Energy Used to Store Data in South Africa

Telkom Group Ltd is a telecommunications company in South Africa. Since the early 1990s they have provided a telephone service, and then later internet access, eventually expanding into other African countries. More recently they have expanded their product offering to include data hosting. Launched in 2009, its data centre operation, Cybernest, based in Bellville, Cape Town stores data for clients, including email archives, cheaper and more securely than they could themselves. The company promotes the security of its operation and its ability to help clients recover from disasters, such as fire and flood, which have destroyed their IT. Rather than store it locally, clients store their information at the Cybernest data centres. The company has six data centres in South Africa, four in Gauteng and two in the Western Cape and employs around 600 IT specialists. Client data is backed up so that, if a disaster hits one centre, a copy is held at another. Many companies cannot afford to do such "off-site" backups themselves.

Cybernest also promote their green credentials. Data centres use an incredible amount of electricity, mostly in the cooling of their components, and any reduction in this has immediate financial and environmental benefits. Cybernest expects to achieve an overall energy saving of 34 per cent a year by embedding green principles into the design of its newest data centre and by using free cooling. Free cooling uses external air temperature to chill water which is then used in removing the heat generated by the data centre. At Cybernest's newest data centre, two cooling modes are in place: the usual chiller system and free air cooling. The latter is used when the weather allows it – when the ambient temperature outside is less than 24 degrees celsius. On these days, cool outside air is filtered in and hot air is vented out. The temperature inside older data centres tends to be uncomfortably cold, because air conditioners chill the entire environment, not just the computers. New-generation centres are more selective. They don't cool everything, only the components that need cooling. Using the principle that hot air rises and cold air sinks, they have alternating hot and cold aisles, with each cold aisle blowing cool air upwards through the floor and a hot aisle above, sucking warm air out through the ceiling. The components needing cooling are positioned to face the cold aisle, ensuring the best use of cool air flowing in and hot air flowing out.

Other energy-efficient techniques in use include eco-friendly forms of un-interruptable power supply which are needed in order to safely shut the computers down in case of power failure. According to Althon Beukes, Cybernest's Executive of Infrastructure Operations, "Some people ask where are the wind turbines and solar panels. The answer is that these solutions aren't yet feasible in a data centre environment. We focus on green technologies that also make business sense."

Discussion Questions

1 What are some of the dangers a company faces when it uses a third party to store and manage its information?

2 Should energy reduction be a priority for all organisations?

Critical Thinking Questions

1 Can you think of other services Cybernest could provide?

2 Do you think clients actually care that Cybernest has green credentials, or are they just interested in the cost of the service?

SOURCES: http://www.cybernest.co.za/cn/index.jsp. Accessed January 6, 2011.
http://www.telkom.co.za. Accessed January 6, 2011.
Data Center Knowledge, "Smart Approaches to Free-Cooling in Data Centers," June 2, 2010. Available from: http://www.datacenterknowledge.com/archives/2010/06/02/smart-approaches-to-free-cooling-in-data-centers/.

Case Two

Aldra Manages Workflow to Support Customisation

Aldra Fenster und Türen GmbH, or Aldra for short, is a leading door and window manufacturer with over 300 dealers in Germany and Scandinavia. Aldra is well known for its precision craftsmanship in manufacturing intricate, custom-designed windows. In the early 1970s, the company developed a unique method of manufacturing windows from plastic. Combined with its customisation service, this cost-saving manufacturing innovation gave Aldra a leg up on the competition. Aldra's custom window design and manufacturing has created challenges in its corporate workflow and information processing. Mass-producing windows and doors in standard sizes is far easier than creating custom designs, where production techniques change from one item to the next. At Aldra, most orders have unique requirements in terms of size, shape, materials, function, and embedded technology. To support custom orders, Aldra must provide considerable flexibility in both its manufacturing processes and its information systems.

Providing customised manufacturing does not excuse Aldra from meeting the tight deadlines imposed by costly construction projects. Aggressive construction schedules rarely allow for the extra time required to produce custom products. Aldra found that the complexities of building its high-quality products were causing confusion in the order processing system and delays in manufacturing, leading to missed deadlines. Order specifications were sometimes incomplete or incorrect, and correcting orders is time consuming. Lack of coordination among departments resulted in additional errors that occasionally resulted in costly idle time on the production line. The lack of coordination also led to errors in calculating manufacturing costs, which reduced profits. Aldra set out to implement a new system that would assist the company in managing its value chain and corporate workflow. Aldra purchased information systems from Infor Corporation that allowed the company to better coordinate efforts across departments. Using the software, Aldra now models its critical core processes (workflows) and then uses the models to improve communication across the value chain.

The models define the specific employees involved in the various stages of the process. The system then generates daily activities for each employee displayed in a particular area on the computer desktop. As activities approach their deadline, they are moved to the top of the list. Employees also receive email notices of new or pressing actions needing attention.

Aldra's new workflow management system depends on a corporate-wide system that stores and manipulates all order details. Top managers can view orders to see how they are progressing through the value chain so that they can intervene when necessary.

Aldra implemented the new system in an unusually short amount of time. The company spent three days installing the system, another three days training managers in how to model workflow processes, and two weeks to model processes and train users. The benefits of the new system were almost immediately apparent. Within weeks, the company's adherence to delivery dates was improved by over 95 per cent. Cost estimates are now reliably calculated. Employees make more productive use of their time, and customers are happy. Aldra is looking to expand the use of its new systems to other areas of its business.

Discussion Questions

1 What problems did Aldra's new information systems address, and what was the root of those problems?

2 How did Aldra's new systems assist employees in being more productive?

Critical Thinking Questions

1 What lessons can be learned from this case in terms of managing information in a value chain?

2 How does an organisation determine when it is worthwhile to invest in a system, such as Aldra's workflow management system?

SOURCES: Infor Staff, "Aldra Fenster und Türen GmbH," Aldra Customer Profile. Available from: www.infor.com/content/casestudies/296661. Accessed December 24, 2009; Infor ERP systems website, accessed December 24, 2009; Aldra website (translated). Available from: www.aldra.de. Accessed December 24, 2009.

Notes

1 Floridi, Luciano, "Information A Very Short Introduction," Oxford University Press, 2010.

2 DiColo, Jerry, "Chip Makers to Benefit From Utility Smart Meters," *The Wall Street Journal,* April 1, 2009, p. B6.

3 BBC, "China's Tianhe-1A crowned supercomputer king". Available from: http://www.bbc.co.uk/news/technology-11766840. Accessed November 16, 2010.

4 Clark, D. and Scheck, J., "High-Tech Companies Take Up Netbooks," *The Wall Street Journal,* January 6, 2009, p. B6.

5 Mossberg, Walter, "Some Favorite Apps," *The Wall Street Journal,* March 26, 2009, p. D1.

6 Staff, "Bringing Technology to the Bush," *The Australian Financial Review,*" August 31, 2009, p. 28.

7 Tham, Irene, "Changing the World, One Laptop at a Time," *The Straits Time,* July 16, 2009.

8 Wildstrom, Stephen, "Touch-Sensitive Desktops," *Business Week,* March 23, 2009, p. 97.

9 Scheck, Justin, "PC Makers Try Google, Challenging Microsoft," *The Wall Street Journal,* April 1, 2009, p. B1.

10 "Adobe Creative Suite 4". Available from: www.adobe.com/products/creativesuite. Accessed December 10, 2009.

11 Wildstrom, Stephen, "Coming at You: 3D on Your PC," *Business Week,* January 19, 2009, p. 65.

12 Hamm, Steve, "Cloud Computing's Big Bang for Business," *Business Week,* June 15, 2009, p. 42.

13 Available from: www.intoweb.com. Accessed January 4, 2011.

14 Weier, Mary Hayes, "Business Gone Mobile," *Information Week,* March 30, 2009, p. 23.

15 Staff, "Nissan Developing Smart Cars," *CNN Online,* March 1, 2005.

16 Rowley, Ian, "Drive, He Thought," *Business Week,* April 20, 2009, p. 10.

17 Staff, "Artificial Neural Networks," *Biotech Business Week,* October 5, 2009, p. 404.

18 Kane, Yukare Iwatani, "Apple Woos Developers With New iPhone," *The Wall Street Journal,* March 18, 2009, p. B6.

19 BBC Tax credit fiasco costs EDS £71m. 22/11/05. Available from: http://news.bbc.co.uk/1/hi/business/4460800.stm. Accessed April 27, 2011.

20 Porter, Michael, "Competitive Strategy," Free Press, 1980.

21 Dong, S., *et al.,* "Information Technology in Supply Chains," *Information Systems Research,* March 2009, p. 18.

22 Huifen, Chen, "Courting the Small Enterprise," *The Business Times,* Singapore, September 22, 2009.

23 Christensen, Clayton, "The Innovator's Dilemma," Harvard Business School Press, 1997, p. 225 and "The Inventor's Solution," Harvard Business School Press, 2003.

24 Bailey, J. and Pearson, W., "Development of a Tool for Measuring and Analyzing Computer User Satisfaction," *Management Science,* 29(5), 1983, p. 530.

25 Chaparro, Barbara, *et al.,* "Using the End-User Computing Satisfaction Instrument to Measure Satisfaction with a website," *Decision Sciences,* May 2005, p. 341.

26 Ilie, V., *et al.,* "Paper Versus Electronic Medical Records," *Decision Sciences,* May 2009, p. 213.

27 Barki, H., *et al.,* "Information System Use-Related Activity," *Information Systems Research,* June 2007, p. 173.

28 Armstrong, Curtis and Sambamurthy, V., "Information Technology Assimilation in Firms," *Information Systems Research,* April 1999, p. 304.

29 Sykes, T. and Venkatesh, V., "Model of Acceptance with Peer Support," *MIS Quarterly,* June 2009, p. 371.

30 Agarwal, Ritu and Prasad, Jayesh, "Are Individual Differences Germane to the Acceptance of New Information Technology?" *Decision Sciences,* Spring 1999, p. 361.

31 Fuller, R. and Denis, A., "Does Fit Matter?" *Information Systems Research,* March 2009, p. 2.

32 D'Amours, M., *et al.,* "Optimization Helps Shermag Gain Competitive Advantage," *Interfaces,* July–August, 2009, p. 329.

33 BBC, "Kodachrome last remaining film roll developed in Kansas". Available from: http://www.bbc.co.uk/news/world-us-canada-1209577. Accessed April 27, 2011.

34 Irani and P.E.D. Love. Evaluating the impact of IT on the Organisation. In: Robert Galliers & Dorothy Leidner (eds) 2003. Strategic Information Management. Butterworth Heinemann

35 Huber, Nick, "Return on Investment: Analysts to Offer Tips on Measuring the Value of IT," *Computer Weekly,* April 26, 2005, p. 20.

36 Friedman, Thomas, "The World Is Flat," Farrar, Straus and Giroux, 2005, p. 488.

37 Balfour, Frederik, "Invasion of the Brain Snatchers," *Business Week,* May 9, 2005, p. 24.

38 Available from: www.europa.eu.int. Accessed January 15, 2006.

39 Smith, Geri, *et al.,* "Central America Is Holding Its Breath," *Business Week,* June 20, 2005, p. 52.

40 Available from: http://www.sice.oas.org/ agreements_e.asp. Accessed January 5, 2011.

CHAPTER 2 CONTENTS

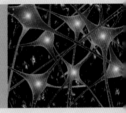

02

Hardware and Software

This chapter will cover SIX main sections and detail the issues implicit within business information systems and how they are based within hardware and software concerns for businesses and organisations.

Principles	Learning Objectives
1. Computer hardware must be carefully selected to meet the evolving needs of the organisation and its supporting information systems.	▉ Identify and discuss the role of the essential hardware components of a computer system. ▉ Identify the characteristics of and discuss the usage of various classes of single-user and multiuser computer systems.
2. The computer hardware industry and users are implementing green computing designs and products.	▉ Define the term green computing and identify the primary goals of this program.
3. Systems and application software are critical in helping individuals and organisations achieve their goals.	▉ Identify and briefly describe the functions of the two basic kinds of software. ▉ Outline the role of the operating system and identify the features of several popular operating systems.
4. Organisations should not develop proprietary application software unless doing so will meet a compelling business need that can provide a competitive advantage.	▉ Discuss how application software can support personal, workgroup and enterprise business objectives. ▉ Identify three basic approaches to developing application software and discuss the pros and cons of each.
5. Organisations should choose a programming language whose functional characteristics are appropriate for the task at hand, considering the skills and experience of the programming staff.	▉ Outline the overall evolution and importance of programming languages and clearly differentiate among the generations of programming languages.
6. The software industry continues to undergo constant change; users need to be aware of recent trends and issues to be effective in their business and personal life.	▉ Identify several key software issues and trends that have an impact on organisations and individuals.

Organisations invest in computer hardware and software to improve worker productivity, increase revenue, reduce costs and provide better customer service. Those that don't may be stuck with outdated hardware and software that is unreliable and cannot take advantage of the latest advances. As a result, obsolete hardware and software can place an organisation at a competitive disadvantage. Managers, no matter what their career field and educational background, are expected to know enough about their business needs to be able to ask tough questions of those recommending the hardware and software to meet those needs. This is especially true in small organisations that might not have information systems specialists. Cooperation and sharing of information between business managers and IT managers is needed to make wise IT investments that yield real business results. Managers in marketing, sales and human resources often help IS specialists assess opportunities to apply hardware and software and evaluate the various options and features. Managers in finance and accounting especially must also keep an eye on the bottom line, guarding against overspending, yet be willing to invest in computer hardware and software when and where business conditions warrant it.

Today's use of technology is practical – it's intended to yield real business benefits. Employing information technology and providing additional processing capabilities can increase employee productivity, expand business opportunities and allow for more flexibility. This chapter discusses the hardware and software components of a computer-based information system (CBIS), beginning with a definition of hardware.

Hardware refers to the physical components of a computer that perform the input, processing, storage and output activities of the computer. When making hardware decisions, the overriding consideration of a business should be how hardware can support the objectives of the information system and the goals of the organisation.

2.1 Computer Systems: Integrating the Power of Technology

To assemble an effective and efficient system, you should select and organise components, while understanding the trade-offs between overall system performance and cost, control and complexity. For instance, in building a car, manufacturers try to match the intended use of the vehicle to its components. Racing cars, for example, require special types of engines, transmissions and tires. Selecting a transmission for a racing car requires balancing how much engine power can be delivered to the wheels (efficiency and effectiveness) with how expensive the transmission is (cost), how reliable it is (control) and how many gears it has (complexity). Similarly, organisations assemble computer systems so that they are effective, efficient and well suited to the tasks that need to be performed.

Because the business needs and their importance vary at different companies, the IS solutions they choose can be quite different.

People involved in selecting their organisation's computer hardware must clearly understand current and future business requirements, so they can make informed acquisition decisions. Consider the following examples of applying business knowledge to reach critical hardware decisions.

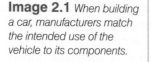

Image 2.1 *When building a car, manufacturers match the intended use of the vehicle to its components.*

2.2 Hardware Components

Computer system hardware components include devices that perform the functions of input, processing, data storage and output (see Figure 2.1).

Figure 2.1 Hardware Components
These components include the input devices, output devices, communications devices, primary and secondary storage devices, and the central processing unit (CPU). The control unit, the arithmetic/logic unit (ALU) and the register storage areas constitute the CPU.

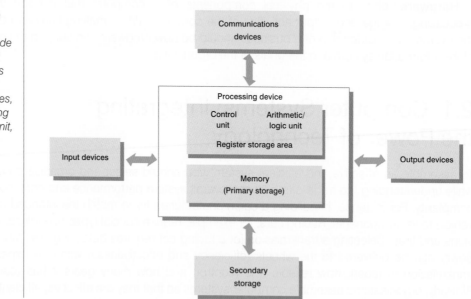

central processing unit (CPU)
The part of the computer that consists of three associated elements: the arithmetic/logic unit, the control unit and the register areas.

The ability to process (organise and manipulate) data is a critical aspect of a computer system in which processing is accomplished by an interplay between one or more of the central processing units and primary storage. Each **central processing unit (CPU)** consists of two primary elements: the arithmetic/logic unit and the control unit. The **arithmetic/logic unit (ALU)** performs mathematical calculations and makes logical comparisons. The **control unit** sequentially accesses program instructions, decodes them and coordinates the flow of data in and out of the ALU, primary storage and even secondary storage and various output devices. Primary memory, which holds program instructions and data, is closely associated with the CPU.

Now that you have learned about the basic hardware components and the way they function, you are ready to examine processing power, speed and capacity. These three attributes determine the capabilities of a hardware device.

arithmetic/logic unit (ALU) The part of the CPU that performs mathematical calculations and makes logical comparisons.

control unit The part of the CPU that sequentially accesses program instructions, decodes them and coordinates the flow of data in and out of the ALU, the registers, the primary storage, and even secondary storage and various output devices.

2.3 Processing and Memory Devices: Power, Speed and Capacity

The components responsible for processing – the CPU and memory – are housed together in the same box or cabinet, called the *system unit*. All other computer system devices, such as the monitor and keyboard, are linked either directly or indirectly into the system unit housing. As discussed previously, achieving IS objectives and organisational goals should be the primary consideration in selecting processing and memory devices. In this section, we investigate the characteristics of these important devices.

Processing Characteristics and Functions

Because efficient processing and timely output are important, organisations use a variety of measures to gauge processing speed. These measures include the time it takes to complete a machine cycle, clock speed and others.

Clock Speed

Each CPU produces a series of electronic pulses at a predetermined rate, called the **clock speed**, which affects machine cycle time. The control unit executes an instruction in accordance with the electronic cycle, or pulses of the CPU "clock." Each instruction takes at least the same amount of time as the interval between pulses. The shorter the interval between pulses, the faster each instruction can be executed. The clock speed for personal computers is in the multiple gigahertz (GHz), or billions of cycles per second, range.

clock speed A series of electronic pulses produced at a predetermined rate that affects machine cycle time.

Physical Characteristics of the CPU

CPU speed is also limited by physical constraints. Most CPUs are collections of digital circuits imprinted on silicon wafers, or chips, each no bigger than the tip of a pencil eraser. To turn a digital circuit within the CPU on or off, electrical current must flow through a medium (usually silicon) from point A to point B. The speed at which it travels between points can be increased by either reducing the distance between the points or reducing the resistance of the medium to the electrical current.

Memory Characteristics and Functions

Located physically close to the CPU (to decrease access time), memory provides the CPU with a working storage area for program instructions and data. The chief feature of memory is that it rapidly provides the data and instructions to the CPU.

Storage Capacity

Like the CPU, memory devices contain thousands of circuits imprinted on a silicon chip. Each circuit is either conducting electrical current (on) or not (off). Data is stored in memory as a combination of on or off circuit states. Usually 8 bits are used to represent a character, such as the letter A. Eight bits together form a **byte (B)**. In most cases, storage capacity is measured in bytes, with 1 byte equivalent to one character of data. The contents of the Library of Congress, with more than 126 million items and 530 miles of bookshelves, would require about 20 petabytes of digital storage. Table 2.1 lists units for measuring computer storage capacity.

byte (B) Eight bits that together represent a single character of data.

Table 2.1 Computer Storage Units

Name	Abbreviation	Number of Bytes
Byte	B	1
Kilobyte	KB	2^{10} or approximately 1024 bytes
Megabyte	MB	2^{20} or 1024 kilobytes (about 1 million)
Gigabyte	GB	2^{30} or 1024 megabytes (about 1 billion)
Terabyte	TB	2^{40} or 1024 gigabytes (about 1 trillion)
Petabyte	PB	2^{50} or 1024 terabytes (about 1 quadrillion)
Exabyte	EB	2^{60} or 1024 petabytes (about 1 quintillion)

Types of Memory

Several forms of memory are available. Instructions or data can be temporarily stored in **random access memory (RAM)**. RAM is temporary and volatile – RAM chips lose their contents if the current is turned off or disrupted (as in a power surge, brownout, or electrical noise generated by lightning or nearby machines). RAM chips are mounted directly on the computer's main circuit board or in chips mounted on peripheral cards that plug into the computer's main circuit board. These RAM chips consist of millions of switches that are sensitive to changes in electric current.

random access memory (RAM) A form of memory in which instructions or data can be temporarily stored.

read-only memory (ROM) A nonvolatile form of memory.

Read-only memory (ROM), another type of memory, is usually non-volatile. In ROM, the combination of circuit states is fixed, and, therefore, its contents are not lost if the power is removed. ROM provides permanent storage for data and instructions that do not change, such as programs and data from the computer manufacturer, including the instructions that tell the computer how to start up when power is turned on.

multiprocessing The simultaneous execution of two or more instructions at the same time.

multicore microprocessor A microprocessor that combines two or more independent processors into a single computer so they can share the workload and improve processing capacity.

Multiprocessing

There are a number of forms of **multiprocessing**, which involves the simultaneous execution of two or more instructions.

Multicore Microprocessor

A **multicore microprocessor** combines two or more independent processors into a single computer, so that they can share the workload and boost processing capacity. A dual-core processor is like a four-lane highway – it can handle up to twice as many cars as its two-lane predecessor without making each car drive twice as fast. In addition, a dual-core processor enables people to perform multiple tasks simultaneously, such as playing a game and burning a CD. Intel, AMD and IBM are battling for leadership in the multicore processor marketplace.

Both Intel and AMD have improved on dual processors by introducing new quad-core chips. The Intel Core i7 integrates four processors onto a single chip and lets them share a common L3 cache.[1] AMD recently launched its quad-core Phenom II X4 Black Edition CPU, which operates at 3.4 GHz. Although the AMD clock speed is slightly faster than the Intel Core i7, comparing clock speed of two CPUs with different architectures means little. The entire computer system must be designed so that the CPU works well with main memory and the other components of the computer. The Intel Core i7 processor surpasses the AMD Phenom processor based on the results of various computing benchmarks.[2] IBM introduced its Power7 chip with eight processing cores. Because each core can process four tasks or threads, the chip provides a 32-core processor. With this powerful processor "electric utilities can move from processing less than one million metres per day, in a typical [power] grid, to more than 85 million reads per day in a smart grid."[3]

Parallel Computing

Another form of multiprocessing, called **parallel processing**, speeds processing by linking several processors to operate at the same time, or in parallel. The most frequent uses for parallel computing include modelling, simulation and analyzing large amounts of data. Parallel computing is used in medicine to develop new imaging systems to complete ultrasound scans in less time with greater accuracy, for example, enabling doctors to provide better diagnosis to patients. Instead of building physical models of new products, engineers can create a virtual model of them and use parallel computing to test how the products work and then change design elements and materials as needed. Clothing designers can simulate the look and movement of new designs on virtual models, reducing the development time for a seasonal clothing collection to just over one month from the traditional six-month period.[4]

parallel computing The simultaneous execution of the same task on multiple processors to obtain results faster.

Grid Computing

Grid computing is the use of a collection of computers, often owned by many people or organisations, to work in a coordinated manner to solve a common problem. Grid computing is one low-cost approach to parallel processing. The grid can include dozens, hundreds, or even thousands of computers that run collectively to solve extremely large parallel processing problems. Key to the success of grid computing is a central server that acts as the grid leader and traffic monitor. This controlling server divides the computing task into subtasks and assigns the work to computers on the grid that have (at least temporarily) surplus processing power. The central server also monitors the processing, and, if a member of the grid fails to complete a subtask, it will restart or reassign the task. When all the subtasks are completed, the controlling server combines the results and advances to the next task until the whole job is completed.

grid computing The use of a collection of computers, often owned by multiple individuals or organisations, to work in a coordinated manner to solve a common problem.

IBM launched the World Community Grid project in 2004 to harness the unused computing power of personal and business computers into a large-scale public computing grid. Researchers at the University of Texas Medical Branch (UTMB) used the computer power of more than 1 million devices attached to the grid to test drug candidates for new and drug-resistant flu strains, such as H1N1. Stan Watowich, the lead researcher at UTMB claims that "we expect to identify new influenza drug candidates in less than a month. We can move from computer calculations into laboratory testing more quickly and with a sharper focus."[5]

2.4 Secondary Storage and Input and Output Devices

As you have seen, memory is an important factor in determining overall computer system power. However, memory provides only a small amount of storage area for the data and instructions the CPU requires for processing. Computer systems also need to store larger amounts of data, instructions and information more permanently than main memory allows. Secondary storage, also called *permanent storage*, serves this purpose.

Compared with memory, secondary storage offers the advantages of nonvolatility, greater capacity and greater economy. Most forms of secondary storage are considerably less expensive than memory (see Table 2.2). Because of the electromechanical processes involved in using secondary storage, however, it is considerably slower than memory. The selection of secondary storage media and devices requires understanding their primary characteristics – access method, capacity and portability.

Table 2.2 Cost Comparison for Various Forms of Data Storage

Description	Cost	Storage Capacity (GB)	Cost per GB
72 GB DAT 72 data cartridge	€11	72	€0.15
50 4.7 GB DVD+R disks	€17	235	€0.07
20 GB 4 mm backup data tape	€5	20	€0.25
500 GB portable hard drive	€87	500	€0.17
25 GB rewritable Blu-ray disc	€8	25	€0.32
9.1 GB write-once, read-many optical disc	€69	9.1	€7.50
4 GB flash drive	€8	4	€2.00
1 TB desktop external hard drive	€91	1000	€0.09
2 GB DDR2 SDRAM memory upgrade	€38	2	€19.00

SOURCE: Office Depot website, *www.officedepot.com*, December 9, 2009.

Access Methods

sequential access A retrieval method in which data must be accessed in the order in which it is stored.

direct access A retrieval method in which data can be retrieved without the need to read and discard other data.

sequential access storage device (SASD) A device used to sequentially access secondary storage data.

Data and information access can be either sequential or direct. **Sequential access** means that data must be accessed in the order in which it is stored. For example, inventory data stored sequentially may be stored by part number, such as 100, 101, 102 and so on. If you want to retrieve information on part number 125, you need to read and discard all the data relating to parts 001 through 124.

Direct access means that data can be retrieved directly, without having to pass by other data in sequence. With direct access, it is possible to go directly to and access the needed data – such as part number 125 – without reading through parts 001 through 124. For this reason, direct access is usually faster than sequential access. The devices used to sequentially access secondary storage data are simply called **sequential access storage devices (SASDs)**;

those used for direct access are called **direct access storage devices (DASDs)**.

direct access storage device (DASD) A device used for direct access of secondary storage data.

Secondary Storage Devices

The most common forms of secondary storage include magnetic tapes, magnetic discs and optical discs. Some of these media (magnetic tape) allow only sequential access, whereas others (magnetic and optical discs) provide direct and sequential access.

Magnetic Tapes

One common secondary storage medium is **magnetic tape**. Similar to the kind of tape found in audio and video cassettes, magnetic tape is a Mylar film coated with iron oxide. Portions of the tape are magnetised to represent bits. Magnetic tape is a sequential access storage medium. Although access is slower, magnetic tape is usually less expensive than disc storage. Magnetic tape is often used to back up disc drives and to store data off-site for recovery in case of disaster. Technology is improving to provide tape storage devices with greater capacities and faster transfer speeds. Large, bulky tape drives have been replaced with much smaller tape cartridge devices measuring a few millimetres in diameter that take up much less floor space and allow hundreds of tape cartridges to be stored in a small area.

magnetic tape A type of sequential secondary storage medium, now used primarily for storing backups of critical organisational data in the event of a disaster.

Magnetic Disks

Magnetic disks are also coated with iron oxide; they can be thin metallic platters (hard disks, see Figure 2.2) or Mylar film (diskettes). As with magnetic tape, magnetic disks represent bits using small magnetised areas. Magnetic disks are direct access storage devices that enable fast data retrieval and are used by companies that need to respond quickly to customer requests. For example, if a manager needs information on the credit history of a customer or the seat availability on a particular flight, the information can be obtained in seconds, if the data is stored on a direct access storage device.

magnetic disc A direct access storage device, with bits represented by magnetised areas.

SOURCE: Courtesy of Seagate Technology.

Figure 2.2 Hard Disc
Hard disks provide direct access to stored data. The read/write head can move directly to the location of a desired piece of data, dramatically reducing access times as compared to magnetic tape.

RAID

Companies' data storage needs are expanding rapidly. Today's storage configurations routinely entail many hundreds of gigabytes. However, putting the company's data online involves a serious business risk – the loss of critical business data can put a corporation out of operation. The concern is that the most critical mechanical components inside a disc storage device – the disc drives, the fans and other input/output devices – can break.

Organisations now require their data-storage devices to be fault tolerant – they can continue with little or no loss of performance in the event of a failure of one or more key components. **Redundant array of independent/inexpensive disks (RAID)** is a method of storing data so that, if a hard drive

redundant array of independent/inexpensive disks (RAID) A method of storing data that generates extra bits of data from existing data, allowing the system to create a "reconstruction map" so that if a hard drive fails, the system can rebuild lost data.

fails, the lost data on that drive can be rebuilt. With this approach, data is stored redundantly on different physical disc drives using a technique called *stripping* to evenly distribute the data. Point360 is a post-production company based in Burbank, California that edits, masters, reformats and archives video files for its TV and film production clients. The firm implemented a RAID storage solution to provide a greater level of security and to manage the increasing amount of storage required by high-definition video and sophisticated visual effect rendering.[6]

Virtual Tape

Virtual tape is a storage technology for less frequently needed data so that it appears to be stored entirely on tape cartridges, although some parts might actually be located on faster hard disks. The software associated with a virtual tape system is sometimes called a *virtual tape server*. Virtual tape can be used with a sophisticated storage-management system that moves data to slower but less costly forms of storage media as people use the data less often. Virtual tape technology can decrease data access time, lower the total cost of ownership and reduce the amount of floor space consumed by tape operations. The IS organisation at Boston Medical Center is responsible for maintaining more than 400 TB of data associated with the operation of this 581-bed academic medical centre. The organisation adopted a virtual tape management system to cope with a 50 per cent annual data growth rate, while keeping data storage costs under control and meeting strict regulatory requirements.[7]

> **virtual tape** A storage device for less frequently needed data so that it appears to be stored entirely on tape cartridges, although some parts of it might actually be located on faster hard disks.

SAN

A **storage area network (SAN)** uses computer servers, distributed storage devices and networks to tie everything together, as shown in Figure 2.3. To increase the speed of storing and retrieving data, high-speed communications channels are often used. Although SAN technology is relatively new, a number of companies are using SAN to successfully and efficiently store critical data. Austar is a major subscription TV provider in Australia that provides digital satellite services to some 713 000 subscribers.[8] The company employs a 60 terabyte SAN to keep a record of every transaction and interaction it has with customers. "It is all valuable information," says CIO Dean Walters. "Through those touch points we generate a lot of intelligence around the mood, openness, and attitudes to service of our customers. Importantly, we learn about a customer's propensity to leave the service."[9]

> **storage area network (SAN)** A special-purpose, high-speed network that provides high-speed connections among data-storage devices and computers over a network.

Figure 2.3 Storage Area Network
A SAN provides high-speed connections between data-storage devices and computers over a network.

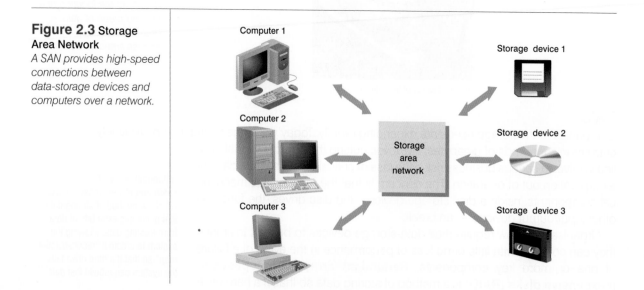

Optical Discs

A common optical disc is the **compact disc read-only memory (CD-ROM)** with a storage capacity of 740 MB of data. After data is recorded on a CD-ROM, it cannot be modified – the disc is "read-only." A CD burner, the informal name for a CD recorder, is a device that can record data to a compact disc. *CD-recordable (CD-R)* and *CD-rewritable (CD-RW)* are the two most common types of drives that can write CDs, either once (in the case of CD-R) or repeatedly (in the case of CD-RW). CD-rewritable (CD-RW) technology allows PC users to back up data on CDs.

compact disc read-only memory (CD-ROM) A common form of optical disc on which data cannot be modified once it has been recorded.

Digital Video Disc

A **digital video disc or digital versatile disc** (DVD) is a CD-ROM look alike with the ability to store about 135 minutes of digital video or several gigabytes of data (see Figure 2.4). Software programs, video games, and movies are common uses for this storage medium.

digital video disc or digital versatile disc A storage medium used to store software, video games and movies.

SOURCE: Courtesy of LaCie USA.

Figure 2.4 Digital Video Disc and Player
DVDs look like CDs but have a greater storage capacity and can transfer data at a faster rate.

DVDs have replaced recordable and rewritable CD discs (CD-R and CD-RW) as the preferred format for sharing movies and photos. Whereas a CD can hold about 740 MB of data, a single-sided DVD can hold 4.7 GB, with double-sided DVDs having a capacity of 9.4 GB. Recordings can be made on record-once discs (DVD-R and DVD+R) or on rewritable discs (DVD-RW, DVD+RW, and DVD-RAM). Not all types of rewritable DVDs are compatible with other types.

The Blu-ray high-definition video disc format based on blue-laser technology stores at least three times as much data as a DVD now holds. The primary use for this new format is in home entertainment equipment to store high-definition video, though this format can also store computer data.

The Holographic Versatile Disc (HVD) is an advanced optical disc technology still in the development stage that would store more data than even the Blu-ray optical disc system. HVD devices are under development with the potential to transfer data at the rate of 1 to 20 GB per second and store up to 6 TB of data on a single optical disc.

Solid State Secondary Storage Devices

Solid state storage devices (SSDs) store data in memory chips rather than magnetic or optical media. These memory chips require less power and provide faster data access than magnetic data-storage devices. In addition, SSDs have few moving parts, so they are less fragile than hard disc drives. All these factors make the SSD a preferred choice for portable computers. Two current disadvantages of SSD are their high cost per GB of data storage (roughly a 5:1 disadvantage compared to hard disks) and lower capacity compared to current hard drives. SSD is a rapidly developing technology, and future improvements will lower their cost and increase their capacity.

A Universal Serial Bus (USB) flash drive is one example of a commonly used SSD (see Figure 2.5). USB flash drives are external to the computer and are removable and rewritable. Most weigh less than an ounce and can provide storage of 1 GB to 64 GB. SanDisc manufactures flash drives that can store up to 64 GB based on technology it calls X4, which stores 4 bits of data in each of the millions of tiny storage elements on a chip called cells.[10]

Figure 2.5 Flash Drive
Flash drives are solid state storage devices.

The overall trend in secondary storage is toward use of direct access methods, higher capacity and increased portability. The business needs and needs of individual users should be considered when selecting a specific type of storage. In general, the ability to store large amounts of data and information and access it quickly can increase organisational effectiveness and efficiency.

Input Devices

Your first experience with computers is usually through input and output devices. These devices are the gateways to the computer system – you use them to provide data and instructions to the computer and receive results from it. Input and output devices are part of a computer's user interface, which includes other hardware devices and software that allow you to interact with a computer system.

As with other computer system components, an organisation should keep their business goals in mind when selecting input and output devices. For example, many restaurant chains use handheld input devices or computerised terminals that let waiters enter orders efficiently and accurately. These systems have also cut costs by helping to track inventory and market to customers.

Literally hundreds of devices can be used for data input, ranging from special-purpose devices used to capture specific types of data to more general-purpose input devices. We will now discuss several.

Personal Computer Input Devices

A keyboard and a computer mouse are the most common devices used for entry of data, such as characters, text and basic commands. Some companies are developing newer keyboards that are more comfortable, adjustable and faster to use. These keyboards, such as the split keyboard by Microsoft and others, are designed to avoid wrist and hand injuries caused by hours of keyboarding. Using the same keyboard, you can enter sketches on the touchpad and text using the keys.

You use a computer mouse to point to and click symbols, icons, menus and commands on the screen. The computer takes a number of actions in response, such as placing data into the computer system.

A keyboard and mouse are two of the most common devices for computer input. Wireless mice and keyboards are now readily available.

SOURCE: Courtesy of Hewlett-Packard Company.

Speech-Recognition Technology

Speech-recognition technology enables a computer equipped with a source of speech input, such as a microphone, to interpret human speech as an alternative means of providing data or instructions to the computer. The most basic systems require you to train the system to recognise your speech patterns or are limited to a small vocabulary of words. More advanced systems can recognise continuous speech without requiring you to break up your speech into discrete words. Very advanced systems used by the government and military can interpret a voice they have never heard and understand a rich vocabulary.

speech-recognition technology Input devices that recognise human speech.

Companies that must constantly interact with customers are eager to reduce their customer support costs, while improving the quality of their service. For example, SBI Funds Management is a fund management organisation in India with more than 5.8 million investors. The organisation deployed a speech-recognition system to replace all the services that live agents used to provide. Besides the cost savings generated by reducing staff, the system will eliminate the need for customers to wait for live agents to become available. Customers interact with the system using their natural voice and do not have to touch keys on their phone keypad.[11]

Digital Cameras

Digital cameras record and store images or video in digital form. When you take pictures, the images are electronically stored in the camera. You can download the images to a computer either directly or by using a flash memory card. After you store the images on the computer's hard disc, you can edit them, send them to another location, paste them into another application, or print them. For example, you can download a photo of your project team captured by a digital camera and then post it on a website or paste it into a project status report. Digital cameras have eclipsed film cameras used by professional photographers for photo quality and features, such as zoom, flash, exposure controls, special effects, and even video-capture capabilities. With the right software, you can add sound and handwriting to the photo.

digital camera An input device used with a PC to record and store images and video in digital form.

Canon, Casio, Nikon, Olympus, Panasonic, Pentax, Sony and other camera manufacturers offer full-featured, high-resolution digital camera models for less than $250. Some manufacturers offer pocket-sized camcorders for less than $150.

Touch-Sensitive Screens

Advances in screen technology allow display screens to function as input, as well as output, devices. By touching certain parts of a sensitive screen, you can execute a program or cause the computer to take an action. Touch-sensitive screens are frequently used at gas stations for customers to select grades of gas and request a receipt, at fast-food restaurants for order clerks to enter customer choices, at information centres in hotels to allow guests to request facts about local eating and drinking establishments, and at amusement parks to provide directions to patrons. They also are used in kiosks at airports and department stores.

Optical Data Readers

You can use a special scanning device called an *optical data reader* to scan documents. The two categories of optical data readers are optical mark recognition (OMR) and optical character recognition (OCR). You use OMR readers for test scoring and other purposes when test takers use pencils to fill in boxes on OMR paper, which is also called a "mark sense form." In comparison, most OCR readers use reflected light to recognise and scan various characters. With special software, OCR readers can convert handwritten or typed documents into digital data. After being entered, this data can be shared, modified and distributed over computer networks to hundreds or thousands of people.

US law in some states requires traffic police to record data about every car they stop. The St. Peters police department decided to comply with this by using OMR technology. The department designed a data card to capture the required data, which the officer fills in during each traffic stop. At the end of each shift, the cards are turned in and scanned. The results are summarised in two forms: an overview report to provide the required data for the state attorney general and a more detailed analysis including charts and graphs to ensure the department is meeting the needs of the citizens.[12]

Magnetic Ink Character Recognition (MICR) Devices

In the 1950s, the banking industry became swamped with paper cheques, loan applications, bank statements and so on. To remedy this overload and process documents more quickly, the industry developed *magnetic ink character recognition (MICR),* a system for reading this data quickly. With MICR, data to help clear and route cheques is placed on the bottom of a cheque or other form using a special magnetic ink. Data printed with this ink using a special character set can be read by both people and computers.

Pen Input Devices

By touching a touch screen with a pen input device, you can activate a command or cause the computer to perform a task, enter handwritten notes and draw objects and figures. Pen input requires special software and hardware. Handwriting recognition software can convert handwriting on the screen into text. The Tablet PC from Microsoft and its hardware partners can transform handwriting into typed text and store the "digital ink" just the way a person writes it. Users can use a pen to write and send email, add comments to Word documents, mark up PowerPoint presentations and even hand-draw charts in a document. That data can then be moved, highlighted, searched and converted into text. If perfected, this interface is likely to become widely used. Pen input is especially attractive if you are uncomfortable using a keyboard. The success of pen input depends on how accurately handwriting can be read and translated into digital form and at what cost.

Radio Frequency Identification

The purpose of a **Radio Frequency Identification (RFID)** system is to transmit data by a mobile device called a tag, which is read by an RFID reader and processed according to the needs of an information system program (see Figure 2.6). One popular application of RFID is to place a microchip on retail items and install in-store readers that track the inventory on the shelves to determine when shelves should be restocked. Recall that the RFID tag chip includes a special form of erasable programmable read-only memory (EPROM) that holds data about the item to

Radio Frequency Identification (RFID) A technology that employs a microchip with an antenna to broadcast its unique identifier and location to receivers.

Figure 2.6 RFID Tag
An RFID tag is small compared to current bar-coded labels used to identify items.

RFID tag

SOURCE: Courtesy of Intermec Technologies Corporation.

which the tag is attached. A radio-frequency signal can update this memory as the status of the item changes. The data transmitted by the tag might provide identification, location information, or details about the product tagged, such as date manufactured, retail price, colour, or date of purchase.

The Newmount Leeville Gold Mine in Nevada uses RFID technology to track miners, equipment and vehicles. RFID tags are placed in the miners' cap lamps and mounted to vehicles and equipment to transmit real-time location data so the company can track where miners are working and quickly locate them in the event of an accident.[13]

Output Devices

Computer systems provide output to decision makers at all levels of an organisation so they can solve a business problem or capitalise on a competitive opportunity. In addition, output from one computer system can provide input into another computer system. The desired form of this output might be visual, audio, or even digital. Whatever the output's content or form, output devices are designed to provide the right information to the right person in the right format at the right time.

Display Monitors

The display monitor is a device used to display the output from the computer. Because early monitors used a cathode-ray tube to display images, they were sometimes called *CRTs*. The cathode-ray tubes generate one or more electron beams. As the beams strike a phosphorescent compound (phosphor) coated on the inside of the screen, a dot on the screen, called a pixel, lights up. A **pixel** is a dot of colour on a photo image or a point of light on a display screen. It appears in one of two modes: on or off. The electron beam sweeps across the screen so that, as the phosphor starts to fade, it is struck and lights up again.

A **plasma display** uses thousands of smart cells (pixels) consisting of electrodes and neon and xenon gases that are electrically turned into plasma (electrically charged atoms and negatively charged particles) to emit light. The plasma display lights up the pixels to form an image based on the information in the video signal. Each pixel is made up of three types of light – red, green and blue. The plasma display varies the intensities of the lights to produce a full range of colours. Plasma displays can produce high resolution and accurate representation of colours to create a high-quality image.

pixel A dot of colour on a photo image or a point of light on a display screen.

plasma display A type of display using thousands of smart cells (pixels) consisting of electrodes and neon and xenon gases that are electrically turned into plasma (electrically charged atoms and negatively charged particles) to emit light.

2

LCD display Flat display that uses liquid crystals – organic, oil-like material placed between two polarisers – to form characters and graphic images on a backlit screen.

organic light-emitting diode (OLED) display Flat display that uses a layer of organic material sandwiched between two conductors, which, in turn, are sandwiched between a glass top plate and a glass bottom plate so that when electric current is applied to the two conductors, a bright, electro-luminescent light is produced directly from the organic material.

LCD displays are flat displays that use liquid crystals – organic, oil-like material placed between two polarisers – to form characters and graphic images on a backlit screen. These displays are easier on your eyes than CRTs, because they are flicker-free, brighter, and they do not emit the type of radiation that concerns some CRT users. In addition, LCD monitors take up less space and use less than half of the electricity required to operate a comparably sized CRT monitor.

Organic light-emitting diode (OLED) uses a layer of organic material sandwiched between two conductors, which, in turn, are sandwiched between a glass top plate and a glass bottom plate. When electric current is applied to the two conductors, a bright, electro-luminescent light is produced directly from the organic material. OLEDs can provide sharper and brighter colours than LCDs and CRTs, and, because they do not require a backlight, the displays can be half as thick as LCDs, and they are flexible. Another big advantage is that OLEDs do not break when dropped. OLED technology can also create 3D video displays by taking a traditional LCD monitor and then adding layers of transparent OLED films to create the perception of depth without the need for 3D glasses or laser optics. The iZ3D monitor is capable of displaying in both 2D and 3D mode. The manufacturer offered a 22-inch version of the monitor at a price of 400 euro to coincide with the debut of *Avatar*, a film directed by James Cameron.

Because most users leave their computers on for hours at a time, power usage is an important factor when deciding which type of monitor to purchase. Although the power usage varies from model to model, LCD monitors generally consume between 35 and 50 per cent less power than plasma screens.[14] OLED monitors use even less power than LCD monitors.

Printers and Plotters

Hard copy is paper output from a device called a printer. Printers with different speeds, features and capabilities are available. Some can be set up to accommodate different paper forms, such as blank cheque forms, invoice forms and so forth. Newer printers allow businesses to create customised, printed output for each customer from standard paper and data input using full colour.

The speed of the printer is typically measured by the number of pages printed per minute (ppm). Like a display screen, the quality, or resolution, of a printer's output depends on the number of dots printed per inch (dpi). A 600-dpi printer prints more clearly than a 300-dpi printer. A recurring cost of using a printer is the inkjet or laser cartridge that is used as pages are printed. Figure 2.7 shows an inkjet printer.

Laser printers are generally faster than inkjet printers and can handle more volume than inkjet printers. Laser printers print 25 to 60 ppm for black and white and 6 to 25 ppm for colour. Inkjet printers that can print 12 to 40 ppm for black and white and 5 to 20 ppm for colour are available for less than $200.

Plotters are a type of hard-copy output device used for general design work. Businesses typically use these devices to generate paper or acetate blueprints, schematics, and drawings of buildings or new products onto paper or transparencies.

Digital Audio Player

digital audio player A device that can store, organise, and play digital music files.

A **digital audio player** is a device that can store, organise and play digital music files. MP3 (MPEG-1 Audio Layer-3) is a popular format for compressing a sound sequence into a very small file, while preserving the original level of sound quality when it is played. By compressing the sound file, it requires less time to download the file and less storage space on a hard drive.

You can use many different music devices about the size of a cigarette pack to download music from the internet and other sources. These devices have no moving parts and can store hours of music. Apple expanded into the digital music market with an MP3 player (the iPod) and the iTunes Music Store, which allows you to find music online, preview it and download it in a way that is safe,

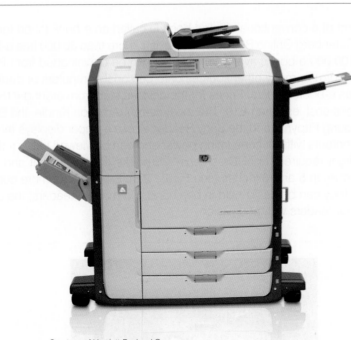

SOURCE: Courtesy of Hewlett-Packard Company.

Figure 2.7 The Hewlett-Packard CM8060 Inkjet Printer

legal and affordable. The Apple iPod has a 2.5-inch screen and can play video, including selected TV shows you can download from the iTunes Music Store. Other MP3 manufacturers include Dell, Sony, Samsung, Iomega and Motorola, whose Rokr product is the first iTunes-compatible phone.

The Apple iPod Touch, with a 3.5-inch wide screen, is a music player that also plays movies and TV shows, displays photos and connects to the internet. You can, therefore, use it to view YouTube videos, buy music online, check email and more. The display automatically adjusts the view when it is rotated from portrait to landscape. An ambient light sensor adjusts brightness to match the current lighting conditions.

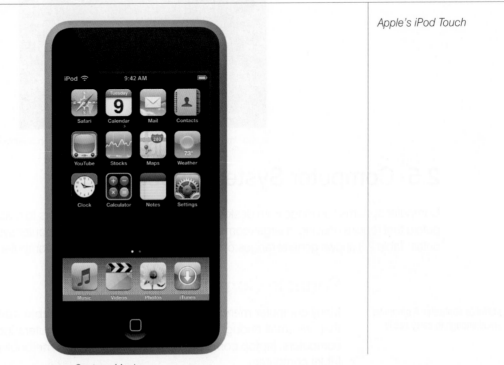

Apple's iPod Touch

SOURCE: Courtesy of Apple.

2

E-Books

The digital media equivalent of a conventional printed book is called an *e-book* (short for electronic book). The Project Gutenberg Online Book Catalogue lists more than 30 000 free e-books and a total of more than 100 000 e-books available. E-books can be downloaded from Project Gutenberg (*www.gutenberg.org*) or many other sources onto personal computers or dedicated hardware devices known as e-book readers. Prices for the devices start from around €150 and downloads of popular books cost less than €10. The most current Amazon Kindle, the Barnes and Nobel Nook, the Samsung Papyrus and the Sony Reader all use e-paper displays that look like printed pages, store contents without consuming power and can be viewed using reflected light rather than the backlight required for LCD screens.[15] E-books are lightweight and come with a display screen of between 5 and 8 inches (see Figure 2.8). E-books are more compact than most paperbacks so they can be easily held in one hand. On many e-readers, the size of the text can be magnified for readers with poor vision.

Figure 2.8 E-book
The speed and convenience of e-books has convinced many people to purchase e-book readers.

SOURCE: Image © 2010, Photosani. Used under licence from Shutterstock.com

2.5 Computer System Types

Computer systems can range from desktop (or smaller) portable computers to massive supercomputers that require housing in large rooms. Let's examine the types of computer systems in greater detail. Table 2.3 shows general ranges of capabilities for various types of computer systems.

Portable Computers

portable computer A computer small enough to carry easily.

Many computer manufacturers offer a variety of **portable computers**, those that are small enough to carry easily. Portable computers include handheld computers, laptop computers, notebook computers, netbook computers and tablet computers.

Table 2.3 Types of Computer Systems

Single-user computer systems can be divided into two groups – portable computers and nonportable computers. Multiple-user computer systems include servers, mainframes and supercomputers.

Factor	Single-User Systems				
	Portable Computers				
	Handheld	**Laptop**	**Notebook**	**Netbook**	**Tablet**
Cost	€100–€300	€400–€1200	€150–€600	€150–€600	€600–€2000
Weight (pounds)	<0.15	<3	<2.5	<1	<2.5
Screen size (inches)	2.4–3.6	13.0–15.0	12.0–14.0	7.0–11.0	11.0–14.0
Typical use	Organise personal data	Improve worker productivity	Improve productivity of highly mobile worker	Access the internet and email	Capture data via pen input, improve worker productivity

Factor	Nonportable Computers			
	Thin Client	**Desktop**	**Nettop**	**Workstation**
Cost	€150–€600	€400–€2000	<€200	€600–€4000
Weight (pounds)	<0.5	<14	<2.5	<16
Screen size (inches)	10.0–15.0	13.0–27.0	Comes w/o monitor	13.0–27.0
Typical use	Enter data and accessthe internet	Improve worker productivity	Replace desktop with small, low-cost, low-energy computer	Perform engineering, CAD, and software development

Factor	Multiple-User Computers		
	Server	**Mainframe**	**Supercomputer**
Cost	€400–€38 000	€80 000	€200 000
Weight (pounds)	>11	>45	>45
Screen size (inches)	n/a	n/a	n/a
Typical use	Perform network and internet applications	Perform computing tasks for large organisations and provide massive data storage	Run scientific applications; perform intensive number crunching

Handheld computers are single-user computers that provide ease of portability because of their small size – some are as small as a credit card. These systems often include a variety of software and communications capabilities. Most can communicate with desktop computers over wireless networks. Some even add a built-in GPS receiver with software that can integrate location data into the application. For example, if you click an entry in an electronic address book, the device displays a map and directions from your current location. Such a computer can also be mounted in your car and serve as a navigation system. One of the shortcomings of handheld computers is that they require a lot of power relative to their size.

handheld computer A single-user computer that provides ease of portability because of its small size.

smartphone A phone that combines the functionality of a mobile phone, personal digital assistant, camera, web browser, email tool and other devices into a single handheld device.

A **smartphone** combines the functionality of a mobile phone, camera, web browser, email tool, MP3 player and other devices into a single handheld device.

laptop computer A personal computer designed for use by mobile users; it is small and light enough to sit comfortably on a user's lap.

A **laptop computer** is a personal computer designed for use by mobile users. It is small and light enough to sit comfortably on a user's lap. Laptop computers use a variety of flat panel technologies to produce a lightweight and thin display screen with good resolution. In terms of computing power, laptop computers can match most desktop computers and come with powerful CPUs, as well as large-capacity primary memory and disc storage. This type of computer is highly popular among students and mobile workers who carry their laptops to meetings and classes. Many personal computer users now prefer a laptop computer over a desktop because of its portability, lower energy usage and smaller space requirements. Starting in 2008, more portable computers were sold in the US than desktop computers.

notebook computer Smaller than a laptop computer, an extremely lightweight computer that weighs less than 3 kilograms and can easily fit in a briefcase.

A **notebook computer** is an extremely lightweight computer that weighs less than 3 kilograms and can easily fit in a briefcase. It is smaller and lighter than a laptop computer. When Eddie Bauer commissioned Dave Hahn, 15-time conqueror of Mount Everest, and a production crew to climb the world's highest peak as a way to promote its line of First Ascent professional climbing gear, the team packed MacBooks notebook computers so they could blog and post photos and a few minutes of video edited on their computers.[16]

netbook computer The smallest, lightest, least expensive member of the laptop computer family.

Netbook computers are the smallest (screen size of 7–10 inches), lightest (around 1 kilogram) and least expensive (€200–€600) members of the laptop computer family. They are great for tasks that do not require a lot of computing power, such as sending and receiving email or accessing the internet. Many mobile workers have purchased them due to their portability and low cost. Netbook computers are not good for users who want to run demanding applications, have many applications open at one time, or need lots of data storage capacity.

tablet computer A portable, lightweight computer with no keyboard that allows you to roam the office, home, or factory floor carrying the device like a clipboard.

Tablet computers are portable, lightweight computers with no keyboard that allow you to roam the office, home, or factory floor carrying the device like a clipboard. You can enter text with a writing stylus directly on the screen thanks to built-in handwriting recognition software. Other input methods include an optional keyboard or speech recognition. Tablet PCs that support input only via a writing stylus are called *slate computers*. The *convertible tablet PC* comes with a swivel screen and can be used as a traditional notebook or as a pen-based tablet PC.[17] Tablet computers are especially popular with students and are frequently used in the healthcare, retail, insurance and manufacturing industries because of their versatility.

The Apple iPad is a tablet computer capable of running the same software that runs on the older Apple iPhone and iPod Touch devices, giving it a library of more than 140 000 applications. It also runs software developed specifically for it. The device has a 9.7-inch screen and an on-screen keypad. It weighs less than 1 kilogram and supports internet access over wireless networks. The initial version cannot support voice communications, nor does it have a built-in camera like the iPhone has.

Nonportable Single-User Computers

Nonportable single-user computers include thin client computers, desktop computers, nettop computers and workstations.

thin client A low-cost, centrally managed computer with essential but limited capabilities and no extra drives (such as CD or DVD drives) or expansion slots.

A **thin client** is a low-cost, centrally managed computer with no extra drives (such as CD or DVD drives) or expansion slots. These computers

Image 2.2 *The iPad is a tablet computer that sits somewhere between a smartphone and a laptop.*

© Tobias Ohls/Alamy.

have limited capabilities and perform only essential applications, so they remain "thin" in terms of the client applications they include. As stripped-down computers, they do not have the storage capacity or computing power of typical desktop computers, nor do they need it for the role they play. With no hard disc, they never pick up viruses or suffer a hard disc crash. Unlike personal computers, thin clients download data and software from a network when needed, making support, distribution and updating of software applications much easier and less expensive.

Tokio Marine and Nichido Fire Insurance Company began deploying some 30 000 thin client systems in 2009 and estimates that the total cost of ownership of the thin clients will be about 30 per cent less than deploying full-fledged computers. In addition, because no data is stored on the thin client systems, the firm will be able to implement a highly secure computing environment that carefully safeguards customer data.[18]

Desktop computers are single-user computer systems that are highly versatile. Named for their size, desktop computers can provide sufficient computing power, memory and storage for most business computing tasks. The Apple iMac is a family of Macintosh desktop computers, first introduced in 1998, in which all the components (including the CPU, the disc drives and so on) fit behind the display screen.

desktop computer A relatively small, inexpensive, single-user computer that is highly versatile.

A **nettop computer** is an inexpensive desktop computer designed to be smaller and lighter and to consume one-tenth the power of a traditional desktop computer.[19] It is designed to perform basic processing tasks, such as internet surfing, document processing and audio/video playback. Unlike netbook computers, nettop computers are not designed to be portable; they come without a monitor, but they may include an optical drive (CD/DVD). Businesses are considering using nettop computers, because they are inexpensive to buy and run, so they can improve an organisation's profitability.

nettop computer An inexpensive desktop computer designed to be smaller, lighter and consume much less power than a traditional desktop computer.

Workstations are more powerful than personal computers but still small enough to fit on a desktop. They are used to support engineering and technical users who perform heavy mathematical computing, computer-aided design (CAD) and other applications requiring a high-end processor. Such users need very powerful CPUs, large amounts of main memory and extremely high-resolution graphic displays. Workstations are typically much more expensive than the average desktop computer. Blue Sky Studios used powerful workstations for

workstation A more powerful personal computer used for mathematical computing, computer-aided design and other high-end processing but still small enough to fit on a desktop.

the rendering of the animated feature *Ice Age: Dawn of the Dinosaurs*. The new workstations provided Blue Sky animators with more powerful design tools to create images for the film in a much shorter time period.[20]

Multiple-User Computer Systems

Multiple-user computers are designed to support workgroups from a small department of two or three workers to large organisations with tens of thousands of employees and millions of customers. Multiple-user systems include servers, mainframe computers and supercomputers.

server A computer used by many users to perform a specific task, such as running network or internet applications.

A **server** is a computer used by many users to perform a specific task, such as running network or internet applications. Servers typically have large memory and storage capacities, along with fast and efficient communications abilities. A web server handles internet traffic and communications. An enterprise server stores and provides access to programs that meet the needs of an entire organisation. A file server stores and coordinates program and data files. Server systems consist of multiuser computers, including supercomputers, mainframes and other servers. Often an organisation will house a large number of servers in the same room where access to the machines can be controlled and authorised support personnel can more easily manage and maintain them from this single location. Such a facility is called a *server farm*.

The amazing 3D images of a futuristic world and the blue creatures from the movie *Avatar* were created by Weta Digital, Ltd., a visual effects company near Wellington, New Zealand. The 3D image rendering was performed on some 4000 Hewlett-Packard blade servers in Weta's 10 000 square foot server farm.[21]

blade server A server that houses many individual computer motherboards that include one or more processors, computer memory, computer storage, and computer network connections.

A **blade server** houses many computer motherboards that include one or more processors, computer memory, computer storage and computer network connections. These all share a common power supply and air-cooling source within a single chassis. By placing many blades into a single chassis and then mounting multiple chassis in a single rack, the blade server is more powerful but less expensive than traditional systems based on mainframes or server farms of individual computers. In addition, the blade server approach requires much less physical space than traditional server farms.

mainframe computer A large, powerful computer often shared by hundreds of concurrent users connected to the machine via terminals.

A **mainframe computer** is a large, powerful computer shared by dozens or even hundreds of concurrent users connected to the machine over a network. The mainframe computer must reside in a data centre with special heating, ventilating and air-conditioning (HVAC) equipment to control temperature, humidity and dust levels. In addition, most mainframes are kept in a secure data centre with limited access to the room. The construction and maintenance of a controlled-access room with HVAC can add hundreds of thousands of euros to the cost of owning and operating a mainframe computer.

The mainframe can handle the millions of daily transactions associated with airline, automobile and hotel/motel reservation systems. It can process the tens of thousands of daily queries necessary to provide data to decision support systems. Its massive storage and input/output capabilities enable it to play the role of a video computer, providing full-motion video to multiple, concurrent users.

supercomputers The most powerful computer systems with the fastest processing speeds.

Supercomputers are the most powerful computers with the fastest processing speed and highest performance. They are *special-purpose machines* designed for applications that require extensive and rapid computational capabilities. Originally, supercomputers were used primarily by government

IBM's Sequoia will be the fastest supercomputer in the world when it becomes operational in 2012 and can perform calculations at the rate of 20 petaflops – equivalent to an astounding 3 million computations by every human on the planet each second!

SOURCE: Courtesy of IBM Corporation.

agencies to perform the high-speed number crunching needed in weather forecasting and military applications. With recent reductions in the cost of these machines, they are now used more broadly for commercial purposes.

2.6 Green Computing

Green computing is concerned with the efficient and environmentally responsible design, manufacture, operation and disposal of IS-related products, including all types of computers, printers and printer materials, including cartridges and toner. Business organisations recognise that going green is in their best interests in terms of public relations, safety of employees and the community at large. They also recognise that green computing presents an opportunity to substantially reduce total costs over the life cycle of their IS equipment. Green computing has three goals: reduce the use of hazardous material, enable companies to lower their power-related costs (including potential cap and trade fees) and enable the safe disposal or recycling of some 700 000 tons of computers each year.

> **green computing** A program concerned with the efficient and environmentally responsible design, manufacture, operation and disposal of IS-related products.

Computer manufacturers, such as Apple, Dell and Hewlett-Packard, have long competed on the basis of price and performance. As the difference among the manufacturers in these two arenas narrows, support for green computing is emerging as a new business strategy for these companies to distinguish themselves from the competition. Apple claims to have the "greenest lineup of notebooks" and is making progress at removing toxic chemicals. Dell's new mantra is to become "the greenest technology company on Earth." Hewlett-Packard highlights its long tradition of environmentalism and is improving its packaging to reduce use of materials. Hewlett-Packard is also urging computer users around the world to shut down their computers at the end of the day to save energy and reduce carbon emissions.

We now turn to the other critical component of effective computer systems – software. Like hardware, software has made great technological leaps in a relatively short time span.

Ethical and Societal Issues

2

Video Game Retailer Owns Customers' Souls

Click-through agreements or "clickwrap" are the terms and conditions users are often presented with before they are able to access an online service or download software. Users are asked to agree to the terms by clicking on a button marked "I Agree" before continuing to access the content. Many of them run to multiple pages and are written in a very dense legal style. As a result, very few people, it seems, actually read them.

Video game seller Gamestation demonstrated this very effectively when it included the following as one of its terms that users had to agree to in order to place an order:

By placing an order via this website on the first day of the fourth month of the year 2010, Anno Domini, you agree to grant us a non-transferable option to claim, for now and for ever more, your immortal soul. Should We wish to exercise this option, you agree to surrender your immortal soul, and any claim you may have on it, within 5 (five) working days of receiving written notification from gamestation.co.uk or one of its duly authorised minions.

The "first day of the fourth month" clearly marks this as an April fools joke. Only 12 per cent spotted the prank and were awarded with a Gamestation gift voucher.

Legal tests of click-through agreements are rare but not unheard of. The case Register.com *vs.* Verio was heard by the US Court of Appeals. Register.com allows internet users to run WHOIS queries to find out the name and contact details of an internet domain. In other words, a user can find out the name, physical address and email address of someone who (or an organisation that) runs a website. Verio is a web development company that designs and builds websites for clients. By using a WHOIS query, a company like Verio can get details from its customers regarding advertisements they were receiving.

Verio developed a software program that would automatically generate WHOIS queries. Register.com began to receive complaints from its customers regarding the advertisements. Register.com claimed that Verio had breached the terms of use of its WHOIS database. Verio responded that the terms were not binding since users could access the database with or without expressing consent to the terms. The court ruled in favour of Register.com, holding that contractual relationships could be formed whether or not users are required to express assent prior to using a product or service:

Nor can Verio argue that it has not assented to Register.com's terms of use. Register.com's terms of use are clearly posted on its website. The conclusion of the terms paragraph states 'by submitting this query, you agree to abide by these terms'. Verio does not argue that it was unaware of these terms, only that it was not asked to click on an icon indicating that it accepted the terms. However, in light of this sentence at the end of Register.com's terms of use, there can be no question that by proceeding to submit a WHOIS query, Verio manifested its assent to be bound by Register.com's terms of use, and a contract was formed and subsequently breached.

The clickwrap agreement had been upheld.

Law firm Steptoe&Johnson has produced advice for software producers who use click-through agreements. It suggests that users should be required to at least scroll through all the text with its response options available only at the bottom, that the text of the agreement be clear and readable in a legible font, that the user should not be able to gain access to the content (product or service) without first assenting to the terms of the agreement, that the user should be able to read the terms at his or her own pace and come back to read them again at any time, that the format and content of the terms must comply with applicable laws and that the accept or reject decision the user is asked to make be clear and unambiguous.

Disucssion Questions

1 Is it reasonable to expect users to read through and agree to a long page of legal text before they can access online content? Does it matter if it's reasonable?

2 What do you think Gamestation was trying to achieve? Do you think it succeeded?

Critical Thinking Questions

1 What are some of the ethical and other issues involved in writing and using a piece of software that automatically makes use of a service that is intended for a human to use, like a WHOIS query?

2 Could you produce some advice for users to complement the advice to companies produced by Steptoe&Johnson?

SOURCES: *http://www.huffingtonpost.com/2010/04/17/gamestation-grabs-souls-o_n_541549.html*; *http://www.icann.org/en/registrars/register.com-verio/decision-23jan04.pdf*; Kunz, Christina; Thayer, Heather; Del Duca, Maureen; and Debrow, Jennifer, 'Click-through agreements: Strategies for avoiding disputes on validity of assent.' Available from: *http://www.steptoe.com/publications/220b.pdf*.

2.7 Overview of Software

As you learned in Chapter 1, software consists of computer program that control the workings of computer hardware. **computer program** are sequences of instructions for the computer. Documentation describes the program functions to help the user operate the computer system. The program displays some documentation on screen, whereas other forms appear in external resources, such as printed manuals. People using commercially available software are usually asked to read and agree to End-User License Agreements (EULAs). After reading the EULA, you normally have to click an "I agree" button before you can use the software, which can be one of two basic types: systems software and application software.

computer program Sequences of instructions for the computer.

SOURCE: © Jim West/Alamy.

Application software has the greatest potential to affect processes that add value to a business, because it is designed for specific organisational activities and functions.

Systems software is the set of programs designed to coordinate the activities and functions of the hardware and various programs throughout the computer system. Each type of systems software is designed for a specific CPU design and class of hardware. Application software consists of programs that help users solve particular computing problems. In most cases, application software resides on the computer's hard disc before it is brought into the computer's main memory and run. Application software can also be stored on CDs, DVDs, and even flash or key chain storage devices that plug into a USB port. An increasing amount of application software is available on the web. Sometimes referred to as a *rich internet application (RIA)*, a web-delivered software application combines hardware resources of the web server and the PC to deliver valuable software services through a web browser interface. Before a person, group, or enterprise decides on the best approach for acquiring application software, they should analyze their goals and needs carefully.

Supporting Individual, Group and Organisational Goals

Every organisation relies on the contributions of individuals, groups and the entire enterprise to achieve business objectives. To help them achieve these objectives, the organisation provides them with specific application software and information systems. One useful way of classifying the many potential uses of information systems is to identify the scope of the problems and opportunities addressed by a particular organisation, called the sphere of influence. For most companies, the spheres of influence are personal, workgroup and enterprise. Table 2.4 shows how various kinds of software support these three spheres.

Table 2.4 Classifying Software by Type and Sphere of Influence

Software	Personal	Workgroup	Enterprise
Systems software	Personal computer and workstation operating systems	Network operating systems	Server and mainframe operating systems
Application software	Word processing, spreadsheet, data-base, graphics	Electronic mail, group scheduling, shared work, collaboration	General ledger, order entry, payroll, human resources

Information systems that operate within the *personal sphere of influence* serve the needs of individual users. These information systems enable users to improve their personal effectiveness, increasing the amount of work that can be done and its quality. Such software is often referred to as *personal productivity software*. For example, MindManager software from Mindjet provides tools to help people diagram complex ideas and projects using an intuitive graphic interface.[22]

A *workgroup* is two or more people who work together to achieve a common goal. A workgroup may be a large, formal, permanent organisational entity, such as a section or department or a temporary group formed to complete a specific project. An information system that operates in the *workgroup sphere of influence* supports a workgroup in the attainment of a common goal. Users of such applications must be able to communicate, interact and collaborate to be successful. People can also use online calendar software, such as Google Calendar, to store personal appointments, as well as to schedule meetings with others.[23]

Information systems that operate within the *enterprise sphere of influence* support the firm in its interaction with its environment. The surrounding environment includes customers, suppliers, shareholders, competitors, special-interest groups, the financial community and government agencies. For example, many enterprises use IBM Cognos software as a centralised web-based system where employees, partners and stakeholders can report and analyze corporate financial data.[24]

Installing and Removing New Software

Before you can use any type of software, it must be installed on a computer. Installing new software usually involves only a few setup steps. Software for personal computers typically comes on CDs or is downloaded from the web.

When possible, it is best to remove software using an add/remove software utility that comes with the operating system or that is part of some utility software, such as Norton System Works and McAfee QuickClean. This will help ensure that all elements of unwanted software are removed.

2.8 Systems Software

Controlling the operations of computer hardware is one of the most critical functions of systems software. Systems software also supports the application programs' problem-solving capabilities. Different types of systems software include operating systems and utility programs.

Operating Systems

An operating system (OS) is a set of computer program that control the computer hardware and act as an interface with application programs (see Figure 2.9). Operating systems can control one computer or multiple computers, or they can allow multiple users to interact with one computer. The various combinations of OSs, computers, and users include the following:

- *Single computer with a single user.* This system is commonly used in a personal computer or a handheld computer that allows one user at a time.

- *Single computer with multiple users.* This system is typical of larger, mainframe computers that can accommodate hundreds or thousands of people, all using the computer at the same time.

- *Multiple computers with multiple users.* This system is typical of a network of computers, such as a home network with several computers attached or a large computer network with hundreds of computers attached around the world.

- *Special-purpose computers.* This type of system is typical of a number of computers with specialised functions, such as those that control sophisticated military aircraft, space shuttles, digital cameras, or home appliances.

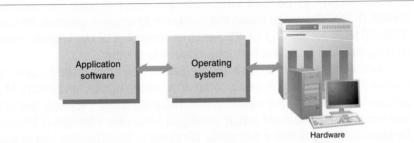

Figure 2.9 The Role of Operating Systems
The role of the operating system is to act as an interface between application software and hardware.

The OS, which plays a central role in the functioning of the complete computer system, is usually stored on disc. After a computer system is started, or "booted up," portions of the OS are transferred to memory as they are needed. You can also boot a computer from a CD, DVD, or

2

even a thumb drive that plugs into a USB port. A storage device that contains some or all of the OS is often called a "rescue disc," because you can use it to start the computer if you have problems with the primary hard disc.

The collection of programs that make up the operating system performs a variety of activities, including the following:

- Performing common computer hardware functions
- Providing a user interface and input/output management
- Providing a degree of hardware independence
- Managing system memory
- Managing processing tasks
- Providing networking capability
- Controlling access to system resources
- Managing files

Common Hardware Functions

All applications must perform certain hardware-related tasks, such as the following:

- Get input from the keyboard or another input device
- Retrieve data from disks
- Store data on disks
- Display information on a monitor or printer

Each of these tasks requires a detailed set of instructions. The OS converts a basic request into the set of detailed instructions that the hardware requires. In effect, the OS acts as an intermediary between the application and the hardware. The typical OS performs hundreds of such tasks, translating each into one or more instructions for the hardware. The OS notifies the user if input or output devices need attention, if an error has occurred and if anything abnormal happens in the system.

User Interface and Input/Output Management

user interface The element of the operating system that allows you to access and command the computer system.

command-based user interface A user interface that requires you to give text commands to the computer to perform basic activities.

graphical user interface (GUI) An interface that displays pictures (icons) and menus that people use to send commands to the computer system.

One of the most important functions of any OS is providing a **user interface**, which allows people to access and interact with the computer system. The first user interfaces for mainframe and personal computer systems were command based.

A **command-based user interface** requires text commands to be given to the computer to perform basic activities. For example, the command ERASE 00TAXRTN would cause the computer to erase or delete a file called 00TAXRTN. RENAME and COPY are other examples of commands used to rename files and copy files from one location to another.

A **graphical user interface (GUI)** displays pictures (called *icons*) and menus that people use to send commands to the computer system. Many people find that GUIs are easier to use, because users intuitively grasp the functions. Today, the most widely used graphical user interface is Windows by Microsoft. As the name suggests, Windows is based on the use of a window, or a portion of the display screen dedicated to a specific application. The screen can display several windows at once. Building on the success of the iPhone, due in no small part to its unique and advanced multitouch user interface, Windows 7 also provides strong support for interacting with its GUI through touch, which has spawned a new generation of PCs being sold with touch displays.

Hardware Independence

To run, applications request services from the OS through a defined **application program interface (API)**, as shown in Figure 2.10. Programmers can use APIs to create application software without understanding the inner workings of the operating system.

application program interface (API) An interface that allows applications to make use of the operating system.

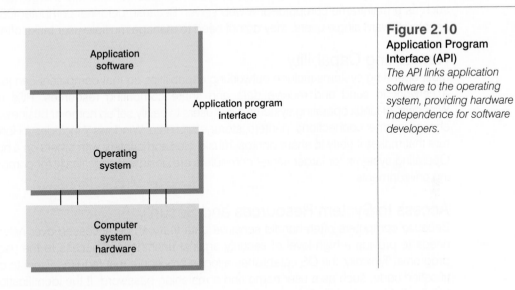

Application software

Application program interface

Operating system

Computer system hardware

Figure 2.10
Application Program Interface (API)
The API links application software to the operating system, providing hardware independence for software developers.

Memory Management

The OS also controls how memory is accessed and maximises available memory and storage. Most newer OSs manage memory better than older OSs. The memory-management feature of many OSs allows the computer to execute program instructions effectively and to speed processing. One way to increase the performance of an old computer is to upgrade to a newer OS and increase the amount of memory.

Most OSs support virtual memory, which allocates space on the hard disc to supplement the immediate, functional memory capacity of RAM. Virtual memory works by swapping programs or parts of programs between memory and one or more disc devices – a concept called paging. This reduces CPU idle time and increases the number of jobs that can run in a given time span.

Processing Tasks

The task-management features of today's OSs manage all processing activities. Task management allocates computer resources to make the best use of each system's assets. Task-management software lets one user run several programs or tasks at the same time (multitasking) and allows several users to use the same computer at the same time (time sharing).

An OS with multitasking capabilities allows a user to run more than one application at the same time. Most computer users take advantage of multitasking OSs without realising how innovative they are. Without having to exit a program, you can work in one application, easily pop into another and then jump back to the first program, picking up where you left off. Better still, while you're working in the *foreground* in one program, one or more other applications can be churning away, unseen, in the *background*, sorting a database, printing a document, or performing other lengthy operations that otherwise would monopolise your computer and leave you staring at the screen unable to perform other work. Multitasking can save users a considerable amount of time and effort.

2

Time sharing allows more than one person to use a computer system at the same time. For example, 15 customer service representatives might be entering sales data into a computer system for a mail-order company at the same time. In another case, thousands of people might be simultaneously using an online computer service to get stock quotes and valuable business news.

The ability of the computer to handle an increasing number of concurrent users smoothly is called *scalability*. This feature is critical for systems expected to handle a large number of users, such as a mainframe computer or a web server. Because personal computer OSs are usually oriented toward single users, they do not need to manage multiple-user tasks often.

Networking Capability

Most operating systems include networking capabilities so that computers can join together in a network to send and receive data and share computing resources. PCs running Mac, Windows, or Linux operating systems allow users to easily set up home or business networks for sharing internet connections, printers, storage and data. Windows 7 includes a HomeGroup feature that makes it easy to share photos, music, files and printers with others on a home network. Operating systems for larger server computers are designed specifically for computer networking environments.

Access to System Resources and Security

Because computers often handle sensitive data that can be accessed over networks, the OS needs to provide a high level of security against unauthorised access to the users' data and programs. Typically, the OS establishes a logon procedure that requires users to enter an identification code, such as a user name and a matching password. If the identification code is invalid or if the password does not match the identification code, the user cannot gain access to the computer. Some OSs require that user passwords change frequently – such as every 20 to 40 days. If the user is successful in logging on to the system, the OS restricts access to only portions of the system for which the user has been authorised. The OS records who is using the system and for how long and reports any attempted breaches of security.

File Management

The OS manages files to ensure that files in secondary storage are available when needed and that they are protected from access by unauthorised users. Many computers support multiple users who store files on centrally located disks or tape drives. The OS keeps track of where each file is stored and who can access them. The OS must determine what to do if more than one user requests access to the same file at the same time. Even on stand-alone personal computers with only one user, file management is needed to track where files are located, what size they are, when they were created and who created them.

Current Operating Systems

Early OSs were very basic. Today, however, more advanced OSs have been developed, incorporating sophisticated features and impressive graphics effects. Table 2.5 classifies a number of current OSs by sphere of influence.

Microsoft PC Operating Systems

Since a small company called Microsoft developed PC-DOS and MS-DOS to support the IBM personal computer introduced in the 1980s, personal computer OSs have steadily evolved. *PC-DOS* and *MS-DOS* had command-driven interfaces that were difficult to learn and use. Each new version of OS has improved the ease of use, processing capability, reliability and ability to support new computer hardware devices.

Table 2.5 Operating Systems Serving Three Spheres of Influence

Personal	Workgroup	Enterprise
Microsoft Windows, Microsoft Windows Mobile	Microsoft Windows Server 2008	Microsoft Windows Server 2008
Mac OS X, Mac OS X iPhone	Mac OS X Server	Linux
Linux	Linux	UNIX
Google Android, Chrome OS	UNIX	IBM i5/OS and z/OS
Palm web OS	IBM i5/OS and z/OS	HP-UX 11i
	HP-UX 11i	

Windows XP was released in fall of 2001. Previous consumer versions of Windows were notably unstable and crashed frequently, requiring frustrating and time-consuming reboots. With XP, Microsoft sought to bring reliability to the consumer.

Microsoft released *Windows Vista* in 2007 with the goal of providing a more secure and stable operating system. The new operating system includes a number of new features. The most advanced versions of Vista include a 3D graphics interface called Aero. However, the system requirements for Windows Vista with Aero require many users to purchase new, more powerful PCs. Another issue was that some software and hardware designed for Windows XP would not run on Vista.

The next version, *Windows 7*, was released in 2009 with improvements and new features. Most analysts classified Windows 7 as "Vista done right."[25] Besides addressing some of the flaws in Windows Vista, Windows 7 introduced new windows manipulation functionality that allows users to more easily find, access and work with information in files. It also features improved home networking capabilities and improved applications. Windows 7 has strong support for touch displays and netbooks, ushering in a new era of mobile computing devices.

Apple Computer Operating Systems

Although IBM system platforms traditionally use one of the Windows OSs and Intel microprocessors (often called *Wintel* for this reason), Apple computers have used non-Intel microprocessors designed by Apple, IBM and Motorola and a proprietary Apple OS – the *Mac OS*. Newer Apple computers, however, use Intel chips. Although Wintel computers hold the largest share of the business PC market, Apple computers are also quite popular, especially in the fields of publishing, education, graphic arts, music, movies and media.

The Apple OSs have also evolved over a number of years and often provide features not available from Microsoft. Recently, however, Windows and Mac platforms have evolved to share many of the same features as they compete for users. In July 2001, Mac OS X was released as an entirely new OS for the Mac based on the UNIX operating system. It included a new user interface, which provided a new visual appearance for users – including luminous and semitransparent elements, such as buttons, scroll bars, windows and fluid animation to enhance the user's experience.

Since its first release, Apple has upgraded OS X several times. Snow Leopard (OS X v10.6) is the most recent version of OS X, released in 2009 to compete with Windows 7 (see Figure 2.11).

Figure 2.11 Mac OS X
Snow Leopard

Snow Leopard includes Time Machine, a powerful backup tool that allows users to view their system as it looked in the past and resurrect deleted files. Snow Leopard also includes multiple desktops, a video chat program that allows users to pose in front of imaginary landscapes, a powerful system search utility and other updated software. Macs are also considered very secure, with no widespread virus or spyware infections to date.

Because Mac OS X runs on Intel processors, Mac users can set up their computer to run both Windows Vista and Mac OS X and select which platform they want to work with when they boot their computer. Such an arrangement is called *dual booting*. Although Macs can dual boot into Windows, the opposite is not true. Apple does not allow OS X to be run on any machine other than an Apple. However, Windows PCs can dual boot with Linux and other OSs.

Linux

Linux, sometimes known as GNU/Linux, is an OS developed by Linus Torvalds in 1991 as a student in Finland. The OS is distributed under the GNU General Public License and its source code is freely available to everyone. It is, therefore, called an open-source operating system. This doesn't mean, however, that Linux and its assorted distributions are necessarily free – companies and developers can charge money for a distribution as long as the source code remains available. Linux is actually only the kernel of an OS, the part that controls hardware, manages files, separates processes and so forth. Several combinations of Linux are available, with various sets of capabilities and applications to form a complete OS. Each of these combinations is called a *distribution* of Linux. Many distributions are available as free downloads.

Linux is available on the internet and from other sources. Popular versions include Red Hat Linux and Caldera OpenLinux. Several large computer vendors, including IBM, Hewlett-Packard and Intel, support the Linux operating system. For example, IBM has hundreds of programmers working with Linux. Linux is a popular OS for servers, distributed systems and even supercomputers. Most computer science and engineering graduates are familiar with Linux, so there is no shortage of programmers and engineers for Linux-based systems. The flexibility of the open architecture also makes it easy to customise Linux for different needs in different environments.

Google has developed its own Linux-based operating system named Chrome OS. Chrome is designed for small mobile computers and netbooks with a focus on accessing web-based information and services such as email, web browsing, social networks and Google online applications.[26]

Workgroup Operating Systems

To keep pace with user demands, the technology of the future must support a world in which network usage, data-storage requirements and data-processing speeds increase at a dramatic rate. This rapid increase in communications and data-processing capabilities pushes the boundaries of computer science and physics. Powerful and sophisticated OSs are needed to run the servers that meet these business needs for workgroups.

Windows Server

Microsoft designed *Windows Server* to perform a host of tasks that are vital for websites and corporate web applications. For example, Microsoft Windows Server can be used to coordinate large data centres. The OS also works with other Microsoft products. It can be used to prevent unauthorised disclosure of information by blocking text and emails from being copied, printed, or forwarded to other people. Microsoft *Windows Server 2008* is the most recent version of Windows Server and delivers benefits, such as a powerful web server management system, virtualisation tools that allow various operating systems to run on a single server, advanced security features and robust administrative support.

UNIX

UNIX is a powerful OS originally developed by AT&T for minicomputers – the predecessors of servers that are larger than PCs and smaller than mainframes. UNIX can be used on many computer system types and platforms, including workstations, servers and mainframe computers. UNIX also makes it much easier to move programs and data among computers or to connect mainframes and workstations to share resources. There are many variants of UNIX – including HP/UX from Hewlett-Packard, AIX from IBM, UNIX SystemV from UNIX Systems Lab, Solaris from Sun Microsystems and SCO from Santa Cruz Operations.

The online marketplace eBay uses Sun Microsystems servers, software, storage and services to run its operations. Sun's Solaris operating system manages eBay's systems, including database servers, web servers, tape libraries and identity management systems. The online auction company found that, when they switched to Sun and Solaris, system performance increased by 20 per cent.[27] The Idaho National Laboratory also uses Solaris to conduct research in their work to design more efficient and safe nuclear reactors.[28]

Red Hat Linux

Red Hat Software offers a Linux network OS that taps into the talents of tens of thousands of volunteer programmers who generate a steady stream of improvements for the Linux OS. The *Red Hat Linux* network OS is very efficient at serving web pages and can manage a cluster of up to eight servers. Linux environments typically have fewer virus and security problems than other OSs. Distributions, such as SuSE and Red Hat, have proven Linux to be a very stable and efficient OS.

Mac OS X Server

The *Mac OS X Server* is the first modern server OS from Apple Computer and is based on the UNIX OS. The most recent version is OS X Server 10.6 Snow Leopard. It includes support for 64-bit processing, along with several server functions and features that allow the easy management of network and internet services, such as email, website hosting, calendar management and sharing, wikis and podcasting.

Information Systems at Work

2

Blended Platforms at LinkedIn

Although Microsoft Windows dominates the business desktop OS market, Macs are beginning to make inroads. The popular business-focused social network, LinkedIn, finds that its employees generally have a strong preference for one operating system over another. Rather than forcing employees to use one standard operating system and compatible software, LinkedIn allows its employees to choose either the Windows or Mac platform and sometimes even Linux.

Big web companies, such as LinkedIn, hire a variety of specialists ranging from web developers and software engineers to graphic artists, designers, accountants and executives. Often professionals from different disciplines prefer one platform over another because of specific software tools designed for that platform.

Macs are especially popular with so-called techies: web developers, software engineers and programmers. They like the Mac platform because of its power and because it is based on the UNIX kernel. UNIX is popular with programmers who like to work from the command line. LinkedIn provides all of its software engineers with state-of-the-art Mac Pros (desktop PCs) and MacBooks (notebook PCs). LinkedIn uses this equipment as an enticement to attract top-of-the-line engineers. According to LinkedIn, "the Mac factor" has a big impact on developers' decisions to join the company. Some developers even set up their Macs to run both Mac OS X and Linux so that they can develop LinkedIn software to run in browsers on the Linux platform.

Artists and graphic designers are typically divided between Windows and Macs depending on what software they prefer to use. Aperture is popular photo-editing software for the Mac. However, Photoshop and other popular graphics software from Adobe are available for both Windows and Mac. Generally speaking, Mac has a long history of appealing to digital media designers. It is especially popular with video and music producers.

For business applications, Microsoft Windows is typically king. It is rare to find a Mac in a business environment. LinkedIn product managers, accountants, human resources managers, executives and other business staff have a choice of Microsoft Windows PCs or Macs. Surprisingly, 68 per cent have chosen Macs. The general popularity of the Mac in Silicon Valley might be why LinkedIn has so many Mac users. Also, Microsoft Office and other business software are available for the Mac platform.

LinkedIn's IT department now provides services to all employees over the dual platform integrated network. Mac is completely compatible with Windows and has no problem sharing files and resources over a network. LinkedIn did not have to modify its network environment to accommodate both Macs and Windows PCs. As an increasing amount of computing takes place online, rather than on the local PC, it is likely that the choice of PC platforms will become less important.

Discussion Questions

1 In what ways is LinkedIn unique in the options it provides its employees and in the choices it allows its employees to make?

2 If LinkedIn required all employees to use the same platform, how might that requirement detract from employee productivity?

Critical Thinking Questions

1 Do you think LinkedIn will serve as a trendsetter, with many businesses following suit?

2 What benefits does standardising around one platform provide for businesses?

SOURCES: Apple staff, 'LinkedIn. Not Just Your Ordinary Network," Apple Business Profiles. Available from: *www.apple.com/business/ profiles/linkedin*. Accessed October 12, 2009; LinkedIn website. Available from: *www.linkedin.com*. Accessed February 11, 2010.

Enterprise Operating Systems

Mainframe computers, often referred to as "Big Iron," provide the computing and storage capacity to meet massive data-processing requirements and offer many users high performance and excellent system availability, strong security and scalability. In addition, a wide range of application software has been developed to run in the mainframe environment, making it possible to purchase software to address almost any business problem. As a result, mainframe computers remain a popular computing platform for mission-critical business applications for many companies. Examples of mainframe OSs include z/OS from IBM, HP-UX from Hewlett-Packard and Linux.

z/OS

The *z/OS* is IBM's first 64-bit enterprise OS. It supports IBM's z900 and z800 lines of mainframes that can come with up to 16 64-bit processors. (The z stands for zero downtime.) The OS provides several new capabilities to make it easier and less expensive for users to run large mainframe computers. The OS has improved workload management and advanced e-commerce security. The IBM zSeries mainframe, like previous generations of IBM mainframes, lets users subdivide a single computer into multiple smaller servers, each of which can run a different application. In recognition of the widespread popularity of a competing OS, z/OS allows partitions to run a version of the Linux OS. This means that a company can upgrade to a mainframe that runs the Linux OS.

Germany's largest health insurance company, AOK, recently replaced its core systems with two IBM mainframe servers running z/OS. The company chose z/OS based on its reputation for high reliability and performance. AOK also uses IBM Tivoli software to assist in automating tasks in the mainframe infrastructure and storage management system. AOK is legally responsible for storing records for 30 years for its more than 25 million policy holders.[29] That level of responsibility requires the highest levels of system reliability.

HP-UX and Linux

HP-UX is a robust UNIX-based OS from Hewlett-Packard designed to handle a variety of business tasks, including online transaction processing and web applications. It supports internet database and a variety of business applications on server and mainframe enterprise system. It can work with Java programs and Linux applications. HP-UX supports Hewlett-Packard's computers and those designed to run Intel's Itanium processors. *Red Hat Enterprise Linux* for IBM mainframe computers is another example of an enterprise operating system.

Operating Systems for Small Computers, Embedded Computers and Special-Purpose Devices

New OSs and other software are changing the way we interact with smartphones, cell phones, digital cameras, TVs and other appliances. These OSs are also called *embedded operating systems*, or just *embedded systems*, because they are typically embedded within a device, such as an automobile, TV recorder, or other device. Embedded software is a multibillion dollar industry. Embedded systems are designed to perform specialised tasks. For example, an automotive embedded system might be responsible for controlling fuel injection. A digital camera's embedded system supports taking and viewing photos and may include a limited set of editing tools. An embedded system controlling an MRI machine controls a powerful magnetic field to acquire 3D images of the body. A GPS device uses an embedded system to help people find their way around town (see Figure 2.12). Some of the more popular OSs for devices are described in the following section.

Figure 2.12 GPS
Devices Use Embedded
Operating Systems
A GPS device uses an embedded system to acquire information from satellites, display your current location on a map and direct you to your destination.

SOURCE: © iStockphoto/Roberta Casaliggi.

Cell Phone Embedded Systems and Operating Systems

Cell phones have traditionally used embedded systems to provide communication and limited personal information management services to users. Symbian is the world's most widely used cell phone embedded OS and has traditionally provided voice and text communication, an address book and a few other basic applications. When RIM introduced the BlackBerry smartphone in 2002, the mobile phone's capabilities were vastly expanded. Since then, cell phone embedded systems have been transformed into full-fledged personal computer OSs, such as the iPhone OS, Google Android and Microsoft Windows Mobile. Even traditional embedded systems, such as Palm OS (now WebOS) and Symbian, have evolved into PC operating systems, with APIs and software development kits that allow developers to design hundreds of applications providing a myriad of mobile services.

Windows Embedded

Windows Embedded is a family of Microsoft OSs included with or embedded into small computer devices. Windows Embedded includes several versions that provide computing power for TV set-top boxes, automated industrial machines, media players, medical devices, digital cameras, PDAs, GPS receivers, ATMs, gaming devices and business devices, such as cash registers. Microsoft Auto provides a computing platform for automotive software, such as Ford Sync. The Ford Sync system uses an in-dashboard display and wireless networking technologies to link automotive systems with cell phones and portable media players (see Figure 2.13).

Figure 2.13 Microsoft
Auto and Ford Sync
The Ford Sync system, developed on the Microsoft Auto operating system, is a communications and entertainment system that allows you to use voice commands with portable devices, such as cell phones and media players.

SOURCE: Sam VarnHagen/FordMotor Co.

Proprietary Linux-Based Systems

Because embedded systems are typically designed for a specific purpose in a specific device, they are usually proprietary, or custom-created and owned by the manufacturer. Sony's Wii, for example, uses a custom-designed OS based on the Linux kernel. Linux is a popular choice for embedded systems, because it is free and highly configurable. In October of 2009, Nokia released the N900 smartphone – the first Linux-based smartphone.[30] Linux has been used in many embedded systems, including e-book readers, ATM machines, mobile phones, networking devices and media players. At least nine distributions of Linux are designed for embedded systems. Linux is a major competitor to Symbian in the cell phone market and Microsoft Embedded in most other markets.

2.9 Utility Programs

Utility programs help to perform maintenance or correct problems with a computer system. For example, some utility programs merge and sort sets of data, keep track of computer jobs being run, compress files of data before they are stored or transmitted over a network (thus saving space and time) and perform other important tasks. Some utility programs can help computer systems run better and longer without problems.

utility program Program that helps to perform maintenance or correct problems with a computer system.

Utility programs can also help to secure and safeguard data. For example, the publishing and motion picture industries use digital rights management (DRM) technologies to prevent copyright-protected books and movies from being unlawfully copied. The files storing the intellectual property are encoded so that software running on e-book readers and media players recognises and plays only legally obtained copies. DRM has been criticised for infringing on the freedom and rights of customers. Record companies have already moved away from DRM technologies in an effort to win the appreciation of their customers.

Although many PC utility programs come installed on computers, you can also purchase utility programs separately. Table 2.6 provides examples of some common types of utilities.

Table 2.6 Examples of Utility Programs

Personal	Workgroup	Enterprise
Software to compress data so that it takes less hard disc space	Software that maintains an archive of changes made to a shared document	Software to archive contents of a database by copying data from disc to tape
Software that assists in determining which files to delete to free up disc space	Software that monitors group activity to determine levels of participation	Software that monitors network traffic and server loads
Antivirus and antispyware software for PCs	Software that reports unsuccessful user logon attempts	Software that reports the status of a particular computer job

2.10 Application Software

Application software applies the power of a computer to give individuals, workgroups and the entire enterprise the ability to solve problems and perform specific tasks. Application programs interact with systems software, and the systems software directs the computer hardware to perform the necessary tasks.

Applications help you perform common tasks, such as creating and formatting text documents, performing calculations, or managing information, though some applications are more specialised. Application software is used throughout the medical profession to save and prolong lives. For example, Swedish Medical Center in Seattle, Washington uses content management software from Oracle to access patient records when and where they are needed.[31]

The functions performed by application software are diverse and range from personal productivity to business analysis. For example, application software can help sales managers track sales of a new item in a test market. Software from IntelliVid monitors video feeds from store security cameras and notifies security when a shopper is behaving suspiciously. Most of the computerised business jobs and activities discussed in this book involve application software. We begin by investigating the types and functions of application software.

Types and Functions of Application Software

proprietary software One-of-a-kind software designed for a specific application and owned by the company, organisation, or person that uses it.

off-the-shelf software Software mass-produced by software vendors to address needs that are common across businesses, organisations, or individuals.

The key to unlocking the potential of any computer system is application software. A company can either develop a one-of-a-kind program for a specific application (called **proprietary software**) or purchase and use an existing software program (sometimes called **off-the-shelf software**). It is also possible to modify some off-the-shelf programs, giving a blend of off-the-shelf and customised approaches. The relative advantages and disadvantages of proprietary software and off-the-shelf software are summarised in Table 2.7.

Table 2.7 A Comparison of Proprietary and Off-the-Shelf Software

Proprietary Software		Off-the-Shelf Software	
Advantages	**Disadvantages**	**Advantages**	**Disadvantages**
You can get exactly what you need in terms of features, reports and so on.	It can take a long time and significant resources to develop required features.	The initial cost is lower, because the software firm can spread the development costs over many customers.	An organisation might have to pay for features that are not required and never used.
Being involved in the development offers control over the results.	In-house system development staff may become hard pressed to provide the required level of ongoing support and maintenance because of pressure to move on to other new projects.	The software is likely to meet the basic business needs – you can analyze existing features and the performance of the package before purchasing.	The software might lack important features, thus, requiring future modification or customisation. This can be very expensive, because users must adopt future releases of the software as well.
You can modify features that you might need to counteract an initiative by competitors or to meet new supplier or customer demands. A merger with or acquisition of another firm also requires software changes to meet new business needs.	The features and performance of software that has yet to be developed present more potential risk.	The package is likely to be of high quality, because many customer firms have tested the software and helped identify its bugs.	The software might not match current work processes and data standards.

Many companies use off-the-shelf software to support business processes. In 2009, Forrester Research reported that 80 per cent of enterprises use Microsoft Office.[32] Key questions for selecting off-the-shelf software include the following: (1) Will the software run on the OS and hardware you have selected? (2) Does the software meet the essential business requirements that have been defined? (3) Is the software manufacturer financially solvent and reliable? and (4) Does the total cost of purchasing, installing and maintaining the software compare favourably to the expected business benefits?

Some off-the-shelf programs can be modified, in effect blending the off-the-shelf and customised approaches. For example, El Camino Hospital in Mountain View, California customised Microsoft's e-health management system, Amalga, to track patients with the H1N1 flu and those that may have been exposed to it.[33]

Another approach to obtaining a customised software package is to use an application service provider. An **application service provider (ASP)** is a company that can provide the software, support and computer hardware on which to run the software from the user's facilities over a network. An ASP can also simplify a complex corporate software package so that it is easier for the users to set up and manage. ASPs provide contract customisation of off-the-shelf software, and they speed deployment of new applications while helping IS managers avoid implementation headaches, reducing the need for many skilled IS staff members and decreasing project start-up expenses. Such an approach allows companies to devote more time and resources to more important tasks. For example, Rapid Advance, a leading cash advance service for small to medium-sized businesses (SMBs), uses Business Objects and Crystal Reports, applications served by SAP, to manage its business intelligence (BI). The system provides real-time access to sales information, business partner information and critical corporate reports.[34]

> **application service provider (ASP)** A company that provides software, support and the computer hardware on which to run the software from the user's facilities over a network.

Using an ASP involves some risks – sensitive information could be compromised in a number of ways, including unauthorised access by employees or computer hackers; the ASP might not be able to keep its computers and network up and running as consistently as necessary; or a disaster could disable the ASP's data centre, temporarily putting an organisation out of business. These are legitimate concerns that an ASP must address.

The high overhead of an ASP designing, running, managing and supporting many customised applications for many businesses has led to a new form of software distribution known as software as a service. **Software as a Service (SaaS)** allows businesses to subscribe to web-delivered business application software by paying a monthly service charge or a per use fee. Like ASP, SaaS providers maintain software on their own servers and provide access to it over the internet. SaaS usually uses a web browser-based user interface. SaaS can reduce expenses by sharing its running applications among many businesses. For example, Sears, JC Penney and Wal-Mart might use customer relationship management software provided by a common SaaS provider. Providing one high-quality SaaS application to thousands of businesses is much more cost-effective than custom designing software for each business.

> **Software as a Service (SaaS)** A service that allows businesses to subscribe to web-delivered business application software by paying a monthly service charge or a per-use fee.

SaaS and new web development technologies have led to a new paradigm in computing called cloud computing. Cloud computing refers to the use of computing resources, including software and data storage, on the internet (the cloud) rather than on local computers. The emergence of powerful web programming languages and techniques, such as AJAX, lets developers create web-based software that rivals traditional installed software. Rather than installing, storing and running software on your own computer, with cloud computing you use the web browser to access software stored and delivered from a web server. Typically, the data generated by the software is also stored on the web server. For example, Tableau software allows users to import database or spreadsheet data to create powerful visualisations that provide useful information.[35] Cloud computing provides the benefit of being able to easily collaborate with others by sharing documents on the internet.

Starbucks used cloud computing services from Salesforce.com when it designed its online community at *www.mystarbucksidea.com*. The site allows Starbucks to converse with its customers to find out how they feel about Starbucks and its products. The customer interactions are stored in a CRM system at Saleforce.com and accessed by Starbucks managers and executives using Salesforce.com's online reporting tools. The cloud computing solution has recorded 77 000 customer suggestions and hundreds of thousands of comments and votes, resulting in 25 new Starbucks products and services.[36]

Personal Application Software

Hundreds of computer applications can help individuals at school, home and work. The features of personal application software are summarised in Table 2.8. In addition to these general-purpose programs, there are literally thousands of other personal computer applications to perform specialised tasks to help you: do your taxes, get in shape, lose weight, get medical advice, write wills and other legal documents, make repairs to your computer, fix your car, write music and edit your pictures and videos. This type of software, often called *user software ox personal productivity software*, includes the general-purpose tools and programs that support individual needs.

Table 2.8 Examples of Personal Application Software

Type of Software	Explanation	Example
Word processing	Create, edit and print text documents	Microsoft Word Corel WordPerfect Google Docs Apple Pages Sun Writer
Spreadsheet	Provide a wide range of built-in functions for statistical, financial, logical, database, graphics, and date and time calculations	Microsoft Excel IBM Lotus 1-2-3 Google Spreadsheet Apple Numbers Sun Calc
Database	Store, manipulate and retrieve data	Microsoft Access IBM Lotus Approach Borland dBASE Sun Base
Graphics	Develop graphs, illustrations and drawings	Adobe Illustrator Adobe FreeHand
Project management	Plan, schedule, allocate and control people and resources (money, time and technology) needed to complete a project according to schedule	Microsoft Project Symantec On Target Scitor Project Scheduler Symantec Time Line
Financial management	Provide income and expense tracking and reporting to monitor and plan budgets (some programs have investment portfolio management features)	Intuit Quicken
Desktop publishing (DTP)	Use with personal computers and high-resolution printers to create high-quality printed output, including text and graphics; various styles of pages can be laid out; art and text files from other programs can also be integrated into published pages	Quark XPress Microsoft Publisher Adobe PageMaker Corel Ventura Publisher Apple Pages

Word Processing

If you write reports, letters, or term papers, word-processing applications can be indispensable. The majority of personal computers in use today have word-processing applications installed. Such applications can be used to create, edit and print documents. Most come with a vast array of features, including those for checking spelling, creating tables, inserting formulas, creating graphics and much more. This book (and most like it) was entered into a word-processing application using a personal computer.

A team of people can use a word-processing program to collaborate on a project. The authors and editors who developed this book, for example, used the Track Changes and Reviewing features of Microsoft Word to track and make changes to chapter files. With these features, you can add comments or make revisions to a document that a coworker can review and either accept or reject.

Spreadsheet Analysis

People use spreadsheets to prepare budgets, forecast profits, analyze insurance programs, summarise income tax data and analyze investments. Whenever numbers and calculations are involved, spreadsheets should be considered. Features of spreadsheets include graphics, limited database capabilities, statistical analysis, built-in business functions and much more (see Figure 2.14). The business functions include calculation of depreciation, present value, internal rate of return and the monthly payment on a loan, to name a few. Optimisation is another powerful feature of many spreadsheet programs. *Optimisation* allows the spreadsheet to maximise or minimise a quantity subject to certain constraints. For example, a small furniture manufacturer that produces chairs and tables might want to maximise its profits. The constraints could be a limited supply of lumber, a limited number of workers that can assemble the chairs and tables, or a limited amount of various hardware fasteners that might be required. Using an optimisation feature, such as Solver in Microsoft Excel, the spreadsheet can determine what number of chairs and tables to produce with labour and material constraints to maximise profits.

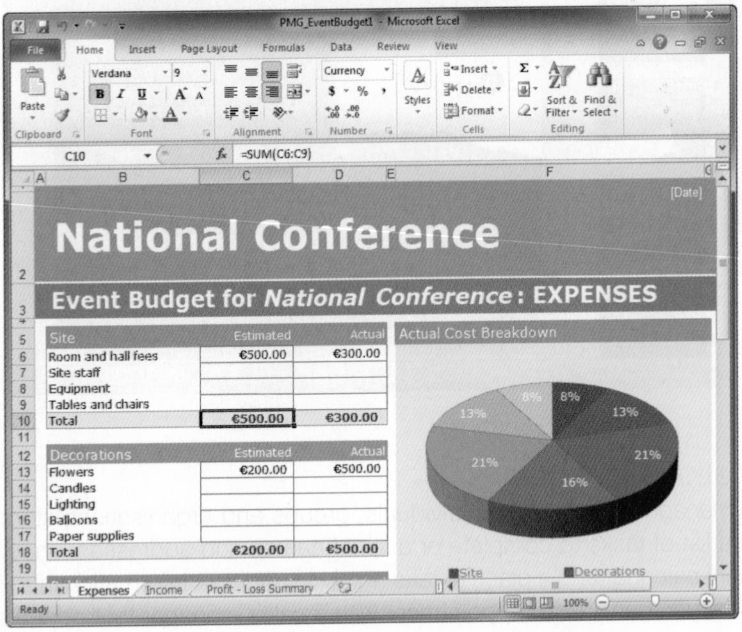

Figure 2.14
Spreadsheet Program
Spreadsheet programs are good for setting up complex calculations.

Database Applications

Database applications are ideal for storing, manipulating and retrieving data. These applications are particularly useful when you need to manipulate a large amount of data and produce reports and documents. Database manipulations include merging, editing and sorting data. The uses of a database application are varied. You can keep track of a CD collection, the items in your apartment, tax records and expenses. A student club can use a database to store names, addresses, phone numbers and dues paid. In business, a database application can help process sales orders, control inventory, order new supplies, send letters to customers and pay employees. Database management systems can be used to track orders, products and customers; analyze weather data to make forecasts for the next several days; and summarise medical research results. A database can also be a front end to another application. For example, you can use a database application to enter and store income tax information and then export the stored results to other applications, such as a spreadsheet or tax-preparation application.

Graphics Programs

With today's graphics programs, it is easy to develop attractive graphs, illustrations and drawings. Graphics programs can be used to develop advertising brochures, announcements and full-colour presentations. If you are asked to make a presentation at school or work, you can use a graphics program to develop and display slides while you are making your talk. A graphics program can be used to help you make a presentation, a drawing, or an illustration (see Figure 2.15). Most presentation graphics programs come with many pieces of *clip art*, such as drawings and photos of people meeting, medical equipment, telecommunications equipment, entertainment and much more.

Figure 2.15
Presentation Graphics Program
Presentation graphics such as Microsoft PowerPoint can produce impressive slides to support a speaker.

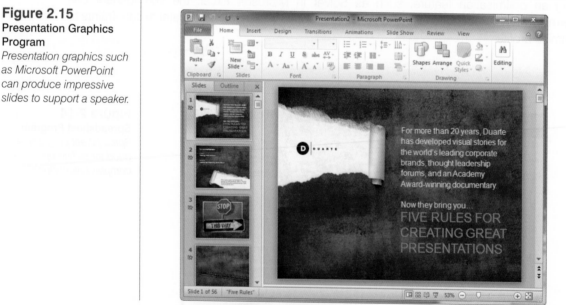

Personal Information Managers

Personal information managers (PIMs) help individuals, groups and organisations store useful information, such as a list of tasks to complete or a list of names and addresses. They usually provide an appointment calendar and a place to take notes. In addition, information in a PIM can be linked. For example, you can link an appointment with a sales manager that appears in the calendar with information on the sales manager in the address book. When you click the appointment in the calendar, information on the sales manager from the address book is automatically opened and displayed on the computer screen. Microsoft Outlook is an example of a PIM software package.

iGoogle and other web portals support PIM by allowing users to access calendars, to-do lists, email, social networks, contacts and other information all from one page.

Some PIMs allow you to schedule and coordinate group meetings. If a computer or handheld device is connected to a network, you can upload the PIM data and coordinate it with the calendar and schedule of others using the same PIM software on the network. You can also use some PIMs to coordinate emails to invite others to meetings. As users receive their invitations, they click a link or button to be automatically added to the guest list.

Software Suites and Integrated Software Packages

A **software suite** is a collection of single programs packaged together in a bundle. Software suites can include a word processor, spreadsheet, database management system, graphics program, communications tool, organiser and more. Some suites support the development of web pages, note taking and speech recognition, whereby applications in the suite can accept voice commands and record dictation. Software suites offer many advantages. The software programs have been designed to work similarly, so after you learn the basics for one application, the other applications are easy to learn and use. Buying software in a bundled suite is cost-effective; the programs usually sell for a fraction of what they would cost individually.

software suite A collection of single programs packaged together in a bundle.

Microsoft Office, Lotus Symphony, Corel WordPerfect Office, Lotus SmartSuite, Oracle StarOffice available for free as OpenOffice.org Apple iWork and Google Apps are examples of popular general-purpose software suites for personal computer users. Each of these software suites includes a spreadsheet program, word processor, database program and graphics presentation software. All can exchange documents, data and diagrams (see Table 2.9). In other words, you can create a spreadsheet and then cut and paste that spreadsheet into a document created using the word-processing application.

Table 2.9 Major Components of Leading Software Suites

Personal Productivity Function	Microsoft Office	Lotus Symphony	Corel WordPerfect Office	Oracle StarOffice	Apple iWork	Google
Word Processing	Word	Documents	WordPerfect	Writer	Pages	Docs
Spreadsheet	Excel	Spreadsheets	Quattro Pro	Calc	Numbers	Spreadsheet
Presentation Graphics	PowerPoint	Presentations	Presentations	Impress	Keynote	Presentation
Database	Access		Paradox	Base		

Zoho, Google and Thinkfree offer free web-based productivity software suites that require no installation on the PC. Adobe has developed Acrobat.com, which features an impressive online suite, including Buzzword for word processing, Tables for spreadsheet and database applications and Presentations for presentation graphics (see Figure 2.16). Documents created with the software can be stored on the web server. Currently, these online applications are not as powerful and robust as installed software, such as Microsoft Office. However, as the technology

Figure 2.16 Web Suites

Adobe Acrobat.com provides a suite of online applications, including Buzzword, with cutting-edge interface designs.

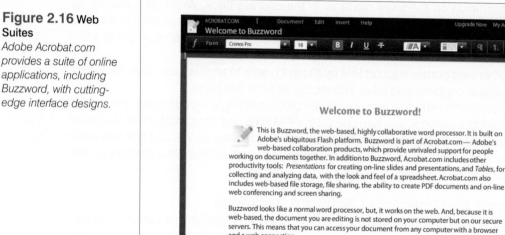

becomes more powerful and network connection speeds increase, users will probably need to install less software on their PCs and turn instead to using software online. After observing this trend, Microsoft responded with an online version of some of its popular Office applications. The online versions of Word, Excel, PowerPoint and OneNote are tightly integrated with their desktop counterparts for easy sharing of documents among computers and collaborators.[37]

Mobile Application Software

Recall that operating systems designed for smartphones include OS X iPhone android and WebOS. The APIs and software development kits designed for these mobile operating systems have given software developers the opportunity to develop applications specifically for mobile use on a small display – and develop they have. Besides the valuable mobile applications that come with the OS, tens of thousands of applications have been developed by third parties for the iPhone. iPhone users download and install these so-called "apps" using Apple's App Store. Many iPhone apps are free; others range in price from 99 pence to hundreds of pounds. Thousands of mobile apps are also available in the Android Market for users of Android handsets. The Palm WebOS has only recently released its software development kit and might soon have many applications available beyond the dozens that are currently available. Table 2.10 lists typical mobile app categories.

Workgroup Application Software

Workgroup application software is designed to support teamwork, whether people are in the same location or dispersed around the world. This support can be accomplished with software known as *groupware* that helps groups of people work together effectively. Microsoft Exchange Server, for example, has groupware and email features. Also called *collaborative software*, the approach allows a team of managers to work on the same production problem, letting them share their ideas and work via connected computer systems. The "Three Cs" rule for successful implementation of groupware is summarised in Table 2.11.

Examples of workgroup software include group scheduling software, electronic mail and other software that enables people to share ideas. Lotus Notes from IBM, for example, lets

Table 2.10 Categories of Mobile Applications for Smart Phones

Category	Description
Books and reference	Access e-books, subscribe to journals, or look up information in Webster's or Wikipedia
Business and finance	Track expenses, trade stocks and access corporate information systems
Entertainment	Access all forms of entertainment, including movies, television programs, music videos and local night life
Games	Play a variety of games from 2D games, such as Pacman and Tetris, to 3D games, such as Need for Speed, Rock Band and The Sims
Health and fitness	Track workout and fitness progress, calculate calories and even monitor your speed and progress from your wirelessly connected Nike shoes
Lifestyle	Find good restaurants, select wine for a meal, record workout progress and more
Music	Find, listen to and create music
News and weather	Access major news and weather providers, including Reuters, AP, the New York Times and the Weather Channel
Photography	Organise, edit, view and share photos taken on your camera phone
Productivity and utilities	Create grocery lists, practice PowerPoint presentations, work on spreadsheets, synchronise with PC files and more
Social networking	Connect with others via major social networks, including Facebook, Twitter and MySpace
Sports	Keep up with your favourite team or track your own golf scores
Travel and navigation	Use the GPS in your smartphone to get turn-by-turn directions, find interesting places to visit, access travel itineraries and more

Table 2.11 Ernst & Young's 'Three Cs' Rule for Groupware

Quality	Description
Convenient	If it's too hard to use, it's not used; it should be as easy to use as the telephone.
Content	It must provide a constant stream of rich, relevant and personalised content.
Coverage	If it isn't conveniently accessible, it might never be used.

companies use one software package and one user interface to integrate many business processes. Lotus Notes can allow a global team to work together from a common set of documents, have electronic discussions using threads of discussion and schedule team meetings. As the program matured, Lotus added services to it and renamed it Domino (Lotus Notes is now the name of the email package), and now an entire third-party market has emerged to build collaborative software based on Domino.

Web-based software is ideal for group use. Because documents are stored on an internet server, anyone with an internet connection can access them easily. Google provides options in its online applications that allow users to share documents, spreadsheets, presentations, calendars and notes with other specified users or everyone on the web. This makes it convenient for several people to contribute to a document without concern for software compatibility or storage. Google also provides a tool for creating web-based forms and surveys. When invited parties fill out the form, the data is stored in a Google spreadsheet (see Figure 2.17).

Figure 2.17 Google Forms

Google forms are used to collect information online and store it in a spreadsheet.

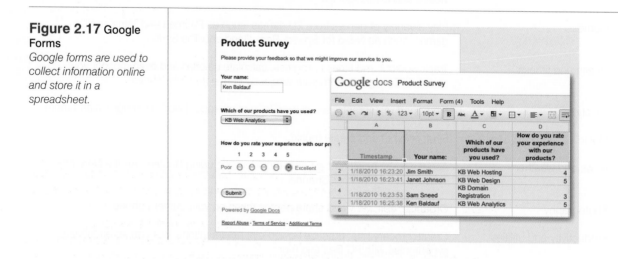

Enterprise Application Software

Software that benefits an entire organisation – enterprise application software – can also be developed specifically for the business or purchased off the shelf. Some software vendors, such as SAP, specialise in developing software for enterprises. One of the first enterprise applications was a payroll program for Lyons Bakeries in England, developed in 1954 on the Leo 1 computer. Many organisations are moving to integrated enterprise software that supports supply chain management (movement of raw materials from suppliers through shipment of finished goods to customers). Following are some applications that can be addressed with enterprise software.

Accounts payable
Accounts receivable
Airline industry operations
Automatic teller systems
Cash-flow analysis
Cheque processing
Credit and charge card administration
Distribution control
Fixed asset accounting
General ledger
Human resource management
Inventory control

Invoicing
Manufacturing control
Order entry
Payroll
Receiving
Restaurant management
Retail operations
Sales ordering
Savings and time deposits
Shipping
Stock and bond management
Tax planning and preparation

Organisations can no longer respond to market changes using nonintegrated information systems based on overnight processing of yesterday's business transactions, conflicting data models and obsolete technology. Wal-Mart and many other companies have sophisticated information systems to speed processing and coordinate communications between stores and their main offices. Many corporations are turning to enterprise resource planning (ERP) software, a set of integrated programs that manage a company's vital business operations for an entire multisite, global organisation. Thus, an ERP system must be able to support many legal entities, languages and currencies. Although the scope can vary from vendor to vendor, most ERP systems provide integrated software to support manufacturing and finance. In addition to these core business processes, some ERP systems might support business functions, such as human resources, sales and distribution. The primary benefits of implementing ERP software include eliminating inefficient systems, easing adoption of improved work processes, improving access to data for operational decision making, standardising technology vendors and equipment and enabling supply chain management. In contrast, small businesses usually do not need complex enterprise application software. They rely on software, such as Intuit QuickBooks and Microsoft Office Small Business Accounting, for accounting and recording keeping.

Application Software for Information, Decision Support and Specialised Purposes

Specialised application software for information, decision support and other purposes is available in every industry. For example, many schools and colleges use Blackboard or other learning management software to organise class materials and grades.[38] Genetic researchers, as another example, are using software to visualise and analyze the human genome. Music executives use decision support software to help pick the next hit song. Sophisticated decision support software is also being used to increase the cure rate for cancer by analyzing about 100 scans of a cancerous tumour to create a 3D view of the tumour. Software can then consider thousands of angles and doses of radiation to determine the best program of radiation therapy. The software analysis takes only minutes, but the results can save years or decades of life for the patient. As you will see in future chapters, information, decision support and specialised systems are used in businesses of all sizes and types to increase profits or reduce costs. But how are all these systems actually developed and built? The answer is through the use of programming languages, discussed next.

2.11 Programming Languages

Both OSs and application software are written in coding schemes called *programming languages*. The primary function of a programming language is to provide instructions to the computer system so that it can perform a processing activity. IS professionals work with **programming languages**, which are sets of keywords, symbols and rules for constructing statements that people can use to communicate instructions to a computer. Programming involves translating what a user wants to accomplish into instructions that the computer can understand and execute. The desire to use the power of information processing efficiently in problem solving has pushed the development of literally thousands of programming languages, but only a few dozen are commonly used today. A brief summary of the various programming language generations is provided in Table 2.12.

programming languages Sets of keywords, symbols and rules for constructing statements that people can use to communicate instructions to a computer.

Although many programming languages are used to write new business applications, more lines of code are written in COBOL in existing business applications than any other

Table 2.12 The Evolution of Programming Languages

Generation	Language	Approximate Development Date	Sample Statement or Action
First	Machine language	1940s	00010101
Second	Assembly language	1950s	MVC
Third	High-level language	1960s	READ SALES
Fourth	Query and database languages	1970s	PRINT EMPLOYEE NUMBER IF GROSS PAY>1000
Beyond Fourth	Natural and intelligent languages	1980s	IF gross pay is greater than 40, THEN pay the employee overtime pay

programming language. Today, programmers often use visual and object-oriented languages. In the future, they will likely be using artificial intelligence languages to a greater extent. In general, these languages are easier for nonprogrammers to use compared with older generation languages.

2.12 Software Issues and Trends

Because software is such an important part of today's computer systems, issues, such as software bugs, licensing and global software support, have received increased attention.

Software Bugs

A software bug is a defect in a computer program that keeps it from performing as it is designed to perform. Some software bugs are obvious and cause the program to terminate unexpectedly. Other bugs are more subtle and allow errors to creep into your work. Computer and software vendors say that as long as people design and program hardware and software, bugs are inevitable. The following list summarises tips for reducing the impact of software bugs.

- Register all software so that you receive bug alerts, fixes and patches.
- Check the manual or read-me files for solutions to known problems.
- Access the support area of the manufacturer's website for patches.
- Install the latest software updates.
- Before reporting a bug, make sure that you can re-create the circumstances under which it occurs.
- After you re-create the bug, call the manufacturer's tech support line.
- Consider waiting before buying the latest release of software to give the vendor a chance to discover and remove bugs. Many schools and businesses don't purchase software until the first major revision with patches is released.

Copyrights and Licences

Most software products are protected by law using copyright or licensing provisions. Those pro-visions can vary, however. In some cases, you are given unlimited use of software on one or two computers. This is typical with many applications developed for personal computers. In other cases, you pay for your usage – if you use the software more, you pay more. This approach is becoming popular with software placed on networks or larger computers. Most of these protections prevent you from copying software and giving it to others without restrictions. Some software now requires that you *register* or *activate* it before it can be fully used. Registration and activation sometimes put software on your hard disc that monitors activities and changes to your computer system.

Software Upgrades

Software companies revise their programs and sell new versions periodically. In some cases, the revised software offers new and valuable enhancements. In other cases, the software uses complex program code that offers little in terms of additional capabilities. In addition, revised software can contain bugs or errors. When software companies stop supporting older software versions or releases, some customers feel forced to upgrade to the newer software. Deciding whether to purchase the newest software can be a problem for corporations and people with a large investment in software. Should the newest version be purchased when it is released? Some users do not always get the most current software upgrades or versions, unless it includes significant improvements or capabilities. Instead, they might upgrade to newer software only when it offers vital new features. Software upgrades usually cost much less than the original pur-chase price.

Global Software Support

Large, global companies have little trouble persuading vendors to sell them software li-cences for even the most far-flung outposts of their company. But can those same vendors provide adequate support for their software customers in all locations? Supporting local op-erations is one of the biggest challenges IS teams face when putting together standardised, company-wide systems. In slower technology growth markets, such as Eastern Europe and Latin America, there may be no official vendor presence at all. Instead, large vendors, such as Sybase, IBM and Hewlett-Packard, typically contract out support for their software to local providers.

One approach that has been gaining acceptance in North America is to outsource global support to one or more third-party distributors. The software-user company may still negotiate its license with the software vendor directly, but it then hands over the global support contract to a third-party supplier. The supplier acts as a middleman between software vendor and user, often providing distribution, support and invoicing. American Home Products Corporation han-dles global support for both Novell NetWare and Microsoft Office applications this way – throughout the 145 countries in which it operates. American Home Products negotiated the agreements directly with the vendors for both purchasing and maintenance, but fulfilment of the agreement is handled exclusively by Philadelphia-based Softsmart, an international supplier of software and services.

In today's computer systems, software is an increasingly critical component. Whatever approach individuals and organisations take to acquire software, it is important for everyone to be aware of the current trends in the industry. Informed users are wise consumers.

Summary

At the start of this chapter, we set out the SIX main principles relating to hardware and software uses within information systems in organisations together with the key learning objectives for each. Now it's time to summarise the chapter by recapping on those SIX principles: can you recall what is important and why about each one?

1 **Computer hardware must be carefully selected to meet the evolving needs of the organisation and its supporting information systems.** Hardware refers to the physical components of a computer that perform the input, processing, storage and output activities of the computer. Processing is performed by an interplay between the central processing unit (CPU) and memory. Primary storage, or memory, provides working storage for program instructions and data to be processed and provides them to the CPU. Together, a CPU and memory process data and execute instructions.

Processing that uses several processing units is called multiprocessing. A multicore processor combines two or more independent processors into a single computer so that they can share the workload and boost processing capacity. Parallel processing involves linking several processors to work together to solve complex problems. Grid computing is the use of a collection of computers, often owned by multiple individuals or organisations, to work in a coordinated manner to solve a common problem.

Computer systems can store large amounts of data and instructions in secondary storage, which is less volatile and has greater capacity than memory. Storage media can be either sequential access or direct access. Common forms of secondary storage include magnetic tape, magnetic disc, video tape, optical disc storage, digital video disc and solid state storage devices. Redundant array of independent/inexpensive disks (RAID) is a method of storing data that allows the system to more easily recover data in the event of a hardware failure. Storage area network (SAN) uses computer servers, distributed storage devices and networks to provide fast and efficient storage.

Input and output devices allow users to provide data and instructions to the computer for processing and allow subsequent storage and output.

These devices are part of a user interface through which humans interact with computer systems. Input and output devices vary widely, but they share common characteristics of speed and functionality.

A keyboard and computer mouse are the most common devices used for entry of data. Speech recognition technology enables a computer to interpret human speech as an alternative means of providing data and instructions. Digital cameras record and store images or video in digital form. Handwriting recognition software can convert handwriting on the screen into text. Radio-frequency identification (RFID) technology employs a microchip, called a tag, to transmit data that is read by an RFID reader. The data transmitted could include facts, such as item identification number, location information, or other details about the item tagged.

Output devices provide information in different forms, from hard copy to sound to digital format. Display monitors are standard output devices; monitor quality is determined by size, number of colours that can be displayed and resolution. Other output devices include printers, plotters and e-books.

Portable single-user computers include handheld computers, laptops, notebook computers, netbook computers and tablet computers. Nonportable single-user computers include thin clients, desktop computers, nettop computers and workstations. Multiple-user computer systems include servers, mainframe computers and supercomputers.

Grid computing is the use of a collection of computers, often owned by many people or organisations, to work in a coordinated manner to solve a common problem. Grid computing is one low-cost approach to parallel processing.

2 **The computer hardware industry and users are implementing green computing designs and products.** Green computing is concerned with the efficient and environmentally responsible design, manufacture, operation and disposal of IS-related products.

Business organisations recognise that going green is in their best interests in terms of public relations, safety of employees and the community at large. They also recognise that green computing presents an opportunity to substantially reduce total costs over the life cycle of their IS equipment.

Green computing has three goals: reduce the use of hazardous material, enable companies to lower their power-related costs and enable the safe disposal or recycling of IS products.

3 **Systems and application software are critical in helping individuals and organisations achieve their goals.** Software consists of programs that control the workings of the computer hardware. The two main categories of software are systems software and application software. Systems software is a collection of programs that interacts between hardware and application software. Application software can be proprietary or off-the-shelf and enables people to solve problems and perform specific tasks.

An operating system (OS) is a set of computer program that controls the computer hardware to support users' computing needs. An OS converts an instruction from an application into a set of instructions needed by the hardware. This intermediary role allows hardware independence. An OS also manages memory, which involves controlling storage access and use by converting logical requests into physical locations and by placing data in the best storage space, perhaps virtual memory.

An OS manages tasks to allocate computer resources through multitasking and time-sharing. With multitasking, users can run more than one application at a time. Timesharing allows more than one person to use a computer system at the same time.

The ability of a computer to handle an increasing number of concurrent users smoothly is called scalability, a feature critical for systems expected to handle a large number of users.

An OS also provides a user interface, which allows users to access and command the computer. A command-based user interface requires text commands to send instructions; a graphical user interface (GUI), such as Windows, uses icons and menus.

Software applications use the OS by requesting services through a defined application program interface (API). Programmers can use APIs to create application software without having to understand the inner workings of the OS. APIs also provide a degree of hardware independence so that the underlying hardware can change without necessarily requiring a rewrite of the software applications.

Over the years, several popular OSs have been developed. These include several proprietary OSs used primarily on mainframes. Windows Vista,

Windows XP and Windows 7 are the most recent Microsoft Windows operating systems. Apple computers use proprietary OSs, such as the Mac OS and Mac OS X. UNIX is a powerful OS that can be used on many computer system types and platforms, from personal computers to mainframe systems. UNIX makes it easy to move programs and data among computers or to connect mainframes and personal computers to share resources. Linux is the kernel of an OS whose source code is freely available to everyone. Several variations of Linux are available, with sets of capabilities and applications to form a complete OS, for example, Red Hat Linux, Caldera Open Linux, and Google Chrome. z/OS and HP-UX are OSs for mainframe computers. Some OSs have been developed to support consumer appliances, such as Palm OS, Windows CE.Net, Windows XP Embedded, Pocket PC and variations of Linux.

Symbian is the world's most widely used cell phone embedded OS and has traditionally provided voice and text communication, an address book and a few other basic applications. When RIM introduced the BlackBerry smartphone in 2002, the mobile phone's capabilities were vastly expanded. Since then, cell phone embedded systems have transformed into full-fledged personal computer OSs, such as the iPhone OS, Google Android and Microsoft Windows Mobile.

4 **Organisations should not develop proprietary application software unless doing so will meet a compelling business need that can provide a competitive advantage.** Application software applies the power of the computer to solve problems and perform specific tasks. One useful way of classifying the many potential uses of information systems is to identify the scope of problems and opportunities addressed by a particular organisation or its sphere of influence. For most companies, the spheres of influence are personal, workgroup and enterprise.

User software, or personal productivity software, includes general-purpose programs that enable users to improve their personal effectiveness, increasing the quality and amount of work that can be done. Software that helps groups work together is often called workgroup application software and includes group scheduling software, electronic mail and other software that enables people to share ideas. Enterprise software that benefits the entire organisation can also be developed or purchased. Many organisations are turning to enterprise resource planning software, a set of integrated programs that manage a company's vital business operations for an entire multisite, global organisation.

Three approaches to developing application software are to build proprietary application software, buy existing programs off the shelf, or use a combination of customised and off-the-shelf application software. Building proprietary software (in-house or on contract) has the following advantages: the organisation will get software that more closely matches its needs; by being involved with the development, the organisation has further control over the results; and the organisation has more flexibility in making changes. The disadvantages include the following: it is likely to take longer and cost more to develop, the in-house staff will be hard pressed to provide ongoing support and maintenance, and there is a greater risk that the software features will not work as expected or that other performance problems will occur.

Purchasing off-the-shelf software has many advantages. The initial cost is lower, there is a lower risk that the software will fail to work as expected and the software is likely to be of higher quality than proprietary software. Some disadvantages are that the organisation might pay for features it does not need, the software might lack important features requiring expensive customisation and the system might require process reengineering.

Some organisations have taken a third approach – customising software packages. This approach usually involves a mixture of the preceding advantages and disadvantages and must be carefully managed.

An application service provider (ASP) is a company that can provide the software, support and computer hardware on which to run the software from the user's facilities over a network. ASPs provide contract customisation of off-the-shelf software, and they speed deployment of new applications while helping IS managers avoid implementation headaches. Use of ASPs reduces the need for many skilled IS staff members and also lowers a project's start-up expenses.

Software as a service, or SaaS, allows business to subscribe to web-delivered business application software by paying a monthly service charge or a per use fee.

Cloud computing refers to the use of computing resources, including software and data storage, on the internet (the cloud) rather than on local computers.

Although hundreds of computer applications can help people at school, home and work, the primary applications are word processing, spreadsheet analysis, database, graphics, and online services. A software suite, such as SmartSuite, WordPerfect, StarOffice, or Office, offers a collection of powerful programs.

5 **Organisations should choose a programming language whose functional characteristics are appropriate for the task at hand, considering the skills and experience of the programming staff.** AU software programs are written in coding schemes called programming languages, which provide instructions to a computer to perform some processing activity. The several classes of programming languages include machine, assembly, high-level, query, and database, and natural and intelligent languages.

Programming languages have changed since their initial development in the early 1950s. In the first generation, computers were programmed in machine language, and the second generation of languages used assembly languages. The third generation consists of many high-level programming languages that use English-like statements and commands. Fourth-generation languages include database and query languages, such as SQL.

Users frequently use fourth generation and higher-level programming languages to develop their own simple programs.

6 **The software industry continues to undergo constant change; users need to be aware of recent trends and issues to be effective in their business and personal life.** Software bugs, software licensing and copyrighting, software upgrades and global software support are all important software issues and trends.

A software bug is a defect in a computer program that keeps it from performing in the manner intended. Software bugs are common, even in key pieces of business software.

Software upgrades are an important source of increased revenue for software manufacturers and can provide useful new functionality and improved quality for software users.

Global software support is an important consideration for large, global companies putting together standardised, company-wide systems. A common solution is outsourcing global support to one or more third-party software distributors.

Review Questions

1   When determining the appropriate hardware components of a new information system, what role must the user of the system play?

2   Identify two basic characteristics of RAM and ROM.

3   What is RFID technology? How does it work?

4   Identify the three components of the CPU and explain the role of each.

5   What is solid state storage technology? What advantages does it offer?

6   Identify and briefly describe the various classes of nonportable single-user computers.

7   Give three examples of recent operating systems.

8   What are the two basic types of software? Briefly describe the role of each.

9   What is cloud computing? What are the pros and cons of cloud computing?

10   What is an application service provider? What issues arise in considering the use of one?

11   What does the acronym API stand for? What is the role of an API?

12   Describe the term *enterprise resource planning (ERP)* system. What functions does such a system perform?

Discussion Questions

1   Briefly discuss the advantages and disadvantages of frequent software upgrades from the perspective of the user of that software. How about from the perspective of the software manufacturer?

2   What would be the advantages for a university computer lab to install thin clients rather than standard desktop personal computers? Can you identify any disadvantages?

3   Which would you rather have – a handheld computer or a tablet computer? Why?

4   If cost were not an issue, describe the characteristics of your ideal computer. What would you use it for? Which operating system would you want it to run?

5   Identify the three spheres of influence and briefly discuss the software needs of each.

6   Identify the two fundamental sources for obtaining application software. Discuss the advantages and disadvantages of each source.

7   Define *Software as a Service*. Discuss some of the pros and cons of using software as a service.

8   In what ways is an operating system for a mainframe computer different from the operating system for a laptop computer? In what ways are they similar?

9   Discuss potential issues that can arise if an organisation is not careful in selecting a reputable service organisation to recycle or dispose of its IS equipment.

10   Briefly explain the difference between grid computing and cloud computing.

Web Exercises

1   Use the internet to research four productivity software suites from various vendors (see *http://en.wikipedia.org/wiki/Office_Suite*). Create a table in a word-processing document to show what applications are provided by the competing suites. Write a few paragraphs on which suite you think best matches your needs and why.

2   Do research on the internet to identify the current state of development and production of

advanced technology secondary storage devices. What are some of the most promising devices? What issues are associated with mass producing these new devices? Write a brief report summarising your findings.

3 Do research on the internet about application software that is used in an industry that is of interest to you. Write a brief report describing how the application software can be used to increase profits or reduce costs.

2

Case One

Electronics Manufacturers Face the Global E-Waste Problem

The world is consuming and discarding increasing amounts of electronics products every year. The United States Environmental Protection Agency estimates that "over 2 billion computers, televisions, wireless devices, printers, gaming systems, and other devices have been sold since 1980." Have you considered where those devices end up when they become obsolete or worn out? It turns out that a large percentage of them are shipped to third-world countries where they are dismantled in salvaging operations that strip out valuable metals and burn the remaining parts. Ghana, Nigeria, Pakistan, India and China have become the world's primary dumpsters for electronics salvaging.

The real problem with electronics waste, or e-waste, lies in the use of toxic heavy materials, such as mercury, cadmium, beryllium and lead, along with PVC plastic and hazardous chemicals like brominated flame retardants (BFR) that are included in electronics components. When dumped in landfills, these toxic components leach into the land over time and are released into the atmosphere. Burning computer components also releases these toxic components into the atmosphere, with deadly results to the people doing the burning in the short term and a gradual eroding of the global environment in the long term.

The third-world countries that salvage electronics rarely take environmental precautions. Children are often used as labour, becoming sick after prolonged exposure to the toxic waste.

Organisations, such as Greenpeace, are going to great lengths to call attention to this global problem. They are encouraging electronics manufacturers to eliminate toxic materials from the products they sell. They also encourage manufacturers to provide incentives for their customers to properly recycle electronics devices when they are through with them. In its annual "Guide to Greener Electronics,"

Greenpeace ranks technology companies on their level of "green-ness" based on the each company's manufacturing and recycling practices. For example, currently Nokia is ranked greenest due to its comprehensive voluntary take-back programs and recycling practices. Samsung is number two, because it removed PVC from its LCD displays, BFR from some of its cell phones and halogen from its chips and semiconductors. Although Nokia and Samsung earned high points from Greenpeace, no company is currently ranked as being 100 per cent green, and most are listed in the red with a lot of improvements still needed.

Some manufacturers are seeing green manufacturing practices as a method of gaining market share. The growing population of environmentally conscious consumers prefers to do business with green businesses. Apple has invested heavily in building its green reputation. It has worked to remove or dramatically reduce the amount of lead in its displays. It has eliminated or reduced dangerous chemicals, including arsenic and mercury and compounds, such as PVC and BFR. Apple operates recycling programs in 93 per cent of the countries where Macs, iPhones and iPods are sold. It even reduced packaging materials to a minimum to save trees and eliminate Styrofoam.

Apple is not unique in its efforts to reduce and safeguard e-waste but is considered the most progressive PC manufacturer by Greenpeace. Most other PC manufacturers are following suit. However, soon "going green" may not be a voluntary decision for electronics manufacturing. Legislation has been proposed in the US to address the e-waste issue. One bill is named the "Electronic Device Recycling Research and Development Act." The bill addresses how to manage current e-waste, develop recycling programs and eliminate the use of toxic materials in electronics. The US has fallen behind other countries in responding to the problem. The European Union has already passed two directives to deal with e-waste: the Restriction on the Use of Hazardous Substances (RoHS) and the Waste Electrical and Electronic Equipment (WEEE).

With increased attention turning toward the e-waste problem, optimism is increasing. One study estimates that, if recycling initiatives continue to expand, the e-waste problem should reach a peak global volume of 73 million metric tons by 2015 and then begin to decline.

Discussion Questions

1 What concerns have been raised over e-waste?

2 What actions can electronics manufacturers take to address the e-waste problem?

Critical Thinking Questions

1 What laws, if any, do you think are necessary to address this problem? Why?

2 How might the global community cooperate to help speed up recovery?

SOURCES: Johnston, Casey, 'Legislation seeks to deal with growing piles of e-waste,' *Ars Technica*. Available from: *http://arstechnica.com*, November 1, 2009; Lombardi, Candace, 'Study: E-waste build-up will plateau by 2015,' CNET news. Available from: *http://news.cnet.com*. Accessed May 6, 2009; Greenpeace E-Waste website. Available from: *www.greenpeace.org/international/campaigns/toxics/electronics*. Accessed January 1, 2010; A Greener Apple web page. Available from: *www.apple.com/hotnews/agreenerapple*. Accessed January 1, 2010.

Case Two

Open Source in South Africa

A South African government council has recommended that official government policy promotes the use of open-source software, by expressing a preference for open source when there is no compelling reason to adopt a proprietary alternative. Their proposal document recommends that the selection criteria for all software by its citizens be based on efficiency, effectiveness and economy of service. It also recommends that the government should use open-source software to promote access to information by it's citizens. South Africa finds it has little influence with proprietary software developers as their products are mostly aimed at other markets. It is acknowledged that this is the same with most open-source projects, but that open source gives users the ability to change and adapt the code. This is something that some groups in South Africa, for instance, the Council for Scientific and Industrial Research, are keen to do.

Others have also seen the potential for open source in South Africa. The "Go Open Source" campaign ran for two years, trying to raise awareness generally and plan for a transition to open source within the South African government. Recently, the organisation providing computing resources to South African school, SchoolNet Namibia, rejected Microsoft's offer to put its Windows operating system in schools, preferring to keep Linux OS. The Department of Agriculture is planning to migrate its infrastructure to one based on open standards.

One of the concerns for moving to open source is the need for skilled developers to do the work. According to Kugan Soobramani, senior manager and government IT officer, "when they talk about open source, everybody says, it's free, it's free, it's free, but it's not free to develop applications – that's where the costs come in."

Unsurprisingly, Microsoft has lobbied against policies favouring or mandating the use of open-source software claiming that decisions should be made according to what is best in the given situation, not going with open source by default. In fact the wording of the council's document allows for this position.

Several years on and the State IT Agency (SITA) is assuming the role of paving the way for open-source migration by finalising standards and conducting pilot projects to make it easier for all to implement open-source software successfully. They also expect all government department websites to be running

2

on open-source software "very soon." A variety of interest groups, such as the local ICT industries, multi-national software vendors, industry associations, academia and civil society, are increasingly lobbying their governments to take action. The suggestions that are being put forward range from mandating the exclusive use and procurement of open-source software to an unregulated free-market approach.

Bridges.org researcher Philipp Schmidt says, however, that one element currently missing from the research and analysis of free software is a practical overview of the areas in which governments can make interventions and the strategic approaches they can take. He also says that many advocacy efforts fail, because open-source proponents fail to address the link between open-source software and broader social and economic development goals. Schmidt recommends an approach to open-source policy-making linked to national development goals and discusses some example development goals and how open-source policies could be shaped to address them. Deployment of open-source software effectively is clearly not as simple as its installation.

Discussion Questions

1 How might open-source software benefit and hinder the South African government?

2 Should all government departments be mandated to use open-source software?

Critical Thinking Questions

1 What are some of the challenges faced by the South African government when purchasing software?

2 What could Soobramani do to reduce development costs?

SOURCES: Go Open Source in South Africa. Available from: *http://www.go-opensource.org/*; Festa, P. 'South Africa considers open source', CNET news, *http://news.cnet.com/*, February 5, 2003; Khan, B. 'Open source gives South African farmers a leg-up', Tectonic, November 22. Available from: 2005; *http://opendotdot.blogspot.com/2009/03/yet-more-open-source-for-south-africa.html*. Accessed January 13, 2011; Toolkit for governments moving to free software. Available from: *http://www.opensourceafrica.org/view_article.php?type=news&id=18*. Accessed January 13, 2011.

Notes

1 Shah, Agam, 'Intel's New Core i7 Chips Surface on Retail Sites,' *Computerworld*, May 27, 2009.

2 Lai, Eric, 'AMD's Latest Quad-Core Phenom CPU Ups Its Game,' *Computerworld*, August 13, 2009.

3 Crothers, Brooke, 'IBM Launches Power7 Chip, Systems,' *Cnet*, February 7, 2010.

4 ACMA Computers, 'Success Stories,' Acma Computers website. Available from: *www.acma.com/acma/Casestudy.asp*. Accessed January 16, 2010.

5 Shread, Paul, 'Big Blue Takes on Swine Flu,' *Grid Computing Planet*, May 12, 2009.

6 Staff, 'Media Distributors Introduces Industry's Most Affordable RAID Storage Solution for Professional Video Production Customers,' Green Technology website. Available from: *http://green.tmcnet.com/news/2009/09/17/4375055.htm*. Accessed September 17, 2009.

7 Data Domain, 'Boston Medical Center Presents on Reducing IT Costs and Simplifying Storage Management Using Data Domain,' Press release, February 20, 2009.

8 Staff, 'Company Profile,' Austar website. Available from: *www.austarunited.com.au/about/profile*. Accessed January 16, 2010.

9 Winterford, Brett, 'Austar Breathes New Life into Old Data,' *itnews for Australian Business*, September 16, 2009.

10 Clark, Don, 'SanDisc Says New Chips Will Lower Production Costs,' *Wall Street Journal*, October 13, 2009.

11 Nuance, 'SBI Mutual Fund Deploys Nuance Powered Technology to Enhance Customer Experience,' Press release. Available from: *www.nuance.com/news/pressreleases/2009/20090721_sbiMutual.asp*. Accessed July 21, 2009.

12 Townsend, Captain Mark, 'Remark-able Story: Remark Office OMR Helps Police Department Meet State Requirements,' Remark Office website. Available from: *www.gravic.com/remark/officeomr/reviews/remark3.html*.

13 Staff, 'Newmont Gold - Leeville Mine In Nevada Goes Digital with MST,' *Mining-Technology.com*. Accessed March 20, 2009.

14 Kondolojy, Amanda, 'LCD Vs Plasma Monitors,' eHow website. Available from: *www.ehow.com/about_4778386_lcd-vs-plasma-monitors.html*. Accessed January 20, 2010.

15 Staff, 'Solar Power – Yes, Life's Good,' *The Daily Contributor*, October 12, 2009.

16 Ion, Florence, 'Into Thin Air - Conquering Mt. Everest with a MacBook,' *Mac|Life*. Available from: *www.maclife.com/print/5013*. Accessed October 2, 2009.

17 Stone, Brad and Vance, Ashlee, 'Just a Touch Away, the Elusive Tablet PC,' *The New York Times*, October 5, 2009.

18 NEC Corporation, 'NEC Deploys One of Japan's Largest Thin Client Systems for Tokio Marine,' Press release. Available from: *www.nec.co.jp/press/en/0909/2901.html*. Accessed September 29, 2009.

19 'Dell Studio Hybrid Intel Dual-Core 2.1 GHz Miniature Desktop (26GB/160GB) $299.99,' Tech Bargains, October 20, 2009.

20 Sun Microsystems, 'Blue Sky Studios Deploys Sun Solution for Ice Age: Dawn of the Dinosaurs Film,' Press release. Available from: *www.sun.com/aboutsun/pr/2009-07/sunflash.20090706.1.xml*. Accessed July 6, 2009.

21 Betts, Mitch, 'Data Center Plays Supporting Role in Avatar,' *Computerworld*, January 18, 2010.

22 Boulton Clint, 'Mindjet MindManager 8 for Mac Integrates with Apple Apps,' *eweek*, January 27, 2010. Available from: *www.eweek.com*.

23 Dunn, Scott, 'Master Your Schedule with Google Calendar,' *PC World*, August 2008, p. 110.

24 IBM staff, 'Leading energy management firm streamlines global reporting, increases synergies, thanks to powerful IBM Cognos solution,' IBM Case Study. Available from: *www-01.ibm.com/software/success/cssdb.nsf/cs/SANS-82GM69?OpenDocument&Site=cognos&cty=en_us*. Accessed February 10, 2010.

25 Pogue, David, 'Windows 7 Keeps the Good, Tries to Fix Flaws,' *NewYork Times*, October 21, 2009.

26 Tweney, Dylan, 'Google Chrome OS: Ditch Your Hard Drives, the Future Is the web,' *Wired*. Available from: *www.wired.com*. Accessed November 19, 2009.

27 Staff, 'eBay Inc.,' Sun Customer Snapshot website. Available from: *www.sun.com/customers/index.xml?c=ebay.xml&submit=Find*. Accessed January 17, 2010.

28 Staff, 'Idaho National Lab,' Sun Customer Snapshot website. Available from: *www.sun.com/customers/index.xml?c=inl.xml&submit=Find*. Accessed January 17, 2010.

29 IBM staff, 'IBM eServer zSeries systems and GDPS help AOK Bavaria create a healthy environment for growth,' IBM Success Stories, May 1, 2009. Available from: *www-01.ibm.com/software/success/cssdb.nsf/CS/JFTD-6VESNY?OpenDocument&Site=eserverzseries&cty=en_us*.

30 Kinnander, Ola, 'Nokia to Roll Out Phone Based on Linux Software,' *Wall Street Journal*, August 28, 2009, Technology Section, p. B4.

31 Oracle staff, 'Swedish Medical Leverages Content Management Solution to Facilitate Patient-centric Care,' Oracle Customer Snapshot. Available from: *www.oracle.com/customers/snapshots/swedish-medical-center-content-management-snapshot.pdf*. Accessed January 17, 2010.

32 Montalbano, Elizabeth, 'Forrester: Microsoft Office in No Danger From Competitors,' PC World, *www.pcworld.com/businesscenter/article/166123/forrester_microsoft_office_in_no_danger_from_competitors.html?tk=nl_dnx_h_crawl*. Accessed June 04, 2009.

33 Montalbano, Elizabeth, 'Amalga Helps Hospital Keep Swine Flu in Check,' *CIO*. Available from: *www.cio.com/article/494533/Amalga_Helps_Hospital_Keep_Swine_Flu_in_Check*. Accessed June 8, 2009.

34 Staff, 'Customer: RapidAdvance,' SAP Case Study. Available from: *www.ondemand.com/ customers/rapidadvance.asp*. Accessed January 17, 2010.

35 Lai, Eric 'Forget mashups: Tableau Software wants data junkies to do the 'viz,'' *Computerworld*. Available from: *www.computerworld.com*. Accessed February 11, 2010.

36 Salesforce staff, 'Powered By Salesforce CRM's Idea Community, My Starbucks Idea Brews Customer Feedback at Starbucks,' Salesforce Success Story. Available from: *www.salesforce.com/customers/distribution-retail/starbucks.jsp*. Accessed January 17, 2010.

37 Burrows, Peter, 'Microsoft Defends Its Empire,' *Businessweek*, July 6, 2009, pg 28.

38 Schaffhauser, Dian, 'Florida Virtual to Extend Use of LMS to Students,' *The Journal*. Available from: *www.thejournal.com*. Accessed January 22, 2010.

CHAPTER 3 CONTENTS

03

Organising Data and Information

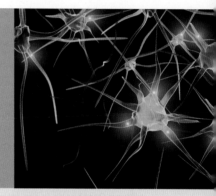

I n this chapter we will look at the THREE main factors you need to understand when considering how business information systems organise and handle data.

Principles

1. Data management and modelling are key aspects of organising data and information.

2. A well-designed and well-managed database is central to almost all information systems and is an extremely valuable tool in supporting decision making.

3. The number and type of database applications will continue to evolve and yield real business benefits.

Learning Objectives

■ Define general data management concepts and terms, highlighting the advantages of the database approach to data management.

■ Describe the relational database model and outline its basic features.

■ Identify the common functions performed by all database management systems and identify popular user database management systems.

■ Identify and briefly discuss current database applications.

Why Learn About Organising Data and Information?

Having had an overview of IS in organisations and examined different types of hardware and software, we now turn to look at using that hardware and software to store and process data. Databases are the heart of almost all IS. A huge amount of data is entered into computer systems every day. In this chapter, you will learn about database management systems and how they can help you. If you become a marketing manager, you can access a vast store of data on existing and potential customers from surveys, web habits, and past purchases. This information can help you sell products and services. If you work in business law, you will have access to past cases and legal opinions from sophisticated legal databases. This information can help you win cases and protect your organisation legally. If you become a human resource (HR) manager, you will be able to use databases to analyze the impact of raises, employee insurance benefits, and retirement contributions on long-term costs to your company. Using database management systems will likely be a critical part of your job. In this chapter, you will see how you can use data mining to extract valuable information to help you succeed. This chapter starts by introducing basic concepts of database management systems. Additional practical instruction on how to use Microsoft Access to set up a database is given on this book's accompanying CD.

3.1 Data Management and Data Modelling

At the centre of almost every information system is a database, used to store data so that it can be processed to provide useful information. A database is used by almost every firm to record a history of that firm's transactions. This historical data can be hugely useful in uncovering patterns and relationships the firm had never even considered before, a practice known as "data mining," something that is explained later in this chapter. The most common type of database is a relational database, so-named because the basic structure for storing data is a table and the word relation is another name for a table. A **relational database** is defined as a series of related tables, stored together with a minimum of duplication to achieve consistent and controlled pool of data.

> **relational database** A series of related tables, stored together with a minimum of duplication to achieve consistent and controlled pool of data.

So a relational database is made up of a number of tables. In loose terms, each table stores the data about someone or something of interest to the firm. This someone or something is known as an **entity**. (We will see later that sometimes the data about one entity is stored in two or more tables, and sometimes the data about two or more entities are stored in one table.) For example, a small business selling office furniture might have a customer table to store all the data about their customers, a supplier table to store information about suppliers, and an order table that records all the orders that are placed by its customers. In this example there are three entities – customer, order, and supplier.

> **entity** A person, place or thing about whom or about which an organisation wants to store data.

The rows in a table collect together all the data about one specific entity. For example, in the customer table, each row stores all the data about one particular customer – Jane Smith, for instance, or Desmond Paton. These rows are known as **records**. The columns in a table are the specific items of data that get stored, for example, first name, surname or telephone number. These columns are known as **fields** or attributes.

> **record** A row in a table; all the data pertaining to one instance of an entity.
>
> **field** A characteristic or attribute of an entity that is stored in the database.

So a database is made up of tables, which are made up of records, which are made up of fields. This is illustrated in Figure 3.1 using the customer table example. Notice that, in the figure, each customer has been given a unique customer number. This is because, as can be seen, there are two customers called Jane Wilson. Both work for the same company and, therefore,

Figure 3.1 The Customer Table for Office Furniture Seller

Customer_Number	First_Name	Surname	Address1	Address2
10	Jane	Wilson	London Road	Oxford
11	John	Smith	Quai d'Orsay	Paris
12	Jane	Wilson	London Road	Oxford
13	Desmond	Paton	Marshall Street	Johannesburg
14	Susan	Haynes	Baker Street	London

3

primary key A field in a table that is unique – each record in that table has a different value in the primary key field. The primary key is used to uniquely identify each record, and to create relationships between tables.

have the same address and phone number. The database needs some way of differentiating between them, and that is the job of the customer number, which is the **primary key**. Every table should have a primary key field used to identify individual records and also to create relationships between tables, something we will examine next.

The advantages and disadvantages of using a relational database to store data are listed in Table 3.1.

Table 3.1 Advantages and Disadvantages of the Database Approach

Advantages	Explanation
Improved strategic use of corporate data	Accurate, complete, up-to-date data can be made available to decision makers where, when, and in the form they need it. The database approach can also give greater visibility to the organisation's data resource.
Reduced data redundancy	Data is organised by the DBMS and stored in only one location. This results in more efficient use of system storage space.
Improved data integrity	With the traditional approach, some changes to data were not reflected in all copies of the data kept in separate files. This is prevented with the database approach, because no separate files contain copies of the same piece of data.
Easier modification and updating	The DBMS coordinates updates and data modifications. Programmers and users do not have to know where the data is physically stored. Data is stored and modified once. Modification and updating is also easier, because the data is stored in only one location in most cases.
Data and program independence	The DBMS organises the data independently of the application program, so the application program is not affected by the location or type of data. Introduction of new data types not relevant to a particular application does not require rewriting that application to maintain compatibility with the data file.
Better access to data and information	Most DBMS have software that makes it easy to access and retrieve data from a database. In most cases, users give simple commands to get important information. Relationships between records can be more easily investigated and exploited, and applications can be more easily combined.
Standardisation of data access	A standardised, uniform approach to database access means that all application programs use the same overall procedures to retrieve data and information.

Table 3.1 *Continued*

Advantages	Explanation
A framework for program development	Standardised database access procedures can mean more standardisation of program development. Because programs go through the DBMS to gain access to data in the database, standardised database access can provide a consistent framework for program development. In addition, each application program need address only the DBMS, not the actual data files, reducing application development time.
Better overall protection of the data	Accessing and using centrally located data is easier to monitor and control. Security codes and passwords can ensure that only authorised people have access to particular data and information in the database, thus ensuring privacy.
Shared data and information resources	The cost of hardware, software, and personnel can be spread over many applications and users. This is a primary feature of a DBMS.
Disadvantages	Explanation
More complexity	DBMS can be difficult to set up and operate. Many decisions must be made correctly for the DBMS to work effectively. In addition, users have to learn new procedures to take full advantage of a DBMS.
More difficult to recover from a failure	With the traditional approach to file management, a failure of a file affects only a single program. With a DBMS, a failure can shut down the entire database.
More expensive	DBMS can be more expensive to purchase and operate. The expense includes the cost of the database and specialised personnel, such as a database administrator, who is needed to design and operate the database. Additional hardware might also be required.

Relationships Between Tables

Consider the customer table (Figure 3.1) and the order table (Figure 3.2) in the office furniture seller's database. It should be obvious that there is a relationship between these two – the firm needs to know which orders have been placed by which customer, otherwise they wouldn't know where to ship the goods or who to charge for them. How this relationship is created in a database is shown in Figure 3.2, which shows the order table. For example, the fourth record in the table is an order for a computer desk. The first field in the table, order number, is the order

Order_Number	Description	Price	Colour	Customer_Number
100	Swivel chair	€89	Black	10
101	Coat rack	€15	Silver	10
102	White board	€23	White	11
103	Computer desk	€150	Brown	13
104	Filing cabinet	€50	Gray	10

Figure 3.2 The Order Table for Office Furniture Seller

table's primary key. Then there are details of what the order is, description, price and colour. The last field on the right hand side is the customer number. This creates the relationship between order and customer – customer 13 has ordered the computer desk. To find out who customer 13 is, look back at Figure 3.1, find 13 in the customer number field, and we see it is Desmond Paton. We also find the delivery address – the desk is being shipped to South Africa. The customer number, in the order table, is known as a **foreign key**.

foreign key When a primary key is posted into another table to create a relationship between the two, it is known as a foreign key.

This is an extremely convenient and useful way of organising data (refer back to Table 3.1). It means, in this case, that the delivery address doesn't have to be stored twice – once with the order and again with the customer details. Storing the same information twice is very bad practice and leads to all sorts of problems. If a customer moves and one address is updated but the other is not, then the firm has useless data – they don't know which address is the correct one. A large part of organising data involves deciding which fields are going to be primary keys and identifying where the foreign keys should be. A process for making that decision is described next.

Designing Relational Databases

This section describes an approach to designing a relational database. A database design is also known as a data model or a database schema. It is a list of all the tables in the database, along with all the fields, with any primary and foreign keys identified. The approach has four stages:

1 Identify all entities.
2 Identify all relationships between entities.
3 Identify all attributes.
4 Resolve all relationships.

If you are trying this approach out for yourself, you are unlikely to get the perfect data model the first time. The approach is iterative, that is, once you do all four stages once, examine the resulting schema. If it doesn't work perfectly, go back to stage one and adjust your list of entities, then go through the rest of the stages again. Do this over and over again until, eventually, a good data model emerges.

Identify Entities

The first step is to identify all the entities you want to store data about. This is usually done by interviewing the firm's managers and staff. If there are too many of them to interview, sometimes database designers will use a questionnaire to get opinions from as many people as possible. If you are designing a database for a student project, you will probably think that this first step is the easy bit, but in fact getting the right list of entities is vital if your data model is to be useful, and it is often not a trivial task, specifically because you have to interview different people and each might give you a different list! This problem is examined more closely in Chapter 8.

Identify Relationships

You next need to identify any relationships that exist between entities. The sort of relationships that you have to identify are relationships that the firm wants to store information about. For example, there might be a relationship between customers and suppliers – some of them might play golf together. However, this is unlikely to be the sort of thing the firm will want to store. The relationship between customers and orders is definitely something that the firm will want to store, so that they can see which customers have placed which orders.

Like identifying entities, identifying relationships between them is not trivial and may take several attempts to get right.

Once you identify a relationship, there are three things you need to document about it: degree, cardinality, and optionality.

The **degree** of a relationship is simply how many entities are involved, and this figure is often two. When the degree is two, it is known as a "binary relationship."

degree The number of entities involved in a relationship.

The **cardinality** of a relationship is whether each entity in the relationship is related to one or more than one of the other entities. For example, going back to the customer-order relationship, each order is placed by just one customer, but each customer can place many orders. Hence, the cardinality in this case is one to many (1 : M). Cardinality for a binary relationship can be one to one (1 : 1), one to many (1 : M) or many to many (M : M).

cardinality In a relationship, cardinality is the number of one entity that can be related to another entity.

Lastly, the **optionality** documents whether the relationship must exist for each entity or whether it is optional. For instance, an order must be placed by a customer – there is no option. An order can't exist unless a customer has placed it! However, a customer can be in the database even though he or she has no current orders, so the relationship is optional for the customer.

optionality If a binary relationship is optional for an entity, that entity doesn't have to be related to the other.

All of the above is documented in an entity-relationship diagram, shown in Figure 3.3.

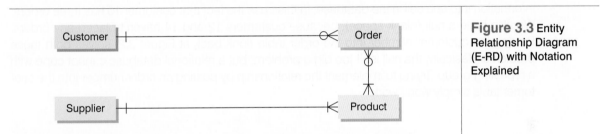

Figure 3.3 Entity Relationship Diagram (E-RD) with Notation Explained

The crow's foot notation means "many," so a supplier supplies many products, but each product is supplied by only one supplier.

The 0 and | represent optionality – a 0 means the relationship is optional so a customer doesn't have to have an order. A | means not-optional (or "obligatory") so an order has to have one (and only one) customer.

It is important to note that the database designer doesn't get to make up the degree, cardinality and optionality herself. These are dictated to her by what are known as the **enterprise rules**, which the designer must uncover by, usually, interviewing staff. An example of the enterprise rules describing the customer-order relationship is as follows:

enterprise rules The rules governing relationships between entities.

■ Each order must be placed by one and only one customer.

■ Each customer can place many orders, but some won't have placed any orders.

Enterprise rules are specific to the firm. For example, consider the relationship between employee and car, which a firm wants to store so it can manage its parking spaces. One employee can own as many cars as he can afford, so does that mean this relationship is one to many? Not necessarily. If the firm has decided that it is only going to store information on one car for each of its employees, then the relationship is one to one, regardless of how many cars each actually owns. The relationship will probably be optional on one side, because not every employee will own a car, but every car in the database will be owned by an employee.

Identify Attributes

The third stage is to identify all the attributes that are going to be stored for each entity. An attribute should be the smallest sensible piece of data that is to be stored. For example, customer name is probably a bad attribute – customer first name and surname would be better (some databases also include title and initial as separate attributes). Why is this? It is so that first name and surname can be accessed separately. For example if you wanted to start a letter to a customer, "Dear John," you would be unable to do this if you had stored the name as "John Smith." In this case, the letter would have to read "Dear John Smith." As before, attributes can be identified by interviewing staff.

Resolve Relationships

The customer-order relationship was implemented by taking the primary key of a customer and posting it as a foreign key in the order table. This is essentially what resolving a relationship means – deciding how to implement it. Sometimes a relationship between two entities will result in three tables being implemented, sometimes one, most often two. There are a series of rules to decide what tables to implement and which primary keys to use as a foreign key.

First, let us examine the customer-order relationship more closely to see why we implemented it the way we did.

If we had taken the order table primary key (order number) and posted it as a foreign key in the customer table, we would have had two problems, both illustrated in Figure 3.4. First, we have a repeating group – that means we would be trying to squeeze more than one piece of information into one cell in the database, in this case the fact that customer 10 has three orders. We also have a null (blank space), because customers 12 and 14 haven't placed any orders. Posting the customer number into the order table (look back at Figure 3.2) solves both those problems. Basically, the null isn't too big a problem, but a relational database cannot cope with a repeating group. Trying to implement the relationship by posting an order number into the customer table simply won't work.

Figure 3.4 Posting Order Number into Customer for Office Furniture Seller

Customer_Number	First_Name	Surname	Address1	Address2	Order_Number
10	Jane	Wilson	London Road	Oxford	100,101,104
11	John	Smith	Quai d'Orsay	Paris	102
12	Jane	Wilson	London Road	Oxford	
13	Desmond	Paton	Marshall Street	Johannesburg	103
14	Susan	Haynes	Baker Street	London	

A full discussion of resolving relationships is beyond the scope of this book. However, there only are six types of binary relationship. Figure 3.5 gives one example of each and explains how to implement it. Note that the figure illustrates the most "elegant" way to resolve each relationship, not necessarily the most efficient in terms of access time. A company with a lot of data would implement their database for speed rather than elegance. What this means in practice is that their database would have some nulls in the foreign keys.

What you should end up with after you resolve each relationship is a list of tables along with all primary and foreign keys identified, such as that shown in Figure 3.6. This could then be implemented using a database management system.

1. One-to-one relationship, obligatory on both sides.

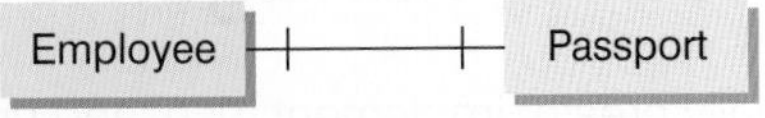

   Employee – Passport

   Each employee must have one and only one passport, each passport must have one and only one employee.

   To resolve this relationship, combine both entities into one table.

2. One-to-one relationship, optional on one side.

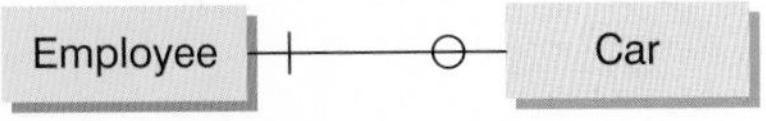

   Employee – Company car

   Each employee might have one and only one company car, each company car is owned by one and only one employee.

   To resolve this relationship, take the primary key from employee and post it as a foreign key in company car.

3. One-to-one relationship, optional on both sides.

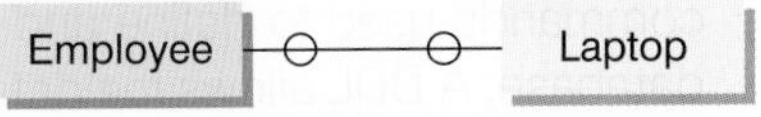

   Employee – Laptop

   Each employee might have one laptop, each laptop might belong to one employee (but some are for general use and, therefore, won't belong to anyone).

   To resolve this relationship, implement three tables – an employee table, a latop table and a new table that we will call "owns." The owns table only has two fields – employee number and laptop number. The primary key of owns is a "composite key" (i.e. it is the employee number and laptop number combined, and each combination of the two is unique).

4. One-to-many relationship, many side obligatory to one side.

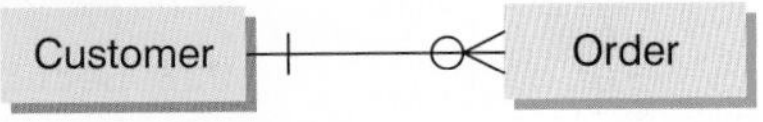

   Customer – Order

   A customer can place many orders, but might have placed no orders, each order must be placed by one and only one employee.

   Resolve this relationship by taking the primary key from customer and posting it as a foreign key in order.

5. One-to-many relationship, many side optional to one side.

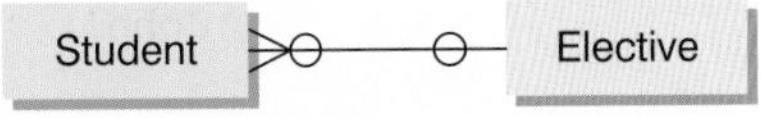

   Student – Elective module

   A student might take one elective module, each module is taken by many students (i.e. the students don't have to take an elective module).

   Most companies would implement this in the same way as Relationship 4. However, the way to avoid nulls in the foreign key is to implement three tables – one for student, one for elective module, and one that we'll call "studies" (as a student studies a module). The studies table just has two fields – student number and module number. The primary key of the studies table is student number (or you could implement a composite key).

6. Many-to-many relationship.

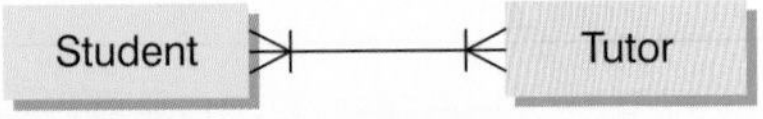

   Student – Tutor

   Each tutor teaches many students, each student is taught by many tutors.

   To resolve this relationship, implement three tables – one for student, one for tutor, and a third we'll call teaches. The teaches table has two fields – student number and tutor number, and its primary key is a composite key (i.e. a combination of student number and tutor number).

Figure 3.5 The Six Types of Binary Relationship

Customer{Customer_Number#, FirstName, Surname, Telephone}

Order{Order_Number#, Description, Price Colour, Customer_Number}

Supplier{Supplier_Number#, Company_Name, Contact_FirstName, Contact_Surname, Telephone}

Figure 3.6 A Database Design (Also Known as a Data Model or a Database Schema)
Primary keys are identified with a # symbol, foreign keys are underlined.

3.2 Database Management Systems

How do we actually create, implement, use, and update a database? The answer is found in the database management system. A DBMS is a group of programs used as an interface between a database and application programs or between a database and the user. The capabilities and types of database systems, however, vary, but generally they provide the following.

Creating and Modifying the Database

Schemas or designs are entered into the DBMS (usually by database personnel) via a data definition language. A **data definition language (DDL)** is a collection of instructions and commands used to define and describe data and relationships in a specific database. A DDL allows the database's creator to describe the data and relationships. Structured Query Language (SQL) is a DDL. Figure 3.7 shows four SQL statements to create a database called Lettings, a table called Landlords and insert a record about John Smith.

data definition language (DDL) A collection of instructions and commands used to define and describe data and relationships in a specific database.

Figure 3.7 SQL as a data definition language

```
CREATE DATABASE Lettings;

USE Lettings;

CREATE TABLE landlords(
Firstname CHAR(10),
Surname CHAR(10),
Telephone CHAR(10));

INSERT INTO landlords(
'John', 'Smith', '123456');
```

data dictionary A detailed description of all the data used in the database.

Another important step in creating a database is to establish a **data dictionary**, a detailed description of all data used in the database. The data dictionary describes all the fields in the database, their range of accepted values, the type of data (such as alphanumeric or numeric), the amount of storage space needed for each, and a note of who can access each and who updates each. Figure 3.8 shows a typical data dictionary entry.

Figure 3.8 A Typical Data Dictionary Entry for the Customer Table for Office Furniture Seller

Attribute	Data Type	Primary Key?	Required?
Customer_Number	Text	Y	Y
First_Name	Text	N	Y
Surname	Text	N	Y
Date_of_Birth	Date	N	N

A data dictionary helps achieve the advantages of the database approach in these ways:

- *Reduced data redundancy:* By providing standard definitions of all data, it is less likely that the same data item will be stored in different places under different names.

For example, a data dictionary reduces the likelihood that the same part number would be stored as two different items, such as PT_NO and PARTNO.

■ *Increased data reliability:* A data dictionary and the database approach reduce the chance that data will be destroyed or lost. In addition, it is more difficult for unauthorised people to gain access to sensitive data and information.

■ *Assists program development:* With a data dictionary, programmers know what data is stored and what data type each field is. This information is valuable when writing programs that make use of the data.

■ *Easier modification of data and information:* The data dictionary and the database approach make modifications to data easier, because users do not need to know where the data is stored. The person making the change indicates the new value of the variable or item, such as part number, that is to be changed. The database system locates the data and makes the necessary change.

Storing and Retrieving Data

One function of a DBMS is to be an interface between an application program and the database. When an application program needs data, it requests that data through the DBMS. Suppose that, to calculate the total price of a new car, a car dealer pricing program needs price data on the engine option – six cylinders instead of the standard four cylinders. The application program, thus, requests this data from the DBMS. In doing so, the application program follows a logical access path. Next, the DBMS, working with various system programs, accesses a storage device, such as disk drives, where the data is stored. When the DBMS goes to this storage device to retrieve the data, it follows a path to the physical location (physical access path) where the price of this option is stored. In the pricing example, the DBMS might go to a disk drive to retrieve the price data for six-cylinder engines. This relationship is shown in Figure 3.9.

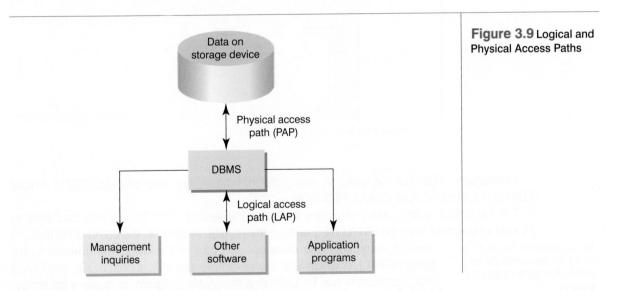

Figure 3.9 Logical and Physical Access Paths

This same process is used if a user wants to get information from the database. First, the user requests the data from the DBMS. For example, a user might give a command, such as LIST ALL OPTIONS FOR WHICH PRICE IS GREATER THAN 200 Euros. This is the logical access path (LAP). Then, the DBMS might go to the options price section of a disk to get the information for the user. This is the physical access path (PAP).

Two or more people or programs attempting to access the same record in the same database at the same time can cause a problem. For example, an inventory control program might attempt to reduce the inventory level for a product by ten units, because ten units, were just shipped to a customer. At the same time, a purchasing program might attempt to increase the inventory level for the same product by 200 units, because more inventory was just received.

concurrency control A method of dealing with a situation in which two or more people need to access the same record in a database at the same time.

Without proper database control, one of the inventory updates might not be correctly made, resulting in an inaccurate inventory level for the product. **Concurrency control** can be used to avoid this potential problem. One approach is to lock out all other application programs from access to a record if the record is being updated or used by another program.

Manipulating Data and Generating Reports

After a DBMS has been installed, employees, managers, and consumers can use it to review reports and obtain important information. Some databases use Query-by-Example (QBE), which is a visual approach to developing database queries or requests (see Figure 3.10).

Figure 3.10 Query by **Example** *Some databases use Query by Example (QBE) to generate reports and information.*

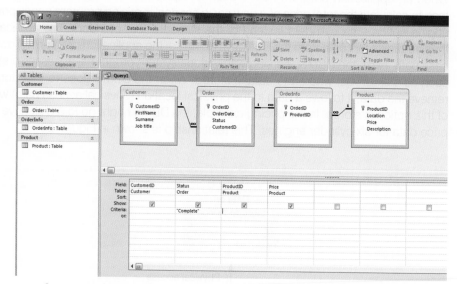

SOURCE: Courtesy of Microsoft Corporation.

Alternatively, SQL can be used to query the database. For example, SELECT * FROM EMPLOYEE WHERE JOB_CLASSIFICATION = "C2".

This will output all employees who have a job classification of "C2." The "*" tells the DBMS to include all columns from the EMPLOYEE table in the results. In general, the commands that are

data manipulation language (DML) The commands that are used to manipulate the data in a database.

used to manipulate the database are part of the **data manipulation language (DML)**, of which SQL is an example. (So SQL is both a DDL and DML.) SQL commands can be used in a computer program, to query a database, which is convenient for programmers.

SQL, which is pronounced like the word "sequel," was developed in the 1970s at the IBM Research Laboratory in San Jose, California. In 1986, the American National Standards Institute (ANSI) adopted SQL as the standard query language for relational databases. Since ANSI's acceptance of SQL, interest in making SQL an integral part of relational databases on both mainframe and personal computers has increased. SQL has many built-in functions, such as average (AVG), find the largest value (MAX), find the smallest value (MIN), and others. Table 3.2 contains examples of SQL commands.

SQL lets programmers learn one powerful query language and use it on systems ranging from PCs to the largest mainframe computers (see Figure 3.11). Programmers and database users also find SQL valuable, because SQL statements can be embedded into many programming languages (discussed in Chapter 4), such as C++, Visual Basic and COBOL. Because SQL uses standardised and simplified procedures for retrieving, storing, and manipulating data in a database system, the popular database query language can be easy to understand and use.

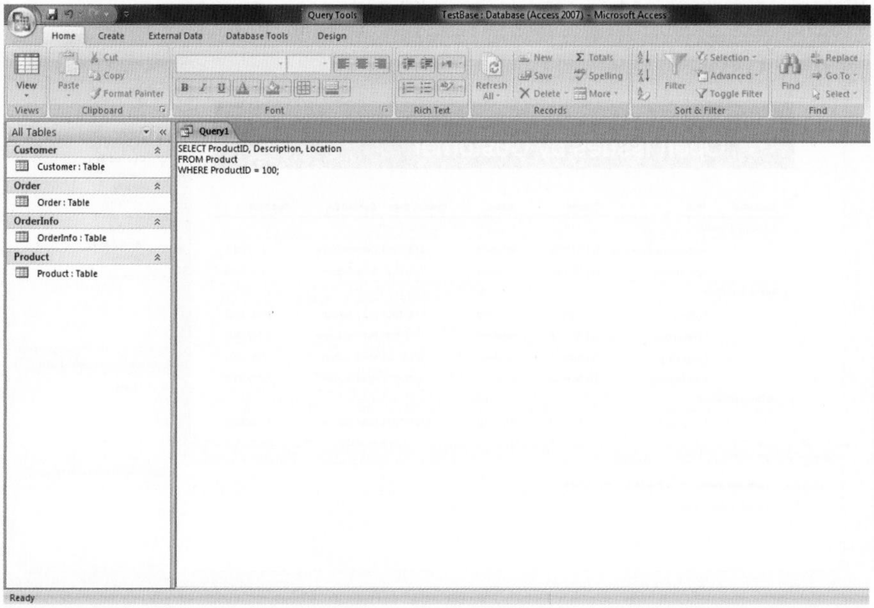

Figure 3.11 Structured Query Language
Structured Query Language (SQL) has become an integral part of most relational databases.

SOURCE: Courtesy of Microsoft Corporation.

Table 3.2 Examples of SQL Commands

SQL Command	Description
SELECT ClientName, Debt FROM Client WHERE Debt > 1000	This query displays all clients (ClientName) and the amount they owe the company (Debt) from a database table called Client for clients who owe the company more than €1000 (WHERE Debt > 1000).
SELECT ClientName, ClientNum, OrderNum FROM Client, Order WHERE Client.ClientNum=Order.ClientNum	This command is an example of a join command that combines data from two tables: the client table and the order table (FROM Client, Order). The command creates a new table with the client name, client number, and order number (SELECT ClientName, ClientNum, OrderNum). Both tables include the client number, which allows them to be joined. This is indicated in the WHERE clause, which states that the client number in the client table is the same as (equal to) the client number in the order table (WHERE Client.ClientNum=Order.ClientNum).
GRANT INSERT ON Client to Guthrie	This command is an example of a security command. It allows Bob Guthrie to insert new values or rows into the Client table.

After a database has been set up and loaded with data, it can produce any desired reports, documents, and other outputs, as shown in Figure 3.12. These outputs usually appear in screen displays or hard-copy printouts. The output-control features of a database program allow you to select the records and fields to appear in reports. You can also make calculations specifically for the report by manipulating database fields. Formatting controls and organisation options (such as report headings) help you to customise reports and create flexible, convenient, and powerful information-handling tools.

Figure 3.12 Database **Output** *A database application offers sophisticated formatting and organisation options to produce the right information in the right format.*

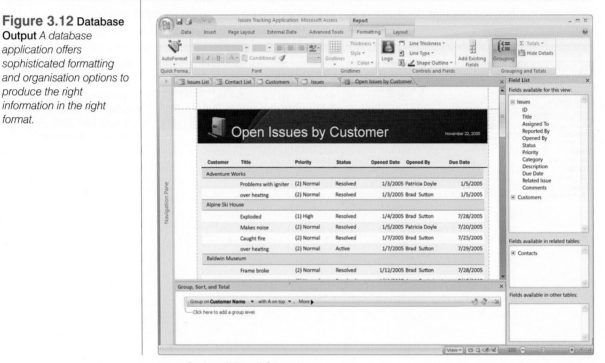

SOURCE: Courtesy of Microsoft Corporation.

A DBMS can produce a wide variety of documents, reports, and other outputs that can help organisations achieve their goals. The most common reports select and organise data to present summary information about some aspect of company operations. For example, accounting reports often summarise financial data, such as current and past-due accounts. Many companies base their routine operating decisions on regular status reports that show the progress of specific orders toward completion and delivery.

A database is central to every business selling over the internet. Amazon, for example, has a huge amount of data that other books sellers must envy, on customers' past purchases, which it uses to make personal recommendations and generate more sales. Each time a returning customer comes back to the website, a report is produced (which becomes part of the webpage itself, something described later in this chapter of their recommendations).

Prezi.com uses a database to store text and images, and then turn them into innovate presentations, to rival the "one slide after another" approach taken by software, such as Microsoft PowerPoint. Prezi gives users a large virtual canvas where they can assemble their material and then navigate through it in whatever order they please. It forgoes the linear presentation model for something much more free-form and creative.[1]

database administrator (DBA)
The role of the database administrator is to plan, design, create, operate, secure, monitor, and maintain databases.

Database Administration

Database systems require a skilled **database administrator (DBA)**. A DBA is expected to have a clear understanding of the fundamental business of the organisation, be proficient in the use of selected database management systems, and stay abreast of emerging technologies and new design approaches. The role of the DBA is to plan, design, create, operate, secure, monitor, and maintain databases. Typically, a DBA has a degree in computer science or management information systems and some on-the-job training with a particular database product or more extensive experience with a range of database products.

The DBA works with users to decide the content of the database – to determine exactly what entities are of interest and what attributes are to be recorded about those entities. Thus, personnel outside of IS must have some idea of what the DBA does and why this function is important. The DBA can play a crucial role in the development of effective information systems to benefit the organisation, employees, and managers.

The DBA also works with programmers as they build applications to ensure that their programs comply with database management system standards and conventions. After the database is built and operating, the DBA monitors operations logs for security violations. Database performance is also monitored to ensure that the system's response time meets users' needs and that it operates efficiently. If there is a problem, the DBA attempts to correct it before it becomes serious.

Some organisations have also created a position called the **data administrator**, a non-technical, but important, role that ensures that data is managed as an important organisational resource. The data administrator is responsible for defining and implementing consistent principles for a variety of data issues, including setting data standards and data definitions that apply across all the databases in an organisation. For example, the data administrator would ensure that a term such as "customer" is defined and treated consistently in all corporate databases. This person also works with business managers to identify who should have read or update access to certain databases and to selected attributes within those databases. This information is then communicated to the database administrator for implementation. The data administrator can be a high-level position reporting to top-level managers.

data administrator A non-technical position responsible for defining and implementing consistent principles for a variety of data issues.

Selecting a Database Management System

The database administrator often selects the database management system for an organisation. The process begins by analyzing database needs and characteristics. The information needs of the organisation affect the type of data that is collected and the type of database management system that is used. Important characteristics of databases include the following:

- *Database size:* The number of records or files in the database.
- *Database cost:* The purchase or lease costs of the database.
- *Concurrent users:* The number of people who need to use the database at the same time (the number of concurrent users).
- *Performance:* How fast the database is able to update records.
- *Integration:* The ability to be integrated with other applications and databases.
- *Vendor:* The reputation and financial stability of the database vendor.

For many organisations, database size doubles about every year or two.[2] Wal-Mart, for example, adds billions of rows of data to its databases every day. Its database of sales and marketing information is approximately 500 terabytes large. According to Dan Phillips, Wal-Mart's vice president of information systems, "Our database grows because we capture data on every item, for every customer, for every store, every day." Wal-Mart deletes data after two years and doesn't track individual customer purchases. Scientific databases are likely the largest in the world. The UK forensic DNA database is vast and NASA's Stanford Linear Accelerator Centre stores about 1000 terabytes of data.[3]

Using Databases with Other Software

Database management systems are often used with other software packages or the internet. A DBMS can act as a front-end application or a back-end application. A front-end application is one that directly interacts with people or users. Marketing researchers often use a database as a front end to a statistical analysis program. The researchers enter the results of market questionnaires or surveys into a database. The data is then transferred to a statistical analysis program to determine the potential for a new product or the effectiveness of an advertising campaign. A back-end application interacts with other programs or applications; it only indirectly interacts with people or users. When people request information from a website, the website can interact with a database (the back end) that supplies the desired information. For example, you can connect to a university website to find out whether the university's library has a book you want to read. The website then interacts with a database that contains a catalogue of library books and articles to determine whether the book you want is available.

3.3 Database Applications

Today's database applications manipulate the content of a database to produce useful information. Common manipulations are searching, filtering, synthesising, and assimilating the data, using a number of database applications. These applications allow users to link the company databases to the internet, set up data warehouses and marts, use databases for strategic business intelligence, place data at different locations, use online processing and open connectivity standards for increased productivity, develop databases with the object-oriented approach, and search for and use unstructured data, such as graphics, audio, and video.

Linking Databases to the Internet

Linking databases to the internet is an incredibly useful application for organisations and individuals. Every e-commerce website uses database technology to dynamically create its webpages, saving vast amounts of efforts. Every time you visit Amazon, for instance, or the South Afrikan fashion retailer Edgars, or one of thousands of other internet businesses, the pages you see are created at that time from a database of product and customer information. This simplifies the maintenance of the website – to add new stock, all that needs to be done is enter a new record in the product table.

Google has scanned over 15 million books using optical character recognition technology, and has stored each book in a huge database.[4] The use of optical character recognition means that users of the service, known as Google Books, can search the actual text rather than having to search on information about the book such as the title or author. Google's technology can scan books at a rate of 1000 pages per hour.[5]

Developing a seamless integration of traditional databases with the internet is often called a "semantic web." A semantic web allows people to access and manipulate a number of traditional databases at the same time through the internet. Many software vendors – including IBM, Oracle, Microsoft, Macromedia, Inline Internet Systems, and Netscape Communications – are incorporating the capability of the internet into their products. Such databases allow companies to create an internet-accessible catalogue, which is nothing more than a database of items, descriptions, and prices.

In addition to the internet, organisations are gaining access to databases through networks to get good prices and reliable service. Connecting databases to corporate websites and networks can lead to potential problems, however. One database expert believes that up to 40 per cent of websites that connect to corporate databases are susceptible to hackers taking complete control of the database. By typing certain characters in a form on some websites, a hacker can issue SQL commands to control the corporate database.

Data Warehouses and Data Centres

The data necessary to make sound business decisions is stored in a variety of locations and formats. This data is initially captured, stored, and managed by transaction processing systems that are designed to support the day-to-day operations of the organisation. For decades, organisations have collected operational, sales, and financial data with their transaction processing systems (explained fully in Chapter 7). The data can be used to support decision making using data warehouses and data mining.

Data Warehouses

A **data warehouse** is a database or a collection of databases that holds business information from many sources in the enterprise, covering all aspects of the company's processes, products, and customers. The data warehouse provides business users with a multidimensional view of the data they need to analyze business conditions. A data warehouse stores historical data that has been extracted from transaction processing systems, as well as data from external sources (see Figure 3.13). This operational and external data is "cleaned" to remove inconsistencies and integrated to create a new information database that is more suitable for business analysis.

data warehouse A database or collection of databases that collects business information from many sources in the enterprise, covering all aspects of the company's processes, products, and customers.

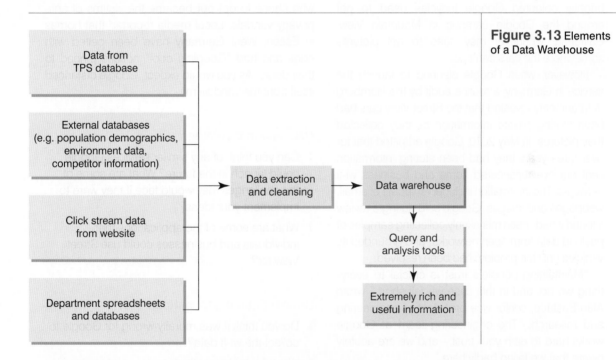

Figure 3.13 Elements of a Data Warehouse

Data from TPS database

External databases (e.g. population demographics, environment data, competitor information)

Click stream data from website

Department spreadsheets and databases

Data extraction and cleansing

Data warehouse

Query and analysis tools

Extremely rich and useful information

Data warehouses typically start out as very large databases, containing millions and even hundreds of millions of data records. As this data is collected from various sources, one data warehouse is built that business analysts can use. To keep it accurate, the data warehouse receives regular updates. Old data that is no longer needed is purged. It is common for a data warehouse to contain from three to ten years of current and historical data. Data-cleaning tools can merge data from many sources to make the warehouse, automate data collection and verification, delete unwanted data, and maintain the data. Data warehouses can also get data from unique sources. Oracle's Warehouse Management software, for example, can accept information from radio frequency identification (RFID) technology, which is being used to tag products as they are shipped or moved from one location to another.[6] A data warehouse can be extremely difficult to establish, with the typical cost exceeding €2 million.

Ethical and Societal Issues

3

Google Has to Navigate More than the World's Streets

Google Street View is a technology that allows users to view pictures taken along many streets all over the world. The technology allows users to navigate via a web browser the locations as if they were driving them. Locations covered include North and South America, many parts of Europe, Australia, parts of the Far East and South Africa. In South Africa the provinces of Gauteng, Northern Cape and the Western Cape are currently included.

To get the images, Google employees drive cars with large cameras fitted to their roofs along the streets of the world, swapping to the distinctive brightly coloured Google tricycles used to get around the Google campus in Mountain View, California, whenever they need to get pictures somewhere the cars can't go.

However, when Google planned to launch the service in Germany, a routine audit by the Hamburg data authority revealed that the Street View cars had been storing private information as they collected their pictures. In May 2010, Google admitted that for over three years they had been storing information sent out over unsecured home and business wi-fi networks. The information included snippets of email, webpages and images. Google said during a review it found it had "been mistakenly collecting samples of payload data from open networks" and grounded its vehicles until the problem had been resolved.

"Maintaining people's trust is crucial to everything we do, and in this case we fell short," wrote Alan Eustace, senior vice president of engineering and research. "The engineering team at Google works hard to earn your trust – and we are acutely aware that we failed badly here."

Google said the problem dated back to 2006 when "an engineer working on an experimental wi-fi project wrote a piece of code that sampled all categories of publicly broadcast wi-fi data."

That code was included in the software the Street View cars used and "quite simply, it was a mistake," said Mr Eustace. "This incident highlights just how publicly accessible, open non-password protected wi-fi networks are today."

In the UK, the information commissioner said that wi-fi data accidentally collected by Google's Street View cars will be deleted within nine months and that there would be no further enquiries into the matter. Deputy commissioner David Smith said that there was no indication that any information collected "had fallen into the wrong hands."

This was not enough for many people in Germany who have opted out of the service. Those who opt out have their houses blurred in the pictures. However, not everyone in Germany was against Google on this issue. Some home-owners who chose to opt out became the victims of anti-privacy vandals. Local media reported that homes in Essen, West Germany have been pelted with eggs and had "Google's cool" notices pinned to their doors. As you would expect, Google distanced itself from the vandalism.

Discussion Questions

1 Can you think of any similar services Google could launch in the future? What are some of the challenges they would face if they were to implement your ideas?

2 What are some of the applications that individuals and businesses could use Street View for?

Critical Thinking Questions

1 Do you think it was morally wrong for Google to collect the wi-fi data?

2 What rights do you think people and businesses should have in relation to Street View?

SOURCES: BBC, "EnglandGoogle admits wi-fi data collection blunder," May 15, 2010. Available from: http://news.bbc.co.uk/1/hi/technology/8684110.stm.
BBC, "Google's wi-fi data to be deleted," November 19, 2010. Available from: http://www.bbc.co.uk/news/technology-11797907.
BBC, "German vandals target Street View opt-out homes," November 24, 2010. Available from: http://www.bbc.co.uk/news/technology-11827862.

Data Centres

Databases, and the systems that manipulate them, can be physically stored on computers as small as a PC or as large as mainframes and data centres. A **data centre** is a climate-controlled building or set of buildings that house database servers and the systems that deliver mission critical information and services. Data centres of large organisations are often distributed among several locations, but a recent trend has many organisations consolidating their data centres into a few large facilities. For example, the US federal government is working to save billions of dollars by consolidating 1100 data centres into a dozen facilities. The project is recognised as the largest data centre consolidation in history.[7]

Data centre A climate-controlled building or set of buildings that house database servers and the systems that deliver mission-critical information and services.

Microsoft recently constructed a €500 million, 36 000-square-metre data centre on 44 acres in San Antonio. Google invested €600 million for a mega data centre in Lenoir, North Carolina, and €750 million for another in Goose Creek, South Carolina. Clearly, storing and managing data is a serious business.

Traditional data centres consist of warehouses filled with row upon row of server racks and powerful cooling systems to compensate for the heat generated by the processors. Microsoft,[8] Google,[9] and others have adopted a new modular data centre approach, which uses large shipping containers like the ones that transport consumer goods around the world. The huge containers, such as the HP POD, are packed with racks of servers prewired and cooled to easily connect and set up. Microsoft recently constructed a 65 000 square-metre data centre in Northlake, Illinois. It is considered to be one of the largest in the world and is filled with 220 shipping containers packed with servers. Microsoft says that a new shipping container can be wheeled into place and connected to the internet within hours[10] (see Figure 3.14).

Figure 3.14
Modular Data Centre
Modular data centres, such as the this one from IBM, use large shipping containers to store racks of servers.

(SOURCE: Courtesy of IBM.)

Modular data centres are becoming popular around the world due to their convenience and efficiencies. Taiwan's Technology Research Institute is working to create standards for modular data centres in shipping containers that they say will reduce the costs of these units by half while increasing ease of use and reducing energy demands.[11]

Although a company's data sits in large super-cooled data centres, the people accessing that data are typically in offices spread across the country or around the world. In fact, the

IS at Work

The Database that Drives the Austrian Turnpike

ASFINAG Maut Service GmbH is the company responsible for planning, financing, building, maintaining, and operating the Austrian turnpike and highway system – all 2100 kilometres of it. As with most European countries, Austria has relied on manually collected tolls to finance its highway system. Recently, the country turned to state-of-the-art database-driven systems to transport its highways into the twenty-first century.

Bernd Datler, head of system development for AS-FINAG Maut Service GmbH, calls it "the world's first fully automated, free-flowing tolling system for commercial vehicles." ASFINAG hired Austrian IS service provider Raiffeisen Informatik GmbH to implement a system that would tag and track more than 700 000 commercial vehicles across Austrian roads, automatically billing each vehicle according to complicated specifications. The database that supports this massive system would have to contend with a variety of data formats and high frequency of data input. It would feed numerous systems to serve a variety of needs. The fully automated, free-flowing tolling system begins with river registration. Drivers can register online, by phone, or at local sales centres. The registration process collects information about the driver, the vehicle, and the company that employs the driver. This information is fed into the database and is accessed by a customer relationship management (CRM) system as needed. Upon registration, drivers are provided with a radio transceiver box that is mounted to the dashboard of the commercial vehicle. The 800 tollgates along Austrian highways were fitted with special microwave receivers that connect with the boxes on drivers' dashboards without the drivers needing to stop. As drivers pass a tollgate, data is continuously collected and entered into the database as transactions. Rather than billing a flat rate, the automated system allows for custom rates to be applied. Fees are calculated based on several criteria, including the size of the vehicle, whether it is full or empty, the time of day, and the vehicle's emission class. These last two criteria can be used to motivate drivers to travel at off-peak times and to use vehicles with low emissions.

The database also collects photographic data. Cameras mounted at tollgates photograph every vehicle to catch unregistered vehicles. The photos are used to see vehicle tags and registration to track down the vehicle's owner. The photo system is also used to collect tolls from noncommercial vehicles that use a registration sticker on the windshield. Drivers can access their toll information online using a web-based portal that delivers real-time reporting. Data is automatically transferred into a data warehouse, where ASFINAG managers have access to powerful business intelligence (BI) tools that allow them to generate reports on highway usage from multiple perspectives. The system manages 2.5 million transactions per week, without the need for any human intervention. Invoices are automatically generated in the customer's native language and are delivered electronically. The system was designed to be interoperable as well, reading not only Austrian-registered vehicles, but also vehicles registered in Switzerland, Germany, and Italy. All in all, the project took more than 100 Raiffeisen Informatik IS professionals 18 months to complete. The team met its deadline and hit its goals in terms of quality, functionality, and costs.

Discussion Questions

1 What unique challenges did the ASFINAG project present for database installation, administration, and security?

2 How does the "world's first fully automated, free-flowing tolling system for commercial vehicles" benefit drivers and the highway system?

Critical Thinking Questions

1 What business functions are supported by the database at ASFINAG?

2 What database applications discussed in the chapter are used in conjunction with the ASFINAG database?

SOURCES: "Raiffeisen Informatik - SAP Software Powers Outsourced Toll-Col-lection System," SAP Customer Success Story. Available from: www.sap.com/solutions/sap-businessobjects/customers. Accessed May 15, 2010; ASFINAG website. Available from: www.asfinag.at/en. Accessed May 15, 2010.

expectation of data centre specialists, such as Hewlett-Packard CEO Mark Hurd, is that, in the near future, the only personnel on duty at data centres will be security guards. Data centres are approaching the point of automation, whereby they can run and manage themselves while being monitored remotely. This is referred to as a "lights out" environment. The State of Vermont recently switched to a lights out approach for nights and weekends, reducing its staff by 40 per cent and significantly reducing costs.[12] HP has moved to automated data centres, reducing its IT staffing needs by 3000.[13]

As data centres continue to expand in terms of the quantity of data that they store and process, their energy demands are becoming an increasingly significant portion of the total energy demands of humanity. Businesses and technology vendors are working to develop green data centres that run more efficiently and require less energy for processing and cooling.

Distributed Databases

Distributed processing involves placing processing units at different locations and linking them via telecommunications equipment. A **distributed database** – a database in which the data is spread across several smaller databases connected through telecommunications devices – works on much the same principle. A user in the London branch of a clothing manufacturer, for example, might make a request for data that is physically located at corporate headquarters in Milan, Italy. The user does not have to know where the data is physically stored (see Figure 3.15).

distributed database A database in which the data is spread across several smaller databases connected via telecommunications devices.

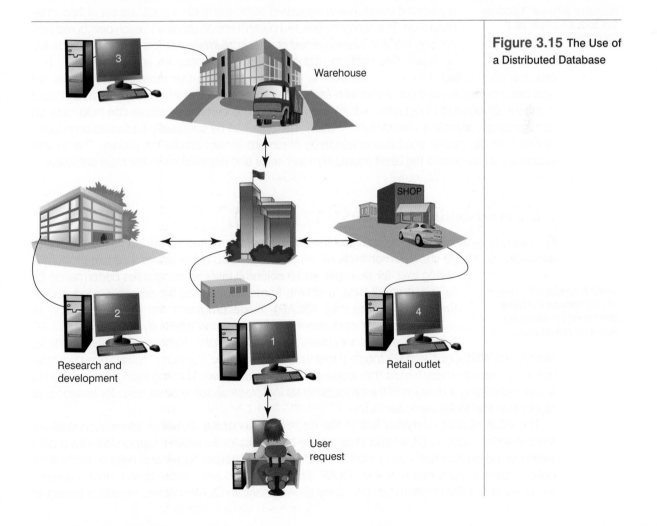

Figure 3.15 The Use of a Distributed Database

Warehouse

SHOP

Research and development

Retail outlet

User request

For the clothing manufacturer, computers might be located at the headquarters, in the research and development centre, in the warehouse, and in a company-owned retail store. Telecommunications systems link the computers so that users at all locations can access the same distributed database no matter where the data is actually stored.

Distributed databases give organisations more flexibility in how databases are organised and used. Local offices can create, manage, and use their own databases, and people at other offices can access and share the data in the local databases. Giving local sites more direct access to frequently used data can improve organisational effectiveness and efficiency significantly. The New York City Police Department, for example, has about 35 000 officers searching for information located in over 70 offices around the city.[14] According to one database programmer, "They had a lot of information available in a lot of different database systems and wanted fingertip access to the information in a very user-friendly front-end." Dimension Data helped the police department by developing an US$11(€8) million system to tie their databases together. "Now, we can send them critical details before they even arrive at the scene," said police commissioner Raymond Kelly. The new distributed database is also easier for police officers to use.

Despite its advantages, distributed processing creates additional challenges in integrating different databases (information integration), maintaining data security, accuracy, timeliness, and conformance to standards.[15] Distributed databases allow more users direct access at different sites; thus, controlling who accesses and changes data is sometimes difficult.[16] Also, because distributed databases rely on telecommunications lines to transport data, access to data can be slower.

replicated database A database that holds a duplicate set of frequently used data.

To reduce telecommunications costs, some organisations build a **replicated database**. A replicated database holds a duplicate set of frequently used data. The company sends a copy of important data to each distributed processing location when needed or at predetermined times. Each site sends the changed data back to update the main database on an update cycle. This process, often called data synchronization, is used to make sure that replicated databases are accurate, up to date, and consistent with each other. A railway, for example, can use a replicated database to increase punctuality, safety, and reliability. The primary database can hold data on fares, routings, and other essential information. The data can be continually replicated and downloaded from the master database to hundreds of remote servers across the country. The remote locations can send back the latest figures on ticket sales and reservations to the main database.

Online Analytical Processing (OLAP)

For nearly two decades, databases and their display systems have provided flashy sales presentations and trade show demonstrations. All you have to do is ask where a certain product is selling well, for example, and a colourful table showing sales performance by region, product type, and time frame appears on the screen. Called **online analytical processing (OLAP)**, these programs are now being used to store and deliver data warehouse information efficiently. The leading OLAP software vendors include Cognos, Comshare, Hyperion Solutions, Oracle, MineShare, WhiteLight, and Microsoft. (Note that, in this context, the word "online" does not refer to the internet – it simply means that a query is made and answered immediately, as opposed to a user submitting a query and the processing taking place at some other time, for instance, at night when the servers are used less.)

online analytical processing (OLAP) Software that allows users to explore data from a number of perspectives.

The value of data ultimately lies in the decisions it enables. Powerful information-analysis tools in areas, such as OLAP and data mining (see Chapter 5), when incorporated into a data warehousing architecture, bring market conditions into sharper focus and help organisations deliver greater competitive value. OLAP provides top-down, query-driven data analysis; data mining provides bottom-up, discovery-driven analysis. OLAP requires repetitive testing of

Table 3.3 Comparison of OLAP and Data Mining

Characteristic	OLAP	Data Mining
Purpose	Supports data analysis and decision making	Supports data analysis and decision making
Type of analysis supported	Top-down, query-driven data analysis	Bottom-up, discovery-driven data analysis
Skills required of user	Must be very knowledgeable of the data and its business context	Must trust in data mining tools to uncover valid and worthwhile hypotheses

user-originated theories; data mining requires no assumptions and instead identifies facts and conclusions based on patterns discovered. OLAP, or multidimensional analysis, requires a great deal of human ingenuity and interaction with the database to find information in the database. A user of a data-mining tool does not need to figure out what questions to ask; instead, the approach is, "here's the data, tell me what interesting patterns emerge." For example, a data-mining tool in a credit card company's customer database can construct a profile of fraudulent activity from historical information. Then, this profile can be applied to all incoming transaction data to identify and stop fraudulent behaviour, which might otherwise go undetected. Table 3.3 compares the OLAP and data-mining approaches to data analysis.

Visual, Audio, and Other Database Systems

Organisations are increasingly finding a need to store large amounts of visual and audio signals in an organised fashion. Credit card companies, for example, enter pictures of charge slips into an image database using a scanner. The images can be stored in the database and later sorted by customer name, printed, and sent to customers along with their monthly statements. Image databases are also used by physicians to store x-rays and transmit them to clinics away from the main hospital. Financial services, insurance companies, and government branches are using image databases to store vital records and replace paper documents. Drug companies often need to analyze many visual images from laboratories. The PetroView database and analysis tool allows petroleum engineers to analyze geographic information to help them determine where to drill for oil and gas. Recently, a visual-fingerprint database was used to solve a 40-year-old murder case in California. Visual databases can be stored in some object-relational databases or special-purpose database systems. Many relational databases can also store graphic content.

Combining and analyzing data from different databases is an increasingly important challenge. Global businesses, for example, sometimes need to analyze sales and accounting data stored around the world in different database systems. Companies, such as IBM, are developing virtual database systems to allow different databases to work together as a unified database system. DiscoveryLink, one of IBM's projects, can integrate biomedical data from different sources. The Centre for Disease Control (CDC) also has the problem of integrating more than 100 databases on various diseases.

In addition to visual, audio, and virtual databases, there are a number of other special-purpose database systems. Spatial data technology involves using a database to store and access data according to the locations it describes and to permit spatial queries and analysis. MapExtreme is spatial technology software from MapInfo that extends a user's database so that it can store, manage, and manipulate location-based data. Police departments, for example, can use this type of software to bring together crime data and map it visually so that patterns are easier to analyze. Police officers can select and work with spatial data at a specified location, within a rectangle, a given radius, or a polygon, such as their area of jurisdiction. For example, a police officer can request a list of all alcohol shops within a two-mile radius of the police station. Builders and insurance companies use spatial data to make decisions related to natural hazards. Spatial data can even be used to improve financial risk management with information stored by investment type, currency type, interest rates, and time.

Object-Oriented and Object-Relational Database Management Systems

An **object-oriented database** uses the same overall approach of object-oriented programming that was first discussed in Chapter 2. With this approach, both the data and the processing instructions are stored in the database. For example, an object-oriented database could store monthly expenses and the instructions needed to compute a monthly budget from those expenses. A traditional DBMS might only store the monthly expenses. In an object-oriented database, a method is a procedure or action. A sales tax method, for example, could be the procedure to compute the appropriate sales tax on an order. A message is a request to execute or run a method. Many object-oriented databases have their own query language, called object query language (OQL), which is similar to SQL, discussed earlier.

object-oriented database A database that stores both data and its processing instructions.

An object-oriented database uses an **object-oriented database management system (OODBMS)** to provide a user interface and connections to other programs. A number of computer vendors sell or lease OODBMS, including eXcelon, Versant, Poet, and Objectivity. Object-oriented databases are used by a number of organisations. Versant's OODBMS, for example, is being used by companies in the telecommunications, financial services, transportation, and defence industries. The Object Data Standard is a design standard by the Object Database Management Group (www.odmg.org) for developing object-oriented database systems.

object-oriented database management system (OODBMS) A group of programs that manipulate an object-oriented database and provide a user interface and connections to other application programs.

An **object-relational database management system (ORDBMS)** provides a complete set of relational database capabilities plus the ability for third parties to add new data types and operations to the database. These new data types can be audio, images, unstructured text, spatial, or time series data that require new indexing, optimisation, and retrieval features. Each of the vendors offering ORDBMS facilities provides a set of application programming interfaces to allow users to attach external data definitions and methods associated with those definitions to the database system. They are essentially offering a standard socket into which users can plug special instructions. DataBlades, Cartridges, and Extenders are the names applied by Oracle and IBM to describe the plug-ins to their respective products. Other plug-ins serve as interfaces to web servers.

object-relational database management system (ORDBMS) A DBMS capable of manipulating audio, video, and graphical data.

Summary

At the start of this chapter we set out the THREE main principles relating to the organisation and handling requirements of data within information systems in organisations, together with the key learning objectives for each. It's now time to summarise the chapter by recapping on those THREE principles: can you recall what is important and why about each one?

1 **Data management and modelling are key aspects of organising data and information.** Data is one of the most valuable resources that a firm possesses. The most common way to organise data is in a relational database. A relational database is made up of tables, each table is made up of records and each record is made up of fields.

Loosely, each table stores information about an entity. An entity is someone or something that the firm wants to store information about. The fields are the characteristics or attributes about the entity that are stored. A record collects together all the fields of a particular instance of an entity. A primary key uniquely identifies each record.

Designing a database involves identifying entities and the relationships between them, as well as the attributes of each entity. There are rules to follow to convert related entities into a data model, a list of all tables to be implemented in the database, with primary and foreign key identified. Basic data manipulations include selecting, projecting, and joining.

2 **A well-designed and well-managed database is central to almost all information systems and is an extremely valuable tool in supporting decision making.** A DBMS is a group of programs used as an interface between a database and its users and other application programs. When an application program requests data from the database, it follows a logical access path. The actual retrieval of the data follows a physical access path. Records can be considered in the same way: A logical record is what the record contains; a physical record is where the record is stored on storage devices. Schemas are used to describe the entire database, its record types, and their relationships to the DBMS. Schemas are entered into the computer via a data definition language, which describes the data and relationships in a specific database. Another tool used in database management is the data dictionary, which contains detailed descriptions of all data in the database.

After a DBMS has been installed, the database can be accessed, modified, and queried via a data manipulation language. A specialised data manipulation language is Structured Query Language (SQL). SQL is used in several popular database packages today and can be installed on PCs and mainframes.

Popular single-user DBMS include Corel Paradox and Microsoft Access. IBM, Oracle, and Microsoft are the leading DBMS vendors.

Selecting a DBMS begins by analyzing the information needs of the organisation. Important characteristics of databases include the size of the database, the number of concurrent users, its performance, the ability of the DBMS to be integrated with other systems, the features of the DBMS, the vendor considerations, and the cost of the database management system.

3 **The number and types of database applications will continue to evolve and yield real business benefits.** Organisations are building data warehouses, which are relational database management systems specifically designed to support management decision making.

Predictive analysis is a form of data mining that combines historical data with assumptions about future conditions to forecast outcomes of events, such as future product sales or the probability that a customer will default on a loan.

Business intelligence is the process of getting enough of the right information in a timely manner and usable form and analyzing it so that it can have a positive effect on business strategy, tactics, or operations. Competitive intelligence is one aspect of business intelligence limited to information about competitors and the ways that information affects strategy, tactics, and operations. Competitive intelligence is not espionage – the use of illegal means to gather information. Counterintelligence describes the steps an organisation takes to protect information sought by "hostile" intelligence gatherers.

With the increased use of telecommunications and networks, distributed databases, which allow multiple users and different sites access to data that may be stored in different physical locations, are gaining in popularity. To reduce telecommunications costs, some organisations build replicated databases, which hold a duplicate set of frequently used data.

Online analytical processing (OLAP) programs are being used to store data and allow users to explore the data from a number of different perspectives.

An object-oriented database uses the same overall approach of object-oriented programming, first discussed in Chapter 4. With this approach, both the data and the processing instructions are stored in the database. An object-relational database management system (ORDBMS) provides a complete set of relational database capabilities, plus the ability for third parties to add new data types and operations to the database. These new data types can be audio, video, and graphical data that require new indexing, optimisation, and retrieval features.

In addition to raw data, organisations are increasingly finding a need to store large amounts of visual and audio signals in an organised fashion. There are also a number of special-purpose database systems.

Review Questions

1 What is an attribute? How is it related to an entity?

2 Define the term "database." How is it different from a database management system?

3 What are the advantages of the database approach?

4 What is a database schema, and what is its purpose?

5 What is the difference between a data definition language (DDL) and a data manipulation language (DML)?

6 How do you resolve a many-to-many relationship?

7 What is a distributed database system?

8 What are the differences between running a query with SQL and Query By Example?

9 What is an ORDBMS? What kind of data can it handle?

10 What is business intelligence? How is it used?

Discussion Questions

1 When designing a database, should a company store all the attributes it possibly can or should it be more selective?

2 Imagine a company could store information about which of its webpages are viewed by visitors the most, which search terms are used to find its website, the order that visitors view the pages on the website and how long is spent looking at each page. What are some of the decisions a company could make using this data?

3 Make a list of the databases in which data about you exists. How is the data in each database captured? Who updates each database and how often? Is it possible for you to request a printout of the contents of your data record from each database? What data privacy concerns do you have?

4 You are the vice president of information technology for a large, multinational consumer packaged goods company (such as Procter and Gamble, Unilever, or Gillette). You must make a presentation to persuade the board of directors to invest €5 million to establish a competitive-intelligence group – including people, data-gathering services, and software tools. What key points do you need to make in favour of this investment? What arguments can you anticipate that others might make?

5 Identity theft, where people steal your personal information, continues to be a threat. Assume that you are the database administrator for a corporation with a large database. What steps would you implement to help you prevent people from stealing personal information from the corporate database?

Web Exercises

1 Use a search engine to find information on specific products for one of the following topics: business intelligence, object-oriented databases, or audio databases. Write a brief report describing what you found, including a description of the database products and the companies that developed them.

2 Use a search engine to find three companies in an industry that interests you that use a database management system. Describe how databases are used in each company. Could the companies survive without the use of a database management system? Why?

Case One

Mega Data Centres and Their Environmental Impact

To keep up with the unprecedented amount of information being generated, businesses need to invest in larger and larger data centres. Many businesses find it more economical to outsource their data centre needs. Dozens of mega data centres are being constructed around the world for a variety of uses. Mega data centres typically cost hundreds of millions of euros and consume acres of property. One of the world's largest was recently constructed for around €300 million by Next Generation Data, outside of Newport in South Wales. The 70 000-square-meter facility has enough space to house 19 000 server racks that each hold a dozen servers. The facility hopes to serve hundreds of businesses, many located in nearby London. Its first two tenants, BT and Logica, signed contracts worth a combined total of about €29 million.

Next Generation Data can provide its customers with certain guarantees of service and data protection. To guard against terrorist attacks, the data centre has "triple-skinned walls, bomb-proof glass, prison-grade perimeter fencing, infrared detection, uses biometric recognition, and employs ex-special forces security guards." The data centre's network is equally protected, and all systems have failback systems to guard against hardware or electrical failure. The biggest environmental impact of mega data centres is their energy consumption for the processing, storage, and cooling required. The data centre for Next Generation Data outside Newport has its own energy substation that provides 90 megavolt-amperes of electrical power. That's roughly equivalent to the requirements of a city of 400 000 people. Multiply this by the dozens of other mega data centres going online, including huge facilities, such as Microsoft's new 65 000-square-metre centre near Chicago, and the energy requirements increase around the world. Adding the energy needs of mega data centres to the increasing energy demands of developing countries with huge populations such as China and India results in unprecedented worldwide energy consumption.

When coal-burning power plants fulfill these energy demands, they add carbon to the atmosphere, which many scientists argue accelerates climate change. A number of efforts are underway to counteract the growing demand for data centres. Hardware manufacturers are producing servers that are more efficient, requiring half the energy as their predecessors to do twice the work. As new data centres go into operation, they are implementing new energy-efficient technologies. Gradually, as old wasteful systems break down, managers will migrate data to new greener systems. The Newport data centre uses fresh air cooling and Energy Star rated equipment to help reduce its impact on the environment. The Environmental Protection Agency has recently released Energy Star standards for servers and is developing standards for enterprise storage as well. Such standards give hardware and software manufacturers targets to shoot for to keep systems running efficiently with less energy.

In light of environmental pressures and public sentiment, many companies are making pledges to reduce the energy requirements of information systems. Disney recently pledged to reduce its electricity consumption by 20 per cent by 2013. By measuring Power Usage Effectiveness (PUE), companies can compare IS equipment power requirements to environmental power requirements. A PUE of 2 – the industry average – indicates that processing and cooling are requiring equal amounts of energy. Disney and others hope to invest in technologies that have significantly lower energy requirements. Google discovered that adjusting thermostats in its data centres up from the frigid 60s to 80 degrees Fahrenheit helped to lower its PUE to 1.5. Without a doubt, data centres will continue consuming increasing amounts of real estate. Through a combination of techniques and technologies that include consolidation, more efficient servers, more effective cooling techniques, and alternative energy sources, expanding data centres can reduce their impact on the environment.

Discussion Questions

1 Why is the increase in data centre construction a concern for the environment?

2 What efforts can help to minimise the impact of data centres on the environment?

Critical Thinking Questions

1 Companies are finding it necessary to weigh the value of storing information against the value of affecting the environment. Write a few paragraphs outlining the importance of both and describing how companies might financially benefit from protecting both.

2 If you were a systems administrator for a data centre, what steps would you take to create and manage a data centre to store the maximum amount of valuable data with the minimum impact on the environment?

SOURCES: Niccolai, James, "750 000-sq.ft. data center opens in Wales," Computerworld, March 15, 2010. Available from: www.computerworld.com; Lawson, Stephen, "EPA drafting Energy Star standards for enterprise storage," Computerworld, May 10, 2010. Available from: www.computerworld.com; Brodkin, Jon, "Disney, Verizon go green in the data center," Computerworld, October 6, 2009. Available from: www.computerworld.com; Niccolai, James, "Google: Crank up the heat in your data center," Computerworld, April 29, 2010. Available from: www.computerworld.com.

Case Two

Handwriting Recognition with Nearest Neighbour

Handwriting recognition is an important application – many touch screen mobile devices allow input in this way. Some of these systems require a learning period, where the device asks the user to write several words, so it can "learn" to recognise its owner's handwriting. What the system is actually doing is building up a database of examples of the user's writing, which it can expand every time the user writes something new. This database then becomes the "training data," which the system uses to recognise new writing. Each character that is written gets stored as a record in the database, with the fields being tiny portions of the screen, perhaps with the value 1 representing if the square is black (blue in the diagram), a 0 if it is blank (green), and values in-between for shades of gray (where the user has lightly touched the screen). The letter T is shown in the right column.

One part of the record in the character table for this T would look like this:

Letter	1,7	2,7	3,7	4,7	5,7	6,7	7,7	1,6	2,6
T	0	1	1	1	1	1	0	0	0

and so on. (The field names are the coordinates of the grid – 1,7 is the top left hand corner, 2,7 is the square beside it, which is the first cell of the horizontal line of the T.)

To see how this might be used to identify a letter T from a letter L, consider the nearest neighbour data mining algorithm. The nearest neighbour can be visualised very easily if there are only two or three fields. Any more fields and it becomes impossible for us to illustrate it. So let's consider the above table, pretending that it only contains three fields – Letter, 1,7 and 2,7. If we had five examples of T and five of L, we could plot out the data on a two dimensional grid as follows:

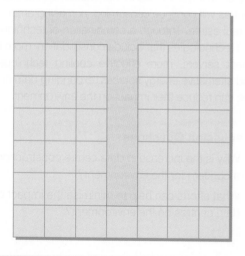

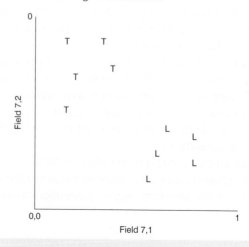

In the figure there are two clear clusters, one for Ts and one for Ls. When the user types a new letter, if it is closest (or "nearest," hence the name) to the T cluster then the computer recognises that letter as a "T." If it is closest to the L cluster, it recognises it as an "L."

Humans can see instantly which datapoint is closest to another, but how does a computer "see" this? Well, the computer can easily calculate the distance between two datapoints using Pythagoras' Theorem.

The nearest neighbour approach is simple to implement but is extremely calculation costly – if there are 1000 examples of letters in the database, then it must perform the Pythagoras calculation 1000 times to find the nearest datapoint. And in the above example there would be only 50 (7 $\times$ 7 plus letter) fields in the table. On a real touch screen, there would be many more than this, although using more sophisticated techniques than nearest neighbour, not all of them would need to be stored.

Questions

1 Why would the nearest neighbour approach not be suitable for handwriting recognition on a real mobile device?

2 Using the web if you have to, remind yourself of Pythagoras' Theorem and the calculation that the computer must do.

Critical Thinking Questions

1 Do you think handwriting is a good way to input data in the first place? Explain your answer.

2 Why can the makers of mobile devices not simply include their own database of handwriting in the system? Why do they need users create their own?

Notes

1 Digital Analog, "prezi – new style of presentation," 26 September, 2010. Available from: http://digitalanalog.in/2010/09/26/prezi-new-style-of-presentation/.

2 Staff, "Data, Data, Everywhere," *Information Week*, January 9, 2006, p. 49.

3 Staff, "Biggest Brother: DNA Evidence," *The Economist*, January 5, 2006.

4 Crawford, James, "On the future of books," 14 October, 2010. Available from: http://booksearch.blogspot.com/2010/10/on-future-of-books.html.

5 Kelly, Kevin, "Scan this book," *New York Times Magazine*, 14 May, 2006.

6 Hall, Mark, "Databases Can't Handle RFID," *Computerworld,* February 7, 2005, p. 8.

7 Miller, Rich, "Feds Commence Huge Data Center Consolidation," Data Center Knowledge, March 1, 2010. Available from: www.datacenterknowledge.com/archives/2010/03/01/feds-commence-huge-data-center-consolidation.

8 Miller, Rich, "Microsoft Goes All-in on Container Data Centers," Data Center Knowledge, December 2, 2008. Available from: www.datacenterknowledge.com/archives/2008/12/02/microsoft-goes-all-in-on-container-data-centers.

9 Miller, Rich, "Google Unveils Its Container Data Center," Data Center Knowledge, April 1, 2009. Available from: www.datacenterknowledge.com/archives/2009/04/01/google-unveils-its-container-data-center.

10 Miller, Rich, "Microsoft to Open Two Massive Data Centers," Data Center Knowledge, June 29, 2009. Available from: www.datacenterknowledge.com.

11 Nystedt, Dan, "Project aims to halve cost of a data center," *InfoWorld*, June 2, 2010. Available from: www.infoworld.com.

12 Lemos, Rob, "Vermont's Lights Out Data Center: No One's Home Nights or Weekends," *CIO*, October 9, 2009.

13 Thibodeau, Patrick, "HP job cuts point to shifting IT skills," *Computerworld*, June 1, 2010. Available from: www.computerworld.com.iHealthBeat, May 14, 2010. Available from: www.ihealthbeat.org/features/2010/personal-health-records-may-not-be-so-personal.aspx.

14 Murphy, David, "Fighting Crime in Real Time," *PC Magazine*, September 28, 2005, p. 70.

15 Kay, Russell, "Enterprise Information Integration," *Computerworld*, September 19, 2005, p. 64.

16 Babcock, Charles, "Protection Gets Granular," *InformationWeek,* September 23, 2005, p. 58.

CHAPTER 4 CONTENTS

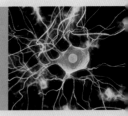

04

Telecommunications, the Internet, Intranets and Extranets

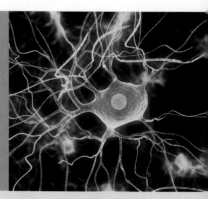

In this chapter, we will look at the FIVE main factors you need to understand when considering how business information systems interact with, and have specific needs of, the internet and web-based communications.

Principles	Learning Objectives
1. A telecommunications system has many fundamental components that must be carefully selected and work together effectively to enable people to meet personal and organisation objectives.	■ Identify and describe the fundamental components of a telecommunications system. ■ Identify several network types and describe the uses and limitations of each. ■ Name three basic processing alternatives for organisations that require two or more computer systems and discuss their fundamental features.
2. The internet provides a critical infrastructure for delivering and accessing information and services.	■ Briefly describe how the internet works, including alternatives for connecting to it and the role of internet service providers.
3. Originally developed as a document-management system, the World Wide Web has grown to become a primary source of news and information, an indispensible conduit for commerce, and a popular hub for social interaction, entertainment and communication.	■ Describe how the World Wide Web works and the use of web browsers, search engines and other web tools.
4. The internet and web provide numerous resources for finding information, communicating and collaborating, socialising, conducting business and shopping, and being entertained.	■ Identify and briefly describe several applications associated with the internet and the web. ■ Outline a process and identify tools used to create web content.
5. Popular internet and web technologies have been applied to business networks in the form of intranets and extranets.	■ Define the terms intranet and extranet and discuss how organisations are using them. ■ Identify several issues associated with the use of networks.

Why Learn About Telecommunications and Networks?

Today's decision makers need to access data wherever it resides. They must be able to establish fast, reliable connections to exchange messages, upload and download data and software, route business transactions to processors, connect to databases and network services, and send output to printers. Regardless of your chosen major or future career field, you will need the communications capabilities provided by telecommunications and networks, including the internet, especially if your work involves the supply chain. Among all business functions, supply chain management might use telecommunications and networks the most, because it requires cooperation and communications among workers in inbound logistics, warehouse and storage, production, finished product storage, outbound logistics, and most importantly, with customers, suppliers and shippers. Many supply chain organisations make use of the web to purchase raw materials, parts and supplies at competitive prices. All members of the supply chain must work together effectively to increase the value perceived by the customer, so partners must communicate well. Other employees in human resources, finance, research and development, marketing and sales positions must also use communications technology to communicate with people inside and outside the organisation. To be a successful member of any organisation, you must be able to take advantage of the capabilities that these technologies offer you. This chapter begins by discussing the importance of effective communications.

4

4.1 An Overview of Telecommunications

Telecommunications refers to the electronic transmission of signals for communications, by such means as telephone, radio and television. Telecommunications is creating profound changes in business, because it lessens the barriers of time and distance. Telecommunications not only is changing the way businesses operate, but the nature of commerce itself. As networks are connected with one another and transmit information more freely, a competitive marketplace demands excellent quality and service from all organisations.

Figure 4.1 shows a general model of telecommunications. The model starts with a sending unit (1), such as a person, a computer system, a terminal, or another device, that originates the message. The sending unit transmits a signal (2) to a modem (3) that can perform many tasks, which can include converting the signal into a different form or from one type to another. The modem then sends the signal through a medium (4). A **telecommunications medium** is any material substance that carries an electronic signal to support communications between a sending and receiving device. Another modem (5) connected to the receiving device

telecommunications medium Any material substance that carries an electronic signal to support communications between a sending and receiving device.

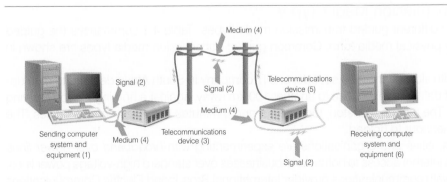

Medium (4)

Signal (2)

Signal (2)

Telecommunications device (5)

Medium (4)

Sending computer system and equipment (1)

Medium (4)

Telecommunications device (3)

Signal (2)

Receiving computer system and equipment (6)

Figure 4.1 Elements of a Telecommunications System *Telecommunications devices relay signals between computer systems and transmission media.*

(6) receives the signal. The process can be reversed, and the receiving unit (6) can send another message to the original sending unit (1). An important characteristic of telecommunications is the speed at which information is transmitted, which is measured in bits per second (bps). Common speeds are in the range of thousands of bits per second (Kbps) to millions of bits per second (Mbps) and even billions of bits per second (Gbps).

Advances in telecommunications technology allow us to communicate rapidly with clients and coworkers almost anywhere in the world. Telecommunications also reduces the amount of time needed to transmit information that can drive and conclude business actions.

Telecommunications technology enables business people to communicate with coworkers and clients from remote locations.

SOURCE: © John Prescott.

Channel Bandwidth

Telecommunications professionals consider the capacity of the communications path or channel when they recommend transmission media for a business. **Channel bandwidth** refers to the rate at which data is exchanged, usually measured in bits per second (bps) – the broader the bandwidth, the more information can be exchanged at one time. **Broadband communications** is a relative term but generally means a telecommunications system that can exchange data very quickly. For example, for wireless networks, broadband lets you send data at a rate greater than 1.5 Mbps. In general, today's organisations need more bandwidth for increased transmission speed to carry out their daily functions.

channel bandwidth The rate at which data is exchanged, usually measured in bits per second (bps).

broadband communications A relative term but generally means a telecommunications system that can exchange data very quickly.

Communications Media

In designing a telecommunications system, the transmission media selected depends on the amount of information to be exchanged, the speed at which data must be exchanged, the level of concern for data privacy, whether or not the users are stationary or mobile, and many other business requirements. Transmission media can be divided into two broad categories: *guided transmission media* in which communications signals are guided along a solid medium and *wireless* in which the communications signal is broadcast over airwaves as a form of electromagnetic radiation.

Guided Transmission Media Types

There are many different guided transmission media types. Table 4.1 summarises the guided media types by physical media form. Common guided transmission media types are shown in Figure 4.2.

Frustrated with slow connection speeds, one IT company in South Africa decided to race uploading 4 GB of data from one office to another 100 km away, against a homing pigeon carrying the same data. The pigeon, Winston, took 1 hour and 8 minutes to fly between the offices. The data took another hour to upload.[1]

Many utilities, cities and organisations are experimenting with *broadband over power lines (BPL)* to provide internet access to homes and businesses over standard high-voltage power lines. IBM is working with communications provider International Broadband Electric Communications

Table 4.1 Guided Transmission Media Types

Media Form	Description	Advantages	Disadvantages
Twisted-pair wire	Twisted pairs of copper wire, shielded or unshielded	Used for telephone service; widely available	Transmission speed and distance limitations
Coaxial cable	Inner conductor wire surrounded by insulation	Cleaner and faster data transmission than twisted-pair wire	More expensive than twisted-pair wire
Fibre-optic cable	Many extremely thin strands of glass bound together in a sheathing; uses light beams to transmit signals	Diameter of cable is much smaller than coaxial; less distortion of signal; capable of high transmission rates	Expensive to purchase and install
Broadband over power lines	Transmitted over standard high-voltage power lines	Can provide internet service to rural areas where cable and phone service may be nonexistent	Can be expensive and may interfere with ham radios and police and fire communications

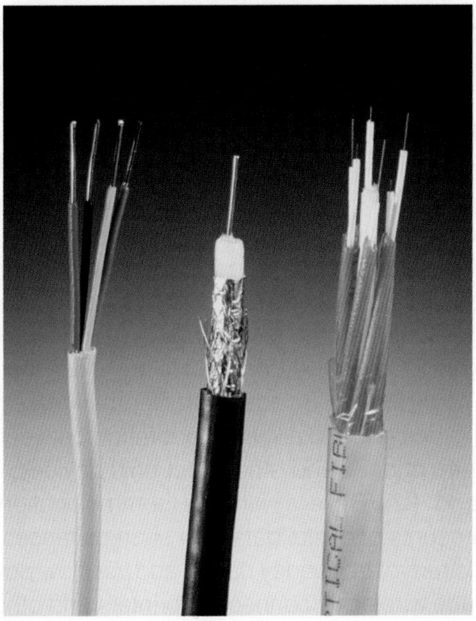

Figure 4.2 Types of Guided Transmission Media *Twisted-pair wire (left), coaxial cable (middle), fibre-optic cable (right)*

SOURCE: © Greg Pease/Getty Images.

to implement BPL networks to provide broadband access to rural residents in Alabama, Indiana, Virginia and Michigan. In addition to providing broadband service to electric customers, this new BPL connectivity will enable electric companies to better monitor, manage and control the reliability of their electric grids.[2]

Wireless Technologies

Wireless communications coupled with the internet are revolutionising how and where we gather and share information, collaborate in teams, listen to music or watch video, and stay in touch with our families and coworkers while on the road. The many advantages and freedom provided by wireless communications are causing many organisations to consider moving to an all-wireless environment.

Wireless telecommunications involves the broadcast of communications in one of three frequency ranges: microwave, radio and infrared, as shown in Table 4.2.

Table 4.2 Frequency Ranges Used for Wireless Communications

Technology	Description	Advantages	Disadvantages
Radio frequency range	Operates in the 3KHz–300 MHz range	Supports mobile users; costs are dropping	Signal highly susceptible to interception
Microwave – terrestrial and satellite frequency range	High-frequency radio signal (300 MHz–300 GHz) sent through atmosphere and space (often involves communications satellites)	Avoids cost and effort to lay cable or wires; capable of high-speed transmission	Must have unobstructed line of sight between sender and receiver; signal highly susceptible to interception
Infrared frequency range	Signals in the 300 GHz to 400 THz frequency range sent through air as lightwaves	Lets you move, remove, and install devices without expensive wiring	Must have unobstructed line of sight between sender and receiver; transmission effective only for short distances

near field communication (NFC)
A very short-range wireless connectivity technology designed for cell phones and credit cards.

Bluetooth A wireless communications specification that describes how cell phones, computers, faxes, printers and other electronic devices can be interconnected over distances of 3–10 metres at a rate of about 2 Mbps.

ultra wideband (UWB) A form of short-range communications that employs extremely short electromagnetic pulses lasting just 50 to 1000 picoseconds that are transmitted across a broad range of radio frequencies of several gigahertz.

Wi-Fi A medium-range wireless telecommunications technology brand owned by the Wi-Fi Alliance.

Some of the more widely used wireless communications options are discussed next.

Near field communication (NFC) is a very short-range wireless connectivity technology designed for cell phones and credit cards. With NFC, consumers can swipe their credit cards or even cell phones within a few centimetres of NFC point-of-sale terminals to pay for purchases.

Bluetooth is a wireless communications specification that describes how mobile phones, computers, printers and other electronic devices can be interconnected over distances of 3–10 metres at a rate of about 2 Mbps. Bluetooth enables users of multifunctional devices to synchronise with information in a desktop computer, send or receive faxes, print, and, in general, coordinate all mobile and fixed computer devices. The Bluetooth technology is named after the tenth century Danish King Harald Blatand, or Harold Bluetooth in English. He had been instrumental in uniting warring factions in parts of what is now Norway, Sweden and Denmark – just as the technology named after him is designed to allow collaboration between differing devices, such as computers, phones and other electronic devices.

Ultra wideband (UWB) is a wireless communications technology that transmits large amounts of digital data over short distances of up to 10 metres using a wide spectrum of frequency bands and very low power. Potential UWB applications include wirelessly connecting printers and other devices to desktop computers or enabling completely wireless home multimedia networks. UWB products are considered too expensive at this time to have broad market appeal, but prices are coming down.[3]

Wi-Fi is a wireless telecommunications technology brand owned by the Wi-Fi Alliance, which consists of about 300 technology companies, including AT&T, Dell, Microsoft, Nokia and Qualcomm. The alliance exists to improve the interoperability of wireless local area network products.

With a Wi-Fi wireless network, the user's computer, smartphone, or other mobile device has a wireless adaptor that translates data into a radio signal and transmits it using an antenna. A wireless access point, which consists of a transmitter with an antenna, receives the signal and decodes it. The access point then sends the information to the internet over a wired connection (see Figure 4.3). When receiving data, the wireless access point takes the information from the internet, translates it into a radio signal and sends it to the device's wireless adaptor. These devices typically come with built-in wireless transmitters and software to enable them to alert the user to the existence of a Wi-Fi network. The area covered by one or more interconnected wireless access points is called a "hot spot." Current Wi-Fi access points have a maximum

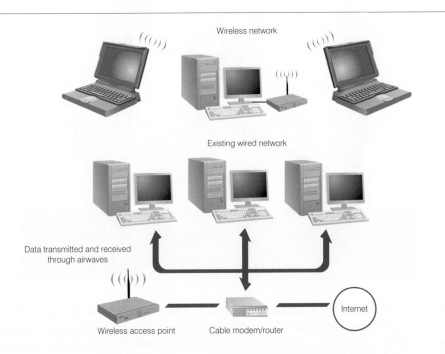

Figure 4.3 Wi-Fi Network

range of about 90 metres outdoors and 30 metres within a dry-walled building. Wi-Fi has proven so popular that hot spots are popping up in places, such as airports, coffee shops, college campuses, libraries and restaurants. Many cities have implemented Wi-Fi based networks for their citizens and government workers.

The availability of free Wi-Fi within a hotel's premises has become very popular with the business traveller. The Aloft and Element hotels, part of the Starwood chain, cater to the extended stay traveller. Both hotels have recently added free Wi-Fi service in their rooms and lobbies. At the other end of the accommodations spectrum, The Four Seasons Hotels and Resorts also offer free Wi-Fi. Many other hotels offer or are considering adding free Wi-Fi.[4]

Microwave Transmission

Microwave is a high-frequency (300 MHz–300 GHz) signal sent through the air. Terrestrial (Earth-bound) microwaves are transmitted by line-of-sight devices, so the line of sight between the transmitter and receiver must be unobstructed. Typically, microwave stations are placed in a series – one station receives a signal, amplifies it and retransmits it to the next microwave transmission tower. Such stations can be located roughly 48 km apart before the curvature of the Earth makes it impossible for the towers to "see" one another. Microwave signals can carry thousands of channels at the same time. Because they are line-of-sight transmission devices, microwave dishes are frequently placed in relatively high locations, such as mountains, towers, or tall buildings.

A communications satellite also operates in the microwave frequency range (see Figure 4.4). The satellite receives the signal from the Earth station, amplifies the relatively weak signal and then rebroadcasts it at a different frequency. The advantage of satellite communications is that satellites can receive and broadcast over large geographic regions. Such problems as the curvature of the Earth, mountains and other structures that block the line-of-sight microwave transmission make satellites an attractive alternative. Geostationary, low-Earth orbit and small mobile satellite stations are the most common forms of satellite communications.

A *geostationary satellite* orbits the Earth directly over the equator, approximately 35000 metres above the Earth, so that it appears stationary. The US National Weather Service relies on the Geostationary Operational Environmental Satellite program for weather imagery and quantitative data to support weather forecasting, severe storm tracking and meteorological research.

A *low earth orbit (LEO) satellite* system employs many satellites, each in an orbit at an altitude of less than 1600 km. The satellites are spaced so that, from any point on the Earth, at any time,

Figure 4.4 Satellite Transmission

Communications satellites are relay stations that receive signals from one Earth station and rebroadcast them to another.

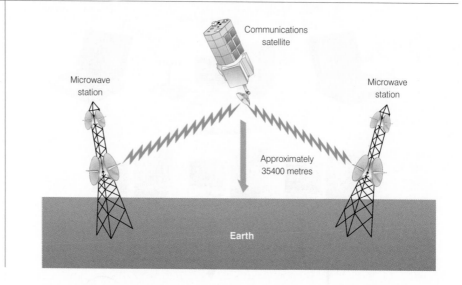

at least one satellite is on a line of sight. Iridium Communications Inc. provides a global communications network that spans the entire Earth using 66 satellites in a near polar orbit at an altitude of 800 km. Calls are routed among the satellites to create a reliable connection between call participants that cannot be disrupted by natural disasters, such as earthquakes, tsunamis, or hurricanes, that knock out ground-based wireless towers and wire or cable-based networks.[5] Iridium phones were the primary source of communication in New Orleans after Hurricane Katrina in 2005 and after the major earthquake in China in 2008.[6]

A *very small aperture terminal* (*VSAT*) is a satellite ground station with a dish antenna smaller than 3 metres in diameter. The US Army is buying thousands of VSATs under a five-year 5 bn Euro contract. Paul Brown, technical adviser for the Defense Communications and Army Transmission Systems, explains: "In a war zone, a soldier who needs to order parts would typically have to get into his vehicle and drive from one outlying camp to another. Providing them with a VSAT solution allows them to stay within the wire of their base and communicate directly to order those parts. VSATs save lives; that's a critical piece."[7]

3G Wireless Communications

3G wireless communications supports wireless voice and broadband speed data communications in a mobile environment. It is called 3G for third generation of solutions for wireless voice and data communications. Additional capabilities include mobile video, mobile e-commerce, location-based services, mobile gaming, and the downloading and playing of songs.

The ITU established a single standard for cellular networks in 1999. The goal was to standardise future digital wireless communications and allow global roaming with a single handset. Called IMT-2000, now referred to as 3G, this standard provides for faster transmission speeds in the range of 2–4 Mbps. Originally, 3G was supposed to be a single, unified, worldwide standard, but the 3G standards effort split into several different standards.

4G Wireless Communications

Fourth-generation broadband mobile wireless is expected to deliver more advanced versions of enhanced multimedia, smooth streaming video, universal access, portability across all types of devices, and, eventually, worldwide roaming capability. 4G will also provide increased data transmission rates in the 20–40 Mbps range.

LTE has the potential to download data at up to 100 Mbps.[8] T-Mobile is also planning a 4G network based on LTE. Telecommunications operator Teliasonera implemented the world's first 4G network. In a public demonstration, the network downloaded a 7 megabyte MP3 file in just one second.[9]

Worldwide Interoperability for Microwave Access (WiMAX)

Worldwide Interoperability for Microwave Access (WiMAX) is the common name for a set of IEEE 802. wireless metropolitan area network standards that support various types of communications access. In many respects, WiMAX operates like Wi-Fi, only over greater distances and at faster transmission speeds. A WiMAX tower connects directly to the internet via a high-bandwidth, wired connection. A WiMAX tower can also communicate with another WiMAX tower using a line-of-sight, microwave link. The distance between the WiMAX tower and an antenna can be as great as 48 km. WiMAX can support data communications at a rate of 70 Mbps. Fewer WiMAX base stations are required to cover the same geographical area than when Wi-Fi technology is used.

Worldwide Interoperability for Microwave Access (WiMAX) The common name for a set of IEEE 802.16 wireless metropolitan area network standards that support various types of communications access.

Clear residential modems provide up to 6 Mbps download speeds, whereas mobile internet customers can expect to receive up to 4 Mbps download speeds. Sprint is working with Intel, Motorola, Nokia and Samsung to provide WiMAX-capable PC cards, gaming devices, laptops, cameras and even phones.

WiMAX is a key component of Intel's broadband wireless strategy to deliver innovative mobile platforms for "anytime, anywhere." Centrino is a marketing initiative from Intel. Intel touts that its Centrino laptops deliver improved performance, have a longer battery life and can access a variety of wireless networks, including WiMAX. Dell, Fujitsu, Lenovo, Panasonic, Samsung and Toshiba are among the manufacturers that produce laptop computers with the Centrino label.[10]

Most telecommunications experts agree that WiMAX is an attractive option for developing countries with little or no wireless telephone infrastructure. However, it is not clear whether WiMAX will be as successful in developed countries, such as the United States, where regular broadband is plentiful and cheap and where 3G wireless networks already cover most major metropolitan areas.

Telecommunications Hardware

Networks require various telecommunications hardware devices to operate, including smartphones, modems, multiplexers, front-end processors, private branch exchanges, switches, bridges, routers and gateways.

Smartphones

A smartphone combines the functionality of a mobile phone, camera, web browser, email tool, MP3 player, and other devices into a single handheld device. For example, the Apple iPhone is a combination mobile phone, widescreen iPod and internet access device capable of supporting email and web browsing. An iPhone user can connect to the internet either via Wi-Fi or AT&T's Edge data network.

Smartphones have their own software operating systems and are capable of running applications that have been created for their particular operating system. As a result, the capabilities of

Apple iPhone *The iPhone is a combination mobile phone, widescreen iPod and internet access device.*

SOURCE: Courtesy of Apple.

smartphones will continue to evolve as new applications become available. The Apple iPhone (iPhone OS), BlackBerry (RIM OS) and Palm (Palm OS) smartphones come with their own proprietary operating systems. The Android, Microsoft Windows Mobile and Symbian operating systems are used on various manufacturers' smartphones.

Smartphone applications are developed by the manufacturers of the handheld device, by the operators of the communications network on which they operate and by third-party software developers. More than 125 000 Apple iPhone applications can be downloaded from the Apple Apps for iPhone online store. BlackBerry, Palm and Android-based phones sell their apps through their own online stores – BlackBerry App World, Palm Pre Applications and Android Market.

The Droid smartphone is manufactured by Motorola and uses the Android operating system from Google. The Nexus One is another smartphone that uses Google's Android mobile operating system. The device is manufactured according to Google's specifications by Taiwan's HTC Corporation. The phone is similar in size and shape to the iPhone but boasts a higher resolution, enhanced 3D graphics, and speech-to-text features that enable the user to dictate Facebook and Twitter updates. The Nexus One can be bought directly from Google over the web and comes "unlocked," meaning it is not restricted to use on a single network provider. As of this writing, Google offers it for use on the T-Mobile network, with later versions expected for use on Verizon, Vodafone and AT&T.[11]

Smartphones come with phone capabilities, a digital camera, video recorder, GPS tracking capability, digital player, internet browser and email tool.

Table 4.3 identifies several common telecommunications hardware devices and describes the function they perform.

Table 4.3 Common Telecommunications Devices

Device	Function
Modem	Translates data from a digital form (as it is stored in the computer) into an analog signal that can be transmitted over ordinary telephone lines.
Fax modem	Facsimile devices, commonly called fax devices, allow businesses to transmit text, graphs, photographs, and other digital files via standard telephone lines. A fax modem is a very popular device that combines a fax with a modem, giving users a powerful communications tool.
Multiplexer	Allows several telecommunications signals to be transmitted over a single communications medium at the same time, thus, saving expensive long-distance communications costs.
PBX	A communications system that manages both voice and data transfer within a building and to outside lines. In a PBX system, switching PBXs can be used to connect hundreds of internal phone lines to a few phone company lines.
Front-end processor	Special-purpose computer that manages communications to and from a computer system serving many people.
Switch	Uses the physical device address in each incoming message on the network to determine which output port it should forward the message to in order to reach another device on the same network
Bridge	Connects one LAN to another LAN that uses the same telecommunications protocol.
Router	Forwards data packets across two or more distinct networks toward their destinations through a process known as routing. Often an internet service provider (ISP) installs a router in a subscriber's home that connects the ISP's network to the network within the home
Bridge	Connects one LAN to another LAN that uses the same telecommunications protocol.

4.2 Networks and Distributed Processing

A **computer network** consists of communications media, devices and software needed to connect two or more computer systems or devices. The computers and devices on the networks are also called *network nodes*. After they are connected, the nodes can share data, information, work processes and allow employees to collaborate on projects. If a company uses networks effectively, it can grow into an agile, powerful and creative organisation, giving it a long-term competitive advantage. Organisations can use networks to share hardware, programs and databases. Networks can transmit and receive information to improve organisational effectiveness and efficiency. They enable geographically separated workgroups to share documents and opinions, which fosters teamwork, innovative ideas and new business strategies.

> **computer network** The communications media, devices and software needed to connect two or more computer systems or devices.

Network Types

Depending on the physical distance between nodes on a network and the communications and services it provides, networks can be classified as personal area, local area, metropolitan area and wide area network.

Personal Area Networks

A **personal area network (PAN)** is a wireless network that connects information technology devices close to one person. With a PAN, you can connect a laptop, digital camera and portable printer without cables. You can download digital image data from the camera to the laptop and then print it on a high-quality printer – all wirelessly. Bluetooth is the industry standard for PAN communications.

> **personal area network (PAN)** A network that supports the interconnection of information technology within a range of 10 meters or so.

Local Area Networks

A network that connects computer systems and devices within a small area, such as an office, home, or several floors in a building, is a **local area network (LAN)**. Typically, LANs are wired into office buildings and factories, as shown in Figure 4.5. Although LANs often use unshielded twisted-pair wire, other media – including fibre-optic cable – is also popular. Increasingly, LANs are using some form of wireless communications. You can build LANs to connect personal computers, laptop computers, or powerful mainframe computers.

> **local area network (LAN)** A network that connects computer systems and devices within a small area, such as an office, home, or several floors in a building.

Docklands Light Railway is one of the first light rail systems in Britain and carries over 67 million passengers per year. Serco Docklands, the operator of the railway, is upgrading its existing LAN to support the railway's rollout of new services and applications, including a novel public address system that services 32 railway stations and is controlled by personal computer workstations at a single control centre. The system will also provide passengers with audio/visual updates to keep track of the comings and goings of the various rail cars.[12]

With more people working at home, connecting home computing devices and equipment into a unified network is on the rise. Small businesses are also connecting their systems and equipment. A home or small business can connect network, computers, printers, scanners and other devices. A person working on one computer, for example, can use data and programs stored on another computer's hard disc. In addition, several computers on the network can

Figure 4.5 Typical LAN

All network users within an office building can connect to each other's devices for rapid communication. For instance, a user in research and development could send a document from her computer to be printed at a printer located in the desktop publishing centre.

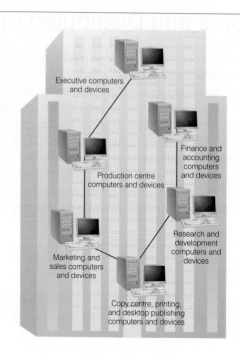

4

share a single printer. To make home and small business networking a reality, many companies are offering standards, devices and procedures.

Metropolitan Area Networks

A **metropolitan area network (MAN)** is a telecommunications network that connects users and their computers in a geographical area that spans a campus or city. A MAN might redefine the many networks within a city into a single larger network or connect several LANs into a single campus LAN. Grupo AMSA S.A. is a privately owned textile manufacturing company located in Lima, Peru. It operates three production plants that are separated by roughly 10 km from one another. The company implemented a MAN to support wireless communications among the three plants. The network provides high-speed data, voice and internet traffic among the locations, enabling effective planning, tracking and controlling of operations at all three facilities.[13]

metropolitan area network (MAN) A telecommunications network that connects users and their computers in a geographical area that spans a campus or city.

Wide Area Networks

A **wide area network (WAN)** is a telecommunications network that connects large geographic regions. A WAN might be privately owned or rented and includes public (shared users) networks. When you make a long-distance phone call or access the internet, you are using a WAN. WANs usually consist of computer equipment owned by the user, together with data communications equipment and telecommunications links provided by various carriers and service providers.

wide area network (WAN) A telecommunications network that connects large geographic regions.

China Datang Corporation is a state-owned corporation with 88 subsidiaries, including several large power generation plants. Its operations span 21 provinces of China and required the implementation of a WAN covering virtually the entire country. The network ensures high-quality voice, video and data communications among the sites connected to the network.[14]

WANs often provide communications across national borders, which involves national and international laws regulating the electronic flow of data across international boundaries, often called *transborder dataflow*. Some countries have strict laws limiting the use of telecommunications and databases, making normal business transactions, such as payroll, costly, slow, or even impossible.

Distributed Processing

When an organisation needs to use two or more computer systems, it can implement one of three basic processing alternatives: centralised, decentralised, or distributed.

With **centralised processing**, all processing occurs in a single location or facility. This approach offers the highest degree of control, because a single centrally managed computer performs all data processing. The Ticketmaster reservation service is an example of a centralised system. One central computer with a database stores information about all events and records the purchases of seats. Ticket clerks at various ticket selling locations can enter order data and print the results, or customers can place orders directly over the internet.

> **centralised processing** An approach to processing wherein all processing occurs in a single location or facility.

With **decentralised processing**, processing devices are placed at various remote locations. Each processing device is isolated and does not communicate with any other processing device. Decentralised systems are suitable for companies that have independent operating units, such as 7-Eleven, where each of its 5800 US stores is managed to meet local retail conditions. Each store has a computer that runs more than 50 business applications, such as cash register operations, gasoline pump monitoring and merchandising.

> **decentralised processing** An approach to processing wherein processing devices are placed at various remote locations.

With **distributed processing**, processing devices are placed at remote locations but are connected to each other via a network. One benefit of distributed processing is that managers can allocate data to the locations that can process it most efficiently. Kroger operates more than 2400 supermarkets, each with its own computer to support store operations, such as customer checkout and inventory management. These computers are connected to a network so that sales data gathered by each store's computer can be sent to a huge data repository on a mainframe computer for efficient analysis by marketing analysts and product supply chain managers.

> **distributed processing** An approach to processing wherein processing devices are placed at remote locations but are connected to each other via a network.

Ongoing terrorist attacks around the world and the heightened sensitivity to natural disasters (such as the 2010 earthquakes in Chile and Haiti and the series of blizzards in the mid-Atlantic and northeast sections of the US in early 2010) have motivated many companies to distribute their workers, operations and systems much more widely, a reversal of the previous trend toward centralisation. The goal is to minimise the consequences of a catastrophic event at one location while ensuring uninterrupted systems availability.

Client/Server Systems

Users can share data through file server computing, which allows authorised users to download entire files from certain computers designated as file servers. After downloading data to a local computer, a user can analyze, manipulate, format and display data from the file.

In **client/server architecture**, multiple computer platforms are dedicated to special functions, such as database management, printing, communications and program execution. These platforms are called servers. Each server is accessible by all computers on the network. Servers can be computers of all sizes; they store both application programs and data files

> **client/server architecture** An approach to computing wherein multiple computer platforms are dedicated to special functions, such as database management, printing, communications and program execution.

and are equipped with operating system software to manage the activities of the network. The server distributes programs and data to the other computers (clients) on the network as they request them. An application server holds the programs and data files for a particular application, such as an inventory database. The client or the server can do the processing.

Telecommunications Software

network operating system (NOS) Systems software that controls the computer systems and devices on a network and allows them to communicate with each other.

A **network operating system (NOS)** is systems software that controls the computer systems and devices on a network and allows them to communicate with each other. The NOS performs similar functions for the network as operating system software does for a computer, such as memory and task management and coordination of hardware. When network equipment (such as printers, plotters and disc drives) is required, the NOS makes sure that these resources are used correctly. Novell NetWare, Windows 2000, Windows 2003 and Windows 2008 are common network operating systems. MySpace, the popular social networking website that offers an interactive, user-submitted network of friends, personal profiles, blogs, music and videos internationally, was one of the first very busy websites to adopt the use of Windows Server 2008.

network-management software Software that enables a manager on a networked desktop to monitor the use of individual computers and shared hardware (such as printers); scan for viruses; and ensure compliance with software licences.

Software tools and utilities are available for managing networks. With **network-management software**, a manager on a networked personal computer can monitor the use of individual computers and shared hardware (such as printers); scan for viruses; and ensure compliance with software licences. Network-management software also simplifies the process of updating files and programs on computers on the network – a manager can make changes through a communications server instead of having to visit each individual computer. In addition, network-management software protects software from being copied, modified, or downloaded illegally. It can also locate telecommunications errors and potential network problems. Some of the many benefits of network-management software include fewer hours spent on routine tasks (such as installing new software), faster response to problems, and greater overall network control.

Now that we have covered many of the basics of telecommunications, let's discuss the use of the internet.

4.3 Use and Functioning of the Internet

The internet is the world's largest computer network; it is actually a collection of interconnected networks, all freely exchanging information using a common set of protocols. (A communications protocol is a set of rules that govern the exchange of information over a communications channel.) The internet began as an experiment linking together research institutes and universities. Over time, more organisations were connected to the internet, followed by homes and businesses, until today, when it is difficult to find a computer that is not connected to the internet. More than 750 million computers, or hosts,[15] make up today's internet, supporting nearly 2 billion users. Those numbers are expected to continue growing.[16] Figure 4.6 shows the staggering growth of the internet, as measured by the number of internet host sites, or domain names. Domain names are discussed later in the chapter.

The internet is truly international in scope, with users on every continent – including Antarctica. Of all the people using the internet, citizens of Asian countries make up 42.4 per cent, Europeans 23.6 per cent and North Americans only 14.4 per cent.[17] China has by far the most internet users at 384 million, which is more people than the total US population, but only

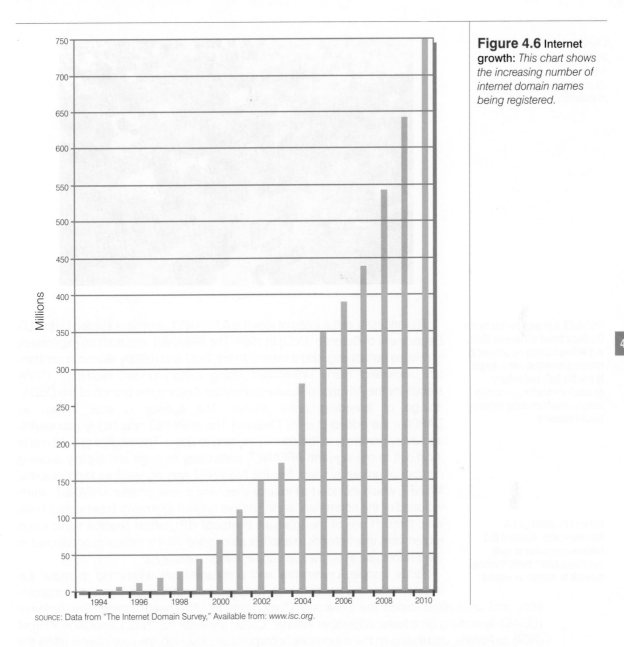

Figure 4.6 Internet growth: *This chart shows the increasing number of internet domain names being registered.*

SOURCE: Data from "The Internet Domain Survey," Available from: *www.isc.org*.

29 per cent of China's total population. Use of the internet is growing around the globe, though at differing rates for each country. For example, most internet use in South Korea is through high-speed broadband connections, and more than 71 per cent of the population is online. In contrast, north of the border in North Korea, the government prohibits internet use and other civil liberties. Being connected to the internet provides global economic opportunity to individuals, businesses and countries.

The freedom of expression provided by the internet has been a source of controversy in many countries. China, for example, blocks internet content that it feels is subversive or threatening to "national unity."[18] Ireland, France, Australia and several other countries have blocked internet access to individuals caught illegally downloading copyrighted material.[19] Other countries have blocked content that is considered blasphemous to their national religions.[20] Even the US has experimented with blocking "indecent" web content.[21] However, the internet includes so many connections that completely controlling its flow of information is next to impossible.

China has more than 384 million internet users online, which is only 29 per cent of its population.

SOURCE: Reuters/Landov.

ARPANET A project started by the US Department of Defense (DoD) in 1969 as both an experiment in reliable networking and a means to link the DoD and military research contractors, including many universities doing military-funded research.

The ancestor of the internet was the **ARPANET**, a project started by the US Department of Defense (DoD) in 1969. The ARPANET was both an experiment in reliable networking and a means to link DoD and military research contractors, including many universities doing military-funded research. (*ARPA* stands for the Advanced Research Projects Agency, the branch of the DoD in charge of awarding grant money. The agency is now known as DARPA – the added D is for *Defense*) The ARPANET was highly successful, and every university in the country wanted to use it. This wildfire growth made it difficult to manage the ARPANET, particularly its large and rapidly growing number of university sites. So, the ARPANET was broken into two networks: MILNET, which included all military sites, and a new, smaller ARPANET, which included all the nonmilitary sites. The two networks remained connected, however, through use of the **Internet Protocol (IP)**, which enables traffic to be routed from one network to another as needed. All the networks connected to the internet use IP, so they all can exchange messages.

Internet Protocol (IP) A communication standard that enables computers to route communications traffic from one network to another as needed.

Today, people, universities and companies are attempting to make the internet faster and easier to use. To speed internet access, a group of corporations and universities called the University Corporation for Advanced Internet Development (UCAID) is working on a faster, alternative internet. Called Internet2 (I2), Next Generation Internet (NGI), or Abilene, depending on the universities or corporations involved, the new internet offers the potential of faster internet speeds, up to 2 Gbps per second or more.[22] In the US, the *National LambdaRail (NLR)* is a cross-country, high-speed (10 Gbps) fibre-optic network dedicated to research in high-speed networking applications.[23] The NLR provides a "unique national networking infrastructure" to advance networking research and next-generation network-based applications in science, engineering and medicine. This new high-speed fibre-optic network will support the ever-increasing need of scientists to gather, transfer and analyze massive amounts of scientific data.

How the Internet Works

In the early days of the internet, the major telecommunications (telecom) companies around the world agreed to connect their networks so that users on all the networks could share information over the internet. The cables, routers, switching stations, communication towers and satellites that make up these networks are the hardware over which internet traffic flows. These large telecom companies are called *network service providers* (*NSPs*). Examples include Verizon, Sprint, British Telecom and AT&T. The combined backbones of these and other NSPs – the fibre-optic cables that span the globe over land and under sea – make up the internet backbone.

The internet transmits data from one computer (called a *host*) to another (see Figure 4.7). If the receiving computer is on a network to which the first computer is directly connected, it can send the message directly. If the receiving and sending computers are not directly connected to the same network, the sending computer relays the message to another computer that can forward it. The message is typically sent through one or more routers to reach its destination. It is not unusual for a message to pass through a dozen or more routers on its way from one part of the internet to another.

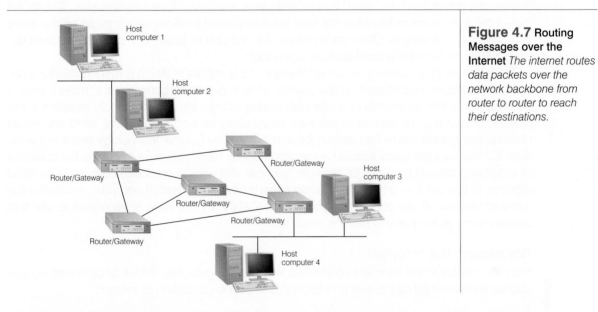

Figure 4.7 Routing Messages over the Internet *The internet routes data packets over the network backbone from router to router to reach their destinations.*

The various telecommunications networks that are linked to form the internet work much the same way – they pass data around in chunks called packets, each of which carries the addresses of its sender and its receiver along with other technical information. The set of rules used to pass packets from one host to another is the IP protocol. Many other communications protocols are used in connection with IP. The best known is the Transmission Control Protocol (TCP). Many people use TCP/IP as an abbreviation for the combination of TCP and IP used by most internet applications. After a network following these standards links to the internet's backbone, it becomes part of the worldwide internet community.

An **IP address** is a 64-bit number (e.g. 208.77.201.209) assigned to each computer to identify it on the internet. The internet will soon be upgraded to IPv6, which uses 128-bit addresses to provide for many more devices.[24] Because people prefer to work with words rather than numbers, a system called the Domain Name System (DNS) was created. Domain names, such as www.cengage.com, are mapped to IP addresses, such as 69.32.133.79, using the DNS. If you type either www.cengage.com or 69.32.133.79 into your web browser, you will access the same website.

IP address A 64-bit number that identifies a computer on the internet.

A **Uniform Resource Locator** (URL) is a web address that specifies the exact location of a web page using letters and words that map to an IP address and a location on the host. The URL gives those who provide information over the internet a standard way to designate where internet resources, such as servers and documents, are located. Consider the URL for Course Technology, http:// www.cengage.com/coursetechnology.

Uniform Resource Locator (URL) A web address that specifies the exact location of a web page using letters and words that map to an IP address and a location on the host.

The "http" specifies the access method and tells your software to access a file using the Hypertext Transport Protocol. This is the primary method for interacting with the internet. In many cases, you don't need to include "http://" in a URL, because it is the default protocol. The "www" part of the address sometimes, but not always, signifies that the address is associated with the World Wide Web service. The URL *www.cengage.com* is the domain name that identifies the internet host site. The part of the address following the domain name – /coursetechnology – specifies an exact location on the host site.

Domain names must adhere to strict rules. They always have at least two parts, with each part separated by a dot (period). For some internet addresses, the far right part of the domain name is the country code, such as au for Australia, ca for Canada, dk for Denmark, fr for France, de (Deutschland) for Germany and jp for Japan. Many internet addresses have a code denoting affiliation categories, such as "com" for business sites and "edu" for education sites. The far left part of the domain name identifies the host network or host provider, which might be the name of a university or business. Other countries outside the United States use different top-level domain affiliations from the ones described in the table.

The Internet Corporation for Assigned Names and Numbers (ICANN) is responsible for managing IP addresses and internet domain names. One of its primary concerns is to make sure that each domain name represents only one individual or entity – the one that legally registers it. For example, if your teacher wanted to use *www.course.com* for a course website, he or she would discover that domain name has already been registered by Course Technology and is not available. ICANN uses companies called *accredited domain name registrars* to handle the business of registering domain names. For example, you can visit *www.namecheap.com*, an accredited registrar, to find out if a particular name has already been registered; if not, you can register the name for around $6 per year. Once you do so, ICANN will not allow anyone else to use that domain name as long as you pay the yearly fee.

Accessing the Internet

You can connect to the internet in numerous ways (see Figure 4.8). Which access method you choose is determined by the size and capability of your organisation or system.

Figure 4.8 Several **Ways to Access the Internet** *Users can access the internet several ways, including using a LAN server, telephone lines, a high-speed service, or a wireless network.*

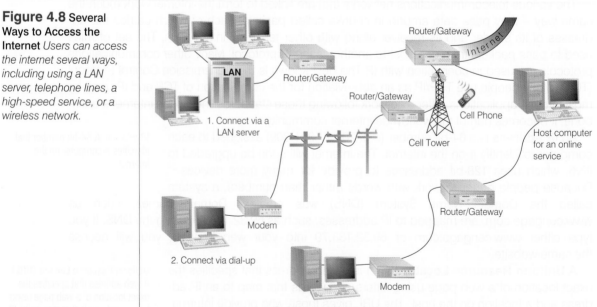

Connect via LAN Server

This approach is used by businesses and organisations that manage a local area network (LAN). By connecting a server on the LAN to the internet using a router, all users on the LAN are provided access to the internet. Business LAN servers are typically connected to the internet at very fast data rates, sometimes in the hundreds of Mbps. In addition, you can share the higher cost of this service among several dozen LAN users to allow a reasonable cost per user.

Connecting via Internet Service Providers

Companies and residences unable to connect directly to the internet through a LAN server must access the internet through an internet service provider. An **Internet service provider (ISP)** is any organisation that provides internet access to people. Thousands of organisations serve as ISPs, ranging from universities that make the internet available to students and faculty, to small internet businesses, to major telecommunications giants, such as BT and Telkom. To connect to the internet through an ISP, you must have an account with the service provider (for which you usually pay) along with software (such as a browser) and devices (such as a computer or smartphone) that support a connection via TCP/IP.

Internet service provider (ISP) Any organisation that provides internet access to people.

The slowest connection provided by ISPs is a dial-up connection. A *dial-up internet connection* uses a modem and standard phone line to "dial-up" and connect to the ISP server. Dial-up is considered the slowest of connections, because it is restricted by the 56 Kbps limitation of traditional phone line service. A dial-up connection also ties up the phone line so that it is unavailable for voice calls. Although dial-up was originally the only way to connect to the internet from home, it is rapidly becoming replaced by high-speed services.

Several "high-speed" internet services are available for home and business. They include cable modem connections from cable television companies, DSL connections from phone companies (a telecommunications service that delivers high-speed internet access to homes and small businesses over the existing phone lines of the local telephone network) and satellite connections from satellite television companies.

In addition to connecting to the internet through wired systems, such as phone lines and television cables, wireless internet over cellular and Wi-Fi networks has become common. Thousands of public Wi-Fi services are available in coffee shops, airports, hotels and elsewhere, where internet access is provided free, for an hourly rate, or for a monthly subscription fee. In 2010, McDonalds became the biggest provider of free wireless in the US when it began offering free Wi-Fi at 11 000 of its 13 000 restaurants.[25] Many businesses have followed suit using free Wi-Fi access as a tool to attract customers. Wi-Fi is even making its way into aircraft, allowing business travellers to be productive during air travel by accessing email and corporate networks.

Mobile phone carriers also provide internet access for handsets, notebooks and tablets. New 4G mobile phone services rival wired high-speed connections enjoyed at home and work. By purchasing data plans, users can connect to these networks with smartphones and computers.

When Apple introduced the iPhone, one of its slogans was the "internet in your pocket." The iPhone serves to prove the popularity of, and potential for, internet services over a handset. Many other smartphones followed hot on the heels of the iPhone offering similar services on all of the cellular networks. More recently, the iPhone 4 brought video calling into vogue, while the iPad and other tablets provided anywhere, anytime access to all types of internet services on a larger display.

Connecting Wirelessly
The iPad connects to the internet over cellular or Wi-Fi networks.

SOURCE: © Stefan Sollfors/Alamy.

Cloud Computing

Cloud computing refers to a computing environment where software and storage are provided as an internet service and accessed with a web browser. As internet connection speeds increase and wireless internet access becomes pervasive, computing activities are increasingly being delivered over the internet rather than from installed software on PCs. Google and Yahoo! store the email of many users, along with calendars, contacts and to-do lists. Facebook provides social interaction and can store personal photos, as can Flickr and a dozen other photo sites. Pandora delivers music, and Hulu and YouTube deliver movies. Google Docs, Microsoft Web Apps, Zoho, 37signals, Flypaper, Adobe Buzzword and others provide web-delivered productivity and information management software. Soon, it seems, most computing will take place on internet servers through the web browser. All your friends, photos, documents, music and media will be available to you from any internet-connected device. This is the world of cloud computing.

The term cloud computing comes from the use of a cloud in network diagrams to represent the internet in an abstract sense (see Figure 4.9). Cloud computing service providers manage their services much like a utility company manages its resources. The processing and storage requirements of all of its clients can be spread over numerous servers. As business grows, more servers are added. If one server fails, others pick up the slack. Cloud computing is extremely scalable and often takes advantage of virtualisation technologies.

Cloud computing offers tremendous advantages to businesses.[26] By outsourcing business information systems to the cloud, a business saves on system design, installation and maintenance. Employees can also access corporate systems from any internet-connected computer using a standard web browser. For example, RezBook is a cloud computing application (app for short) designed by Urbanspoon for the iPad to manage reservations for restaurants. Staff in a restaurant use their iPads to access the system stored on an internet server to check for open tables, track each table's progress through a meal, and store and access customer reservations.[27] Some companies, including Microsoft and Google, provide free online storage (with capacity limitations) for access from any internet-connected computer. Dropbox, SugarSync and others include file backup and synchronisation services to their cloud storage offerings.

A related concept is Software as a Service (SaaS). Using cloud computing, application service providers (ASPs) provide access for their clients to software. This means the clients don't

Figure 4.9 Cloud Computing *Cloud computing uses applications and resources delivered via the web.*

SOURCE: Image copyright 2010, Helder Almeida. Used under licence from Shutterstock.com.

Ethical and Societal Issues

Danger in the Cloud

The general public has embraced cloud computing more readily than many businesses. Millions of people trust cloud computing technologies from Google to store their email, appointment calendars and address books. They trust Facebook to store their photos and personal information. Businesses have been more hesitant to trust internet firms with their valuable corporate information – and with good cause.

Cloud computing services do fail, leaving users unable to access programs or data. It is not uncommon for Google, Twitter, Microsoft, Facebook and other online companies to experience server outages. In other cases, cloud computing services have lost customer data. Perhaps the most notable was the catastrophe with T-Mobile's Sidekick smartphone service. In October 2009, T-Mobile informed its thousands of Sidekick users that it had lost their data and might not be able to recover it. It advised the users not to turn off their cell phones, as the data stored on them would be irrecoverable. The Sidekick uses a cloud computing data service from a Microsoft subsidiary ironically named Danger, Inc. to back up user data from smartphones. The data

stored includes user contacts, calendars, notes, photos, text messages and other data typically stored on mobile phones. The cloud storage system for this data failed and had no backup system in place. As angry Sidekick users posted comments online, the failure gained the attention of businesses and consumers.

In the end, much of the data was recovered, and those who lost data were compensated with a US $100 credit. Still, the incident is considered a black eye for T-Mobile and cloud computing. Similar incidents, such as Gmail outages, cause businesses to be leery about trusting cloud computing with important data.

The City of Los Angeles recently decided to trust Google and its online applications rather than using traditional software, such as Microsoft Office. The decision was not made lightly. The US $75 million contract came with several stipulations. Google has agreed to pay a considerable penalty if a security breach occurs. Google is legally responsible for any release of data in violation of a nondisclosure agreement. The city's data must also be encrypted,

(continued)

stored on a dedicated server and kept in the US with limited access.

Such assurances are essential if cloud computing is going to live up to its potential for businesses. Microsoft is lobbying the US Congress to create new laws designed to offer protection for data stored in the cloud and to enact stiffer penalties for hackers who attempt to illegally access it. Microsoft hopes that government support for cloud computing will spread globally so that data can be safe wherever it is stored within the global business infrastructure. This would mean companies around the world that provide outsourced cloud storage will be held accountable by the same laws that govern US firms. "We need a free trade agreement for data," says Brad Smith, senior vice president and general counsel at Microsoft.

Without government assistance, open standards and international cooperation, some fear that cloud computing will be controlled by two or three big companies, leaving smaller companies unable to compete. Users may be locked into one service provider's proprietary system. Open standards, on the other hand, would allow customers to easily transfer their cloud computing services from one company to another. Smith calls for cloud computing vendors to band together to establish open standards for data storage that provide transparency for security and privacy. "Simply put, it should not be enough for service providers simply to say that their services are private and secure," Smith said. "There needs to be some transparency about why this is the case."

Jonathan Rochelle, a group product manager at Google, suggests that cloud computing isn't any more dangerous than storing data on your own PC or server. "While it feels more comfortable, the same way the money under your mattress feels more comfortable, it may not be the best way to manage your information," suggests Rochelle. The point is that the public is willing to trust banks and companies with their financial well being, so why not trust the companies that provide cloud computing services with your information?

Discussion Questions

1 Would you be comfortable storing all of your data, including personal data, media and professional data, in the cloud rather than on your own PC? Why or why not?

2 What assurances and practices do you feel are necessary from cloud computing firms to earn the trust of businesses and the public?

Critical Thinking Questions

1 What role can government(s) play in helping cloud computing realise its potential?

2 Why do you think Microsoft, a company that has been historically opposed to open standards, is now lobbying for them?

SOURCES : Weinschenk, Carl, 'T-Mobile Resumes Sidekick Sales Despite Costly Risk.' NewsFactor. Available from: *www.newsfactor.com/story.xhtml? story_id=70139&full_skip=1*. Accessed November 17, 2009; Resende, Patricia, 'L.A. Cloud Contract Goes to Google Over Microsoft,' NewsFactor. Available from: *www.newsfactor.com/story.xhtml?story_id=69765*. Accessed October 28, 2009; Thibodeau, Patrick, 'Microsoft Seeks Legal Protections for Data Stored in Cloud,' *CIO*. Available from: *www.cio.com/article/520724/Microsoft_Seeks_Legal_Protections_for_ Data_Stored_in_Cloud?source=rss_all*. Accessed January 21, 2010; Gross, Grant, 'Microsoft calls for cloud computing transparency,' *ITWorld*. Available from: *www.itworld.com/government/93452/microsoft-calls-cloud- computing-transparency?utm_source=feedburner&utm_medium= feed&utm_campaign=Feed%3A+Itworld Today+%28ITworld+Today%29*. Accessed January 20, 2010; Dunn, John E., 'Internet Heading for "Perfect Storm,"' *CIO*. Available from: *www.cio.com/article/ 519770/Internet_ Heading_for_Perfect_Storm_?source=rss_all*. Accessed January 20, 2010.

have to install and maintain the software themselves. Salesforce.com is an example of SaaS as applied to customer relationship management (CRM). Salesforce.com services more than 50 000 businesses, providing hundreds of CRM applications for a wide variety of business types. Employees of those businesses can access customer data from desktops, notebooks and cell phones using a web browser. Businesses that use Salesforce.com don't have to worry about supporting complicated CRM software on their servers, installing updates and security patches, and troubleshooting problems. The SaaS provider manages it all.

The popularity of netbooks, small notebook computers designed primarily for accessing web applications, and nettops, their desktop equivalent, are an indication of the direction of computing. As cloud computing grows, the power and storage capacity of users' computers can diminish. High-speed wireless access and a decent keyboard and display are all you really need for computing in the cloud.

4.4 The World Wide Web

The World Wide Web was developed by Tim Berners-Lee at CERN, the European Organisation for Nuclear Research in Geneva. He originally conceived of it as an internal document-management system. From this modest beginning, the web has grown to become a primary source of news and information, an indispensible conduit for commerce, and a popular hub for social interaction, entertainment and communication.

How the Web Works

Although the terms internet and web are often used interchangeably, technically, the two are different technologies. The internet is the infrastructure on which the web exists. The internet is made up of computers, network hardware, such as routers and fibre-optic cables, software and the TCP/IP protocols. The **Web**, on the other hand, consists of server and client software, the hypertext transfer protocol (http), standards and mark-up languages that combine to deliver information and services over the internet.

> **Web** Server and client software, the hypertext transfer protocol (http), standards, and mark-up languages that combine to deliver information and services over the internet.

The web was designed to make information easy to find and organise. It connects billions of documents, which are now called web pages, stored on millions of servers around the world. These are connected to each other using **hyperlinks**, specially denoted text or graphics on a web page, that, when clicked, open a new web page containing related content. Using hyperlinks, users can jump between web pages stored on various web servers – creating the illusion of interacting with one big computer. Because of the vast amount of information available on the web and the wide variety of media, the web has become the most popular means of information access in the world today.

> **hyperlink** Highlighted text or graphics in a web document that, when clicked, opens a new web page containing related content.

In short, the web is a hyperlink-based system that uses the client/server model. It organises internet resources throughout the world into a series of linked files, called pages, accessed and viewed using web client software called a **Web browser**. Internet Explorer, Firefox, Chrome, Safari and Opera are five popular web browsers (see Figure 4.10). A collection of pages on one particular topic, accessed under one web domain, is called a website. The web was originally designed to support formatted text and pictures on a page. It has evolved to support many more types of information and communication including user interactivity, animation and video. Web plug-ins help provide additional features to standard websites. Adobe Flash and Real Player are examples of web plug-ins.

> **Web browser** Web client software, such as Internet Explorer, Firefox, Chrome, Safari and Opera, used to view web pages.

Hypertext Markup Language (HTML) is the standard page description language for web pages. HTML is defined by the World Wide Web Consortium (referred to as "W3C") and has developed through numerous revisions. It is currently in its fifth revision – HTML5. HTML tells the browser how to display font characteristics, paragraph formatting, page layout, image placement, hyperlinks and the content of a web page. HTML uses **tags**, which are codes that tell the browser how to format the text or graphics: as a heading, list, or body text, for example. Website creators "mark up" a page by placing HTML tags before and after one or more words. For example, to have the browser display a sentence as a heading, you place the <h1> tag at the start of the sentence and an </h1> tag at the end of the sentence. When you view this page in your browser, the sentence is displayed as a heading. HTML also provides tags to import objects stored in files, such as photos, pictures, audio and movies, into a web page. In short, a web page is made up of three components: text, tags and references to files. The text is your web page content, the tags are codes that mark the way words will be displayed and the references to files insert photos and media into the web page at specific locations. All HTML tags are enclosed in a set of angle

> **Hypertext Markup Language (HTML)** The standard page description language for web pages.
>
> **HTML tags** Codes that tell the web browser how to format text – as a heading, as a list, or as body text – and whether images, sound and other elements should be inserted.

Figure 4.10 Mozilla **Firefox** *web browsers, such as Firefox, let you access internet resources, such as this customisable web portal from Google.*

brackets (< and >), such as <h2>. The closing tag has a forward slash in it, such as </b> for closing bold. Consider the following text and tags:

```
<html>
<head>
<title>Table of Contents</title>
<link href='style.css' rel='stylesheet' type='text/css' />
</head>
<body style='background-colour:#333333'>
<div id='container'>
<p><img src='header.png' width='602' height='78' /></p>
<h1 align=center>Fundamentals of Business Information Systems</h1>
<ol>
<li>An Overview</li>
<li>Information Technology Concepts</li>
<li>Business Information Systems</li>
<li>Systems Development</li>
<li>Information Systems in Business and Society</li>
</ol>
</div>
</body>
</html>
```

The <html> tag identifies this as an HTML document. HTML documents are divided into two parts: the <head> and the <body>. The <body> contains everything that is viewable in the web browser window, and the <head> contains related information, such as a <title> to place on the browser's title bar. The background colour of the page is specified in the <body> tag using a hexadecimal code. The heading "Fundamentals of Business Information Systems" is identified as the largest level 1 heading with the <h1> tag, typically a 16–18 point font, centred on the page. The <ol> tag indicates an ordered list, and the <li> tags indicate list items. The resulting web page is shown in Figure 4.11.

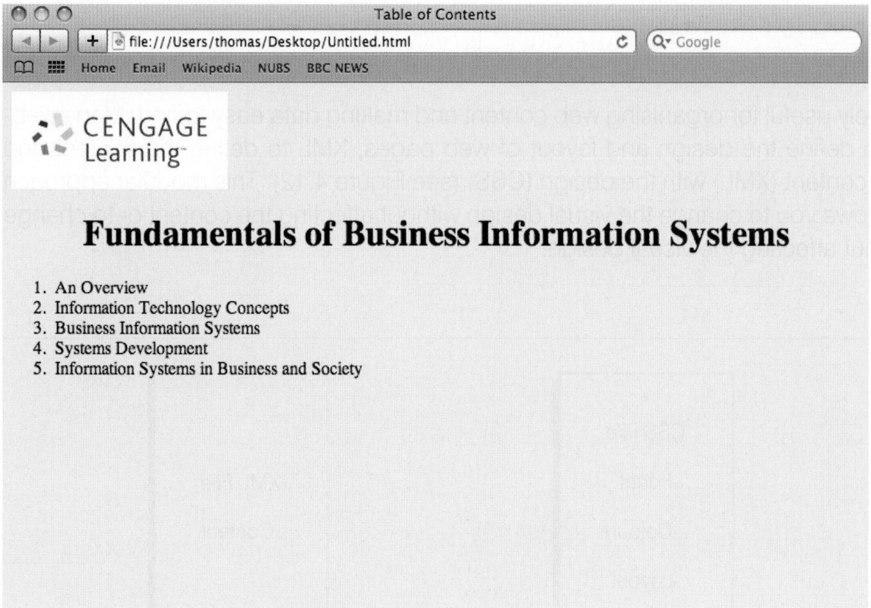

Figure 4.11 HTML Code Interpreted by a Browser *The example HTML code as interpreted by the Safari web browser on a Mac.*

Although HTML is the standard page description language for web pages, some other web standards have become nearly equal to HTML in importance, including Extensible Markup Language (XML), Cascading Style Sheets (CSS) and Wireless Markup Language (WML).

Extensible Markup Language (XML) is a markup language for web documents containing structured information, including words and pictures. XML does not have a predefined tag set. With HTML, for example, the <hl> tag always means a first-level heading. The content and formatting are contained in the same HTML document. XML web documents contain the content of a web page. The formatting of the content is contained in a style sheet. A few typical instructions in XML follow:

Extensible Markup Language (XML) The markup language designed to transport and store data on the web.

```
<book>
<chapter>Hardware</chapter>
<topic>Input Devices</topic>
<topic>Processing and Storage Devices</topic>
<topic>Output Devices</topic>
</book>
```

A **Cascading Style Sheet (CSS)** is a file or portion of an HTML file that defines the visual appearance of content in a web page. Using CSS is convenient, because you only need to define the technical details of the page's appearance once, rather than in each HTML tag. For example, the visual

Cascading Style Sheet (CSS) A markup language for defining the visual design of a web page or group of pages.

appearance of the preceding XML content may be contained in the following style sheet. This style sheet specifies that the chapter title "Hardware" is displayed on the web page in a large Arial font (18 points). "Hardware" will also appear in bold blue text. The "Input Devices" title will appear in a smaller Arial font (12 points) and italic red text.

```
chapter: (font-size: 18pt; colour: blue; font-weight: bold;
display: block; font-family: Arial;

margin-top: 10pt; margin-left: 5pt)

topic: (font-size: 12pt; colour: red; font-style: italic; display:
block; font-family: Arial;

margin-left: 12pt)
```

XML is extremely useful for organising web content and making data easy to find. Many websites use CSS to define the design and layout of web pages, XML to define the content and HTML to join the content (XML) with the design (CSS) (see Figure 4.12). This modular approach to web design allows you to change the visual design without affecting the content or to change the content without affecting the visual design.

Figure 4.12 XML, CSS, and XHTML *Today's websites are created using XML to define content, CSS to define the visual style and XHTML to put it all together.*

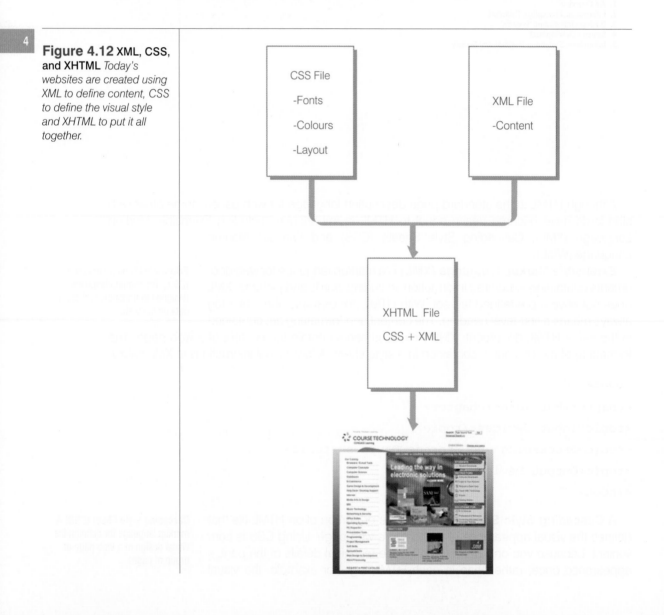

Web Programming Languages

Several programming languages are key to the web. Java, for example, is an object-oriented programming language from Sun Microsystems based on the C++ programming language, which allows small programs called *applets* to be embedded within an HTML document. When the user clicks the appropriate part of an HTML page to retrieve an applet from a web server, the applet is downloaded onto the client workstation, where it begins executing. Unlike other programs, Java software can run on any type of computer. Programmers use Java to make web pages come alive, adding splashy graphics, animation and real-time updates.

In addition to Java, companies use a variety of other programming languages and tools to develop websites. JavaScript, VBScript and ActiveX (used with Internet Explorer) are internet languages used to develop web pages and perform important functions, such as accepting user input. *Hypertext Preprocessor*, or *PHP*, is an open-source programming language. PHP code or instructions can be embedded directly into HTML code. Unlike some other internet languages, PHP can run on a web server, with the results being transferred to a client computer. PHP can be used on a variety of operating systems, including Microsoft Windows, Macintosh OS X, HP-UX and others. It can also be used with a variety of database management systems, such as DB2, Oracle, Informix, MySQL and many others. These characteristics – running on different operating systems and database management systems and being an open-source language – make PHP popular with many web developers.

Web Services

Web services consist of standards and tools that streamline and simplify communication among websites, promising to revolutionise the way we develop and use the web for business and personal purposes. Internet companies, including Amazon, eBay and Google, are now using web services. Amazon, for example, has developed Amazon Web Services (AWS) to make the contents of its huge online catalogue available to other websites or software applications.

The key to web services is XML. Just as HTML was developed as a standard for formatting web content into web pages, XML is used within a web page to describe and transfer data between web service applications.

Developing Web Content

The art of web design involves working within the technical limitations of the web and using a set of tools to make appealing designs. A number of products make developing and maintaining web content easier. Microsoft, for example, has introduced a development and web services platform called .NET. The .NET platform allows developers to use different programming languages to create and run programs, including those for the web. The .NET platform also includes a rich library of programming code to help build XML web applications. Bubbler is another example of a web design and building tool. Bubbler helps you obtain a domain name, develop attractive web pages by dragging and dropping features and options, host your website and maintain it. Other web publishing packages include Homestead QuickSites and JobSpot (see Figure 4.13).

After you create web pages, your next step is to place, or publish, the content on a web server. Popular publishing options include using ISPs, free sites and web hosting. Web hosting services provide space on their web servers for people and businesses that don't have the financial resources, time, or skills to host their own websites. A web host can charge €10 or more per month, depending on services. Some web hosting sites include domain name registration, web authoring software, and activity reporting and monitoring of the website. Some ISPs also provide limited web space, typically 1 to 6 MB, as part of their monthly fee. If more disc space is needed,

Figure 4.13 **Creating Web Pages** *Microsoft Expression web makes web design nearly as easy as using a word processor.*

SOURCE: Courtesy of Microsoft Corporation.

additional fees are charged. Free sites offer limited space for a website. In return, free sites often require the user to view advertising or agree to other terms and conditions.

Some web developers are creating programs and procedures to combine two or more web applications into a new service, called a *mashup*. A mashup is named for the process of mixing two or more hip-hop songs into one song. Map applications, such as Google Maps, provide tool kits that allow them to be combined with other web applications. For example, Google Maps can be used in conjunction with Twitter to display the location where various tweets were posted. Likewise, Google Maps combined with Flickr can overlay photos of specific geographic locations.

4.5 Internet and Web Applications

The types of internet and web applications available are vast and ever expanding. The most common and popular uses for the internet and web can be categorised as publishing information, assisting users in finding information, supporting communication and collaboration, building online community, providing software applications, providing a platform for expressing ideas and opinions, delivering media of all types, providing a platform for commerce, and supporting travel and navigation.

Online Information Sources

The web has become the most popular medium for distributing and accessing information. Consumers increasingly rely on online resources to ease and inform major life events, such as weddings, buying a home, changing jobs and having a baby. The web has become the most popular source for daily news, surpassing newspapers and television. Academic researchers use the web to share their findings with others in their field; most academic publications have moved from paper to the web. Businesses rely on the web for storing and delivering corporate information internally to employees and externally to business partners, customers and the press. The web has become the first place people look when faced with a challenge or question.

News and Opinion

The web is a powerful tool for keeping informed about local, state, national, and global news. It allows the public to actively research issues and become more knowledgeable about current events. Traditional news media deliver the news through television, radio, and newspapers. These media provide the news that they consider to be of interest to the general public. Items of special or unique interest may be replaced with more general stories. In contrast, the web has an abundance of special-interest coverage. It also provides the capacity to provide deeper analysis of the subject matter. For example, during military conflicts overseas, online news services provide news articles in text, audio, and video coverage. Clicking links allows you to drill down and find out more about geographic regions by viewing maps, for example; you could also link to historical coverage of international relations and learn about the battle equipment being deployed.

Most newspaper, radio and television news services have expanded to provide online news coverage. Text and photos are supported by the HTML standard. Video, sometimes called a webcast, and audio are provided in the browser through plug-in technology and in podcasts (see Figure 4.14). Bringing the news to the web is eliminating the lines of distinction between traditional newspaper, radio and television news sources.

Figure 4.14 News **Webcast** *Online news is available in text, audio, and video formats, providing the ability to drill down into stories.*

SOURCE: © Chris Ridley – Internet Stock/Alamy.

While traditional news sources migrate to the web, new sources are emerging from online companies. News websites from Google, Yahoo!, Digg and Newsvine provide the most popular or interesting news stories from a variety of news sources.

In a trend some refer to as social journalism or citizen journalism, ordinary citizens are more involved in reporting the news than ever before. The online community is taking journalism into its hands and reporting the news from each person's perspective using an abundance of online tools. Although social journalism provides important news not available elsewhere, its sources may not be as reliable as mainstream media sources. It is sometimes difficult to discern news from opinion. News from nonprofessional journalists, reporting without the strict guidelines of formal news agencies, may be biased, misrepresented, mistaken, or perhaps even deliberately misleading. Many citizen journalists would be quick to point out that mainstream media may also be biased in its reporting of the news.

Education and Training

As a tool for sharing information and a primary repository of information on all subjects, the web is ideally suited for education and training. Advances in interactive web technologies further support important educational relationships between teacher and student and among students. The web can play a major role in education from pre-K through adult continuing education. In today's highly competitive and rapidly changing professional environments, more professionals are turning to the web to learn skills that will enhance their professional value.

Even before children enter school, they are engaged with educational content on the web at sites, such as http://bbb.co.uk/cbeebies. Primary schools use the web to inform parents of school schedules and activities. Teachers give elementary school students research exercises in the classroom and at home that use web resources. By high school, students have integrated the web into daily study habits. Teachers manage class web pages that contain information and links for students to use in homework exercises.

Most college-level courses rely on the web to enhance learning. Educational support products, such as Blackboard, provide an integrated web environment that includes virtual chat for class members; a discussion group for posting questions and comments; access to the class syllabus and agenda, student grades and class announcements; and links to class-related material. Some course websites even deliver filmed lectures using webcasting technology. Such environments can complement the traditional classroom experience or be the sole method of course delivery.

Conducting classes over the web with no physical class meetings is called *distance education*. Many colleges and universities offer distance education classes, which provide a convenient method for nontraditional students to attend college. Nontraditional students include older students who have job or family obligations that might otherwise prohibit them from attending college. Distance education offers them a way of working through class material on a flexible schedule. Some schools offer entire degree programs through distance education.

In a program it calls Open Courseware, the Massachusetts Institute of Technology (MIT) offers all of its courses free online. Students who take courses via Open Courseware do not earn credit toward a degree or have access to teachers, but they can benefit from the knowledge gained. Since MIT's move online, many other schools have followed suit. Organisations, such as the Open Courseware Consortium and the Centre for Open Sustainable Learning, have been established to support open education around the world.

Business Information

Businesses often use internet and web-based systems for knowledge management within the enterprise. Information systems within the organisation may be accessed through web portals and dashboards that provide a single source for all business-related news and information. Such portals may extend beyond the walls of the office to notebooks and smartphones through internet connections.

Providing news and information about a business and its products through the company's website and online social media can assist in increasing a company's exposure to the general public and improving its reputation. Providing answers to common product questions and customer support online can help keep customers coming back for more. For example, natural food company Kashi uses its website to promote healthy living, with a blog about leading a natural lifestyle, recipes, tools for dieters and personal stories from Kashi employees. The website helps build community around the Kashi brand and promotes awareness of Kashi's philosophy and products.[28]

Personal and Professional Advice and Support

Websites now support every subject and activity of importance. As people confront life's challenges, they can find web resources that can educate and prepare them to succeed. Examples include *www.theknot.com*, which provides information and advice about getting married; *www.whattoexpect.com* provides information and support for expectant parents; and the housing and urban development website at *www.hud.gov* provides all the information a prospective home buyer needs.

Online forums and support groups provide information and access to resources for every disease. For example, *www.LiveStrong.org* provides free support resources for cancer victims. Many physicians and hospitals provide abundant educational information online to assist their patients.

The web is an excellent source of job-related information. People looking for their first jobs or seeking information about new job opportunities can find a wealth of information on the web. Search engines, such as Google or Bing, can be a good starting point for searching for specific companies or industries. You can use a directory on Yahoo's home page, for example, to explore industries and careers. Most medium and large companies have websites that list open positions, salaries, benefits and people to contact for further information. The IBM website, *www.ibm.com*, has a link to "Jobs." When you click this link, you can find information on jobs with IBM around the world. Some sites can help you develop a résumé and assist you during your job search. They can also help you develop an effective cover letter for a résumé, prepare for a job interview, negotiate an employment contract and more. In addition, several internet sites specialise in helping you find job information and even apply for jobs online, including *www.monster.com, www.hotjobs.com* and *www.careerbuilder.com*.

Search Engines and Web Research

The fundamental purpose of the web is to make it easier to find related documents from diverse internet sources by following hyperlinks. However, the web has become so large that many complain of information overload, or the inability to find the information they need due to the overabundance of information. To relieve the strain of information overload, web developers have provided web search engines to help organise and index web content.

A **search engine** is a valuable tool that enables you to find information on the web by specifying words or phrases known as keywords, which are related to a topic of interest. You can also use operators, such as OR and NOT, for more precise search results.

> **search engine** A valuable tool that enables you to find information on the web by specifying words that are key to a topic of interest, known as keywords.

Search engines have become the biggest application on the web. Search giant Google has become one of the world's most profitable companies, with more than €16.5 billion in annual revenue. Web search has become such a profitable business, because it's the one application that everyone uses. Search engine companies make money through advertisements. Because everyone uses search, advertisers are keen to pay to have their ads posted on search pages.

Most search engines use an automated approach that scours the web with "bots" (automated programs) called spiders that follow all web links in an attempt to catalogue every web page by topic. Each web page is analyzed and ranked using unique algorithms and the resulting information is stored in a database. Google maintains more than 4 billion indexed web pages on 30 clusters of up to 2000 computers each, totalling over 30 petabytes of data.

A keyword search at Yahoo!, Bing, or Google isn't a search of the web but rather a search of a database that stores information about web pages. The database is continuously checked and refreshed so that it is an accurate reflection of the current status of the web.

The Bing and Cuil search engines have attempted to innovate with their design. Bing refers to itself as a decision engine, providing more than just a long list of links in its search results. Bing also includes media – music, videos and games – in its search results[29] (see Figure 4.15). Cuil takes it one step further with easy-to-navigate search results and tabs that show related topics.

Figure 4.15 Microsoft
Bing Decision Engine
*Microsoft calls its search
engine a decision engine to
distinguish it from other
search software.*

SOURCE: *www.bing.com.*

Search engines have become important to businesses as tools to draw visitors to the business' website. Many businesses invest in search engine optimisation (SEO) – a process for driving traffic to a website by using techniques that improve the site's ranking in search results. SEO is based on the understanding that web page links listed on the first page of search results, as high on the list as possible, have a far greater chance of being clicked. SEO professionals study the algorithms employed by search engines, altering the web page contents and other variables to improve the page's chance of being ranked number one. SEO professionals use *web analytics software* to study detailed statistics about visitors to their sites.

In addition to search engines, you can use other internet sites to research information. Wikipedia, an encyclopedia with more than 3.3 million English-language entries created and edited by millions of users, is another example of a website that can be used to research information (see Figure 4.16). In Hawaiian, *wiki* means quick, so a wikipedia provides quick access to information. The website is both open source and open editing, which means that people can add or edit entries in the encyclopedia at any time. Besides being self-regulating, Wikipedia articles are vetted by around 1700 administrators. However, even with so many administrators, it is possible that some entries are inaccurate and biased.

Figure 4.16 Wikipedia
*Wikipedia captures the
knowledge of tens of
thousands of experts.*

New features   Log in / create account

Article   Discussion   Read   Edit   View history   Search

WIKIPEDIA
The Free Encyclopedia

Main page
Contents
Featured content
Current events
Random article

▼ Interaction
  About Wikipedia
  Community portal
  Recent changes
  Contact Wikipedia
  Donate to Wikipedia
  Help

▶ Toolbox

▶ Print/export

Information system

From Wikipedia, the free encyclopedia

Not to be confused with information systems (discipline).

An **Information System** (IS) is any combination of information technology and people's activities using that technology to support operations, management, and decision-making.[1] In a very broad sense, the term *information system* is frequently used to refer to the interaction between people, algorithmic processes, data and technology. In this sense, the term is used to refer not only to the information and communication technology (ICT) an organization uses, but also to the way in which people interact with this technology in support of business processes[2].

Some make a clear distinction between information systems, ICT and business processes. Information systems are distinct from information technology in that an information system is typically seen as having an ICT component. Information systems are also different from business processes. Information systems help to control the performance of business processes [3].

CS, SE, IS, IT, & Customer Venn
Diagram where functionality spans left and design spans right stemming from discovery.

SOURCE: *en.wikipedia.org.*

Although Wikipedia is the best-known, general-purpose wiki, many other wikis are designed for special purposes. Wikimedia, the nonprofit organisation behind Wikipedia, has wikis for books, news, media and open learning. Zoho, Wikispaces, Wetpaint and others provide tools to create wikis for any use. Wiki.com is a search engine designed for searching thousands of wikis. A wiki can be used in an enterprise to enable the sharing of information between employees, training for new employees, or customer support for products.[30]

Besides online card catalogues, libraries typically provide links to public and sometimes private research databases on the web. Online research databases allow visitors to search for information in thousands of journal, magazine and newspaper articles. Information database services are valuable, because they offer the best in quality and convenience. They conveniently provide full-text articles from reputable sources over the web. College and public libraries typically subscribe to many databases to support research. One of the most popular private databases is LexisNexis Academic Universe. LexisNexis provides access to full-text documents from over 5900 news, business, legal, medical and reference publications. You can access the information through a standard keyword search engine (see Figure 4.17).

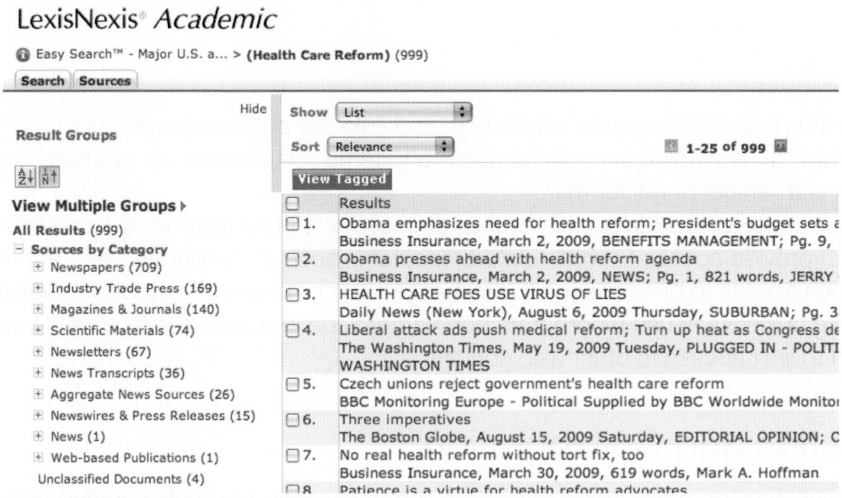

Figure 4.17 LexisNexis
A search at LexisNexis on "Health Care Reform" yields hundreds of full-text articles.

SOURCE: *www.lexisnexis.com.*

Web Portals

A **web portal** is a web page that combines useful information and links and acts as an entry point to the web – they typically include a search engine, a subject directory, daily headlines and other items of interest. Many people choose a web portal as their browser's home page (the first page you open when you begin browsing the web), so the two terms are used interchangeably. Portals provide a convenient starting point for web exploration in a general or a specific context. They allow users to have convenient access to their most frequently used web resources.

Many web pages have been designed to serve as web portals. iGoogle, Yahoo!, AOL and MSN are examples of horizontal portals; "horizontal" refers to the fact that these portals cover a wide range of topics. My Yahoo! and iGoogle allow users to custom design their page, selecting from hundreds of widgets – small applications that deliver information and services. Yahoo also integrates with Facebook so that Facebook users can access their friends and news streams from the My Yahoo portal[31] (see Figure 4.18).

web portal A web page that combines useful information and links and acts as an entry point to the web – they typically include a search engine, a subject directory, daily headlines and other items of interest. Many people choose a web portal as their browser's home page (the first page you open when you begin browsing the web).

Figure 4.18 MyYahoo!
Personalised Portal
*Personalised portals
contain custom designs
and widgets.*

SOURCE: *www.yahoo.com.*

Vertical portals are pages that provide information and links for special-interest groups. For example, the portal at *www.iVillage.com* focuses on items of interest to women, and *www.AskMen.com* is a vertical portal for men.

Many businesses set up corporate portals for their employees. Corporate portals (sometimes called dashboards) provide access to work-related resources, such as corporate news and information, along with access to business tools, databases and communication tools to support collaboration. Some businesses use a corporate portal to provide employees with work-related online content and to limit access to other web content.

Communication and Collaboration

The internet and web provide many applications for communication and collaboration. From text-based applications, such as email, to telepresence systems that use high-definition video and audio that allow individuals from around the world to meet around a table, internet communications supports many levels of communication.

The many forms of internet communication include instant messaging, chat, virtual chat, blogging, microblogging, status updates, internet phone, video chat and conferencing, virtual chat and web conferencing. When selecting a communication method, first consider the importance of the exchange and what needs to be shared. The most effective and meaningful communications are typically the least convenient. Although the value of an in-person, face-to-face meeting should not be underestimated, many communications benefit from the convenience provided by the internet.

Email

Email is a useful form of internet communication that supports text communication, HTML content and sharing documents as email attachments. Email is accessed through web-based systems or through dedicated email applications, such as Outlook and Thunderbird. Email can also be distributed through enterprise systems to desktop computers, notebook computers, and smartphones.

Many people use online email services, such as Hotmail, MSN and Gmail, to access email (see Figure 4.19). Online email services store messages on the server, so users need to be

Gmail Calendar Documents Web Reader more ▼   kbaldauf@gmail.com | ⚖ | Settings | Help | Sign out

Gmail
by Google

Search Mail   Search the Web   Show search options / Create a filter

Compose Mail

Inbox (25)	Florida Auto Insurance - flsfautoinsurance.com/tallahassee - Switch & Save on Auto Insurance Find an
Buzz 💬	Archive Report spam Delete Move to ▼ Labels ▼ More actions ▼ Refresh 1 - 50 of
Starred ☆	Select: All, None, Read, Unread, Starred, Unstarred

Figure 4.19 Gmail
Gmail is one of several free online email services.

☆ Yahoo!	»	You've successfully linked your Facebook account to Yahoo
☆ Momemtary Lapse Driving .	»	[SPAM] At this moment you require - It is surprising just how
☆ Learning, Education and .	»	From Ayesha Habeeb Omer, Ph.D and other Learning, Edu
☆ Facebook	»	Facebook Birthday Reminders for Week of June 14th - face
☆ Audible.com	»	Sale Ends Soon - You Pick What's on Sale - This email was
☆ LinkedIn Connections	»	Ryan DeGrote has accepted your LinkedIn invitation - LinkedIn
☆ list	»	Calvin and Hobbes 06/13/2010 - GoComics-logo Comics Edit
☆ Grant Peeples	»	6000 miles in June - Email not displaying correctly? View in b
☆ ComputationWorld 2010	»	Deadline Extension || ComputationWorld 2010: November
☆ GoDaddy.com		My Go Daddy Statement - June 2010 - NOTICE: To ensure d
☆ Amazon.com	»	Amazon.com: New Releases in Business & Investing Book

ACCOMPLISHMENTS
CONFERENCES
CPATH (2)
EWC2
EWC2/DESIGN
EWC2/PROBLEMS
FRIENDS (4)
GAMING
IDC

Sent Mail
Drafts (9)

connected to the internet to view, send and manage email. Other people prefer to use software, such as Microsoft Outlook, Apple Mail, or Mozilla Thunderbird, which retrieve email from the server and deliver it to the user's PC. Post Office Protocol (POP) is used to transfer messages from email servers to your PC. Email software typically includes more information management features than online email services and let you save your email on your own PC, making it easier to manage and organise messages and to keep the messages private and secure. Another protocol, called Internet Message Access Protocol (IMAP), allows you to view email using Outlook or other email software without downloading and storing the messages locally. Some users prefer this method, because it allows them to view messages from any internet-connected PC.

Business users that access email from smartphones, such as the BlackBerry, take advantage of a technology called push email. Push email uses corporate server software that transfers, or pushes, email to the handset as soon as it arrives at the corporate email server. To the BlackBerry user, it appears as though email is delivered directly to the handset. Push email allows the user to view email from any mobile or desktop device connected to the corporate server. This arrangement allows users flexibility in where, when, and how they access and manage email.

BlackBerry users have instant access to email sent to their business accounts.

SOURCE: Courtesy of Marvin Woodyatt/Photoshot/Landov.

Instant Messaging

Instant messaging is online, real-time communication between two or more people who are connected to the internet (see Figure 4.20). With instant messaging, participants build buddy lists, or contact lists, that let them see which contacts are currently logged on to the internet and available to chat. You can send messages to one of your on-line buddies, which opens a small dialog box on your buddy's computer and allows the two of you to chat via the keyboard. Although chat typically involves exchanging text messages with one other person, more advanced forms of chat are emerging. Today's instant messaging software supports not only text messages, but also sharing images, sounds, files and voice communications. Popular instant messaging services include America Online Instant Messenger (AIM), MSN Messenger, Google Talk and Yahoo!.

instant messaging A method that allows two or more people to communicate online in real time using the internet.

Figure 4.20 Instant Messaging *Instant messaging lets you converse with another internet user by exchanging messages instantaneously.*

SOURCE: © Spencer C. Grant/PhotoEdit.

Microblogging, Status Updates and News Feeds

Twitter is a web application that allows members to report on what they are doing throughout the day. Referred to as a microblogging service, Twitter allows users to send short text updates (up to 140 characters) from a cell phone or web account to their Twitter followers. Although Twitter has been hugely successful for personal use, businesses are finding value in the service as well. Businesspeople use Twitter to stay in close touch with associates by sharing their location and activities throughout the day. Businesses also find Twitter to be a rich source of consumer sentiment that can be tapped to improve marketing, customer relations and product development. Many businesses have a presence on Twitter, dedicating personnel to communicate with customers by posting announcements and reaching out to individual users. Village Books, an independent bookstore, uses Twitter to build relationships with its customers and to make them feel part of their community.[32]

The popularity of Twitter has caused social networks, such as Facebook, LinkedIn and MySpace, to include Twitter-like news feeds. Previously referred to as Status Updates, Facebook users share their thoughts and activities with their friends by posting messages to Facebook's News Feed.

Conferencing

Some internet technologies support real-time online conferencing. Teleconferences have been a popular form of remote conferencing for many years. Participants dial into a common phone number to share a multi-party phone conversation. The internet has made it possible for those involved in teleconferences to share computer desktops. Using services, such as WebEx or

GoToMeeting, conference participants log on to common software that allows them to broadcast their computer display to the group. This is quite useful for presenting with PowerPoint, demonstrating software, training, or collaborating on documents. Participants verbally communicate by phone or PC microphone. Some conferencing software uses web cams to broadcast video of the presenter and group participants.

Telepresence takes video conferencing to the ultimate level. Telepresence systems, such as those from Cisco and HP, use high-resolution video and audio with high-definition displays to make it appear that conference participants are actually sitting around a table (see Figure 4.21). Participants enter a telepresence studio where they sit at a table facing display screens that show other participants from a variety of geographic locations. Cameras and microphones collect high-quality video and audio at all locations and transmit them over high-speed network connections to provide an environment that replicates actual physical presence. Document cameras and computer software are used to share views of computer screens and documents with all participants.

Figure 4.21 Halo **Collaboration Meeting Room** *HP's Halo telepresence system allows people at various locations to meet as though they were gathered around a table.*

SOURCE: Courtesy of Hewlett-Packard.

You don't need to be a big business to enjoy the benefits of video conversations. Free software is available to make video chat easy to use for anyone with a computer, a web cam and a high-speed internet connection. Online applications, such as Google Chat and Microsoft Messenger, support video connections between web users. For spontaneous, random video chat with strangers, you can use *www.Chatroulette.com* and internet Conga Line.[33] Software, such as Apple iChat and Skype, provide computer-to-computer video chat so users can speak to each other face to face. In addition to offering text, audio, and video chat on computers, Skype offers its video phone service over internet-connected TVs. Recent internet-connected sets from Panasonic and Samsung ship with the Skype software preloaded. You attach a web cam to your TV to video-chat from your sofa.

Web 2.0 and the Social Web

Over the past several years, the web has evolved from a one-directional resource where users only obtain information to a two-directional resource where users obtain and contribute information. Consider websites such as YouTube, Wikipedia and Facebook, as examples. The web has also grown in power to support full-blown software applications, such as Google Docs, and is

Web 2.0 The web as a computing platform that supports software applications and the sharing of information among users.

becoming a computing platform itself. These two major trends in how the web is used and perceived have created dramatic changes in how people, businesses and organisations use the web, creating a paradigm shift to **Web 2.0**.

The original web, now referred to as Web 1.0, provided a platform for technology-savvy developers and the businesses and organisations that hired them to publish information for the general public to view. The introduction of user-generated content supported by Wikipedia, blogging and podcasting made it clear that those using the web were also interested in contributing to its content. This led to the development of websites with the sole purpose of supporting user-generated content and user feedback.

Websites, such as YouTube and Flickr, allow users to share video and photos with other people, groups and the world. Microblogging sites, such as Twitter, allow people to post thoughts and ideas throughout the day for friends to read. Social bookmarking sites, such as *www.digg.com* and *www.delicious.com,* allow users to pool their votes to determine what online news stories and web pages are most interesting at any given time of the day. Similarly, Epinions and many retail websites allow consumers to voice their opinions about products. All of these popular websites serve as examples of how the web has transformed to become the town square where people share information, ideas and opinions; meet with friends; and make new acquaintances.

Businesses can observe social network users to determine their tastes and interests. Such data can be mined to discover consumer trends to guide product design and offerings.[34] Consumer information can also be used for targeted advertising.[35]

Some businesses are including social networking features in their products. The use of social media in business is called Enterprise 2.0. Enterprise 2.0 applications, such as Salesforce's Chatter, bring Facebook-like interaction to the workplace. Employees post profiles, making it easy to find colleagues with knowledge that is useful to the work environment. News feeds provide a constant patter of interaction and discussion around work-related topics. Although many see Enterprise 2.0 applications as revitalising forces in the workplace, others worry that they are distracting.[36]

Rich Internet Applications

The introduction of powerful web-delivered applications, such as Google Docs, Adobe Photoshop Express, Xcerion web-based OS and Microsoft Office Web Apps, have elevated the web from an online library to a platform for computing. Many of the computer activities traditionally provided through software installed on a PC can now be carried out using rich internet applications (RIAs) in a web browser without installing any software. A **rich internet application** is software that has the functionality and complexity of traditional application software, but runs in a web browser and does not require local installation (see Figure 4.22). RIAs are the result of continuously improving programming languages and platforms designed for the web.

rich internet application (RIA) Software that has the functionality and complexity of traditional application software, but does not require local installation and runs in a web browser.

Blogging and Podcasting

A **web log**, typically called a **blog**, is a website that people can create and use to write about their observations, experiences and opinions on a wide range of topics. The community of blogs and bloggers is often called the *blogosphere*. A *blogger* is a person who creates a blog, whereas *blogging* refers to the process of placing entries on a blog site. A blog is like a journal. When people post information to a blog, it is placed at the top of the blog page. Blogs can include links to external information and an area for comments submitted by visitors. Video content can also be placed on the internet using the same approach as a blog. This is often called a *video log* or *vlog*.

Web log (blog) A website that people can create and use to write about their observations, experiences and opinions on a wide range of topics.

Figure 4.22 Rich Internet Application
SlideRocket is a rich internet application for creating vibrant online presentations.

SOURCE: www.sliderocket.com.

Internet users may subscribe to blogs using a technology called Really Simple Syndication (RSS). RSS is a collection of web technologies that allow users to subscribe to web content that is frequently updated. With RSS, you can receive a blog update without actually visiting the blog website. You can also use RSS to receive other updates on the internet, for example, from news websites, such as *nyt.com*, which provides the daily news from the New York Times. Software used to subscribe to RSS feeds is called *aggregator software*. Google Reader is a popular aggregator for subscribing to blogs. Blog search engines include Technorati, Feedster and Blogdigger. You can also use Google to locate a blog.

A corporate blog can be useful for communicating with customers, partners and employees. However, companies and their employees need to be cautious about the legal risks of blogging. Blogging can expose a corporation and its employees to charges of defamation, copyright and trademark infringement, invasion of privacy and revealing corporate secrets.

A *podcast* is an audio broadcast over the internet. The name podcast originated from Apple's iPod combined with the word *broadcast*. A podcast is like an audio blog. Using PCs, recording software and microphones, you can record podcast programs and place them on the internet. Apple's iTunes provides free access to tens of thousands of podcasts, sorted by topic and searchable by keyword (see Figure 4.23). After you find a podcast, you can download it to your PC (Windows or Mac), to an MP3 player, such as the iPod, or any smartphone. You can also subscribe to podcasts using RSS software included in iTunes and other digital audio software.

People and corporations can use podcasts to listen to audio material, increase revenues, or advertise products and services. You can listen to podcasts of radio programs, while you are driving, walking, making a meal, or doing most other activities. Colleges and universities often use blogs and podcasts to deliver course material to students.

Online Media and Entertainment

Music, movies, television program episodes, user-generated videos, e-books, and audio books are all available online to download and purchase or stream.

Figure 4.23 iTunes
Podcasts *iTunes provides free access to tens of thousands of podcasts.*

content streaming A method for transferring large media files over the internet so that the data stream of voice and pictures plays more or less continuously as the file is being downloaded.

Content streaming is a method of transferring large media files over the internet so that the data stream of voice and pictures plays more or less continuously as the file is being downloaded. For example, rather than wait for an entire 5 MB video clip to download before they can play it, users can begin viewing a streamed video as it is being received. Content streaming works best when the transmission of a file can keep up with the playback of the file.

Music

The internet and the web have made music more accessible than ever, with artists distributing their songs through online radio, subscription services and download services. The web has had a dramatic impact on the music industry, causing unprecedented changes in marketing and distribution. Digital distribution has allowed artists to distribute music directly to fans without the need for record companies. It has also opened the door to music piracy and illegal distribution of music that is legally protected by copyright.

Internet radio is similar to local AM and FM radio, except that it is digitally delivered to your computer over the internet, providing many more choices of stations. For example, Live365 provides access to thousands of radio stations in more than 200 musical genre categories. Some stations charge a subscription fee, but most do not.

Compressed music formats, such as MP3, have made music swapping over the internet a convenient and popular activity. File-sharing software, such as BitTorrent, provide a means by which some music fans copy and distribute music, often without consideration of copyright laws. The result is a popular music distribution system that is largely illegal and difficult to control and cuts deeply into the recording industry's profits. In addition, it is not always safe to swap files with strangers. Downloaded music files may actually be viruses renamed to look like MP3 files. Music industry giants have pulled together to win back customers by offering legal and safe electronic music distribution at a reasonable price that provides services and perks not offered by file-sharing networks.

Several legal music download services are available. Apple's iTunes was one of the first online music services to find success. Microsoft, Amazon.com, Wal-Mart and other retailers also sell music online. Downloaded music may include digital rights management (DRM) technology that prevents or limits the user's ability to make copies and play the music on multiple players.

Movies, Video and Television

With increasing amounts of internet bandwidth going to more homes, streaming video and television are becoming commonplace. Once content with small, low-quality YouTube videos, the public now craves professionally produced video. Some are connecting their computers to high-definition television sets to access television and even motion picture quality programming. The web and TV are rapidly merging into a single integrated system available from home entertainment systems, PCs and mobile phones. Many television stations provide much of their content online, after it has been shown for TV audiences first. The BBC's iPlayer, for instance, allows viewers the chance to "catch-up" on programs they have missed.

Television is expanding to the web in leaps and bounds. Websites, such as Hulu, and internet-based television platforms like Joost provide television programming from hundreds of providers, including most mainstream television networks. Joost attracts an estimated 67 million viewers per month.[37] Hulu provides a premium service, called Hulu Plus, that provides an extended menu of programming to iPhones, iPads, TVs and more for $6 per month. Hulu CEO Jason Kilar says the service compliments rather than replaces cable TV. But most analysts agree that it's only a matter of time until cable is challenged by internet-based television programming.[38] Many TV networks offer online full-length streamed episodes of popular programs, including season premieres that are released before airing on television. Clicker.com serves as a television guide to most online programming.

Motion pictures are also making their way to internet distribution. Subscription services, such as LoveFilm, allow members to rent DVDs by mail or stream movies over the web to their computers. Apple iTunes users can rent or purchase movies from the iTunes store and download them to a computer.

No discussion of internet video would be complete without mentioning YouTube. YouTube supports the online sharing of user-created videos. Every day, people upload hundreds of thousands of videos to YouTube and view hundreds of millions of these videos. YouTube videos are relatively short and cover a wide range of categories from the nonsensical to college lectures (see Figure 4.24). Other video streaming sites include Google Video, Yahoo! Video, Metacafe and AOL Video.

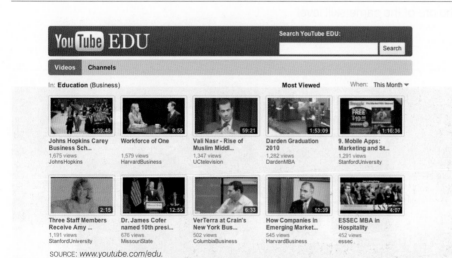

SOURCE: www.youtube.com/edu.

Figure 4.24 YouTube EDU *YouTube EDU provides thousands of educational videos from hundreds of universities.*

E-Books and Audio Books

An e-book is a book stored digitally, rather than on paper, and read on a display using e-book reader software. E-books have been available for quite a while, nearly as long as computers. However, it wasn't until the introduction of Amazon's eBook reading device, the Kindle, in 2007 that they gained more widespread acceptance. Several features of the Kindle appeal to the general public. First, the Kindle features ePaper, a display that does not include backlighting like traditional displays. Some feel that ePaper is less harsh on your eyes than using a backlit display. Second, the Kindle is light and compact, similar in size and weight to a paperback book, but thinner than most books. Finally, Amazon created a vast library of eBooks that could be purchased and downloaded to the Kindle over whispernet – a wireless network provided free of charge by Sprint.

As an eBook reader, the Apple's iPad functions much like the Kindle; however, the iPad provides thousands of applications in addition to e-books. Apple offers users much the same selection of books as Kindle users. Amazon has even developed a Kindle application that runs on the iPad so users can access their Kindle libraries on the iPad.

Google has partnered with libraries to digitise more than 10 million books in its Google Books Library Project. A Google search includes searching for information in its Google Books Library. Google Books includes digital copies of in-copyright books, out-of-copyright books and books from publishers with whom Google has partnered. Search results from Google Books may include snippets of information about the book and where to buy it, or, in the case of out-of-copyright books, the entire contents. Google has made an effort to open its own eBook store, but so far they've been blocked by US courts because of worries that Google would obtain monopoly power over the industry.

Online Games

Many video games are available online. They include single-user, multiuser and massively multi-user games. The web offers a multitude of games for all ages. From Nickelodeon's Sponge Bob games to solitaire to massively multiplayer online role-playing games (MMORPG), a wide variety of offerings suits every taste (see Figure 4.25). Of course, the web provides a medium for downloading single-player games to your desktop, notebook, handheld, or cell phone device, but the power of the web is most apparent with multiplayer games.

Game consoles, such as the Wii, Xbox and PlayStation, provide multiplayer options for online gaming over the internet. Subscribers can play with or against other subscribers in 3D virtual environments. They can even talk to each other using a microphone headset. Microsoft's Xbox LIVE provides features that allow users to keep track of their buddies online and match up with other players who are of the same skill level.

Figure 4.25 Blizzard's **World of Warcraft** *World of Warcraft is an extremely popular massively multiplayer online role-playing game.*

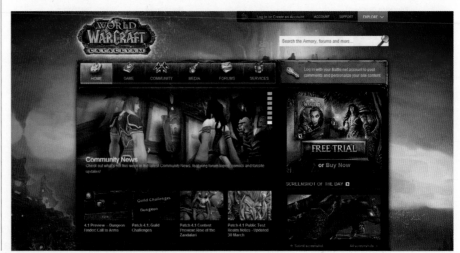

SOURCE: Reproduced with permission © Blizzard Entertainment.

Shopping Online

Many online shopping options are available to web users. E-tail stores – online versions of retail stores – provide access to many products that may be unavailable in local stores. JCPenney, Target, Wal-Mart and many others only carry a percentage of their actual inventory in their stores. You can find additional products at their online stores. To add to their other conveniences, many websites offer free shipping and pickup for returned items that don't fit or otherwise meet a customer's needs.

Like your local shopping mall, cybermalls provide access to a collection of stores that aim to meet your every need. Cybermalls are typically aligned with popular web portals, such as Yahoo!, AOL and MSN. Websites, such as mySimon.com, DealTime.com, PriceSCAN.com, PriceGrabber.com and NexTag.com, provide product price quotations from numerous e-tailers to help you to find the best deal. An app for Android smartphones, called Compare Everywhere, allows users to compare the price of an item offered by many retailers.

Online clearinghouses, web auctions and marketplaces provide a platform for businesses and individuals to sell their products and belongings. Online clearinghouses, such as uBid.com, provide a method for manufacturers to liquidate stock and for consumers to find a good deal. Outdated or overstocked items are put on the virtual auction block, and users bid on the objects. The highest bidder(s) when the auction closes gets the merchandise – often for less than 50 per cent of the advertised retail price.

The most popular online auction or marketplace is *www.eBay.com* (see Figure 4.26). eBay provides a public platform for global trading where anyone can buy, sell, or trade practically anything. eBay offers a wide variety of features and services that enable members to buy and sell on the site quickly and conveniently. Buyers have the option to purchase items at a fixed price or in auction-style format, where the highest bid wins the product. Information about auction items on eBay includes how much time is left in the auction, the current highest bid, as well as details about the item and seller. On any given day, millions of items are listed on eBay across thousands of categories.

Craigslist is a network of online communities that provides free online classified advertisements. It is a popular online marketplace for purchasing items from local individuals. Many shoppers turn to Craigslist, rather than going to the classifieds in the local paper.

Figure 4.26 eBay
eBay.com provides an online marketplace where anyone can buy, sell, or trade practically anything.

SOURCE: © Ian Dagnall/Alamy.

Businesses benefit from shopping online as well. *Global supply management (GSM)* online services provide methods for businesses to find the best deals on the global market for raw materials and supplies needed to manufacture their products. *Electronic exchanges* provide an industry-specific web resource created to deliver a convenient centralised platform for B2B e-commerce among manufacturers, suppliers and customers. You can read more about this topic in Chapter 5.

Travel, Geolocation and Navigation

Travel websites, such as *www.travelocity.com*, *www.expedia.com* and *www.priceline.com*, help travellers find the best deals on flights, hotels, car rentals, vacation packages, and cruises. Priceline offers a slightly different approach from Travelocity and Expedia. It allows shoppers to name a price they're willing to pay for a ticket and then works to find an airline that can meet that price. After flights have been reserved, travellers can use these websites to book hotels and rental cars, often at discounted prices.

Travel agencies, resorts, airlines, cruise lines and all businesses associated with travel have a strong online presence. Map websites, such as Bing Maps and Google Maps, are invaluable for finding your way to and around destinations; you can even view your destination from street view (see Figure 4.27). Websites like *www.tripit.com* allow you to organise all of your travel plans, including flights, car rentals, hotel reservations, restaurants and landmarks in one easy-to-access web page. Today, most travel begins on the web.

Google Maps also provides extensive location-specific business information, satellite imagery, up-to-the-minute traffic reports and Street View. Street View is the result of Google employees driving the streets of the world's cities in vehicles with high-tech camera gear, taking 360-degree images. These images are integrated into Google Maps to allow users to get a "street view" of an area that can be manipulated as if they were actually walking down the street looking around. Bing Maps takes it a step further with high-resolution aerial photos and street-level 3D photographs.

Figure 4.27 Bing Maps
Mapping software, such as Bing Maps, provide streetside views of Times Square.

SOURCE: *www.bing.com/maps*.

Information Systems at Work

Selling Real Estate with Google Maps

The REA Group, headquartered in Australia, started its business in 1995 with $24 000 AUD (Australian dollars) and the belief that the web would grow to become a dominant tool for the real estate industry. The company worked with Australian realtors to develop effective online real estate advertising. Before long, its website, *www.realestate.com.au*, became the most popular real estate portal in Australia. Today, the REA Group has 18 web portals and operations in 12 countries, including Belgium, France, Germany, Hong Kong, Italy, Luxembourg, New Zealand and the United Kingdom, with an annual revenue of more than AUD $156 million.

As online map software, such as Google Maps, arrived on the scene, the REA Group immediately saw its potential for the real estate market. CEO Simon Baker believes that shoppers want to see as much information about a property as possible before contacting an agent. The REA Group purchased simple mapping software to add to its real estate web portals. Unfortunately, the software was slow to load, and key features, such as zooming in and out, worked inconsistently in different web browsers. Even worse, the software failed to plot some coordinates accurately.

Fortunately, mapping technology improved over time, and the REA Group became impressed with the features provided by Google Maps. In particular, the company appreciated that Google Maps could be customised to meet the needs of the real estate industry and could easily be embedded into web pages. The REA Group dropped their previous mapping technology and moved to Google Maps.

The API Premier version of Google Maps allows businesses to associate information with map coordinates. Google Maps embedded in *www.realestate .com.au* allows shoppers to see home locations on a map using a map view, a satellite view, hybrid view, terrain view, or street view. Shoppers can click the house icons on the map to view details and price. Google Maps also provides detailed property boundary lines. Those shopping for real estate can combine Google Maps and interior photos of the home to get a fairly thorough inspection before taking time for a physical visit. The REA Group believes

that the embedded map is the most important feature of the online shopping experience.

Additionally, shoppers can perform structured and geographic searches for property. They can also use the embedded Google search bar to look for nearby schools, restaurants, attractions and businesses. The REA Group plans to extend the capabilities of Google Maps with an assortment of overlays that provide information on a particular geographic region.

After the REA Group added Google Maps to its Australian site, it witnessed a steady boost in traffic and sales leads. Rather than competing with real estate agents, the software provides the agents with well-informed customers ready to buy, allowing the agents to make more sales with less effort. More recently, the company has rolled out the technology to its UK and Luxembourg sites and is currently continuing to extend the software to its remaining sites.

In 2009, the REA Group provided more than 1.5 billion maps through its real estate portals, making it one of the largest map providers in the world. CEO Simon Baker says that "With the mapping technology from Google, we're able to enhance the user experience, increase site stickiness, and improve the quality and accuracy of the data being displayed."

Discussion Questions

1 How has Google Maps improved the online shopping experience for visitors to *www.realestate.com.au*?

2 How does Google Maps help real estate agents in their work?

Critical Thinking Questions

1 What might the REA Group have done to avoid the problems it experienced with its first mapping software?

2 How might a company like the REA Group make money?

SOURCES: Staff, 'Global real estate portal network adds Google Maps to enhance customers' house hunting experience,' Google Maps Case Study. Available from: *www.google.com/ enterprise/maps/reagroup.html*. Accessed January 23, 2010; The REA Group website. Available from: *www.rea-group.com*. Accessed January 24, 2010; *realestate.com.au*. Accessed January 24, 2010.

4.6 Intranets and Extranets

An intranet is an internal corporate network built using internet and World Wide Web standards and products. Employees of an organisation use it to gain access to corporate information. After getting their feet wet with public websites that promote company products and services, corporations are seizing the web as a swift way to streamline – even transform – their organisations. These private networks use the infrastructure and standards of the internet and the World Wide Web. Using an intranet offers one considerable advantage: Many people are already familiar with internet technology, so they need little training to make effective use of their corporate intranet.

An intranet is an inexpensive yet powerful alternative to other forms of internal communication, including conventional computer setups. One of an intranet's most obvious virtues is its ability to reduce the need for paper. Because web browsers run on any type of computer, the same electronic information can be viewed by any employee. That means that all sorts of documents (such as internal phone books, procedure manuals, training manuals and requisition forms) can be inexpensively converted to electronic form on the web and be constantly updated. An intranet provides employees with an easy and intuitive approach to accessing information that was previously difficult to obtain. For example, it is an ideal solution to providing information to a mobile salesforce that needs access to rapidly changing information.

A growing number of companies offer limited network access to selected customers and suppliers. Such networks are referred to as extranets, which connect people who are external to the company. An **extranet** is a network that links selected resources of the intranet of a company with its customers, suppliers, or other business partners. Again, an extranet is built around web technologies.

extranet A network based on web technologies that links selected resources of a company's intranet with its customers, suppliers, or other business partners.

Security and performance concerns are different for an extranet than for a website or network-based intranet. User authentication and privacy are critical on an extranet so that information is protected. Obviously, the network must perform well to provide quick response to customers and suppliers.

Secure intranet and extranet access applications usually require the use of a *virtual private network (VPN)*, a secure connection between two points on the internet. VPNs transfer information by encapsulating traffic in IP packets and sending the packets over the internet, a practice called **tunnelling**. Most VPNs are built and run by ISPs. Companies that use a VPN from an ISP have essentially outsourced their networks to save money on wide area network equipment and personnel.

tunnelling The process by which VPNs transfer information by encapsulating traffic in IP packets over the internet.

Summary

At the start of this chapter, we set out the FIVE main principles relating to how business information systems use the internet and other web-based communication systems together with the key learning objectives for each. Now it's time to summarise the chapter by recapping on those FIVE principles: can you recall what is important and why about each one?

1 **A telecommunications system has many fundamental components that must be carefully** selected and work together effectively to enable people to meet personal and organisation objectives. Telecommunications refers to the electronic transmission of signals for communications, including telephone, radio and television. Telecommunications is creating profound changes in business, because it removes the barriers of time and distance.

The elements of a telecommunications system include the sending and receiving devices, modems, the transmission media and the message. The sending unit transmits a signal to a modem, which performs a number of functions, such as converting the signal into a different form or from one type to another. The modem then sends the signal through a medium, which is anything that carries an electronic signal and serves as an interface between a sending device and a receiving device. The signal is received by another modem that is connected to the receiving computer. The process can then be reversed, and another message can pass from the receiving unit to the original sending unit. A communications channel is the transmission medium that carries a message from the source to its receivers.

The telecommunications media that physically connect data communications devices can be divided into two broad categories: guided transmission media in which a communications signal travels along a solid medium and wireless media in which the communications signal is sent over airwaves. Guided transmission media include twisted-pair wire cable, coaxial cable, fibre-optic cable and broadband over power lines. Wireless telecommunications involves the broadcast of communications in one of three frequency ranges: microwave, radio and infrared.

Wireless communications options include near field communications, Bluetooth, ultra wideband, Wi-Fi, 3G, 4G and WiMAX.

Telecommunications uses various devices, including smartphones, modems, multiplexers, PBXs, front-end processors, switches, bridge, routers and gateways.

The effective use of networks can turn a company into an agile, powerful and creative organisation, giving it a long-term competitive advantage. Networks let users share hardware, programs and databases across the organisation. They can transmit and receive information to improve organisational effectiveness and efficiency. They enable geographically separated workgroups to share documents and opinions, which fosters teamwork, innovative ideas and new business strategies.

The physical distance between nodes on the network and the communications and services provided by the network determines whether it is called a personal area network (PAN), local area network (LAN), metropolitan area network (MAN), or a wide area network (WAN).

The electronic flow of data across international and global boundaries is often called transborder data flow.

When an organisation needs to use two or more computer systems, it can follow one of three basic data processing strategies: centralised, decentralised, or distributed.

A client/server system is a network that connects a user's computer (a client) to one or more server computers (servers). A client is often a PC that requests services from the server, shares processing tasks with the server and displays the results.

A communications protocol is a set of rules that govern the exchange of information over a communications channel.

A network operating system controls the computer systems and devices on a network, allowing them to communicate with one another. Network-management software enables a manager to monitor the use of individual computers and shared hardware, scan for viruses and ensure compliance with software licences.

2 **The internet provides a critical infrastructure for delivering and accessing information and services.** The internet is truly international in scope, with users on every continent. It is the world's largest computer network. Actually, it is a collection of interconnected networks, all freely exchanging information. The internet transmits data from one computer (called a host) to another. The set of conventions used to pass packets from one host to another is known as the Internet Protocol (IP). Many other protocols are used with IP. The best known is the Transmission Control Protocol (TCP). TCP is so widely used that many people refer to the internet protocol as TCP/IP, the combination of TCP and IP used by most internet applications. Each computer on the internet has an assigned IP address for easy identification. A Uniform Resource Locator (URL) is a web address that specifies the exact location of a web page using letters and words that map to an IP address and a location on the host.

Cloud computing refers to a computing environment where software and storage are provided as an internet service and accessed with a web browser. Computing activities are increasingly being delivered over the internet rather than from installed software on PCs. Cloud computing offers tremendous advantages to businesses. By outsourcing business information systems to the cloud, a business saves on system design, installation, and maintenance. Employees can also access corporate systems from any internet-connected computer using a standard web browser.

People can connect to the internet backbone in several ways: via a LAN whose server is an internet host, or via a dial-up connection, high-speed service, or wireless service. An internet service provider is any company that provides access to the internet. To use this type of connection, you must have an account with the service provider and software that allows a direct link via TCP/IP.

3 Originally developed as a document-management system, the World Wide Web has grown to become a primary source of news and information, an indispensible conduit for commerce, and a popular hub for social interaction, entertainment and communication. The web is a collection of tens of millions of servers that work together as one in an internet service providing information via hyperlink technology to billions of users worldwide. Thanks to the high-speed internet circuits connecting them and hyperlink technology, users can jump between web pages and servers effortlessly – creating the illusion of using one big computer. Because of its ability to handle multimedia objects and hypertext links between distributed objects, the web is emerging as the most popular means of information access on the internet today.

As a hyperlink-based system that uses the client/server model, the web organises internet resources throughout the world into a series of linked files, called pages, accessed and viewed using web client software, called a web browser. Internet Explorer, Firefox, Chrome, Opera and Safari are popular web browsers. A collection of pages on one particular topic, accessed under one web domain, is called a website.

Hypertext Markup Language (HTML) is the standard page description language for web pages. The HTML tags let the browser know how to format the text. HTML also indicates where images, sound and other elements should be inserted. Some newer web standards are gaining in popularity, including Extensible Markup Language (XML), Cascading Style Sheets (CSS) and Wireless Markup Language (WML).

Web 2.0 refers to the web as a computing platform that supports software applications and the sharing of information between users. The web is changing from a one-directional resource where users find information to a two-directional resource where users find and share information. The web has also grown in power to support complete software applications and is becoming a computing platform in and of itself. A rich internet application (RIA) is software that has the functionality and complexity of traditional application software, but runs in a web browser and does not require local installation. Java, PHP, AJAX, MySQL, .NET and web application frameworks are all used to create interactive web pages

4 The internet and web provide numerous resources for finding information, communicating and collaborating, socialising, conducting business and shopping, and being entertained. The most common and popular uses for the internet and web can be categorised as publishing information, assisting users in finding information, supporting communication and collaboration, building online community, providing software applications, providing a platform for expressing ideas and opinions, delivering media of all types, providing a platform for commerce, and supporting travel and navigation.

The web has become the most popular medium for distributing and accessing information. It is a powerful tool for keeping informed about local, state, national, and global news. As a tool for sharing information and a primary repository of information on all subjects, the web is ideally suited for education and training. Museums, libraries, private businesses, government agencies, and many other types of organisations and individuals offer educational materials online for free or a fee. Many businesses use the web browser as an interface to corporate information systems. Websites have sprung up to support every subject and activity of importance.

A search engine is a valuable tool that enables you to find information on the web by specifying words that are key to a topic of interest – known as keywords. Some search companies have experimented with human-powered and human-assisted search. In addition to search engines, you can use other internet sites to research information. Wikipedia, an encyclopedia with more than 3.3 million English-language entries created and edited by millions of users, is another example of a website that can be used to research information. There are other wikis that are designed for special purposes. Online research is also greatly assisted by traditional resources that have migrated from libraries to websites, such as online databases.

A web portal is a web page that combines useful information and links and acts as an entry point to the web – the first page you open when you begin browsing the web. A web portal typically includes a search engine, a subject directory, daily headlines and other items of interest. They can be general or specific in nature.

The internet and web provide many applications for communication and collaboration. Email is an incredibly useful form of internet communication that not only supports text communication, but also supports HTML content and sharing documents as email attachments. Instant messaging is online, real-time communication between two or more people who are connected to the internet. Referred to as a microblogging service, Twitter allows users to send short text updates (up to 140 characters long) from a cell phone or the web to their Twitter followers. There are a number of internet technologies that support real-time online conferencing. The internet has made it possible for those involved in teleconferences to share computer desktops. Using services, such as WebEx or GoToMeeting, conference participants log on to common software that allows them to broadcast their computer display to the group. Telepresence systems, such as those from Cisco and HP, use high-resolution video and audio with high-definition displays to make it appear that conference participants are actually sitting around a table.

Websites, such as YouTube and Flickr, allow users to share video and photos with other people, groups, and the world. Microblogging sites, such as Twitter, allow people to post thoughts and ideas throughout the day for friends to read. Social bookmarking sites, such as www.digg.com and www.delicious.com, allow users to pool their votes to determine what online news stories and web pages are most interesting at any given time of the day. Similarly, Epinions and many retail websites allow consumers to voice their opinions about products. Social networking websites provide web-based tools for users to share information about themselves with people on the web and to find, meet and converse with other members.

Many of the computer activities traditionally provided through software installed on a PC can now be carried out using RIAs in a web browser without installing any software. RIAs are the result of continuously improving programming languages and platforms designed for the web.

A web log, or blog, is a website that people can create and use to write about their observations, experiences and opinions on a wide range of topics. Internet users may subscribe to blogs using a technology called Really Simple Syndication (RSS). RSS is a collection of web technologies that allow users to subscribe to web content that is frequently updated. With RSS, you can receive a blog update without actually visiting the blog website. A *podcast* is an audio broadcast over the internet.

Like news and information, all forms of media and entertainment have followed their audiences online. The internet and the web have made music more accessible than ever, with artists distributing their songs through online radio, subscription services and download services. With increasing amounts of internet bandwidth going to more homes, streaming video and television are becoming commonplace. E-books have been available for quite a while, nearly as long as computers. eBook reading devices are gaining in user acceptance. Online games include the many different types of single-user, multiuser and massively multiuser games played on the internet and the web.

Many online shopping options are available to web users. E-tail stores – online versions retail stores – provide access to many products that may be unavailable in local stores. Like your local shopping mall, cybermalls provide access to a collection of stores that aim to meet your every need. Online clearinghouses, web auctions and marketplaces provide a platform for businesses and individuals to sell their products and belongings.

The web has had a profound effect on the travel industry and the way people plan and prepare for trips. From getting assistance with short trips across town to planning long holidays abroad, travellers are turning to the web to save time and money and overcome much of the risk involved in visiting unknown places. Mapping and geolocation tools are among the most popular and successful web applications. MapQuest, Google Maps and Bing Maps are examples. Geo-tagging is technology that allows for tagging information with an associated location.

5 **Popular internet and web technologies have been applied to business networks in the form of intranets and extranets.** An intranet is an internal corporate network built using internet and World Wide Web standards and products. Because web browsers run on any type of computer, the same electronic information can be viewed by any

employee. That means that all sorts of documents can be converted to electronic form on the web and can constantly be updated.

An extranet is a network that links selected resources of the intranet of a company with its customers, suppliers, or other business partners. It is also built around web technologies. Security and performance concerns are different for an extranet than for a website or network-based intranet. User authentication and privacy are critical on an extranet. Obviously, the network must perform well to provide quick response to customers and suppliers.

Review Questions

1 What is meant by broadband communications?

2 Describe the elements and steps involved in the telecommunications process.

3 What is a telecommunications protocol?

4 What are the names of the three primary frequency ranges used in wireless communications?

5 What is VPN? How do organisations use this technology?

6 What is the difference between near field communication and ultra wideband?

7 What is the difference between Wi-Fi and WiMAX communications?

8 What roles do the bridge, router, gateway and switch play in a network?

9 Distinguish between a PAN, LAN, MAN and WAN.

10 What is TCP/IP? How does it work?

11 Explain the naming conventions used to identify internet host computers.

12 What is a web browser? Provide four examples.

13 What is cloud computing?

14 Briefly describe three ways to connect to the internet. What are the advantages and disadvantages of each approach?

15 What is an internet service provider? What services do they provide?

16 How do web application frameworks assist web developers?

17 What is a podcast?

18 What is content streaming?

19 What is instant messaging?

20 What is the web? Is it another network like the internet or a service that runs on the internet?

21 What is a URL and how is it used?

22 What is an intranet? Provide three examples of the use of an intranet.

23 What is an extranet? How is it different from an intranet?

Discussion Questions

1 Why is an organisation that employs centralised processing likely to have a different management decision-making philosophy than an organisation that employs distributed processing?

2 What are the pros and cons of distributed processing versus centralised processing for a large retail chain?

3 Social networks are being widely used today. Describe how this technology could be used in a business setting. Are there any drawbacks or limitations to using social networks in a business setting?

4 Why is it important to have an organisation that manages IP addresses and domain names?

5 What are the benefits and risks involved in using cloud computing?

6 Describe how a company could use a blog and podcasting.

7 What are the defining characteristics of a Web 2.0 site?

8 Name four forms of internet communication describing the benefits and drawbacks of each.

9 What social concerns surround geolocation technologies?

10 One of the key issues associated with the development of a website is getting people to visit it. If you were developing a website, how would you inform others about it and make it interesting enough that they would return and tell others about it?

11 Downloading music, radio and video programs from the internet is easier than in the past, but some companies are still worried that people will illegally obtain copies of this programming without paying the artists and producers royalties. If you were an artist or producer, what would you do?

12 Briefly summarise the differences in how the internet, a company intranet and an extranet are accessed and used.

Web Exercises

1 Do research on the web to identify the latest 4G communications developments. In your opinion, which carrier's 4G network (AT&T, Sprint Nextel, T-Mobil, or Verizon) is the most widely deployed? Write a short report on what you found.

2 Research some of the potential disadvantages of using the internet, such as privacy, fraud, or unauthorised websites. Write a brief report on what you found.

3 Set up an account on *www.twitter.com* and invite a few friends to join. Use Twitter to send messages to your friends on their cell phones, keeping everyone posted on what you are doing throughout the day. Write a review of the service to submit to your instructor.

Case One

Processing Petabytes at CERN and Around the World

Founded in 1954, the CERN laboratory sits astride the Franco–Swiss border near Geneva. CERN, the European Organisation for Nuclear Research, is one of the world's largest and most respected centres for scientific research. Its business is fundamental physics, finding out what the universe is made of and how it works. CERN is the home of the recently completed Large Hadron Collider, a 27-km-long particle accelerator used in physics experiments to study the basic constituents of matter and learn about the laws of Nature.

A by-product of these experiments is data. Lots of data.

When particles collide, a 7000-tonne device called the ATLAS detector monitors what happens, looking at the new particles that are created. Scientists are hoping ATLAS will one day detect the Higgs boson particle, the only particle predicted by the standard model of particle physics that has not already been observed. According to parameters set by the physicists, particles pass through ATLAS, while microprocessors convert their path and energies into electronic signals, discarding the majority (199 999 out of every 200 000) and keeping only those that look promising. Even by discarding this many, ATLAS, still creates 19 GB of data every minute. In 2010, ATLAS generated enough data to fill a stack of CDs 14 km long. That rate of data production outstrips any other scientific effort. Physicists deal with this data flood with a divide-and-conquer approach. Data from ATLAS are sent to a vast global network known as the Worldwide LHC Computer Grid. Nature magazine's Geoff Brumfiel says that the grid is as great a technological advance as the collider itself. Distributed across 34 countries and with 150 petabytes of disc space, the grid allows for analyses that would push the most powerful supercomputers to the edge.

From the ATLAS detector, the data are sent to CERN's computing centre where selected collisions are reconstructed. Dedicated fibre-optic links then carry the data to 11 data centres spread across the globe, one of which is in the Rutherford Appleton Laboratory at Oxford, UK. Here, scientists divide up the data by the kinds of particles they want to study. "Particle physics is a bit like investigating a mid-air collision. Nobody is there to witness it; instead the debris is painstakingly collected and reassembled to give investigators hints as to what happened," says Mr Brumfiel.

At the next level down, more computer centres request data analyses from the 11 data centres so that they can provide storage and access to the data for other users. When a request for an analysis is made, the grid pulls the data from centres like the one at Oxford, then parcels the data into thousands of separate pieces and spreads it across the network. When complete, an email is sent to the person who made the request telling him or her the results are ready.

Things don't always run smoothly. Air-conditioning units have become clogged shutting down centres, road workers have severed the fibre-optic cable and a fire brought down a data centre in Taiwan for months. The entire system relies on goodwill: "We have no line management over these people whatsoever," says Jamie Shiers, a group leader in CERN's computing centre, in reference to the people who work at the data centres and smaller computer centres.

Discussion Questions

1 How could a project as complex as the Worldwide LHC Computer Grid operate "on goodwill?"

2 What are some of the challenges the designers of the Worldwide LHC Computer Grid faced when creating it?

Critical Thinking Questions

1 This project was created mostly using public funding. Do you feel this was money well spent?

2 How could the data produced be archived for future generations of scientists and historians to examine?

SOURCES: Brumfiel, Geoff, 'Down the petabyte highway,' Nature 469(7330), January 20, 2011.
European Organisation for Nuclear Research. Available from: http://public.web.cern.ch/public/. Accessed January 28, 2011.

Case Two

Barriers to Enterprise 2.0

Web 2.0 and social media, such as Facebook, Wikipedia and YouTube, have transformed life for many people, providing new ways to connect with friends and share information and media.

The use of Web 2.0 technologies and social media in the enterprise has been dubbed Enterprise 2.0. In most instances, Enterprise 2.0 is an extension of a corporate intranet; it is sealed off for access to employees only. VPN technology may be used to allow employee access from any internet-connected device using a corporate login.

Some companies have been extremely successful with the implementation of Enterprise 2.0. Cisco, one of the world's largest technology companies, has implemented Enterprise 2.0 for its 65 000 employees. Cisco is the global leader in the design, manufacturing, and sales of networking and communications technologies and services. Cisco created a Facebook-like application for its employees to assist in finding subject matter experts within the organisation. Like Facebook users, Cisco employees create profiles within the system that include their professional areas of expertise. When other employees need assistance with a problem, a quick search of the system will lead them to an expert within the organisation.

Cisco also provides a video wiki used for training on different products and technologies and a Wikipedia-like application for sharing knowledge across the Enterprise. A number of mash-up applications have been developed to draw information from the main Enterprise 2.0 applications to address specific needs. For example, one mash-up can be used to quickly contact technical support staff.

Initially, Cisco experienced some cultural pushback in the planning stage of its Enterprise 2.0 applications. A highly sceptical group of engineers thought that the company was wasting resources on needless technologies. Ultimately, the technologies have created real improvements for Cisco's business models.

Cisco is in a vast minority of companies that have successfully implemented Enterprise 2.0; however, it is likely that many companies will be following Cisco's lead. Traditional business culture often acts as a barrier to the adoption of Web 2.0 technologies. There is often a prevailing notion that posting to social networks is wasting time, rather than being productive, and doesn't constitute "real work." In reality, people are most productive when interacting with networks of colleagues.

Another barrier to Enterprise 2.0 is a concern that social networks act as gateways to chaos, generating an unmanageable amount of mostly worthless data. The response to this argument is to provide tools that allow users to filter out the junk to get an optimal signal-to-noise ratio. Those that have been successful with Enterprise 2.0 find that getting users to generate as much noise and activity as possible creates the most valuable information to mine.

Yet another barrier to implementing Enterprise 2.0 is fear that the social network will be used as a "digital soapbox for disgruntled employees." This issue, as with the others, can be handled with proper management of the system and employees. If employees have grounds for complaining, management can more easily address those issues through the open forum of a social network.

In general, Enterprise 2.0 has been slow to take off due to an inability to easily show a return on investment. Social networks within an enterprise provide a soft return that is sometimes difficult to quantify. Successful Enterprise 2.0 implementations typically have two things in common: they are built to support key business processes, and they are not expected to show an ROI.

Discussion Questions

1 What Web 2.0 applications can provide benefits to employees in a business environment?

2 What barriers exist in some businesses that hamper the adoption of Enterprise 2.0?

Critical Thinking Questions

1 How might an information system administrator make a case for the implementation of Enterprise 2.0 when no ROI can be easily demonstrated?

2 In a large global enterprise, how might Enterprise 2.0 applications be organised so as to provide local benefits as well as global benefits?

SOURCES : Bennett, Elizabeth, 'Web 2.0 in the Enterprise 2.0,' CIO Insight, July 13, 2009; Gardner, W. David, 'Enterprise 2.0: How Cloud Computing Is Challenging CIOs,' Information Week, June 15, 2010. Available from: www.informationweek.com.

Notes

1 BBC, 'SA pigeon 'faster than broadband,' September 10 , 2009. Available from: *http://news.bbc.co.uk/1/hi/8248056.stm*.

2 Reed, Brad, 'IBM Uses BPL to Extend Broadband Coverage to Rural Areas,' *Network World*, February 18, 2009.

3 Fleishman, Greg, 'UWB Groups Shutters, Sends Tech to Bluetooth, USB Groups,' *Ars Technica*, March 16, 2007.

4 Staff, 'Hotel Chatter Annual Wi-Fi Report 2009.' Available from: *www.hotelchatter.com/special/Best_WiFi_Hotels_2009*. Accessed January 6, 2010.

5 Iridium Everywhere web page. Available from: *www.iridium.com/about/globalnetwork.php*. Accessed November 18, 2009.

6 Wells, Jane, 'Iridium Satellite Is Back and Ready for Liftoff.' Available from: *CNBC.com*. Accessed February 26, 2009.

7 Rosenberg, Barry, 'VSAT Proves Crucial to Battlefield Communications,' *Defense Systems*, June 5, 2009.

8 Staff, 'AT&T Promises Formal 4G Service in 2011,' *electronista*, February 17, 2009.

9 Staff, 'Success Stories – Teliasonera in Norway Pioneers the 4G Wireless Broadband Services in the World,' Huawei website. Available from: *www.huawei.com/publications/view.do?id=6035&cid=11341&pid=2043*. Accessed March 12, 2010.

10 'Intel to Launch Centrino WiMAX 6250 Codenamed Kilmer Peak in Q1 2010,' Going *Wimax.com*. Available from: *www.goingwimax.com/intel-to-launch-centrino-wimax-6250-codenamed kilmer-peak-in-q1-2010*. Accessed November 10, 2009.

11 Jaroslovsky, Rich, 'Google Phone Threatens Droid More than iPhone: Rich Jaroslovsky,' *BusinessWeek*, January 11, 2010.

12 Staff, 'Docklands Light Railway on Track for Growth with New Cisco LAN and VoIP-Based Public Address System,' *New Blaze*, February 10, 2009.

13 Staff, 'Netkrom Customer Success Stories Metropolitan Backbone Network,' *www.netkrom.com/success_stories_lima.html*. Accessed December 29, 2009.

14 Staff, 'NE20 Serves Datang Power WAN.' Available from: *www.huawei.com/products/datacomm/catalog.do?id=361*. Accessed December 29, 2009.

15 The ISC Domain Survey. Available from: *http://www.isc.org/solutions/survey*. Accessed June 8, 2010.

16 Internet Usage Statistics. Available from: *http://www.internetworldstats.com/stats.htm*. Accessed June 8, 2010.

17 Internet Usage World Stats website. Available from: *www.internetworldstats.com*. Accessed June 8, 2010.

18 McDonald, Scott, 'China Vows to Keep Blocking Online Content,'" NewsFactor, June 8, 2010. Available from: *www.newsfactor.com*.

19 Anderson, Nate, 'Internet disconnections come to Ireland, starting today,' *Ars Technica*, May 24, 2010. Available from: *www.arstechnica.com*.

20 Greene, Patrick Allen, "Pakistan blocks Facebook over 'Draw Mohammed Day,' CNN, May 19, 2010. Available from: *www.cnn.com*.

21 'Communications Decency Act,' Wikipedia. Available from: *http://en.wikipedia.org*. Accessed July 3, 2010.

22 Internet2 website. Available from: *www.internet2.edu*. Accessed June 8, 2010.

23 National LambdaRail website. Available from: *www.nlr.net*. Accessed June 8, 2010.

24 Miller, Rich, 'Facebook Begins Deploying IPv6,' Data Center Knowledge, June 10, 2010. Available from: *www.datacenterknowledge.com*.

25 Levine, Barry, 'You Want Wi-Fi with That? McDonalds to Make Wi-Fi Free,' NewsFactor, December 16, 2009. Available from: *www.newsfactor.com*.

26 Gaskin, James, 'Clouds Now Strong Enough to Support Your Business,' *Computerworld*. Available from: *www.computerworld.com*. Accessed October 6, 2009.

27 Schonfeld, Erick, 'Urbanspoon Wants to Challenge OpenTable With Its Rezbook iPad App,' TechCrunch. Available from: *www.techcrunch.com*, May 19, 2010.

28 Kashi website. Available from: *www.kashi.com*. Accessed July 6, 2010.

29 Pegoraro, Rob, 'Bing adds music, videos, games,' *The Washington Post*. Available from: *http://voices.washingtonpost.com*. Accessed June 23, 2010.

30 Porter, Alan, 'Getting over the barriers to wiki adoption,' *Ars Technica*. Available from: *www.arstechnica.com*. Accessed February 13, 2010.

31 Noyes, Katherine, 'Facebook Quickens Yahoo's Pulse,' E-Commerce Times. Available from: *www.ecommercetimes.com*. Accessed June 7, 2010.

4

32 Cohen, Jason, 'Socializing the Storefront, Part 1: Give Them Something to Talk About,' E-Commerce Times. Available from: *www.ecommercetimes.com*. Accessed June 21, 2010.

33 Butcher, Mike, 'Internet Conga Line – a new take on ChatRoulette which feels safer,' TechCrunch. Available from: *www.techcrunch.com*. Accessed June 23, 2010.

34 Naone, Erica, 'Getting a Grip on Online Buzz,' Technology Review. Available from: *www.technologyreview.com*. Accessed February 9, 2010.

35 Wauters, Robin, 'Measuring The Value Of Social Media Advertising,' TechCrunch. Available from: *www.techcrunch.com*. Accessed April 20, 2010.

36 Nakano, Chelsi, 'Enterprise 2.0 Roll-up: Social Computing Is Destroying the Enterprise, Yet Solutions Arrive in Waves,' CRM Newswire. Available from: *www.crmnewswire.com*. Accessed June 24, 2010.

37 Wauters, Robin, 'Joost Video Network Stuns with Big Reach: 67 Million Viewers Per Month,' TechCrunch. Available from: *www.techcrunch.com*. Accessed April 14, 2010.

38 Hollister, Sean, 'Hulu CEO: We're "complimentary" to cable,' Engadget. Available from: *www.engadget.com*. Accessed July 1, 2010.

4

CHAPTER 5 CONTENTS

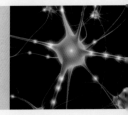

05

Operational Systems

In this chapter we will look at the FOUR main factors you need to understand as part of this topic covering operational systems, and the value of enterprise resource planning systems within businesses.

Principles

1. A company that implements an enterprise resource planning system is creating a highly integrated set of systems, which can lead to many business benefits.

2. An organisation must have information systems that support the routine, day-to-day activities that occur in the normal course of business and help a company add value to its products and services.

3. Traditional transaction processing systems support the various business functions of organisations that have not yet implemented enterprise resource planning systems.

4. Electronic and mobile commerce allow transactions to be made by the customer, with less need for sales staff, and open up new opportunities for conducting business.

Learning Objectives

▪ Identify the challenges multinational corporations must face in planning, building, and operating their transaction processing systems.

▪ Discuss the advantages and disadvantages associated with the implementation of an enterprise resource planning system.

▪ Identify the basic activities and business objectives common to all transaction processing systems.

▪ Identify key control and management issues associated with transaction processing systems.

▪ Describe the inputs, processing, and outputs for the transaction processing systems associated with the order processing, purchasing, and accounting business functions.

▪ Define e- and m-commerce and describe various forms of e-commerce.

Why Learn About Operational Systems?

You might recall from Chapter 1 that operational systems support the day-to-day running of a firm. Operational systems, such as transaction processing systems (TPS), allow firms to buy and sell. Without systems to perform these functions, the firm could not operate. Organisations today are moving from a collection of nonintegrated transaction processing systems to highly integrated enterprise resource planning systems to perform routine business processes and maintain records about them. These systems support a wide range of business activities associated with supply chain management and customer relationship management (as mentioned in Chapter 1). Although they were initially thought to be cost-effective only for very large companies, even small and mid-sized companies are now implementing these systems to reduce costs and improve service.

Employees who work directly with customers – whether in sales, customer service, or marketing – require high-quality transaction processing systems and their associated information to provide good customer service. Companies selling online need electronic and mobile commerce software to allow customer to perform transactions. No matter what your role, it is very likely that you will provide input to or use the output from your organisation's systems. Your effective use of these systems will be essential to raise the productivity of your firm, improve customer service, and enable better decision making. Thus, it is important that you understand how these systems work and what their capabilities and limitations are. This chapter begins by discussing the various TPS of a typical organisation and also covers the use of systems to provide a set of integrated and coordinated systems to meet the needs of the firm.

5.1 Introduction

This and the next two chapters describe the main types of business information systems. This chapter looks at those systems that manage the day-to-day running of the firm. Without them an organisation couldn't operate. They include systems that sell products and services to customers (transaction processing systems), systems that buy materials from suppliers (supply chain management systems), systems that help manage after after sales service (customer relationship management systems) and systems that maintain tax records (accounting systems). Chapter 6 looks at systems used by the organisation to manage its longer term operations and make decisions about product offerings and marketing campaigns. Chapter 7 looks at more specialised systems, including robotics and artificial intelligence.

Often, especially with the systems described in this chapter and the next, the output from one of the systems described is the input to another of the systems described. Therefore, an alternative approach to having separate systems do these jobs, is to have one enterprise wide system that does all of them. This is the enterprise resource planning (ERP) approach, which is described in this chapter. ERP doesn't really fit into either the day-to-day running category or the long term planning category as it does both. The decision to include it in this chapter rather than the next is fairly arbitrary. Also there is no agreed minimum set of tasks that a system has to perform in order for it to be classed as an ERP. However, the expectation is that an ERP does some of the tasks described in this chapter and some of the tasks described in the next chapter. One way of looking at the material in these chapters is that, if an organisation has an ERP, then the other systems described are sub-systems of their ERP. If an organisation does not have an ERP, then the systems described are stand-alone information systems in their own right.

5.2 Enterprise Resource Planning

Enterprise resource planning (ERP) systems evolved from materials requirement planning systems (MRP) that tied together the production planning, inventory control, and purchasing business functions for manufacturing organisations. Many organisations recognised that their legacy transaction processing systems lacked the integration needed to coordinate activities and share valuable information across all the business functions of the firm. As a result, costs were higher and customer service poorer than desired. As a result, firms are scrapping large parts of their existing information systems and converting to new ERP systems. Large organisations, specifically members of the Fortune 1000, were the first to take on the challenge of implementing ERP. An ERP is a system that manages an entire company's vital business information. Many firms consider themselves to have an ERP if the system manages most, rather than all, of their information.

Enterprise resource planning
A system that manages an entire company's vital business information.

Advantages of ERP

Increased global competition, new needs of executives for control over the total cost and product flow through their enterprises, and ever-more-numerous customer interactions drive the demand for enterprise-wide access to real-time information. ERP offers integrated software from a single vendor to help meet those needs. The primary benefits of implementing ERP include improved access to data for operational decision making, elimination of inefficient or outdated systems, improvement of work processes, and technology standardisation. ERP vendors have also developed specialised systems for specific applications and market segments.

Improved Access to Data for Operational Decision Making

ERP systems operate via an integrated database, using one set of data to support all business functions. The systems can support decisions on optimal sourcing or cost accounting, for instance, for the entire enterprise or business units from the start, rather than gathering data from multiple business functions and then trying to coordinate that information manually or reconciling data with another application. The result is an organisation that looks seamless, not only to the outside world but also to the decision makers who are deploying resources within the organisation. The data is integrated to facilitate operational decision making and allows companies to provide greater customer service and support, strengthen customer and supplier relationships, and generate new business opportunities.

Flambeau produces a wide range of plastic products and employs thousands of workers in eight manufacturing locations worldwide. It has grown through acquisition and, out of necessity, was running multiple, disparate legacy information systems that drew data from multiple databases. The firm had to resort to the use of spreadsheets to manually track critical business information used for cost and inventory control. This inevitably led to errors and poor decision making. Finally, the company implemented an ERP system to deliver timely, consistent data for both production and financial management purposes. Flambeau has used the system to lower its inventory costs, better manage its production operations, and provide access to a single set of data used to run the business.[1]

Elimination of Costly, Inflexible Legacy Systems

Adoption of an ERP system enables an organisation to eliminate dozens or even hundreds of separate systems and replace them with a single, integrated set of applications for the entire enterprise. In many cases, these systems are decades old, the original developers are long gone, and the systems are poorly documented. As a result, the systems are extremely difficult to fix when they break, and adapting them to meet new business needs takes too long. They become an anchor around the organisation that keeps it from moving ahead and remaining competitive. An ERP system helps match the capabilities of an organisation's information systems to its business needs – even as these needs evolve.

Improvement of Work Processes

Competition requires companies to structure their business processes to be as effective and customer oriented as possible. ERP vendors do considerable research to define the best business processes. They gather requirements of leading companies within the same industry and combine them with research findings from research institutions and consultants. The individual application modules included in the ERP system are then designed to support these best practices, the most efficient and effective ways to complete a business process. Thus, implementation of an ERP system ensures good work processes based on best practices. For example, for managing customer payments, the ERP system's finance module can be configured to reflect the most efficient practices of leading companies in an industry. This increased efficiency ensures that everyday business operations follow the optimal chain of activities, with all users supplied the information and tools they need to complete each step.

With 22 000 employees serving 4.7 million customers and generating revenue of 14 billion Euros, Achmea is the largest insurance company in the Netherlands. The company had grown rapidly through acquisition and had evolved to using a mix of manual data collection and reporting processes. The company converted to an ERP system to standardise on a set of industry best practices, streamlined work processes, and sophisticated data analysis tools across all divisions and operating companies. As a result, the company could reduce staffing levels in some areas of the business by as much as 30 per cent, thus, improving productivity and cutting costs. In addition, the time required to complete month-end financial reporting was reduced by 30 per cent, with an increase in the accuracy and reliability of the data.[2]

Upgrade of Technology Infrastructure

When implementing an ERP system, an organisation has an opportunity to upgrade the information technology (hardware, operating systems, databases, etc.) that it uses. While centralizing and formalizing these decisions, the organisation can eliminate the hodgepodge of multiple hardware platforms, operating systems, and databases it is currently using – most likely from a variety of vendors. Standardising on fewer technologies and vendors reduces ongoing maintenance and support costs, as well as the training load for those who must support the infrastructure.

Barloworld Handling UK is the United Kingdom distributor of Hyster forklifts. It also provides parts and service through 26 service locations that field customer service calls, schedule and dispatch field techs, and manage the ordering and delivery of parts. This highly decentralised service operation resulted in inefficient work processes, high costs, and inconsistent service levels. Barloworld reengineered its service operations to squeeze out waste and inefficiency. Service techs were issued handheld computers programmed to follow the new work processes. The handheld devices could also access work orders, equipment information, and inventory data held in the firm's ERP database. By integrating mobile devices with improved work processes and access to ERP data, the firm achieved "paperless, real-time data entry; immediate parts lookup and availability checks with overnight delivery; time sheets completed as work progresses; and automatic dispatch of work orders," according to Robert S. Tennant, the firm's CIO. The number of service locations was reduced from 26 to 6, service tech efficiency was increased by 10 per cent, and annual revenue increased by more than €500 000.[3]

Disadvantages of ERP Systems

Unfortunately, implementing ERP systems can be difficult and can disrupt current business practices. Some of the major disadvantages of ERP systems are the expense and time required for implementation, the difficulty in implementing the many business process changes that accompany the ERP system, the problems with integrating the ERP system with other systems, difficulty in loading data into the new system, the risks associated with making a major commitment to a single vendor, and the risk of implementation failure.

Expense and Time in Implementation

Getting the full benefits of ERP takes time and money. Although ERP offers many strategic advantages by streamlining a company's TPSs, large firms typically need three to five years and spend tens of millions of dollars to implement a successful ERP system.

Difficulty Implementing Change

In some cases, a company has to radically change how it operates to conform to the ERP's work processes – its best practices. These changes can be so drastic to long-time employees that they retire or quit, rather than go through the change. This exodus can leave a firm short of experienced workers. Sometimes, the best practices simply are not appropriate for the firm and cause great work disruptions.

Difficulty Integrating with Other Systems

Most companies have other systems that must be integrated with the ERP system, such as financial analysis programs, e-commerce operations, and other applications. Many companies have experienced difficulties making these other systems operate with their ERP system.

Other companies need additional software to create these links.

Difficulty in Loading Data into New ERP System

A major amount of work is required to load existing data from various sources into the new ERP database. The new ERP system may have the capability to store hundreds or even thousands of data items (e.g. customer name, bill to address, product description, etc.). The data items that will be required depend on the scope of ERP implementation. If certain processes or transactions are not included within the scope of implementation, there will be less data to load.

Data mapping is the examination of each data item required for the new ERP system and determining where that data item will come from. Although most of the data for the new system will come from the files of existing legacy systems, some data items may need to be pulled from manual systems or may even need to be created for the new system. Data cleanup is required because the legacy systems are likely to contain data that is inaccurate, incomplete, or inconsistent. For example, the same customer may be listed multiple times in existing customer files with varying bill to addresses, or products may appear in the existing inventory files that have not been produced for years. Data loading can be performed either by using data conversion software that reads the old data and converts it into a format for loading it into the database or by end users entering data via the input screens of the new system.

Risks in Using One Vendor

The high cost to switch to another vendor's ERP system makes it extremely unlikely that a firm will do so. After a company has adopted an ERP system, the vendor has less incentive to listen and respond to customer concerns. The high cost to switch also increases risk – in the event the ERP vendor allows its product to become outdated or goes out of business. Selecting an ERP system involves not only choosing the best software product, but also the right long-term business partner. It was unsettling for many companies that had implemented PeopleSoft, J.D. Edwards, or Siebel Systems enterprise software when these firms were acquired by Oracle.

Risk of Implementation Failure

Implementing an ERP system for a large organisation is extremely challenging and requires tremendous amounts of resources, the best IS and businesspeople, and plenty of management support. Unfortunately, large ERP installations occasionally fail, and problems with an ERP implementation can require expensive solutions. The following list provides tips for avoiding many common causes for failed ERP implementations:

- Assign a full-time executive to manage the project.
- Appoint an experienced, independent resource to provide project oversight and to verify and validate system performance.
- Allow sufficient time for transition from the old way of doing things to the new system and new processes.
- Plan to spend a lot of time and money training people.
- Define metrics to assess project progress and to identify project-related risks.
- Keep the scope of the project well defined and contained to essential business processes.
- Be wary of modifying the ERP software to conform to your firm's business practices.

ERP for Small and Medium-Size Enterprises (SMEs)

It is not only large Fortune 1000 companies that are successful in implementing ERP. SMEs (both for-profit and not-for-profit) can achieve real business benefits from their ERP efforts. Many of the SMEs elected to implement open-source ERP systems. With open-source software, anyone can see and modify the source code to customise it to meet their needs. Such systems are much less costly to acquire and are relatively easy to modify to meet business needs. A wide range of organisations can perform the system development and maintenance.

Table 5.1 lists some of the open-source ERP systems geared for SMEs.

The following sections outline systems that can be considered as sub-systems of an ERP, or as information systems in their own right.

Table 5.1 Open-Source ERP Systems

Vendor	ERP Solutions
Apache	Open for Business ERP
Compiere	Compiere Open Source ERP
Openbravo	Openbravo Open Source ERP
WebERP	WebERP

5.3 Transaction Processing Systems

Every organisation has many transaction processing systems (TPS). These systems include order processing, inventory control, payroll, accounts payable, accounts receivable, and the general ledger, to name just a few. The input to these systems includes basic business transactions, such as a customer placing an order, an employee purchasing supplies, a customer payment, and an employee signing on and off at the start and end of a day. The processing activities include data collection, data editing, data correction, data manipulation, data storage, and document production. The result of processing business transactions is that the organisation's records are updated to reflect the status of the operation at the time of the last processed transaction.

A TPS also has a second important function – it collects data which is input to other essential information systems – management information systems, decision support systems, and other special-purpose information systems (all discussed in the following chapters). A transaction processing system serves as the foundation for these other systems. These higher-level systems require the basic business transaction data captured by the TPS.

Transaction processing systems support routine operations in the business. The amount of support for decision making that a TPS directly provides managers and workers is low.

Because TPS often perform activities related to customer contacts – such as order processing and invoicing – these information systems play a critical role in providing value to the customer. For example, by capturing and tracking the movement of each package, shippers, such as FedEx, can provide timely and accurate data on the exact location of a package. Shippers and receivers can access an online database and, by providing the air bill number of a package, find the package's current location. If the package has been delivered, they can see who signed for it (a service that is especially useful in large companies where packages can become "lost" in internal distribution systems and mailrooms). Such a system provides the basis for added value through improved customer service (see Figure 5.1).

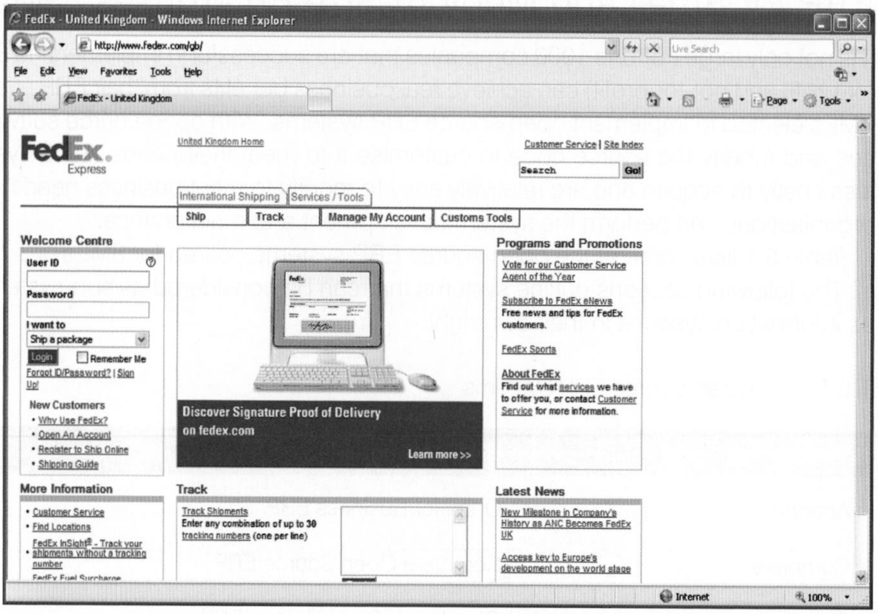

Figure 5.1
FedEx adds value to its service by providing timely and accurate data online on the exact location of a package.

Traditional Transaction Processing Methods and Objectives

With **batch processing systems**, business transactions are accumulated over a period of time and prepared for processing as a single unit or batch (see Figure 5.2a). Transactions are accumulated for the appropriate length of time needed to meet the needs of the users of that system. For example, it might be important to process invoices and customer payments for the accounts receivable system daily. On the other hand, the payroll system might process data weekly to create cheques, update employee earnings records, and distribute labour costs. The essential characteristic of a batch processing system is that there is some delay between an event and the eventual processing of the related transaction to update the organisation's records.

batch processing system A form of data processing where business transactions are accumulated over a period of time and prepared for processing as a single unit or batch.

online transaction processing (OLTP) A form of data processing where each transaction is processed immediately, without the delay of accumulating transactions into a batch.

With **online transaction processing (OLTP)**, each transaction is processed immediately, without the delay of accumulating transactions into a batch (see Figure 5.2b). Consequently, at any time, the data in an online system

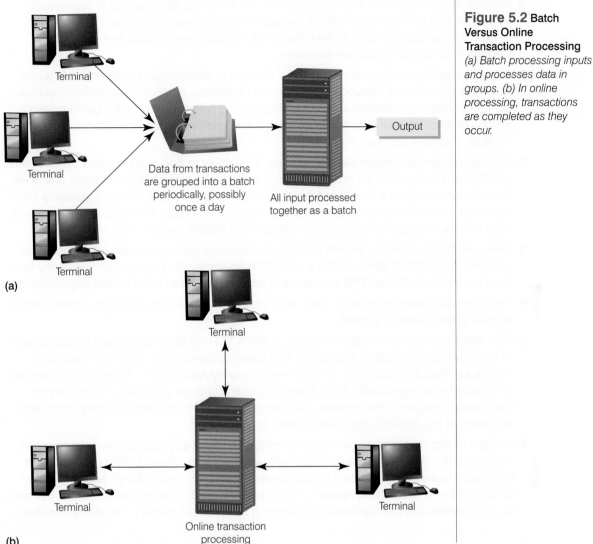

Figure 5.2 Batch Versus Online Transaction Processing *(a) Batch processing inputs and processes data in groups. (b) In online processing, transactions are completed as they occur.*

reflects the current status. This type of processing is essential for businesses that require access to current data, such as airlines, ticket agencies, and stock investment firms. Many companies find that OLTP helps them provide faster, more efficient service, one way to add value to their activities in the eyes of the customer. Increasingly, companies are using the internet to capture and process transaction data, such as customer orders and shipping information, from e-commerce applications.

Although the technology is advanced enough, TPS applications do not always run using online processing. For many applications, batch processing is more appropriate and cost effective. Payroll transactions and billing are typically done via batch processing. Specific goals of the organisation define the method of transaction processing best suited for the various applications of the company.

Because of the importance of transaction processing, organisations expect their TPS to accomplish a number of specific objectives, some of which are listed next. Depending on the specific nature and goals of the organisation, any of these objectives might be more important than others.

■ *Process data generated by and about transactions.* The primary objective of any TPS is to capture, process, and update databases of business data required to support routine business activities. Utilities, telecommunications companies, and financial-services organisations especially are under pressure to process ever-larger volumes of online transactions.

- *Maintain a high degree of accuracy and integrity.* Ensuring that the data is processed accurately and completely is critical, because reports generated by the TPS are used to execute key operational activities, such as filling customer orders and scheduling shipments to various customer locations.

- *Avoid processing fraudulent transactions.* Related to data integrity is the need to avoid processing fraudulent transactions. Standard Chartered, a London-based international bank, recently implemented anti-money-laundering software to monitor banking transactions against terrorist watch lists and flag transactions between individuals, organisations, or countries deemed high risk.[4]

- *Produce timely user responses and reports.* The ability to conduct business transactions quickly can be essential for an organisation's bottom line. For instance, if bills (invoices) are sent to customers a few days later than planned, payment is delayed, possibly forcing the firm to seek costly short-term borrowing to avoid cash flow problems. As a result, firms employ monitoring systems to measure and ensure system performance.

- *Increase labour efficiency.* Before businesses used computers, manual processes often required rooms full of administrators and office equipment to process the necessary business transactions. Today, TPS substantially reduce these and other labour requirements.

- *Help improve customer service.* Another objective of a TPS is to assist an organisation in providing fast, efficient service.

- *Help build and maintain customer loyalty.* A firm's TPS are often the means for customers to communicate. Customer interaction with these systems must, therefore, keep customers satisfied and returning. A recent web study by Allulent, Inc., found that 55 per cent of consumers surveyed said that a frustrating online shopping experience diminishes their overall opinion of that retailer. Surprisingly, nearly 33 per cent said they might stop shopping at the retailer's brick-and-mortar store as well.[5]

- *Achieve competitive advantage.* A goal common to almost all organisations is to gain and maintain a competitive advantage (discussed in Chapter 2). When a TPS is developed or modified, the personnel involved should carefully consider the significant and long-term benefits the new or modified system might provide. Table 5.2 summarises some of the ways that companies can use transaction processing systems to achieve competitive advantage.

Table 5.2 Examples of Transaction Processing Systems for Competitive Advantage

Competitive Advantage	Example
Customer loyalty increased	Customer interaction system to monitor and track each customer interaction with the company
Superior service provided to customers	Tracking systems that customers can access to determine shipping status
Better relationship with suppliers	Internet marketplace to allow the company to purchase products from suppliers at discounted prices
Superior information gathering	Order configuration system to ensure that products ordered will meet customers' objectives
Costs dramatically reduced	Warehouse management system employing RFID technology to reduce labour hours and improve inventory accuracy
Inventory levels reduced	Collaborative planning, forecasting, and replenishment to ensure the right amount of inventory is in stores

Transaction Processing Activities

TPS capture and process data of fundamental business transactions. This data is used to update databases and to produce a variety of reports people both within and outside the enterprise use. The business data goes through a **transaction processing cycle** that includes data collection, data editing, data correction, data manipulation, data storage, and document production (see Figure 5.3).

transaction processing cycle The process of data collection, data editing, data correction, data manipulation, data storage, and document production.

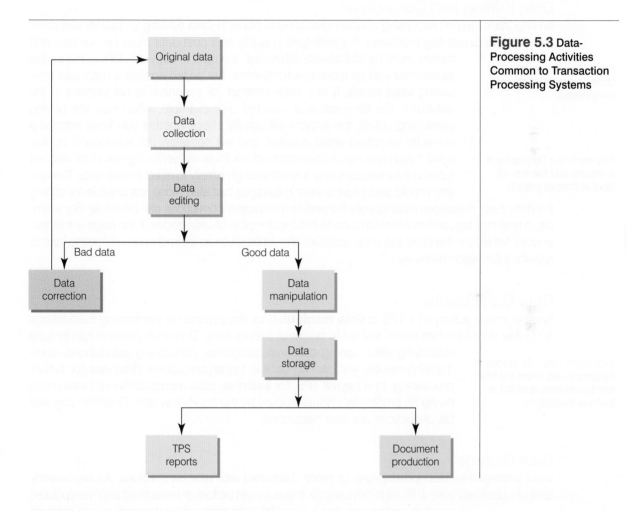

Figure 5.3 Data-Processing Activities Common to Transaction Processing Systems

Data Collection

Capturing and gathering all data necessary to complete the processing of transactions is called **data collection**. In some cases, it can be done manually, such as by collecting handwritten sales orders or a customer typing in their credit card details on a web page. In other cases, data collection is automated via special input devices, such as barcode scanners and RFID readers.

data collection Capturing and gathering all data necessary to complete the processing of transactions.

   Data collection begins with a transaction (e.g. taking a customer order) and results in data that serves as input to the TPS. Data should be captured at its source and recorded accurately in a timely fashion, with minimal manual effort and in an electronic or digital form that can be directly entered into the computer. This approach is called "source data automation." An example of source data automation is a barcode reader at a supermarket that speeds the checkout process. Using barcodes is quicker and more accurate than having a shop assistant enter codes manually at the cash register. The product ID for each item is determined automatically, and its price is retrieved from the item database. This TPS uses the price data to determine the customer's bill. It also updates the shop's inventory database and its database of purchases. This data is then used by the shop's management information systems to generate reports (to be discussed in Chapter 6).

Data Editing and Correction

An important step in processing transaction data is to perform **data editing** for validity and completeness to detect any problems. For example, quantity and cost data must be numeric and names must be alphabetic; otherwise, the data is not valid. Often, the codes associated with an individual transaction are edited against a database containing valid codes. If any code entered (or scanned) is not present in the database, the transaction is rejected. For example, when you are buying something online, the system will usually check whether you have entered a correctly formatted email address and will not allow the transaction to proceed if you have not. A **data correction** involves reentering data that was not typed or scanned properly. It is not enough simply to reject invalid data. The system should also provide error messages that alert those responsible for editing the data. Error messages must specify the problem so proper corrections can be made. For example, a scanned barcode must match a code in a master table of valid codes. If the code is misread or does not exist in the table, the shop assistant should be given an instruction to rescan the item or type the information manually.

data editing The process of checking data for validity and completeness.

data correction The process of re-entering data that was not typed or scanned properly.

5

Data Manipulation

Another major activity of a TPS is **data manipulation**, the process of performing calculations and other data transformations related to business transactions. Data manipulation can include classifying data, sorting data into categories, performing calculations, summarising results, and storing data in the organisation's database for further processing. In a payroll TPS, for example, data manipulation includes multiplying an employee's hours worked by the hourly pay rate. Overtime pay and tax deductions are also calculated.

data manipulation The process of performing calculations and other data transformations related to business transactions.

Data Storage

Data storage involves updating one or more databases with new transactions. As has already been emphasised several times in this chapter, this data can be further processed and manipulated by other systems so that it is available for management reporting and decision making. Thus, although transaction databases can be considered a by-product of transaction processing, they have a pronounced effect on nearly all other information systems and decision-making processes in an organisation.

data storage The process of updating one or more databases with new transactions.

Document Production and Reports

Document production involves generating output records, documents, and reports. These can be hard-copy paper reports or displays on computer screens (sometimes referred to as "soft copy"). Printed paycheques, for example, are hard-copy documents produced by a payroll TPS, whereas an outstanding balance report for invoices might be a soft-copy report displayed by an accounts receivable TPS.

document production The process of generating output records and reports.

Information Systems at Work

Mobile Wallets the World Over

The mobile phone is increasingly being considered as a remote control to the digital world. Banks, marketing agencies, those in the entertainment industry, and a host of other businesses are focused on creating useful m-commerce (discussed later in this chapter) applications that will increase revenues. The ability to carry out transactions from any location at any time using a mobile phone is revolutionizing the manner in which some people conduct our day-to-day activities.

For instance, take the case of Wizzit. About 16 million South Africans, over half of the adult population, have no bank account. However, 30 per cent of these people do have mobile phones. With mobile banking, they could use their mobile phones to send money to relatives, pay for goods and services, check balances and pay bills. Wizzit, is trying to get them to do just that. Wizzit, a division of the South African Bank of Athens, describes itself as a virtual bank and, as such, it has no branches. Since it started at the end of 2004, it now has over 50 000 customers. This means that many South Africans now no longer have to carry cash around, which can be risky. In addition, many relatives who have left the country can send money home securely, quickly and cheaply. This is making a big difference to poorer people who rely on their families abroad. Money sent home from ex-patriots is a key part of South Africa's economy. Even for those who already have a bank account, mobile banking will mean they no longer have to travel to (often distant) bank branches, something that takes on average 30 minutes and costs around 15 rand for busfare. According to Consultative Group to Assist the Poor (CGAP), a Wizzit account can be one-third cheaper than an equivalent account at one of South Africa's big retail banks. A CGAP survey found customers use Wizzit, because it is cheap, safe, convenient, and fast.

Meanwhile in the UK, mobile phone operator Orange is about to roll out what it claims is the UK's first mobile payments service.

The service sees the phone operator partnering with payments firm Barclaycard. Unlike the Wizzit service that allows users to "text" money from one account to another, Orange mobile phones will come equipped with wireless payment chips. Businesses that have the technology to let customers pay in this way include Pret a Manger, Little Chef and the National Trust. More are joining them, especially for the 2012 Olympics. The London games is seen as an epicentre for contactless payments, with sponsors, such as Visa and Transport for London, heavily involved in so-called Near Field Communication, the short range wireless technology that underpins many wireless payment systems.

David Chan, chief executive of Barclaycard's consumer division, thinks there is a natural fit between the phone and the wallet. "I believe that future generations will find it surprising that early this century we were still carrying separate items to buy goods and to communicate with each other," he said.

However, not everyone is happy with the spread of mobile banking. In Somali, Islamist group al-Shabab has ordered mobile phone companies to stop their popular money transfer services, saying they are "unIslamic." Mobile phone banking was introduced in the northern Somaliland region in 2009 and has now spread across the country. Al-Shabab and its allies control much of southern Somalia, and one mobile phone company official said he had "no option but to obey" the order. Al-Shabab says mobile phone banking could expose Somalia to interference by Western countries. However, some observers believe the ban may be intended to block a rival to the traditional money transfer systems, known as hawala, which al-Shabab can tax more easily. The ban has been widely condemned.

(continued)

Discussion Questions

1 Why is a mobile account considered "safe?" In your opinion is the Wizzit approach any safer than the one taken by Orange?

2 List the ways in which you use a mobile phone and the ways in which you use a PC. Which activities that you currently perform on a PC could be transferred to a mobile phone and which could not? Why?

Critical Thinking Questions

1 What concerns would you have about using your mobile phone in this way? How could

Wizzit and other providers overcome these fears?

2 How could Governments encourage or, in the case of Somali, discourage the use of mobile banking?

SOURCES: The Economist, 'Phoney finance.' Available from: http://www.economist.com/finance/displaystory.cfm?story_id=8089667, October 26, 2006. Accessed June 14, 2007; Consultative Group to Assist the Poor, 'Mobile Phone Banking and Low-Income Customers, Evidence from South Africa.' Available from: http://www.cgap.org/publications/mobilephonebanking.pdf. Accessed June 14, 2007; BBC, "Orange customers of Everything Everywhere get mobile payments", 27 January 2011. Available from: http://www.bbc.co.uk/news/technology-12287009; BBC, "Al-Shabab bans mobile phone money transfers in Somalia", 18 October 2010. Available from: http://www.bbc.co.uk/news/world-africa-11566247.

In addition to major documents, such as cheques and invoices, most TPS provide other useful management information and decision support, such as printed or on-screen reports that help managers and employees perform various activities. A report showing current inventory is one example; another might be a document listing items ordered from a supplier to help an administrator check the order for completeness when it arrives. A TPS can also produce reports required by law, such as tax statements.

5.4 Traditional Transaction Processing Applications

This section presents an overview of several common transaction processing systems that support the order processing, purchasing, and accounting business functions (see Table 5.3).

Table 5.3 Systems that Support Order Processing, Purchasing, and Accounting Functions

Order Processing	Purchasing	Accounting
Order processing	Inventory control (raw materials, packing materials, spare parts, and supplies)	Budget
Sales configuration	Purchase order processing	Accounts receivable
Shipment planning	Receiving	Payroll
Shipment execution	Accounts payable	Asset management
Inventory control (finished product)		General ledger
Accounts receivable		

Order Processing Systems

The traditional TPS for order processing include order entry, sales configuration, shipment planning, shipment execution, inventory control, and accounts receivable. Running these systems efficiently and reliably is critical to an enterprise. Figure 5.4 is a system-level flowchart that shows the various systems and the information that flows among them. Table 5.4 summarises the input, processing, and output (IPO) of the essential systems that include the traditional order processing systems.

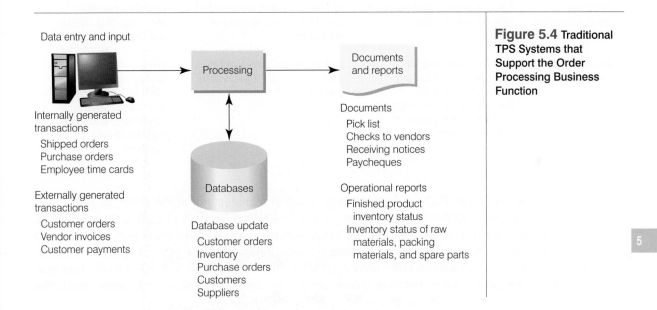

Figure 5.4 Traditional TPS Systems that Support the Order Processing Business Function

Table 5.4 IPO of the Traditional TPS Systems that Support Order Processing

System	Input	Processing	Output
Order entry	Customer order information via a variety of means: data entry by sales rep, customer input, mail, phone, e-commerce, or computer to computer via EDI or XML formats	Order is checked for completeness and accuracy. On-hand inventory is checked to ensure each item can be shipped in the quantity ordered or a substitute item is suggested	An open order record
Sales configuration	Customer order information including model and options desired	Review customer order information and ensure the configuration will meet the customer's needs; suggest additional options and features when appropriate	Revised customer order
Shipment planning	Open orders (i.e. orders received but not yet shipped)	Determine which open orders will be filled when and from which location each order will be shipped to minimise delivery costs and meet customer desired delivery dates	Pick list for each order to be filled from each shipping location showing the items and quantities needed to fill the order

(continued)

Table 5.4 *Continued*

System	Input	Processing	Output
Shipment execution	Pick list and data entered by warehouse operations personnel as they fill the order	Data entered by warehouse operations personnel captured and used to update record of what was shipped to the customer	A shipped order record specifying exactly what was shipped to the customer – this can be different than what was ordered
Inventory control (finished product)	Record of each item picked to fill a customer order	Inventory records are updated to reflect current quantity of each item	Updated inventory database and various management reports
Accounts receivable	Shipped order records received from shipment execution that show precisely what was shipped on each order; payments from customers	Determine amount owed by each customer for each order placed	Invoice statement containing details of each order and its associated costs; customers' accounts receivable data is updated

Beaulieu Group, LLC., is the third-largest carpet manufacturer in the world. Its major customers include US home improvement chains The Home Depot and Lowe's Companies. Its most popular brands are Beaulieu, Coronet, Hollytex, and Laura Ashley Home. In an effort to stream line its traditional order processing process, the firm equipped 250 of its commercial accounts sales staff with an order entry application that runs on a Pocket PC. With the new system, salespeople enter customer orders, access the company's pricing databases, and make

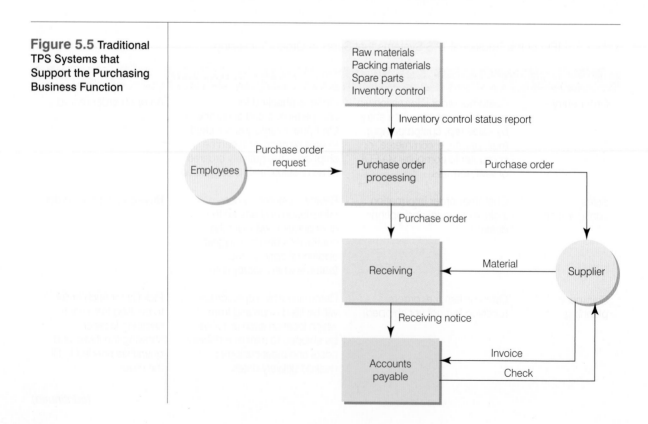

Figure 5.5 Traditional TPS Systems that Support the Purchasing Business Function

changes to orders over a wireless network. If a wireless connection cannot be made at the customer's site, the salesperson can enter orders on the Pocket PC and then transmit the data later when communications can be established. The new process has improved the way salespeople interact with customers and reduced the time they spend filling out paperwork. Previously, orders had to be written out at a customer's site and then sent to the company's central office, where clerical workers keyed them into an order processing system. As a result, the salespeople spent too much time on administrative work entering and correcting orders and not enough time selling.

Purchasing Systems

The traditional TPS that support the purchasing business function include inventory control, purchase order processing, receiving, and accounts payable (see Figure 5.5). Table 5.5 shows the input, processing, and output associated with this collection of systems. Figure 5.6 shows how RFID technology is helping inventory control.

Table 5.5 IPO for the Traditional TPS Systems that Support Purchasing

System	Input	Processing	Output
Inventory control	Records reflecting any increase or decrease in the inventory of specific items of raw materials, packing materials, or spare parts	Withdrawals are subtracted from inventory counts of specific items; additions are added to the inventory count	The inventory record of each item is updated to reflect its current count
Purchase order processing	Inventory records, employee-prepared purchase order requests, information on preferred suppliers	Items that need to be ordered are identified, quantities to be ordered are determined, qualified supplier with whom to place the order is identified	Purchase orders are placed with preferred suppliers for items
Receiving	Information on the quantity and quality of items received	Receipt is matched to purchase order, input data is edited for accuracy and completeness	Receiving report is created, inventory records are updated to reflect new receipts
Accounts payable	Purchase orders placed, information on receipts, supplier invoices	Supplier invoice matched to original purchase order and receiving report	Payment generated to supplier

Accounting Systems

The primary **accounting systems** include the budget, accounts receivable, payroll, asset management, and general ledger (see Figure 5.7). Table 5.6 shows the input, processing, and output associated with these systems.

accounting systems Systems that include budget, accounts receivable, payroll, asset management, and general ledger.

Transaction Processing Systems for Small and Medium-Size Enterprises (SMEs)

Many software packages provide integrated transaction processing system solutions for small and medium-size enterprises (SMEs), wherein small is an enterprise with fewer than 50 employees and medium is one with fewer than 250 employees. These systems are

Figure 5.6 *Many companies use RFID tags to shorten order processing time and improve inventory accuracy*

SOURCE: © Marc F. Henning/Alamy.

Figure 5.7 Traditional TPS Systems that Support the Accounting and Finance Business Function

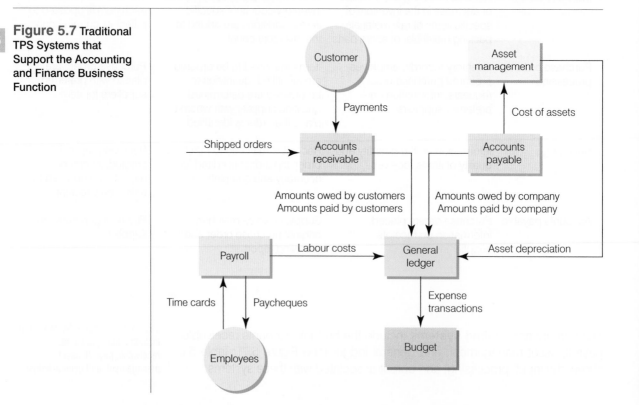

typically easy to install, easy to operate, and have a low total cost of ownership with an initial cost of a few hundred to a few thousand dollars. Such solutions are highly attractive to firms that have outgrown their current software but cannot afford a complex, high-end integrated system solution. Table 5.7 presents some of the dozens of such software solutions available.

Table 5.6 IPO for the Traditional TPS Systems that Support Accounting

System	Input	Processing	Output
Budget	Amounts budgeted for various categories of expense	Accumulates amount spent in each budget category	Budget status report showing amount under/over budget
Accounts receivable	Shipment records specifying exactly what was shipped to a customer	Determines amount to be paid by customer including delivery costs and taxes	Customer bills and monthly statements, management reports summarising customer payments
Payroll	Number of hours worked by each employee, employee pay rate, employee tax and withholding information	Calculates employee gross pay and net pay and amount to be withheld for various taxing agencies and employee benefit programs	Payroll cheque and stub, payroll register (a summary report of all payroll transactions),W-2 forms
Asset management	Data regarding the purchase of capital assets	Calculates depreciation and net value of all corporate assets	Listing of all assets showing purchase price and current value after depreciation
General ledger	All transactions affecting the financial standing of the firm	Posts financial transactions to appropriate accounts specified in the firms chart of accounts	Financial reports such as the profit and loss statement, balance sheet

Table 5.7 Sample of Integrated TPS Solutions for SMEs

Vendor	Software	Type of TPS Offered	Target Customers
AccuFund	AccuFund	Financial reporting and accounting	Nonprofit, municipal, and government organisations
OpenPro	OpenPro	Complete ERP solution, including financials, supply chain management, e-commerce, customer relationship management, and retail POS system	Manufacturers, distributors, and retailers
Intuit	QuickBooks	Financial reporting and accounting	Manufacturers, professional services, contractors, nonprofits, and retailers
Sage	Timberline	Financial reporting, accounting, and operations	Contractors, real estate developers, and residential builders
Redwing	TurningPoint	Financial reporting and accounting	Professional services, banks, and retailers

5.5 Electronic and Mobile Commerce

Electronic Commerce

Electronic commerce is conducting a business transaction (e.g. distribution, buying, selling, and servicing) electronically over computer networks, primarily the internet but also extranets, and corporate networks.

electronic commerce Conducting business transactions (e.g. distribution, buying, selling, and servicing) electronically over computer networks such as the internet, extranets, and corporate networks.

Business activities that are strong candidates for conversion to e-commerce are paper based, time-consuming, and inconvenient for customers. Thus, some of the first business processes

business-to-consumer (B2C) e-commerce A form of e-commerce in which customers deal directly with an organisation and avoid intermediaries.

that companies converted to an e-commerce model were those related to buying and selling. Integrated e-commerce systems directly link a firm's website, which allows customers to place orders with its order processing system. This is the traditional **business-to-consumer (B2C) e-commerce** model.

Early business-to-consumer (B2C) e-commerce pioneers competed with the traditional "bricks-and-mortar" retailers. For example, in 1995, Amazon.com challenged well-established US booksellers Waldenbooks and Barnes and Noble. Although Amazon did not become profitable until 2003, the firm has grown from selling only books on a US website to selling a wide variety of products (including clothes, CDs, DVDs, home and garden supplies, and consumer electronic devices) on international websites in Canada, China, France, Germany, Japan, and the UK.[6] The reasons people shop online rather than go to high street shops include convenience, because there is often a wider product range available online, and because costs are often less online. In addition, many sellers personalise their web pages

B2Me A form of e-commerce where the business treats each customer as a separate market segment. Typical B2Me features include customising a website for each customer, perhaps based on their previous purchases and personalised (electronic) marketing literature.

for each individual customer, something high street shops cannot do (see Figure 5.8). This personalisation is sometimes called **B2Me e-commerce**. By using B2C e-commerce to sell directly to consumers, producers or providers of consumer products can eliminate the middlemen, or intermediaries, between them and the consumer. In many cases, this squeezes costs and inefficiencies out of the supply chain and can lead to higher profits and lower prices for consumers.[7] The elimination of intermediate organisations between the producer and the consumer is called "disintermediation."

Figure 5.8 A Screenshot from Amazon.co.uk with a Personal Shopper's Tab and Product Recommendations

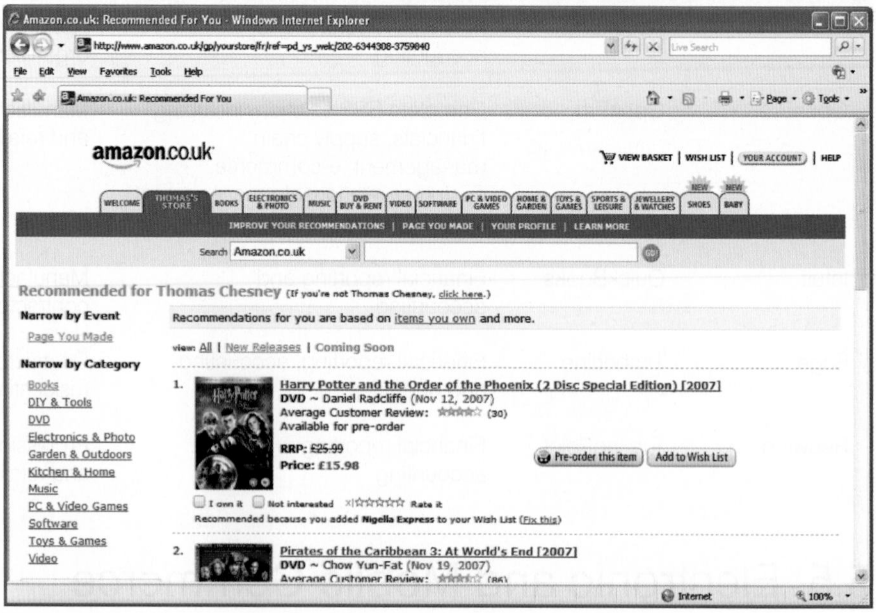

Dell is an example of a manufacturer that has successfully embraced this model to achieve a strong competitive advantage. People can specify their own unique computer online and Dell assembles the components and ships the computer directly to the consumer within five days. Dell does not inventory computers and does not sell through intermediate resellers or distributors. The savings are used to increase Dell's profits and reduce consumer prices.

Business-to-business (B2B) e-commerce is a subset of e-commerce where all the participants are organisations. B2B e-commerce is a useful tool for connecting business partners in a virtual supply chain to cut resupply times and reduce costs. Many travel agents specialise in organising business travel. Business Travel Direct in the UK provide flight and hotel bookings, tailoring their service for business customers. The sort of things B2B travel agents must deal with that high street agents may not are, for example, that the person who purchases the flight tickets may not be the person who will be travelling and the decision on whether to travel may be made by a group, rather than an individual.

business-to-business (B2B) e-commerce A subset of e-commerce where all the participants are organisations.

Consumer-to-consumer (C2C) e-commerce is another subset of e-commerce that involves consumers selling directly to other consumers. eBay is an example of a C2C e-commerce site; customers buy and sell items directly to each other through the site. Founded in 1995, eBay has become one of the most popular websites in the world, where 181 million users buy and sell items valued at many billions of euros.[8] Other popular online auction websites include Craigslist, uBid, Yahoo! Auctions, Onsale, WeBidz, and many others. The growth of C2C is responsible for reducing the use of the classified pages of a newspaper to advertise and sell personal items.

consumer-to-consumer (C2C) e-commerce A subset of e-commerce that involves consumers selling directly to other consumers.

E-government is the use of information and communications technology to simplify the sharing of information, speed formerly paper-based processes, and improve the relationship between citizen and government. Government-to-consumer (G2C), government-to-business (G2B), and government-to-government (G2G) are all forms of e-government, each with different applications. For example, citizens can use G2C applications to submit their tax returns online, apply for planning permission, and submit e-petitions. G2B applications support the purchase of materials and services from private industry by government procurement offices, enable firms to bid on government contracts, and help businesses receive current government regulations related to their operations. G2G applications are designed to improve communications among the various levels of government.

e-government The use of information and communications technology to simplify the sharing of information, speed formerly paper-based processes, and improve the relationship between citizen and government.

Mobile Commerce

Mobile commerce (m-commerce) relies on the use of wireless devices, such as personal digital assistants, mobile phones, and smartphones, to transact. Handset manufacturers, such as HTC, Plan and Sony Ericsson, are working with communications carriers, such as Orange, to develop wireless devices, related technology, and services. In addition, content providers and mobile service providers are working together more closely than ever. Content providers recognise that customers want access to their content whenever and wherever they go, and mobile service providers seek out new forms of content to send over their networks.

In most Western European countries, communicating via wireless devices is common, and consumers are much more willing to use m-commerce. Japanese consumers are generally enthusiastic about new technology and are much more likely to use mobile technologies for making purchases.

For m-commerce to work effectively, the interface between the wireless device and its user needs to improve to the point that it is nearly as easy to purchase an item on a wireless device as it is to purchase it on a home computer. In addition, network speed must improve so that users do not become frustrated. Security is also a major concern, particularly in two areas: the security of the transmission itself and the trust that the transaction is being made with the

Ethical and Societal Issues

Google Pulls Out of China

Companies that serve customers around the world often need to make adjustments so that the products and services that they provide adhere to local laws. Conforming to the local laws of the countries in which you do business is not typically a major issue, unless those laws contradict the company's ethical values. Such was the case when Google decided to pull out of China.

The story begins in December of 2009 when Google and dozens of other companies and government organisations were the targets of a cyberattacks originating in China. The purpose of the attack was to gain access to the accounts of Chinese dissidents and journalists. For Google, the attack served as the final straw to building tensions between Google and the Chinese government. For years the Chinese government had required Google to filter search results served to Chinese citizen – a requirement that Google regards as unethical. China also occasionally required Google's China office to provide account information of Chinese bloggers that had criticised the government. In some cases, the information provided by Google reportedly resulted in arrests and torture. After it was clear to Google that the December attack could not have occurred without government sponsorship, Google laid down an ultimatum: Google would continue operations in China only if it was allowed to provide unfiltered search results. Google used the hacking incident as a lever to raise the ethical concerns it has with Chinese laws. China responded to the hacking allegation by downplaying the incident and reiterating that all businesses in China are bound to uphold Chinese laws. After months of closed-door negotiations, with China holding firm to its stance, Google closed the doors on its search engine in China, following through on its promise. But, rather than eliminating its filters on google.cn and risking the arrest of its China-based employees, Google redirected requests for google.cn to its Hong Kong search engine, google.com.hk, where it maintains unfiltered Chinese-language search results. Shortly after the

switch, China was quick to apply its own censoring filters to the internet DNS servers that feed its country. Google's decision to close google.cn was shocking because of the large monetary sacrifice that Google has made. China has the world's largest population and has one of the most rapidly growing economies. Google has given up a large competitive advantage in exchange for a cleaner conscience. Google's move is causing many companies that do business in China to reevaluate their own motivations and convictions.

So far, although many have applauded Google's decision, only a few have followed suit. Popular web hosting company GoDaddy stopped registering domain names for the .cn domain. That decision came after the Chinese government demanded personal information about people who had purchased domain names from GoDaddy. Microsoft has stated that it intends to continue growing its business in China. Even Google continues other operations in China and looks forward to robust sales of Google Android phones in China in coming years. China isn't the only country where Google censors content based on government-imposed policies. Google has posted the site www .google.com/governmentrequests that lists governments that require Google to censor content. Brazil, Germany, India, the UK, South Korea, and the US rank high on the list. Granted, censorship is sometimes justified, such as in cases where it protects populations from physical harm. However, many feel that it is not justified when it is used to silence dissident opinions, such as in China. Increasingly, technology companies, such as Google and internet service providers, are assuming responsibility for policing internet content. Google's stance against China's censorship has shown that the company is clearly uncomfortable with its role as a censor and causes some to wonder if it may not follow up with changes in policy elsewhere. Google's chief legal officer wrote that the China issue "goes to the heart of a much bigger global debate about freedom of speech." Google's experience in China provides an extreme example of the considerations faced by technology companies providing services abroad. Similar considerations are faced by all kinds of international companies, at varying levels of complexity every day. Although most companies comply with local laws and customs in the countries in which they operate without complaint, Google chose to use its financial power and influence to make a statement about its company's ethical position on political censorship.

Discussion Questions

1 What constraints imposed by China combined to cause Google to close its Chinese search engine?

2 What pressures might cause businesses to set aside ethical considerations to do business in China?

Critical Thinking Questions

1 Some have argued that Google's exit from China might have actually harmed the growth of democracy around the world. How might Google have positively influenced democracy if it had stayed in China?

2 What constraints might China place on a business like Wal-Mart, or India place on a restaurant like McDonalds? How do those constraints differ from those placed on Google in China?

SOURCES: Perez, Juan Carlos, "Google stops censoring in China," Computerworld, March 22, 2010. Available from: www.computerworld.com; Gross, Grant, "GoDaddy to stop registering .cn domain names," Computerworld, March 24, 2010. Available from: www.computerworld.com; Naone, Erica, "Google and Censorship," Technology Review, March 26, 2010. Available from: www.technologyreview.com; Wills, Ken, "China state media accuses Google of political agenda," Reuters, March 21, 2010. Available from: www.reuters.com.

intended party. Encryption can provide secure transmission. Digital certificates can ensure that transactions are made between the intended parties.

The handheld devices used for m-commerce have several limitations that complicate their use. Their screens are small, perhaps no more than a few square centimetres, and might be able to display only a few lines of text. Their input capabilities are limited to a few buttons, so entering data can be tedious and error prone. They have less processing power and less bandwidth than desktop computers, which are usually hardwired to a high-speed LAN. They also operate on limited-life batteries. For these reasons, it is currently impossible to directly access many websites with a handheld device. Web developers must rewrite web applications so that users with handheld devices can access them.

5.6 Electronic and Mobile Commerce Applications

E-commerce and m-commerce are being used in innovative and exciting ways. This section examines a few of the many B2B, B2C, C2C, and m-commerce applications in the retail and wholesale, manufacturing, marketing, investment and finance, and auction arenas.

Retail and Wholesale

E-commerce is being used extensively in retailing and wholesaling. **Electronic retailing**, sometimes called e-tailing, is the direct sale of products or services by businesses to consumers through electronic shops, which are typically designed around the familiar electronic catalogue and shopping cart model. Tens of thousands of electronic retail websites sell a wide range. In addition, cyber shopping centres, or "cybermalls," are another means to support retail shopping. A cybermall is a single website that offers many products and services at one internet

electronic retailing (e-tailing) The direct sale from business to consumer through electronic storefronts, typically designed around an electronic catalogue and shopping cart model.

location. An internet cybermall pulls multiple buyers and sellers into one virtual place, easily reachable through a web browser. For example, Cybermall New Zealand (www.cybermall.co.nz) is a virtual shopping mall that offers retail shopping, travel, and infotainment products and services.

A key sector of wholesale e-commerce is spending on manufacturing, repair, and operations (MRO) of goods and services – from simple office supplies to mission-critical equipment, such as the motors, pumps, compressors, and instruments that keep manufacturing facilities running smoothly. MRO purchases often approach 40 per cent of a manufacturing company's total revenues, but the purchasing system can be haphazard, without automated controls. In addition to these external purchase costs, companies face significant internal costs resulting from outdated and cumbersome MRO management processes. For example, studies show that a high percentage of manufacturing downtime is often caused by not having the right part at the right time in the right place. The result is lost productivity and capacity. E-commerce software for plant operations provides powerful comparative searching capabilities to enable managers to identify functionally equivalent items, helping them spot opportunities to combine purchases for cost savings. Comparing various suppliers, coupled with consolidating more spending with fewer suppliers, leads to decreased costs. In addition, automated workflows are typically based on industry best practices, which can streamline processes.

Manufacturing

One approach taken by many manufacturers to raise profitability and improve customer service is to move their supply chain operations onto the internet. Here they can form an **electronic exchange** to join with competitors and suppliers alike, using computers and websites to buy and sell goods, trade market information, and run back-office operations, such as inventory control, as shown in Figure 5.9. With such an exchange, the business centre is not a physical building but a network-based location where business interactions occur. This approach has greatly speeded up the movement of raw materials and finished products among all members of the business community, thus, reducing the amount of inventory that must be maintained. It has also led to a much more competitive marketplace and lower prices. Private exchanges are owned and operated by a single company. The owner uses the exchange to trade exclusively with established business partners. Public exchanges are owned and operated by industry groups. They provide services and a common technology platform to their members and are open, usually for a fee, to any company that wants to use them.

electronic exchange An electronic forum where manufacturers, suppliers, and competitors buy and sell goods, trade market information, and run back-office operations.

Several strategic and competitive issues are associated with the use of exchanges. Many companies distrust their corporate rivals and fear they might lose trade secrets through participation in such exchanges. Suppliers worry that the online marketplaces and their auctions will drive down the prices of goods and favour buyers. Suppliers also can spend a great deal of money in the setup to participate in multiple exchanges. For example, more than a dozen new exchanges have appeared in the oil industry, and the printing industry has more than 20 online marketplaces. Until a clear winner emerges in particular industries, suppliers are more or less forced to sign on to several or all of them. Yet another issue is potential government scrutiny of exchange participants – when competitors get together to share information, it raises questions of collusion or antitrust behaviour.

Many companies that already use the internet for their private exchanges have no desire to share their expertise with competitors. At the US shopping giant Wal-Mart, the world's number-one retail chain, executives turned down several invitations to join exchanges in the retail and consumer goods industries. Wal-Mart is pleased with its in-house exchange, Retail Link, which connects the company to 7000 worldwide suppliers that sell everything from toothpaste to furniture.

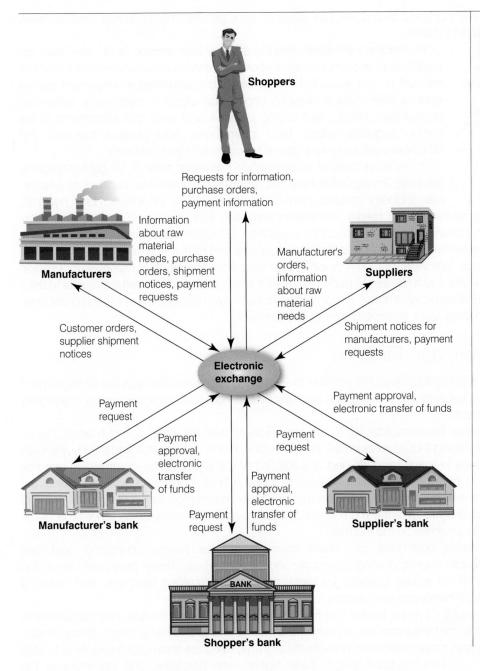

Figure 5.9 Model of an Electronic Exchange

Marketing

The nature of the web allows firms to gather much more information about customer behaviour and preferences than they could using other marketing approaches. Marketing organisations can measure many online activities as customers and potential customers gather information and make their purchase decisions. Analysis of this data is complicated because of the web's interactivity and because each visitor voluntarily provides or refuses to provide personal data, such as name, address, email address, telephone number, and demographic data. Internet advertisers use the data they gather to identify specific portions of their markets and target them with tailored advertising messages. This practice, called **market segmentation**, divides the pool of potential customers into subgroups, which are usually defined

market segmentation The identification of specific markets to target them with advertising messages.

in terms of demographic characteristics, such as age, gender, marital status, income level, and geographic location.

technology-enabled relationship management is a new twist on establishing direct customer relationships made possible when firms promote and sell on the web. Technology-enabled relationship management occurs when a firm obtains detailed information about a customer's behaviour, preferences, needs, and buying patterns and uses that information to set prices, negotiate terms, tailor promotions, add product features, and otherwise customise its entire relationship with that customer.

technology-enabled relationship management Occurs when a firm obtains detailed information about a customer's behaviour, preferences, needs, and buying patterns and uses that information to set prices, negotiate terms, tailor promotions, add product features, and otherwise customise its entire relationship with that customer.

In the past, market segmentation has been difficult for B2B marketers, because firmographic data (i.e. addresses, financials, number of employees, industry classification code) was difficult to obtain. Now, however, Nielsen, the marketing and media information company, has developed its Business-Facts database that provides this information for more than 13 million businesses. Using this data, analysts can estimate potential sales for each business and rank it against all other prospects and customers. Windstream Communications, a telecommunications company with 3 million customers, worked with Nielsen to perform a market segmentation and used the results to drive its marketing strategy. As a result, direct mail response rates have risen more than 50 per cent, and telemarketing sales increased almost 500 per cent.[9]

Investment and Finance

The internet has revolutionised the world of investment and finance. Perhaps the changes have been so great because this industry had so many built-in inefficiencies and so much opportunity for improvement.

The brokerage business adapted to the internet faster than any other arm of finance. The allure of online trading that enables investors to do quick, thorough research and then buy shares in any company in a few seconds and at a fraction of the cost of a full-commission firm has brought many investors to the web. In spite of the wealth of information available online, the average consumer buys stocks based on a tip or a recommendation, rather than as the result of research and analysis. It is the more sophisticated investor that really takes advantage of the data and tools available on the internet.[10]

Online banking customers can check balances of their savings, chequing, and loan accounts; transfer money among accounts; and pay their bills. These customers enjoy the convenience of not writing cheques by hand, tracking their current balances, and reducing expenditures on envelopes and stamps.

All of the country's major banks and many of the smaller banks enable their customers to pay bills online; many support bill payment via a mobile phone or other wireless device. Banks are eager to gain more customers who pay bills online, because such customers tend to stay with the bank longer, have higher cash balances, and use more of the bank's products.

electronic bill presentment A method of billing whereby a vendor posts an image of your statement on the internet and alerts you by email that your bill has arrived.

The next advance in online bill paying is **electronic bill presentment**, which eliminates all paper, right down to the bill itself. With this process, the vendor posts an image of your statement on the internet and alerts you by email that your bill has arrived. You then direct your bank to pay it.

Auctions

eBay has become synonymous with online auctions for both private sellers and small companies. However, hundreds of online auction sites cater to newcomers to online auctions and to unhappy eBay customers. The most frequent complaints are increases in fees and problems with unscrupulous buyers.

Price Comparison

A growing number of companies provide a mobile phone service that enables shoppers to compare prices and products on the web. Google Product Search works for iPhone and Android handsets. The shopper enters the name of the product into the Google search field and clicks "See Shopping Results" to display a list of suppliers and prices. You can also request consumer reviews and technical specifications for a specific choice. Frucall allows users to enter the bar code of a product, and then it finds and displays the best online prices for any product with that bar code. You can also read reviews or purchase the item immediately by clicking a button.[11]

Anywhere, Anytime Applications of Mobile Commerce

Because m-commerce devices usually have a single user, they are ideal for accessing personal information and receiving targeted messages for a particular consumer. Through m-commerce, companies can reach individual consumers to establish one-to-one marketing relationships and communicate whenever it is convenient – in short, anytime and anywhere. Following are just a few examples of potential m-commerce applications:

■ Banking customers can use their wireless handheld devices to access their accounts and pay their bills.

■ Clients of brokerage firms can view stock prices and company research, as well as conduct trades to fit their schedules.

■ Information services, such as financial news, sports information, and traffic updates, can be delivered to people whenever they want.

■ On-the-move retail consumers can place and pay for orders instantaneously.

■ Telecommunications service users can view service changes, pay bills, and customise their services.

■ Retailers and service providers can send potential customers advertising, promotions, or coupons to entice them to try their services as they move past their place of business.

The most successful m-commerce applications suit local conditions and people's habits and preferences. Most people do their research online and then buy offline at a local retailer. As a result, a growing market for local search engines is designed to answer the question, "where do I buy product x at a brick-and-mortar retailer near me?" Consumers provide their post code and begin by asking a basic question – "What local shops carry a particular category of items" (e.g. flat-panel televisions). Consumers typically don't start searching knowing that they want a specific model of Panasonic flat-panel TV. The local search engine then provides a list of local stores, including those with a website and those without, that sell this item.

As with any new technology, m-commerce will only succeed if it provides users with real benefits. Companies involved in m-commerce must think through their strategies carefully and ensure that they provide services that truly meet customers' needs.

Advantages of Electronic and Mobile Commerce

According to the Council of Supply Chain Management Professionals, "Supply Chain Management encompasses the planning and management of all activities involved in sourcing and procurement, conversion, and all logistics management activities. Importantly, it also includes coordination and collaboration with channel partners, which can be suppliers, intermediaries, third-party service providers, and customers."[12] Conversion to an e-commerce driven supply chain provides businesses with an opportunity to achieve operational excellence by enabling consumers and companies to gain a global reach to worldwide markets, reduce the cost of doing business, speed the flow of goods and information, increase the accuracy of order processing and order fulfilment, and improve the level of customer service.

- *Global reach.* E-commerce offers enormous opportunities. It allows manufacturers to buy at a low cost worldwide, and it offers enterprises the chance to sell to a global market right from the very start-up of their business. Moreover, e-commerce offers great promise for developing countries, helping them to enter the prosperous global marketplace and, hence, helping reduce the gap between rich and poor countries.

- *Reduce costs.* By eliminating or reducing time-consuming and labour-intensive steps throughout the order and delivery process, more sales can be completed in the same period and with increased accuracy. With increased speed and accuracy of customer order information, companies can reduce the need for inventory – from raw materials, to safety stocks, to finished goods – at all the intermediate manufacturing, storage, and transportation points.

- *Speed the flow of goods and information.* When organisations are connected via e-commerce, the flow of information is accelerated because of the already established electronic connections and communications processes. As a result, information can flow easily, directly, and rapidly from buyer to seller.

- *Increased accuracy.* By enabling buyers to enter their own product specifications and order information directly, human data-entry error on the part of the supplier is eliminated.

- *Improve customer service.* Increased and more detailed information about delivery dates and current status can increase customer loyalty. In addition, the ability to consistently meet customers' desired delivery dates with high-quality goods and services eliminates any incentive for customers to seek other sources of supply.

Production and Supply Chain Management Systems

Production and Supply Chain Management Systems follow a systematic process for developing a production plan that draws on the information available in the ERP or TPS database.

The process starts with sales forecasting to develop an estimate of future customer demand. This initial forecast is at a fairly high level with estimates made by product group, rather than by each individual product item. The sales forecast extends for months into the future. The sales forecast might be developed using an ERP sub-system or a specialised forecasting system. Many organisations are moving to a collaborative process with major customers to plan future inventory levels and production, rather than relying on an internally generated sales forecast. The sales and operations plan takes demand and current inventory levels into account and determines the specific product items that need to be produced and when to meet the forecast future demand. Production capacity and any seasonal variability in demand must also be considered. The result is a high-level production plan that balances market demand to production capacity. Panasonic and other companies have outsourced the development of a sales and operation plan to i2 Technologies in India. Best Buy, a major Panasonic customer, collects information on sales of Panasonic items at its shops' checkout stations and sends the data to i2. i2 processes the data and sends manufacturing recommendations to Panasonic, which become the basis for factory schedules.[13]

Demand management refines the production plan by determining the amount of weekly or daily production needed to meet the demand for individual products. The output of the demand management process is the master production schedule, which is a production plan for all finished goods.

Detailed scheduling uses the production plan defined by the demand management process to develop a detailed production schedule specifying production scheduling details, such as which item to produce first and when production should be switched from one item to another. A key decision is how long to make the production runs for each product. Longer production runs reduce the number of machine setups required, thus, reducing production costs. Shorter production runs generate less finished product inventory and reduce inventory holding costs.

Materials requirement planning determines the amount and timing for placing raw material orders with suppliers. The types and amounts of raw materials required to support the planned production schedule are determined based on the existing raw material inventory and the bill of materials, or BOM, a sort of "recipe" of ingredients needed to make each product item. The quantity of raw materials to order also depends on the lead time and lot sizing. Lead time is the time it takes from the time a purchase order is placed until the raw materials arrive at the production facility. Lot size has to do with discrete quantities that the supplier will ship and the amount that is economical for the producer to receive and/or store. For example, a supplier might ship a certain raw material in batches of 80 000 units. The producer might need 95 000 units. A decision must be made to order one or two batches.

Purchasing uses the information from materials requirement planning to place purchase orders for raw materials and transmit them to qualified suppliers. Typically, the release of these purchase orders is timed so that raw materials arrive just in time to be used in production and minimise warehouse and storage costs. Often, producers will allow suppliers to tap into data via an extranet that enables them to determine what raw materials the supplier needs, thus, minimising the effort and lead time to place and fill purchase orders.

Production uses the detailed schedule to plan the details of running and staffing the production operation.

5.7 Customer Relationship Management

A **customer relationship management (CRM)** system helps a company manage all aspects of customer encounters, including marketing and advertising, sales, customer service after the sale, and programs to keep and retain loyal customers (see Figure 5.10). The goal of CRM is to understand and anticipate the needs of current and potential customers to increase customer retention and loyalty, while optimizing the way that products and services are sold. Businesses implementing CRM systems report business benefits, such as improved customer satisfaction, increased customer retention, reduced operating costs, and the ability to meet customer demand.

customer relationship management (CRM) system
A system that helps a company manage all aspects of customer encounters, including marketing and advertising, sales, customer service after the sale, and programs to retain loyal customers.

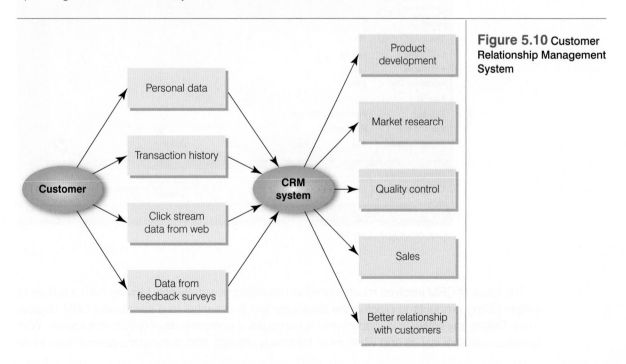

Figure 5.10 Customer Relationship Management System

CRM software automates and integrates the functions of sales, marketing, and service in an organisation. The objective is to capture data about every contact a company has with a customer through every channel and store it in the CRM system so the company can truly understand customer actions. CRM software helps an organisation build a database about its customers that describes relationships in sufficient detail so that management, salespeople, customer service providers – and even customers – can access information to match customer needs with product plans and offerings, remind them of service requirements, and know what other products they have purchased. Figure 5.11 shows contact manager software from SAP that fills this CRM role.

Figure 5.11 SAP
Contact Manager

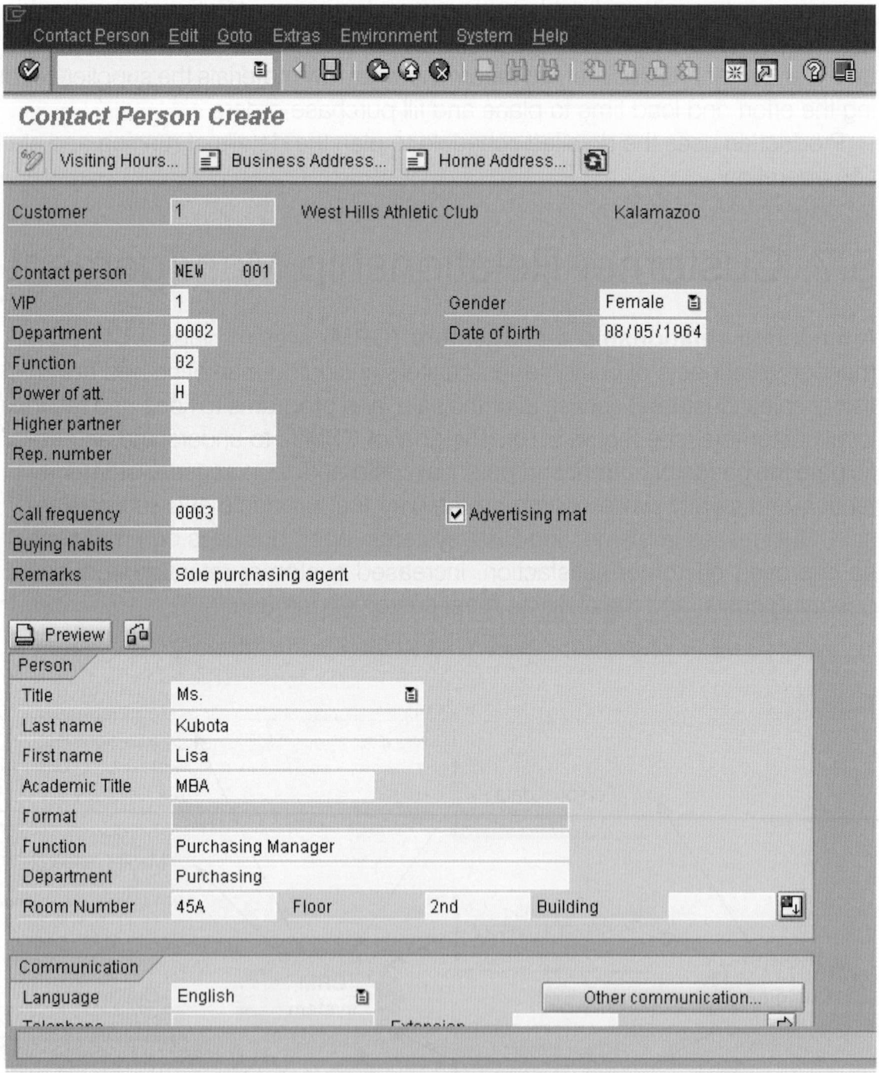

SOURCE: Copyright © by SAP AG.

The focus of CRM involves much more than installing new software. Moving from a culture of simply selling products to placing the customer first is essential to a successful CRM deployment. Before any software is loaded onto a computer, a company must retrain employees. Who handles customer issues and when must be clearly defined, and computer systems need to be integrated so that all pertinent information is available immediately, whether a customer calls a sales representative or customer service representative. In addition to using stationary computers, most CRM systems can now be accessed via wireless devices.

5.8 Financial and Managerial Accounting Systems

The general ledger is the main accounting record of a business. It is often divided into different categories, including assets, liabilities, revenue, expenses, and equity. These categories, in turn, are subdivided into sub-ledgers to capture details, such as cash, accounts payable, accounts receivable, and so on. "When used as an ERP sub-system, input to the general ledger occurs simultaneously with the input of a business transaction to a specific module." Here are several examples of how this occurs:

- An order administrator records a sale and the ERP system automatically creates an accounts receivable entry indicating that a customer owes money for goods received.
- A buyer enters a purchase order and the ERP system automatically creates an accounts payable entry in the general ledger registering that the company has an obligation to pay for goods that will be received at some time in the future.
- A dock worker enters a receipt of purchased materials from a supplier and the ERP system automatically creates a general ledger entry to increase the value of inventory on hand.
- A production worker withdraws raw materials from inventory to support production and the ERP system generates a record to reduce the value of inventory on hand.

Thus, the ERP system captures transactions entered by workers in all functional areas of the business. The ERP system then creates the associated general ledger record to track the financial impact of the transaction. This set of records is an extremely valuable resource that companies can use to support financial accounting and managerial accounting.

Financial accounting consists of capturing and recording all the transactions that affect a company's financial state and then using these documented transactions to prepare financial statements to external decision makers, such as stockholders, suppliers, banks, and government agencies. These financial statements include the profit and loss statement, balance sheet, and cash flow statement. They must be prepared in strict accordance to rules and guidelines of the governing agencies.

All transactions that affect the financial state of the firm are captured and recorded in a database. This data is used in the financial and managerial accounting system to prepare any financial statements that are required and can also be used to perform various analyses, such as generating a forecasted profit and loss statement to assess the firm's future profitability.

5.9 Data Mining and Business Intelligence

The data that are generated by operational systems, such as the ones described in this chapter, are often analyzed by a process known as **data mining**. Data mining the process of analyzing data to try to discover patterns and relationships within the data. Like gold mining, data mining sifts through mountains of data to find a few nuggets of valuable information. There are a number of data mining tools and techniques. Supermarket giant Tesco's success has been attributed in part to the

Data mining The process of analyzing data to try to discover patterns and relationships within the data.

way it used data mining techniques to analyze its Clubcard data. The Clubcard allows Tesco to match individual purchases with information about the customers who purchased them (i.e. age, address, gender etc.) This allowed Tesco to decide on what product mix it should have in each store, what new products it could successfully introduce and how high they could set prices before customer would go elsewhere.[14]

For example, association rules algorithms were created specifically to analyze shopping basket data in order to answer questions, such as, if someone buys eggs, how likely is it that they will also buy cheese? This information could be used by Tesco to help design the layout the goods in the best configuration in their store. Data mining is used extensively in marketing to improve customer retention; identify cross-selling opportunities; manage marketing campaigns; market, channel, and pricing analysis; and customer segmentation analysis (especially one-to-one marketing). An example of data mining software is shown in Figure 5.12.

Figure 5.12 Data Mining Software

Rattle from Togaware is a free graphical interface to the powerful data analysis software R.

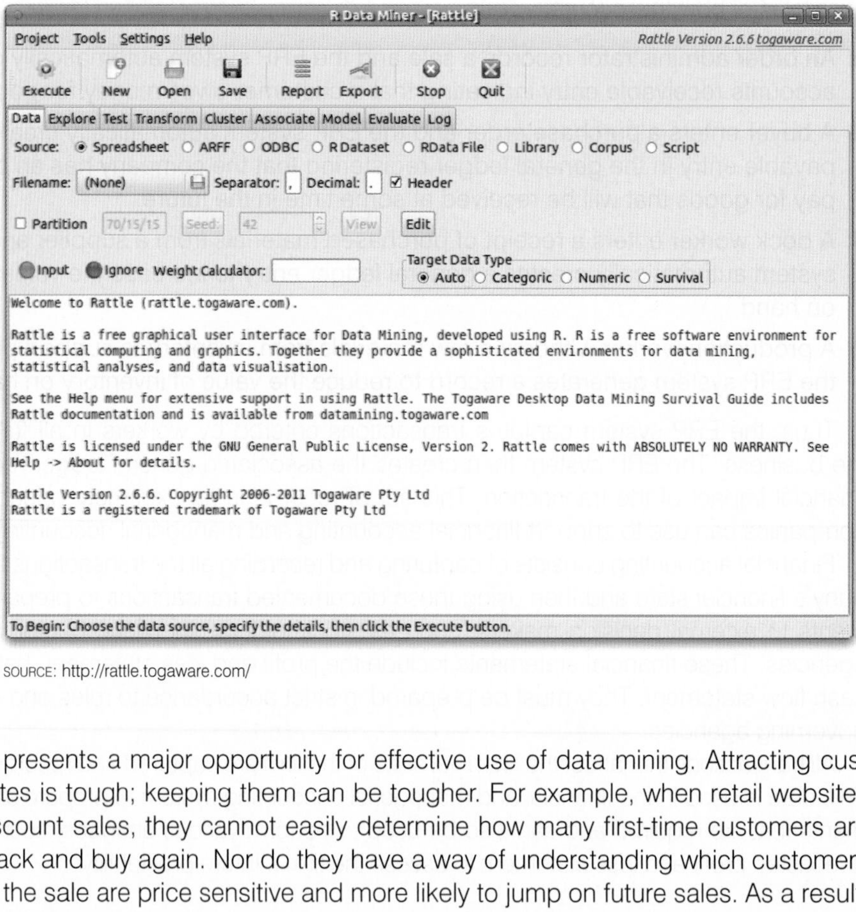

SOURCE: http://rattle.togaware.com/

E-commerce presents a major opportunity for effective use of data mining. Attracting customers to websites is tough; keeping them can be tougher. For example, when retail websites launch deep-discount sales, they cannot easily determine how many first-time customers are likely to come back and buy again. Nor do they have a way of understanding which customers acquired during the sale are price sensitive and more likely to jump on future sales. As a result, companies are gathering data on user traffic through their websites and storing that data in databases. This data is then analyzed using data-mining techniques to personalise and customise websites, and develop sales promotions targeted at specific customers.

business intelligence The process of gathering enough of the right information in a timely manner and usable form and analyzing it to have a positive impact on business strategy, tactics, or operations.

Traditional DBMS vendors are well aware of the great potential of data mining. Thus, companies, such as Oracle, Sybase, Tandem, and Red Brick Systems, are all incorporating data-mining functionality into their products. Table 5.8 summarises a few of the most frequent applications for data mining.

Closely linked to the concept of data mining is the use of databases for business-intelligence purposes. **Business intelligence** (BI) involves gathering enough of the right information in a timely manner and usable

Table 5.8 Common Data-Mining Applications

Application	Description
Branding and positioning of products and services	Enable the strategist to visualise the different positions of competitors in a given market using performance (or other) data on dozens of key features of the product and then to condense all that data into a perceptual map of only two or three dimensions
Customer churn	Predict current customers who are likely to switch to a competitor
Direct marketing	Identify prospects most likely to respond to a direct marketing campaign (such as a direct mailing)
Fraud detection	Highlight transactions most likely to be deceptive or illegal
Market basket analysis	Identify products and services that are most commonly purchased at the same time (e.g. nail polish and lipstick)
Market segmentation	Group customers based on who they are or on what they prefer
Trend analysis	Analyze how key variables (e.g. sales, spending, and promotions) vary over time

form and analyzing it so that it can be used to have a positive effect on business strategy, tactics, or operations. Business intelligence turns data into useful information that is then distributed throughout an enterprise. **Competitive intelligence** is one aspect of business intelligence and is limited to information about competitors and the ways that knowledge affects strategy, tactics, and operations. Competitive intelligence is a critical part of acompany's ability to see and respond quickly and appropriately to the changing marketplace. Competitive intelligence is not espionage, the use of illegal means to gather information. In fact, almost all the information a competitive-intelligence professional needs can be collected by examining published information sources, conducting interviews, and using other legal, ethical methods. Using a variety of analytical tools, a skilled competitive-intelligence professional can by deduction fill the gaps in information already gathered. The term **counterintelligence** describes the steps an organisation takes to protect information sought by "hostile" intelligence gatherers. One of the most effective counterintelligence measures is to define "trade secret" information relevant to the company and control its dissemination.

competitive intelligence One aspect of business intelligence limited to information about competitors and the ways that knowledge affects strategy, tactics, and operations.

counterintelligence The steps an organisation takes to protect information sought by "hostile" intelligence gatherers.

5.10 International Issues Associated with Operational Systems

Operational systems must support businesses that interoperate with customers, suppliers, business partners, shareholders, and government agencies in multiple countries. Different languages and cultures, disparities in IS infrastructure, varying laws and customs rules, and multiple currencies are among the challenges that must be met by an operational system of a multinational company. The following sections highlight these issues.

Different Languages and Cultures

Teams composed of people from several countries speaking different languages and familiar with different cultures might not agree on a single work process. In some cultures, people do not routinely work in teams in a networked environment. Despite these complications, many multinational companies can establish close connections with their business partners and roll out standard IS applications for all to use. However, sometimes they require extensive and costly customisation. For example, even though English has become a standard business language among executives and senior managers, many people within organisations do not speak English. As a result, software might need to be designed with local language interfaces to ensure the successful implementation of a new system. Other customisations will also be needed; date fields for example: the European format is day/month/year, Japan uses year/month/day, and the US date format is month/day/year. Sometimes, users might also have to implement manual processes to override established formatting to enable systems to function correctly.

Disparities in Information System Infrastructure

The lack of a robust or a common information infrastructure can also create problems. For example, much of Latin America lags behind the rest of the world in internet usage, and online marketplaces are almost nonexistent there. This gap makes it difficult for multinational companies to get online with their Latin American business partners. Even something as mundane as the fact that the power plug on a piece of equipment built in one country might not fit into the power socket of another country can affect the infrastructure.

Varying Laws and Customs Rules

Numerous laws can affect the collection and dissemination of data. For example, labour laws in some countries prohibit the recording of worker performance data. Also, some countries have passed laws limiting the transborder flow of data linked to individuals. Specifically, European Community Directive 95/96/EC of 1998 requires that any company doing business within the borders of the 25 European Union member nations protect the privacy of customers and employees. It bars the export of data to countries that do not have data-protection standards comparable to the European Union's.

Trade custom rules between nations are international laws that set practices for two or more nations' commercial transactions. They cover imports and exports and the systems and procedures dealing with quotas, visas, entry documents, commercial invoices, foreign trade zones, payment of duty and taxes, and many other related issues. For example, the North American Free Trade Agreement (NAFTA) of 1994 created trade custom rules to address the flow of goods throughout the North American continent. Most of these custom rules and their changes over time create headaches for people who must keep systems consistent with the rules.

Multiple Currencies

The enterprise system of multinational companies must conduct transactions in multiple currencies. To do so, a set of exchange rates is defined, and the information systems apply these rates to translate from one currency to another. The systems must be current with foreign currency exchange rates, handle reporting and other transactions, such as cash receipts, issue vendor payments and customer statements, record retail store payments, and generate financial reports in the currency of choice.

Summary

At the start of this chapter we set out the FOUR main principles relating to how businesses use enterprise resource planning systems to create improvements in their operations and, in some cases, lead to whole new business opportunities together with the key learning objectives for each. It's now time to summarise the chapter by recapping on those FOUR principles: can you recall what is important and why about each one?

1. **A company that implements an enterprise resource planning system is creating a highly integrated set of systems, which can lead to many business benefits.** Enterprise resource planning (ERP) software supports the efficient operation of business processes by integrating activities throughout a business, including sales, marketing, manufacturing, logistics, accounting, and staffing. Implementation of an ERP system can provide many advantages, including providing access to data for operational decision making; elimination of costly, inflexible legacy systems; providing improved work processes; and creating the opportunity to upgrade technology infrastructure. Some of the disadvantages associated with an ERP system are that they are time consuming, difficult, and expensive to implement.

   Although the scope of ERP implementation can vary from firm to firm, most firms use ERP systems to support production and supply chain management, customer relationship management and sales ordering, and financial and managerial accounting.

   The production and supply chain management process starts with sales forecasting to develop an estimate of future customer demand. This initial forecast is at a fairly high level with estimates made by product group rather than by each individual product item. The sales and operations plan takes demand and current inventory levels into account and determines the specific product items that need to be produced and when to meet the forecast future demand. Demand management refines the production plan by determining the amount of weekly or daily production needed to meet the demand for individual products. Detailed scheduling uses the production plan defined by the demand management process to develop a detailed production schedule specifying production scheduling details, such as which item to

produce first and when production should be switched from one item to another. Materials requirement planning determines the amount and timing for placing raw material orders with suppliers. Purchasing uses the information from materials requirement planning to place purchase orders for raw materials and transmit them to qualified suppliers. Production uses the detailed schedule to plan the details of running and staffing the production operation.

Numerous complications arise that multinational corporations must address in planning, building, and operating their TPS. These challenges include dealing with different languages and cultures, disparities in IS infrastructure, varying laws and customs rules, and multiple currencies.

2. **An organisation must have information systems that support the routine, day-to-day activities that occur in the normal course of business and help a company add value to its products and services.** Transaction processing systems (TPS) are at the heart of most information systems in businesses today. A TPS is an organised collection of people, procedures, software, databases, and devices used to capture fundamental data about events that affect the organisation (transactions). All TPS perform the following basic activities: data collection, which involves the capture of source data to complete a set of transactions; data editing, which checks for data validity and completeness; data correction, which involves providing feedback of a potential problem and enabling users to change the data; data manipulation, which is the performance of calculations, sorting, categorizing, summarising, and storing data for further processing; data storage, which involves placing transaction data into one or more databases; and document production, which involves outputting records and reports.

   The methods of transaction processing systems include batch and online. Batch processing involves the collection of transactions into batches, which are entered into the system at regular intervals as a group. Online transaction processing (OLTP) allows transactions to be entered as they occur.

   Organisations expect TPS to accomplish a number of specific objectives, including processing data generated by and about transactions, maintaining a high degree of accuracy and information integrity, compiling accurate and timely reports and documents, increasing labour efficiency, helping provide increased and enhanced service, and building and maintaining customer loyalty. In some situations, an effective TPS can help an organisation gain a competitive advantage.

3. **Traditional TPS support the various business functions of organisations that have not yet implemented enterprise resource planning systems.** Many organisations conduct ongoing TPS audits to prevent accounting irregularities or loss of data privacy. The audit can be performed by the firm's internal audit group or by an outside auditor for greater objectivity.

The traditional TPS systems that support the order processing business functions include order entry, sales configuration, shipment planning, shipment execution, inventory control, and accounts receivable.

The traditional TPS that support the purchasing function include inventory control, purchase order processing, accounts payable, and receiving.

The traditional TPS that support the accounting business function include the budget, accounts receivable, payroll, asset management, and general ledger.

4. **Electronic and mobile commerce allow transactions to be made by the customer, with less need for sales staff, and open up new opportunities for conducting business.** E-commerce is the conducting of business activities electronically over networks. Business-to-business (B2B) e-commerce allows manufacturers to buy at a low cost worldwide, and it offers enterprises the chance to sell to a global market. Business-to-consumer (B2C) e-commerce enables organisations to sell directly to consumers, eliminating intermediaries. In many cases, this squeezes costs and inefficiencies out of the supply chain and can lead to higher profits and lower prices for consumers. Consumer-to-consumer (C2C) e-commerce involves consumers selling directly to other consumers. Online auctions are the chief method by which C2C e-commerce is currently conducted.

Mobile commerce is the use of wireless devices, such as PDAs, mobile phones, and smartphones, to facilitate the sale of goods or services – anytime, anywhere. The market for m-commerce in North America is expected to mature much later than in Western Europe and Japan. Although some industry experts predict great growth in this arena, several hurdles must be overcome, including improving the ease of use of wireless devices, addressing the security of wireless transactions, and improving network speed. M-commerce provides a unique opportunity to establish one-on-one marketing relationships and support communications anytime and anywhere.

Review Questions

1 Describe the difference between a TPS and an ERP system.

2 Describe how data correction might happen in a TPS.

3 List two B2Me features a firm could add to its website.

4 List and explain four different types of e-commerce.

5 Identify and briefly describe three limitations that complicate the use of handheld devices used for m-commerce.

6 What is source data automation? Give an example.

7 What makes implementing an ERP complicated?

8 How could data mining techniques help a supermarket judge the success of a marketing promotion?

9 Define the term competitive intelligence? How could such intelligence be gathered?

10 Describe two services a government could implement online.

Discussion Questions

1 What do you think are the biggest barriers to wide-scale adoption of m-commerce by consumers? Who do you think is working on solutions to these problems and what might the solutions entail?

2 If a customer prints an order form downloaded from a website, completes it using a black pen, and faxes it off to a company, does this constitute e-commerce? Why or why not?

3 What could a firm do to protect itself from competitive intelligence?

4 What are some of the ethical issues surrounding data mining?

Web Exercises

1 Search for information about the data mining software Rattle. Write a report summarising the features it provides.

2 Do research on the web and identify the most popular ERP system solution for small- and medium-sized businesses. Why is this solution the most popular? Develop a one-page report or send an email message to your instructor about what you found.

Case One

Nike Empowers Customers with Online Customisation

Shopping and selling online provide sellers and buyers with an intimate environment in which to do business. Through the use of dynamic websites that are designed to uniquely appeal to each visitor, electronic retailers, or e-tailers, can provide customers with exactly what they desire. Unlike bricks-and-mortar retail shops with promotions designed to appeal to the lowest common denominator, e-tailers can provide visitors with an environment customised to their tastes and interests. For example, frequent Amazon shoppers are not surprised when they are greeted at Amazon's website by name and shown only items that are likely to appeal to them.

Customisation, or B2Me, is a powerful tool for online businesses selling to individual consumers and to other businesses. Customisation eliminates the frustration consumers feel when they must navigate through massive amounts of unrelated information to find items of interest. Consider, for example, searching the Sunday newspaper for advertisements and coupons of interest or the percentage of commercials on network TV that are for products that actually appeal to you.

Realising the power of customisation and providing shoppers with exactly what they are looking for has inspired Nike and other companies to take advantage of the concept. Going beyond customising the online shopping experience, Nike is empowering shoppers to custom-design the products themselves. Visitors to the recently upgraded Nikeid

.com website can design their own footwear, sports apparel, sports bags, balls, and wristwatches. For example, you can select colours from an extensive palette for the nine elements of a Nike athletic shoe, including a base colour and colours for the tip and heel, lining, tongue, and even the famous Nike swoosh. Furthermore, you can emboss the shoe with your name or slogan and add a national symbol or flag to the heel tab.

Market analysts believe that the appeal of product customisation will increase over time, especially to young shoppers. "It is really a democratic desire," said Sharon Lee, co-founder of a Los Angeles-based consumer research and trend consulting company called Look-Look, Inc. "Every person wants to say this is much more me and I'm not part of this kind of mass culture." Customisation also connects shoppers more closely with a brand and helps companies attract fickle but lucrative young shoppers by giving them the power to put their personal stamp on what they purchase.

The level of customisation provided by Nike is only made possible through e-commerce technologies and supply chain management. E-commerce systems stream the order information from Nike's website to Nike's order processing system and from there to Nike's suppliers and manufacturers, all within seconds of the moment the order is placed. Nike's manufacturing process has been adjusted to accommodate individual products in addition to mass production of its stock items. The result is a wider and happier customer base that is getting exactly what it wants.

Questions

1 Is Nike, by allowing their customers to customise their footwear, really doing B2Me? Are they not customising the product, rather than the website? Is this distinction important?

2 Is B2Me a tactic only suitable in certain industries? If so, what are some of them?

3 What are some of the privacy issues associated with B2Me?

4 It is often said that one of the main advantages small businesses have is that they know their customers more intimately than larger businesses do. Is B2Me eroding this advantage? Explain your answer.

SOURCES: Kahn, Michael, 'Nike Says Just Do It Yourself,' *Reuters*. Available from: www.reuters.com, May 30, 2005; Hallett, Vicky, 'Satisfied Customisers,' *US News & World Report*, November 21, 2005; *DIVERSIONS*, Vol. 139, No. 19; p. D2, D4, or www.lexis-nexis.com. Nike Customisation (website). Available from: http://nikeid.nike.com/nikeid/, May 04, 2006.

Case Two

Dubai Bank Improves Customer Satisfaction with CRM

Dubai Bank is one of the top Islamic banks based in Dubai, United Arab Emirates, with 25 branches across the UAE and total assets of AED 14.4 billion. Banking is a highly competitive business in Dubai, a city of glass-and-steel skyscrapers and state-of-the-art massive engineering projects, rooted in oil money and growing in leaps and bounds. Banks work hard to win over customers with lavish obbies, financial incentives, and impeccable customer service. As Dubai Bank grew over time, adding services and customers, it became apparent that the bank needed a way to easily gather customer information. Dubai Bank customers often had data spread across three separates databases – one for account information, another for credit card information, and yet another for investments and loans. If customers held multiple bank accounts, separate database records were created and even more information was duplicated. The complexity of customer information systems caused Dubai Bank agents frustration in finding information and setting up new accounts. Even worse was the aggravation it caused valuable customers. If a customer phoned customer service with a question, the agent might have had to access eight systems to collect customer information, leaving the customer waiting on the line. If the customer followed up the next day with a visit to the bank, the teller would have had no knowledge of the previous discussion with customer service, further aggravating the customer.

When customers set up a new account, agents were required to fill out multiple applications. Credit checks needed to be performed manually. With this level of customer service, Dubai Bank was having a difficult time keeping customers. Faizal Eledath, chief information officer at Dubai Bank, recognised the need for an enterprise-wide customer relationship management (CRM) system. He sought a system that would integrate all customer records into one cohesive system, providing agents and managers detailed information about each customer through a single interface.

Dubai Bank is recognised as an Islamic institution that strictly adheres to the Shari'a principles – that is, the sacred law of Islam. These principles include conducting business with the highest level of transparency, integrity, fairness, respect, and care. Dubai Bank's information systems would need to support its Islamic principles. Dubai Bank hired information systems consultant Veripark to assist in building the ideal CRM for the bank. Dubai made its choice based on positive past experiences it shared with Veripark and the Microsoft products it represents. Veripark selected Microsoft Dynamics CRM package that integrates all critical operational banking systems, including credit cards, data warehouse, wealth management, and risk systems, into the CRM. The new CRM provides bank representatives with a 360-degree view of the customer, whereby information can be entered and accessed through a single interface. Veripark customised the package to comply with Islamic banking regulations. Business process automation is programmed into the system to further assist the bank in its strict adherence to Shari'a principles.

The new CRM system records information from all customer interactions with the bank. If a customer makes a withdrawal from an ATM, it is recorded in the CRM. When a customer phones customer service, notes are recorded in the system as well. Whenever a customer has a need, a bank representative can easily review the customer's history and quickly recommend a course of action. Since the installation of its new CRM system, both customers and bank agents are much happier. Customer service agents can now provide speedy service, because information is provided in one interface rather than eight. New accounts are created in a quarter of the time previously required. Compliance with Islamic banking requirements is assured and automated, without involving additional effort on the part of bank officials or agents. Most importantly, Dubai Bank knows and understands its customers more deeply and can use that information to provide services and implement programs that increase customer satisfaction.

Discussion Questions

1 What conditions brought Dubai Bank to the realisation that it could benefit from a CRM system?

2 How did the CRM system make life easier for Dubai Bank agents and customers?

Critical Thinking Questions

1 Dubai Bank had regulation imposed on it by the Islamic faith that affected its information systems. What types of regulations are imposed on US banks that have a similar impact?

2 How can the information collected by a CRM system be used to gain insight and boost a business' profits? Provide some examples.

SOURCES: Microsoft Staff, "Dubai Bank," Microsoft Case Studies, March 26, 2010. Available from: www.microsoft.com/casestudies/Case_Study_Detail.aspx?cases-tudyid=4000006766; Dubai Bank website. Available from: www.dubaibank.ae. Accessed May.

5

Notes

1 "Customer Success Stories: Plastic Manufacturer Sets Higher Standards of Performance with Rapid ERP Implementation of ERP from IQMS." Available from: www.iqms.com/company/flambeau/index.html. Accessed April 9, 2010.

2 "Achmea Transforms Financial Reporting with SAP and IBM," March 11, 2010. Available from: www-01.ibm.com/software/success/cssdb.nsf/CS/STRD-83ELTK?OpenDocument&Site=corp&cty=en_us. Accessed April 9, 2010.

3 "Barloworld Handling UK Driving Optimal Performance with Mobile Technology." Available from: www.google.com/search?q=Barloworld+Handling+UK+Driving+Optimal+Performance+&rls=com.microsoft:en-us:IE-SearchBox&ie=UTF-8&oe=UTF-8&sourceid=ie7&rlz=1I7ADBF_en. Accessed April 9, 2010.

4 Marlin, Steven, 'Bank Deploys Anti-Money Laundering System,' Information Week, October 11, 2005.

5 Sullivan, Laurie, 'Bad Online Shopping Experiences Are Bad for Business,' Information Week, January 24, 2005.

6 Perez, Juan Carlos, 'Amazon Turns 10, Helped by Strong Tech, Service,' Computerworld, July 15, 2005.

7 Javed, Naseem, 'Move Over B2B, B2C – It's M2E Time,' E-Commerce Times, August 17, 2005.

8 'Investor Relations,' eBay website. Available from: http://investor.ebay.com/fundamentals.cfm. Accessed May 4, 2006.

9 Mancini, Michael, "B2B Discovers Market Segmentation," NielsenWire, November 2, 2009, blog .nielsen.com/nielsenwire/consumer/b2b-discovers-market-segmentation. Accessed March 3, 2010.

10 Rosencrance, Linda, 'Survey: User Satisfaction with E-Commerce Sites Rises Slightly,' Computerworld, February 21, 2006.

11 Frucall website. Available from: www.frucall.com. Accessed March 27, 2010.

12 Council of Supply Chain Management Professionals (website). Available from: www.cscmp.org/Website/AboutCSCMP/Definitions/Definitions.asp.

13 Anthes, Gary, 'Sidebar: It's All Global Now,' Computerworld, February 20, 2006.

14 Humby, Clive, Hunt, Terry and Phillips, Tim. "Scoring Points: How Tesco is Winning Customer Loyalty," 2003, Kogan Page.

CHAPTER 6 CONTENTS

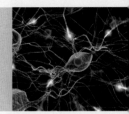

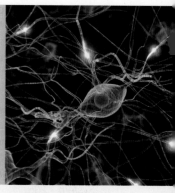

Management Information and Decision Support Systems

In this chapter we will look at the FOUR main factors you need to understand when working through how this topic covers management information systems and decision support systems and how crucial these are to running an effective business.

Principles

1. Good decision making and problem-solving skills are the key to developing effective information and decision support systems.

2. A management information system (MIS) must provide the right information to the right person in the right format at the right time.

3. Decision support systems (DSS) support decision making effectiveness when faced with unstructured or semi-structured business problems.

4. Specialised support systems, such as group support systems (GSS) and executive support systems (ESS), use the overall approach of a DSS in situations such as group and executive decision making.

Learning Objectives

▨ Define the stages of decision making.

▨ Discuss the importance of implementation and monitoring in problem solving.

▨ Explain the uses of MIS and describe their inputs and outputs.

▨ Discuss information systems in the functional areas of business organisations.

▨ List and discuss important characteristics of DSS that give them the potential to be effective management support tools.

▨ Identify and describe the basic components of a DSS.

▨ State the goals of a GSS and identify the characteristics that distinguish it from a DSS.

▨ Identify the fundamental uses of an ESS and list the characteristics of such a system.

Why Learn About Management Information Systems and Decision Support Systems?

The previous chapter looked at systems at the operational level of a firm. This chapter considers systems higher up, at the tactical and strategic levels. The true potential of information systems in organisations is in helping employees make more informed decisions, something that is supported by both management information and decision support systems. Transportation coordinators can use management information reports to find the least expensive way to ship products to market and to solve bottlenecks. A bank or credit union can use a group support system to help it determine who should receive a loan. Shop managers can use decision support systems to help them decide what and how much inventory to order to meet customer needs and increase profits. An entrepreneur who owns and operates a temporary storage company can use vacancy reports to help determine what price to charge for new storage units. Everyone wants to be a better problem solver and decision maker. This chapter shows you how information systems can help. It begins with an overview of decision making and problem solving.

6.1 Decision Making and Problem Solving

Organisations need to make good decisions. In most cases, strategic planning and the overall goals of the organisation set the course for decision making, helping employees and business units achieve their objectives and goals. Often, information systems also assist with strategic planning, helping top management make better decisions.

In business, one of the highest compliments you can receive is to be recognised by your colleagues and peers as a "real problem solver." Problem solving is a critical activity for any business organisation. After identifying a problem, you begin the problem-solving process with decision making. A well-known model developed by Herbert Simon divides the **decision-making phase** of the problem-solving process into three stages: intelligence, design, and choice. This model was later incorporated by George Huber into an expanded model of the entire problem-solving process (see Figure 6.1).

decision-making phase The first part of problem solving, including three stages: intelligence, design, and choice.

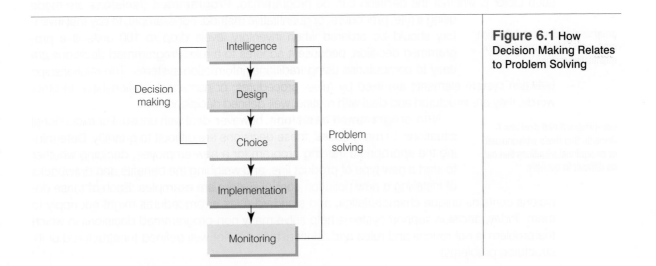

Figure 6.1 How Decision Making Relates to Problem Solving

The three stages of decision making – intelligence, design, and choice – are augmented by implementation and monitoring to result in problem solving.

intelligence stage The first stage of decision making, in which potential problems or opportunities are identified and defined.

The first stage in the problem-solving process is the **intelligence stage**. During this stage, you identify and define potential problems or opportunities. For example, you might learn about the need for an intervention or change in an unsatisfactory situation. During the intelligence stage, you also investigate resource and environmental constraints. For example, if you were a French farmer, during the intelligence stage, you might explore the possibilities of shipping apples from your farm to shops in Ireland. The perishability of the fruit and the maximum price that consumers in Ireland are willing to pay for the fruit are problem constraints. Aspects of the problem environment that you must consider include import/export laws regarding the shipment of food products.

design stage The second stage of decision making, in which alternative solutions to the problem are developed.

In the **design stage**, you develop alternative solutions to the problem. In addition, you evaluate the feasibility of these alternatives. In the fruit shipping example, you would consider the alternative methods of shipment, including the transportation times and costs associated with each.

choice stage The third stage of decision making, which requires selecting a course of action.

problem solving A process that goes beyond decision making to include the implementation and monitoring stages.

The last stage of the decision-making phase, the **choice stage**, requires selecting a course of action. Here you might select the method of shipping fruit by air as the solution. The choice stage would then conclude with selection of an air carrier. As you will see later, various factors influence choice; the act of choosing is not as simple as it might first appear.

implementation stage A stage of problem solving in which a solution is put into effect.

Problem solving includes and goes beyond decision making. It also includes the **implementation stage**, when the solution is put into effect. For example, if your decision is to ship fruit to Ireland as air freight using a specific air freight company, implementation involves informing your farming staff of the new activity, getting the fruit to the airport, and actually shipping the product.

monitoring stage The final stage of the problem-solving process in which decision makers evaluate the implementation.

The final stage of the problem-solving process is the **monitoring stage**. In this stage, decision makers evaluate the implementation to determine whether the anticipated results were achieved and to modify the process in light of new information. Monitoring can involve feedback and adjustment. For example, you might need to change your air carrier if they regularly have shipping delays.

Programmed versus Non-Programmed Decisions

In the choice stage, various factors influence the decision maker's selection of a solution. One such factor is whether the decision can be programmed. **Programmed decisions** are made using a rule, procedure, or quantitative method. For example, to say that inventory should be ordered when inventory levels drop to 100 units is a programmed decision, because it adheres to a rule. Programmed decisions are easy to computerise using traditional information systems. The relationships between system elements are fixed by rules, procedures, or numerical relationships. In other words, they are structured and deal with routine, well-defined decisions.

programmed decision A decision made using a rule, procedure, or quantitative method.

non-programmed decision A decision that deals with unusual or exceptional situations that can be difficult to quantify.

Non-programmed decisions, however, deal with unusual or exceptional situations. In many cases, these decisions are difficult to quantify. Determining the appropriate training program for a new employee, deciding whether to start a new type of product line, and weighing the benefits and drawbacks of installing a new pollution control system are examples. Each of these decisions contains unique characteristics, and standard rules or procedures might not apply to them. Today, decision support systems help solve many non-programmed decisions in which the problem is not routine and rules and relationships are not well defined (unstructured or ill-structured problems).

Optimisation, Satisficing, and Heuristic Approaches

In general, computerised decision support systems can either optimise or satisfice. An optimisation model finds the best solution, usually the one that will best help the organisation meet its goals.[1] For example, an optimisation model can find the appropriate number of products that an organisation should produce to meet a profit goal, given certain conditions and assumptions. Optimisation models use problem constraints. A limit on the number of available work hours in a manufacturing facility is an example of a problem constraint. Some spreadsheet programs, such as Microsoft Excel, have optimising features (see Figure 6.2). A business, such as an appliance manufacturer, can use an optimisation program to reduce the time and cost of manufacturing appliances and increase profits. Optimisation software also allows decision makers to explore various alternatives.

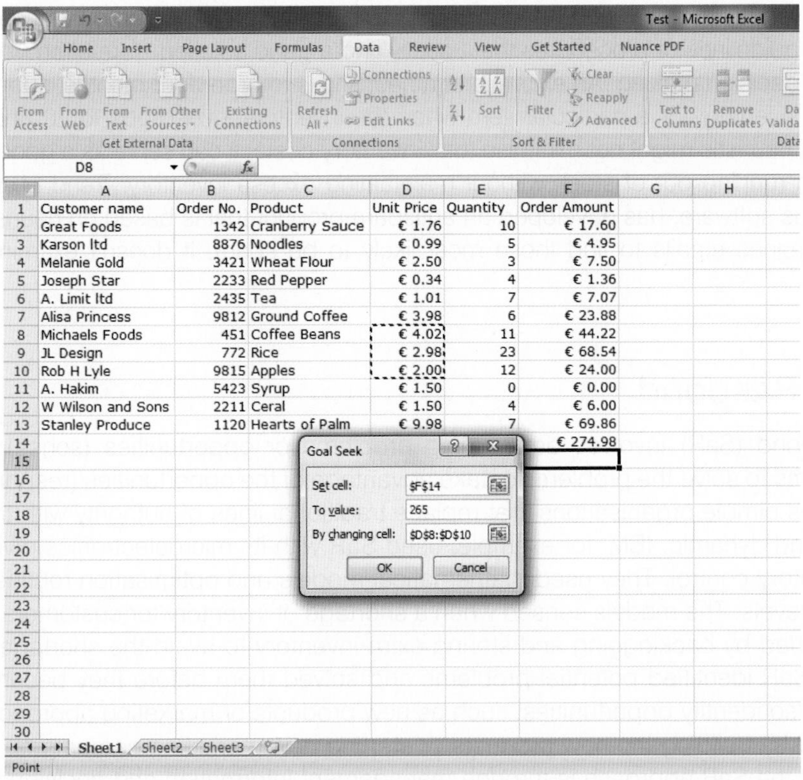

Figure 6.2 Microsoft **Excel Goal Seek**
Microsoft Excel has a number of features that allow 'what-if' analysis of data.

Used with permission from Microsoft.

For example, an optimisation model can find the best route to ship products to markets, given certain conditions and assumptions. StatoilHydro, a Norwegian oil and natural gas organisation, used optimisation software called GassOpt that not only helped the organisation minimise shipping costs for natural gas, but also helped executives determine new shipping routes.[2] The optimisation application has saved the organisation, which is partially owned by the country of Norway, about €2 billion since its development. Laps Care is an information system that used optimisation to assign medical personnel to home healthcare patients in Sweden while minimising healthcare costs. The optimisation system has improved the quality of medical care delivered to the elderly.[3] The system has also improved healthcare efficiency by 10 to 15 per cent and lowered costs by more than 20 million euros. In another case, Xerox has developed an optimisation system to increase printer productivity and reduce costs, called Lean Document Production (LDP) solutions.[4] The optimisation routine was able to reduce labour costs by 20 to 40 per cent in some cases. Marriott international used optimisation to help determine the optimal price of a group or block of rooms. The optimisation routine helped Marriott increase revenues and profits as a result.[5]

A **satisficing model** is one that finds a good – but not necessarily the best – problem solution. Satisficing is usually used because modelling the problem properly to get an optimal decision would be too difficult, complex, or costly. Satisficing normally does not look at all possible solutions but only at those likely to give good results. Consider a decision to select a location for a new manufacturing plant. To find the optimal (best) location, you must consider all cities in Europe. A satisficing approach is to consider only five or ten cities that might satisfy the company's requirements. Limiting the options might not result in the best decision, but it will likely result in a good decision, without spending the time and effort to investigate all cities. Satisficing is a good alternative modelling method, because it is sometimes too expensive to analyze every alternative to find the best solution.

Heuristics, often referred to as "rules of thumb" – commonly accepted guidelines or procedures that usually find a good solution – are often used in decision making. An example of a heuristic is to order four months' supply of inventory for a particular item when the inventory level drops to 20 units or less; although this heuristic might not minimise total inventory costs, it can serve as a good rule of thumb to avoid running out of stock without maintaining excess inventory. Trend Micro, a provider of antivirus software, has developed an antispam product that is based on heuristics. The software examines emails to find those most likely to be spam. It doesn't examine all emails.

Sense and Respond

Sense and Respond (SaR) involves determining problems or opportunities (sense) and developing systems to solve the problems or take advantage of the opportunities (respond).[6] SaR often requires nimble organisations that replace traditional lines of authority with those that are flexible and dynamic. IBM, for example, used SaR with its microelectronics division to help with inventory control. They used mathematical models and optimisation routines to control inventory levels. The models sensed when a shortage of inventory for customers was likely and responded by backlogging and storing extra inventory to avoid the shortages. In this application, SaR identified potential problems and solved them before they became a reality. SaR can also identify opportunities, such as new products or marketing approaches, and then respond by building the new products or starting new marketing campaigns. One way to implement the SaR approach is through management information and decision support systems, discussed next.

6.2 An Overview of Management Information Systems

A management information system (MIS) is an integrated collection of people, procedures, databases, hardware, and software that provides managers and decision makers with information to help achieve organisational goals. The primary purpose of an MIS is to help an organisation achieve its goals by providing managers with insight into the regular operations of the organisation so that they can control, organise, and plan more effectively. One important role of the MIS is to provide the right information to the right person in the right format at the right time.

In short, an MIS provides managers with information, typically in reports, that supports effective decision making and provides feedback on daily operations. For example, a manager might request a report of weekly sales, broken down by area. On the basis of this information, she might decide to redistribute her mobile sales staff to have greater coverage in one place, less in another.

Figure 6.3 shows the role of MIS within the flow of an organisation's information. Note that business transactions can enter the organisation through traditional methods or via the internet or an extranet connecting customers and suppliers to the firm's ERP or transaction processing systems. The use of MIS spans all levels of management. That is, they provide support to and are used by employees throughout the organisation.

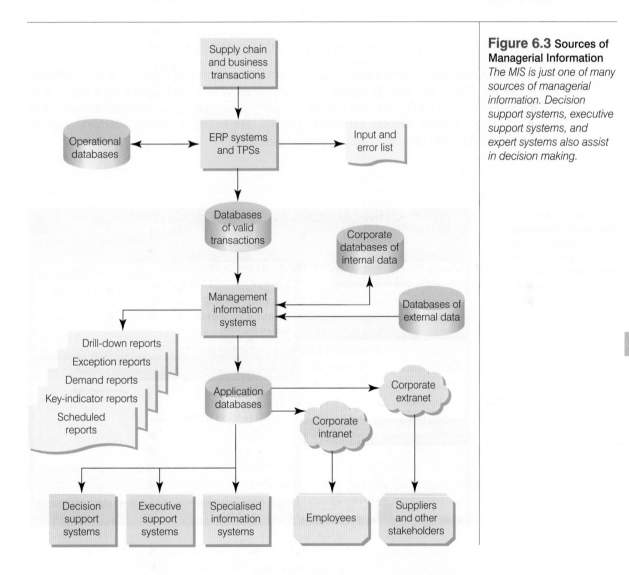

Figure 6.3 Sources of Managerial Information
The MIS is just one of many sources of managerial information. Decision support systems, executive support systems, and expert systems also assist in decision making.

Inputs to a Management Information System

As shown in Figure 6.3, data that enters an MIS originates from both internal and external sources, including the company's supply chain. The most significant internal data sources for an MIS are the organisation's various transaction processing systems. As discussed in Chapter 5, companies also use data warehouses and data marts to store valuable business information. Other internal data comes from specific functional areas throughout the firm.

External sources of data can include customers, suppliers, competitors, and stockholders whose data is not already captured by the TPS, as well as other sources, such as the internet. In addition, many companies have implemented extranets to link with selected suppliers and other business partners to exchange data and information.

The MIS uses the data obtained from these sources and processes it into information more usable by managers, primarily in the form of predetermined reports. For example, rather than simply obtaining a chronological list of sales activity over the past week, a national sales manager might obtain his organisation's weekly sales data in a format that allows him to see sales activity by region, by local sales representative, by product, and even in comparison with last year's sales.

Outputs of a Management Information System

The output of most management information systems is a collection of reports that are distributed to managers. These can include tabulations, summaries, charts, and graphs (see Figure 6.4). Management reports can come from various company databases, data warehouses, and other sources. These reports include scheduled reports, key-indicator reports, demand reports, exception reports, and drill-down reports (see Figure 6.5).

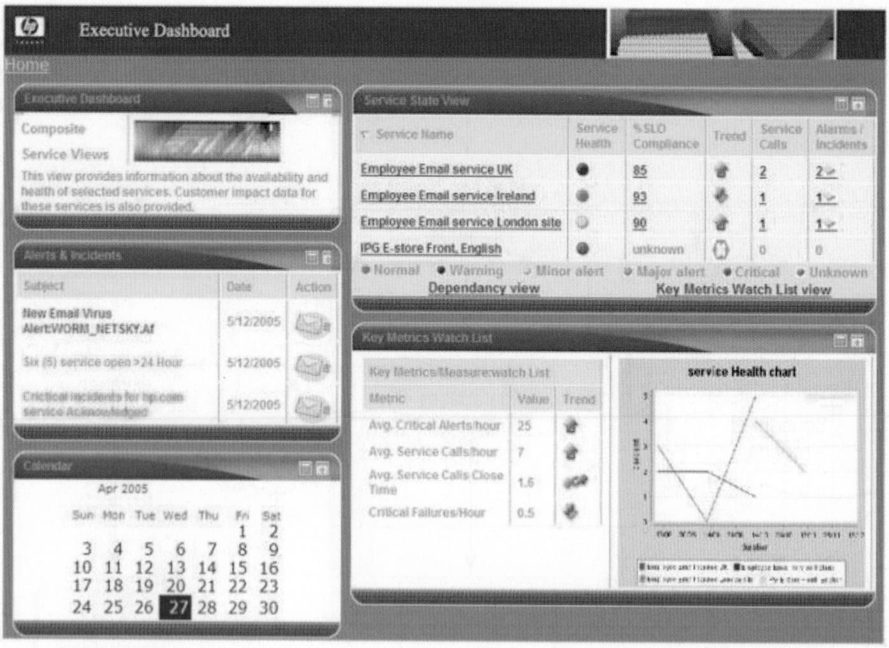

Figure 6.4 An Executive Dashboard
This MIS reporting system puts many kinds of real-time information at managers' fingertips to aid in decision making.

Scheduled Reports

scheduled report A report produced periodically, or on a schedule, such as daily, weekly, or monthly.

Scheduled reports are produced periodically, or on a schedule, such as daily, weekly, or monthly. For example, a production manager could use a weekly summary report that lists total payroll costs to monitor and control labour and job costs. A manufacturing report generated once per day to

Figure 6.5 Reports Generated by an MIS
The types of reports are (a) scheduled, (b) key indicator, (c) demand, (d) exception, and (e–h) drill down.

(a) Scheduled Report

Daily Sales Detail Report

Prepared: 08/10/08

Order #	Customer ID	Salesperson ID	Planned Ship Date	Quantity	Item #	Amount
P12453	C89321	CAR	08/12/08	144	P1234	€3214
P12453	C89321	CAR	08/12/08	288	P3214	€5660
P12454	C03214	GWA	08/13/08	12	P4902	€1224
P12455	C52313	SAK	08/12/08	24	P4012	€2448
P12456	C34123	JMW	08/13/08	144	P3214	€720
....	....	....	....	....	....	....

(b) Key-Indicator Report

Daily Sales Key-Indicator Report

	This Month	Last Month	Last Year
Total Orders Month to Date	€1808	€1694	€1914
Forecasted Sales for the Month	€2406	€2224	€2608

(c) Demand Report

Daily Sales by Salesperson Summary Report

Prepared: 08/10/08

Salesperson ID	Amount
CAR	€42 345
GWA	€38 950
SAK	€22 100
JWN	€12 350
....	....
....	....

(d) Exception Report

Daily Sales Exception Report—Orders Over €10 000

Prepared: 08/10/08

Order #	Customer ID	Salesperson ID	Planned Ship Date	Quantity	Item #	Amount
P12345	C89321	GWA	08/12/08	576	P1234	€12 856
P22153	C00453	CAR	08/12/08	288	P2314	€28 800
P23023	C32832	JMN	08/11/08	144	P2323	€14 400
....	....	....	....	....	....	....
....	....	....	....	....	....	....

monitor the production of a new item is another example of a scheduled report. Other scheduled reports can help managers control customer credit, performance of sales representatives, inventory levels, and more.

A **key-indicator report** summarises the previous day's critical activities and is typically available at the beginning of each workday. These reports can summarise inventory levels, production activity, sales volume, and the like.

key-indicator report A summary of the previous day's critical activities; typically available at the beginning of each workday.

Figure 6.5 *Continued*

(e) First-Level Drill-Down Report

Earnings by Quarter (Millions)

		Actual	Forecast	Variance
2nd Qtr.	2008	€12.6	€11.8	6.8%
1st Qtr.	2008	€10.8	€10.7	0.9%
4th Qtr.	2008	€14.3	€14.5	−1.4%
3rd Qtr.	2008	€12.8	€13.3	−3.8%

(f) Second-Level Drill-Down Report

Sales and Expenses (Millions)

Qtr: 2nd Qtr. 2008	Actual	Forecast	Variance
Gross Sales	€110.9	€108.3	2.4%
Expenses	€ 98.3	€ 96.5	1.9%
Profit	12.6	€ 11.8	6.8%

(g) Third-Level Drill-Down Report

Sales by Division (Millions)

Qtr: 2nd Qtr. 2008	Actual	Forecast	Variance
Beauty Care	€ 34.5	€ 33.9	1.8%
Health Care	€ 30.0	€ 28.0	7.1%
Soap	€ 22.8	€ 23.0	−0.9%
Snacks	€ 12.1	€ 12.5	−3.2%
Electronics	€ 11.5	€ 10.9	5.5%
Total	€110.9	€108.3	2.4%

(h) Fourth-Level Drill-Down Report

Sales by Product Category (Millions)

Qtr: 2nd Qtr. 2008 Division: Health Care	Actual	Forecast	Variance
Toothpaste	€12.4	€10.5	18.1%
Mouthwash	€ 8.6	€ 8.8	−2.3%
Over-the-Counter Drugs	€ 5.8	€ 5.3	9.4%
Skin Care Products	€ 3.2	€ 3.4	−5.9%
Total	€30.0	€28.0	7.1%

SOURCE: George W. Reynolds, *Information Systems for Managers* (3rd ed.), St. Paul, MN: West Publishing Co., 1995.

Key-indicator reports are used by managers and executives to take quick, corrective action on significant aspects of the business.

Demand Reports

demand report A report developed to give certain information at someone's request.

Demand reports are developed to give certain information upon request. In other words, these reports are produced on demand. Like other reports discussed in this section, they often come from an organisation's database system. For example, an executive might want to know the production status of a particular item; a demand report can be generated to provide the requested information by querying the company's database. Suppliers and customers can also use demand reports. FedEx, for example, provides demand reports on its website to allow its customers to track packages from their source to their final destination. Other examples of demand reports include reports requested by executives to show the hours worked by a particular employee, total sales to date for a product, and so on. Today, many demand reports are generated from the internet or by using cloud computing.[7]

Exception Reports

Exception reports are reports that are automatically produced when a situation is unusual or requires management action. For example, a manager might set a parameter that generates a report of all items that have been purchased and then returned by more than five customers. Such items may need to be looked at to identify any production problem, for instance. As with key-indicator reports, exception reports are most often used to monitor aspects important to an organisation's success. In general, when an exception report is produced, a manager or executive takes action. Parameters, or trigger points, for an exception report should be set carefully. Trigger points that are set too low might result in too many exception reports; trigger points that are too high could mean that problems requiring action are overlooked. For example, if a manager wants a report that contains all projects over budget by €1000 or more, the system might retrieve almost every company project. The €1000 trigger point is probably too low. A trigger point of €10 000 might be more appropriate.

exception report A report automatically produced when a situation is unusual or requires management action.

Drill-Down Reports

Drill-down reports provide increasingly detailed data about a situation. Through the use of drill-down reports, analysts can see data at a high level first (such as sales for the entire company), then at a more detailed level (such as the sales for one department of the company), and then a very detailed level (such as sales for one sales representative). Managers can drill down into more levels of detail to individual transactions if they want. Boehringer Ingelheim, a large German drug company with thousands of employees in 60 countries, uses a variety of drill-down reports so it can respond rapidly to changing market conditions. Managers can drill down into more levels of detail to individual transactions if they want.

drill-down report A report providing increasingly detailed data about a situation.

6

Developing Effective Reports

Management information system reports can help managers develop better plans, make better decisions, and obtain greater control over the operations of the firm, but, in practice, the types of reports can overlap. For example, a manager can demand an exception report or set trigger points for items contained in a key-indicator report. In addition, some software packages can be used to produce, gather, and distribute reports from different computer systems. Certain guidelines should be followed in designing and developing reports to yield the best results. Table 6.1 explains some of these guidelines.

Table 6.1 Guidelines for Developing MIS Reports

Guidelines	Reason
Tailor each report to user needs	The unique needs of the manager or executive should be considered, requiring user involvement and input.
Spend time and effort producing only reports that are useful	After being instituted, many reports continue to be generated even if no one uses them anymore.
Pay attention to report content and layout	Prominently display the information that is most desired. Do not clutter the report with unnecessary data. Use commonly accepted words and phrases. Managers can work more efficiently if they can easily find desired information.
Use management-by-exception reporting	Some reports should be produced only when a problem needs to be solved or an action should be taken.
Set parameters carefully	Low parameters might result in too many reports; high parameters mean valuable information could be overlooked.
Produce all reports in a timely fashion	Outdated reports are of little or no value.
Periodically review reports	Review reports at least once per year to make sure they are still needed. Review report content and layout. Determine whether additional reports are needed.

6.3 Functional MIS

Most organisations are structured along functional lines or areas. This functional structure is usually apparent from an organisation chart. Some traditional functional areas are finance, manufacturing, marketing, and human resources, among others. The MIS can also be divided along those functional lines to produce reports tailored to individual functions (see Figure 6.6).

Financial Management Information Systems

A **financial MIS** provides financial information not only for executives, but also for a broader set of people who need to make better decisions on a daily basis. Financial MIS are used to streamline reports of transactions. Most financial MIS perform the following functions:

financial MIS A management information system that provides financial information not only for executives, but also for a broader set of people who need to make better decisions on a daily basis.

- Integrate financial and operational information from multiple sources, including the internet, into a single system.

- Provide easy access to data for both financial and nonfinancial users, often through the use of a corporate intranet to access corporate web pages of financial data and information.

- Make financial data immediately available to shorten analysis turnaround time.

- Enable analysis of financial data along multiple dimensions – time, geography, product, plant, customer.

- Analyze historical and current financial activity.

- Monitor and control the use of funds over time.

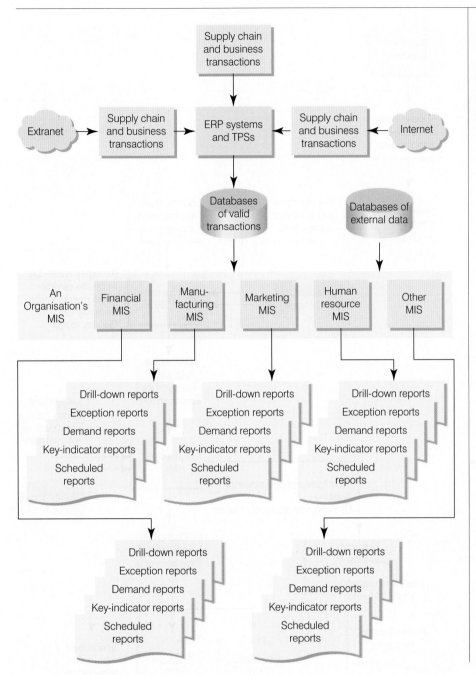

Figure 6.6 An Organisation's MIS
The MIS is an integrated collection of functional information systems, each supporting particular functional areas.

Figure 6.7 shows typical inputs, function-specific subsystems, and outputs of a financial MIS, including profit and loss, auditing, and uses and management of funds.

Financial MIS are used to compute revenues, costs, and profits and for **auditing**. Auditing involves analyzing the financial condition of an organisation and determining whether financial statements and reports produced by the financial MIS are accurate. Financial MIS are also used to manage funds. Internal uses of funds include purchasing additional inventory, updating plants and equipment, hiring new employees, acquiring other companies, buying new computer systems, increasing marketing and advertising, purchasing raw materials or land, investing in new products, and increasing research and development. External uses of funds are

auditing analyzing the financial condition of an organisation and determining whether financial statements and reports produced by the financial MIS are accurate.

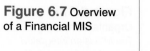

Figure 6.7 Overview of a Financial MIS

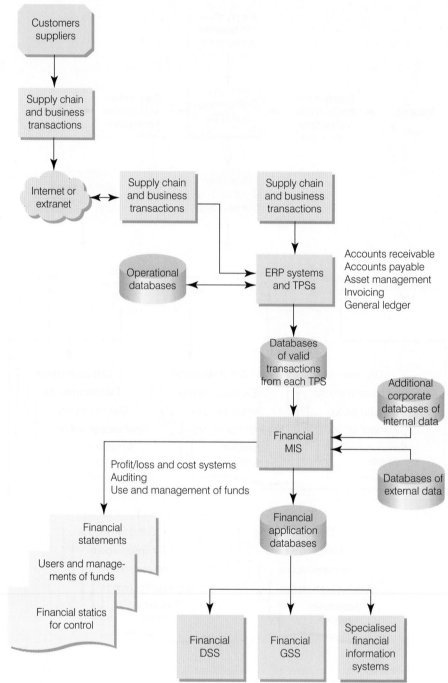

typically investment related. Companies often invest excess funds in such external revenue generators as bank accounts, stocks, bonds, bills, notes, futures, options, and foreign currency using financial MIS.

Manufacturing Management Information Systems

More than any other functional area, advances in information systems have revolutionised manufacturing. As a result, many manufacturing operations have been dramatically improved over the last decade. Also, with the emphasis on greater quality and productivity, having an effective manufacturing process is becoming even more critical. The use of computerised systems is emphasised at all levels of manufacturing – from the shop floor to the executive suite. People and small businesses, for example, can benefit from manufacturing MIS that once were only available to large corporations. Personal fabrication systems, for example, can make circuit boards, precision parts, radio tags, and more.[8] Personal fabrication systems include precise machine tools, such as milling machines and cutting tools and sophisticated software. The total system can cost €15 000. For example, in a remote area of Norway, Maakon Karlson uses a personal fabrication system that makes radio tags to track sheep and other animals. The use of the internet has also streamlined all aspects of manufacturing. Figure 6.8 gives an overview of some of the manufacturing MIS inputs, subsystems, and outputs.

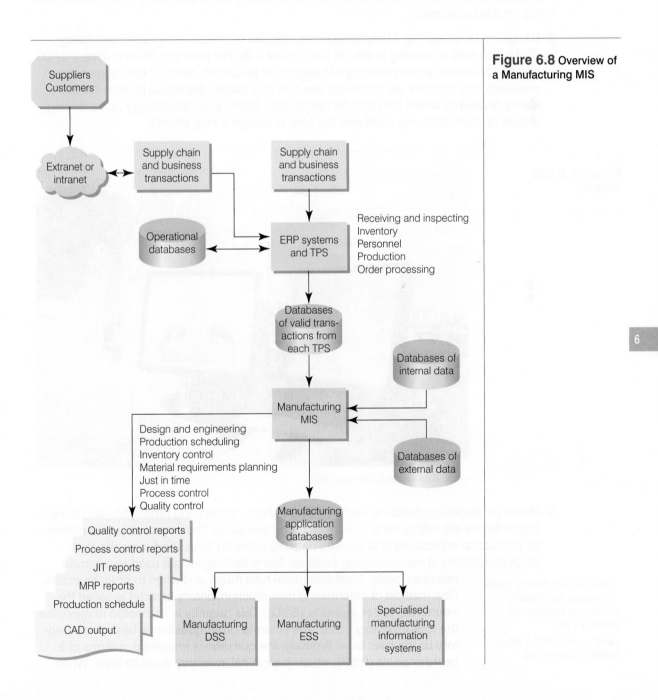

Figure 6.8 Overview of a Manufacturing MIS

The manufacturing MIS subsystems and outputs monitor and control the flow of materials, products, and services through the organisation. As raw materials are converted to finished goods, the manufacturing MIS monitors the process at almost every stage. New technology could make this process easier. Using specialised computer chips and tiny radio transmitters, companies can monitor materials and products through the entire manufacturing process. Car manufacturers, who convert raw steel, plastic, and other materials into a finished automobile, also monitor their manufacturing processes. Auto manufacturers add thousands of dollars of value to the raw materials they use in assembling a car. If the manufacturing MIS also lets them provide additional services, such as customised paint colours, on any of their models, it has added further value for customers. In doing so, the MIS helps provide the company the edge that can differentiate it from competitors. The success of an organisation can depend on the manufacturing function. Some common information subsystems and outputs used in manufacturing are discussed next.

■ *Design and engineering.* Manufacturing companies often use computer-aided design (CAD) with new or existing products (see Figure 6.9). For example, Boeing uses a CAD system to develop a complete digital blueprint of an aircraft before it ever begins its manufacturing process. As mock-ups are built and tested, the digital blueprint is constantly revised to reflect the most current design. Using such technology helps Boeing reduce its manufacturing costs and the time to design a new aircraft.

Figure 6.9 CAD Software

SOURCE: © Ian Lishman/Juice Images/Corbis.

■ *Master production scheduling and inventory control.* Scheduling production and controlling inventory are critical for any manufacturing company. The overall objective of master production scheduling is to provide detailed plans for both short-term and long-range scheduling of manufacturing facilities. Many techniques are used to minimise inventory costs. Most determine how much and when to order inventory. One method of determining how much inventory to order is called the **economic order quantity (EOQ)**. This quantity is calculated to minimise the total inventory costs. The when-to-order question is based on inventory usage over time. Typically, the question is answered in terms of a **reorder point (ROP)**, which is a critical inventory quantity level. When

economic order quantity (EOQ) The quantity that should be reordered to minimise total inventory costs.

reorder point (ROP) A critical inventory quantity level.

the inventory level for a particular item falls to the reorder point, or critical level, the system generates a report so that an order is immediately placed for the EOQ of the product. Another inventory technique used when the demand for one item depends on the demand for another is called **material requirements planning (MRP)**. The basic goal of MRP is to determine when finished products, such as automobiles or airplanes, are needed and then to work backward to determine deadlines and resources needed, such as engines and tires, to complete the final product on schedule. **Just-in-time (JIT) inventory** and manufacturing is an approach that maintains inventory at the lowest levels without sacrificing the availability of finished products. With this approach, inventory and materials are delivered just before they are used in a product. A JIT inventory system would arrange for a car windscreen to be delivered to the assembly line just before it is secured to the automobile, rather than storing it in the manufacturing facility while the car's other components are being assembled. JIT, however, can result in some organisations running out of inventory when demand exceeds expectations.[9]

material requirements planning (MRP) A set of inventory-control techniques that help coordinate thousands of inventory items when the demand of one item is dependent on the demand for another.

just-in-time (JIT) inventory A philosophy of inventory management in which inventory and materials are delivered just before they are used in manufacturing a product.

■ *Process control.* Managers can use a number of technologies to control and streamline the manufacturing process. For example, computers can directly control manufacturing equipment, using systems called **computer-aided manufacturing (CAM)**. CAM systems can control drilling machines, assembly lines, and more. **Computer-integrated manufacturing (CIM)** uses computers to link the components of the production process into an effective system. CIM's goal is to tie together all aspects of production, including order processing, product design, manufacturing, inspection and quality control, and shipping. A **flexible manufacturing system (FMS)** is an approach that allows manufacturing facilities to rapidly and efficiently change from making one product to another. In the middle of a production run, for example, the production process can be changed to make a different product or to switch manufacturing materials. By using an FMS, the time and cost to change manufacturing jobs can be substantially reduced, and companies can react quickly to market needs and competition.

computer-aided manufacturing (CAM) A system that directly controls manufacturing equipment.

computer-integrated manufacturing (CIM) Using computers to link the components of the production process into an effective system.

flexible manufacturing system (FMS) An approach that allows manufacturing facilities to rapidly and efficiently change from making one product to making another.

■ *Quality control and testing.* With increased pressure from consumers and a general concern for productivity and high quality, today's manufacturing organisations are placing more emphasis on **quality control**, a process that ensures that the finished product meets the customers' needs. Information systems are used to monitor quality and take corrective steps to eliminate possible quality problems.

quality control A process that ensures that the finished product meets the customers' needs.

Marketing Management Information Systems

A **marketing MIS** supports managerial activities in product development, distribution, pricing decisions, promotional effectiveness, and sales forecasting. Marketing functions are increasingly being performed on the internet. Many companies are developing internet marketplaces to advertise and sell products. Estée Lauder and Sony have developed a sitcom called Sufie's Diary on an internet site to entertain young viewers and advertise Clinique, a popular Estée Lauder cosmetic, along with various Sony products.[10] The amount spent on online advertising is worth billions of euros annually. Software can measure how many customers see the advertising. Some companies use software products to analyze customer loyalty. Some marketing departments are actively using blogs to publish company related information and interact with customers.[11]

marketing MIS An information system that supports managerial activities in product development, distribution, pricing decisions, and promotional effectiveness.

Customer relationship management (CRM) programs, available from some ERP vendors, help a company manage all aspects of customer encounters. CRM software can help a company collect customer data, contact customers, educate customers on new products, and sell products to customers through a website. An airline, for example, can use a CRM system to notify customers about flight changes. Yet, not all CRM systems and marketing sites on the internet are successful. Customisation and ongoing maintenance of a CRM system can be expensive. Figure 6.10 shows the inputs, subsystems, and outputs of a typical marketing MIS.

Figure 6.10 Overview of a Marketing MIS

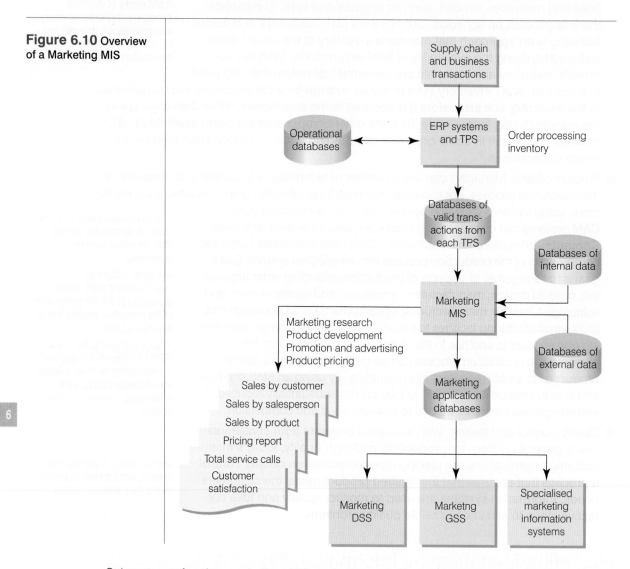

Subsystems for the marketing MIS include marketing research, product development, promotion and advertising, and product pricing. These subsystems and their outputs help marketing managers and executives increase sales, reduce marketing expenses, and develop plans for future products and services to meet the changing needs of customers.

- *Marketing research.* The purpose of marketing research is to conduct a formal study of the market and customer preferences. Computer systems are used to help conduct and analyze the results of surveys, questionnaires, pilot studies, and interviews.

- *Product development.* Product development involves the conversion of raw materials into finished goods and services and focuses primarily on the physical attributes of the product. Many factors, including plant capacity, labour skills, engineering factors, and materials are important in product development decisions. In many cases, a computer program analyzes these various factors and selects the appropriate mix of labour, materials, plant and equipment, and engineering designs. Make-or-buy decisions can also be made with the assistance of computer programs.

■ *Promotion and advertising.* One of the most important functions of any marketing effort is promotion and advertising. Product success is a direct function of the types of advertising and sales promotion done. Increasingly, organisations are using the internet to advertise and sell products and services.

■ *Product pricing.* Product pricing is another important and complex marketing function. Retail price, wholesale price, and price discounts must be set. Most companies try to develop pricing policies that will maximise total sales revenues. Computers are often used to analyze the relationship between prices and total revenues.

■ *Sales analysis.* Computerised sales analysis is important to identify products, sales personnel, and customers that contribute to profits and those that do not. Several reports can be generated to help marketing managers make good sales decisions (see Figure 6.11). The sales-by-product report lists all major products and their sales for

(a) Sales-by-product

Product	August	September	October	November	December	Total
Product 1	34	32	32	21	33	152
Product 2	156	162	177	163	122	780
Product 3	202	145	122	98	66	633
Product 4	345	365	352	341	288	1691

(b) Sales-by-salesperson

Salesperson	August	September	October	November	December	Total
Jones	24	42	42	11	43	162
Kline	166	155	156	122	133	732
Lane	166	155	104	99	106	630
Miller	245	225	305	291	301	1367

(c) Sales-by-customer

Customer	August	September	October	November	December	Total
Ang	234	334	432	411	301	1712
Braswell	56	62	77	61	21	277
Celec	1202	1445	1322	998	667	5634
Jung	45	65	55	34	88	287

Figure 6.11 Reports Generated to Help Marketing Managers Make Good Decisions
(a) This sales-by-product report lists all major products and their sales for the period from August to December. (b) This sales-by-salesperson report lists total sales for each salesperson for the same time period. (c) This sales-by-customer report lists sales for each customer for the period. Like all MIS reports, totals are provided automatically by the system to show managers at a glance the information they need to make good decisions.

6

a period of time, such as a month. This report shows which products are doing well and which need improvement or should be discarded altogether. The sales-by-salesperson report lists total sales for each salesperson for each week or month. This report can also be subdivided by product to show which products are being sold by each salesperson. The sales-by-customer report is a tool that can be used to identify high- and low-volume customers.

Human Resource Management Information Systems

A **human resource MIS (HRMIS)**, also called a personnel MIS, is concerned with activities related to previous, current, and potential employees of the organisation. Because the personnel function relates to all other functional areas in the business, the human resource (HR) MIS plays a valuable role in ensuring organisational success. Increasingly, the HRMIS is being used to oversee and manage part-time, virtual work teams and job sharing, in additional to traditional job titles and duties.[12] Some of the activities performed by this important MIS include workforce analysis and planning, hiring, training, job and task assignment, and many other personnel-related issues. An effective HRMIS allows a company to keep personnel costs at a minimum, while serving the required business processes needed to achieve corporate goals. Although human resource information systems focus on cost reduction, many of today's HR systems concentrate on hiring and managing existing employees to get the total potential of the human talent in the organisation. According to the High Performance Workforce Study conducted by Accenture, the most important HR initiatives include improving worker productivity, improving adaptability to new opportunities, and facilitating organisational change. Figure 6.12 shows some of the inputs, subsystems, and outputs of the HRMIS.

human resource MIS (HRMIS)
An information system that is concerned with activities related to employees and potential employees of an organisation, also called a personnel MIS.

Human resource subsystems and outputs range from the determination of human resource needs and hiring through retirement and outplacement. Most medium and large organisations have computer systems to assist with human resource planning, hiring, training and skills inventorying, and wage and salary administration. Outputs of the human resource MIS include reports, such as human resource planning reports, job application review profiles, skills inventory reports, and salary surveys.

- ■ *Human resource planning.* One of the first aspects of any HRMIS is determining personnel and human needs. The overall purpose of this MIS subsystem is to put the right number and kinds of employees in the right jobs when they are needed. Effective human resource planning can require computer programs, such as SPSS and SAS, to forecast the future number of employees needed and anticipating the future supply of people for these jobs.

- ■ *Personnel selection and recruiting.* If the human resource plan reveals that additional personnel are required, the next logical step is recruiting and selecting personnel. Companies seeking new employees often use computers to schedule recruiting efforts and trips and to test potential employees' skills. Many companies now use the internet to screen for job applicants. Applicants use a template to load their Curriculum Vitaes onto the internet site. HR managers can then access these CVs and identify applicants they are interested in interviewing.

- ■ *Training and skills inventory.* Some jobs, such as programming, equipment repair, and tax preparation, require very specific training for new employees. Other jobs may require general training about the organisational culture, orientation, dress standards, and expectations of the organisation. When training is complete, employees often take computer-scored tests to evaluate their mastery of skills and new material.

- ■ *Scheduling and job placement.* Employee schedules are developed for each employee, showing his or her job assignments over the next week or month. Job placements are

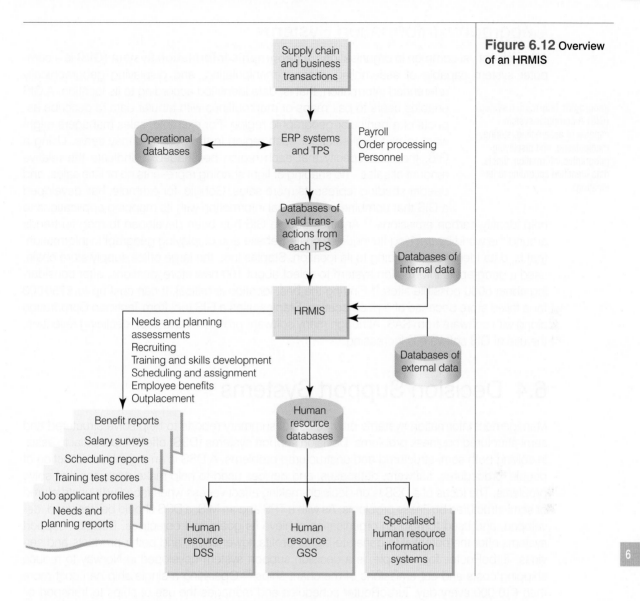

Figure 6.12 Overview of an HRMIS

often determined based on skills inventory reports, which show which employee might be best suited to a particular job. Sophisticated scheduling programs are often used in the airline industry, the military, and many other areas to get the right people assigned to the right jobs at the right time.

■ *Wage and salary administration.* Another HRMIS subsystem involves determining salaries and benefits, including medical insurance and pension payments. Wage data, such as industry averages for positions, can be taken from the corporate database and manipulated by the HRMIS to provide wage information reports to higher levels of management.

■ *Outplacement.* Employees leave a company for a variety of reasons. Outplacement services are offered by many companies to help employees make the transition. Outplacement can include job counseling and training, job and executive search, retirement and financial planning, and a variety of severance packages and options. Many employees use the internet to plan their future retirement or to find new jobs, using job sites, such as www.jobs.co.za in South Africa or www.jobsite.co.uk in the UK.

Geographic Information Systems

Although not yet common in organisations, a **geographic information system (GIS)** is a computer system capable of assembling, storing, manipulating, and displaying geographically referenced information, that is, data identified according to its location. A GIS enables users to pair maps or map outlines with tabular data to describe aspects of a particular geographic region. For example, sales managers might want to plot total sales for each region in the countries they serve. Using a GIS, they can specify that each region be shaded to indicate the relative amount of sales – no shading or light shading represents no or little sales, and deeper shading represents more sales. Google, for example, has developed a GIS that combines geothermal information with its mapping applications to help identify carbon emissions.[13] Another Google GIS has been developed to map flu trends around the world by tracking flu inquiries on its website and displaying geographic information, that is, data identified according to its location. Staples Inc., the large office supply store chain, used a geographic information system to select about 100 new store locations, after considering about 5000 possible sites.[14] Finding the best location is critical. It can cost up to €750 000 for a failed store because of a poor location. Staples uses a GIS tool from Tactician Corporation along with software from SAS. Although many software products have seen declining revenues, the use of GIS software is increasing.

> **geographic information system (GIS)** A computer system capable of assembling, storing, manipulating, and displaying geographic information, that is, data identified according to its location.

6.4 Decision Support Systems

Management information systems provide useful summary reports to help solve structured and semi-structured business problems. Decision support systems (DSS) offer the potential to assist in solving both semi-structured and unstructured problems. A DSS is an organised collection of people, procedures, software, databases, and devices used to help make decisions that solve problems. The focus of a DSS is on decision-making effectiveness when faced with unstructured or semi-structured business problems. As with a TPS and an MIS, a DSS should be designed, developed, and used to help an organisation achieve its goals and objectives. Decision support systems offer the potential to generate higher profits, lower costs, and better products and services. TurboRouter, for example, is a decision support system developed in Norway to reduce shipping costs and cut emissions of merchant ships.[15] Operating a single ship can cost more than €10 000 every day. TurboRouter schedules and manages the use of ships to transport oil and other products to locations around the world. Billerud, a paper mill company in Sweden, used a DSS optimisation program to control a bleaching process that reduced the need for certain chemicals by 10 per cent and saved the company about 2 million euros annually.[16]

Decision support systems, although skewed somewhat toward the top levels of management, are used at all levels. To some extent, today's managers at all levels are faced with less structured, nonroutine problems, but the quantity and magnitude of these decisions increase as a manager rises higher in an organisation. Many organisations contain a tangled web of complex rules, procedures, and decisions. DSS are used to bring more structure to these problems to aid the decision-making process. In addition, because of the inherent flexibility of decision support systems, managers at all levels are able to use DSS to assist in some relatively routine, programmable decisions in lieu of more formalised management information systems.

Capabilities of a Decision Support System

Developers of decision support systems strive to make them more flexible than management information systems and to give them the potential to assist decision makers in a variety of situations. DSS can assist with all or most problem solving phases, decision frequencies, and different degrees of problem structure. DSS approaches can also help at all levels of the decision-making process. A single DSS might provide only a few of these capabilities, depending on its uses and scope.

■ *Support for problem solving phases.* The objective of most decision support systems is to assist decision makers with the phases of problem solving. As previously discussed, these phases include intelligence, design, choice, implementation, and monitoring. A specific DSS might support only one or a few phases. By supporting all types of decision-making approaches, a DSS gives the decision maker a great deal of flexibility in getting computer support for decision-making activities.

■ *Support for different decision frequencies.* Decisions can range on a continuum from one-of-a-kind to repetitive decisions. One-of-a-kind decisions are typically handled by an ad hoc DSS. An **ad hoc DSS** is concerned with situations or decisions that come up only a few times during the life of the organisation; in small businesses, they might happen only once. For example, a company might need to change the layout of its open plan offices. Repetitive decisions are addressed by an institutional DSS. An **institutional DSS** handles situations or decisions that occur more than once, usually several times per year or more. An institutional DSS is used repeatedly and refined over the years. For example, a DSS used to assist help desk staff solve employees' computer problems and queries.

ad hoc DSS A DSS concerned with situations or decisions that come up only a few times during the life of the organisation.

institutional DSS A DSS that handles situations or decisions that occur more than once, usually several times per year or more. An institutional DSS is used repeatedly and refined over the years.

■ *Support for different problem structures.* As discussed previously, decisions can range from highly structured and programmed to unstructured and non-programmed.

Highly structured problems are straightforward, requiring known facts and relationships. **Semi-structured or unstructured problems**, on the other hand, are more complex. The relationships among the pieces of data are not always clear, the data might be in a variety of formats, and it is often difficult to manipulate or obtain. In addition, the decision maker might not know the information requirements of the decision in advance.

highly structured problems Problems that are straightforward and require known facts and relationships.

semi-structured or unstructured problems More complex problems in which the relationships among the pieces of data are not always clear, the data might be in a variety of formats, and the data is often difficult to manipulate or obtain.

■ *Support for various decision-making levels.* Decision support systems can provide help for managers at different levels within the organisa-tion. Operational managers can get assistance with daily and routine decision making. Tactical decision makers can use analysis tools to ensure proper plan-ning and control. At the strategic level, DSS can help managers by providing analysis for long-term decisions requiring both internal and external information (see Figure 6.13).

Figure 6.13 Decision-Making Level *Strategic managers are involved with long-term decisions, which are often made infrequently. Operational managers are involved with decisions that are made more frequently.*

A Comparison of DSS and MIS

A DSS differs from an MIS in numerous ways, including the type of problems solved, the support given to users, the decision emphasis and approach, and the type, speed, output, and development of the system used. Table 6.2 lists brief descriptions of these differences. You should note that entity resource planning systems include both MIS and DSS (and, as discussed in Chapter 5, TPS).

Table 6.2 Comparison of DSS and MIS

Factor	DSS	MIS
Problem Type	A DSS can handle unstructured problems that cannot be easily programmed.	An MIS is normally used only with structured problems.
Users	A DSS supports individuals, small groups, and the entire organisation. In the short run, users typically have more control over a DSS.	An MIS supports primarily the organisation. In the short run, users have less control over an MIS.
Support	A DSS supports all aspects and phases of decision making; it does not replace the decision maker – people still make the decisions.	This is not true of all MIS systems – some make automatic decisions and replace the decision maker.
Emphasis Approach	A DSS emphasises actual decisions and decision-making styles. A DSS is a direct support system that provides interactive reports on computer screens.	An MIS usually emphasises information only. An MIS is typically an indirect support system that uses regularly produced reports.
Speed	Because a DSS is flexible and can be implemented by users, it usually takes less time to develop and is better able to respond to user requests.	An MIS response time is usually longer.
Output	DSS reports are usually screen oriented, with the ability to generate reports on a printer.	An MIS, however, typically is oriented towards printed reports and documents.
Development	DSS users are usually more directly involved in its development. User involvement usually means better systems that provide superior support. For all systems, user involvement is the most important factor for the development of a successful system.	An MIS is frequently several years old and often was developed for people who are no longer performing the work supported by the MIS.

Components of a Decision Support System

dialogue manager A user interface that allows decision makers to easily access and manipulate the DSS and to use common business terms and phrases.

At the core of a DSS are a database and a model base. In addition, a typical DSS contains a user interface, also called **dialogue manager**, that allows decision makers to easily access and manipulate the DSS and to use common business terms and phrases. Finally, access to the internet, networks, and other computer-based systems permits the DSS to tie into other powerful systems, including the TPS or function-specific subsystems. internet software agents, for example, can be used in creating powerful decision support systems. Figure 6.14 shows a conceptual model of a DSS, although specific DSS might not have all these components.

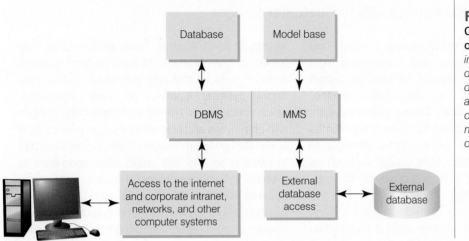

Figure 6.14
Conceptual Model of a DSS *DSS components include a model base; database; external database access; and access to the internet and corporate intranet, networks, and other computer systems.*

The Database

The database management system allows managers and decision makers to perform qualitative analysis on the company's vast stores of data in databases, data warehouses, and data marts (discussed in Chapter 3). DSS tap into vast stores of information contained in the corporate database, retrieving information on inventory, sales, personnel, production, finance, accounting, and other areas.[17] Data mining and business intelligence, introduced in Chapter 5, are often used in DSS. Airline companies, for example, use a DSS to help it identify customers for round-trip flights between major cities. The DSS can be used to search a data warehouse to contact thousands of customers who might be interested in an inexpensive flight. A casino can use a DSS to search large databases to get detailed information on patrons. It can tell how much each patron spends per day on gambling and more. Opportunity International uses a DSS to help it make loans and provide services to tsunami victims and others in need around the world.[18] According to the information services manager of Opportunity International, "We need to pull all the data . . . to one central database that we can analyze, and we need a way to get that information back out to people in the field." DSS can also be used in emergency medical situations to make split-second, life-or-death treatment decisions.[19]

A database management system can also connect to external databases to give managers and decision makers even more information and decision support. External databases can include the internet, libraries, government databases, and more. The combination of internal and external database access can give key decision makers a better understanding of the company and its environment.

The Model Base

In addition to the data, a DSS needs a model of how elements of the data are related, in order to help make decisions. The **model base** allows managers and decision makers to perform quantitative analysis on both internal and external data.[20] The model base gives decision makers access to a variety of models so that they can explore different scenarios and see their effects. Ultimately, it assists them in the decision-making process. Procter & Gamble, maker of Pringles potato chips, Pampers nappies, and hundreds of other consumer products, use DSS to streamline how raw materials and products flow from its suppliers to its customers, saving

model base Part of a DSS that provides decision makers access to a variety of models and assists them in decision making.

Information Systems at Work

Southwest Airlines Applies MIS to Customer Service

Perhaps one of the most frustrating parts of long distance travel is dealing with unexpected flight delays, which can be caused by weather, aircraft mechanical problems, overbooked flights, or other unexpected circumstances. Delays strand travelers away from their destinations for hours or sometimes even for days. Some airlines make attempts to notify passengers about flight delays as soon as they become evident in hopes of saving the passenger needless waiting.

Southwest Airlines has been doing this for years. Southwest prides itself on clever, unique approaches to customer service that it calls "The Southwest Way." The airline makes special efforts to satisfy customers that have been inconvenienced. Fred Taylor is Southwest's Senior Manager of Proactive Customer Service Communications. The New York Times has nicknamed Fred Southwest's "Chief Apology Officer." It's Fred's job to make sure customers who experience difficulties are left with options that leave them feeling satisfied. When Fred found out that Southwest was given a low score for its flight notification service in a Wall Street Journal poll, he took action. Although information systems are typically credited for providing business managers and decision makers with information they can use, they also supply information that customers can use. Information generated by MIS and DSS can act as a service to a company's customers, such as with Google Search, or as a value added, such as UPS package tracking. Another example is Amazon, which uses information about purchases customers have made on the Amazon website to recommend other products that might interest them. Fred Taylor of Southwest Airlines wanted to empower his customers with up-to-the-minute reports on flight information. Not only would his system notify travelers of flight delays, but also of gate changes, opportunities to upgrade, cancellations and rescheduling, and other information that can assist travelers with their preparations. Fred decided that the best way to inform passengers of preflight information was by phone. Southwest does not have access to all passengers' email addresses or cell phone numbers, so it cannot depend on email or text messaging. It does, however, have access to all customers' phone numbers. Fred and his team reviewed a dozen services that offer automated phone messaging systems. It settled on Varolii Corporation, which specialises in helping companies stay in touch with employees and customers through personalised automated phone messages. Fred and his team had to develop an MIS that pulled information from its reservation database provided by Sabre reservations systems and from Southwest's own database that manages flight information. The output of the MIS needed to be a report containing passenger names and phone numbers of those who had reservations on flights that were changed, along with details about the disruption. This information had to be delivered in a format that Varolii's system could take as input. The reports also had to be generated quickly so that passengers received the notification as it was delivered to Southwest personnel. In the early testing of the system, Fred received a call from a flustered gate attendant who had a line of passengers asking about a gate change notification. The passengers had received notification before the attendant! After that, a slight delay was programmed into the system to make sure that the information was disseminated to the right people at the right time.

As Fred and his crew rolled out the new system, they included a failsafe to make sure no misinformation was mistakenly sent to passengers. Each notification requires a human review prior to sending the information to Varolii for phoning. Once a notification gets approved, customers' phones ring within seconds. Upon answering, the customer hears a chime, indicating an automated message, and a personable voice that proclaims, "This is Southwest Airlines calling." The message continues with details on flight information and advice on how to proceed and ends with the offer to connect the customer to a service representative. Southwest is now collecting travelers' cell phone numbers and email addresses so it can extend its service to other forms of communication. Its Chief Apology Officer continues to explore new ways to apply information systems to making customers happy.

Discussion Questions

1 What were the unique aspects and requirements of Southwest's customer notification MIS?

2 How does this information assist Southwest in gaining a competitive advantage?

Critical Thinking Questions

1 In what other ways could airline information systems assist with increasing customer satisfaction?

2 Many banks use Varolii's phone service for notifying customers who are late making loan payments. What are the benefits and drawbacks of using automated communications systems compared to human communication?

SOURCES: Carr, David, "Southwest Upgrades Customer Service," CIO Insight, August 31, 2009. Available from: www.cioinsight.com/index2.php?option= content&task=view&id=882809&pop=1&hide_ads=1&page=0&hide_js=1; Southwest Airlines website. Available from: www.southwest.com. Accessed March 24, 2010; Varolii website www.varolii.com. Accessed March 24, 2010.

millions of euros.[21] Scientists and mathematicians also use DSS.[22] DSS can be excellent at predicting customer behaviours.[23] Most banks, for example, use models to help forecast which customers will be late with payments or might default on their loans.

The models and algorithms used in a DSS are often reviewed and revised over time.[24] As a result of Hurricane Katrina in the US, for example, American insurance companies plan to revise their models about storm damage and insurance requirements.[25]

Model management software (MMS) is often used to coordinate the use of models in a DSS, including financial, statistical analysis, graphical, and project-management models. Depending on the needs of the decision maker, one or more of these models can be used (see Table 6.3).

model management software
Software that coordinates the use of models in a DSS.

Table 6.3 Model Management Software

DSS often use financial, statistical, graphical, and project-management models

Model Type	Description	Software
Financial	Provides cash flow, internal rate of return, and other investment analysis	Spreadsheet, such as Microsoft Excel
Statistical	Provides summary statistics, trend projections, hypothesis testing, and more	Statistical program, such as SPSS or SAS
Graphical	Assists decision makers in designing, developing, and using graphic displays of data and information	Graphics programs, such as Microsoft PowerPoint
Project Management	Handles and coordinates large projects; also used to identify critical activities and tasks that could delay or jeopardise an entire project if they are not completed in a timely and cost-effective fashion	Project management software, such as Microsoft Project

The User Interface or Dialogue Manager

The user interface or dialogue manager allows users to interact with the DSS to obtain information. It assists with all aspects of communications between the user and the hardware and software that constitute the DSS. In a practical sense, to most DSS users, the user interface is the DSS. Upper-level decision makers are often less interested in where the information came from or how it was gathered than that the information is both understandable and accessible.

6.5 Group Support Systems

group support system (GSS)
Software application that consists of most elements in a DSS, plus software to provide effective support in group decision making; also called "group decision support system."

The DSS approach has resulted in better decision making for all levels of individual users. However, many DSS approaches and techniques are not suitable for a group decision-making environment. Although not all workers and managers are involved in committee meetings and group decision-making sessions, some tactical and strategic-level managers can spend more than half their decision-making time in a group setting. Such managers need assistance with group decision making. A **group support system (GSS)**, also called a group decision support system, consists of most of the elements in a DSS, plus software to provide effective support in group decision-making settings (see Figure 6.15).[26]

Figure 6.15
Configuration of a GSS
A GSS contains most of the elements found in a DSS, plus software to facilitate group member communications.

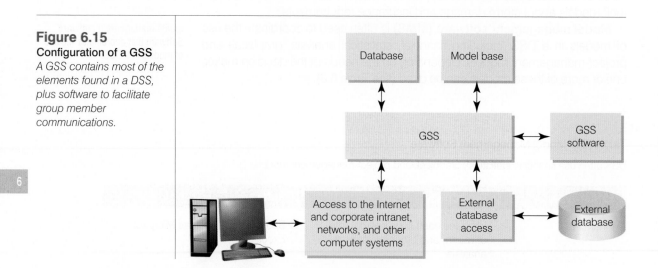

Group support systems are used in most industries. Architects are increasingly using GSS to help them collaborate with other architects and builders to develop the best plans and to compete for contracts. Manufacturing companies use GSS to link raw material suppliers to their own company systems.

Characteristics of a GSS that Enhance Decision Making

It is often said that two heads are better than one. When it comes to decision making, GSS unique characteristics have the potential to result in better decisions. Developers of these systems try to build on the advantages of individual support systems while adding new approaches, unique to group decision making. For example, some GSS can allow the exchange of information and expertise among people without direct face-to-face interaction.

Ethical and Societal Issues

Can search query trends provide the basis for an accurate, reliable model of real-world phenomena?

Google is the world's most popular search engine replacing for many people traditional fact finding exercises, such as using the phone book, going to a library, talking to a friend and watching the news. Every search term that is entered in a Google search is stored and used later by Google to provide new products and services. In 2008, Google wondered if their data could provide another service: early detection of outbreaks of disease.

When a user types a search term into Google, Google know roughly the physical location that user is in. If a user starts searching for an optician it is a reasonable guess that they are about to have an eye check up. If they start searching for back pain remedies, it is a reasonable guess that they or someone they know has a sore back. If they start searching for information about flu-like symptoms and flu remedies, it is a reasonable guess that they or someone they know has the flu. If a lot of users start searching for information about the flu, then it is a reasonable guess that a flu epidemic is on the way.

Google performed a test of this idea using historical data from 2007–2008. (These dates might not sound very "historical," but the point is that, since the events have already happened, Google knows whether an outbreak occurred, and they can see whether their system actually worked.) They gathered together all the flu-related search terms and the locations they came from and compared this with data from the US Centers for Disease Control and Prevention (CDC). The CDC data showed where patients went to their doctor and were diagnosed with the flu. The number of people going to their doctor was highly correlated with the number of flu search terms in the same area. Their idea worked!

With this system, Google claims to be able to estimate how much flu is circulating in different countries and regions around the world, but they want it to complement rather than replace traditional disease surveillance. Their website claims, "traditional flu surveillance is very important, but most health

agencies focus on a single country or region and only update their estimates once per week. Google Flu Trends is currently available for a number of countries around the world and is updated every day, providing a complement to these existing systems."

For health professionals, this is an exciting development, because early detection of a disease outbreak can reduce the number of people affected. If a new strain of flu virus emerges under certain conditions, a pandemic could ensue with the potential to cause millions of deaths. Google's up-to-date flu estimates may enable public health officials and health professionals to better respond to seasonal epidemics and pandemics.

Classifying this system is difficult, and the case highlights the growing tendency for systems to be integrated (see Chapter 5). The user interface of the search engine itself is a transaction processing system, with the transaction being a search term in exchange for search results. The behind the scenes work that the search engine does is a closely guarded secret, but it is some sort of data mining system used to produce the most relevant search results for a given search term. The inclusion of the location Flu Trends data turns the entire thing into a crude geographic information system. The reports and charts that Google puts on its Flu Trends webpages are produced by what would be called a management information system, and if the data were ever used to decide how to fight an outbreak it would be considered a decision support system.

Although not yet available in the UK, the service is available in South Africa – the first African country to be added – and throughout much of Europe.

However, although many think it is still valuable, some researchers are not convinced. A study at the University of Washington found that, when compared to the Centers for Disease Control's national surveillance of influenza lab tests, data from Google Flu Trends is 25 per cent less accurate at estimating rates of lab-confirmed influenza infections.

(continued)

Discussion Questions

1 What sort of system is this? How is it best described?

2 What else do you think search terms be used to predict?

Critical Thinking Questions

1 Does a user's search term, that is, the data that they type into the search engine, belong to them or Google?

2 Google search engine is a free service that people choose to use. Should Google be allowed to capture whatever data about its users that it can, or should there be restrictions?

SOURCES: Available from: http://www.google.org/flutrends/about/how.html. Accessed 9 Febuary 2011. CNET news, "Google Flu Trends: Take with grain of salt", 17 May 2010. Available from: http://news.cnet.com/8301-27083_3-20005150-247.html.

The following sections describe some characteristics that can improve and enhance decision making.

■ *Design for groups.* The GSS approach acknowledges that special procedures, devices, and approaches are needed in group decision-making settings. These procedures must foster creative thinking, effective communications, and good group decision-making techniques.

■ *Ease of use.* Like an individual DSS, a GSS must be easy to learn and use. Systems that are complex and hard to operate will seldom be used. Many groups have less tolerance than do individual decision makers for poorly developed systems.

■ *Flexibility.* Two or more decision makers working on the same problem might have different decision-making styles and preferences. Each manager makes decisions in a unique way, in part because of different experiences and cognitive styles. An effective GSS not only has to support the different approaches that managers use to make decisions, but also must find a means to integrate their different perspectives into a common view of the task at hand.

■ *Decision-making support.* A GSS can support different decision-making approaches, such as **brainstorming**, the **group consensus approach** or the **nominal group technique**.

■ *Anonymous input.* Many GSS allow anonymous input, where group members do not know which of them is giving the input. For example, some organisations use a GSS to help rank the performance of managers. Anonymous input allows the group decision makers to concentrate on the merits of the input without considering who gave it. In other words, input given by a top-level manager is given the same consideration as input from employees or other members of the group. Some studies have shown that groups using anonymous input can make better decisions and have superior results compared with groups that do not use anonymous input. Anonymous input, however, can result in flaming, where an unknown team member posts insults or even obscenities on the GSS.

■ *Reduction of negative group behaviour.* One key characteristic of any GSS is the ability to suppress or eliminate group behaviour that is counterproductive or harmful to effective decision making. In some group settings, dominant individuals can take over the discussion, which can prevent other members of the group from presenting creative alternatives. In other cases, one or two group members can sidetrack or

6

brainstorming A decision-making approach that often consists of members offering ideas "off the top of their heads."

group consensus approach A decision-making approach that forces members in the group to reach a unanimous decision.

nominal group technique A decision-making approach that encourages feedback from individual group members, and the final decision is made by voting, similar to the way public officials are elected.

subvert the group into areas that are non-productive and do not help solve the problem at hand. Other times, members of a group might assume they have made the right decision without examining alternatives – a phenomenon called "groupthink." If group sessions are poorly planned and executed, the result can be a tremendous waste of time. GSS designers are developing software and hardware systems to reduce these types of problems. Procedures for effectively planning and managing group meetings can be incorporated into the GSS approach. A trained meeting facilitator is often employed to help lead the group decision-making process and to avoid groupthink.

■ *Parallel communication.* With traditional group meetings, people must take turns addressing various issues. One person normally talks at a time. With a GSS, every group member can address issues or make comments at the same time by entering them into a PC or workstation. These comments and issues are displayed on every group member's PC or workstation immediately. Parallel communication can speed meeting times and result in better decisions.

■ *Automated recordkeeping.* Most GSS can keep detailed records of a meeting automatically. Each comment that is entered into a group member's PC or workstation can be recorded. In some cases, literally hundreds of comments can be stored for future review and analysis. In addition, most GSS packages have automatic voting and ranking features. After group members vote, the GSS records each vote and makes the appropriate rankings.

A picture showing a meeting using GSS is shown in Figure 6.16.

Figure 6.16 GSS
A group using a GSS.

© Dmitriy Shironosov/Shutterstock.com.

GSS Software

GSS software, often called groupware or workgroup software, helps with joint work group scheduling, communication, and management. Software from Autodesk, for example, has GSS capabilities that allow group members to work together on the design of manufacturing facilities, buildings, and other structures. Designers, for example, can use Autodesk's Buzzsaw Professional Online Collaboration Service, which works with AutoCAD, a design and engineering software product from Autodesk.

One popular package, IBM's Lotus Notes, can capture, store, manipulate, and distribute memos and communications that are developed during group projects. Some companies standardise on messaging and collaboration software, such as Lotus Notes. Lotus Connections is a feature of Lotus Notes that allows people to post documents and information on the internet. The feature is similar to popular social networking sites, such as Facebook, LinkedIn, and MySpace, but is designed for business use. Microsoft has invested billions of dollars in GSS software to incorporate collaborative features into its Office suite and related products. Office Communicator, for example, is a Microsoft product developed to allow better and faster collaboration. Other GSS software packages include Collabnet, OpenMind, and TeamWare. All of these tools can aid in group decision making. Shared electronic calendars can be used to coordinate meetings and schedules for decision-making teams. Using electronic calendars, team leaders can block out time for all members of the decision-making team.

A number of additional collaborative tools are available on the internet. Sharepoint (www.microsoft.com), WebOffice (www.weboffice.com), and BaseCamp (www.basecamphq.com) are just a few examples. Fuze Meeting (www.fuzemeeting.com) provides video collaboration tools on the internet.[27] The service can automatically bring participants into a live chat, allow workers to share information on their computer screens, and broadcast video content in high definition. Twitter (www.twitter.com) and Jaiku (www.jaiku.com) are internet sites that some organisations use to help people and groups stay connected and coordinate work schedules. Yammer (www.yammer.com) is similar to Twitter but aimed at business rather than social use (see Figure 6.17). Sermo (www.sermo.com) is a social networking site used by doctors to collaborate with other doctors, share their medical experiences, and even help make diagnoses. Teamspace (www.teamspace.com) is yet another collaborative software package that assists teams to successfully complete projects. Many of these internet packages embrace the use of Web 2.0 technologies. Some executives, however, worry about security and corporate compliance issues with any new technology.

Figure 6.17
Yammer is a microblogging site aimed at professional rather than social use.

In addition to stand-alone products, GSS software is increasingly being incorporated into existing software packages. Today, some transaction processing and enterprise resource planning packages include collaboration software. Some ERP producers (see Chapter 5), for example, have developed groupware to facilitate collaboration and to allow users to integrate applications from other vendors into the ERP system of programs. In addition to groupware, GSS use a number of tools discussed previously, including the following:

- Email, instant messaging (IM), and text messaging (TM)
- Video conferencing
- Group scheduling
- Project management
- Document sharing

6.6 Executive Support Systems

Because top-level executives often require specialised support when making strategic decisions, many companies have developed systems to assist executive decision making. This type of system, called an **executive support system (ESS)**, is a specialised DSS that includes all hardware, software, data, procedures, and people used to assist senior-level executives within the organisation. In some cases, an ESS, also called an executive information system (EIS), supports decision making of members of the board of directors, who are responsible to stockholders.

executive support system (ESS)
Specialised DSS that includes all hardware, software, data, procedures, and people used to assist senior-level executives within the organisation.

An ESS is a special type of DSS, and, like a DSS, an ESS is designed to support higher-level decision making in the organisation. The two systems are, however, different in important ways. DSS provide a variety of modelling and analysis tools to enable users to thoroughly analyze problems – that is, they allow users to answer questions. ESS present structured information about aspects of the organisation that executives consider important. In other words, they allow executives to ask the right questions.

The following are general characteristics of ESS:

- *Are tailored to individual executives.* ESS are typically tailored to individual executives; DSS are not tailored to particular users. They present information in the preferred format of that executive.
- *Are easy to use.* A top-level executive's most critical resource can be his or her time. Thus, an ESS must be easy to learn and use and not overly complex.
- *Have drill-down abilities.* An ESS allows executives to drill down into the company to determine how certain data was produced. Drilling down allows an executive to get more detailed information if needed.
- *Support the need for external data.* The data needed to make effective top-level decisions is often external – information from competitors, the federal government, trade associations and journals, consultants, and so on. An effective ESS can extract data useful to the decision maker from a wide variety of sources, including the internet and other electronic publishing sources.
- *Can help with situations that have a high degree of uncertainty.* Most executive decisions involve a high degree of uncertainty. Handling these unknown situations using modelling and other ESS procedures helps top-level managers measure the amount of risk in a decision.
- *Have a future orientation.* Executive decisions are future oriented, meaning that decisions will have a broad impact for years or decades. The information sources to support future-oriented decision making are usually informal – from organising golf partners to tying together members of social clubs or civic organisations.

■ *Are linked with value-added business processes.* Like other information systems, executive support systems are linked with executive decision making about value-added business processes.

Capabilities of Executive Support Systems

The responsibility given to top-level executives and decision makers brings unique problems and pressures to their jobs. The following is a discussion of some of the characteristics of executive decision making that are supported through the ESS approach. ESS take full advantage of data mining, the internet, blogs, podcasts, executive dashboards, and many other technological innovations. As you will note, most of these decisions are related to an organisation's overall profitability and direction. An effective ESS should have the capability to support executive decisions with components, such as strategic planning and organising, crisis management, and more.

■ *Support for defining an overall vision.* One of the key roles of senior executives is to provide a broad vision for the entire organisation. This vision includes the organisation's major product lines and services, the types of businesses it supports today and in the future, and its overriding goals.

strategic planning Determining long-term objectives by analyzing the strengths and weaknesses of the organisation, predicting future trends, and projecting the development of new product lines.

■ *Support for strategic planning.* ESS also support **strategic planning**. Strategic planning involves determining long-term objectives by analyzing the strengths and weaknesses of the organisation, predicting future trends, and projecting the development of new product lines. It also involves planning the acquisition of new equipment, analyzing merger possibilities, and making difficult decisions concerning downsizing and the sale of assets if required by unfavourable economic conditions.

■ *Support for strategic organising and staffing.* Top-level executives are concerned with organisational structure. For example, decisions concerning the creation of new departments or downsizing the labour force are made by top-level managers. Overall direction for staffing decisions and effective communication with labour unions are also major decision areas for top-level executives. ESS can be employed to help analyze the impact of staffing decisions, potential pay raises, changes in employee benefits, and new work rules.

■ *Support for strategic control.* Another type of executive decision relates to strategic control, which involves monitoring and managing the overall operation of the organisation. Goal seeking can be done for each major area to determine what performance these areas need to achieve to reach corporate expectations. Effective ESS approaches can help top-level managers make the most of their existing resources and control all aspects of the organisation.

■ *Support for crisis management.* Even with careful strategic planning, a crisis can occur. Major disasters, including hurricanes, tornadoes, floods, earthquakes, fires, and terrorist activities, can totally shut down major parts of the organisation. Handling these emergencies is another responsibility for top-level executives. In many cases, strategic emergency plans can be put into place with the help of an ESS. These contingency plans help organisations recover quickly if an emergency or crisis occurs.

Decision making is a vital part of managing businesses strategically. IS systems, such as information and decision support, group support, and executive support systems, help employees by tapping existing databases and providing them with current, accurate information. The increasing integration of all business information systems can help organisations monitor their competitive environment and make better-informed decisions. Organisations can also use specialised business information systems, discussed in Chapters 7 and 8, to achieve their goals.

Summary

At the start of this chapter we set out the FOUR main principles relating to how businesses regard management information systems and decision support systems and how crucial these are to running an effective business together with the key learning objectives for each. It's now time to summarise the chapter by recapping on those FOUR principles: can you recall what is important and why about each one?

1 **Good decision making and problem-solving skills are the key to developing effective information and decision support systems.** Every organisation needs effective decision making and problem solving to reach its objectives and goals. Problem solving begins with decision making. A well-known model developed by Herbert Simon divides the decision-making phase of the problem-solving process into three stages: intelligence, design, and choice. During the intelligence stage, potential problems or opportunities are identified and defined. Information is gathered that relates to the cause and scope of the problem. Constraints on the possible solution and the problem environment are investigated. In the design stage, alternative solutions to the problem are developed and explored. In addition, the feasibility and implications of these alternatives are evaluated. Finally, the choice stage involves selecting the best course of action. In this stage, the decision makers evaluate the implementation of the solution to determine whether the anticipated results were achieved and to modify the process in light of new information learned during the implementation stage.

Decision making is a component of problem solving. In addition to the intelligence, design, and choice steps of decision making, problem solving also includes implementation and monitoring. Implementation places the solution into effect. After a decision has been implemented, it is monitored and modified if needed.

Decisions can be programmed or non-programmed. Programmed decisions are made using a rule, procedure, or quantitative method. Ordering more inventory when the level drops to 100 units or fewer is an example of a programmed decision. A non-programmed decision deals with unusual or exceptional situations. Determining the best training program for a new employee is an example of a non-programmed decision.

Decisions can use optimisation, satisficing, or heuristic approaches. Optimisation finds the best solution. Optimisation problems often have an objective, such as maximising profits given production and material constraints. When a problem is too complex for optimisation, satisficing is often used. Satisficing finds a good, but not necessarily the best, decision. Finally, a heuristic is a "rule of thumb" or commonly used guideline or procedure used to find a good decision.

2 **A management information system (MIS) must provide the right information to the right person in the right format at the right time.** A management information system is an integrated collection of people, procedures, databases, and devices that provides managers and decision makers with information to help achieve organisational goals. An MIS can help an organisation achieve its goals by providing managers with insight into the regular operations of the organisation so that they can control, organise, and plan more effectively and efficiently. The primary difference between the reports generated by the TPS and those generated by the MIS is that MIS reports support managerial decision making at the higher levels of management.

Data that enters the MIS originates from both internal and external sources. The most significant internal sources of data for the MIS are the organisation's various TPSs and ERP systems. Data warehouses and data marts also provide important input data for the MIS. External sources of data for the MIS include extranets, customers, suppliers, competitors, and stockholders.

The output of most MIS is a collection of reports that are distributed to managers. Management information systems have a number of common characteristics, including producing scheduled, demand, exception, and drill-down reports; producing reports with fixed and standard formats; producing hard-copy and soft-copy reports; using internal data stored in organisational computerised databases; and having reports developed and implemented by IS personnel or end users.

Most MIS are organised along the functional lines of an organisation. Typical functional management information systems include financial, manufacturing, marketing, human resources, and other specialised systems. Each system is composed of inputs, processing subsystems, and outputs.

3 **Decision support systems (DSS) support decision making effectiveness when faced with unstructured or semi-structured business problems.** DSS characteristics include the ability to handle large amounts of data; obtain and process data from different sources; provide report and presentation flexibility; support drill-down analysis; perform complex statistical analysis; offer textual and graphical orientations; support optimisation, satisficing, and heuristic approaches; and perform what-if, simulation, and goal-seeking analysis.

DSS provide support assistance through all phases of the problem-solving process. Different decision frequencies also require DSS support. An ad hoc DSS addresses unique, infrequent decision situations; an institutional DSS handles routine decisions. Highly structured problems, semi-structured problems, and unstructured problems can be supported by a DSS. A DSS can also support different managerial levels, including strategic, tactical, and operational managers. A common database is often the link that ties together a company's TPS, MIS, and DSS.

The components of a DSS are the database, model base, user interface or dialogue manager, and a link to external databases, the internet, the corporate intranet, extranets, networks, and other systems. The database can use data warehouses and data marts. Access to other computer-based systems permits the DSS to tie into other powerful systems, including the TPS or function-specific subsystems.

4 **Specialised support systems, such as group support systems (GSS) and executive support systems (ESS), use the overall approach of a DSS in situations, such as group and executive decision making.** A group support system (GSS) consists of most of the elements in a DSS, plus software to provide effective support in group decision-making settings. GSS are typically easy to learn and use and can offer specific or general decision-making support. GSS software, also called "groupware," is specially designed to help generate lists of decision alternatives and perform data analysis. These packages let people work on joint documents and files over a network.

The frequency of GSS use and the location of the decision makers will influence the GSS alternative chosen. The decision room alternative supports users in a single location who meet infrequently. Local area networks can be used when group members are located in the same geographic area and users meet regularly. Teleconferencing is used when decision frequency is low and the location of group members is distant. A wide area network is used when the decision frequency is high and the location of group members is distant.

Executive support systems (ESS) are specialised decision support systems designed to meet the needs of senior management. They serve to indicate issues of importance to the organisation, indicate new directions the company might take, and help executives monitor the company's progress. ESS are typically easy to use, offer a wide range of computer resources, and handle a variety of internal and external data. In addition, the ESS performs sophisticated data analysis, offers a high degree of specialisation, and provides flexibility and comprehensive communications abilities. An ESS also supports individual decision-making styles. Some of the major decision-making areas that can be supported through an ESS are providing an overall vision, strategic planning and organising, strategic control, and crisis management.

Review Questions

1 What is a "satisficing model?" Describe a situation when it should be used.

2 What is the difference between a programmed decision and a non-programmed decision? Give several examples of each.

3 What are the basic kinds of reports produced by an MIS? Summarise the differences between them.

4 What are the functions performed by a financial MIS?

5 Describe the functions of a marketing MIS.

6 What is the difference between decision making and problem solving?

7 What is a geographic information system? What can it be used for?

8 Describe the difference between a structured and an unstructured problem and give an example of each.

9 What is the difference between what-if analysis and goal-seeking analysis?

10 What is an executive support system? Identify three fundamental uses for such a system.

Discussion Questions

1 How can management information systems be used to support the objectives of the business organisation?

2 How can a strong financial MIS provide strategic benefits to a firm?

3 You have been hired to develop a management information system and a decision support system for a manufacturing company. Describe what information you would include in printed reports and what information you would provide using a screen-based decision support system.

4 You have been hired to develop group support software. Describe the features you would include in your new GSS software.

5 The use of ESS should not be limited to the executives of the company. Do you agree or disagree? Why?

Web Exercises

1 Use a search engine, such as Yahoo! or Google, to explore two or more companies that produce and sell MIS or DSS software. Describe what you found and any problems you had in using search engines on the internet to find information. You might be asked to develop a report or send an email message to your instructor about what you found.

2 Use the internet to explore two or more software packages that can be used to make group decisions easier. Summarise your findings in a report.

Case One

Amenities Inc. Gets a Grip on Pachinko Information

Just as Las Vegas has its casinos and slot machines, Japan has pachinko parlors and pachinko machines. Pachinko is a game played on vertical boards where small metal balls are flung to the top and cascade down through numerous metal pins. If a ball happens to land in one of the cups, points are scored and more balls are released. Winning scores collect prizes. Amenities Inc. owns 16 pachinko parlors in Japan, as well as cinemas, karaoke booths, bowling alleys, and restaurants. In 2005, Amenities became the first in the pachinko industry to adopt an ERP system to manage its data and provide useful information for business decision making. In 2008, Amenities installed a business intelligence platform to further benefit from the information it gathered about its businesses and customers. More recently, Amenities began a quest to organise and display information in a manner that better supports strategic decision making.

Until recently, Amenities used a decision-making process referred to as the plan-do-check-act (PDCA) approach. This is a model based on the scientific method that begins with a hypothesis (plan), tested by an experiment (do), followed by an examination of results (check), and adjustments applied based on observations (act), which cycles back to the planning stage. Amenities realised that the PDCA approach was not ideal for the strategic decisions it needed to make in the pachinko industry. It thought that a more appropriate model was the observe, orient, decide, and act (OODA) approach. OODA is used by the military in combat operations and in business to gain advantages in tough competitive markets. The OODA model is designed to defeat an adversary and survive. It depends on ongoing observation and analysis of a situation. It requires an information system that can supply up-to-the minute information about the business, its competitors, and the environment in which it operates. Over the years, Amenities had built such an information system. Now it needed to focus on getting relevant data to its decision makers.

Amenities purchased three software packages intended to deliver the right information to the right people at the right time in the right format. SAP BusinessObjects Web Intelligence software is designed to allow decision makers to access business reports through a web browser interface. SAP BusinessObjects Live Office software is designed to obtain and analyze data directly in Microsoft Excel and Word. Xcelsius software is designed to provide a dashboard that graphically displays key indicators. This was combined with Crystal Reports software that provides additional visual reporting tools. Armed with this arsenal of MIS tools, Amenities CIO Kazuo Yoshida set out to deliver useful information to its decision makers. For corporate executives, a dashboard was designed that included three key indicator charts and meters: profits and losses, sales amounts, and customer amounts. The charts were integrated with the company's groupware so that every time executives check email or collaborate online, they get a quick glimpse of the company's current health. If the graphs indicate anything unusual, an executive can click the graph to drill down into more detailed information.

Lower-ranked business managers within Amenities have a similar dashboard showing key indicators that include bar graphs for sales, profits, and expenses with goals and current status listed side by side. The layout allows managers to easily see their current degree of success in achieving key indicators and corporate goals. Managers also have access to interactive forms that allow them to submit daily reports to head-quarters. Amenities' new information delivery system provides its decision makers with up-to-the-minute corporate information. If a competitor launches a one-day promotion, managers can react before midday. Executives can quickly react to significant sales declines by launching ad-hoc promotional events. Unexpected sales increases allow executives to recognise new opportunities and quickly take advantage of them. With its ERP system, business intelligence system, and reporting tools in place, Amenities will continue to refine the manner in which it delivers valuable information to individuals who are able to act upon it and improve its position in the market.

Discussion Questions

1   What information system components did Amenities use to get the right information to the right people at the right time in the right format?

2   Why did Amenities decide to combine its dashboard charts and meters with its groupware?

Critical Thinking Questions

1   What advantages did Amenities think it could gain by adopting an OODA approach to decision making?

2   How might real-time and continuous access to key-indicator data influence a business' decision making?

SOURCES: SAP Staff, "Amenities – Sap Software Optimises Decision, Making And Information Quality," SAP Success Stories. Available from: www.sap.com/solutions/sap-businessobjects/sme/reporting-dashboarding/customers/index.epx. Accessed March 23, 2010.

Case Two

V-Commerce and Micro-Business Entrepreneurs

Second Life is a virtual world, a persistent computer-based environment where many users can interact, represented in world by their avatar. The virtual world concept began as a platform for game playing but has emerged into a more general mode of social and commercial interaction. Some commentators are predicting that virtual world-like interfaces will become the dominant means of internet information access. Google, for instance, recently experimented with tools to enable users to embed 3D environments in web-pages, although the service has now been discontinued.

Second Life has around 10 million registered user accounts, and at any time around 30 000 users are logged in. The world is not exactly a game and is perhaps better described as an "arena of creativity." Its developers, Linden Lab, have created an environment where users can create whatever they can

SOURCE: Courtesy of Second Life © Linden Labs.

imagine. To enable users to accomplish this goal, the interface allows for the creation of objects that can be programmed with behaviour. An example is building an object to look like a car, and then programming it so an avatar can drive it like a car. Second Life is unusual among virtual worlds in that the intellectual property of any object built by a user belongs to that user. The interface also allows for the immediate and costless exchange of money between users in the form of the Linden dollar, which has a floating exchange rate with the US dollar. Objects can likewise be swapped between users. Together these features mean that products can be designed and built by one user, then sold and delivered to another user. This is known as virtual world commerce or v-commerce.

V-commerce has been commented on in The Economist: "of about 10m objects created, about 230 000 are bought and sold every month in the in-world currency, Linden dollars, which is exchangeable for hard currency. Second Life already has about 7000 profitable 'businesses,' where avatars supplement or make their living from their in world creativity. The top ten in-world entrepreneurs are making average profits of just over US$200 000 a year."

A typical v-commerce transaction proceeds as follows. An avatar enters a shop to browse goods for sale. Second Life shops are usually designed to look similar to real world shops, with pictures of products on the walls, and sometimes objects set out on display. There may be a shop keeper avatar present, although frequently there is not. When the user wishes to purchase an item, they right click on it or its picture and select the menu option "Buy." They are asked to confirm, and, if they do, the appropriate amount of Linden dollars are transferred immediately from the buyer's account to the seller's account and the object is transferred into the buyer's inventory. Personal details, such as postal address and credit card number, are not swapped – in fact, discounting avatar name, the seller and buyer can remain entirely anonymous to each other. V-commerce can involve the sale of "real" goods, by which is meant something that could be used outside of Second Life. If the good can be digitised, such as a song or a short story, then it can be sold and delivered inside the world; for example, shops selling real photographs can easily be found. Otherwise the item could be delivered through the post the same as any other physical object bought online, although no one is doing this yet. Reebok came close by allowing users to customise and purchase a pair of virtual shoes for their avatar, then purchase identical, real shoes for themselves, although the "real" part of the purchase happened on a traditional E-commerce website reached from a link inside Second Life.

V-commerce entrepreneurs are taking advantage of the Second Life interface to set up businesses almost risk free with minimal investment from themselves, at least in terms of money – they are still investing a lot of time. These entrepreneurs are running "micro-businesses," businesses tiny numbers of employees, typically zero. (A business with zero employees is one that is run in someone's spare time.)

Most v-commerce shops sell things that can be used inside the virtual world, such as avatar clothes, tattoos and vehicles. Some sell escort services (someone who will spend time with you). Some people are making enough money doing this to live on, but for most people it is a hobby. That is not to say it's all fun. One Second Life entrepreneur designs jewellery and has products in 105 outlets. Managing all of that is no small task, and it certainly isn't all fun. Tasks include designing and building the shops, designing and building the products, taking pictures of the products for the shop and other forms of advertising, promoting the products, sorting the inventory, paying land rent each month and finally managing customer service. The operation is designed to run itself, but new users often get stuck and need advice, even on something simple like opening the box the products come in. Typically, managing this is done outside of Second Life using a spreadsheet. Some Second Life entrepreneurs even pay taxes (in the real world) and have to produce information about their income.

The skills needed to do all of this are very relevant in the real world. Ian Hughes, Consulting IT Specialist with 18 years experience at IBM, says that virtual worlds extend to more than just entertainment or corporate communication. "They show business process models in actions," he says. Talking about virtual world games, he goes on, "The formidable organisational skills needed to run a game team or guild, organise raids involving perhaps 40 people and co-ordinate their different abilities to defeat a game's strongest foes are all relevant to work."

Discussion Questions

1 If you have experience of playing computer games, list the skills (if any) you learned while playing. Are any relevant to your study?

2 Do you think v-commerce is play or work?

Critical Thinking Questions

1 Are people who run v-commerce shops really business owners? Why or why not?

2 Is selling products for use by an avatar a sustainable business? Explain your answer.

SOURCES: The Economist, "Living a second life", 28 September 2006. Available from: http://www.economist.com/node/7963538?story_id=7963538. http://eightbar.co.uk/about/epredator/. Accessed 10 February 2010.

Notes

1 Gnanlet, A., et al., "Sequential and Simultaneous Decision Making for Optimizing Health Care," *Decision Sciences*, May 2009, p. 295.

2 Romo, Frode, et al., "Optimizing the Norwegian Natural Gas Production and Transport," *Interfaces*, January–February 2009, p. 46.

3 Eveborn, P., et al., "Operations Research Improves Quality and Efficiency in Home Care," *Interfaces*, January 2009, p. 18.

4 Rai, S., et al., "LDP – O.R. Enhanced Productivity Improvements for the Printing Industry," *Interfaces*, January 2009, p. 69.

5 Hormby, S., et al., "Marriott International Increases Revenue by Implementing a Group Pricing Optimizer," Interfaces, January–February, 2010, p. 47. October 12, 2009, p. 4.

6 Kapoor, S., et al., 'A Technical Framework for Sense-and-Respond Business Management', *IBM Systems Journal,* Vol. 44, 2005, p. 5.

7 Jackson-Higgins, Kelly, 'Jive Wikis Meet SAP Analytics," *Information Week*, July 6, 2009, p. 15.

8 Port, Otis, 'Desktop Factories,' *Business Week,* May 2, 2005, p. 22.

9 Wysocki, Bernard, et al., 'Just-In-Time Inventories Make U.S. Vulnerable in a Pandemic,' *Wall Street Journal,* January 12, 2006, p. A1.

10 Fong, Mei, "Clinique, Sony Star in Web Sitcom," *The Wall Street Journal*, March 27, 2009, p. B4.

11 Richmond, Rita, 'Blogs Keep Internet Customers Coming Back,' *Wall Street Journal,* March 1, 2005, p. B8.

12 Moy, Patsy, "Sharing Just the Job For Women," *The Standard*, October 12, 2009.

13 Hardy, Quentin, "High Network Individual," *Forbes*, March 16, 2009, p. 20.

14 Anthes, Gary, 'Beyond Zip Codes,' *Computerworld,* September 19, 2005, p. 56.

15 Christiansen, et al., "An Ocean of Opportunities," *OR/MS Today*, April 2009, p. 26.

16 Flisberg, Patrik, et al., "Billerud Optimizes Its Bleaching Process," *Interfaces*, March–April 2009, p. 119. p. 36.

[17] Havenstein, Heather, 'Celtics Turn to Data Analytics Tools for Help Pricing Tickets,' *Computerworld,* January 9, 2006, p. 43.

[18] Havenstein, Heather, 'Business Intelligence Tools Help Nonprofit Group Make Loans to Tsunami Victims,' *Computerworld,* March 14, 2005, p. 19.

[19] Rubenstein, Sarah, 'Next Step Toward Digitized Health Records,' *Wall Street Journal,* May 9, 2005, p. B1.

[20] Bhattacharya, K., et al., 'A Model-Driven Approach to Industrializing Discovery Processes in Pharmaceutical Research,' *IBM Systems Journal,* Vol. 44, No. 1, 2005, p. 145.

[21] Anthes, Gary, 'Modelling Magic,' *Computerworld,* February 7, 2005, p. 26.

[22] Port, Otis, 'Simple Solutions,' *Business Week,* October 3, 2005, p. 24.

[23] Mitchell, Robert, 'Anticipation Game,' *Computerworld,* June 13, 2005, p. 23.

[24] Aston, Adam, 'The Worst Isn't Over,' *Business Week,* January 16, 2006, p. 29.

[25] Babcock, Charles, 'A New Model for Disasters,' *Information Week,* October 10, 2005, p. 47.

[26] Majchrak, Ann, et al., 'Perceived Individual Collaboration Know-How Development Through Information Technology-Enabled Contextualization,' *Information Systems Research,* March 2005, p. 9.

[27] Stern, Zack, "Collaboration Online with Fuze Meeting Service," *PC World*, March 2009, p. 34.

6

CHAPTER 7 CONTENTS

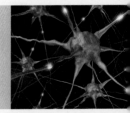

Knowledge Management and Specialised Information Systems

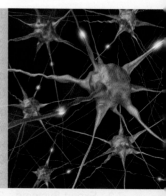

In this chapter we will look at the FOUR main factors you are going to have to understand fully when considering how businesses and organisations use systems to share information between managers and employees, and the benefits and issues inherent in such systems.

Principles

1. Knowledge management systems allow organisations to share knowledge and experience among their managers and employees.

2. Artificial intelligence systems form a broad and diverse set of systems that can replicate human decision making for certain types of well-defined problems.

3. Expert systems can enable a novice to perform at the level of an expert but must be developed and maintained very carefully.

4. Virtual reality systems can reshape the interface between people and information technology by offering new ways to communicate information, visualise processes, and express ideas creatively.

Learning Objectives

▪ Describe the role of the chief knowledge officer (CKO).

▪ List some of the tools and techniques used in knowledge management.

▪ Define the term "artificial intelligence" and state the objective of developing artificial intelligence systems.

▪ List the characteristics of intelligent behaviour and compare the performance of natural and artificial intelligence systems for each of these characteristics.

▪ Identify the major components of the artificial intelligence field and provide one example of each type of system.

▪ List the characteristics and basic components of expert systems.

▪ Identify at least three factors to consider in evaluating the development of an expert system.

▪ Outline and briefly explain the steps for developing an expert system.

▪ Identify the benefits associated with the use of expert systems.

▪ Define the term "virtual reality" and provide three examples of virtual reality applications.

▪ Discuss examples of specialised systems for organisational and individual use.

| Why Learn About Knowledge Management and Specialised Information Systems? | Knowledge management systems are used in almost every industry. If you are a manager, you might use a knowledge management system to support decisive action to help you correct a problem. If you are a production manager at a car company, you might oversee robots, a specialised information system, that attach windscreens to cars or paint body panels. As a young stock trader, you might use a system called a neural network to uncover patterns and make money trading stocks and stock options. As a marketing manager |

for a PC manufacturer, you might use virtual reality on a website to show customers your latest laptop and desktop computers. If you are in the military, you might use computer simulation as a training tool to prepare you for combat. In a petroleum company, you might use an expert system to determine where to drill for oil and gas. You will see many additional examples of using these information systems throughout this chapter. Learning about these systems will help you discover new ways to use information systems in your day-to-day work.

7.1   Knowledge Management Systems

Defining knowledge is difficult. One useful definition is that knowledge is the awareness and understanding of a set of information and the ways that information can be made useful to support a specific task or reach a decision. Knowing the procedures for ordering more inventory to avoid running out is an example of knowledge. In a sense, information tells you what has to be done (low inventory levels for some items), whereas knowledge tells you how to do it (make two important phone calls to the right people to get the needed inventory shipped overnight). A knowledge management system (KMS) is an organised collection of people, procedures, software, databases, and devices used to create, store, share, and use the organisation's knowledge and experience.[1]

Overview of Knowledge Management Systems

Like the other systems discussed throughout this book, knowledge management systems attempt to help organisations achieve their goals. For businesses, this usually means increasing profits or reducing costs. For nonprofit organisations, it can mean providing better customer service or providing special needs to people and groups. Many types of firms use KMS to increase profits or reduce costs. According to a survey of CEOs, firms that use KMS are more likely to innovate and perform better.[2]

A KMS stores and processes knowledge. This can involve different types of knowledge. Explicit knowledge is objective and can be measured and documented in reports, papers, and rules. For example, knowing the best road to take to minimise drive time from home to the office when a major motorway is closed due to an accident is explicit knowledge. It can be documented in a report or a rule, as in "If the A453 is closed, take the M1 to junction 25 and from there to the office." Tacit knowledge, on the other hand, is hard to measure and document and typically is not objective or formalised. Knowing the best way to negotiate with a foreign government about nuclear disarmament or deal with a volatile hostage situation often requires a lifetime of experience and a high level of skill. These are examples of tacit knowledge. It is difficult to write a detailed report or a set of rules that would always work in every hostage situation. Many organisations actively attempt to convert tacit knowledge to explicit knowledge to make the knowledge easier to measure, document, and share with others.

In a well-known *Harvard Business Review* paper called "The Knowledge Creating Company" (from the November–December 1991 issue), Ikujiro Nonaka describes four ways in which knowledge can be created.

1   When an individual learns directly from another individual, in an apprentice type relationship, tacit knowledge is created from tacit knowledge.

2 When two pieces of explicit knowledge are combined. For example, a website mash-up could be considered an example of this type of new knowledge. (Mash-ups were described in Chapter 6 as the combining of information from two or more web pages onto one web page.)

3 When an expert writes a book teaching others, explicit knowledge is being created from tacit knowledge.

4 When someone reads that book, and (eventually) becomes an expert themselves, tacit knowledge has been created by explicit knowledge.

A diverse set of technologies can help capture, create and share knowledge. Expert systems (subsequently discussed in this chapter) can be used to share explicit knowledge. Blogs can be used to share tacit knowledge. Data mining algorithms (see Chapter 5) can be used to discover new knowledge.

Obtaining, Storing, Sharing and Using Knowledge

Knowledge workers are people who create, use, and disseminate knowledge. They are usually professionals in science, engineering, or business and belong to professional organisations. Other examples of knowledge workers include writers, researchers, educators, and corporate designers. The **chief knowledge officer (CKO)** is a top-level executive who helps the organisation work with a KMS to create, store, and use knowledge to achieve organisational goals. The CKO is responsible for the organisation's KMS and typically works with other executives and directors, including the managing director, finance director, and others. Obtaining, storing, sharing, and using knowledge is the key to any KMS.[3] Using a KMS often leads to additional knowledge creation, storage, sharing, and usage. A meteorologist, for example, might develop sophisticated mathematical models to predict the path and intensity of hurricanes. Business professors often conduct research in marketing strategies, management practices, corporate and individual investments and finance, effective accounting and auditing practices, and much more. Drug companies and medical researchers invest billions of euros in creating knowledge on cures for diseases. Although knowledge workers can act alone, they often work in teams to create or obtain knowledge.

chief knowledge officer (CKO)
A top-level executive who helps the organisation use a KMS to create, store, and use knowledge to achieve organisational goals.

Some organisations and professions use communities of practice (COP) to create, store, and share knowledge. A COP is a group of people dedicated to a common discipline or practice, such as open-source software, auditing, medicine, or engineering. A group of oceanographers investigating climate change or a team of medical researchers looking for new ways to treat lung cancer are examples of COPs. COPs excel at obtaining, storing, sharing, and using knowledge. A study of knowledge workers in a large insurance company showed that a COP shares information better, solves problems more collaboratively, and is more committed to sharing best practices.[4]

After knowledge is created, it is often stored in a "knowledge repository." The knowledge repository can be located both inside and outside the organisation. Some types of software can store and share knowledge contained in documents and reports. Adobe Acrobat PDF files, for example, allow you to store corporate reports, tax returns, and other documents and send them to others over the internet. You can use hardware devices and software to store and share audio and video material.[5] Traditional databases and data warehouses, discussed in Chapter 3, are often used to store the organisation's knowledge. Specialised knowledge bases in expert systems, discussed later in the chapter, can also be used.

Because knowledge workers often work in groups or teams, they can use collaborative work software and group support systems to share knowledge. Intranets and password-protected internet sites also provide ways to share knowledge. The social services department of Surrey Council in the UK, for example, use an intranet to help it create and manipulate knowledge.[6] Because knowledge can be critical in maintaining a competitive advantage, businesses should be careful in how they share it. Although they want important decision makers inside and outside the organisation to have complete and easy access to knowledge, they also need to protect knowledge from competitors and others who shouldn't see it. As a result, many businesses use patents, copyrights, trade secrets, internet firewalls, and other measures to keep prying eyes from seeing important knowledge that is often expensive and hard to create.

In addition to using information systems and collaborative software tools to share knowledge, some organisations use nontechnical approaches. These include corporate retreats and gatherings, sporting events, informal knowledge worker lounges or meeting places, kitchen facilities, day-care centres, and comfortable workout centres.

Using a knowledge management system begins with locating the organisation's knowledge. This is often done using a knowledge map or directory that points the knowledge worker to the needed knowledge. Drug companies have sophisticated knowledge maps that include database and file systems to allow scientists and drug researchers to locate previous medical studies. Lawyers can use powerful online knowledge maps, such as the legal section of Lexis-Nexis to research legal opinions and the outcomes of previous cases. Medical researchers, university professors, and even textbook authors use Lexis-Nexis to locate important knowledge. Organisations often use the internet or corporate web portals to help their knowledge workers find knowledge stored in documents and reports. The following are examples of profit and nonprofit organisations that use knowledge and knowledge management systems.

China Netcom Corporation uses KM software from Autonomy Corporation to search the records of up to 100 million telecommunications customers and create knowledge about its customers and marketing operations.[7]

Feilden, Clegg, Bradley, and Aedas, an architectural firm, uses KM to share best practices among its architects.[8] According to one designer, "Knowledge management was one of those ideas that sprang up in the 1990s, along with fads, such as total quality management and the concept of the learning organisation. But knowledge management (KM) appears to have had staying power, and it is still firmly on the business agenda."

Munich Re Group, a German insurance organisation, uses KM to share best practices and knowledge.[9] "It was always important to us that knowledge management isn't just an IT platform," said Karen Edwards, knowledge management consultant in Munich Re's Knowledge Management Center of Competence in Munich, Germany. "The Munich Re people, they really were the assets. They're the things you try to bring together."

Technology to Support Knowledge Management

KMS use a number of tools discussed throughout this book. An effective KMS is based on learning new knowledge and changing procedures and approaches as a result.[10] A manufacturing company, for example, might learn new ways to program robots on the factory floor to improve accuracy and reduce defective parts. The new knowledge will likely cause the manufacturing company to change how it programs and uses its robots. In Chapter 5, we investigated the use of data mining and business intelligence. These powerful tools can be important in capturing and using knowledge. Enterprise resource planning tools, such as SAP, include knowledge management features.[11] We have also seen how groupware could improve group decision making and collaboration. Groupware can also be used to help capture, store, and use knowledge. Wiki technology, which allows a number of people to collectively edit a website, is another tool that can be used to collect and disseminate peoples' knowledge. Lastly, of course, hardware, software, databases, telecommunications, and the internet, discussed in Chapters 2–4, are important technologies used to support knowledge management systems.

Hundreds of companies provide specific KM products and services.[12] In addition, researchers at colleges and universities have developed tools and technologies to support knowledge management[13] (see Figure 7.1). Companies, such as IBM, have many knowledge management tools in a variety of products, including Lotus Notes and Domino.[14] Lotus Notes is a collection of software products that help people work together to create, share, and store important knowledge

Figure 7.1 Knowledge Management Technology

Lotus Sametime helps people communicate, collaborate, and share ideas in real time.

Sam Curman/Chicago/Renovations - Started: 9:03:04 PM

File   Edit   View   Actions   Help

Kelly Hardart - Chicago, IL USA
Sales Representative
Work: (617) 555-6782
Local Time:11:04 A

Sam Curman	Good morning Kelly.	09:03:04 A
	‹ Are you available to discuss the presentation today?	
	‹ Just let me know when you're free, I'm hoping to wrap	
	‹ this up before noon. 🙂	
	‹ Does that sound reasonable?	
Kelly Hardart	Hi Sam!	09:04:58 A
	‹ Sure, noon is a good time for me.	
Sam Curman	Excellent!	09:05:11 A
Kelly Hardart	Oh no! I forgot I have a lunch meeting with **Larry!**	09:06:27 A
	Would you be able to meet at 1:00 instead?	
Sam Curman	Okay, let me check my calendar.	09:06:54 A
	‹ I prefer to meet earlier than later.	
	:: Sam Curman is away from the computer ::	09:15:33 A
	:: Sam Curman is now available ::	10:22:15 A
Kelly Hardart	Okay.	10:12:45 A
	‹ Yes, 2:00 works for me. I'll send you an invite.	
	‹ Do you think we should invite Monifa? I think she will	
	have some valuable insight on the presentaion?	

A&   ✎   T T̂ Ť   **B** *i* u   🙂▾   abⱿc

Hey Sam, I'm going to schedule a follow up meeting to discuss the feedback.
I seeem to remember you saying that you are you on vacation the week of the
17th? If so, I will be sure to schedule a meeting the week after.

Send

Kelly is typing a message

SOURCE: Courtesy of IBM Corporation.

and business documents. Its knowledge management features include domain search, content mapping, and Lotus Sametime shown in Figure 7.1. Domain search allows people to perform sophisticated searches for knowledge in Domino databases using a single simple query. Content mapping organises knowledge by categories, like a table of contents for a book. Lotus Sametime helps people communicate, collaborate, and share ideas in real time. Lotus Domino Document Manager, formerly called Lotus Domino, helps people and organisations store, organise, and retrieve documents.[15] The software can be used to write, review, archive, and publish documents throughout the organisation. Morphy Richards, a leading supplier of small home appliances in the UK, uses Domino for email, collaboration, and document management.[16] According to one executive, "Rather than relying on groups of employees emailing each other, we are putting in place a business application through which documents will formally flow – to improve the efficiency of the supply chain and create more transparent working practices."

Microsoft offers a number of knowledge management tools, including Digital Dashboard, based on the Microsoft Office suite.[17] Digital Dashboard integrates information from different sources, including personal, group, enterprise, and external information and documents. "Microsoft has revolutionised the way that people use technology to create and share information. The company is the clear winner in the knowledge management business," according to Rory Chase, managing director of Teleos, an independent knowledge management research company based in the UK. Other tools from Microsoft include Web Store Technology, which uses wireless technology to deliver knowledge to any location at any time; Access Workflow Designer,

Table 7.1 Additional Knowledge Management Organisations and Resources

Company	Description	Website
CortexPro	Knowledge management collaboration tools	www.cortexpro.com
Delphi Group	A knowledge management consulting company	www.delphigroup.com
Knowledge Management Resource Centre	Knowledge management sites, products and services, magazines, and case studies	www.kmresource.com
Knowledge Management Solutions, Inc.	Tools to create, capture, classify, share, and manage knowledge	www.kmsi.us
Knowledge Management Web Directory	A directory of knowledge management websites	www.knowledge-manage.com
KnowledgeBase	Content creation and management	www.knowledgebase.net
Law Clip Knowledge Manager	A service that collects and organises text, weblinks, and more from law-related websites	www.lawclip.com
Knowledge Management Consortium International	Offers knowledge management training and support	www.kmci.org/index.html

which helps database developers create effective systems to process transactions and keep work flowing through the organisation; and related products. Table 7.1 lists additional knowledge management products.

In addition to these tools, several artificial intelligence, discussed next, can be used in a KMS.

7.2 Artificial Intelligence

At a Dartmouth College conference in 1956, John McCarthy proposed the use of the term artificial intelligence (AI) to describe computers with the ability to mimic or duplicate the functions of the human brain. Advances in AI have since led to systems to recognise complex patterns.[18] Many AI pioneers attended this first conference; a few predicted that computers would be as "smart" as people by the 1960s. This prediction has not yet been realised and there is a debate about whether it actually ever could be, however, the benefits of artificial intelligence in business and research can be seen today, and the research continues.

Artificial intelligence systems include the people, procedures, hardware, software, data, and knowledge needed to develop computer systems and machines that demonstrate characteristics of intelligence. Researchers, scientists, and experts on how human beings think are often involved in developing these systems.

artificial intelligence systems People, procedures, hardware, software, data, and knowledge needed to develop computer systems and machines that demonstrate characteristics of intelligence.

In Febuary 2011, IBM supercomputer Watson took part in televised quiz show Jeopardy, playing against two of the show's most successful winners. After a three night marathon on the show, Watson emerged victorious to win a US $1 million prize.[19] The victory, however, was about more than money. It was about ushering in a new era in computing, where machines will increasingly be able to learn and understand what humans are really asking them for.

The Nature of Intelligence

From the early AI pioneering stage, the research emphasis has been on developing machines with **intelligent behaviour**. Machine intelligence, however, is hard to achieve. Some of the specific characteristics of intelligent behaviour include the ability to do the following:

intelligent behaviour The ability to learn from experiences and apply knowledge acquired from experience, handle complex situations, solve problems when important information is missing, determine what is important, react quickly and correctly to a new situation, understand visual images, process and manipulate symbols, be creative and imaginative, and use heuristics.

■ *Learn from experience and apply the knowledge acquired from experience.* Learning from past situations and events is a key component of intelligent behaviour and is a natural ability of humans, who learn by trial and error. This ability, however, must be carefully programed into a computer system. Today, researchers are developing systems that can learn from experience.[20] For instance, computerised AI chess software can learn to improve while playing human competitors. In one match, Garry Kasparov competed against a personal computer with AI software developed in Israel, called Deep Junior. This match was a 3–3 tie, but Kasparov picked up something the machine would have no interest in – €500 000. The 20 questions (20Q) website, www.20q.net, is another example of a system that learns.[21] The website is an artificial intelligence game that learns as people play (see Figure 7.2).

Figure 7.2 20Q
20Q is an online game where users play the popular game, Twenty Questions, against an artificial intelligence foe.

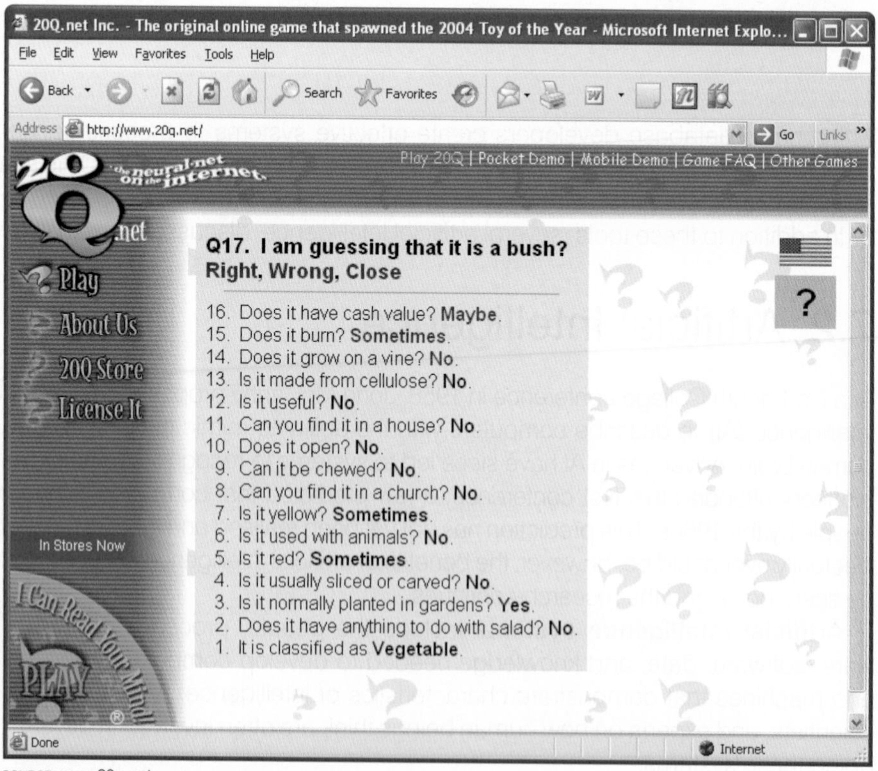

SOURCE: www.20q.net.

■ *Handle complex situations.* People are often involved in complex situations. World leaders face difficult political decisions regarding terrorism, conflict, global economic conditions, hunger, and poverty. In a business setting, top-level managers and executives must handle a complex market, challenging competitors, intricate government regulations, and a demanding workforce. Even human experts make mistakes in dealing with these situations. Developing computer systems that can handle perplexing situations requires careful planning and elaborate computer programming.

■ *Solve problems when important information is missing.* The essence of decision making is dealing with uncertainty. Often, decisions must be made with too little information or inaccurate information, because obtaining complete information is too costly or even impossible. Today, AI systems can make important calculations, comparisons, and decisions even when information is missing.

■ *Determine what is important.* Knowing what is truly important is the mark of a good decision maker. Developing programs and approaches to allow computer systems and machines to identify important information is not a simple task.

■ *React quickly and correctly to a new situation.* A small child, for example, can look over a ledge or a drop-off and know not to venture too close. The child reacts quickly and correctly to a new situation. Computers, on the other hand, do not have this ability without complex programming.

■ *Understand visual images.* Interpreting visual images can be extremely difficult, even for sophisticated computers. Moving through a room of chairs, tables, and other objects can be trivial for people but extremely complex for machines, robots, and computers. Such machines require an extension of understanding visual images, called a **perceptive system**. Having a perceptive system allows a machine to approximate the way a person sees, hears, and feels objects. Military robots, for example, use cameras and perceptive systems to conduct reconnaissance missions to detect enemy weapons and soldiers. Detecting and destroying them can save lives.

perceptive system A system that approximates the way a person sees, hears, and feels objects.

■ *Process and manipulate symbols.* People see, manipulate, and process symbols every day. Visual images provide a constant stream of information to our brains. By contrast, computers have difficulty handling symbolic processing and reasoning. Although computers excel at numerical calculations, they aren't as good at dealing with symbols and three-dimensional objects. Recent developments in machine-vision hardware and software, however, allow some computers to process and manipulate symbols on a limited basis.

■ *Be creative and imaginative.* Throughout history, people have turned difficult situations into advantages by being creative and imaginative. For instance, when defective mints with holes in the middle were shipped, an enterprising entrepreneur decided to market these new mints as "LifeSavers" instead of returning them to the manufacturer. Ice cream cones were invented at the St. Louis World's Fair when an imaginative store owner decided to wrap ice cream with a waffle from his grill for portability. Developing new and exciting products and services from an existing (perhaps negative) situation is a human characteristic. Computers cannot be imaginative or creative in this way, although software has been developed to enable a computer to write short stories.

■ *Use heuristics.* For some decisions, people use heuristics (rules of thumb arising from experience) or even guesses. In searching for a job, you might rank the companies you are considering according to profits per employee. Today, some computer systems, given the right programs, obtain good solutions that use approximations instead of trying to search for an optimal solution, which would be technically difficult or too time consuming.

This list of traits only partially defines intelligence. Unlike the terminology used in virtually every other field of IS research in which the objectives can be clearly defined, the term "intelligence" is a formidable stumbling block. One of the problems in AI is arriving at a working definition of real intelligence against which to compare the performance of an AI system.

Developing a link between the human brain and the computer is another exciting area that touches all aspects of artificial intelligence. Called Brain Computer Interface (BCI), the idea is to directly connect the human brain to a computer and have human thought control computer activities.[22] Two exciting studies conducted at the Massachusetts General Hospital in Boston will attempt to use a chip called BrainGate to connect a human brain to a computer. If successful, the BCI experiment will allow people to control computers and artificial arms and legs through thought alone. The objective is to give people without the ability to speak or move (called Locked-in Syndrome) the ability to communicate and move artificial limbs using advanced BCI technologies. Honda Motors has developed a BCI system that allows a person to complete certain operations, like bending a leg, with 90 per cent accuracy.[23] The new system uses a special helmet that can measure and transmit brain activity to a computer.

The Difference Between Natural and Artificial Intelligence

Since the term "artificial intelligence" was defined in the 1950s, experts have disagreed about the difference between natural and artificial intelligence. Can computers be programed to have common sense? Profound differences separate natural from artificial intelligence, but they are declining in number (see Table 7.2). One of the driving forces behind AI research is an attempt to understand how people actually reason and think. Creating machines that can reason is possible only when we truly understand our own processes for doing so.

Table 7.2 A Comparison of Natural and Artificial Intelligence

	Natural Intelligence (Human)		Artificial Intelligence (Machine)	
Ability to	Low	High	Low	High
Use sensors (see hear, touch, smell)		√	√	
Be creative and imaginative		√	√	
Learn from experience		√	√	
Adapt to new situations		√	√	
Afford the cost of acquiring intelligence		√	√	
Acquire a large amount of external information		√		√
Use a variety of information sources		√		√
Make complex calculations	√			√
Transfer information	√			√
Make a series of calculations rapidly and accurately	√			√

The Major Branches of Artificial Intelligence

AI is a broad field that includes several specialty areas, such as expert systems, robotics, vision systems, natural language processing, learning systems, and neural networks. Many of these areas are related; advances in one can occur simultaneously with or result in advances in others.

Social Networking IS at Work

Organisations Gain Valuable Intelligence from Social Networking Sites

You might not think of your favourite social networking site as a knowledge management system, but chances are some companies do. For many people, the moment they realised the power of social networks was when they first heard about David Carroll.

Dave Carroll's music group, Sons of Maxwell, was setting off to start their tour of Nebraska when airport baggage handlers damaged one of their guitars. So began a year-long tussle between Dave and the airline, trying without success to get compensation. Inspired by frustration, Dave wrote and recorded a song about the experience, made a music video for it, uploaded it to YouTube and within three days it had been seen by half a million people. Within a month it was up to five million. All of a sudden the airline had a public relations nightmare on their hands with thousands of other unhappy customers coming forward to complain.

Similar things are happening all over the world. In the UK, the communications team of a multinational retailer was taken by surprise when journalists called to ask about huge technical problems they were having in half their UK stores. If the team had been monitoring Twitter they would have known what was going on.

"The boundaries between news and social media are getting more and more fuzzy," says Jorn Lyseggen, chief executive of Meltwater Group, an online media monitoring company. "Social media is like a toddler, but nobody yet knows what promise that toddler holds," he says.

A rapidly growing number of companies like Meltwater Group and Alterian is offering help. Alterian assists clients manage their customer relations by "combining campaign management, web content management, email and social media monitoring tools to help marketers be more insightful, engaging and accountable than ever before, by sending the best, most relevant message at the right time – regardless of channel." Their social media database currently holds about nine billion postings, with 50 million more added every day. At the most basic, these tools measure the volume of social media chatter. For example, researchers at Hewlett Packard have demonstrated that they can accurately predict a Hollywood movie's box office takings by counting how often it is mentioned on Twitter before it opens.

Social media is quickly becoming a customer relationship management system, as companies have "for the first time access to people's minds in real-time," says Jorn Lyseggen. The tools on offer provide companies with dashboards that show trends, hot topics, the reach of brands, customer mood and how competitors are doing.

Most companies are still cagey about showing off their dashboards. After all, this is their reputation laid bare, although what they see is hardly a secret: anybody (with enough money) can subscribe to a social media analytics service and do the very same research. Social media may be popular, but in reality "only a few firms get it, it's of peripheral interest for most," says Tom Austin at technology consultancy Gartner. Few realise that using social media has become much more than customer service and reputation management.

Used carefully, it allows companies to build passion for their products and services. Most importantly, it can act as an early warning system when something goes wrong. If your system tells you that your customers are unhappy about a product or service, it can be mission critical that the tool immediately alerts the team in charge of it. It also makes business sense.

And what about Dave Carroll? He ended up thanking the airline for the creative outlet they gave him. "We had a pile of laughs making the recording and the video," he said. He probably sold a few records too.

Discussion Questions

1   If a company needs Twitter to alert them to a problem, then is something not very wrong in the first place?

(continued)

7

2 As well as movie success, what else could be predicted with Twitter posts?

2 Once the music video was on YouTube, how could the airline have responded to minimise the problem?

Critical Thinking Questions

1 How should companies use social networking sites for public relations? What would good and bad practice look like?

SOURCES: www.alterian.com/ourcompany/. Accessed 17 January 2011; www.davecarrollmusic.com/ubg/story/. Accessed 17 January 2011; BBC, "Why companies watch your every Facebook and Twitter move", 3 October 2010. Available from: http://www.bbc.co.uk/news/business-11450923.

Expert Systems

expert system Hardware and software that stores knowledge and makes inferences, similar to a human expert.

An **expert system** consists of hardware and software that stores knowledge and makes inferences, similar to those of a human expert. Because of their many business applications, expert systems are discussed in more detail in their own section later in this chapter.

Robotics

Robotics involves developing mechanical or computer devices that can paint cars, make precision welds, and perform other tasks that require a high degree of precision or are tedious or hazardous for human beings. Some robots are mechanical devices that don't use the AI features discussed in this chapter. Others are sophisticated systems that use one or more AI features or characteristics, such as the vision systems, learning systems, or neural networks discussed later in the chapter. For many businesses, robots are used to do the "three Ds" – dull, dirty, and dangerous jobs.[24] Manufacturers use robots to assemble and paint products. The NASA shuttle crash of the early 2000s, for example, has led some people to recommend using robots instead of people to explore space and perform scientific research (see Figure 7.3). Some robots, such as Sony's Aibo, can be used for companionship (see Figure 7.4). Contemporary robotics combine both high-precision machine capabilities and sophisticated controlling software. The controlling software in robots is what is most important in terms of AI.

robotics Mechanical or computer devices that perform tasks requiring a high degree of precision or that are tedious or hazardous for humans.

The field of robotics has many applications, and research into these unique devices continues. The following are a few examples:

■ IRobot is a company that builds a number of robots, including the Roomba Floorvac for cleaning floors and the PackBot, an unmanned vehicle used to assist and protect soldiers.[25] Manufacturers use robots to assemble and paint products.

■ The Porter Adventist Hospital in Denver, Colorado, uses a US $90 000 Da Vinci Surgical System to perform surgery on prostate cancer patients.[26] The robot has multiple arms that hold surgical tools. According to one doctor at Porter, "The biggest advantage is it improves recovery time. Instead of having an eight-inch incision, the patient has a 'band-aid' incision. It's much quicker."

■ DARPA (The Defence Advanced Research Project Agency) sponsors the DARPA Grand Challenge, a 212 km (132 mile) race over rugged terrain for computer-controlled cars.[27]

■ Because of an age limit on camel jockeys, the state of Qatar decided to use robots in its camel races.[28] Developed in Switzerland, the robots have a human shape and only weigh 27 kg (59 lb). The robots use global positioning systems (GPS), a microphone to deliver voice commands to the camel, and cameras. A camel trainer uses a joystick to control the robot's movements on the camel. Camel racing is very popular in Qatar.

Figure 7.3 Robots in **Space** *Robots can be used in situations that are hazardous or inaccessible to humans. The ExoMars Rover – the European Space Agency's first field biologist on Mars.*

SOURCE: ESA.

■ In military applications, robots are becoming real weapons. The US Air Force is developing a smart robotic jet fighter. Often called "unmanned combat air vehicles" (UCAVs), these robotic war machines, such as the X-45A, will be able to identify and destroy targets without human pilots. UCAVs send pictures and information to a central command centre and can be directed to strike military targets. These new machines extend the current Predator and Global Hawk technologies the military used in Afghanistan after the September 11th, 2001 terrorist attacks.

Although robots are essential components of today's automated manufacturing and military systems, future robots will find wider applications in banks, restaurants, homes, doctors' offices, and hazardous working environments, such as nuclear stations. The Repliee Q1 and Q2 robots from Japan are ultra-humanlike robots or androids that can blink, gesture, speak, and even appear to breathe (see Figure 7.5).[29] Microrobotics is a developing area. Also called micro-electro-mechanical systems (MEMS), microrobots are the size of a grain of salt and can be used in a

Figure 7.4 Aibo
*Sony has stopped making
this robot puppy.*

SOURCE: Chris Willson/Alamy.

person's blood to monitor the body and for other purposes in air bags, cell phones, refrigerators, and more.

If you would like to try to make a robot, Lego Mindstorms is a good place to start (see Figure 7.6).

Vision Systems

Another area of AI involves **vision systems**. Vision systems include hardware and software that permit computers to capture, store, and manipulate visual images.

vision systems The hardware and software that permit computers to capture, store, and manipulate visual images.

For example, vision systems can be used with robots to give these machines "sight." Factory robots typically perform mechanical tasks with no visual stimuli. Robotic vision extends the capability of these systems, allowing the robot to make decisions based on visual input. Generally, robots with vision systems can recognise black and white and some grey shades but do not have good colour or three-dimensional vision. Other systems concentrate on only a few key features in an image, ignoring the rest. Another potential application of a vision system is fingerprint analysis.

Figure 7.5 The Repliee
Q2 Robot from Japan

SOURCE: Karl F. MacDorman. A student in the Intelligent Robotics Laboratory at Osaka University, Japan, shaking hands with Repliee Q2, an android robot developed by the Intelligent Robotics Laboratory and Kokoro Co., Ltd.

Even with recent breakthroughs in vision systems, computers cannot see and understand visual images the way people can.

Natural Language Processing and Voice Recognition

As discussed in Chapter 4, **natural language processing** allows a computer to understand and react to statements and commands made in a "natural" language, such as English. In some cases, voice recognition is used with natural language processing. Voice recognition involves converting sound waves into words. Dragon Systems' Naturally Speaking uses continuous voice recognition, or natural speech, allowing the user to input data into the computer by speaking at a normal pace without pausing between words. The spoken words are transcribed immediately onto the computer screen (see Figure 7.7). After converting sounds into words, natural language processing systems can be used to react to the words or commands by performing a variety of tasks. Brokerage services are a perfect fit for voice-recognition and natural language processing technology to replace the existing "press 1 to buy or sell shares" touchpad telephone menu system. People buying and selling use a vocabulary too varied for easy access through menus and touchpads, but still small enough for software to process in real time. Several brokerages – including Charles Schwab & Company, Fidelity Investments, DLJdirect, and TD Waterhouse Group – offer these services. These systems use voice recognition and natural language processing to let customers access retirement accounts, check balances, and find stock quotes. Eventually, the technology may allow people to make transactions using voice commands over the phone and to use search engines to have their questions answered through the brokerage firm's call centre. One of the big advantages is that the number of calls routed to the customer service department drops considerably after new voice features are added. That is desirable to brokerages, because it helps them staff their call centres correctly – even in volatile markets. Whereas a typical person uses a vocabulary of about 20 000 words or less, voice-recognition software can have a built-in vocabulary of 85 000 words. Some companies claim that

natural language processing
Processing that allows the computer to understand and react to statements and commands made in a 'natural' language, such as English.

Figure 7.6 Lego
Mindstorms *The kit
contains a programmable
brick, Lego bricks, motors
and sensors to build
robots. The robot can be
programed in a range of
languages, including Java
and Visual Basic, as well as
Lego's own easy to master
RCX Code.*

voice-recognition and natural language processing software is so good that customers forget
they are talking to a computer and start discussing the weather or sports results.

Learning Systems

learning systems A combination
of software and hardware that
allows the computer to change
how it functions or reacts to
situations based on feedback it
receives.

Another part of AI deals with **learning systems**, a combination of software and
hardware that allows a computer to change how it functions or reacts to situations based on feedback it receives. For example, some computerised games
have learning abilities. If the computer does not win a game, it remembers not to
make the same moves under the same conditions again. Tom Mitchell, director
of the Center for Automated Learning and Discovery at Carnegie Mellon

Figure 7.7 Dragon Systems' Naturally Speaking

University, is experimenting with two learning software packages that help each other learn.[30] He believes that two learning software packages that cooperate are better than separate learning packages. Mitchell's learning software helps internet search engines do a better job in finding information. Learning systems software requires feedback on the results of actions or decisions. At a minimum, the feedback needs to indicate whether the results are desirable (winning a game) or undesirable (losing a game). The feedback is then used to alter what the system will do in the future.

Neural Networks

An increasingly important aspect of AI involves **neural networks**, also called "neural nets." A neural network is a computer system that can act like or simulate the functioning of a human brain. The systems use massively parallel processors in an architecture that is based on the human brain's own mesh-like structure. In addition, neural network software simulates a neural network using standard computers. Neural networks can process many pieces of data at the same time and learn to recognise patterns. Some of the specific abilities of neural networks include discovering relationships and trends in large databases and solving complex problems for which all the information is not present.

> **neural network** A computer system that attempts to simulate the functioning of a human brain.

A particular skill of neural nets is analyzing detailed trends. Large amusement parks and banks use neural networks to determine staffing needs based on customer traffic – a task that requires precise analysis, down to the half-hour. Increasingly, businesses are using neural nets to help them navigate ever-thicker forests of data and make sense of a myriad of customer traits and buying habits. One application, for example, would be to track the habits of insurance customers and predict which ones will not renew a policy. Staff could then suggest to an insurance agent what changes to make in the policy to persuade the consumer to renew it. Some pattern-recognition software uses neural networks to analyze hundreds of millions of bank, brokerage, and insurance accounts involving a trillion euros to uncover money laundering and other suspicious money transfers.

Ethical and Societal Issues

Knowledge Sharing Website Takes Whistleblowing to a New Level

SOURCE: © Luxio/Alamy.

A "wiki" is a website that anyone, or a selected group of people, can edit. Wikis are an excellent knowledge management tool. They allow people to document and disseminate their knowledge, and add to the knowledge other people have documented. The most famous example is Wikipedia, "the free encyclopedia that anyone can edit."

Almost as famous is another site, Wikileaks. Citizens have always desired accountability and transparency in their elected officials, to be secure in the knowledge that they are doing a good job and working for the good of their nation. Use of new information laws, such as the Freedom of Information Act in the UK, have raised public awareness that this does not always appear to be the case. One Freedom of Information request revealed the frivolous expenses claimed by members of parliament, and Wikileaks aims to bring important news and information like this to the public by providing an innovative, secure and anonymous way for sources to "leak" information.

Wikileaks is no longer actually a wiki-like Wikipedia in that it is not edited directly and collaboratively, although that is how it was originally designed. Instead, the name is probably kept for historical reasons and now refers to the fact that members of the public can anonymously submit material they wish to make public. The material is vetted and verified by Wikileaks' accredited journalists and then published as downloadable files. In that sense the Wikileaks website is a knowledge sharing site. Wikileaks itself, however, is more than a website. It is a not-for-profit media organisation whose members base their work on the defence of freedom of speech and improving humanity's com-

mon historical record. It was supposedly started by Chinese dissidents, journalists, mathematicians and startup company technologists from the US, Taiwan, Europe, Australia and South Africa, but is now represented in the media by Julian Assange.

Whoever they are, they certainly know how to create headlines. They have received a number of media awards and have published sensitive information about torture, suppression of free speech, financial corruption, abuse and religious cults. More famously, in 2010, they released detailed correspondence between the US State Department and its diplomats. The content included unguarded comments from diplomats about the host countries of their embassies and information about US intelligence and counterintelligence actions. Since this happened, lawyers for Wikileaks have stated that they believe they are being watched by security services, and several companies severed ties with Wikileaks, including the company that provided its web server. (In a twist, a group of internet activists called Anonymous then targeted these companies with denial of service attacks.) At the time of writing, Julian Assange is on bail in the UK, waiting to hear the outcome of a request for extradition by Sweden.

Despite all this, the organisation does seem to be having an effect. Information published by Wikileaks has been partially credited with starting the 2010–2011 revolution in Tunisia which saw their unpopular president standing down. However, according to BBC reporter Bill Thompson its ultimate impact might be something else: "Wikileaks has exposed the inadequacies in the way governments control their internal flow of information, and organisations dedicated to transparency and disclosure will observe the tactics used to shut it down and adapt accordingly. But the state can learn, too, and has the resources to implement what it learns. I fear that Wikileaks is as likely to usher in an era of more effective control as it is to sweep away the authoritarian regimes that Julian Assange opposes."

Discussion Questions

1 What do you feel the impact of whistleblowing organisations, such as Wikileaks, will be?

2 Should governments be worried by organisations such as Wikileaks?

Critical Thinking Questions

1 What role has the internet played in empowering citizens? Many governments claim to have e-government initiatives. Review what is available in your country – does this put power into the hands of the people? What more could your government do?

2 Can you think of a way in which people can be given accountability and transparency from their elected officials without going to the extremes Wikileaks has?

SOURCES: web.archive.org/web/20080314204422/http://www.wikileaks.org/wiki/Wikileaks:About. Accessed 16 January 2011; www.guardian.co.uk/media/2010/dec/05/julian-assange-lawyers-being-watched. Accessed 16 January 2011; wikileaks.ch/About.html. Accessed 16 January 2011; www.bbc.co.uk/news/technology-12007616. Accessed 16 January 2011.

Other Artificial Intelligence Applications

A few other artificial intelligence applications exist in addition to those just discussed. A **genetic algorithm**, also called a genetic program, is an approach to solving large, complex problems in which many repeated operations or models change and evolve until the best one emerges. The first step is to change or vary competing solutions to the problem. This can be done by changing the parts of a program or by combining different program segments into a new program. The second step is to select only the best models or algorithms, which continue to evolve. Programs or program segments that are not as good as others are discarded, similar to natural selection or "survival of the fittest," in which only the best species survive. This process of variation and natural selection continues until the genetic algorithm yields the best possible solution to the original problem. For example, some investment firms use genetic algorithms to help select the best stocks or bonds. Genetic algorithms are also used in computer science and mathematics. Genetic algorithms can help companies determine which orders to accept for maximum profit. This approach helps companies select the orders that will increase profits and take full advantage of the company's production facilities. Genetic algorithms are also being used to make better decisions in developing inputs to neural networks.

genetic algorithm An approach to solving large, complex problems in which a number of related operations or models change and evolve until the best one emerges.

An **intelligent agent** (also called an "intelligent robot" or "bot") consists of programs and a knowledge base used to perform a specific task for a person, a process, or another program. Like a sports agent who searches for the best sponsorship deals for a top athlete, an intelligent agent often searches to find the best price, schedule, or solution to a problem. The programs used by an intelligent agent can search large amounts of data as the knowledge base refines the search or accommodates user preferences. Often used to search the vast resources of the internet, intelligent agents can help people find information on an important topic or the best price for a new digital camera. Intelligent agents can also be used to make travel arrangements, monitor incoming email for viruses or junk mail, and coordinate meetings and schedules of busy executives. In the human resources field, intelligent agents help with online training. The software can look ahead in training materials and know what to start next.

intelligent agent Programs and a knowledge base used to perform a specific task for a person, a process, or another program; also called intelligent robot or bot.

7

7.3 Expert Systems

An expert system outputs a recommendation based on answers given to it by users (who are not experts in the field). The intention of the system is to capture the expert's knowledge and make it available to those who lack this knowledge. Expert systems have been developed to diagnose medical conditions, resolve engineering problems, and solve energy problems. They have also been used to design new products and systems, develop innovative insurance products, determine the best use of timber, and increase the quality of healthcare (see Figure 7.8). Like human experts,

Figure 7.8 **Using a Credit Card** *Credit card companies often use expert systems to determine credit limits for credit cards.*

SOURCE: © Don Bayley/iStock.

expert systems use heuristics, or rules of thumb, to arrive at conclusions or make suggestions. The research conducted in AI during the past two decades is resulting in expert systems that explore new business possibilities, increase overall profitability, reduce costs, and provide superior service to customers and clients.

When to Use Expert Systems

Sophisticated expert systems can be difficult, expensive, and time consuming to develop. The following is a list of factors that normally make expert systems worth the expenditure of time and money. Develop an expert system, if it can do any of the following:

- Provide a high potential payoff or significantly reduce downside risk
- Capture and preserve irreplaceable human expertise
- Solve a problem that is not easily solved using traditional programming techniques
- Develop a system that is more consistent than human experts
- Provide expertise needed at a number of locations at the same time or in a hostile environment that is dangerous to human health
- Provide expertise that is expensive or rare
- Develop a solution faster than human experts can
- Provide expertise needed for training and development to share the wisdom and experience of human experts with many people

Components of Expert Systems

An expert system consists of a collection of integrated and related components, including a knowledge base, an inference engine, an explanation facility, a knowledge base acquisition facility, and a user interface. A diagram of a typical expert system is shown in Figure 7.9.

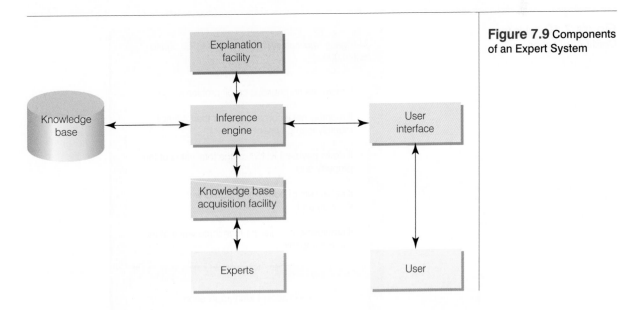

Figure 7.9 Components of an Expert System

The Knowledge Base

The knowledge base stores all relevant information, data, rules, cases, and relationships that the expert system uses. A knowledge base is a natural extension of a database (presented in Chapter 5) and an information and decision support system (presented in Chapter 8).

A knowledge base must be developed for each unique application. For example, a medical expert system contains facts about diseases and symptoms. The following are some tools and techniques that can be used to create a knowledge base.

■ *Assembling human experts.* One challenge in developing a knowledge base is to assemble the knowledge of multiple human experts. Typically, the objective in building a knowledge base is to integrate the knowledge of people with similar expertise (for example, many doctors might contribute to a medical diagnostics knowledge base).

■ *Fuzzy logic.* Another challenge for expert system designers and developers is capturing knowledge and relationships that are not precise or exact. Instead of the yes/no, or true/false, conditions of typical computer decisions, fuzzy logic allows shades of grey, or what is known as "fuzzy sets." Fuzzy logic rules help computers evaluate the imperfect or imprecise conditions they encounter and make educated guesses based on the probability of correctness of the decision.

■ *Rules.* A rule is a conditional statement that links conditions to actions or outcomes. In many instances, these rules are stored as **IF-THEN statements**, such as "IF a certain set of network conditions exists, THEN a certain network problem diagnosis is appropriate." In an expert system for a weather forecasting operation, for example, the rules could state that if certain temperature patterns exist with a given barometric pressure and certain previous weather patterns over the last 24 hours, then a specific forecast will be made, including temperatures, cloud coverage, and wind-chill factor. Figure 7.10 shows how to use expert system rules in determining whether a person should receive a mortgage loan from a bank. These rules can be placed in almost any standard program language, discussed in Chapter 4, using "IF-THEN" statements or into special expert systems shells, discussed later in the chapter. In general, as the number of rules that an expert system knows increases, the precision of the expert system also increases.

IF-THEN statements Rules that suggest certain conclusions.

Figure 7.10 Rules for a Credit Application

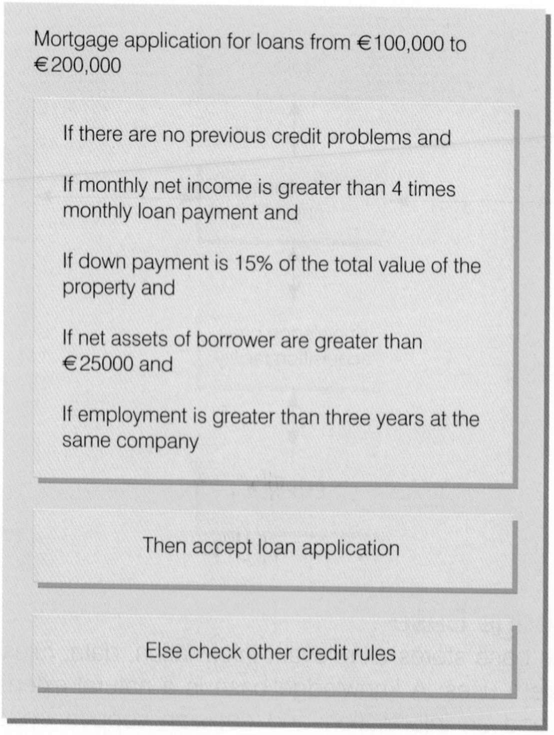

Mortgage application for loans from €100,000 to €200,000

If there are no previous credit problems and

If monthly net income is greater than 4 times monthly loan payment and

If down payment is 15% of the total value of the property and

If net assets of borrower are greater than €25000 and

If employment is greater than three years at the same company

Then accept loan application

Else check other credit rules

■ *Cases.* An expert system can use cases in developing a solution to a current problem or situation. This process involves (1) finding cases stored in the knowledge base that are similar to the problem or situation at hand and (2) modifying the solutions to the cases to fit or accommodate the current problem or situation.

The Inference Engine

The overall purpose of an **inference engine** is to seek information and relationships from the knowledge base and to provide answers, predictions, and suggestions the way a human expert would. In other words, the inference engine is the component that delivers the expert advice. To provide answers and give advice, expert systems can use backward and forward chaining. **Backward chaining** is the process of starting with conclusions and working backward to the supporting facts. If the facts do not support the conclusion, another conclusion is selected and tested. This process is continued until the correct conclusion is identified. **Forward chaining** starts with the facts and works forward to the conclusions. Consider the expert system that forecasts future sales for a product. Forward chaining starts with a fact, such as "The demand for the product last month was 20 000 units." With the forward-chaining approach, the expert system searches for rules that contain a reference to product demand. For example, "IF product demand is over 15 000 units, THEN check the demand for competing products." As a result of this process, the expert system might use information on the demand for competitive products. Next, after searching additional rules, the expert system might use information on personal income or national inflation rates. This process continues until the expert system can reach a conclusion using the data supplied by the user and the rules that apply in the knowledge base.

inference engine Part of the expert system that seeks information and relationships from the knowledge base and provides answers, predictions, and suggestions the way a human expert would.

backward chaining The process of starting with conclusions and working backward to the supporting facts.

forward chaining The process of starting with the facts and working forward to the conclusions.

The Explanation Facility

An important part of an expert system is the **explanation facility**, which allows a user or decision maker to understand how the expert system arrived at certain conclusions or results. A medical expert system, for example, might reach the conclusion that a patient has a defective heart valve given certain symptoms and the results of tests on the patient. The explanation facility allows a doctor to find out the logic or rationale of the diagnosis made by the expert system. The expert system, using the explanation facility, can indicate all the facts and rules that were used in reaching the conclusion. This facility allows doctors to determine whether the expert system is processing the data and information correctly and logically.

explanation facility Component of an expert system that allows a user or decision maker to understand how the expert system arrived at certain conclusions or results.

The Knowledge Acquisition Facility

A difficult task in developing an expert system is the process of creating and updating the knowledge base. In the past, when more traditional programming languages were used, developing a knowledge base was tedious and time consuming. Each fact, relationship, and rule had to be programed into the knowledge base. In most cases, an experienced programer had to create and update the knowledge base.

Today, specialised software allows users and decision makers to create and modify their own knowledge bases through the **knowledge acquisition facility**. The purpose of the knowledge acquisition facility is to provide a convenient and efficient means for capturing and storing all components of the knowledge base. Knowledge acquisition software can present users and decision makers with easy-to-use menus. After entering the appropriate attributes, the knowledge acquisition facility correctly stores information and relationships in the knowledge base, making the knowledge base easier and less expensive to set up and maintain. Knowledge

knowledge acquisition facility Part of the expert system that provides convenient and efficient means of capturing and storing all the components of the knowledge base.

acquisition can be a manual process or a mixture of manual and automated procedures. Regardless of how the knowledge is acquired, the knowledge base must be validated and updated frequently to make sure that it is still accurate.

The User Interface

Specialised user interface software is employed for designing, creating, updating, and using expert systems. The main purpose of the user interface is to make an expert system easier for users and decision makers to develop and use. At one time, skilled computer personnel created and operated most expert systems; today, the user interface permits decision makers to develop and use their own expert systems. Because expert systems place more emphasis on directing user activities than do other types of systems, text-oriented user interfaces (using menus, forms, and scripts) might be more common in expert systems than the graphical interfaces often used with DSS. Here is a typical user interface between a user and the expert system for a credit application:

> **EXPERT SYSTEM:** Are there any previous credit problems?
> **USER:** No.
> **EXPERT SYSTEM:** Is the applicant's net income greater than four times the monthly loan payment?
> **USER:** Yes.
> **EXPERT SYSTEM:** Is the down payment greater than 15 per cent of the property value?
> **USER:** Yes.
> **EXPERT SYSTEM:** Are the net assets of the borrower greater than €25 000?
> **USER:** Yes.
> **EXPERT SYSTEM:** Has the borrower worked more than three years at the same company?
> **USER:** Yes.
> **EXPERT SYSTEM:** Accept the loan application.

Expert Systems Development

Like other computer systems, expert systems require a systematic development approach for best results. This approach includes determining the requirements for the expert system, identifying one or more experts in the area or discipline under investigation, constructing the components of the expert system, implementing the results, and maintaining and reviewing the complete system.

Participants in Developing and Using Expert Systems

domain The area of knowledge addressed by the expert system.

domain expert The individual or group who has the expertise or knowledge one is trying to capture in the expert system.

Because of the time and effort involved in the task, an expert system is developed to address only a specific area of knowledge. This area of knowledge is called the **domain**. The **domain expert** is the person or group with the expertise or knowledge the expert system is trying to capture. The domain expert (individual or group) usually can do the following:

- ■ Recognise the real problem.
- ■ Develop a general framework for problem solving.
- ■ Formulate theories about the situation.
- ■ Develop and use general rules to solve a problem.
- ■ Know when to break the rules or general principles.
- ■ Solve problems quickly and efficiently.
- ■ Learn from experience.
- ■ Know what is and is not important in solving a problem.
- ■ Explain the situation and solutions of problems to others.

A **knowledge engineer** is a person who has training or experience in the design, development, implementation, and maintenance of an expert system, including training or experience with expert system shells. The **knowledge user** is the person or group who uses and benefits from the expert system. Knowledge users do not need any previous training in computers or expert systems.

knowledge engineer A person who has training or experience in the design, development, implementation, and maintenance of an expert system.

knowledge user The person or group who uses and benefits from the expert system.

Expert Systems Development Tools and Techniques

Theoretically, expert systems can be developed from any programming language. Since the introduction of computer systems, programming languages have become easier to use, more powerful, and increasingly able to handle specialised requirements. In the early days of expert systems development, traditional high-level languages, including Pascal, FORTRAN, and COBOL, were used (see Figure 7.11). LISP was one of the first special languages developed and used for expert system applications. PROLOG was also developed to build expert systems. Since the 1990s, however, other expert system products (such as shells) have become available that remove the burden of programming, allowing nonprogramers to develop and benefit from the use of expert systems.

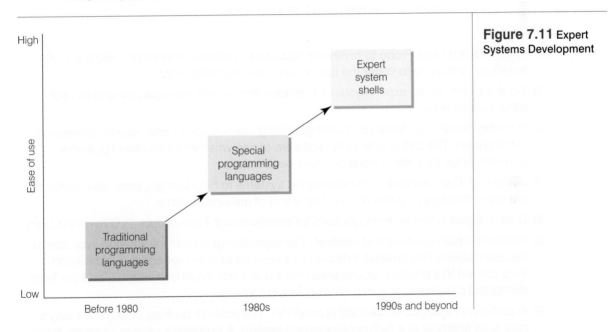

Figure 7.11 Expert Systems Development

An expert system shell is a collection of software packages and tools used to design, develop, implement, and maintain expert systems. Expert system shells are available for both personal computers and mainframe systems. Some shells are inexpensive, costing less than €400. In addition, off-the-shelf expert system shells are complete and ready to run. The user enters the appropriate data or parameters, and the expert system provides output to the problem or situation.

Some expert system products can analyze LAN networks, monitor air quality in commercial buildings, and evaluate oil and drilling operations. Table 7.3 lists a few expert system products.

Applications of Expert Systems and Artificial Intelligence

Expert systems and artificial intelligence have wide applications in business and government. A list of applications, some of which have already been mentioned, is given next.

■ *Credit granting and loan analysis.* Many banks employ expert systems to review a customer's credit application and credit history data from credit bureaus to make a decision on whether to grant a loan or approve a transaction. KPMG Peat Marwick uses an expert

Table 7.3 Popular Expert System Products

Name of Product	Application and Capabilities
Financial Adviser	Analyzes financial investments in new equipment, facilities, and the like; requests the appropriate data and performs a complete financial analysis
G2	Assists in oil and gas operations. Transco, a British company, uses it to help in the transport of gas to more than 20 million commercial and domestic customers
HazMat Loader	Analyzes hazardous materials in truck shipments
LSI Indicator	Helps determine property values; developed by one of the largest residential title and closing companies
MindWizard	Enables development of compact expert systems ranging from simple models that incorporate business decision rules to highly sophisticated models; PC-based and inexpensive
RAMPART	Analyzes risk. The US General Services Administration uses it to analyze risk to the approximately 8000 federal buildings it manages

system called Loan Probe to review its reserves to determine whether sufficient funds have been set aside to cover the risk of some uncollectible loans.

■ *Stock picking.* Some expert systems help investment professionals pick stocks and other investments.

■ *Catching cheats and terrorists.* Some gambling casinos use expert system software to catch cheats. The CIA is testing the software to see whether it can detect possible terrorists when they make hotel or airline reservations.

■ *Budgeting.* Car companies can use expert systems to help budget, plan, and coordinate prototype testing programs to save hundreds of millions of euros.

■ *Games.* Some expert systems are used for entertainment. For example, 20Q (www.20Q.net).

■ *Information management and retrieval.* The explosive growth of information available to decision makers has created a demand for devices to help manage the information. Bots can aid this process. Businesses might use a bot to retrieve information from large distributed databases or a vast network like the internet.

■ *AI and expert systems embedded in products.* The antilock braking system on today's cars is an example of a rudimentary expert system. A processor senses when the tyres are beginning to skid and releases the brakes for a fraction of a second to prevent the skid. AI researchers are also finding ways to use neural networks and robotics in everyday devices, such as toasters, alarm clocks, and televisions.

■ *Plant layout and manufacturing.* FLEXPERT is an expert system that uses fuzzy logic to perform plant layout. The software helps companies determine the best placement for equipment and manufacturing facilities. Expert systems can also spot defective welds during the manufacturing process. The expert system analyzes radiographic images and suggests which welds could be flawed.

■ *Hospitals and medical facilities.* Some hospitals use expert systems to determine a patient's likelihood of contracting cancer or other diseases. Hospitals, pharmacies, and other healthcare providers can use CaseAlert by MEDecision to determine possible high-risk or high-cost patients. MYCIN is an early expert system developed at Stanford University to analyze blood infections. UpToDate is another expert system used to diagnose patients. To help doctors in the diagnosis of thoracic pain, MatheMEDics has developed

THORASK, a straightforward, easy-to-use program, requiring only the input of carefully obtained clinical information. The program helps the less experienced to distinguish the three principal categories of chest pain from each other. It does what a true medical expert system should do without the need for complicated user input. The user answers basic questions about the patient's history and directed physical findings, and the program immediately displays a list of diagnoses. The diagnoses are presented in decreasing order of likelihood, together with their estimated probabilities. The program also provides concise descriptions of relevant clinical conditions and their presentations, as well as brief suggestions for diagnostic approaches.

■ *Help desk and assistance.* Customer service help desks use expert systems to provide timely and accurate assistance. The automated help desk frees up staff to handle more complex needs while still providing more timely assistance for routine calls.

■ *Employee performance evaluation.* An expert system developed by Austin-Hayne, called Employee Appraiser, provides managers with expert advice for use in employee performance reviews and career development.

■ *Virus detection.* IBM is using neural network technology to help create more advanced software for eradicating computer viruses, a major problem in businesses. IBM's neural network software deals with "boot sector" viruses, the most prevalent type, using a form of artificial intelligence that generalises by looking at examples. It requires a vast number of training samples, which, in the case of antivirus software, are fragments of virus code.

■ *Repair and maintenance.* ACE is an expert system used by AT&T to analyze the maintenance of telephone networks. IET-Intelligent Electronics uses an expert system to diagnose maintenance problems related to aerospace equipment. General Electric Aircraft Engine Group uses an expert system to enhance maintenance performance levels at all sites and improve diagnostic accuracy.

■ *Shipping.* CARGEX cargo expert system is used by Lufthansa, a German airline, to help determine the best shipping routes.

■ *Marketing.* CoverStory is an expert system that extracts marketing information from a database and automatically writes marketing reports.

■ *Warehouse optimisation.* United Distillers uses an expert system to determine the best combinations of liquor stocks to produce its blends of Scotch whiskey. This information is then supplemented with information about the location of the casks for each blend. The system optimises the selection of required casks, keeping to a minimum the number of "doors" (warehouse sections) from which the casks must be taken and the number of casks that need to be moved to clear the way. Other constraints must be satisfied, such as the current working capacity of each warehouse and the maintenance and restocking work that may be in progress.

7.4 Virtual Reality

The term "virtual reality" was initially coined by Jaron Lanier, founder of VPL Research, in 1989. Originally, the term referred to immersive virtual reality in which the user becomes fully immersed in an artificial, three-dimensional world that is completely generated by a computer. Immersive virtual reality can represent any three-dimensional setting, real or abstract, such as a building, an archaeological excavation site, human anatomy, a sculpture, or a crime scene reconstruction. Through immersion, the user can gain a deeper understanding of the virtual world's behaviour and functionality.

A virtual reality system enables one or more users to move and react in a computer-simulated environment. Virtual reality simulations require special interface devices that transmit the sights, sounds, and sensations of the simulated world to the user. These devices can also record and send the speech and movements of the participants to the simulation program, enabling users to sense and manipulate virtual objects much as they would real objects. This natural style of interaction gives the participants the feeling that they are immersed in the simulated world. For example, a car manufacturer can use virtual reality to help it simulate and design factories.

A related term is "augmented reality," which refers to the combination of computer generated data (images, sounds, etc.) with stimuli from the real world. For example, an augmented reality system might project instructions onto the user's eye, on top of the real world images they are seeing, so they could look at both at the same time.

Interface Devices

To see in a virtual world, often the user wears a head-mounted display (HMD) with screens directed at each eye. The HMD also contains a position tracker to monitor the location of the user's head and the direction in which the user is looking. Using this information, a computer generates images of the virtual world – a slightly different view for each eye – to match the direction that the user is looking and displays these images on the HMD. Many companies sell or rent virtual-reality interface devices, including Virtual Realities (www.vrealities.com), Amusitronix (www.amusitronix.com), I-O Display Systems (www.i-glassesstore.com), and others. With current technology, virtual-world scenes must be kept relatively simple so that the computer can update the visual imagery quickly enough (at least ten times per second) to prevent the user's view from appearing jerky and from lagging behind the user's movements.

The Electronic Visualisation Laboratory at the University of Illinois at Chicago introduced a room constructed of large screens on three walls and the floor on which the graphics are projected. The CAVE®, as this room is called, provides the illusion of immersion by projecting stereo images on the walls and floor of a room-sized cube. Several persons wearing light-weight stereo glasses can enter and walk freely inside the CAVE®. A head-tracking system continuously adjusts the stereo projection to the current position of the leading viewer (see Figure 7.12).

Figure 7.12 *Military personnel design systems in an immersive CAVE® environment.*

Users hear sounds in the virtual world through speakers mounted above or behind the screens. Spatial audio is possible, allowing for position tracking. When a sound source in virtual space is not directly in front of or behind the user, the computer transmits sounds to arrive at one ear a little earlier or later than at the other and to be a little louder or softer and slightly different in pitch.

The haptic interface, which relays the sense of touch and other physical sensations in the virtual world, is the least developed and perhaps the most challenging to create. Currently, with the use of a glove and position tracker, the computer locates the user's hand and measures finger movements. The user can reach into the virtual world and handle objects; however, it is difficult to realise sensations of a person tapping a hard surface, picking up an object, or running a finger across a textured surface. Touch sensations also have to be synchronised with the sights and sounds of the user's experience.

Forms of Virtual Reality

Aside from immersive virtual reality, which just has been discussed, virtual reality can also refer to applications that are not fully immersive, such as mouse-controlled navigation through a three-dimensional environment on a graphics monitor, stereo viewing from the monitor via stereo glasses, stereo projection systems, and others (see Figure 7.13).

Figure 7.13 The PowerWall

SOURCE: Courtesy of Fakespace Systems, Inc.

Some virtual reality applications allow views of real environments with superimposed virtual objects. Motion trackers monitor the movements of dancers or athletes for subsequent studies in immersive virtual reality. Telepresence systems (such as telemedicine and telerobotics) immerse a viewer in a real world that is captured by video cameras at a distant location and allow for the remote manipulation of real objects via robot arms and manipulators. Many believe that virtual reality will reshape the interface between people and information technology by offering new ways to communicate information, visualise processes, and express ideas creatively.

Virtual Reality Applications

You can find thousands of applications of virtual reality, with more being developed as the cost of hardware and software declines and people's imaginations are opened to the potential of virtual reality. The following are a few virtual reality applications in medicine, education and training, business, and entertainment (see Figure 7.14).

Figure 7.14 Virtual
Reality Applications
Virtual reality has been used to increase real estate sales in several powerful ways. RealSpace Vision Communication, for example, helps real estate developers showcase their properties with virtual reality tours.

SOURCE: Courtesy of RealSpace Vision Communication Inc.

Medicine

Barbara Rothbaum, the director of the Trauma and Recovery Program at Emory University School of Medicine and cofounder of Virtually Better, uses an immersive virtual reality system to help in the treatment of anxiety disorders. One VR program, called SnowWorld, helps treat burn patients. Using VR, the patients can navigate through icy terrain and frigid waterfalls. VR helps, because it gets a patient's mind off the pain.

Education and Training

Virtual environments are used in education to bring exciting new resources into the classroom. According to the founder of Mantis Development Corporation, a software company that specialised in digital media and virtual reality, "In order to learn, you need to engage the mind, and immersive education is engaging." In development for more than 10 years, *3D Rewind Rome* is a virtual reality show developed at a virtual reality lab at University of California Los Angeles (UCLA) (see Image 7.1). The show is historically accurate with more than 7000 reconstructed buildings on a background of realistic landscape. The Archaeology Technologies Laboratory at North Dakota State University has developed a 3D virtual reality system that displays an eighteenth-century American Indian village.

Virtual technology has also been applied by the military. To help with aircraft maintenance, a virtual reality system has been developed to simulate an aircraft and give a user a sense of touch, while computer graphics provide a sense of sight and sound. The user sees, touches, and manipulates the various parts of the virtual aircraft during training. The Virtual Aircraft Maintenance System simulates real-world maintenance tasks that are routinely performed on the AV8B vertical takeoff and landing aircraft used by the US Marines. Also, the Pentagon is using a virtual reality training lab to prepare for a military crisis. The virtual reality system simulates various war scenarios.

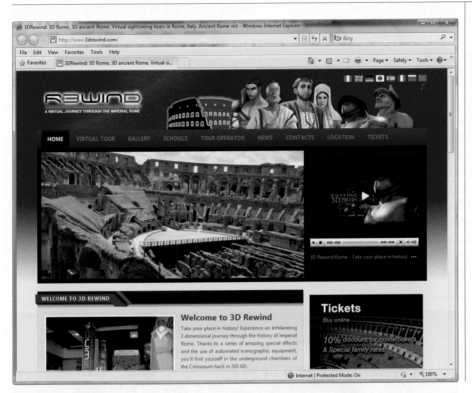

SOURCE: www.3drewind.com.

Image 7.1 *3D Rewind Rome is based on more than ten years of research by archaeologists and historians coordinated by the University of California, Los Angeles.*

Business and Commerce

Virtual reality has been used in all areas of business. Boeing used virtual reality to help it design and manufacture airplane parts and new planes, including the 787 Dreamliner. Boeing used 3D PLM from Dassault Systems. One healthcare institution used Second Life to create a virtual hospital when it started construction of a real multimillion dollar hospital (see Image 7.2). The purpose of the Second Life virtual hospital was to show clients and staff the layout and capabilities of the new hospital. Second Life has also been used in business and recruiting. Second Life (*www.secondlife.com*) also allows people to play games, interact with avatars, and build

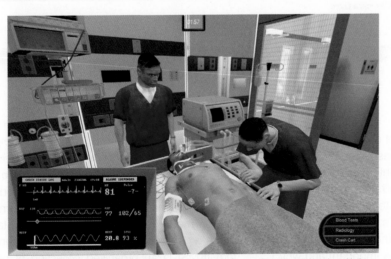

SOURCE: Pulse!! is a research project of Texas A&M University-Corpus Christi in collaboration with the Office of Naval Research and Breakaway Ltd.

Image 7.2 *Although it looks like a video game, Pulse!! is a serious training tool for nurses and physicians developed by Breakaway.*

structures, such as homes. A number of companies are using VR in advertising. Pizza chain Papa John's used VR as an advertising tool. It placed a VR image on many of its pizza boxes. When the image is viewed by a web camera on a computer, a standard keyboard can be used to manipulate images of a Chevrolet Camaro on the computer screen. It is a moving image of the Camaro that the founder of Papa John's sold to start his pizza company.

Entertainment

Computer-generated image technology, or CGI, has been around since the 1970s. Many movies use this technology to bring realism to the silver screen, including *Avatar, Finding Nemo, Spider-Man II, and Star Wars Episode II – Attack of the Clones*. A team of artists rendered the roiling seas and crashing waves of *Perfect Storm* almost entirely on computers, using weather reports, scientific formulas, and their imagination. Other films that have used CGI technology include Dinosaur with its realistic talking reptiles, *Titan A.E.*'s beautiful 3D spacescapes, and the casts of computer-generated crowds and battles in *Gladiator* and *The Patriot*. CGI can also be used for sports simulation to enhance the viewers' knowledge and enjoyment of a game. SimCity (*http://simcity.ea.com/*), a virtual reality game, allows people to experiment with decisions related to urban planning.

Image 7.3 *SimCity simulates urban planning by letting you create, build, and run a virtual city.*

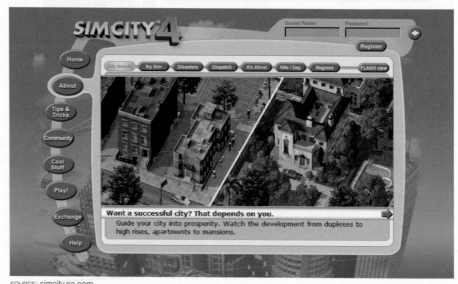

SOURCE: simcity.ea.com.

Summary

At the start of this chapter we set out the FOUR main principles relating to how businesses and organisations use systems to share information between managers and employees and the benefits and issues inherent in such systems together with the key learning objectives for each. It's now time to summarise the chapter by recapping on those FOUR principles: can you recall what is important and why about each one?

1. **Knowledge management systems allow organisations to share knowledge and experience among their managers and employees.** Knowledge is an awareness and understanding of a set of information and the ways that information can be made useful to support a specific task or reach a decision. A knowledge management system (KMS) is an organised collection of people, procedures, software, databases, and devices used

to create, store, share, and use the organisation's knowledge and experience. Explicit knowledge is objective and can be measured and documented in reports, papers, and rules. Tacit knowledge is hard to measure and document and is typically not objective or formalised.

Knowledge workers are people who create, use, and disseminate knowledge. They are usually professionals in science, engineering, business, and other areas. The chief knowledge officer (CKO) is a top-level executive who helps the organisation use a KMS to create, store, and use knowledge to achieve organisational goals. Obtaining, storing, sharing, and using knowledge is the key to any KMS. The use of a KMS often leads to additional knowledge creation, storage, sharing, and usage. Many tools and techniques can be used to create, store, and use knowledge. These tools and techniques are available from IBM, Microsoft, and other companies and organisations.

2. **Artificial intelligence systems form a broad and diverse set of systems that can replicate human decision making for certain types of well-defined problems.** The term artificial intelligence is used to describe computers with the ability to mimic or duplicate the functions of the human brain. The objective of building AI systems is not to replace human decision making completely, but to replicate it for certain types of well-defined problems.

Intelligent behaviour encompasses several characteristics, including the abilities to learn from experience and apply this knowledge to new experiences; handle complex situations and solve problems for which pieces of information might be missing; determine relevant information in a given situation, think in a logical and rational manner, and give a quick and correct response; and understand visual images and process symbols. Computers are better than people at transferring information, making a series of calculations rapidly and accurately, and making complex calculations, but human beings are better than computers at all other attributes of intelligence.

Artificial intelligence is a broad field that includes several key components, such as expert systems, robotics, vision systems, natural language processing, learning systems, and neural networks. An expert system consists of the hardware and software used to produce systems that behave as a human expert would in a specialised field or area (e.g. credit analysis). Robotics uses mechanical or computer devices to perform tasks that require a high degree of precision or are tedious or hazardous for humans (e.g. stacking cartons on a pallet). Vision systems include hardware and software that permit computers to capture, store, and manipulate images and pictures (e.g. face-recognition software). Natural language processing allows the computer to understand and react to statements and commands made in a "natural" language, such as English. Learning systems use a combination of software and hardware to allow a computer to change how it functions or reacts to situations based on feedback it receives (e.g. a computerised chess game). A neural network is a computer system that can simulate the functioning of a human brain (e.g. disease diagnostics system). A genetic algorithm is an approach to solving large, complex problems in which a number of related operations or models change until the best one emerges.

3. **Expert systems can enable a novice to perform at the level of an expert but must be developed and maintained very carefully.** An expert system consists of a collection of integrated and related components, including a knowledge base, an inference engine, an explanation facility, a knowledge acquisition facility, and a user interface. The knowledge base is an extension of a database, discussed in Chapter 5, and an information and decision support system, discussed in Chapter 8. It contains all the relevant data, rules, and relationships used in the expert system. The rules are often composed of IF-THEN statements, which are used for drawing conclusions. Fuzzy logic allows expert systems to incorporate facts and relationships into expert system knowledge bases that might be imprecise or unknown.

The inference engine processes the rules, data, and relationships stored in the knowledge base to provide answers, predictions, and suggestions the way a human expert would. Two common methods for processing include backward and forward chaining. Backward chaining starts with a conclusion, then searches for facts to support it; forward chaining starts with a fact, then searches for a conclusion to support it.

The explanation facility of an expert system allows the user to understand what rules were used in arriving at a decision. The knowledge acquisition facility helps the user add or update knowledge in the knowledge base. The user interface makes it easier to develop and use the expert system.

The people involved in the development of an expert system include the domain expert, the knowledge engineer, and the knowledge users. The domain expert is the person or group who has the expertise or knowledge being captured for the system. The knowledge engineer is the developer whose job is to extract the expertise from the domain expert. The knowledge user is the person who benefits from the use of the developed system.

The steps involved in the development of an expert system include: determining requirements, identifying experts, constructing expert system components, implementing results, and maintaining and reviewing the system.

Expert systems can be implemented in several ways. A fast way to acquire an expert system is to purchase an expert system shell or existing package. The shell program is a collection of software packages and tools used to design, develop, implement, and maintain expert systems.

The benefits of using an expert system go beyond the typical reasons for using a computerised processing solution. Expert systems display "intelligent" behaviour, manipulate symbolic information and draw conclusions, provide portable knowledge, and can deal with uncertainty. Expert systems can be used to solve problems in many fields

or disciplines and can assist in all stages of the problem-solving process.

4. **Virtual reality systems can reshape the interface between people and information technology by offering new ways to communicate information, visualise processes, and express ideas creatively.** A virtual reality system enables one or more users to move and react in a computer-simulated environment. Virtual reality simulations require special interface devices that transmit the sights, sounds, and sensations of the simulated world to the user. These devices can also record and send the speech and movements of the participants to the simulation program. Thus, users can sense and manipulate virtual objects much as they would real objects. This natural style of interaction gives the participants the feeling that they are immersed in the simulated world.

Virtual reality can also refer to applications that are not fully immersive, such as mouse-controlled navigation through a three-dimensional environment on a graphics monitor, stereo viewing from the monitor via stereo glasses, stereo projection systems, and others. Some virtual reality applications allow views of real environments with superimposed virtual objects. Virtual reality applications are found in medicine, education and training, and entertainment.

Review Questions

1 Define the term "artificial intelligence."

2 What is a vision system? Discuss two applications of such a system.

3 What is natural language processing? What are the three levels of voice recognition?

4 Describe three examples of the use of robotics. How can a microrobot be used?

5 What is an expert system shell?

6 Under what conditions is the development of an expert system likely to be worth the effort?

7 Identify the basic components of an expert system and describe the role of each.

8 What is virtual reality? Give several examples of its use.

9 Describe the roles of the domain expert, the knowledge engineer, and the knowledge user in expert systems.

10 Describe three applications of expert systems or artificial intelligence.

Discussion Questions

1 What are the requirements for a computer to exhibit human-level intelligence? How long will it be before we have the technology to design such computers? Do you think we should push to try to accelerate such a development? Why or why not?

2 Describe how you might encourage your employees to share their knowledge with one another. What technologies might you use and why?

3 Describe how natural language processing could be used in a university setting.

4 What is the purpose of a knowledge base? How is one developed?

5 Imagine that you are developing the rules for an expert system to select the strongest candidates for a medical school. What rules or heuristics would you include?

Web Exercises

1 Use the internet to find information about the use of robotics. Describe three examples of how this technology is used.

2 This chapter discussed several examples of expert systems. Search the internet for two examples of the use of expert systems. Which one has the greatest potential to increase profits? Explain your choice.

Case One

Manchester Police Turn to Twitter

Launched in 2006, Twitter is a micro-blogging social networking website that lets users publish up to 140 characters of news for their friends at a time. Author Steven Johnson described the experience as, "Twitter revolves around the principle of followers. When you choose to follow another Twitter user, that user's tweets appear in reverse chronological order on your main Twitter page. If you follow 20 people, you'll see a mix of tweets scrolling down the page: breakfast-cereal updates, interesting new links, music recommendations, even musings on the future of education." Conventional blogging, essentially publishing a diary online, has long been seen as a knowledge capture and sharing tool. Some people are wondering whether Twitter could be used in a similar way.

In October 2010, one of the UK's biggest police forces decided to publish information about every incident it dealt with in a 24 hour period on Twitter. Greater Manchester Police used the technology to give the public an idea about their officers' workloads. Chief Constable Peter Fahy said it would also give politicians an idea of the kind of incidents "not recognised in league tables and measurements."

By 3 pm on the chosen day, the Twitter page had been updated with more than 1300 calls from members of the public. Among them was a report of a man holding a baby over a bridge (which turned out to actually be a man carrying a dog) and a complaint about someone smoking on a flight into Manchester Airport. Other incidents included suspected shoplifters, aggressive drivers, nuisance phone calls and more seriously a child was injured in a crash.

Mr Fahy said, "Policing is often seen in very simple terms, with cops chasing robbers and locking them up. However, the reality is that this accounts for only part of the work they have to deal with. A lot of what we do is dealing with social problems, such as missing children, people with mental health problems and domestic abuse. Often these incidents can be incredibly complex and need a lot of time, resources and expertise."

Discussion Questions

1 What benefits do you think Manchester police got from doing this?

2 What other organisations could benefit from using Twitter to inform the general public about what they do?

Critical Thinking Questions

1 Do you think Twitter is a useful knowledge sharing technology? Why or why not?

2 What other technologies could be used to connect the public with the police?

SOURCES: BBC, "Twitter feed for all Greater Manchester Police work", 14 October 2010. Available from: http://www.bbc.co.uk/news/uk-england-manchester-11537806; Johnson, S. "How Twitter Will Change the Way We Live", 5 June 2009. Available from: http://www.time.com/time/printout/0,8816,1902604,00.html.

Case Two

MITRE Taps the Brain Trust of Top US Experts

MITRE Corporation is responsible for managing the Research and Development (R&D) Centers for the US Department of Defense, the Federal Aviation Administration, the Internal Revenue Service, US Department of Veterans Affairs, and the Department of Homeland Security. MITRE also researches new technologies that may assist in solving its clients' problems.

More than 7000 scientists, engineers, and support specialists work in labs managed by MITRE, and most have masters or doctoral degrees. Staff members are engaged in hundreds of different projects across the company. Each staff member possesses valuable technical, operational, and domain knowledge that MITRE wants to tap to its full value and potential. When knowledge management (KM) systems came on the scene in the mid-1990s, MITRE immediately saw the benefit for its researchers and has been tinkering with KM ever since. With so many research specialists engaged across its labs, the value of tapping each other's knowledge and collaborating on projects is immense. However, it's a challenge to interact efficiently with low overhead, while researchers are simultaneously working on hundreds of separate projects. For KM, MITRE takes a gradual learn-while-you-go approach.

MITRE's first step in providing KM was to simply track its research staff. A people locator was developed as part of the larger MITRE Information Infrastructure (MII). The people locator works like an electronic phone book, identifying which employees worked on which assignments over time. The system drew information from the existing project management systems and human resource systems. Using the people locator, staff could find colleagues with useful knowledge based on previous work or the sponsoring organisation. As MITRE researchers used the people finder, developers refined the system based on user feedback. Over time, they introduced additional capabilities. For example, they added an Expertise Finder to help find researchers with expertise in special areas. MITRE also included a library of best practices for systems engineering and project management in the system. MITRE experimented with technology exchange meetings and an annual Innovation Exchange, which allowed researchers to share their successes with colleagues.

When they found new technologies and ideas useful, developers added them to the KM system. More recently, MITRE has experimented with Web 2.0 technologies similar to Facebook and Wikipedia for its KM system. MITRE's approach to KM has been evolutionary. New ideas are piloted, and those proven valuable and viable are its unique approach to KM as a journey with continuous improvements.

Discussion Questions

1 Why is KM extremely valuable in areas of R&D?

2 How do the different components of MITRE's KM system assist in spreading knowledge throughout its labs and in storing knowledge for use in the future?

Critical Thinking Questions

1 What unique challenges do R&D labs provide for KM implementation?

2 What is the benefit of MITRE's evolutionary approach to KM?

SOURCES: Swanborg, Rick, "Mitre's Knowledge Management Journey," CIO, February 27, 2009. Available from: www.cio.com; "About MITRE," MITRE website. Available from: www.mitre.org/about. Accessed January 31, 2010.

Notes

[1] Kimble, Chris, et al., 'Dualities, Distributed Communities of Practice and Knowledge Management,' *Journal of Knowledge Management,* Vol. 9, 2005, p. 102.

[2] Darroch, Jenny, 'Knowledge Management, Innovation, and Firm Performance,' *Journal of Knowledge Management,* Vol. 9, 2005, p. 101.

3 Thurm, Scott, 'Companies Struggle to Pass on Knowledge that Workers Acquire,' *Wall Street Journal,* January 23, 2006, p. B1.

4 Hemmasi, M. and Csanda C., "The Effectiveness of Communities of Practice," *Journal of Managerial Issues,*" Summer 2009, p. 262.

5 Woods, Ginny Parker, 'Sony Sets Its Sights on Digital Books,' *Wall Street Journal,* February 16, 2006, p. B3.

6 Skok, Walter, et al., 'Evaluating the Role and Effectiveness of an Intranet in Facilitating Knowledge Management: A Case Study at Surrey County Council,' *Information and Management,* July 2005, p. 731.

7 Staff, 'Autonomy Links with Blinkx to Offer Search Facilities in China,' *ComputerWire,* Issue 5228, July 19, 2005.

8 Staff, 'eArchitect: Share and Enjoy.' *Building Design,* June 17, 2005, p. 24.

9 Zolkos, Rodd, 'Sharing the Intellectual Wealth,' *BI Industry Focus,* March 1, 2005, p. 12.

10 Hsiu-Fen, Lin, et al., 'Impact of Organizational Learning and Knowledge Management Factors on E-Business Adoption,' *Management Decision,* Vol. 43, 2005, p. 171.

11 Pelz-Sharpe, Alan, 'Document Management and Content Management Tucked Away in Several SAP Products,' *Computer Weekly,* August 2, 2005, p. 26.

12 McKellar, Hugh, '100 Companies That Matter in Knowledge Management,' *KM World,* March 2005, p. 18.

13 Sambamurthy, V., et al., 'Special Issue of Information Technologies and Knowledge Management,' *MIS Quarterly,* June 2005, p. 193.

14 Kajmo, David, 'Knowledge Management in R5.' Available from: www-128.ibm.com/ developerworks/lotus/library/ ls-Knowledge_Management/index.html.

15 Staff, 'IBM Lotus Domino Document Manager.' Available from: www.lotus.com/lotus/offering4.nsf/ wdocs/domdochome.

16 Staff, 'Morphy Richards Integrates Its Global Supply Chain with Lotus Domino.' Available from: www-306.ibm.com/software/success/cssdb.nsf/cs/ DNSD-6EUNJ7? OpenDocument&Site=lotus.

17 Staff, 'Survey Rates Microsoft Number One in Knowledge Management Efforts.' Available from: www.microsoft.com/presspass/features/ 1999/11-22award.mspx.

18 Quain, John, 'Thinking Machines, Take Two,' *PC Magazine,* May 24, 2005, p. 23.

19 BBC, "IBM's Watson supercomputer crowned Jeopardy king," 17 January 2011. Available from: www.bbc.co.uk/news/technology-12491688.

20 Markoff, John, "IBM Computer Program to Take on Jeopardy," *The New York Times,* April 27, 2009, p. 11.

21 20Q (website). Available from: www.20q.net.

22 Staff, "Mind-Machine Meld: Brain-Computer Interfaces for ALS, Paralysis," *Alzheimer Research Forum,* June 22, 2009. Available from: www.alzforum.org/new/detail.asp?id=2173. Accessed July 21, 2009.

23 Rowley, Ian, "Drive, He Thought," *Businessweek,* April 20, 2009, p. 10.

24 Staff, 'Send in the Robots,' *Fortune,* January 24, 2005, p. 140.

25 iRobot (website). Available from: www.irobot.com.

26 Freeman, Diane, 'RobotDoc,' *Rocky Mountain News,* June 27, 2005, p. 1B.

27 DARPA Grand Challenge. Available from: http:// en.wikipedia.org/wiki/Darpa_grand_challenge.

28 El-Rashidi, Yasime, 'Ride'em Robot,' *Wall Street Journal,* October 3, 2005, p. A1.

29 Chamberlain, Ted, 'Ultra-Lifelike Robot Debuts in Japan,' *National Geographic News,* June 10, 2005.

30 Anthes, Gary, '*Self Taught,*' *Computerworld,* February 6, 2006, p. 28.

CHAPTER 8 CONTENTS

08

Systems Development

This chapter will cover SIX main sections in considering the subject of systems development so that you will be able to see exactly how organisations approach the critical questions around auditing current systems, and implementing changed or replacement systems as a result.

Principles

1. Effective systems development requires a team effort of stakeholders, users, managers, systems development specialists and various support personnel, and it starts with careful planning.

2. Systems development often uses different approaches and tools, such as traditional development, prototyping, rapid application development, end-user development, computer-aided software engineering, and object-oriented development to select, implement and monitor projects.

3. Systems development starts with investigation and analysis of existing systems.

4. Designing new systems or modifying existing ones should always be aimed at helping an organisation achieve its goals.

5. The primary emphasis of systems implementation is to make sure that the right information is delivered to the right person in the right format at the right time.

6. Maintenance and review add to the useful life of a system but can consume large amounts of resources, so they benefit from the same rigorous methods and project management techniques applied to systems development.

Learning Objectives

- Identify the key participants in the systems development process and discuss their roles.
- Define the term *information systems planning* and discuss the importance of planning a project.

- Discuss the key features, advantages and disadvantages of the traditional, prototyping, rapid application development and end-user systems development life cycles.
- Discuss the use of computer-aided software engineering (CASE) tools and the object-oriented approach to systems development.

- State the purpose of systems investigation.
- Discuss the importance of performance and cost objectives.
- State the purpose of systems analysis and discuss some of the tools and techniques used in this phase of systems development.

- State the purpose of systems design and discuss the differences between logical and physical systems design.
- Discuss the use of environmental design in the systems development process.

- State the purpose of systems implementation and discuss the various activities associated with this phase of systems development.

- State the importance of systems and software maintenance and discuss the activities involved.
- Describe the systems review process.

Why Learn About Systems Development?

Throughout this book, you have seen many examples of the use of information systems in a variety of careers. A manager at a hotel chain can use an information system to look up client preferences. An entrepreneur can use systems development to build a new information systems and a new business. An accountant at a manufacturing company can use an information system to analyze the costs of a new plant. A sales representative for a music store can use an information system to determine which CDs to order and which to discount because they are not selling. Information systems have been designed and implemented for almost every career and industry. An individual can use systems development to create applications for smartphones and other mobile devices for profit or enjoyment. But where do you start to acquire these systems or have them developed? How can you work with IS personnel, such as systems analysts and computer programmers, to get what you need to succeed on the job? This chapter gives you the answer. You will see how you can initiate the systems development process and analyze your needs with the help of IS personnel. In this chapter, you will learn how your project can be planned, aligned with corporate goals, rapidly developed and much more. We start with an overview of the systems development process.

When an organisation needs to accomplish a new task or change a work process, how does it do so? It develops a new system or modifies an existing one. Systems development is the activity of creating or modifying systems. It refers to all aspects of the process – from identifying problems to solve or opportunities to exploit to implementing and refining the chosen solution.

8.1 An Overview of Systems Development

In today's businesses, managers and employees in all functional areas work together and use business information systems. As a result, they are helping with development and, in many cases, leading the way. Users might request that a systems development team determine whether they should purchase a few PCs or create an attractive website using the tools discussed in Chapter 4. In another case, an entrepreneur might use systems development to build an internet site to compete with large corporations. A number of individuals, for example, have developed applications for Apple's iPhone that are sold on Apple's applications store (App Store).[1] According to Steve Jobs, one of the founders of Apple Computer, "The App Store is like nothing the industry has ever seen before in both scale and quality. With 1.5 billion apps downloaded, it is going to be very hard for others to catch up." This chapter provides you with a deeper appreciation of the systems development process for individuals and organisations.

Participants in Systems Development

Effective systems development requires a team effort. The team usually consists of stakeholders, users, managers, systems development specialists and various support personnel. This team, called the *development team*, is responsible for determining the objectives of the information system and delivering a system that meets these objectives. Selecting the best IS team for a systems development project is critical to project success.[2] A *project* is a planned collection of activities that achieves a goal, such as constructing a new manufacturing plant or developing a new decision support system. Nevsun Resources, a Canadian mining operation, used a software package called Unifier to oversee its large African mining operations.[3] The company used the project-management software to obtain real-time reviews of its mining projects in remote areas.

8

stakeholders People who, either themselves or through the organisation they represent, ultimately benefit from the systems development project.

users People who will interact with the system regularly.

In the context of systems development, **stakeholders** are people who, either themselves or through the organisation they represent, ultimately benefit from the systems development project. **Users** are people who will interact with the system regularly. They can be employees, managers, or suppliers. For large-scale systems development projects in which the investment in and value of a system can be high, it is common for senior-level managers, including the functional vice presidents (of finance, marketing and so on), to be part of the development team.

Because stakeholders ultimately benefit from the systems development project, they often work with others in developing a computer application.

SOURCE: © Jacob Wackerhausen/ iStockphoto.

Depending on the nature of the systems project, the development team might include systems analysts and programmers, among others. A **systems analyst** is a professional who specialises in analyzing and designing business systems. One popular magazine rated a systems analyst job as one of the 50 best jobs in the US.[4] Systems analysts play various roles while interacting with the stakeholders and users, management, vendors and suppliers, external companies, programmers and other IS support personnel (see Figure 8.1). Like an architect developing blueprints for a new building, a systems analyst develops detailed plans for the new or modified system. The **programmer** is responsible for modifying or developing programs to satisfy user requirements. Like a contractor constructing a new building or renovating an existing one, the programmer takes the plans from the systems analyst and builds or modifies the necessary software.

systems analyst A professional who specialises in analyzing and designing business systems.

programmer A specialist responsible for modifying or developing programs to satisfy user requirements.

Individual Systems Developers and Users

For decades, systems development was oriented towards corporations and corporate teams or groups. The major participants were discussed above. Although this continues to be an important part of systems development, we are seeing individual systems developers and users to a greater extent.

An *individual systems developer* is a person that performs all of the systems development roles, including systems analyst, programmer, technical specialist and other roles described

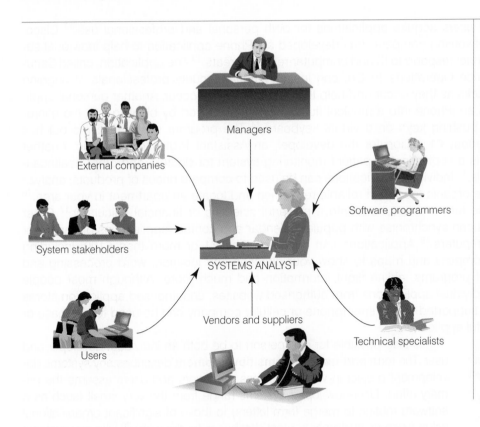

Figure 8.1 Role of the Systems Analyst
The systems analyst plays an important role in the development team and is often the only person who sees the system in its totality. The one-way arrows in this figure do not mean that there is no direct communication between other team members. These arrows just indicate the pivotal role of the systems analyst – a person who is often called on to be a facilitator, moderator, negotiator and interpreter for development activities.

Managers

External companies

System stakeholders

SYSTEMS ANALYST

Users

Vendors and suppliers

Software programmers

Technical specialists

in the above section. Although individual systems developers can create applications for a group or entire organisation, many specialise in developing applications for individuals. A large number of these applications are available for smartphones and other handheld computing devices. Individual developers from around the world, for example, are using the steps of systems development to create unique applications for the iPhone.[5] In addition, Apple has special tools for iPhone application developers, including GPS capabilities, turn-by-turn directions, instant messaging, cut-and-paste features, and audio streaming, to make it easier for people to craft unique applications.[6] Apple is also allowing systems developers to charge users in a variety of ways, including fixed prices and subscription fees through Apple's App Store. Ted Sullivan, for example, has developed a free download he hopes to make available on Apple's App Store called Game Changer.[7] The application will collect baseball statistics from kids' baseball games and send them to the iPhones of parents, relatives and others. Sullivan hopes to make millions of dollars from advertisers and monthly subscription fees for the service. Before an individual developer can have his or her application placed or sold on Apple's application store, however, Apple must approve or select the application.[8] Apple has tens of thousands of applications that can be downloaded and used. Other companies also have application stores. BlackBerry has an application store, called App World, and Google has Android Market store.[9] Google also has a systems development tool called Wave that lets individual developers collaborate and communicate with others in creating documents.[10] Other people can add text, multimedia and a variety of applications to a document. According to a Wave cofounder, "We're banking on Wave having a very large impact, but a lot of it depends on our ability to explain this to users. That's part of the reason why we're putting this out early to developers." Some applications, such as Google's Secure Data Connector, allow data to be downloaded from secure corporate databases, including customer and supplier information.[11]

Individual users acquire applications for both personal and professional use.[12] Cisco, the large networking company, has developed an iPhone application to help individual security personnel respond to IS and computer-related threats.[13] The application, called Security Intelligence Operations To Go, can instantly notify security professionals of ongoing security attacks as they occur and help them recover if they occur. Another personal application turns an iPhone into a musical flute that can be played by blowing into the microphone and pushing keys on a virtual keyboard.[14] The program costs 99 cents but has generated about €1 million for the developer, an Assistant Professor of Music. Another application is a sophisticated patient monitoring system for doctors and other healthcare professionals.[15] Individual applications can be used to compare prices of products, analyze loans, locate organic food, find reliable repairmen and locate an apartment in your area.[16] You can also turn a smartphone into a powerful scientific or financial calculator.[17] Other applications can synchronise with popular calendar and contact applications on laptop or desktop computers.[18] Applications can cost less than €1 or more than €100, including games, a compass and maps to show your direction and location, word-processing and spreadsheet programs, airline flight information and much more. Although most people purchase individual applications from authorised websites, unauthorised application stores that are not supported by the smartphone or cellular company can be used to purchase or acquire useful applications.[19]

end-user systems development
Any systems development project in which the primary effort is undertaken by a combination of business managers and users.

It is also possible for one person to be both an individual developer and user. The term **end-user systems development** describes any systems development project in which business managers and users assume the primary effort. User-developed systems range from the very small (such as a software routine to merge form letters) to those of significant organisational value (such as customer contact databases for the web).[20] Like any systems developer, individual developers and end users should follow the approach and techniques of the systems development process described in this chapter. Even if you develop your own applications, you will likely want to have an IS department develop applications for you that are too complex or time consuming to develop on your own. In this case, you will be involved in initiating systems development, discussed next.

Many end users today are demonstrating their systems development capability by designing and implementing their own PC-based systems.

SOURCE: India Today Group/Getty Images.

Information Systems Planning and Aligning Corporate and IS Goals

Information systems planning and aligning corporate and IS goals are important aspects of any systems development project. Achieving a competitive advantage is often the overall objective of systems development.

The term **information systems planning** refers to translating strategic and organisational goals into systems development initiatives (see Figure 8.2).[21] Proper IS planning ensures that specific systems development objectives support organisational goals. Long-range planning can also be important and result in getting the most from a systems development effort. It can also align IS goals with corporate goals and culture, which is discussed next.

> **information systems planning**
> Translating strategic and organisational goals into systems development initiatives.

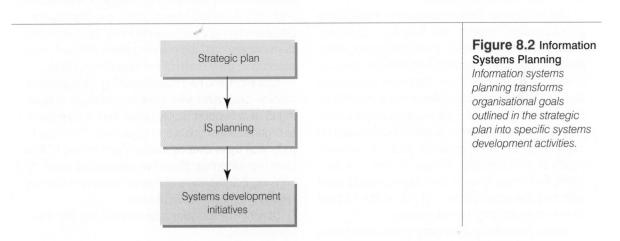

Figure 8.2 Information Systems Planning
Information systems planning transforms organisational goals outlined in the strategic plan into specific systems development activities.

Aligning organisational goals and IS goals is critical for any successful systems development effort.[22] Because information systems support other business activities, IS staff and people in other departments need to understand each other's responsibilities and tasks. Most corporations have profits and return on investment (ROI), first introduced in Chapter 1, as primary goals. According to the chief technology officer for the Financial Industry Regulatory Authority, "ROI is a key metric for technology initiatives, and the business case needs to include both initial development costs and subsequent maintenance costs."[23] Another difficult aspect of aligning corporate and IS goals is the changing nature of business goals and priorities.[24]

8.2 Systems Development Life Cycles

The systems development process is also called a *systems development life cycle (SDLC)*, because the activities associated with it are ongoing. As each system is built, the project has timelines and deadlines, until at last the system is installed and accepted. The life of the system continues as it is maintained and reviewed. If the system needs significant improvement beyond the scope of maintenance, if it needs to be replaced because of a new generation of technology, or if the IS needs of the organisation change significantly, a new project will be initiated and the cycle will start over.

The Traditional Systems Development Life Cycle

Traditional systems development efforts can range from a small project, such as purchasing an inexpensive computer program to a major undertaking. The steps of traditional systems

Information Systems at Work

Hess Information Systems Take the Long View

Hess Corporation is a global energy company engaged in the exploration for and production of crude oil and natural gas. Hess has offices in 18 countries across six continents, with key headquarters in Houston, London, Kuala Lumpur (Malaysia) and Woodbridge (New Jersey).

Like most smart, mature companies, Hess aligns its information systems with long-term organisational goals and strategies. The focus on long-term, however, was further emphasised with the arrival of a new CIO, Jeff Steinhorn. Steinhorn discovered that the Hess information systems group had historically taken a short-term approach to project planning. The company had its IS personnel focused on supporting near-term initiatives and the separate needs of each business division. No one was analyzing how these smaller short-term projects were assisting the company as a group at the highest level to meet its long-term objectives.

Although this short-sighted approach served Hess adequately during the years that the company was focused solely on the oil business, it became more important as the company diversified for IS to assist in high-level long-term goals. In the past decade, Hess has expanded into natural gas and electricity. It was clear to Steinhorn that the company's IS initiatives needed to support and connect the organisation's more diverse interests over the long haul.

Bobby Cameron at Forrester Research says that Steinhorn's predicament is not unique. The majority of new CIOs find themselves addressing the same problem. This is the result of the recent trend of organisations moving to use IS in ways important to the organisation as a whole. Although businesses have traditionally called upon IS to support various initiatives, enterprise IS is a current force that drives business processes and spurs innovation. With this in mind, more and more IS initiatives are aligned with high-level, long-term organisational goals.

Steinhorn began by centralising the data source that fed all information systems. Since IS projects had been conducted in each business division, the divisions weren't sharing important information, such as customer records and market information.

A central data store would eliminate data redundancy and improve data accuracy.

Next, Steinhorn set out to develop a five-year IS strategic plan. Once established, Steinhorn had to work to gain senior management approval. Senior management was resistant to change, and Steinhorn had not yet proved himself within the organisation. Steinhorn brought some of the Hess' best regarded IS managers onto the planning team and, with their assistance, gained senior management support.

Steinhorn also had trouble gaining the support of division executives who were accustomed to viewing IS as a support facility rather than a contributor to organisational goals and objectives. Steinhorn finally won them over by selling them on the ROI of longterm planning. Steinhorn persuaded them by showing that the costs of his plan were one-tenth as much as the benefits would return.

Steinhorn's five-year plan was divided into three components:

Business or "B" projects that assisted in improving business processes, reducing costs, and increasing revenue.

Enabler or "E" projects that provided decision makers with information that enabled them to make better decisions, including business intelligence and analytical systems.

Process or "P" projects that assisted the IS group in organising and standardising its own work processes.

Within nine months of Steinhorn's five-year plan, 17 projects had been kicked off and seven were completed. This included a major upgrade of the company's SAP retail energy system.

Under its "P" project category, Steinhorn's group developed standardised systems for application development, project management and IS governance. Steinhorn also implemented a performance tracking and scorecard system with which project success could be gauged. These advances in IS project management dramatically improved the quality and efficiency of the IS team's work.

With each successful project, Steinhorn's efforts are gaining increased support across Hess. The three divisions of Hess – oil, gas and electricity – have become more interested in working together. Approaching IS from a long-term, enterprise level "has really elevated the decision-making to help decide where it's best to invest IT dollars to get the greatest returns," says William Hanna, vice president of electric operations at Hess and a program sponsor for the IT strategic planning initiative.

Discussion Questions

1   What challenges did Steinhorn face when he took the job as CIO of Hess?

2   Why are many businesses switching to a long-term, enterprisewide emphasis for IS projects?

Critical Thinking Questions

1   How did Steinhorn organise IS projects under his five-year plan? What other categories of projects might you have included?

2   Why did Steinhorn face resistance from top-level managers and executives? What smart moves did he make to win them over?

SOURCES: 'Amerada Hess Uses SAP Oil & Gas to Reduce Cost of Joint-Venture Activity,' SAP Customer Implementation Success. Accessed May 23, 2010. Available from: *www.sap.com/industries/oil-gas/pdf/ 50026246.pdf*; Hess website. Accessed May 23, 2010. Available from: *www.hess.com*; Hoffman, Thomas, 'Hess builds a project pipeline with long-term vision,' *Computerworld*, April 7, 2008. Available from: *www.computerworld.com/s/article/314711/ Building_an_IT_Project_ Pipeline?taxonomyId=74& pageNumber=1.*

development might vary from one company to the next, but most approaches have five common phases: investigation, analysis, design, implementation, and maintenance and review (see Figure 8.3).

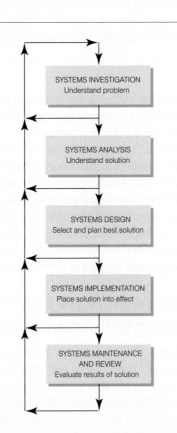

Figure 8.3 The Traditional Systems Development Life Cycle
Sometimes, information learned in a particular phase requires cycling back to a previous phase.

In the systems **investigation phase**, potential problems and opportunities are identified and considered in light of the goals of the business. Systems investigation attempts to answer the questions "What is the problem, and is it worth solving?" The primary result of this phase is a defined development

systems investigation The systems development phase during which problems and opportunities are identified and considered in light of the goals of the business.

project for which business problems or opportunity statements have been created, to which some organisational resources have been committed and for which systems analysis is recommended. **Systems analysis** attempts to answer the question "What must the information system do to solve the problem?" This phase involves studying existing systems and work processes to identify strengths, weaknesses and opportunities for improvement. The major outcome of systems analysis is a list of requirements and priorities. **Systems design** seeks to answer the question "How will the information system do what it must do to obtain the problem solution?" The primary result of this phase is a technical design that either describes the new system or describes how existing systems will be modified. The system design details system outputs, inputs and user interfaces; specifies hardware, software, database, telecommunications, personnel and procedure components; and shows how these components are related. **Systems implementation** involves creating or acquiring the various system components detailed in the systems design, assembling them and placing the new or modified system into operation. An important task during this phase is to train the users. Systems implementation results in an installed, operational information system that meets the business needs for which it was developed. It can also involve phasing out or removing old systems, which can be difficult for existing users, especially when the systems are free.

The purpose of **systems maintenance and review** is to ensure that the system operates as intended and to modify the system so that it continues to meet changing business needs. As shown in Figure 8.3, a system under development moves from one phase of the traditional SDLC to the next.

systems analysis The systems development phase that attempts to answer the question "What must the information system do to solve the problem?"

systems design The systems development phase that defines how the information system will do what it must do to obtain the problem solution.

systems implementation The systems development phase involving the creation or acquisition of various system components detailed in the systems design, assembling them and placing the new or modified system into operation.

systems maintenance and review The systems development phase that ensures the system operates as intended and modifies the system so that it continues to meet changing business needs.

Prototyping

Prototyping takes an iterative approach to the systems development process.[25] During each iteration, requirements and alternative solutions to the problem are identified and analyzed, new solutions are designed and a portion of the system is implemented. Users are then encouraged to try the prototype and provide feedback (see Figure 8.4). Prototyping begins with creating a preliminary model of a major subsystem or a scaled-down version of the entire system. For example, a prototype might show sample report formats and input screens. After they are developed and refined, the prototypical reports and input screens are used as models for the actual system, which can be developed using an end-user programming language, such as Visual Basic. The first preliminary model is refined to form the second- and third-generation models, and so on until the complete system is developed (see Figure 8.5).

prototyping An iterative approach to the systems development process in which, at each iteration, requirements and alternative solutions to a problem are identified and analyzed, new solutions are designed and a portion of the system is implemented.

Rapid Application Development, Agile Development and Other Systems Development Approaches

Rapid application development (RAD) employs tools, techniques and methodologies designed to speed application development. These tools can also be used to make systems development projects more flexible and agile to be able to rapidly change with changing conditions and environments.[26] Vendors, such as Computer Associates International, IBM and Oracle, market products targeting the RAD market. Rational Software, a division of IBM, has a RAD tool called Rational Rapid Developer to make developing large Java programs and applications easier and faster. Rational allows both systems developers and users to collaborate on systems development projects using Team Concert, which is like a social networking site for IBM developers and users.[27] Locus Systems, a program developer, used a RAD

rapid application development (RAD) A systems development approach that employs tools, techniques and methodologies designed to speed application development.

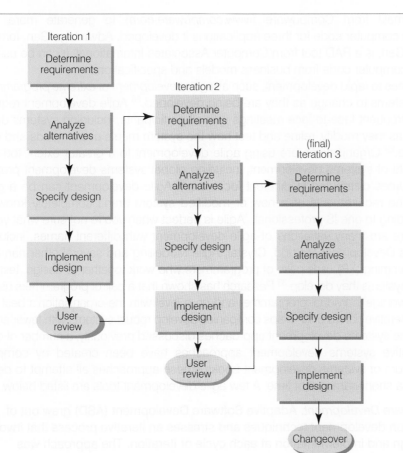

Figure 8.4 Prototyping

Prototyping is an iterative approach to systems development.

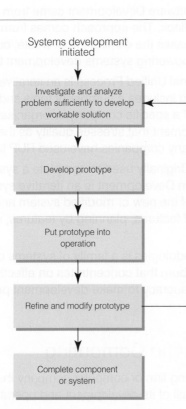

Figure 8.5 Refining during Prototyping

Each generation of prototype is a refinement of the previous generation based on user feedback.

tool called OptimalJ from Compuware (*www.compuware.com*) to generate more than 60 per cent of the computer code for three applications it developed. Advantage Gen, formerly known as COOL:Gen, is a RAD tool from Computer Associates International. It can be used to rapidly generate computer code from business models and specifications.

Other approaches to rapid development, such as *agile development* or *extreme programming (XP)*, allow the systems to change as they are being developed.[28] Agile development requires cooperation and frequent face-to-face meetings with all participants, including systems developers and users, as they modify, refine and test how the system meets users' needs and what its capabilities are.[29] Organisations are using agile development to a greater extent today to improve the results of systems development, including global systems development projects requiring IS resources distributed in different locations.[30] Agile development can be a good approach when the requirements of a new or modified system aren't completely known in advance.[31] According to one IS professional, "Agile is perfect when you're not sure what you're getting into." There are many variations of agile development with different names, including Dynamic Systems Development Method, Crystal, Agile Modelling and several other names.[32]

Extreme programming (XP) uses pairs of programmers who work together to design, test and code parts of the systems they develop.[33] Research has shown that a pair of programmers usually outperforms the average individual programmer and on a level with the organisation's best programmers.[34] The iterative nature of XP helps companies develop robust systems with fewer errors.

In addition to the systems development approaches discussed previously, a number of other agile and innovative systems development approaches have been created by computer vendors and authors of systems development books. These approaches all attempt to deliver better systems in a shorter amount of time. A few agile development tools are listed below.

- *Adaptive Software Development.* Adaptive Software Development (ASD) grew out of rapid application development techniques and stresses an iterative process that involves analysis, design and implementation at each cycle or iteration. The approach was primarily developed by James Highsmith.

- *Lean Software Development.* Lean Software Development came from a book with the same title by Mary and Tom Poppendieck. The approach comes from lean manufacturing practices used by Toyota and stresses the elimination of waste, continuous learning, just-in-time decision making and empowering systems development teams.[35]

- *Rational Unified Process (RUP).* Rational Unified Process is an iterative systems development approach developed by IBM and includes a number of tools and techniques that are typically tailored to fit the needs of a specific company or organisation. RUP uses an iterative approach to software development that stresses quality as the software is changed and updated over time.[36] Many companies have used RUP to their advantage.[37]

- *Feature-Driven Development (FDD).* Originally used to complete a systems development project at a large bank, Feature-Driven Development is an iterative systems development approach that stresses the features of the new or modified system and involves developing an overall model, creating a list of features, planning by features, designing by features and building by features.[38]

- *Crystal Methodologies.* Crystal Methodologies is a family of systems development approaches developed by Alistair Cockburn that concentrates on effective team work and the reduction of paperwork and bureaucracy to make development projects faster and more efficient.

Outsourcing and On-Demand Computing

Many companies hire an outside consulting firm or computer company that specialises in systems development to take over some or all of its development and operations activities.[39] The drug company Pfizer, for example, used outsourcing to allow about 4000 of its employees to outsource some of their jobs to other individuals or companies around the globe.[40] Vodafone used outsourcing to help it innovate and find creative solutions in providing wireless services.[41] According its chief executive, "We were a bit naive thinking everything could be done in-house."

Small and medium-sized firms are using outsourcing to a greater extent today to cut costs and acquire needed technical expertise that would be difficult to afford with in-house personnel.[42] According to one outsourcing expert, "The downturn is making it harder for companies to tie outsourcing to broader goals than basic cost cutting." The market for outsourcing services for small and medium-sized firms is expected to increase by 15 per cent annually through 2012 and beyond. Reducing costs, obtaining state-of-the-art technology, eliminating staffing and personnel problems, and increasing technological flexibility are reasons that companies have used the outsourcing and on-demand computing approaches.

A number of companies and nonprofit organisations offer outsourcing and on-demand computing services – from general systems development to specialised services. IBM's Global Services, for example, is one of the largest full-service outsourcing and consulting services.[43] IBM has consultants located in offices around the world and generates over €50 billion in revenues each year. Electronic Data Systems (EDS) is another large company that specialises in consulting and outsourcing.[44] EDS has approximately 140 000 employees in almost 60 countries and more than 9000 clients worldwide. EDS, which was acquired by Hewlett-Packard, generates over €20 billion annually.[45] Accenture is another company that specialises in consulting and outsourcing.[46] The company has more than 75 000 employees in 47 countries with annual revenues that exceed €15 billion. Wipro Technologies, headquartered in India, is another worldwide outsourcing company with more than €3 billion in annual revenues.[47] Amazon, the large online retailer of books and other products, will offer on-demand computing to individuals and other companies of all sizes, allowing them to use Amazon's computer expertise and database capacity. Individuals and companies will only pay for the computer services they use (see Figure 8.6).

Figure 8.6 Outsourcing
With consultants located in offices around the world, including Russia, China and Israel, IBM offers outsourcing services and generates over €50 billion in revenues each year.

Source: LAIF/Redux.

8.3 Factors Affecting Systems Development Success

Successful systems development means delivering a system that meets user and organisational needs – on time and within budget. Achieving a successful systems development project, however, can be difficult.

Getting users and stakeholders involved in systems development is critical for most systems development projects. Some researchers believe that how a systems development project is managed and run is one of the best indicators of systems development success.[48] Having the support of top-level managers is also important. In addition to user involvement and top management support, other factors can contribute to successful systems development efforts – at a reasonable cost. These factors are discussed next.

Degree of Change

A major factor that affects the quality of systems development is the degree of change associated with the project. The scope can vary from enhancing an existing system to major reengineering. The project team needs to recognise where they are on this spectrum of change.

Continuous Improvement versus Reengineering

As discussed in Chapter 1, continuous improvement projects do not require a lot of changes or retraining of people; thus, they have a high degree of success.[49] Typically, because continuous improvements involve minor improvements, these projects also have relatively modest benefits. On the other hand, reengineering involves fundamental changes in how the organisation conducts business and completes tasks. The factors associated with successful reengineering are similar to those of any development effort, including top management support, clearly defined corporate goals and systems development objectives, and careful management of change. Major reengineering projects tend to have a high degree of risk but also a high potential for major business benefits (see Figure 8.7).

Figure 8.7
The degree of change can greatly affect the probability of a project's success.

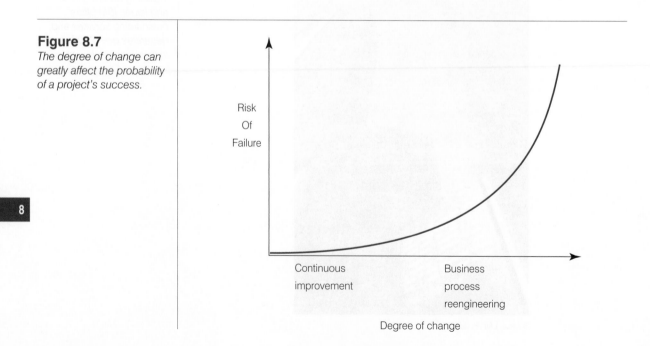

Managing Change

The ability to manage change is critical to the success of systems development. New systems inevitably cause change. Unfortunately, not everyone adapts easily, and the increasing complexity of systems can multiply the problems. Some systems developers believe that system complexity is a major cause of systems development failures.[50] Managing change requires the ability to recognise existing or potential problems (particularly the concerns of users) and deal with them before they become a serious threat to the success of the new or modified system. Here are several of the most common problems that often need to be addressed as a result of new or modified systems:

- Fear that the employee will lose his or her job, power, or influence within the organisation
- Belief that the proposed system will create more work than it eliminates
- Reluctance to work with "computer people"
- Anxiety that the proposed system will negatively alter the structure of the organisation
- Belief that other problems are more pressing than those solved by the proposed system or that the system is being developed by people unfamiliar with "the way things need to get done"
- Unwillingness to learn new procedures or approaches

The Importance of Planning

The bigger the project, the more likely that poor planning will lead to significant problems. Many companies find that large systems projects fall behind schedule, go over budget and do not meet expectations. Although proper planning cannot guarantee that these types of problems will be avoided, it can minimise the likelihood of their occurrence. Good systems development is not automatic. Certain factors contribute to the failure of systems development projects. These factors and the countermeasures to eliminate or alleviate the problem are summarised in Table 8.1.

Table 8.1 Project Planning Issues Frequently Contributing to Project Failure

Factor	Countermeasure
Solving the wrong problem	Establish a clear connection between the project and organisational goals
Poor problem definition and analysis	Follow a standard systems development approach
Poor communication	Set up communications procedures and protocols
Project is too ambitious	Narrow the project focus to address only the most important business opportunities
Lack of top management support	Identify the senior manager who has the most to gain from the success of the project and recruit this person to champion the project
Lack of management and user involvement	Identify and recruit key stakeholders to be active participants in the project
Inadequate or improper system design	Follow a standard systems development approach

Organisational experience with the systems development process is also an important factor for systems development success.[51] The *Capability Maturity Model (CMM)* is one way to measure this experience.[52] It is based on research done at Carnegie Mellon University and work by the Software Engineering Institute (SEI). CMM is a measure of the maturity of the software development process in an organisation. CMM grades an organisation's systems development maturity using five levels: initial, repeatable, defined, managed and optimised.

Use of Project Management Tools

Project management involves planning, scheduling, directing and controlling human, financial and technological resources for a defined task whose result is achievement of specific goals and objectives. Corporations and nonprofit organisations use these important tools and techniques.

A **project schedule** is a detailed description of what is to be done. Each project activity, the use of personnel and other resources, and expected completion dates are described. A **project milestone** is a critical date for the completion of a major part of the project. The completion of program design, coding, testing and release are examples of milestones for a programming project. The **project deadline** is the date the entire project is to be completed and operational – when the organisation can expect to begin to reap the benefits of the project.

project schedule A detailed description of what is to be done.

project milestone A critical date for the completion of a major part of the project.

project deadline The date the entire project is to be completed and operational.

critical path Activities that, if delayed, would delay the entire project.

In systems development, each activity has an earliest start time, earliest finish time and slack time, which is the amount of time an activity can be delayed without delaying the entire project. The **critical path** consists of all activities that, if delayed, would delay the entire project. These activities have zero slack time. Any problems with critical-path activities will cause problems for the entire project. To ensure that critical-path activities are completed in a timely fashion, formalised project management approaches have been developed. Tools, such as Microsoft Project, are available to help compute these critical project attributes.

Although the steps of systems development seem straightforward, larger projects can become complex, requiring hundreds or thousands of separate activities. For these systems development efforts, formal project management methods and tools become essential. A formalised approach called **Programme Evaluation and Review Technique (PERT)** creates three time estimates for an activity: shortest possible time, most likely time and longest possible time. A formula is then applied to determine a single PERT time estimate. A **Gantt chart** is a graphical tool used for planning, monitoring and coordinating projects; it is essentially a grid that lists activities and deadlines. Each time a task is completed, a marker, such as a darkened line, is placed in the proper grid cell to indicate the completion of a task (see Figure 8.8).

Programme Evaluation and Review Technique (PERT) A formalised approach for developing a project schedule.

Gantt chart A graphical tool used for planning, monitoring and coordinating projects.

Both PERT and Gantt techniques can be automated using project management software. Project management software helps managers determine the best way to reduce project completion time at the least cost. Several project management software packages are identified in Table 8.2.

Table 8.2 Selected Project Management Software

Software	Vendor
OpenPlan	Welcom (*www.welcom.com*)
Microsoft Project	Microsoft (*www.microsoft.com*)
Unifier	Skire (*www.skire.com*)

PROJECT PLANNING DOCUMENTATION		Page 1 of 1	
System Warehouse Inventory System (Modification)		Date 12/10	
System — Scheduled activity ▬ Completed activity	Analyst Cecil Truman	Signature	

Activity*	Individual assigned	Week 1	2	3	4	5	6	7	8	9	10	11	12	13	14
R – Requirements definition															
R.1 Form project team	VP, Cecil, Bev	▬													
R.2 Define obj. and constraints	Cecil		▬												
R.3 Interview warehouse staff for requirements report	Bev			▬▬											
R.4 Organise requirements	Team					─▬									
R.5 VP review	VP, Team					─▬									
D – Design															
D.1 Revise program specs.	Bev						─▬								
D. 2. 1 Specify screens	Bev						─								
D. 2. 2 Specify reports	Bev							─▬							
D. 2. 3 Specify doc. changes	Cecil							─							
D. 4 Management review	Team								─						
I — Implementation															
I. 1 Code program changes	Bev									─					
I. 2. 1 Build test file	Team									─					
I. 2. 2 Build production file	Bev										─				
I. 3 Revise production file	Cecil									─					
I. 4. 1 Test short file	Bev								─						
I. 4. 2 Test production file	Cecil											─			
I. 5 Management review	Team												─		
I. 6 Install warehouse**															
I. 6. 1 Train new procedures	Bev												─		
I. 6. 2 Install	Bev												─		
I. 6. 3 Management review	Team														─

*Weekly team reviews not shown here
**Report for warehouses 2 through 5

Figure 8.8 Sample Gantt Chart
A Gantt chart shows progress through systems development activities by putting a bar through appropriate cells.

Use of Computer-Aided Software Engineering (CASE) Tools

Computer-aided software engineering (CASE) tools automate many of the tasks required in a systems development effort and encourage adherence to the SDLC, thus, instilling a high degree of rigour and standardisation to the entire systems development process. Oracle Designer by Oracle (*www. oracle.com*) and Visible Analyst by Visible Systems Corporation (*www.visible. com*) are examples of CASE tools. Oracle Designer is a CASE tool that can help systems analysts automate and simplify the development process for database systems. Other CASE tools include Embarcadero Describe (*www.embarcadero.com*), Popkin Software (*www.popkin.com*), Rational Software (part of IBM) and Visio (a charting and graphics program) from Microsoft.

computer-aided software engineering (CASE) Tools that automate many of the tasks required in a systems development effort and encourage adherence to the SDLC.

8

CASE tools that focus on activities associated with the early stages of systems development are often called *upper-CASE* tools. These packages provide automated tools to assist with systems investigation, analysis and design activities. Other CASE packages, called *lower-CASE* tools, focus on the later implementation stage of systems development and can automatically generate structured program code.

Object-Oriented Systems Development

The success of a systems development effort can depend on the specific programming tools and approaches used. As mentioned in Chapter 2, object-oriented (OO) programming languages allow the interaction of programming objects – that is, an object consists of both data and the actions that can be performed on the data. So, an object could be data about an employee and all the operations (such as payroll, benefits and tax calculations) that might be performed on the data.

Chapter 2 discussed a number of programming languages that use the object-oriented approach, including Visual Basic, C++ and Java. These languages allow systems developers to take the OO approach, making program development faster and more efficient, resulting in lower costs. Modules can be developed internally or obtained from an external source. After a company has the programming modules, programmers and systems analysts can modify them and integrate them with other modules to form new programs.

object-oriented systems development (OOSD) An approach to systems development that combines the logic of the systems development life cycle with the power of object-oriented modelling and programming.

Object-oriented systems development (OOSD) combines the logic of the systems development life cycle with the power of object-oriented modelling and programming.[53] OOSD follows a defined systems development life cycle, much like the SDLC. The life cycle phases are usually completed with many iterations. Object-oriented systems development typically involves the following tasks:

■ *Identifying potential problems and opportunities within the organisation that would be appropriate for the OO approach.* This process is similar to traditional systems investigation. Ideally, these problems or opportunities should lend themselves to the development of programs that can be built by modifying existing programming modules.

■ *Defining what kind of system users require.* This analysis means defining all the objects that are part of the user's work environment (object-oriented analysis). The OO team must study the business and build a model of the objects that are part of the business (such as a customer, an order or a payment). Many of the CASE tools discussed in the previous section can be used, starting with this step of OOSD.

■ *Designing the system.* This process defines all the objects in the system and the ways they interact (object-oriented design). Design involves developing logical and physical models of the new system by adding details to the object model started in analysis.

■ *Programming or modifying modules.* This implementation step takes the object model begun during analysis and completed during design and turns it into a set of interacting objects in a system. Object-oriented programming languages are designed to allow the programmer to create classes of objects in the computer system that correspond to the objects in the actual business process. Objects, such as customer, order and payment, are redefined as computer system objects – a customer screen, an order entry menu or a euro sign icon. Programmers then write new modules or modify existing ones to produce the desired programs.

■ *Evaluation by users.* The initial implementation is evaluated by users and improved. Additional scenarios and objects are added, and the cycle repeats. Finally, a complete, tested and approved system is available for use.

■ *Periodic review and modification.* The completed and operational system is reviewed at regular intervals and modified as necessary.

8.4 Systems Investigation

As discussed earlier in the chapter, systems investigation is the first phase in the traditional SDLC of a new or modified business information system. The purpose is to identify potential problems and opportunities and consider them in light of the goals of the company. In general, systems investigation attempts to uncover answers to the following questions:

- What primary problems might a new or enhanced system solve?
- What opportunities might a new or enhanced system provide?
- What new hardware, software, databases, telecommunications, personnel or procedures will improve an existing system or are required in a new system?
- What are the potential costs (variable and fixed)?
- What are the associated risks?

Initiating Systems Investigation

Because systems development requests can require considerable time and effort to implement, many organisations have adopted a formal procedure for initiating systems development, beginning with systems investigation. The **systems request form** is a document that is filled out by someone who wants the IS department to initiate systems investigation. This form typically includes the following information:

systems request form A document filled out by someone who wants the IS department to initiate systems investigation.

- Problems in or opportunities for the system
- Objectives of systems investigation
- Overview of the proposed system
- Expected costs and benefits of the proposed system

The information in the systems request form helps to rationalise and prioritise the activities of the IS department. Based on the overall IS plan, the organisation's needs and goals, and the estimated value and priority of the proposed projects, managers make decisions regarding the initiation of each systems investigation for such projects.

Feasibility Analysis

A key step of the systems investigation phase is **feasibility analysis**, which assesses technical, economic, legal, operational and schedule feasibility (see Figure 8.9). **Technical feasibility** is concerned with whether the hardware, software and other system components can be acquired or developed to solve the problem.

Economic feasibility determines whether the project makes financial sense and whether predicted benefits offset the cost and time needed to obtain them. Economic feasibility can involve cash flow analysis, such as that done in internal rate of return (IRR) or total cost of ownership (TCO) calculations, first discussed in Chapter 1. Spreadsheet programs, such as Microsoft Excel, have built-in functions to compute internal rate of return and other cash flow measures.

Legal feasibility determines whether laws or regulations can prevent or limit a systems development project. Legal feasibility involves an analysis of existing and future laws to determine the likelihood of legal action against the systems development project and the possible consequences.

feasibility analysis Assessment of the technical, economic, legal, operational and schedule feasibility of a project.

technical feasibility Assessment of whether the hardware, software and other system components can be acquired or developed to solve the problem.

economic feasibility The determination of whether the project makes financial sense and whether predicted benefits offset the cost and time needed to obtain them.

legal feasibility The determination of whether laws or regulations may prevent or limit a systems development project.

Figure 8.9 Technical, Economic, Legal, Operational and Schedule Feasibility

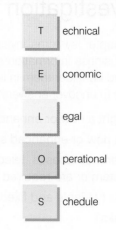

T echnical

E conomic

L egal

O perational

S chedule

operational feasibility The measure of whether the project can be put into action or operation.

Operational feasibility is a measure of whether the project can be put into action or operation. It can include logistical and motivational (acceptance of change) considerations. Motivational considerations are important, because new systems affect people and data flows and can have unintended consequences. As a result, power and politics might come into play, and some people might resist the new system.

schedule feasibility The determination of whether the project can be completed in a reasonable amount of time.

Schedule feasibility determines whether the project can be completed in a reasonable amount of time – a process that involves balancing the time and resource requirements of the project with other projects.

Object-Oriented Systems Investigation

The object-oriented approach can be used during all phases of systems development, from investigation to maintenance and review. Consider a boat rental business in Maui, Hawaii in which the owner wants to computerise its operations, including renting boats to customers and adding new boats into the rental program (see Figure 8.10). As you can see, the boat rental clerk rents boats to customers and adds new boats to the current inventory available for rent. The stick figure is an example of an *actor*, and the ovals each represent an event, called a *use case*. In our example, the actor (the boat rental clerk) interacts with two use cases (rent boats to customers and add new boats to inventory). The use case diagram is part of the Unified Modeling Language (UML) that is used in object-oriented systems development.

Figure 8.10 Use Case Diagram for a Boat Rental Application

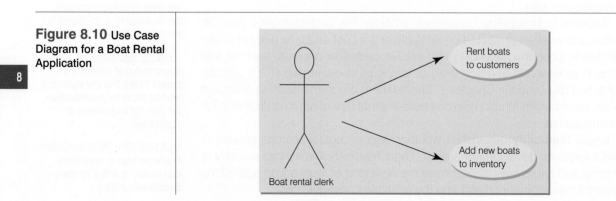

The Systems Investigation Report

The primary outcome of systems investigation is a **systems investigation report**, also called a *feasibility study*. This report summarises the results of systems investigation and the process of feasibility analysis and recommends a course of action: Continue on into systems analysis, modify the project in some manner, or drop it. A typical table of contents for the systems investigation report is shown in Figure 8.11.

systems investigation report A summary of the results of the systems investigation and the process of feasibility analysis and recommendation of a course of action.

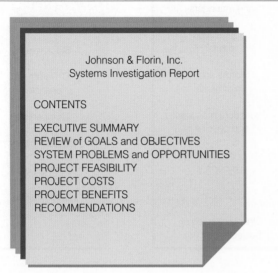

Johnson & Florin, Inc.
Systems Investigation Report

CONTENTS

EXECUTIVE SUMMARY
REVIEW of GOALS and OBJECTIVES
SYSTEM PROBLEMS and OPPORTUNITIES
PROJECT FEASIBILITY
PROJECT COSTS
PROJECT BENEFITS
RECOMMENDATIONS

Figure 8.11 A Typical Table of Contents for a Systems Investigation Report

The systems investigation report is reviewed by senior management, often organised as an advisory committee, or **steering committee**, consisting of senior management and users from the IS department and other functional areas. These people help IS personnel with their decisions about the use of information systems in the business and give authorisation to pursue further systems development activities. After review, the steering committee might agree with the recommendation of the systems development team or suggest a change in project focus to concentrate more directly on meeting a specific company objective. Another alternative is that everyone might decide that the project is not feasible and cancel the project.

steering committee An advisory group consisting of senior management and users from the IS department and other functional areas.

8.5 Systems Analysis

After a project has been approved for further study, the next step is to answer the question "What must the information system do to solve the problem?" The overall emphasis of analysis is gathering data on the existing system, determining the requirements for the new system, considering alternatives within these constraints and investigating the feasibility of the solutions. The primary outcome of systems analysis is a prioritised list of systems requirements.

Data Collection

The purpose of data collection is to seek additional information about the problems or needs identified in the systems investigation report. During this process, the strengths and weaknesses of the existing system are emphasised.

Identifying Sources of Data

Data collection begins by identifying and locating the various sources of data, including both internal and external sources (see Figure 8.12).

Figure 8.12 Internal and External Sources of Data for Systems Analysis

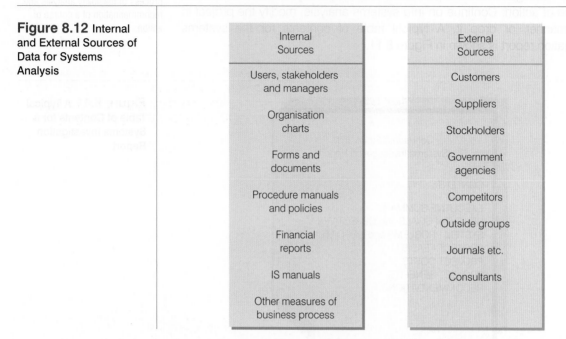

Internal Sources	External Sources
Users, stakeholders and managers	Customers
Organisation charts	Suppliers
	Stockholders
Forms and documents	Government agencies
Procedure manuals and policies	Competitors
	Outside groups
Financial reports	Journals etc.
IS manuals	Consultants
Other measures of business process	

Collecting Data

After data sources have been identified, data collection begins. Figure 8.13 shows the steps involved. Data collection might require a number of tools and techniques, such as interviews, direct observation and questionnaires.

Figure 8.13 The Steps in Data Collection

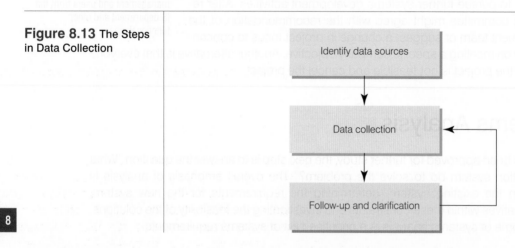

Identify data sources

Data collection

Follow-up and clarification

structured interview An interview in which the questions are written in advance.

unstructured interview An interview in which the questions are not written in advance.

Interviews can either be structured or unstructured. In a **structured interview**, the questions are written in advance. In an **unstructured interview**, the questions are not written in advance; the interviewer relies on experience in asking the best questions to uncover the inherent problems of the existing system.

With **direct observation**, one or more members of the analysis team directly observe the existing system in action.

When many data sources are spread over a wide geographic area, **questionnaires** might be the best method. Like interviews, questionnaires can be either structured or unstructured. In most cases, a pilot study is conducted to fine-tune the questionnaire. A follow-up questionnaire can also capture the opinions of those who do not respond to the original questionnaire.

> **direct observation** Directly observing the existing system in action by one or more members of the analysis team.
>
> **questionnaires** A method of gathering data when the data sources are spread over a wide geographic area.

Data Analysis

The data collected in its raw form is usually not adequate to determine the effectiveness of the existing system or the requirements for the new system. The next step is to manipulate the collected data so that the development team members who are participating in systems analysis can use the data. This manipulation is called **data analysis**. Data and activity modelling and using data-flow diagrams and entity-relationship diagrams are useful during data analysis to show data flows and the relationships among various objects, associations and activities. Other common tools and techniques for data analysis include application flowcharts, grid charts, CASE tools and the object-oriented approach.

> **data analysis** The manipulation of collected data so that the development team members who are participating in systems analysis can use the data.

Data Modelling

Data modelling, first introduced in Chapter 3, is a commonly accepted approach to modelling organisational objects and associations that employ both text and graphics. How data modelling is employed, however, is governed by the specific systems development methodology.

Data modelling is most often accomplished through the use of entity-relationship (ER) diagrams. Recall from Chapter 3 that an entity is a generalised representation of an object type – such as a class of people (employee), events (sales), things (desks) or places (city) – and that entities possess certain attributes. Objects can be related to other objects in many ways. An entity-relationship diagram, such as the one shown in Figure 8.14a, describes a number of objects and the ways they are associated. An ER diagram (or any other modelling tool) cannot by itself fully describe a business problem or solution, because it lacks descriptions of the related activities. It is, however, a good place to start, because it describes object types and attributes about which data might need to be collected for processing.

Activity Modelling

To fully describe a business problem or solution, the related objects, associations and activities must be described. Activities in this sense are events or items that are necessary to fulfill the business relationship or that can be associated with the business relationship in a meaningful way.

Activity modelling is often accomplished through the use of data-flow diagrams. A **data-flow diagram (DFD)** models objects, associations and activities by describing how data can flow between and around various objects. DFDs work on the premise that every activity involves some communication, transference or flow that can be described as a data element. DFDs describe the activities that fulfill a business relationship or accomplish a business task, not how these activities are to be performed. That is, DFDs show the logical sequence of associations and activities, not the physical processes. A system modelled with a DFD could operate manually or could be computer based; if computer based, the system could operate with a variety of technologies.

> **data-flow diagram (DFD)** A model of objects, associations and activities that describes how data can flow between and around various objects.

DFDs are easy to develop and easily understood by nontechnical people. Data-flow diagrams use four primary symbols, as illustrated in Figure 8.14b.

8

Figure 8.14 Data and Activity Modelling

(a) An entity-relationship diagram. (b) A data-flow diagram. (c) A semantic description of the business process.

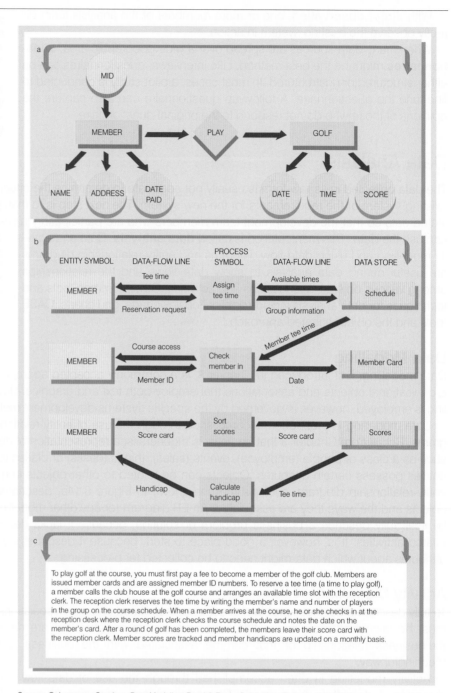

SOURCE: G. Lawrence Sanders, *Data Modeling*, Boyd & Fraser Publishing, Danvers, MA: 1995.

data-flow line Arrows that show the direction of data element movement.

process symbol Representation of a function that is performed.

entity symbol Representation of either a source or destination of a data element.

- *Data flow.* The **data-flow line** includes arrows that show the direction of data element movement.

- *Process symbol.* The **process symbol** reveals a function that is performed. Computing gross pay, entering a sales order, delivering merchandise and printing a report are examples of functions that can be represented with a process symbol.

- *Entity symbol.* The **entity symbol** shows either the source or the destination of the data element. An entity can be, for example, a customer who initiates a sales order, an employee who receives a paycheck or a manager who receives a financial report.

■ *Data store.* A **data store** reveals a storage location for data. A data store is any computerised or manual data storage location, including magnetic tape, discs, a filing cabinet, or a desk.

data store Representation of a storage location for data.

Comparing entity-relationship diagrams with data-flow diagrams provides insight into the concept of top-down design. Figures 8.14a and b show an entity-relationship diagram and a data-flow diagram for the same business relationship – namely, a member of a golf club playing golf. Figure 8.14c provides a brief description of the business relationship for clarification.

Requirements Analysis

The overall purpose of **requirements analysis** is to determine user, stakeholder and organisational needs. For an accounts payable application, the stakeholders could include suppliers and members of the purchasing department. Questions that should be asked during requirements analysis include the following:

requirements analysis The determination of user, stakeholder and organisational needs.

■ Are these stakeholders satisfied with the current accounts payable application?

■ What improvements could be made to satisfy suppliers and help the purchasing department?

Asking Directly

One the most basic techniques used in requirements analysis is asking directly. **Asking directly** is an approach that asks users, stakeholders and other managers about what they want and expect from the new or modified system. This approach works best for stable systems in which stakeholders and users clearly understand the system's functions. The role of the systems analyst during the analysis phase is to critically and creatively evaluate needs and define them clearly so that the systems can best meet them.

asking directly An approach to gather data that asks users, stakeholders and other managers about what they want and expect from the new or modified system.

Critical Success Factors

Another approach uses critical success factors (CSFs). As discussed earlier, managers and decision makers are asked to list only the factors that are critical to the success of their area of the organisation.[54] A CSF for a production manager might be adequate raw materials from suppliers; a CSF for a sales representative could be a list of customers currently buying a certain type of product. Starting from these CSFs, the system inputs, outputs, performance and other specific requirements can be determined.

The IS Plan

As we have seen, the IS plan translates strategic and organisational goals into systems development initiatives. The IS planning process often generates strategic planning documents that can be used to define system requirements. Working from these documents ensures that requirements analysis will address the goals set by top-level managers and decision makers (see Figure 8.15). There are unique benefits to applying the IS plan to define systems requirements. Because the IS plan takes a long-range approach to using information technology within the

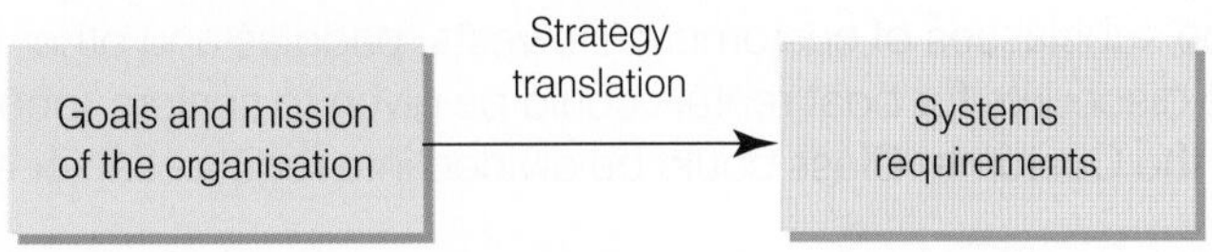

Figure 8.15 Converting Organisational Goals into Systems Requirements

organisation, the requirements for a system analyzed in terms of the IS plan are more likely to be compatible with future systems development initiatives.

Requirements Analysis Tools

A number of tools can be used to document requirements analysis, including CASE tools. As requirements are developed and agreed on, entity-relationship diagrams, data-flow diagrams, screen and report layout forms, and other types of documentation are stored in the CASE repository. These requirements might also be used later as a reference during the rest of systems development or for a different systems development project.

Object-Oriented Systems Analysis

The object-oriented approach can also be used during systems analysis. Like traditional analysis, problems or potential opportunities are identified during object-oriented analysis. Identifying key participants and collecting data are still performed. But, instead of analyzing the existing system using data-flow diagrams and flowcharts, an object-oriented approach is used.

The section "Object-Oriented Systems Investigation" introduced a boat rental example. A more detailed analysis of that business reveals that there are two classes of boats: single boats for one person and tandem boats that can accommodate two people. With the OO approach, a class is used to describe different types of objects, such as single and tandem boats. The classes of boats can be shown in a generalisation/specialisation hierarchy diagram (see Figure 8.16). BoatItem is an object that will store the boat identification number (ID) and the date the boat was purchased (Date Purchased).

Figure 8.16
Generalisation/Specialisation Hierarchy Diagram for Single and Tandem Boat Classes

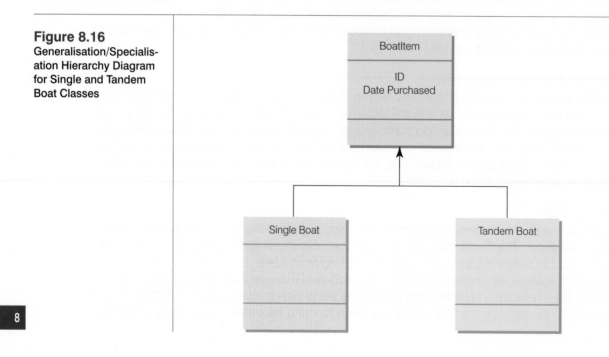

Of course, there could be subclasses of customers, life vests, paddles and other items in the system. For example, price discounts for boat rentals could be given to seniors (people over 65 years) and students. Thus, the Customer Class could be divided into regular, senior and student customer subclasses.

The Systems Analysis Report

Systems analysis concludes with a formal systems analysis report. It should cover the following elements:

■ The strengths and weaknesses of the existing system from a stakeholder's perspective

■ The user/stakeholder requirements for the new system (also called the *functional requirements*)

■ The organisational requirements for the new system

■ A description of what the new information system should do to solve the problem

Suppose analysis reveals that a marketing manager thinks a weakness of the existing system is its inability to provide accurate reports on product availability. These requirements and a preliminary list of the corporate objectives for the new system will be in the systems analysis report. Particular attention is placed on areas of the existing system that could be improved to meet user requirements. The table of contents for a typical report is shown in Figure 8.17.

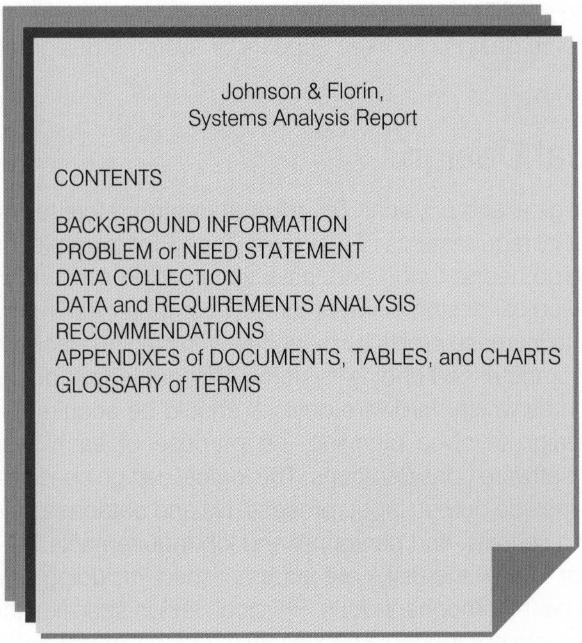

Figure 8.17 A Typical Table of Contents for a Report on an Existing System

Johnson & Florin,
Systems Analysis Report

CONTENTS

BACKGROUND INFORMATION
PROBLEM or NEED STATEMENT
DATA COLLECTION
DATA and REQUIREMENTS ANALYSIS
RECOMMENDATIONS
APPENDIXES of DOCUMENTS, TABLES, and CHARTS
GLOSSARY of TERMS

The systems analysis report gives managers a good understanding of the problems and strengths of the existing system. If the existing system is operating better than expected or the necessary changes are too expensive relative to the benefits of a new or modified system, the systems development process can be stopped at this stage. If the report shows that changes to another part of the system might be the best solution, the development process might start over, beginning again with systems investigation. Or, if the systems analysis report shows that it will be beneficial to develop one or more new systems or to make changes to existing ones, systems design, which is discussed next, begins.

8.6 Systems Design

The purpose of **systems design** is to answer the question "How will the information system solve a problem?" The primary result of the systems design phase is a technical design that details system outputs, inputs and user

systems design The stage of systems development that answers the question "How will the information system do what is necessary to solve a problem?"

interfaces; specifies hardware, software, databases, telecommunications, personnel and procedures; and shows how these components are related. The new or modified system should take advantage of the latest developments in technology. Many companies, for example, are using cloud computing, where applications are run on the internet instead of being developed and run within the company or organisation.[55] One advantage of using cloud computing is easier management of information systems, because everything is in one place on the internet. General Electric, for example, is developing a "private" cloud that can only be accessed and used by General Electric's employees and managers.[56] According to General Electric's CTO, "You get efficiencies when you start to manage that as a single entity. You can flex that capacity across applications, back it up, monitor it, and manage it as one entity." There are, however, potential disadvantages of a systems development effort that relies on cloud computing.[57] One important risk is security. Organisations may not know who is able to hack into the internet and get access to their sensitive and critical data.[58] Another risk is availability. If the internet site that is providing the cloud computing application is unavailable or having technical problems, critical applications may not be available. Some cloud computing users have also complained about slow access and execution times for applications that are run using a cloud computing environment on the internet.[59]

Systems design is typically accomplished using the tools and techniques discussed earlier in this chapter. Depending on the specific application, these methods can be used to support and document all aspects of systems design. Two key aspects of systems design are logical and physical design.

Logical and Physical Design

Design has two dimensions: logical and physical. The **logical design** refers to what the system will do. It describes the functional requirements of a system. Today, for example, many stock exchanges, large hedge funds and institutional stock investors include speed as a critical logical design element for new computer trading systems.[60] The objective is to increase profits by being faster in placing electronic trades than traditional computerised trading systems. Without logical design, the technical details of the system (such as which hardware devices should be acquired) often obscure the best solution. Logical design involves planning the purpose of each system element, independent of hardware and software considerations. The logical design specifications that are determined and documented include output, input, process, file and database, telecommunications, procedures, controls and security, and personnel and job requirements.

logical design A description of the functional requirements of a system.

The **physical design** refers to how the tasks are accomplished, including how the components work together and what each component does. Physical design specifies the characteristics of the system components necessary to put the logical design into action. In this phase, the characteristics of the hardware, software, database, telecommunications, personnel, and procedure and control specifications must be detailed. These physical design components were discussed in Part 2 on technology. The New York Stock Exchange, for example, has developed a physical design to build a large facility the size of several football fields to house super fast trading systems that can be used by large hedge funds and institutional investors to get the speed they specified in their logical designs.[61]

physical design The specification of the characteristics of the system components necessary to put the logical design into action.

Object-Oriented Design

Logical and physical design can be accomplished using either the traditional approach or the object-oriented approach to systems development. Both approaches use a variety of design models to document the new system's features and the development team's understandings and agreements. Many organisations today are turning to OO development because of its increased flexibility. This section outlines a few OO design considerations and diagrams.

Using the OO approach, you can design key objects and classes of objects in the new or updated system.[62] This process includes considering the problem domain, the operating environment and the user interface. The problem domain involves the classes of objects related to solving a problem or realising an opportunity. In our Maui, Hawaii, boat rental shop example discussed earlier in the chapter and referring back to the generalisation/specialisation hierarchy showing classes we presented there, BoatItem in Figure 8.16 is an example of a problem domain object that will store information on boats in the rental program. The operating environment for the rental shop's system includes objects that interact with printers, system software, and other software and hardware devices. The user interface for the system includes objects that users interact with, such as buttons and scroll bars in a Windows program.

During the design phase, you also need to consider the sequence of events that must happen for the system to function correctly. For example, you might want to design the sequence of events for adding a new boat to the rental program. The event sequence is often called a *scenario*, and it can be diagrammed in a sequence diagram (see Figure 8.18).

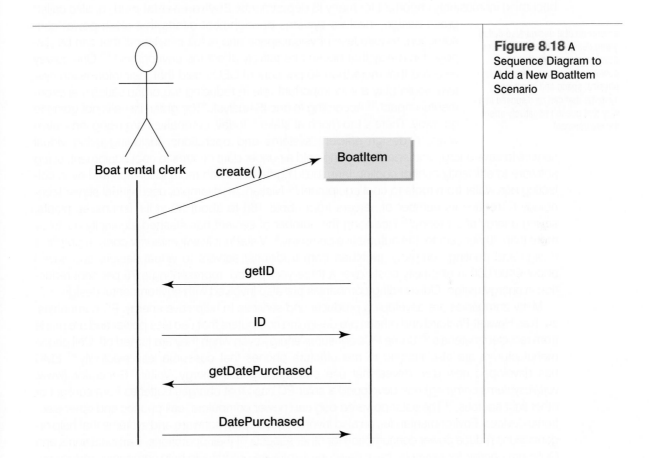

Figure 8.18 A Sequence Diagram to Add a New BoatItem Scenario

You read a sequence diagram starting at the top and moving down.

1 The Create arrow at the top is a message from the boat rental clerk to the BoatItem object to create information on a new boat to be placed into the rental program.

2 The BoatItem object knows that it needs the ID for the boat and sends a message to the clerk requesting the information. See the getID arrow.

3 The clerk then types the ID into the computer. This is shown with the ID arrow. The data is stored in the BoatItem object.

4 Next, BoatItem requests the purchase date. This is shown in the getDatePurchased arrow.

5 Finally, the clerk types the purchase date into the computer. The data is also transferred to BoatItem object. This is shown in the DatePurchased arrow at the bottom of Figure 8.18.

This scenario is only one example of a sequence of events. Other scenarios might include entering information about life jackets, paddles, suntan lotion and other accessories. The same types of use case and generalisation/specialisation hierarchy diagrams can be created for each event, and additional sequence diagrams will also be needed.

8.7 Environmental Design Considerations

Developing new systems and modifying existing ones in an environmentally sensitive way is becoming increasingly important for many IS departments. **Environmental design**, also called *green design*, involves systems development efforts that slash power consumption, require less physical space and result in systems that can be disposed in a way that doesn't negatively affect the environment.[63] One survey revealed that more than 40 per cent of CEOs said that their information system would play a very important role in reducing the organisation's environmental impact.[64] According to one IS analyst, "The green issue is not going to go away. There's too much at stake." Today, companies are using innovative ways to design efficient systems and operations, including using virtual servers to save energy and space, pushing cold air under data centres to cool equipment, using software to efficiently control cooling fans, building facilities with more insulation and even collecting rain water from roofs to cool equipment.[65] Nissan, for example, used virtual server technology to reduce its number of servers from about 160 to about 30 in its Tennessee plants, saving energy and money.[66] Reducing the number of servers has slashed electricity costs by more than 30 per cent for the automotive company.[67] VistaPrint (*www.vistaprint.com*), a graphics design and printing company, switched from traditional servers to virtual servers and saved about €400 000 in electricity costs over a three-year period, representing a 75 per cent reduction in energy usage. Outsourcing companies are also involved with environmental design.

> **environmental design** Also called *green design*, it involves systems development efforts that slash power consumption, require less physical space and result in systems that can be disposed in a way that doesn't negatively affect the environment.

Many companies are developing products and services to help save energy. PC companies, such as Hewlett-Packard and others, are designing computers that use less power and are made from recycled materials.[68] Some PCs consume energy even when they are turned off. Cell phone manufacturers are also starting to manufacture phones that consume less electricity.[69] EMC has developed new disc drives that use substantially less energy. Voltaic Generator (*www.voltaicsystems.com/bag*) has developed a solar PC case that charges batteries from sunlight or other light sources.[70] The solar-powered bag can power computers, cell phones and other electronic devices. Environmental design also involves developing software and systems that help organisations reduce power consumption for other aspects of their operations. Carbonetworks and Optimum Energy, for example, have developed software products to help companies reduce energy costs by helping them determine when and how to use electricity. UPS developed its own software to reduce the miles its trucks and other vehicles drive by routing them more efficiently. The new software helped UPS cut million of miles per year, slash fuel costs and reduce carbon emissions. Hewlett-Packard, Dell Computer and others have developed procedures and machines to dispose of old computers and computer equipment in environmentally friendly ways.[71] VenJuvo (*www.venjuvo.com*) and other companies also recycle old electronics equipment and offer cash in some cases, depending on the age and type of equipment.[72] Old computers and computer equipment are fed into machines that shred them into small pieces and sort them into materials that can be reused. The process is often called *green death*.

SOURCE: www.dell.com/recycle.

Companies, such as Hewlett-Packard and Dell Computer, dispose of old computers and computer equipment in environmentally friendly ways.

Generating Systems Design Alternatives

Generating systems design alternatives often involves getting the involvement of a single vendor or multiple vendors.[73] If the new system is complex, the original development team might want to involve other personnel in generating alternative designs. In addition, if new hardware and software are to be acquired from an outside vendor, a formal request for proposal (RFP) can be made.

Request for Proposals

The **request for proposal (RFP)** is a document that specifies in detail required resources, such as hardware and software. The RFP is an important document for many organisations involved with large, complex systems development efforts. Smaller, less-complex systems often do not require an RFP. A company that is purchasing an inexpensive piece of software that will run on existing hardware, for example, might not need to go through a formal RFP process.

In some cases, separate RFPs are developed for different needs. For example, a company might develop separate RFPs for hardware, software and database systems. The RFP also communicates these needs to one or more vendors, and it provides a way to evaluate whether the vendor has delivered what was expected. In some cases, the RFP is part of the vendor contract. The Table of Contents for a typical RFP is shown in Figure 8.19.

> **request for proposal (RFP)** A document that specifies in detail required resources such as hardware and software.

Evaluating and Selecting a Systems Design

Evaluating and selecting the best design involves achieving a balance of system objectives that will best support organisational goals. Normally, evaluation and selection involves both a preliminary and a final evaluation before a design is selected.

A **preliminary evaluation** begins after all proposals have been submitted. The purpose of this evaluation is to dismiss unwanted proposals. Several vendors can usually be eliminated by investigating their proposals and comparing them with the original criteria. The **final evaluation** begins with a detailed investigation of the proposals offered by the remaining vendors. The vendors should be asked to make a final presentation and to fully demonstrate the system. The demonstration should be as close to actual operating conditions as possible.

> **preliminary evaluation** An initial assessment whose purpose is to dismiss the unwanted proposals; begins after all proposals have been submitted.
>
> **final evaluation** A detailed investigation of the proposals offered by the vendors remaining after the preliminary evaluation.

8

Figure 8.19 A Typical Table of Contents for a Request for Proposal

Johnson & Florin,
Systems Investigation Report

Contents

COVER PAGE (with company name and contact person)
BRIEF DESCRIPTION of the COMPANY
OVERVIEW of the EXISTING COMPUTER SYSTEM
SUMMARY of COMPUTER-RELATED NEEDS and/or PROBLEMS
OBJECTIVES of the PROJECT
DESCRIPTION of WHAT IS NEEDED
HARDWARE REQUIREMENTS
PERSONNEL REQUIREMENTS
COMMUNICATIONS REQUIREMENTS
PROCEDURES to BE DEVELOPED
TRAINING REQUIREMENTS
MAINTENANCE REQUIREMENTS
EVALUATION PROCEDURES (how vendors will be judged)
PROPOSAL FORMAT (how vendors should respond)
IMPORTANT DATES (when tasks are to be completed)
SUMMARY

The Design Report

System specifications are the final results of systems design. They include a technical description that details system outputs, inputs and user interfaces, as well as all hardware, software, databases, telecommunications, personnel, and procedure components and the way these components are related. The specifications are contained in a **design report**, which is the primary result of systems design. The design report reflects the decisions made for systems design and prepares the way for systems implementation. The contents of the design report are summarised in Figure 8.20.

design report The primary result of systems design, reflecting the decisions made and preparing the way for systems implementation.

Figure 8.20 A Typical Table of Contents for a Systems Design Report

Johnson & Florin,
Systems Design Report

Contents

PREFACE
EXECUTIVE SUMMARY of SYSTEMS DESIGN
REVIEW of SYSTEMS ANALYSIS
MAJOR DESIGN RECOMMENDATIONS
    Hardware design
    Software design
    Personnel design
    Communications design
    Database design
    Procedures design
    Training design
    Maintenance design
SUMMARY of DESIGN DECISIONS
APPENDICES
GLOSSARY of TERMS
INDEX

8.8 Systems Implementation

After the information system has been designed, a number of tasks must be completed before the system is installed and ready to operate. This process, called systems implementation, includes hardware acquisition, programming and software acquisition or development, user preparation, hiring and training of personnel, site and data preparation, installation, testing, start-up and user acceptance. The typical sequence of systems implementation activities is shown in Figure 8.21.

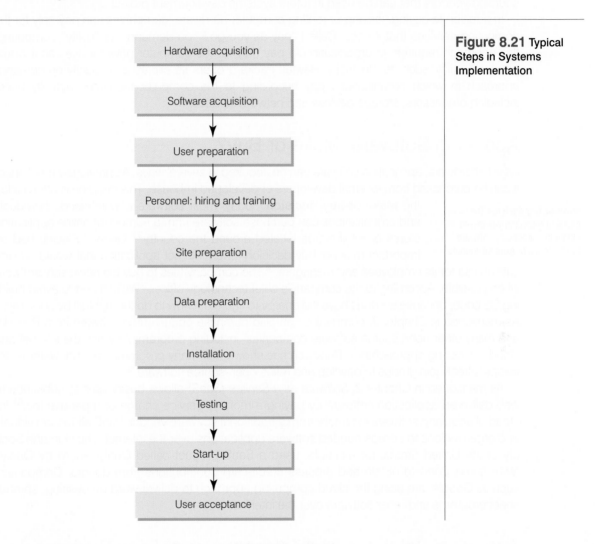

Figure 8.21 Typical Steps in Systems Implementation

Acquiring Hardware from an IS Vendor

To obtain the components for an information system, organisations can purchase, lease, or rent computer hardware and other resources from an IS vendor. An *IS vendor* is a company that offers hardware, software, telecommunications systems, databases, IS personnel or other computer-related resources. Types of IS vendors include general computer manufacturers (such as IBM and Hewlett-Packard), small computer manufacturers (such as Dell and Sony), peripheral equipment manufacturers (such as Epson and SanDisk), computer dealers and distributors (such as PC World), and chip makers (such as Intel and AMD). Some of the most successful vendors include IBM (hardware and other services), Oracle (databases), Apple (personal computers), Microsoft (software), Accenture (IS consulting) and many others.[74] In addition,

8

many new hardware vendors provide specialised equipment and services.[75] Venture capital firms have invested hundreds of millions of euros in new hardware vendors. Hardware vendors can provide very small or very large systems. Many companies have multiple hardware vendors, but managing them can be difficult.[76] Different vendors must compete against each other to get an outsourcing contract with the organisation. Then, the selected vendors must work together to develop an effective information system at a good price. Open communications among the outsourcing vendors is critical. Each vendor's work and pricing should be transparent and available to all the other outsourcing vendors. Over time, it is best to have a set of trusted, reliable outsourcing vendors that can be used in future systems development projects.

In addition to buying, leasing or renting computer hardware, companies can pay only for the computing services that it uses. Called "pay-as-you-go," "on-demand," or "utility" computing, this approach requires an organisation to pay only for the computer power it uses as it would pay for a utility, such as electricity. Hewlett-Packard offers its clients a "capacity-on-demand" approach in which organisations pay according to the computer resources actually used, including processors, storage devices and network facilities.

Acquiring Software: Make or Buy?

As with hardware, application software can be acquired in several ways. As previously mentioned, it can be purchased from external developers or developed in-house. This decision is often called

make-or-buy decision The decision regarding whether to obtain the necessary software from internal or external sources.

the **make-or-buy decision**. Today, most software is purchased. Individuals and organisations can purchase software from a number of online application stores or retail stores located around the country.[77] General Electric had an important make-or-buy decision for an internet application that would provide critical data for its employees and managers.[78] The company tries to buy the necessary software when possible. According to the company's chief technology officer, "We're trying to avoid building GE code, because we don't have the energy to figure out how to do this right all by ourselves." As mentioned in Chapter 2, companies can also purchase open-source software from Red Hat and many other open-source software companies, including programs that use the internet and cloud computing approaches.[79] Research has shown that many programmers and systems developers freely join groups to develop and refine open-source software.[80]

As mentioned in Chapter 2, *Software as a Service (SaaS)* allows businesses to subscribe to web-delivered application software by paying a monthly service charge or a per-use fee.[81] Instead of acquiring software externally from a traditional software vendor, SaaS allows individuals and organisations to access needed software applications over the internet. The Humane Society of the United States, for example, used a SaaS product called QualysGuard by Qualys (*www.qualys.com*) to obtain and process credit-card contributions from donors. Companies, such as Google, are using the cloud computing approach to deliver word processing, spreadsheet programs and other software over the internet.

Acquiring Database and Telecommunications Systems

Because databases are a blend of hardware and software, many of the approaches discussed earlier for acquiring hardware and software also apply to database systems, including open-source databases. *Virtual databases and database as a service (DaaS)* are popular ways to acquire database capabilities.[82] Sirius XM Radio, Bank of America and Southwest Airlines, for example, use the DaaS approach to manage many of their database operations from the internet.[83] In another case, a brokerage company was able to reduce storage capacity by 50 per cent by using database virtualisation.

With the increased use of e-commerce, the internet, intranets and extranets, telecommunications is one of the fastest-growing applications for today's organisations. Like database systems, telecommunications systems require a blend of hardware and software. For personal

Ethical and Societal Issues

Medical Centre Moves Patient Records to Cloud

Beth Israel Deaconess Medical Center (BID) is a large teaching hospital associated with Harvard Medical School that serves Boston and surrounding communities. BID is one of the top four recipients of biomedical research funding from the National Institutes for Health, winning nearly US$200 million annually.

Moving to an electronic health record system (EHRS) has been a priority for BID for years. In 2008, long before the federal government offered stimulus funds for EHRS, BID rolled out its own EHRS. BID was motivated to move to an EHRS by requirements imposed by insurance companies. So-called pay-for-performance insurance plans require highly detailed and real-time documentation that is possible only through EHRS.

BID knew its 300 physicians would approve an EHRS, but earning the approval of the 900 other physicians associated with BID, but not employed by BID, was a bigger challenge. Many of those 900 physicians own small practices with limited resources. Along with their staff, they work ten-hour days, processing 40 patients a day, and have little time to invest in learning new technology. BID decided to invest in an EHRS for its own physicians, gambling that its associated physicians would eventually witness the value of an EHRS and buy in.

BID evaluated many EHRSs, weighing the benefits against the drawbacks. The systems analysts designing the EHRS were at a disadvantage, because they didn't know exactly how many physicians and medical records the system would need to accommodate. They needed a system that could be scaled to match the amount of data. For this reason, they decided on a SaaS cloud computing system.

The solution came from a company named eClinicalWorks, which licences its software to BID and provides the hosted service. The hosted service runs on virtual servers that make it easy to add more storage and processing resources as they are needed, without any interruption to service. For example, BID recently updated its security to a stronger form of encryption. The upgrade placed too much strain on the servers, so BID spent US$20 000 to add more virtual resources to the service provider's hosted servers.

The same scenario without virtualisation would have cost BID US$325 000 for additional hardware. This is a convincing argument in support of both virtualisation and SaaS cloud computing services.

The medical industry has unique information security requirements placed on it by local and federal governments designed to provide patient privacy. Because of this, the move to EHRSs has been slow. The system designed by eClinicalWorks uses a thin client device that connects to PCs to encrypt medical data as it leaves the PC and decrypt data as it arrives. Other than that, the system requires no complicated software or set up, and it runs in a standard web browser. The system also has an offline mode, so that records can be accessed even when clients are not connected to the network. Each time computers connect to eClinicalWorks, the records are synchronised with records on the server.

Because eClinicalWorks is easy to set up and use, BID associates are more likely to join the system. There are many other incentives as well. Besides the obvious convenience of access to medical records anywhere anytime, the EHRS also provides record keeping automation. Medical practices often hire several employees just to process the paperwork required by Medicaid and private insurers. The EHRS automates those processes, dramatically reducing the need for staff. BID has made the EHRS a requirement for associates who want to take advantage of the medical centre's administrative, clinical and technical support.

BID associates have been quick to see the benefits of the eClinicalWorks EHRS and are migrating to the new system. No longer do BID patients have to fill out forms in triplicate every time they visit a new physician or specialist. No longer do BID physicians have to dig through file cabinets for patient records – they have access to them anywhere, anytime on their tablet computers. No longer does staff have to work full time filling out insurance claims. The eClinicalWorks EHRS provides all of these services, and, because it is hosted in the cloud, maintenance is not a concern for BID information systems staff.

8

computer systems, the primary piece of hardware is a modem. For client/server and mainframe systems, the hardware can include multiplexers, concentrators, communications processors and a variety of network equipment. Communications software will also have to be acquired from a software company or developed in-house. Again, the earlier discussion on acquiring hardware and software also applies to the acquisition of telecommunications hardware and software. As discussed earlier in this chapter and previous chapters, individuals and organisations are increasingly using the internet and cloud computing to implement many new systems development efforts.[84] Systems analysts and programmers are also starting to use the internet to develop applications.[85] Scott Schroeder and his company, Rabble +Rouser, developed an application that contained over 200 recipes for barbecues for iPhone users.[86] The $4.99 application was one of the best-selling applications at Apple's application store.

User Preparation

User preparation is the process of readying managers, decision makers, employees, other users and stakeholders for the new systems. This activity is an important but often ignored area of systems implementation. When a new operating system or application software package is implemented, user training is essential. In some cases, companies decide not to install the latest software, because the amount of time and money needed to train employees is too much. Because user training is so important, some companies provide training for their clients, including in-house, software, video, internet and other training approaches.

user preparation The process of readying managers, decision makers, employees, other users and stakeholders for new systems.

Providing users with proper training can help ensure that the information system is used correctly, efficiently and effectively.

SOURCE: © iStock/fredfroese.

IS Personnel: Hiring and Training

Depending on the size of the new system, an organisation might have to hire and, in some cases, train new IS personnel. An IS manager, systems analysts, computer programmers, data entry operators and similar personnel might be needed for the new or modified system.

Site Preparation

The location of the new system needs to be prepared, a process called **site preparation**. For a small system, site preparation can be as simple as rearranging the furniture in an office to make room for a computer. With a larger system, this process is not so easy, because it can require special wiring and air conditioning. A special floor, for example, might have to be built under which the cables connecting the various computer components are placed, and a new security system might be needed to protect the equipment. Today, developing IS sites that are energy efficient is important for most systems development implementations. Security is also important for site preparation.[87] One company, for example, installed special security kiosks that let visitors log on and request a meeting with a company employee. The employee can see the visitor on his or her computer screen and accept or reject the visitor. If the visitor is accepted, the kiosk prints a visitor pass.

Site preparation Preparation of the location of a new system.

Data Preparation

Data preparation, or **data conversion**, involves making sure that all files and databases are ready to be used with new computer software and systems. If an organisation is installing a new payroll program, the old employee-payroll data might have to be converted into a format that can be used by the new computer software or system. After the data has been prepared or converted, the computerised database system or other software will then be used to maintain and update the computer files.

data preparation, or data conversion Making sure all files and databases are ready to be used with new computer software and systems.

Installation

Installation is the process of physically placing the computer equipment on the site and making it operational. Although normally the manufacturer is responsible for installing computer equipment, someone from the organisation (usually the IS manager) should oversee the process, making sure that all equipment specified in the contract is installed at the proper location. After the system is installed, the manufacturer performs several tests to ensure that the equipment is operating as it should.

installation The process of physically placing the computer equipment on the site and making it operational.

Testing

Good testing procedures are essential to make sure that the new or modified information system operates as intended.[88] Inadequate testing can result in mistakes and problems. Problems with a project to consolidate data centre servers, for example, resulted in more than 160 000 internet sites being shut down. The company that was trying to consolidate its database servers was hosting the internet sites. Some internet sites were down for more than six days. Better testing may have prevented these types of problems. Several forms of testing should be used, including testing each program (**unit testing**), testing the entire system of programs (**system testing**), testing the application with a large amount of data (**volume testing**) and testing all related systems together (**integration testing**), as well as conducting any tests required by the user (**acceptance testing**).

unit testing Testing of individual programs.

system testing Testing the entire system of programs.

volume testing Testing the application with a large amount of data.

integration testing Testing all related systems together.

acceptance testing Conducting any tests required by the user.

8

Start-Up

Start-up, also called *cutover*, begins with the final tested information system. When start-up is finished, the system is fully operational. Start-up can be critical to the success of the organisation. If not done properly, the results can be disastrous. In one case, a small manufacturing company decided to stop an accounting service used to send out bills on the same day they were going to start their own program to send out bills to customers. The manufacturing company wanted to save money by using their own billing program developed by an employee. The new program didn't work, the accounting service wouldn't help, because they were upset about being terminated, and the manufacturing company wasn't able to send out any bills to customers for more than three months. The manufacturing company almost went bankrupt.

start-up The process of making the final tested information system fully operational.

Various start-up approaches are available (see Figure 8.22). **Direct conversion** (also called *plunge* or *direct cutover*) involves stopping the old system and starting the new system on a given date. Direct conversion is usually the least desirable approach because of the potential for problems and errors when the old system is shut off and the new system is turned on at the same instant.

direct conversion (also called *plunge* or *direct cutover*) Stopping the old system and starting the new system on a given date.

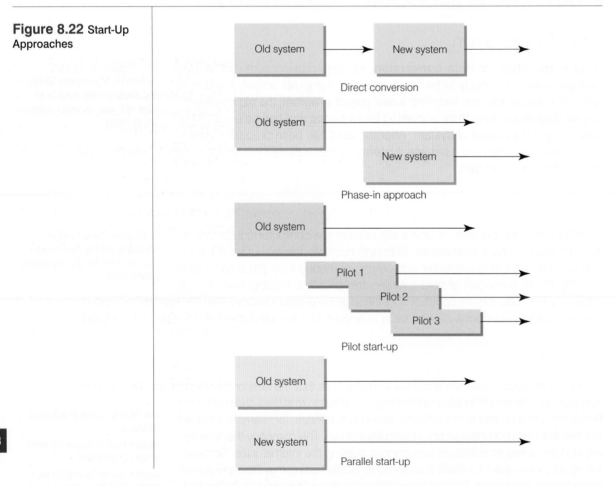

Figure 8.22 Start-Up Approaches

The **phase-in approach** is a popular technique preferred by many organisations. In this approach, sometimes called a *piecemeal approach*, components of the new system are slowly phased in while components of the old one are slowly phased out. When everyone is confident that the new system is performing as expected, the old system is completely phased out. This gradual replacement is repeated for each application until the new system is running every application. In some cases, the phase-in approach can take months or years.

Pilot start-up involves running the new system for one group of users rather than all users. For example, a manufacturing company with many retail outlets throughout the country could use the pilot start-up approach and install a new inventory control system at one of the retail outlets. When this pilot retail outlet runs without problems, the new inventory control system can be implemented at other retail outlets.

Parallel start-up involves running both the old and new systems for a period of time. The output of the new system is compared closely with the output of the old system, and any differences are reconciled. When users are comfortable that the new system is working correctly, the old system is eliminated.

> **phase-in approach** Slowly replacing components of the old system with those of the new one. This process is repeated for each application until the new system is running every application and performing as expected; also called a *piecemeal approach*.

> **pilot start-up** Running the new system for one group of users rather than all users.

> **parallel start-up** Running both the old and new systems for a period of time and comparing the output of the new system closely with the output of the old system; any differences are reconciled. When users are comfortable that the new system is working correctly, the old system is eliminated.

User Acceptance

Most mainframe computer manufacturers use a formal **user acceptance document** – a formal agreement the user signs stating that a phase of the installation or the complete system is approved. This is a legal document that usually removes or reduces the IS vendor's liability for problems that occur after the user acceptance document has been signed. Because this document is so important, many companies get legal assistance before they sign the acceptance document. Stakeholders can also be involved in acceptance testing to make sure that the benefits to them are indeed realised.

> **user acceptance document** A formal agreement signed by the user that states that a phase of the installation or the complete system is approved.

8.9 Systems Operation and Maintenance

Systems operation involves all aspects of using the new or modified system in all kinds of operating conditions. Getting the most out of a new or modified system during its operation is the most important aspect of systems operations for many organisations. Throughout this book, we have seen many examples of information systems operating in a variety of settings and industries. Thus, we will not cover the operation of an information system in detail in this section. To provide adequate support, many companies use a formal help desk. A *help desk* consists of people with technical expertise, computer systems, manuals and other resources needed to solve problems and give accurate answers to questions. If you are having trouble with your PC and call a toll-free number for assistance, you might reach a help desk in India, China, or another country.

> **systems operation** Use of a new or modified system.

Systems maintenance involves checking, changing and enhancing the system to make it more useful in achieving user and organisational goals. Organisations can perform systems maintenance in house or they can hire outside companies to perform maintenance for them.[89] Many companies that use database systems from Oracle or SAP, for example, often hire these companies to maintain their database systems. Systems maintenance is important for individuals groups and organisations. Individuals, for example, can use the internet, computer vendors and independent maintenance companies, including YourTechOnline.com (*www.yourtechonline.com*), Geek Squad (*www.geeksquad.com*), PC Pinpoint (*www.pcpinpoint.com*) and others. Organisations often have personnel dedicated to maintenance.

> **systems maintenance** A stage of systems development that involves checking, changing and enhancing the system to make it more useful in achieving user and organisational goals.

Software maintenance for purchased software can be 20 per cent or more of the purchase price of the software annually.[90] Although some CIOs complain about the high cost of software maintenance, others believe it is worth the cost. According to one CIO, "We've never viewed maintenance as a black hole you put your money into. Maintenance is part of the game." The maintenance process can be especially difficult for older software. A *legacy system* is an old system that might have been patched or modified repeatedly over time. An old payroll program in COBOL developed decades ago and frequently changed is an example of a legacy system. Legacy systems can be very expensive to maintain, and it can be difficult to add new features to some legacy systems. With about 11 million lines of older computer code, a large railroad company wasn't able to add the new features customers wanted.[91] At some point, it becomes less expensive to switch to new programs and applications than to repair and maintain the legacy system. Maintenance costs for older legacy systems can be 50 per cent of total operating costs in some cases.

8.10 Systems Review

Systems review, the final step of systems development, is the process of analyzing systems to make sure that they are operating as intended. The systems review process often compares the performance and benefits of the system as it was designed with the actual performance and benefits of the system in operation. The Transportation Security Agency (TSA), for example, used an approach called the *Idea Factory*, to review current information systems and recommend new ones or changes to existing systems.[92] According to the systems development director for TSA, "Often, the people on the front lines have the best ideas because they're the ones who interact with passengers." The Idea Factory was featured on the White House website.[93] In some cases, a formal audit of the application can be performed, using internal and external auditors.[94] Systems review can be performed during systems development, resulting in halting the new systems while they are being built because of problems.

systems review The final step of systems development, involving the analysis of systems to make sure that they are operating as intended.

System Performance Measurement

Systems review often involves monitoring the system, called **system performance measurement**. The number of errors encountered, the amount of memory required, the amount of processing or CPU time needed and other problems should be closely observed. If a particular system is not performing as expected, it should be modified, or a new system should be developed or acquired. Comcast, the large cable provider, used Twitter to get user feedback on the performance of its information systems and all of its operations.[95] Some Comcast executives believe that using Twitter is like an "early-warning-system" that alerts Comcast to potential problems before they become serious and hurt system performance.

system performance measurement Monitoring the system – the number of errors encountered, the amount of memory required, the amount of processing or CPU time needed and other problems.

System performance products have been developed to measure all components of the information system, including hardware, software, database, telecommunications and network systems. IBM Tivoli OMEGAMON can monitor system performance in real time.[96] Precise Software Solutions has system performance products that provide around-the-clock performance monitoring for ERP systems, Oracle database applications and other programs.[97] HP also offers a software tool called Business Technology Optimisation (BTO) software to help companies analyze the performance of their computer systems, diagnose potential problems and take corrective action if needed.[98] When properly used, system performance products can quickly and efficiently locate actual or potential problems.

system performance products Software that measures all components of the computer-based information system, including hardware, software, database, telecommunications and network systems.

Measuring a system is, in effect, the final task of systems development. The results of this process can bring the development team back to the beginning of the development life cycle, where the process begins again.

Summary

At the start of this chapter, we set out the SIX main principles relating to how businesses and organisations tackle systems development, discussing how they approach the critical questions around auditing current systems and implementing changed or replacement systems as a result together with the key learning objectives for each. Now it's time to summarise the chapter by recapping on those SIX principles: can you recall what is important and why about each one?

1. **Effective systems development requires a team effort of stakeholders, users, managers, systems development specialists and various support personnel, and it starts with careful planning.** The systems development team consists of stakeholders, users, managers, systems development specialists and various support personnel. The development team is responsible for determining the objectives of the information system and delivering to the organisation a system that meets its objectives.

A systems analyst is a professional who specialises in analyzing and designing business systems. The programmer is responsible for modifying or developing programs to satisfy user requirements. Other support personnel on the development team include technical specialists, either IS department employees or outside consultants. Depending on the magnitude of the systems development project and the number of IS systems development specialists on the team, the team may also include one or more IS managers.

An individual systems developer is a person that performs all of the systems development roles, including systems analyst, programmer, technical specialist and other roles described in the above section. Although individual systems developers can create applications for a group or entire organisation, many specialise in developing applications for individuals. Individual users acquire applications for both personal and professional use. It is also possible for one person to be both an individual developer and a user. The term end-user systems development describes any systems development project in which business managers and users assume the primary effort.

Information systems planning refers to the translation of strategic and organisational goals into systems development initiatives. Benefits of IS planning include a long-range view of information technology use and better use of IS resources. Planning requires developing overall IS objectives; identifying IS projects; setting priorities and selecting projects; analyzing resource requirements; setting schedules, milestones and deadlines; and developing the IS planning document.

2. **Systems development often uses different approaches and tools, such as traditional development, prototyping rapid application development, end-user development, computeraided software engineering and object-oriented development to select, implement and monitor projects.** The five phases of the traditional SDLC are investigation, analysis, design, implementation, and maintenance and review. Systems investigation involves identifying potential problems and opportunities and considering them in light of organisational goals. Systems analysis seeks a general understanding of the solution required to solve the problem; the existing system is studied in detail, and weaknesses are identified. Systems design involves creating new or modified system requirements. Systems implementation encompasses programming, testing, training, conversion and operation of the system. Systems operation involves running the system once it is implemented. Systems maintenance and review entails monitoring the system and performing enhancements or repairs.

Prototyping is an iterative development approach that involves defining the problem, building the initial version, having users utilise and evaluate the initial version, providing feedback and incorporating suggestions into the second version. Rapid application development (RAD) uses tools and techniques designed to speed application development. Its use reduces paper-based documentation, automates program source code generation and facilitates user participation in development activities. An agile, or extreme programming, approach allows systems to change as they are being developed. RAD makes extensive use of the joint application development

8

(JAD) process to gather data and perform requirements analysis. JAD involves group meetings in which users, stakeholders and IS professionals work together to analyze existing systems, propose possible solutions and define the requirements for a new or modified system.

The use of automated tools enables detailed development, tracking and control of the project schedule. Effective use of these tools enables a project manager to deliver a highquality system and to make intelligent trade-offs among cost, schedule and quality. CASE tools can automate many of the systems development tasks, thus, reducing the time and effort required to complete them while ensuring good documentation. With the object-oriented systems development (OOSD) approach, a project can be broken down into a group of objects that interact. Instead of requiring thousands or millions of lines of detailed computer instructions or code, the systems development project might require a few dozen or maybe a hundred objects.

3. **Systems development starts with investigation and analysis of existing systems.** In most organisations, a systems request form initiates the investigation process. This form typically includes the problems in or opportunities for the system, objectives of systems investigation, overview of the proposed system, and expected costs and benefits of the proposed system. The systems investigation is designed to assess the feasibility of implementing solutions for business problems. An investigation team follows up on the request and performs a feasibility analysis that addresses technical, economic, legal, operational and schedule feasibility. Object-oriented systems investigation is being used to a greater extent today. As a final step in the investigation process, a systems investigation report should be prepared to document relevant findings.

Systems analysis is the examination of existing systems, which begins once approval for further study is received from management. Additional study of a selected system allows those involved to further understand the system's weaknesses and potential improvement areas. An analysis team is assembled to collect and analyze data on the existing system.

Data collection methods include observation, interviews and questionnaires. Data analysis manipulates the collected data to provide information. Data modelling is used to model organisational objects and associations using text and graphical diagrams.

It is most often accomplished through the use of entity-relationship (ER) diagrams. Activity modelling is often accomplished through the use of data-flow diagrams (DFDs), which model objects, associations and activities by describing how data can flow between and around various objects. DFDs use symbols for data flows, processing, entities, and data stores. The overall purpose of requirements analysis is to determine user and organisational needs. Object-oriented systems analysis also involves diagramming techniques, such as a generalisation/specialisation hierarchy diagram.

4. **Designing new systems or modifying existing ones should always be aimed at helping an organisation achieve its goals.** The purpose of systems design is to prepare the detailed design needs for a new system or modifications to an existing system. Logical systems design refers to the way the various components of an information system will work together. Physical systems design refers to the specification of the actual physical components.

If new hardware or software will be purchased from a vendor, a formal request for proposal (RFP) is needed. The RFP outlines the company's needs; in response, the vendor provides a written reply. Organisations have three alternatives for acquiring computer systems: purchase, lease, or rent. RFPs from various vendors are reviewed and narrowed down to the few most likely candidates. Near the end of the design stage, an organisation prohibits further changes in the design of the system. The design specifications are then said to be frozen. After the vendor is chosen, contract negotiations can begin. One of the most important steps in systems design is to develop a good contract if new computer facilities are being acquired. The final step is to develop a design report that details the outputs, inputs and user interfaces. It also specifies hardware, software, databases, telecommunications, personnel, procedure components and the way these components are related.

Environmental design, also called green design, involves systems development efforts that slash power consumption, take less physical space and result in systems that can be disposed in a way that doesn't negatively affect the environment. A number of companies are developing products and services to help save energy. Environmental design also deals with how companies are developing systems to dispose of old equipment. The US government is also involved in environmental

8

design. It has a plan to require federal agencies to purchase energy-efficient computer systems and equipment. The plan would require federal agencies to use the Electronic Product Environmental Assessment Tool (EPEAT) to analyze the energy usage of new systems. The US Department of Energy rates products with the Energy Star designation to help people select products that save energy and are friendly to the environment.

5. **The primary emphasis of systems implementation is to make sure that the right information is delivered to the right person in the right format at the right time.** The purpose of systems implementation is to install a system and make everything, including users, ready for its operation. Systems implementation includes hardware acquisition, software acquisition or development, user preparation, hiring and training of IS personnel, site and data preparation, installation, testing, start-up and user acceptance. Hardware acquisition requires purchasing, leasing, or renting computer resources from a vendor. Increasingly, companies are using service providers to acquire software, internet access and other IS resources.

Software can be purchased from external vendors or developed in house – a decision termed the *make-or-buy decision*. Implementation must also address database and telecommunications systems, user preparation and IS personnel requirements. User preparation involves readying managers, employees and other users for the new system. New IS personnel may need to be hired, and users must be well trained in the system's functions. The physical site of the system must be prepared, and any existing data to be used in the new system must be converted to the new format. Hardware is installed during the implementation step. Testing includes program (unit) testing, systems testing, volume testing, integration testing and acceptance testing.

Start-up begins with the final tested information system. When start-up is finished, the system is fully operational. There are a number of different start-up approaches. Direct conversion (also called *plunge* or *direct cutover*) involves stopping the old system and starting the new system on a given date. With the phase-in approach, sometimes called a *piecemeal approach*, components of the new system are slowly phased in while components of the old one are slowly phased out. When everyone is confident that the new system is performing as expected, the old system is completely phased out. Pilot start-up involves running the new system for one group of users rather than all users. Parallel start-up involves running both the old and new systems for a period of time. The output of the new system is compared closely with the output of the old system, and any differences are reconciled. When users are comfortable that the new system is working correctly, the old system is eliminated. The final step of implementation is user acceptance.

6. **Maintenance and review add to the useful life of a system but can consume large amounts of resources, so they benefit from the same rigorous methods and project management techniques applied to systems development.** Systems operation is the use of a new or modified system. Systems maintenance involves checking, changing and enhancing the system to make it more useful in obtaining user and organisational goals. Maintenance is critical for the continued smooth operation of the system. Some major reasons for maintenance are changes in business processes; new requests from stakeholders, users and managers; bugs or errors in the program; technical and hardware problems; corporate mergers and acquisitions; government regulations; change in the operating system or hardware; and unexpected events, such as terrorist attacks.

Systems review is the process of analyzing systems to make sure that they are operating as intended. It involves monitoring systems to be sure they are operating as designed.

Review Questions

1 What is the goal of information systems planning? What steps are involved in IS planning?

2 What are the steps of the traditional systems development life cycle?

3 What is the difference between systems investigation and systems analysis? Why is it important to identify and remove errors early in the systems development life cycle?

4 What is end-user systems development? What are the advantages and disadvantages of end-user systems development?

5 What is the result or outcome of systems analysis? What happens next?

6 What is prototyping?

7 What are the steps of object-oriented systems development?

8 What is an RFP? What is typically included in one? How is it used?

9 What activities go on during the user preparation phase of systems implementation?

10 How can SaaS be used in software acquisition?

11 What are some of the reasons for program maintenance?

Discussion Questions

1 Why is it important for business managers to have a basic understanding of the systems development process?

2 Briefly describe the role of a system user in the systems investigation and systems analysis stages of a project.

3 You have decided to become an IS entrepreneur and develop applications for the iPhone and other PDAs. Describe what applications you would develop and how you would do it.

4 Imagine that your firm has never developed an information systems plan. What sort of issues between the business functions and IS organisation might exist?

5 How important are communications skills to IS personnel? Consider this statement: "IS personnel need a combination of skills – one-third technical skills, one-third business skills and one-third communications skills." Do you think this is true? How would this affect the training of IS personnel?

6 You have been hired to perform systems investigation for a French restaurant owner in a large metropolitan area. She is thinking of opening a new restaurant with a state-of-the-art computer system that would allow customers to place orders on the internet or at Kiosks at restaurant tables. Describe how you would determine the technical, economic, legal, operational and schedule feasibility for the restaurant and its new computer system.

7 You have been hired to design a computer system for a small business. Describe how you could use environmental design to reduce energy usage and the computer's impact on the environment.

8 Identify the various forms of testing used. Why are there so many different types of tests?

9 Assume that you have a personal computer that is several years old. Describe the steps you would use to perform a systems review to determine whether you should acquire a new PC.

Case One

LEGO Builds Information Systems from Modular Blocks

SOURCE: © Анареn Савнн/iStock.

LEGO blocks are one of the best-known toys in the world. Founded in 1932 in Denmark by the Kirk Kristiansen family, which still owns the company, the LEGO Group has grown to 8000 employees, providing fun-building toys to children in more than 130 countries. The word "LEGO" is derived from an abbreviation of the two Danish words "leg godt," which translates to "play well." Children can "play well" with LEGO blocks because of the modular framework, which allows children to explore their creativity and solve problems. Recently, LEGO has enjoyed a resurgence of popularity. The company has experienced growing net profits over the past decade, with 2009 annual net profits increasing by 63 per cent to DKK 2204 million. LEGO is building and riding its tidal wave of success by diversifying and growing its product line. Its popular LEGO and DUPLO blocks take advantage of the latest media fads by offering kits for popular titles, such as Star Wars, Toy Story, SpongeBob and Space Police. Its Bionicle line is popular with older children and its Mindstorms computer-driven robots (see Chapter 7) appeal to technically and scientifically minded children and adults. Adults also enjoy LEGO's more complicated kits, such as its Architecture line.

Recently, LEGO expanded its activities into software games that duplicate their physical block packages in virtual reality software. The company has also launched LEGO Universe – a massively multiplayer online game. The LEGO Group has even opened discovery centres featuring educational LEGO activities and theme parks featuring more than 50 LEGO-themed rides, shows and attractions in Denmark, the UK, the US and Germany. By continuously reshaping itself, LEGO has reenergised its brand, leading to unprecedented growth for the company.

The rapid growth of the LEGO Group has provided substantial challenges for its information systems. Until recently, its mainframe-based enterprise system could not provide the flexibility to keep up with the rapid changes of the toy market. LEGO systems engineers were tasked with upgrading LEGO systems to handle the company's growth and diverse business model. LEGO required a system that could support the needs of a large enterprise while being flexible and nimble enough to accommodate rapid change. Esben Viskum, senior director of the LEGO Service Centre, defines rapid change as the ability to "respond to the market quickly, using short product development processes without losing control of cost and quality, and being able to manage both people and operations effectively and efficiently."

After considering the problem, LEGO systems analysts decided that the best system for the task would need to be as modular and standardised as the LEGO blocks themselves. A modular standardised model would make it possible for the company to quickly expand into new markets.

The LEGO system analysts team spent months evaluating LEGO's current systems and data to determine the exact needs for the new system. Next, the team performed numerous feasibility studies to confirm that they could build the new system within their economic, technical, operational and time constraints.

Because the new system would be large and comprehensive, the LEGO team would require the assistance of information system market leaders. LEGO selected SAP as the software foundation of its enterprise-wide systems. This foundation included SAP ERP human capital management software and SAP product lifecycle management software. Esben Viskum defines these as "business-critical" solutions.

LEGO selected IBM for the system infrastructure, including servers and storage. Esben Viskum says that IBM provided the "best way to deliver robust operations, and provide a repeatable template for each new LEGO venture." The resulting system clearly supports LEGO's corporate goals. According to Viskum, LEGO wants to become "a much larger business, with the products, sales, and infrastructure to become truly robust." Its new enterprise systems will allow it to do just that. LEGO plans to expand with new sales offices, manufacturing plants and retail shops. The SAP/IBM system provides a cookie-cutter approach to stamping out new business extensions with information systems that support local operations integrated into the system.

LEGO's investment of €45 million in its new systems is estimated to produce business benefits of €150 million – a threefold payback. The savings result from improved information delivery, which provides managers with better control and allows executives to respond more quickly and effectively to opportunities and problems.

Discussion Questions

1 Why would a toy company started in 1932 have to be able respond to the market quickly?

2 Why are human capital management software and product lifecycle management software critical for LEGO?

Critical Thinking Questions

1 "LEGO's investment of €45 million in its new systems is estimated to produce business

benefits of €150 million." What are some of the challenges involved in making such an estimate?

2 Explain what is meant by a "cookie-cutter approach" to extending the system.

SOURCES: 'LEGO creates model business success with SAP and IBM,' IBM success stories, May 19, 2010. Available from: http://www-01 .ibm.com/software/success/cssdb.nsf/CS/STRD-85KGS6; OpenDocument&Site=bladecenter&cty=en_us; 'LEGO – about us.' Available from: http://www.lego.com/eng/info. Accessed May 23, 2010.

Case Two

Russian Sporting Goods Chain Scales Up Budgeting System

The Sportmaster Group is the largest sporting goods chain in Eastern Europe. It handles Sportlandia and Columbia brands and more than 200 other trademarks, including its own.

When Sportmaster was established, its CIO decided to build a budget planning system in house. The system was built with Excel spreadsheets and was well suited for a young startup business. But in recent years, with stores spread across Eastern Europe, the executives at Sportmaster Group wanted to gain better control of their budgets and use their financial information to make wise strategic decisions. Due to the large amount of data involved, using the current Excel-based system had become burdensome, and the information provided was too limited to support corporate needs.

In the process of system maintenance and review, Sportmaster realised that to move to the next stage of growth, it needed to move to information systems used by large global corporations. In researching packages from a variety of vendors, the company settled on software from Cognos, an IBM company. To customise the Cognos software for its own needs, Sportmaster hired a company named IBS. Sportmaster chose IBS, because it was a certified Cognos vendor and had experience working with Russian companies.

IBS consultants met with Sportmaster executives and information systems staff to discuss the expectations for the new budget analysis system. They worked on site so they could test prototypes on actual corporate data and have their progress reviewed by Sportmaster to confirm that they were on target.

The resulting system met the following goals defined by Sportmaster. According to the Cognos case study, the system could perform the following tasks:

- Create a basic gross profit budget
- Create budgets for investment activity, including opening new stores and capital investments
- Create an operating expenses budget for all corporate divisions, including more than "500 centres of responsibility"
- Create specialised budgets, including a consolidated Revenue and Expenditure Budget, a Cash-Flow Budget, and a Balance Sheet of Payables and Receivables
- Create a Revenue and Expenditure Budget for the divisions
- Integrate with external accounting systems

Sportmaster used a parallel start-up method, introducing the new budget planning and accounting system, keeping the old system available as a backup. After six months of successful use and a few tweaks to perfect the system, the company now fully depends on the new system and is enjoying its benefits. Sportmaster can access highly detailed budget reports that assist in making strategic decisions. The process for creating budget reports has been simplified, and the duration of the budget cycle is shortened. Operations that used to take days are now accomplished in near real time. Most important is that the reliability of the data is improved so that budget errors are minimised.

Discussion Questions

1 What motivated Sportmaster to start an IS project to build a new budget planning and accounting system?

2 What steps did the development team take to make sure that the project was completed in minimum time while meeting the company's needs?

Critical Thinking Questions

1 How can the level of detail of the information provided by a budget planning and accounting system affect a company's decision-making capability?

2 Why do you think Sportmaster decided to outsource the systems development project rather than work in house?

SOURCES: Cognos Staff, 'Sportmaster Group,' Cognos Case Study. Available from: *www-01.ibm.com/software/success/cssdb.nsf/CS/ ABRR-7WEBZ3?OpenDocument&Site=corp&cty=en_us*. Accessed March 3, 2010.

Notes

[1] Kane, Y., 'Seeking Fame in Apple's Sea of Apps,' *The Wall Street Journal*, July 15, 2009, p. B1.

[2] Anderson, Howard, 'Project Triage: Skimpy Must Die,' *Information Week*, March 16, 2009, p. 14.

[3] Soat, John, 'IT leaders are wrestling with how to bring informal collaboration into rigorous processes,' *Information Week*, July 20, 2009, p. 17.

[4] Rosato, Donna, 'The 50 Best Jobs in America,' *Money*, November 2009, p. 88.

[5] Kane, Yukare Iwatani, 'Apple Woos Developers with New iPhone,' *The Wall Street Journal*, March 18, 2009, p. B6.

[6] Kane, Y., 'Apple Woos Developers with New iPhone Tools,' *The Wall Street Journal*, March 18, 2009, p. B6.

[7] Woolsey, Matt, 'New Ball Game,' *Forbes*, March 2, 2009, p. 50.

[8] O'Brien, Jeffrey, 'The Wizards of Apps,' *Fortune*, May 25, 2009, p. 29.

[9] Reena, J. and Burrows, P., 'An All-Out Online Assault on the iPhone,' *BusinessWeek*, April 6, 2009, p. 74.

[10] Albro, Edward, 'Google's Wave,' *PC World*, August 2009, p. 14.

[11] Weier, Mary H., 'Google Tries to Make App Engine Practical,' *Information Week*, April 13, 2009, p. 13.

[12] MacMillan, D., et al., 'The App Economy,' *BusinessWeek*, November 2, 2009, p. 45.

[13] Perez, Marin, 'The iPhone as IT Security Tool,' *Information Week*, November 30, 2009, p. 18.

[14] Boudreau, John, 'iPhone Has Musical Hit,' *The Tampa Tribune*, March 30, 2009, p. 8.

[15] Wildstorm, Stephen, 'The Unstoppable iPhone,' *BusinessWeek*, June 29, 2009, p. 63.

[16] Mossberg W. and Bhehret K., 'A Shopping Trip to the App Store for Your iPhone,' *The Wall Street Journal*, July 23, 2009, p. D1.

[17] Pressman, Aaron, 'Figuring Your Finances,' *BusinessWeek*, December 15, 2008, p. 78.

[18] Wildstrom, Stephan, 'A Stroll Through iPhone App Store,' *BusinessWeek*, July 28, 2009, p. 74.

[19] Kane, Y., 'Breaking Apple's Grip on the iPhone,' *The Wall Street Journal*, March 6, 2009, p. B1.

[20] Aedo, I., et al., 'End User Oriented Strategies,' *Information Processing & Management*, January 2010, p. 11.

[21] Cordoba, J., 'Critical Reflection in Planning Information Systems,' *Information Systems Journal*, March 2009, p. 123.

[22] Preston, D. and Karahanna, E., 'Antecedents of IS Strategic Alignment,' *Information Systems Research*, June 2009, p. 159.

[23] Colburn, M., 'CIO Profiles,' *Information Week*, March 16, 2009, p. 16.

[24] Evans, Bob, 'Stop Aligning IT with the Business,' *Information Week*, January 19, 2009, p. 68.

[25] Web, Warren, 'Prototyping Kit Shortens Embedded-Systems- Development Schedule,' *EDN*, April 9, 2009, p. 8.

[26] Goodhue, D., et al., 'Addressing Business Agility Challenges with Enterprise Systems,' *MIS Quarterly Executive*, June 2009, p. 73.

[27] Babcock, Charles, 'IBM Adds Social Networking to Rational Team Development,' *Information Week*, June 2, 2009, p. 24.

[28] Vidgen, R., et al., 'Coevolving Systems and the Organization of Agile Software Development,' *Information Systems Research*, September 2009, p. 355.

[29] Tubbs, Jerry, 'Team Building Goes Viral,' *Information Week*, February 22, 2010, p. 47.

[30] Sarker, Saonee and Sarker, Suprateek, 'Exploring Agility in Distributed Information Systems Development Teams,' *Information Systems Research*, September 2009, p. 440.

[31] Erickson, J., 'Agile Development,' *Information Week*, April 27, 2009, p. 31.

[32] Conboy, Kieran, 'Agility from First Principles,' *Information Systems Research*, September, 2009, p. 329.

[33] Tolfo, C., et al., 'The Influence of Organizational Culture on the Adoption of Extreme Programming,' *The Journal of Systems and Software*', November 2008, p. 1955.

[34] Balijepally, V., et al., 'Are Two Heads Better Than One for Software Development?' *MIS Quarterly*, March 2009, p. 91.

35 West, Dave, 'Agile Processes Go Lean,' *Information Week*, April 27, 2009, p. 32.

36 'The Rational Unified Process.' Available from: *www-306.ibm.com/software/awdtools/rup/support*. Accessed June 2, 2008.

37 'Rational Case Studies.' Available from: *www-01.ibm.com/software/success/cssdb.nsf/softwareL2VW?OpenView&Start=1&Count=30&RestrictToCategory=rational_RationalUnifiedProcess*. Accessed June 2, 2008.

38 Kettunen, Petri, 'Adopting Key Lesson from Agile Manufacturing to Software Product Development,' *Technovation*, June 2009, p. 408.

39 Weier, M., 'How GM's CIO Looks at IT Restructuring,' *Information Week*, June 8, 2009, p. 20.

40 McGregor, Jena, 'The Chore Goes Offshore,' *BusinessWeek*, March 23, 2009, p. 50.

41 Capell, Kerry, 'Vodafone: Embracing Open Source with Open Arms,' *BusinessWeek*, April 20, 2009, p. 52.

42 McGee, M., 'Pay for Performance,' *Information Week*, March 23, 2009, p. 32.

43 IBM website. Available from: *www.ibm.com*. Accessed June 2, 2008.

44 EDS website. Available from: *www.eds.com*. Accessed June 2, 2008.

45 Scheck, J. and Worthen, B., 'Hewlett-Packard Takes Aim at IBM,' *The Wall Street Journal*, May 4, 2008, p. B1.

46 Accenture website. Available from: *www.accenture.com*. Accessed June 2, 2008.

47 Sheth, N., 'Wipro Sets Outsourcing Sights on Emerging Markets,' *The Wall Street Journal*, May 13, 2009, p. B4B.

48 Tiwana, A., 'Governance-Knowledge Fit in Systems Development Projects,' *Information Systems Research*, June 2009, p. 180.

49 Pereira, Rudy, 'Embrace a Culture of Continuous Improvement,' *Credit Union Magazine,* October 2009, p. 62.

50 Betts, Mitch, 'The No. 1 Cause of IT Failure: Complexity,' *Computerworld*, December 21, 2009, p. 4.

51 Capability Maturity Model for Software home page. Available from: *www.sei.cmu.edu*. Accessed June 2, 2008.

52 Shang, S., et al., 'Understanding the Effectiveness of the Capability Maturity Model,' *Total Quality Management & Business Excellence,'* Vol. 20, 2009, p. 219.

53 Staff, 'An Object-Oriented Graphical Modeling for Power System Analysis,' *International Journal of Modeling & Simulation*, Vol. 29, 2009, p. 71.

54 Sebora, T., et al., 'Critical Success Factors for E-Commerce Entreprenership,' *Small Business Economics*, March, 2009, p. 303.

55 Babcock, Charles, 'Hybrid Clouds,' *Information Week*, September 7, 2009, p. 15.

56 Hoover, Nicholas, 'GE Puts the Cloud Model to the Test,' *Information Week*, April 13, 2009, p. 32.

57 Wildstrom, Stephen, 'What to Entrust to The Cloud,' *BusinessWeek*, April 6, 2009, p. 89.

58 Greenberg, Andy, 'No Phishing Zone,' *Forbes*, April 27, 2009.

59 Healey, M., 'Beat the Slow Commotion,' *Information Week*, March 23, 2009, p. 40.

60 Patterson S. and Ng, S., 'NYSE's Fast-Trade Hub,' *The Wall Street Journal*, July 30, 2009, p. C1.

61 Patterson, S. and Ng, S., 'NYSE's Fast-Trade Hub,' *The Wall Street Journal*, July 30, 2009, p. C1.

62 Marew, T., et al., 'Tactics Based Approach for Integrating Non-Functional Requirements in Object-Oriented Analysis and Design,' *Journal of Systems and Software*, October 2009, p. 1642.

63 Bustillo, Miguel, 'Wal-Mart to Assign New Green Ratings,' *The Wall Street Journal*, July 16, 2009, p. B1.

64 Pratt, Mary, 'Slow-Growing Green,' *Computerworld*, January 1, 2009, p. 13.

65 Campbell, S. and Jeronimo, M., 'Virtual Machines, Real Productivity,' *Information Week*, January 26, 2009, p. 40.

66 Babcock, Charles, 'Nissan Assembly Lines Roll With Fewer Servers,' *Information Week*, July 6, 2009, p. 17.

67 Pratt, Mary, 'Birth of an Energy Star,' *Computerworld*, August 31, 2009, p. 24.

68 Carlton, Jim, 'The PC Goes on an Energy Diet,' *The Wall Street Journal*, September 8, 2009, p. R8.

69 Mies, Ginny, 'Green Phones,' *PC World*, September 2009, p. 28.

70 Voltaic Generator. Available from: *www.voltaicsystems.com/bag_generator.shtml*. Accessed August 17, 2009.

71 Randall, David, 'Be Green and Make A Buck,' *Forbes*, March 2, 2009, p. 40.

72 Mossberg, Walter, 'Where Old Gadgets Go to Breathe New Life,' *The Wall Street Journal*, August 13, 2009, p. D8.

73 Worthen, Ben, 'Oracle Targets a New Rival: IBM,' *The Wall Street Journal*, October 15, 2009, p. B4.

74 Staff, 'The Infotech 100,' *BusinessWeek*, June 1, 2009, p. 39.

75 Conry-Murray, A., 'Engines of Innovation,' *Information Week*, April 20, 2009, p. 30.

76 Poston, R., et al., 'Managing the Vendor Set,' *MIS Quarterly Executive*, June 2009, p. 45.

77 Wingfield, Nick, 'Microsoft Seeks to Take A Bite Out Of Apple With New Stores,' *The Wall Street Journal*, October 15, 2009, p. B1.

78 Hoover, Nicholas, 'GE Puts the Cloud Model to the Test,' *Information Week*, April 13, 2009, p. 32.

79 Babcock, Charles, 'Red Hat to Certify Cloud-Ready Applications,' *Information Week*, July 6, 2009, p. 14.

80 Hahn, J., et al., 'Emergence of New Project Teams from Open Source Software Developer Networks,' *Information Systems Research*, September 2008, p. 369.

81 Crosman, Penny, 'SaaS Gains Street Traction,' *Wall Street & Technology*, September 1, 2008, p. 37.

82 IT Redux website. Available from: *http://itredux.com/office-20/database/?family=Database*. Accessed August 1, 2009.

83 Lai, Eric, 'Cloud database vendors: What, us worry about Microsoft?' *Computerworld,* March 12, 2008. Available from: *www.computerworld.com/action/article.do?command=viewArticleBasic&articleId=9067979&pageNumber=1*.

84 Foley, John, 'Gold in the Clouds,' *Information Week*, September 28, 2009, p. 24.

85 Babcock, 'Charles, 'Platform As A Service,' *Information Week*, October 5, 2009, p. 18.

86 Vuong, Andy, 'Denver Developers Hatch iPhone Apps,' *The Summit Daily News*, September 12, 2009, p. A19.

87 Hoover, N., 'Tough Call,' *Information Week*, February 23, 2009, p. 21.

88 Morrison, Scott, 'Co-Op Field-Tests Software,' *The Wall Street Journal*, October 28, 2009, p. B5A.

89 Hodgson, J., 'Rethinking Software Support,' *The Wall Street Journal*, March 12, 2009, p. B8.

90 Weier, M., 'Numbers Crunch,' *Information Week*, January 26, 2009, p. 25.

91 Hoffman, Thomas, 'Railroad Crossing,' *Computerworld*, December 21, 2009, p. 22.

92 Hoover, N. and Foley, J., 'Feds on the Edge,' *Information Week*, July 6, 2009, p. 19.

93 The Idea factory. Available from: *www.whitehouse.gov/open/innovations/IdeaFactory*. Accessed August 21, 2009.

94 Kelly, C., 'Getting an F and Turning It Into Fun,' *Computerworld*, May 26, 2008, p. 32.

95 Weier, Mary, 'Comcast Team Tweets to Track, Douse Flames,' *Information Week*, March 30, 2009, p. 20.

96 *www.ibm.com/software/tivoli/products*. Accessed August 1, 2009.

97 *www.precise.com*. Accessed August 1, 2009.

98 *https://h10078.www1.hp.com/cda/hpms/display/main/hpms_home.jsp?zn=bto&cp=1_4011_100__*. Accessed August 1, 2009.

CHAPTER 9 CONTENTS

09

Security, Privacy and Ethical Issues in Information Systems

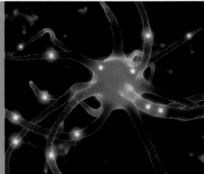

This chapter will cover THREE principles when considering the issues implicit within Business Information Systems that surround the areas of privacy, security and personal health and safety of those who design and use such systems.

Principles

1. Policies and procedures must be established to avoid computer waste and mistakes.

2. Computer crime is a serious and rapidly growing area of concern requiring management attention.

3. Jobs, equipment, and working conditions must be designed to avoid negative health effects.

Learning Objectives

- Describe some examples of waste and mistakes in an IS environment, their causes, and possible solutions.
- Identify policies and procedures useful in eliminating waste and mistakes.
- Discuss the principles and limits of an individual's right to privacy.

- Explain the types and effects of computer crime.
- Identify specific measures to prevent computer crime.

- List the important effects of computers on the work environment.
- Identify specific actions that must be taken to ensure the health and safety of employees.
- Outline criteria for the ethical use of information systems.

Why Learn About Security, Privacy and Ethical Issues in Information Systems?

Our last chapter will look at security, privacy, and ethical issues, something that has been in the background right throughout this book. A wide range of nontechnical issues associated with the use of information systems provide both opportunities and threats to modern organisations. The issues span the full spectrum – from preventing computer waste and mistakes, to avoiding violations of privacy, to complying with laws on collecting data about customers, to monitoring employees. If you become a member of a human resources, information systems, or legal department within an organisation, you will likely be charged with leading the rest of the organisation in dealing with these and other issues covered in this chapter. As a user of information systems, especially the internet, it is in your own self-interest to become well versed on these issues. You need to know about the topics in this chapter to help avoid or recover from crime, fraud, privacy invasion, or other potential problems.

9.1 Computer Waste and Mistakes

Computer-related waste and mistakes are major causes of computer problems, contributing as they do to unnecessarily high costs and lost profits. Computer waste involves the inappropriate use of computer technology and resources. It includes employees wasting computer resources and time by playing games and surfing the web, sending unnecessary email, printing documents and other material that is then not read, developing systems that are not used to their full extent, and discarding old hardware when it could be recycled or given to charity. UK-based Computers for Charities for instance, will collect old technology, wipe clean any data stored on them and deliver them to charities where they are still useful. Junk email, also called spam, and junk faxes also cause waste. People receive hundreds of email messages and faxes advertising products and services not wanted or requested. Not only does this waste time, but it also wastes paper and computer resources. Worse yet, spam messages often carry attached files with embedded viruses that can cause networks and computers to crash or allow hackers to gain unauthorised access to systems and data.[1] Spam is considered a serious enough problem that the US Department of Justice has prosecuted prolific spammers for violation of the CAN-SPAM Act. This law allows the sending of most email spam, as long as it adheres to three basic forms of compliance related to how receivers can unsubscribe, content of the email, and the sending behaviour. Since the act was passed in 2003, several people have been convicted and sentenced to up to six years in jail or up to a US $1 million fine.[2] When waste is identified, it typically points to one common cause: the improper management of information systems and resources.

Computer-related mistakes refer to errors, failures, and other computer problems that make computer output incorrect or not useful, caused mostly by human error. Despite many people's distrust, computers themselves rarely make mistakes. Even the most sophisticated hardware cannot produce meaningful output if users do not follow proper procedures. Mistakes can be caused by unclear expectations and a lack of feedback. Or a programmer might develop a program that contains errors. In other cases, a data-entry administrator might enter the wrong data. Unless errors are caught early and prevented, the speed of computers can intensify mistakes. As information technology becomes faster, more complex, and more powerful, organisations and computer users face increased risks of experiencing the results of computer-related mistakes. Consider the following examples:

■ A software program used by the Mine Safety and Health Administration to identify patterns of safety violations failed to flag eight problems at the Upper Big Branch mine in West Virginia, where 29 workers died in an explosion. Officials claimed the error did not have an impact on the accident, because improvements had already been made without the computer-generated warnings; nevertheless, the failure of the system is deeply disturbing.[3]

■ A computer problem caused all the ATM machines throughout United Arab Emirates to close down for an hour on a busy Saturday.[4]

■ A computer problem caused a computer in Berkeley to mistakenly conclude that an earthquake of magnitude 5.0 hit the Napa area of northern California, causing "a flurry of activity" at the US Geological Survey and the news media.[5]

■ On May 6, 2010, the Dow Jones Industrial Average plunged more than 1000 points in less than half an hour for no apparent reason other than a massive overreaction by automatic computer trading programs.[6]

Preventing Computer-Related Waste and Mistakes

To remain profitable in a competitive environment, organisations must use all resources wisely. Preventing computer-related waste and mistakes like those just described should, therefore, be a goal. To achieve it involves (1) establishing, (2) implementing, (3) monitoring, and (4) reviewing effective policies and procedures.

Establishing Policies and Procedures

The first step to prevent computer-related waste is to establish policies and procedures regarding efficient acquisition, use, and disposal of systems and devices. Most companies have implemented stringent policies on the acquisition of computer systems and equipment, including requiring a formal justification statement before computer equipment is purchased, definition of standard computing platforms (e.g. operating system, type of computer chip, minimum amount of RAM, etc.), and the use of preferred vendors for all acquisitions.

Prevention of computer-related mistakes begins by identifying the most common types of errors, of which there are surprisingly few. Types of computer-related mistakes include the following:

■ Data-entry or data-capture errors

■ Errors in computer programs

■ Errors in handling files, including formatting a disk by mistake, copying an old file over a newer one, and deleting a file by mistake

■ Mishandling of computer output

■ Inadequate planning for and control of equipment malfunctions

■ Inadequate planning for and control of environmental difficulties (e.g. electrical problems, humidity problems, etc.)

■ Installing computing capacity inadequate for the level of activity on corporate websites

■ Failure to provide access to the most current information by not adding new and not deleting old URL links

Training programs for individuals and workgroups and manuals and documents on how computer systems are to be maintained and used can help prevent problems. Other preventative measures include needing approval of certain systems and applications before they are implemented and used to ensure compatibility and cost-effectiveness and a requirement that documentation and descriptions of certain applications be submitted to a central office, including all cell formulas for spreadsheets and a description of all data elements and relationships in a database system (which, as we saw in Chapter 3, is already recorded in the data dictionary). After companies have planned and developed policies and procedures, they must consider how best to implement them.

Sometimes, computer error combines with human procedural errors to lead to the loss of human life. In March 2003, a Patriot missile battery on the Kuwait border accidentally shot down a British Royal Air Force Tornado GR-4 aircraft that was returning from a mission over Iraq. Two British pilots were killed in the incident. Many defence industry experts think the accident was caused by problems with the Patriot's radar combined with human error.

Implementing Policies and Procedures

Implementing policies and procedures to minimise waste and mistakes varies according to the type of business. Most companies develop such policies and procedures with advice from the firm's internal auditing group or its external auditing firm. The policies often focus on the implementation of source data automation and the use of data editing to ensure data accuracy and completeness and the assignment of responsibility for data accuracy within each information system. Some useful policies to minimise waste and mistakes include the following:

- Changes to critical tables, HTML, and URLs should be tightly controlled, with all changes authorised by responsible owners and documented.
- A user manual should be available that covers operating procedures and documents the management and control of the application.
- Each system report should indicate its general content in its title and specify the time period it covers.
- The system should have controls to prevent invalid and unreasonable data entry.
- Controls should exist to ensure that data input, HTML, and URLs are valid, applicable, and posted in the right time frame.
- Users should implement proper procedures to ensure correct input data.

Training is another key aspect of implementation. Many users are not properly trained in using applications, and their mistakes can be very costly. One home in the small town of Valparaiso, in the US, fairly valued at $88 550, was incorrectly recorded in the county's computer system as being worth over $290 million. The erroneous figure was used to forecast future income from property taxes. When the error was uncovered, the local school district and government agencies were forced to slash their budgets by $2 million, because they found they wouldn't be getting the tax money after all.[7]

Monitoring Policies and Procedures

To ensure that users throughout an organisation are following established procedures, the next step is to monitor routine practices and take corrective action if necessary. By understanding what is happening in day-to-day activities, organisations can make adjustments or develop new procedures. Many organisations implement internal audits to measure actual results against established goals, such as percentage of end-user reports produced on time, percentage of data-input errors detected, number of input transactions entered per eight-hour shift, and so on.

The Société Générale scandal in France is a classic example of an individual employee circumventing internal policies and procedures. A low-level trader earning €2000 per month on the arbitrage desk at the French bank created a series of fraudulent and unauthorised investment transactions that built a position of more than €50 billion in European stock index futures. Eventually the house of cards collapsed, causing the bank to lose more than €5 billion – even though a compliance officer at the bank had been alerted months in advance not once, but twice that something unusual was going on. Since the scandal, the bank has taken several steps to improve its internal policies and procedures, tighten computer security, and adopt a more realistic approach to the potential for fraud.[8]

Information Systems at Work

Panic Button App

SOURCE: © Carmen Martínez Banús/iStock.

Facebook has grown to be one of the most popular and influential online businesses. The enormously successful online social network has roughly half a billion members and more than a billion US dollars in annual revenue, earned primarily from advertisements. Facebook's slogan is "Giving people the power to share and make the world more open and connected." Facebook's mission, combined with its popularity and influence, has often put the company in the hot seat when it comes to privacy and security concerns.

In 2010, police chief constables from across England and Wales signed a letter asking the company to install a panic button, aimed primarily at children using the site, that they could use to report suspected paedophiles to CEOP. CEOP is the Child Exploitation and Online Protection Centre, which is dedicated to eradicating the sexual abuse of children. They are part of UK policing and aim to track and bring offenders to account either directly or in partnership with local and international forces.

Facebook had previously resisted such calls, opting instead to put links to organisations, including CEOP, on its reporting pages. CEOP's chief, Jim Gamble, said the matter had become urgent after a teenager was murdered by a man she met on the site. He said, "In our view, Facebook are experts at creating a fantastic online environment, but they are not experts in law enforcement, the power of deterrents and the reassurance it brings for mums and dads."

The "panic button" in question was already used by other websites. Clicking on it takes people to a site that details how to handle cyberbullying, hacking, viruses, distressing material and inappropriate sexual behaviour.

Three months after the letter, and after much negotiation with CEOP, Facebook announced it would allow a "panic button" application on its site. Jim Gamble said, "By adding this application, Facebook users will have direct access to all the services that sit behind our ClickCeop button which should provide reassurance to every parent with teenagers on the site."

Facebook's head of communications in the UK, Sophy Silver, told BBC News that the new app would integrate reporting into both Facebook and CEOP's systems. "Both sides are happy as to where we have got," she said. "We still have the Facebook reporting system and by having a pre-packaged application that users play an active part in, you not only help keep them safe, it makes all of their friends aware too, and acts as a viral awareness campaign."

Discussion Questions

1 List some of the dangers you can see for children using social networking sites (you should be able to come up with a range of different ideas). How would you educate children about the dangers you have identified?

2 Is there anything else Facebook could do to protect child users?

Critical Thinking Questions

1 Should an organisation like CEOP's be limited to the online world? Is there not a need to cover the real world too?

2 How could someone verify that a person they are contacting online is actually who they claim to be?

SOURCES: BBC, "Facebook urged to add panic button at meeting with Ceop," 12 April 2010. Available from: http://news.bbc.co.uk/1/hi/uk/8614787.stm.
BBC, "Facebook unveils child safety 'panic button,'" 11 July 2010. Available from: http://news.bbc.co.uk/1/hi/technology/10572375.stm.
http://www.ceop.police.uk/About-Us/. Accessed 28 Febuary 2011.

Reviewing Policies and Procedures

The final step is to review existing policies and procedures and determine whether they are adequate. During review, people should ask the following questions:

- Do current policies cover existing practices adequately? Were any problems or opportunities uncovered during monitoring?
- Is the organisation planning any new activities in the future? If so, does it need new policies or procedures, and who will handle them and what must be done?
- Are contingencies and disasters covered?

This review and planning allows companies to take a proactive approach to problem solving, which can enhance a company's performance, such as by increasing productivity and improving customer service. Information systems professionals and users still need to be aware of the misuse of resources throughout an organisation. Preventing errors and mistakes is one way to do so. Another is implementing in-house security measures and legal protections to detect and prevent a dangerous type of misuse: computer crime.

9.2 Computer Crime

According to the British Home Office, in 2004, debit and credit card fraud over the internet cost the UK £117 million. During the same period, 77 per cent of medium to large businesses reported virus attacks, costing £27.8 million, whereas 17 per cent suffered financial fraud, costing £133 million. The term computer crime covers a wide variety of activities, including these. Some more examples are listed next, and then some types of computer crime are discussed.

- A 20-year-old man was sentenced to 57 months in prison for hijacking more than 400 000 PCs over the internet and turning them into a "botnet" or "zombie network," a network of personal computers used to perform a task without the owner's knowledge. He then would rent the zombie network out to spyware distributors, hackers, and spammers to use in performing work.[9]

■ Russian organised crime extorted untold thousands of euros from firms doing business on the internet by demanding €7000 or more for protection from being hit by a denial-of-service attack on their website. Some firms bought the "protection;" some of those that did not were attacked.[10]

■ A British information systems expert accessed a series of computer networks used by the US Army, Navy, Air Force, and Department of Defence, searching for what he called "suppressed technology." US authorities claimed he caused more than $700 000 of damage.[11]

■ The UK government's tax credit website, which allowed qualifying citizens to claim tax benefits, was shut down in 2005, because it was being targeted by organised gangs claiming many millions of pounds from the government.[12]

Identify Theft

Identity theft is one of the fastest growing crimes. It is a crime where an imposter obtains key pieces of personal identification information, such as date of birth, address, national insurance number, and mother's maiden name, and uses them to open bank accounts, get credit cards, loans, benefits, and documents, such as passports and driving licences, in the victim's name. In other cases, the identity thief uses personal information to gain access to the person's existing accounts. Typically, the thief changes the mailing address on an account and runs up a huge bill before the person whose identity has been stolen realises there is a problem. The internet has made it easier for an identity thief to use the stolen information, because transactions can be made without any personal interaction. The UK Home Office has a website, http://www.identitytheft.org.uk/, to advise its citizens and help victims. A wide range of methods are used by the perpetrators of these crimes that it makes investigating them difficult. Frequently, a critical computer password has been talked out of a person or guessed based on a knowledge of the person a practice called **social engineering**. For example, many people use the name of their pet as their password. Many teenagers use the name of their favourite pop artist. Alternatively, the attackers might simply go through the person's rubbish, looking for a disgarded utility bill or bank statement. In addition, over 2000 websites offer the digital tools – for free – that will let people snoop, crash computers, hijack control of a machine, or retrieve a copy of every keystroke.

social engineering Using one's social skills to get computer users to provide you with information to access an information system or its data.

Image 9.1 *Many people shred their sensitive paper waste to protect themselves from identify theft.*

Another popular method to get information is "shoulder surfing" – the identity thief simply stands next to someone at a public office, such as the passport office, or even when filling in a form to join a video rental shop, such as Blockbuster, and watches as the person fills out personal information on a form. The same thing can happen at a bank ATM where the attacker simply watches the person enter their PIN or at a shop when the victim is using their credit card to make a purchase.

Consumers can help protect themselves by regularly checking their credit reports, following up with creditors if their bills do not arrive on time, not revealing any personal information in response to unsolicited email or phone calls, and shredding bills and other documents that contain sensitive information.[13]

Cyberterrorism

Government officials and IS security specialists have documented a significant increase in internet probes and server scans since early 2001. A growing concern among authorities is that such intrusions are part of an organised effort by cyberterrorists to map potential security holes in critical systems. A **cyberterrorist** is someone who intimidates or coerces a government or organisation to advance their political or social objectives by launching computer-based attacks against computers, networks, and the information stored on them. Attacks would likely be aimed at critical infrastructure, which includes telecommunications, energy, banking and finance, water systems, government operations, and emergency services. Successful cyberattacks against the facilities that provide these services could cause widespread and massive disruptions to the normal function of a society.

cyberterrorist Someone who intimidates or coerces a government or organisation to advance his or her political or social objectives by launching computer-based attacks against computers, networks, and the information stored on them.

A similar term, "cyberwar," is arguably not a crime but involves a country or state attacking another using the same techniques as a cyberterrorist. The Stuxnet virus was first detected in June 2010 by a security firm based in Belarus. Some researchers claim that the virus is so complex it could only have been written by a nation in order to attack another nation. Experts believe the target was probably infrastructure, such as power stations in Iran.[14]

Illegal Access and Use

Crimes involving illegal system access and use of computer services are a concern to both government and business. Since the outset of information technology, computers have been plagued by criminal crackers. A **cracker**, often called a hacker, although this term has a range of meanings, is a computer-savvy person who attempts to gain unauthorised or illegal access to computer systems. Often they are "just looking" but could also be trying to corrupt files, steal data, or even transfer money. In many cases, crackers are people who are looking for fun and excitement – the challenge of beating the system. **Script kiddies** admire crackers, but have little technical savvy. They are crackers who download programs, called "scripts," that automate the job of breaking into computers. **Insiders** are employees, disgruntled or otherwise, working solo or in concert with outsiders to compromise corporate systems.

cracker A person who enjoys computer technology and spends time learning and using computer systems.

script kiddie A cracker with little technical savvy who downloads programs called scripts, which automate the job of breaking into computers.

insider An employee, disgruntled or otherwise, working solo or in concert with outsiders to compromise corporate systems.

Catching and convicting criminal hackers remains a difficult task. The method behind these crimes is often hard to determine. Even if the method behind the crime is known, tracking down the criminals can take a lot of time.

Data and information are valuable corporate assets. The intentional use of illegal and destructive programs to alter or destroy data is as much a crime as destroying tangible goods. The most common of these programs are viruses and worms, which are software programs that, when loaded into a computer system, will destroy, interrupt, or cause errors in processing. Such programs are also called "malware." Internet security firm McAfee released virus threat definition number 200 000 in July 2006 and predicted that there would be twice that many viruses within two years.[15] McAfee also predicts the increased connectivity of smartphones will lead to serious and widespread attacks on these devices. "… a mobile threat targeting several (smartphone) operating systems could infect up to 200 million connected smartphones simultaneously because the majority of these devices do not currently have mobile security protection installed."[16]

virus A computer program file capable of attaching to disks or other files and replicating itself repeatedly, typically without the user's knowledge or permission.

A **virus** is a computer program file capable of attaching to disks or other files and replicating itself repeatedly, typically without the user's knowledge or permission. Some viruses attach to files, so, when the infected file executes, the virus also executes. Other viruses sit in a computer's memory and infect files as the computer opens, modifies, or creates the files. They are often disguised as games or images with clever or attention-grabbing titles, such as "Boss, naked." Some viruses display symptoms, and some viruses damage files and computer systems. The m00p virus gang, for example, conspired to infect computers with a virus that would turn each infected machine into a zombie machine under their control. The zombie network could then be used to spread viruses and other malware across the internet, without the owners of the compromised computers even being aware.[17] Hoax viruses can also be a problem. A hoax virus is a message, usually distributed by email, warning recipients to carry out a procedure on their computer to protect themselves from a "virus threat," when the procedure itself is actually doing the damage. Typically, a hoax virus encourages people to delete an important systems file. The message will encourage people to forward it on to all their contacts.

worm A parasitic computer program that can create copies of itself on the infected computer or send copies to other computers via a network.

Worms are computer programs that replicate but, unlike viruses, do not infect other computer program files. Worms can create copies on the same computer or can send the copies to other computers via a network. Worms often spread via Internet Relay Chat (IRC). For example, the MyDoom worm, also known as Shimgapi and Novarg, started spreading in January 2004 and quickly became the most virulent email worm ever. The worm arrived as an email with an attachment with various names and extensions, including .exe, .scr, .zip, and .pif. When the attachment executed, the worm sent copies of itself to other email addresses stored in the infected computer. The first version of the virus, MyDoom.A, was designed to attack The SCO Group Inc.'s website. A later variant, dubbed MyDoom.B, was designed to enable similar denial-of-service attacks against the Microsoft website. The B variant also included a particularly nasty feature in that it blocked infected computers from accessing sites belonging to vendors of antivirus products. Infected email messages carrying the MyDoom worm have been intercepted from over 142 countries and, at one time, accounted for one in every 12 email messages.

Trojan horse A malicious program that disguises itself as a useful application and purposefully does something the user does not expect.

A **Trojan horse** program is a malicious program that disguises itself as a useful application and purposefully does something the user does not expect. Trojans are not viruses, because they do not replicate, but they can be just as destructive. Many people use the term to refer only to nonreplicating malicious programs, thus, making a distinction between Trojans and viruses. A German language email, for example, was used to spread a Trojan horse that steals passwords and logon details of customers' online bank accounts and then relays them back to a remote server. The malware tried to get users to install the Trojan horse by disguising itself as a software patch for a new flaw in Microsoft software.[18] Spyware is often spread using the Trojan hourse method. Spyware is software that records all manner of personal information about users and forwards it to the spyware's owner, all without the user's consent. Name, address, credit card numbers, and passwords can all be collected by spyware, as can information on web browsing behaviour, which would be valuable and useful for marketing.

A logic bomb is a type of Trojan horse that executes when specific conditions occur. Triggers for logic bombs can include a change in a file by a particular series of keystrokes or at a specific time or date.

A variant is a modified version of a virus that is produced by the virus's author or another person who amends the original virus code. If changes are small, most antivirus products will also detect variants. However, if the changes are significant, the variant might go undetected by antivirus software.

In some cases, a virus or a worm can completely halt the operation of a computer system or network for days or longer until the problem is found and repaired. In other cases, a virus or a worm can destroy important data and programs. If backups are inadequate, the data and programs might never be fully functional again. The costs include the effort required to identify and neutralise the virus or worm and to restore computer files and data, as well as the value of business lost because of unscheduled computer downtime.

As a result of the increasing threat of viruses and worms, most computer users and organisations have installed **antivirus programs** on their computers. Such software runs in the background to protect your computer from dangers lurking on the internet and other possible sources of infected files. Some antivirus software is even capable of repairing common virus infections automatically, without interrupting your work. The latest virus definitions are downloaded automatically when you connect to the internet, ensuring that your PC's protection is current. To safeguard your PC and prevent it from spreading viruses to your friends and coworkers, some antivirus software scans and cleans both incoming and outgoing email messages. Table 9.1 lists some of the most popular antivirus software.

antivirus program Software that runs in the background to protect your computer from dangers lurking on the internet and other possible sources of infected files.

Table 9.1 Antivirus Software

Antivirus Software	Software Manufacturer	Website
Symantec's Norton AntiVirus 2005	Symantec	www.symantec.com
McAfee Virus Scan	McAfee	www.mcafee.com
Panda Antivirus Platinum	Panda Software	www.pandasoftware.com
Vexira Antivirus	Central Command	www.centralcommand.com
Sophos Antivirus	Sophos	www.sophos.com
PC-cillin	Trend Micro	www.trendmicro.com

Proper use of antivirus software requires the following steps:

1 Install antivirus software. These programs should automatically check for viruses each time you boot up your computer or insert a disk or CD, and some even monitor all email and file transmissions and copying operations.

2 Ensure the antivirus software updates often. New viruses are created all the time, and antivirus software suppliers are constantly updating their software to detect and take action against these new viruses. The software should itself check for updates regularly, without the need for an instruction from the user.

3 Scan all removable media, including CDs, before copying or running programs from them. Hiding on disks or CDs, viruses often move between systems. If you carry document or program files on removable media between computers at school or work and your home system, always scan them.

4　Install software only from a sealed package or secure website of a known software company. Even software publishers can unknowingly distribute viruses on their program disks or software downloads. Most scan their own systems, but viruses might still remain.

5　Follow careful downloading practices. If you download software from the internet or a bulletin board, check your computer for viruses immediately after completing the transmission.

6　If you detect a virus, take immediate action. Early detection often allows you to remove a virus before it does any serious damage.

Despite careful precautions, viruses can still cause problems. They can elude virus-scanning software by lurking almost anywhere in a system. Future antivirus programs might incorporate "nature-based models" that check for unusual or unfamiliar computer code. The advantage of this type of virus program is the ability to detect new viruses that are not part of an antivirus database.

Hoax, or false, viruses are another problem. Crackers sometimes warn the public of a new and devastating virus that doesn't actually exist just to create fear. Companies sometimes spend hundreds of hours warning employees and taking preventative action against a nonexistent virus. Security specialists recommend that IS personnel establish a formal paranoia policy to thwart virus panic among gullible end users. Such policies should stress that, before users forward an email alert to colleagues, they should send it to the help desk or the security team. The corporate intranet can be used to explain the difference between real viruses and fakes, and it can provide links to websites to set the record straight.

Be aware that virus writers also use known hoaxes to their advantage. For example, AOL4FREE began as a hoax virus warning. Then, a hacker distributed a destructive Trojan attached to the original hoax virus warning. Always remain vigilant and never open a suspicious attachment.[19]

Equipment Theft

During illegal access to computer systems, data can be stolen. In addition to theft of data and software, all types of computer systems and equipment have been stolen from offices. Mobile computers, such as laptops and smartphones, are especially easy for thieves to take. Very often the data stored on these devices is more valuable than the device itself. Pop star Natasha Bedingfield had her laptop, which contained music and lyrics to some of her new material, stolen. An MI5 agent's laptop containing sensitive government information was stolen at Paddington train station in London, and a senior British Army official's laptop was taken at Heathrow Airport.[20] To fight computer crime, many companies use devices that disable the disk drive and/or lock the computer to the desk (see Figure 9.1).

Software and Internet Software Piracy

Like books and movies – other intellectual properties – software is protected by copyright laws. Often, people who would never think of plagiarising another author's written work have no qualms about using and copying software programs they have not paid for. Such illegal duplicators are called "pirates;" the act of illegally duplicating software is called **software piracy**.

software piracy The act of illegally duplicating software.

Technically, software purchasers are granted the right only to use the software under certain conditions; they don't really own the software. Licences vary from program to program and can authorise as few as one computer or one person to use the software or as many as several hundred network users to share the application across the system. Making additional copies, or loading the software onto more than one machine, might violate copyright law and be considered piracy.

Figure 9.1 Locking a Laptop to a Desk

SOURCE: © ghassem khosrownia/Istock.

The Business Software Alliance estimates that the software industry loses over €8 billion per year in revenue to software piracy annually. Half the loss comes from Asia, where China and Indonesia are the biggest offenders. In Western Europe, annual piracy losses range between 1.5 and 2 billion euros. Although the rate of software piracy is quite high in Latin America and Central Europe, those software markets are so small that the monetary losses are considerably lower. Overall, it is estimated that 35 per cent of the world's software is pirated.[21]

Internet-based software piracy occurs when software is illegally downloaded from the internet. It is the most rapidly expanding type of software piracy and the most difficult form to combat. The same purchasing rules apply to online software purchases as for traditional purchases. Internet piracy can take several forms, including the following:

■ Pirate websites that make software available for free or in exchange for uploaded programs

■ Internet auction sites that offer counterfeit software, which infringes copyrights

■ Peer-to-peer networks, which enable unauthorised transfer of copyrighted programs

Computer-Related Scams

People have lost hundreds of thousands of euros on property, travel, stock, and other business scams. Now, many of these scams are being perpetrated with computers. Using the internet, scam artists offer get-rich-quick schemes involving bogus property deals, tout "free" holidays with huge hidden costs, commit bank fraud, offer fake telephone lotteries, sell worthless penny stocks, and promote illegal tax-avoidance schemes.

Over the past few years, credit card customers of various banks have been targeted by scam artists trying to get personal information needed to use their credit cards. The scam typically works by sending an email to many thousands of people, asking them to click on a link that seems to direct users to a bank's website and to fill in essential security information. Some of the recipients will probably be customers of the bank. At the site, they are asked for their full debit and credit card number and expiration date, their name, address, and other personal information. The problem is that the website customers are directed to is a fake site operated by someone trying to gain access to that information. This form of scam is called "phishing." The website used is often extremely similar to the bank's real website and may contain links to the real site. During November 2005, the Anti-Phishing Working Group received 16 882 unique reports of phishing attacks aimed at the consumers of 93 different brands – this was double the number of reports received the previous November.[22]

In the weeks following Hurricane Katrina in the US, the FBI warned that over half the Hurricane Katrina aid sites it checked were registered to people outside the US and likely to be fraudulent. A 20-year-old man was charged with setting up websites designed to look like those of the American Red Cross and other organisations accepting donations to help the victims. He then sold these to "would-be scammers" for about $140 each. For his trouble, this person is facing 50 years in prison and a fine of $1 million.[23]

The following is a list of tips to help you avoid becoming a scam victim:

- Don't agree to anything in a high-pressure meeting or seminar. Insist on having time to think it over and to discuss things with your spouse, your partner, or even your solicitor. If a company won't give you the time you need to check it out and think things over, you don't want to do business with it. A good deal now will be a good deal tomorrow; the only reason for rushing you is if the company has something to hide.

- Don't judge a company based on appearances. Professional-looking websites can be created and published in a matter of days. After a few weeks of taking money, a site can vanish without a trace in just a few minutes. You might find that the perfect money-making opportunity offered on a website was a money-maker for the crook and a money-loser for you.

- Avoid any plan that pays commissions simply for recruiting additional distributors. Your primary source of income should be your own product sales. If the earnings are not made primarily by sales of goods or services to consumers or sales by distributors under you, you might be dealing with an illegal pyramid.

- Beware of "hills," people paid by a company to lie about how much they've earned and how easy the plan was to operate. Check with an independent source to make sure that you aren't having the wool pulled over your eyes.

- Beware of a company's claim that it can set you up in a profitable home-based business but that you must first pay up front to attend a seminar and buy expensive materials. Frequently, seminars are high-pressure sales pitches, and the material is so general that it is worthless.

- If you are interested in starting a home-based business, get a complete description of the work involved before you send any money. You might find that what you are asked to do after you pay is far different from what was stated in the ad. You should never have to pay for a job description or for needed materials.

- Get in writing the refund, buy-back, and cancellation policies of any company you deal with. Do not depend on oral promises.

- If you need advice about an online solicitation or if you want to report a possible scam, contact your country's computer crime unit. In the UK, you can find more information at www.direct.gov.uk or www.met.police.uk/computercrime.

9.3 Preventing Computer-Related Crime

Because of increased computer use, greater emphasis is placed on the prevention and detection of computer crime. Many countries have passed data laws governing how data can be stored, processed, and transferred and laws on computer crime. Some believe that these laws are not effective, because companies do not always actively detect and pursue computer crime, security is inadequate, and convicted criminals are not severely punished. However, all over the world, private users, companies, employees and public officials are making individual and group efforts to curb computer crime, and recent efforts have met with some success.

Crime Prevention by the State

In the UK, the Computer Misuse Act of 1990, which criminalises unauthorised access to computer systems, and the Data Protection Act of 1984 (expanded in 1998), which governs when and how data about individuals can be stored and processed, have been passed. Many countries have passed similar laws.

In the UK, the Home Office is charged with tackling computer crime with some police forces having a "cyber crime" unit. The Information Commissioner's Office is in charge of the UK's independent authority set up to protect personal information (and, as we shall see later in this chapter, to promote access to official information). The UK also has an organisation dedicated to fighting specific types of computer crime. The Child Exploitation and Online Protection Centre (CEOP) tackles child sex abuse, especially where it has been facilitated in some way by the internet.

Crime Prevention by Organisations

Companies are also taking crime-fighting efforts seriously. Many businesses have designed procedures and specialised hardware and software to protect their corporate data and systems. Specialised hardware and software, such as encryption devices, can be used to encode data and information to help prevent unauthorised use. Encryption is the process of converting an original electronic message into a form that can be understood only by the intended recipients. A key is a variable value that is applied using an algorithm to a string or block of unencrypted text to produce encrypted text or to decrypt encrypted text. Encryption methods rely on the limitations of computing power for their effectiveness – if breaking a code requires too much computing power, even the most determined code crackers will not be successful. The length of the key used to encode and decode messages determines the strength of the encryption algorithm.

Public-key infrastructure (PKI) enables users of an unsecured public network, such as the internet, to securely and privately exchange data through the use of a public and a private cryptographic key pair that is obtained and shared through a trusted authority. PKI is the most common method on the internet for authenticating a message sender or encrypting a message. PKI uses two keys to encode and decode messages. One key of the pair, the message receiver's public key, is readily available to the public and is used by anyone to send that individual encrypted messages. The second key, the message receiver's private key, is kept secret and is known only by the message receiver. Its owner uses the private key to decrypt messages – convert encoded messages back into the original message. Knowing a person's public key does not enable you to decrypt an encoded message to that person.

> **public-key infrastructure (PKI)** A means to enable users of an unsecured public network, such as the internet, to securely and privately exchange data through the use of a public and a private cryptographic key pair that is obtained and shared through a trusted authority.

Using **biometrics** is another way to protect important data and information systems. Biometrics involves the measurement of one of a person's traits, whether physical or behavioural. Biometric techniques compare a person's unique characteristics against a stored set to detect differences between them. Biometric systems can scan fingerprints, faces, handprints, irises, and retinal images to prevent unauthorised access to important data and computer resources. Most of the interest among corporate users is in fingerprint technology, followed by face recognition. Fingerprint scans hit the middle ground between price and effectiveness (see Figure 9.2). Iris and retina scans are more accurate, but they are more expensive and involve more equipment.

> **biometrics** The measurement of one of a person's traits, whether physical or behavioural.

Co-op Mid Counties is the first UK retailer to implement a payment by biometrics system with fingerprint readers supplied by the US company Pay By Touch. The system is installed in just three of its stores in Oxford, but, if successful, the system will be expanded to all of its 150 stores. To use the system, customers must register with Co-op Mid Counties by providing a photo ID and submit to fingerprinting. In addition to providing improved security, the system

Figure 9.2 Fingerprint Authentication *Fingerprint authentication devices provide security in the PC environment by using fingerprint information instead of passwords.*

SOURCE: © Jochen Tack/Alamy.

takes less time to process a payment – three seconds compared with seven seconds for traditional payment approval methods.[24]

As employees move from one position to another at a company, they can build up access to multiple systems if inadequate security procedures fail to revoke access privileges. It is clearly not appropriate for people who have changed positions and responsibilities to still have access to systems they no longer use. To avoid this problem, many organisations create role-based system access lists so that only people filling a particular role (e.g. line manager) can access a specific system.

Crime-fighting procedures usually require additional controls on the information system. Before designing and implementing controls, organisations must consider the types of computer-related crime that might occur, the consequences of these crimes, and the cost and complexity of needed controls. In most cases, organisations conclude that the trade-off between crime and the additional cost and complexity weighs in favour of better system controls. Having knowledge of some of the methods used to commit crime is also helpful in preventing, detecting, and developing systems resistant to computer crime (see Table 9.2). Some companies actually hire former criminals to thwart other criminals.

Although the number of potential computer crimes appears to be limitless, the actual methods used to commit crime are limited. The following list provides a set of useful guidelines to protect your computer from criminal hackers.

- Install strong user authentication and encryption capabilities on your firewall.
- Install the latest security patches, which are often available at the vendor's website.
- Disable guest accounts and null user accounts that let intruders access the network without a password.
- Do not provide overfriendly logon procedures for remote users (e.g. an organisation that used the word "welcome" on their initial logon screen found they had difficulty prosecuting a criminal hacker).
- Restrict physical access to the server and configure it so that breaking into one server won't compromise the whole network.

Table 9.2 Common Methods Used to Commit Computer Crimes

Methods	Examples
Add, delete, or change inputs to the computer system	Delete records of absences from class in a student's school records
Modify or develop computer programs that commit the crime	Change a bank's program for calculating interest to make it deposit rounded amounts in the criminal's account
Alter or modify the data files used by the computer system	Change a student's grade from C to A
Operate the computer system in such a way as to commit computer crime	Access a restricted government computer system
Divert or misuse valid output from the computer system	Steal discarded printouts of customer records from a company trash bin
Steal computer resources, including hardware, software, and time on computer equipment	Make illegal copies of a software program without paying for its use
Offer worthless products for sale over the internet	Send email requesting money for worthless hair growth product
Blackmail executives to prevent release of harmful information	Eavesdrop on organisation's wireless network to capture competitive data or scandalous information
Blackmail company to prevent loss of computer-based information	Plant logic bomb and send letter threatening to set it off unless paid considerable sum

- ■ Give each application (email, FTP, and domain name server) its own dedicated server.
- ■ Turn audit trails on.
- ■ Consider using caller ID.
- ■ Install a corporate firewall between your corporate network and the internet.
- ■ Install antivirus software on all computers and regularly download vendor updates.
- ■ Conduct regular IS security audits.
- ■ Verify and exercise frequent data backups for critical data.

Companies are also joining together to fight crime. The Software and Information Industry Alliance (SIIA) was the original antipiracy organisation, formed and financed by many of the large software publishers. Microsoft financed the formation of a second antipiracy organisation, the Business Software Alliance (BSA). The BSA, through intense publicity, has become the more prominent organisation. Other software companies, including Apple, Adobe, Hewlett-Packard, and IBM, now contribute to the BSA.

Crime Prevention by Individuals

A number of individuals – victims, former criminals, concerned parents – have set up websites offering support for those worried about computer crime and advice on how to fight it.

Using Managed Security Service Providers (MSSPs)

Keeping up with computer criminals – and with new regulations – can be daunting for organisations. Criminal hackers are constantly poking and prodding, trying to breach the security defences of companies. For most small and mid-sized organisations, the level of in-house network security expertise needed to protect their business operations can be quite costly to acquire and maintain. As a result, many are outsourcing their network security operations to managed security service providers (MSSPs), such as Counterpane, Guardent, Internet Security Services, Riptech, and Symantec. MSSPs monitor, manage, and maintain network security for both hardware and software. These companies provide a valuable service for IS departments drowning in reams of alerts and false alarms coming from virtual private networks (VPNs); antivirus, firewall, and intrusion detection systems; and other security monitoring systems. In addition, some provide vulnerability scanning and web blocking/filtering capabilities.

Preventing Crime on the Internet

As mentioned in Chapter 6, internet security can include firewalls and many methods to secure financial transactions. A firewall can include both hardware and software that act as a barrier between an organisation's information system and the outside world. Some systems have been developed to safeguard financial transactions on the internet.

To help prevent crime on the internet, the following steps can be taken:

1 Develop effective internet usage and security policies for all employees.
2 Use a stand-alone firewall (hardware and software) with network monitoring capabilities.
3 Deploy intrusion detection systems, monitor them, and follow up on their alarms.
4 Monitor managers and employees to make sure that they are using the internet for business purposes.
5 Use internet security specialists to perform audits of all internet and network activities.

Even with these precautions, computers and networks can never be completely protected against crime. One of the biggest threats is from employees. Although firewalls provide good perimeter control to prevent crime from the outside, procedures and protection measures are needed to protect against computer crime by employees. Passwords, identification numbers, and tighter control of employees and managers also help prevent internet-related crime.

9.4 Privacy

Privacy is a big issue for many people. When information is computerised and can be processed and transferred easily, augmented and collated, summarised and reported, privacy concerns mushroom. The European Union has a data-protection directive that requires firms transporting data across national boundaries to have certain privacy procedures in place. This directive affects virtually any company doing business in Europe, and it is driving much of the attention being given to privacy in the US.

Privacy and the Government

Many people are suspicious of the government when it comes to information that is stored about them. In the UK, the government is currently introducing an identity card scheme, which, it is claimed, will help fight international terrorism and identify theft and other fraud. The card would be linked to a database, which would hold names, addresses, and biometric information on all citzens. Expected to cost many billions of euros, some people have pledged never to carry them, claiming that the scheme would create a "big brother" society. Many of these fears are unfounded, although the debate does highlight a lack of trust in the state.

Many governments are in fact quite open about the information that they store. Numerous countries have implemented some sort of freedom of information legistration. In South Africa, it is the Promotion of Access to Information Act. In the UK, it is the Freedom of Information Act. Similar laws have been passed throughout Europe.

The UK Freedom of Information Act governs all data that is not about an individual, in any public organisation, including government, local councils, schools, universities and hospitals. The Act basically states that all such organisations must give out whatever information is requested of them, as long as it is not about an individual (which is protected under the Data Protection Act) or some other sensitive information. So for example, you would be able to ask your university how many people achieved A grades in one of your modules last year (this information is probably published on the students' portal anyway). However, you couldn't request information about a professor's salary. You could, though, ask for information about lecturers' pay scales (which again is already freely available from the relevant union's website).

Privacy at Work

The right to privacy at work is an important issue. Currently, the rights of workers who want their privacy and the interests of companies that demand to know more about their employees are in conflict. Recently, companies that have been monitoring their workers have raised concerns. For example, workers might find that they are being closely monitored via computer technology. These computer-monitoring systems tie directly into workstations; specialised computer programs can track every keystroke made by a user. This type of system can determine what workers are doing while at the keyboard. The system also knows when the worker is not using the keyboard or computer system. These systems can estimate what people are doing and how many breaks they are taking. Needless to say, many workers consider this close supervision very dehumanising.

Email Privacy

Email also raises some interesting issues about work privacy. A company has the right to look at any data stored on its servers, which includes its email servers and, therefore, all messages sent by or to its employees. Many companies routinely store all emails sent or received for several years and many employees have lost their jobs for forwarding inappropriate messages. Others have sent embarassing messages that have been forwarded exponentially by recipients who pass the "joke" on to their friends. A solicitor at a London firm, for example, sent one message to some friends about his girlfriend's sexual preferences and a week later the message had been distributed to over a million people, through many blue chip firms.[25]

Privacy and the Internet

Some people assume that there is no privacy on the internet and that you use it at your own risk. Others believe that companies with websites should have strict privacy procedures and be accountable for privacy invasion. Regardless of your view, the potential for privacy invasion on the internet is huge. People wanting to invade your privacy could be anyone from criminal hackers to marketing companies to corporate bosses. Email is a prime target, as discussed previously. When you visit a website, information about you and your computer can be captured. When this information is combined with other information, companies can know what you read, what products you buy, and what your interests are. According to an executive of an internet software monitoring company, "It's a marketing person's dream."

Most people who buy products on the web say it's very important for a site to have a policy explaining how personal information is used, and the policy statement must make people feel comfortable and be extremely clear about what information is collected and what will and will not be done with it. However, many websites still do not prominently display their privacy policy or implement practices completely consistent with that policy. The real issue that internet users need to be concerned with is "what content providers want with their personal information." If a site requests that you provide your name and address, you have every right to know why and what will be done with it. If you buy something and provide a shipping address, will it be sold to other retailers? Will your email address be sold on a list of active internet shoppers? And if so, you should realise that it's no different than the lists compiled from the orders you place with catalogue retailers – you have the right to be taken off any mailing list.

These same questions can be asked of internet chat rooms that require you to register before you can post messages. It is important for the forum moderators to know who is posting, but users should also have confidence that their information will not be misused.

A potential solution to some consumer privacy concerns is the screening technology called the **Platform for Privacy Preferences (P3P)** being proposed to shield users from sites that don't provide the level of privacy protection they desire. Instead of forcing users to find and read through the privacy policy for each site they visit, P3P software in a computer's browser will download the privacy policy from each site, scan it, and notify the user if the policy does not match his or her preferences. (Of course, unethical marketers can post a privacy policy that does not accurately reflect the manner in which the data is treated.) The World Wide Web Consortium (W3C), an international industry group whose members include Apple, Commerce One, Ericsson, and Microsoft, is supporting the development of P3P.

Platform for Privacy Preferences (P3P) A screening technology that shields users from websites that don't provide the level of privacy protection they desire.

A social network service employs the web and software to connect people for whatever purpose. There are thousands of such networks, which have become popular among teenagers. Most allow one to easily create a user profile that provides personal details, photos, even videos that can be viewed by other visitors to the website. Some of the websites have age restrictions or require that a parent register their preteen by providing a credit card to validate the parent's identity. Teens can provide information about where they live, go to school, their favourite music, and interests in hopes of meeting new friends. Unfortunately, they can also meet ill-intentioned strangers at these sites. Many documented encounters involve adults masquerading as teens, attempting to meet young people for illicit purposes. Parents are advised to discuss potential dangers, check their children's profiles, and monitor their activities at such websites.

Whenever someone registers a domain name, such as www.mydomain.co.uk, the name and address given during registration becomes public information and can be seen by simply running a "whois" query, which can be easily done on many websites. Parents should be aware of this before they let their children have their own web page.

Fairness in Information Use

Selling information to other companies can be so lucrative that many companies will continue to store and sell the data they collect on customers, employees, and others. When is this information storage and use fair and reasonable to the people whose data is stored and sold? Do people have a right to know about data stored about them and to decide what data is stored and used? As shown in Table 9.3, these questions can be broken down into four issues that should be addressed: knowledge, control, notice, and consent.

In the UK, the Data Protection Act governs the answers to these questions. The act relates to data about individuals and states that:

1 Personal data shall be processed fairly and lawfully.

2 Companies must have a reason for collecting and storing the data – they can't arbitrarily start hoarding it, and they cannot process it in any manner incompatible with that reason.

Table 9.3 The Right to Know and the Ability to Decide

Fairness Issues	Database Storage	Database Usage
The right to know	Knowledge	Notice
The ability to decide	Control	Consent

Knowledge. Should people know what data is stored about them? In some cases, people are informed that information about them is stored in a corporate database. In others, they do not know that their personal information is stored in corporate databases

Control. Should people be able to correct errors in corporate database systems? This is possible with most organisations, although it can be difficult in some cases

Notice. Should an organisation that uses personal data for a purpose other than the original purpose notify individuals in advance? Most companies don't do this

Consent. If information on people is to be used for other purposes, should these people be asked to give their consent before data on them is used? Many companies do not give people the ability to decide if information on them will be sold or used for other purposes

3 The data collected shall be adequate, relevant, and not excessive in relation to the reason for collecting it.

4 Companies must make an effort to ensure the data is accurate and, where necessary, up to date.

5 The data will not be stored for longer than necessary.

6 All of the above apply to processing the data, not just collecting and storing it.

7 Companies must take steps to ensure that the data is secure.

8 The data must not be transferred to somewhere that does not have a similar law on processing it.

The act allows individuals to access information stored about them and, if necessary, have the data updated or deleted. Similar laws have been implemented throughout Europe.

Even though privacy laws for private organisations are not very restrictive, most organisations are very sensitive to privacy issues and fairness. They realise that invasions of privacy can hurt their business, turn away customers, and dramatically reduce revenues and profits. Consider a major international credit card company. If the company sold confidential financial information on millions of customers to other companies, the results could be disastrous. In a matter of days, the firm's business and revenues could be reduced dramatically. Therefore, most organisations maintain privacy policies, even though they are not required by law. Corporate privacy policies should address a customer's knowledge, control, notice, and consent over the storage and use of information. They can also cover who has access to private data and when it can be used.

Multinational companies face an extremely difficult challenge in implementing data-collection and dissemination processes and policies because of the multitude of differing country or regional statutes. A good database design practice is to assign a single unique identifier to each customer – so that each has a single record describing all relationships with the company across all its business units. That way, the organisation can apply customer privacy preferences consistently throughout all databases. Failure to do so can expose the organisation to legal risks – aside from upsetting customers who opted out of some collection practices.

Individual Efforts to Protect Privacy

Many people are taking steps to increase their own privacy protection. Some of the steps that you can take to protect personal privacy include the following:

- If you are concerned about what information a company is holding on you, use the Data Protection Act (or your country's equivalent) to find out what is stored about you in existing databases.

- Be careful when you share information about yourself. Don't share information unless it is absolutely necessary.

- Be vigilant in insisting that your doctor, bank, or financial institution not share information about you with others without your written consent.

- Be proactive to protect your privacy. For instance, you could get an unlisted phone number and think twice about registering for a service if it means you must supply a postal address. Consider registering for the telephone preference and mail preference services in your country (which stops commercial calls and post). In the UK the address is www.tpsonline.org.uk.

- When purchasing anything from a website, make sure that you safeguard your credit card numbers, passwords, and personal information. Do not do business with a site unless you know that it handles credit card information securely (look for https:// in the address bar). Do not provide personal information without reviewing the site's data privacy policy.

When some people give over personal information, they change it slightly somehow, maybe changing their name from John T. Smith to John R. Smith. Then in the future, if they get contacted as John R. Smith from an unknown source, they know which company the information must have come from and can take the appropriate steps.

9.5 The Work Environment

The use of computer-based information systems has changed the makeup of the workforce. Jobs that require IS literacy have increased, and many less-skilled positions have been eliminated. Corporate programs, such as re-engineering and continuous improvement, bring with them the concern that, as business processes are restructured and information systems are integrated within them, the people involved in these processes will be removed.

However, the growing field of computer technology and information systems has opened up numerous avenues to professionals and nonprofessionals of all backgrounds. Enhanced telecommunications has been the impetus for new types of business and has created global markets in industries once limited to domestic markets. Even the simplest tasks have been aided by computers, making cash registers faster, smoothing order processing, and allowing people with disabilities to participate more actively in the workforce. As computers and other IS components drop in cost and become easier to use, more workers will benefit from the increased productivity and efficiency provided by computers. However, information systems can raise other concerns.

Health Concerns

Organisations can increase employee effectiveness by paying attention to the health concerns in today's work environment. For some people, working with computers can cause occupational stress. Anxieties about job insecurity, loss of control, incompetence, and demotion are just a few of the fears workers might experience. In some cases, the stress can become so severe that workers might sabotage computer systems and equipment. Monitoring employee stress can alert companies to potential problems. Training and counselling can often help the employee and deter problems.

Computer use can affect physical health as well. Strains, sprains, tendonitis, tennis elbow, the inability to hold objects, and sharp pain in the fingers can result. Also common is repetitive strain injuries (RSI), including carpal tunnel syndrome (CTS), which is the aggravation of the pathway for nerves that travel through the wrist (the carpal tunnel). CTS involves wrist pain, a feeling of tingling and numbness, and difficulty grasping and holding objects. It can be caused by many factors, such as stress, lack of exercise, and the repetitive motion of typing on a computer keyboard. Decisions on workers' compensation related to repetitive stress injuries have been made both for and against employees.

Other work-related health hazards involve emissions from improperly maintained and used equipment. Some studies show that poorly maintained laser printers can release ozone into the air; others dispute the claim. Numerous studies on the impact of emissions from display screens have also resulted in conflicting theories. Although some medical authorities believe that long-term exposure can cause cancer, studies are not conclusive at this time. In any case, many organisations are developing conservative and cautious policies.

Most computer manufacturers publish technical information on radiation emissions from their CRT monitors, and many companies pay close attention to this information. In addition, adjustable chairs and workstations should be supplied if employees request them.

Avoiding Health and Environmental Problems

Many computer-related health problems are caused by a poorly designed work environment. The computer screen can be hard to read, with glare and poor contrast. Desks and chairs can also be uncomfortable. Keyboards and computer screens might be fixed in place or difficult to move. The hazardous activities associated with these unfavourable conditions are collectively referred to as "work stressors." Although these problems might not be of major concern to casual users of computer systems, continued stressors, such as repetitive motion, awkward posture and eyestrain, can cause more serious and long-term injuries. If nothing else, these problems can severely limit productivity and performance (see Figure 9.3).

Figure 9.3 **Repetitive Strain Injury** *Research has shown that developing certain ergonomically correct habits can reduce the risk of RSI when using a computer.*

ergonomics The science of designing machines, products, and systems to maximise the safety, comfort, and efficiency of the people who use them.

The science of designing machines, products, and systems to maximise the safety, comfort, and efficiency of the people who use them, called **ergonomics**, has suggested some approaches to reducing these health problems. The slope of the keyboard, the positioning and design of display screens, and the placement and design of computer tables and chairs have been carefully studied. Flexibility is a major component of ergonomics and an important feature of computer devices. People come in many sizes, have differing preferences, and require different positioning of equipment for best results. Some people, for example, want to place the keyboard in their laps; others prefer it on a solid table. Because of these individual differences, computer designers are attempting to develop systems that provide a great deal of flexibility. In fact, the revolutionary design of Apple's iMac computer came about through concerns for users' comfort, and, after using basically the same keyboard design for over a decade, Microsoft introduced a new split keyboard called the Natural Ergonomic Keyboard 4000. The keyboard provides improved ergonomic features, such as improved angles that reduce motion and how much you must stretch your fingers when you type. The design of the keyboard also provides more convenient wrist and arm postures, which make typing more convenient for users.[26]

Computer users who work at their machines for more than an hour per day should consider using LCD screens, which are much easier on your eyes than CRT screens. If you stare at a CRT screen all day long, your eye muscles can get fatigued from all the screen flicker and bright backlighting of the monitor. LCD screens provide a much better viewing experience for your eyes by virtually eliminating flicker, while still being bright without harsh incandescence.[27]

In addition to steps taken by hardware manufacturing companies, computer users must also take action to reduce strain injury and develop a better work environment. For example, when working at a workstation, the top of the monitor should be at or just below eye level. Your wrists and hands should be in line with your forearms, with your elbows close to your body and supported. Your lower back needs to be well supported. Your feet should be flat on the floor. Take an occasional break to get away from the keyboard and screen. Stand up and stretch while at your workplace. Do not ignore pain or discomfort. Many workers ignore early signs of strain injury, and, as a result, the problem becomes much worse and more difficult to treat.

Ethical and Societal Issues

Is the Internet Eating Our Brains?

Since the rise of the web, many have become concerned that humanity is becoming overly dependent on technology and the internet. Others have countered that the benefits of the internet far outweigh any dependency concerns. Researchers at the University of Maryland asked 200 students to do without all digital media for one full day. The results of the study were startling. Many students in the study exhibited "signs of withdrawal, craving and anxiety" as their 24 hours of digital isolation ticked by. The psychological reactions were very similar to those of individuals with chemical addictions. Students complained of feeling cut off from family and friends. Text messaging, emailing, and Facebook posts allow students to feel continuously connected to friends who provide support and comfort. Losing those connections left students feeling isolated and out of touch. Interacting with their social networks defined these students' daily lives and existence.

Although the American Psychiatric Association does not recognise internet addiction as a formal disorder, it is clear that it is becoming an affliction of today's connected lifestyle. A small private clinic in Redmond, Washington named ReSTART, is one of several support centers that assist individuals who suffer from excessive use of digital technologies. Elsewhere in the world, internet addiction is classified as a more serious problem. In South Korea, perhaps the most wired country in the world, the government is restricting access to popular online video games. This action was taken in response to numerous reports of out-of-control teens who refuse to log off their online games. South Korea has classified 2 million people as "internet addicts." The government has started an educational program in grade schools to discourage students from obsessive internet indulgence similar to programs used to discourage students from taking drugs.

Is our increasing use of the internet an addiction or a natural evolution? Some see it as a positive progression for human kind, allowing us to pool our resources to accomplish more, whereas others think that it is eating our brains. In his book "The Shallows: What the internet is Doing to Our Brains," Nicholas Carr makes the case that internet use is damaging the way we think. Carr believes that, as we jump around the web from topic to topic, we are rewiring our brains and reducing our ability to concentrate, remember, and reason.

The internet represents a major societal change, and such major change always brings with it concern and criticism. Consider the words of English author Barnaby Rich 400 years ago regarding the mass production of books: "One of the great diseases of this age is the multitude of books that doth so overcharge the world that it is not able to digest the abundance of idle matter that is every day hatched and brought into the world."

Whether or not internet addiction exists as a mental disorder, humanity would be wise to consider its dependency on the internet and the implications of the loss of electronic technologies due to natural or economic disaster or military attack. How might a society survive the loss of essential network infrastructure or the electric grid?

Discussion Questions

1 In what manner are individuals becoming dependent on the internet and digital technologies?

2 At what point do you think internet use might be classified as an addiction? Do you know of anyone who you would classify as an internet addict?

Critical Thinking Questions

1 Why do you think internet addiction has become such a problem in South Korea? Do you think the same destiny awaits other countries as we become increasingly digitally connected?

2 What action can be taken so that our dependency on the internet poses less of a threat to our survival?

SOURCES: Slew, Walden, "US students suffering from internet addiction: study," Reuters. Available from: www.reuters.com, April 23, 2010; Yoon, Sangwon, "South Korea Cracks Dwn on Internet Addiction," NewsFactor. Available from: www.newsfactor. com, April 23, 2010; Johnston, Casey, "College students struggle to go without media for 24 hours," Ars Technica. Available from: www.arstechnica.com, April 23, 2010; Snyder, Bill, "Nicholas Carr: The internet is hurting our brains," Computerworld. Available from: www.computerworld.com, June 21, 2010.

9.6 Ethical Issues in Information Systems

As you've seen throughout the book in our Ethical and Societal Issues boxes, ethical issues deal with what is generally considered right or wrong. As we have seen, laws do not provide a complete guide to ethical behaviour. Just because an activity is defined as legal does not mean that it is ethical. As a result, practitioners in many professions subscribe to a **code of ethics** that states the principles and core values that are essential to their work and, therefore, govern their behaviour. The code can become a reference point for weighing what is legal and what is ethical. For example, doctors adhere to varying versions of the 2000-year-old Hippocratic Oath, which medical schools offer as an affirmation to their graduating classes.

Some IS professionals believe that their field offers many opportunities for unethical behaviour. They also believe that unethical behaviour can be reduced by top-level managers developing, discussing, and enforcing codes of ethics. Various IS-related organisations and

code of ethics A code that states the principles and core values that are essential to a set of people and, therefore, govern their behaviour.

associations promote ethically responsible use of information systems and have developed useful codes of ethics. The British Computer Society has a code of ethics and professional conduct that can be used to help guide the actions of IS professionals. These guidelines can also be used for those who employ or hire IS professionals to monitor and guide their work and can be seen at www.bcs.org.

The mishandling of the social issues discussed in this chapter – including waste and mistakes, crime, privacy, health, and ethics – can devastate an organisation. The prevention of these problems and recovery from them are important aspects of managing information and information systems as critical corporate assets. Increasingly, organisations are recognising that people are the most important component of a computer-based information system and that long-term competitive advantage can be found in a well-trained, motivated, and knowledgeable workforce.

Summary

At the start of this chapter we set out the THREE main principles relating to issues of personal health & safety, security and keeping privacy secure online together with the key learning objectives for each. It's now time to summarise the chapter by recapping on those THREE issues: can you recall what is important and why about each one?

1. **Policies and procedures must be established to avoid computer waste and mistakes.** Computer waste is the inappropriate use of computer technology and resources in both the public and private sectors. Computer mistakes relate to errors, failures, and other problems that result in output that is incorrect and without value. Waste and mistakes occur in government agencies, as well as corporations. At the corporate level, computer waste and mistakes impose unnecessarily high costs for an information system and drag down profits. Waste often results from poor integration of IS components, leading to duplication of efforts and overcapacity. Inefficient procedures also waste IS resources, as does thoughtless disposal of useful resources and misuse of computer time for games and personal processing jobs. Inappropriate processing instructions, inaccurate data entry, mishandling of IS output, and poor systems design all cause computer mistakes.

A less dramatic, yet still relevant, example of waste is the amount of company time and money employees can waste playing computer games, sending unimportant email, or accessing the internet. Junk email, also called spam, and junk faxes also cause waste.

Preventing waste and mistakes involves establishing, implementing, monitoring, and reviewing effective policies and procedures. Careful programming practices, thorough testing, flexible network interconnections, and rigorous backup procedures can help an information system prevent and recover from many kinds of mistakes. Companies should develop manuals and training programs to avoid waste and mistakes. Company policies should specify criteria for new resource purchases and user-developed processing tools to help guard against waste and mistakes.

2. **Computer crime is a serious and rapidly growing area of concern requiring management attention.** Some crimes use computers as tools (e.g. to manipulate records, counterfeit money and documents, commit fraud via telecommunications links, and make unauthorised electronic transfers of money). Identity theft is a crime in which an imposter obtains key pieces of personal identification information to impersonate someone else. The information is then used to obtain credit, merchandise, and services in the name of the victim or to provide the thief with false credentials.

A cyberterrorist is someone who intimidates or coerces a government or organisation to advance his or her political or social objectives by launching computer-based attacks against computers, networks, and the information stored on them. A cracker, or criminal hacker, is a computer-savvy person who attempts to gain unauthorised access to computer systems to steal passwords, corrupt files and programs, and even transfer money. Script kiddies are crackers with little technical savvy. Insiders are employees, disgruntled or otherwise, working solo or in concert with outsiders to compromise corporate systems.

Computer crimes target computer systems and include illegal access to computer systems, alteration and destruction of data and programs by viruses (system, application, and document), and simple theft of computer resources. A virus is a program that attaches itself to other programs. A worm functions is an independent program, replicating its own program files until it destroys other systems and programs or interrupts the operation of computer systems and networks. Malware is a general term for software that is harmful or destructive. A Trojan horse program is a malicious program that disguises itself as a useful application and purposefully does something the user does not expect. A logic bomb is designed to "explode" or execute at a specified time and date.

Because of increased computer use, greater emphasis is placed on the prevention and detection of computer crime. Antivirus software is used to detect the presence of viruses, worms, and logic bombs. Use of an intrusion detection system (IDS) provides another layer of protection in the event that an intruder gets past the outer security layers – passwords, security procedures, and corporate firewall. It monitors system and network resources and notifies network security personnel when it senses a possible intrusion. Many small and midsized organisations are outsourcing their network security operations to managed security service providers (MSSPs), which monitor, manage, and maintain network security hardware and software.

Software and internet piracy might represent the most common computer crime. Computer scams have cost people and companies thousands of euros. Computer crime is also an international issue.

Many organisations and people help prevent computer crime. Security measures, such as using passwords, identification numbers, and data encryption, help to guard against illegal computer access, especially when supported by effective control procedures. Public-key infrastructure (PKI) enables users of an unsecured public network, such as the internet, to securely and privately exchange data through the use of a public and a private cryptographic key pair that is obtained and shared through a trusted authority. The use of biometrics, involving the measurement of a person's unique characteristics, such as the iris, retina, or voice pattern, is another way to protect important data and information systems. Virus-scanning software identifies and removes damaging computer programs. Although most companies use data files for legitimate, justifiable purposes, opportunities for invasion of privacy abound. Privacy issues are a concern with government agencies, email use, corporations, and the internet. A business should develop a clear and thorough policy about privacy rights for customers, including database access. That policy should also address the rights of employees, including electronic monitoring systems and email. Fairness in information use for privacy rights emphasises knowledge, control, notice, and consent for people profiled in databases. People should know about the data that is stored about them and be able to correct errors in corporate database systems. If information on people is to be used for other purposes, they should be asked to give their consent beforehand. Each person has the right to know and the ability to decide. Platform for Privacy Preferences (P3P) is a screening technology that shields users from websites that don't provide the level of privacy protection they desire.

3. **Jobs, equipment, and working conditions must be designed to avoid negative health effects.** Computers have changed the makeup of the workforce and even eliminated some jobs, but they have also expanded and enriched employment opportunities in many ways. Computers and related devices can affect employees' emotional and physical health. Some critics blame computer systems for emissions of ozone and electromagnetic radiation.

The study of designing and positioning computer equipment, called ergonomics, has suggested some approaches to reducing these health problems. Ergonomic design principles help to reduce harmful effects and increase the efficiency of an information system. The slope of the keyboard, the positioning and design of display screens, and the placement and design of computer tables and chairs are essential for good health. Good practice includes keeping good posture, not ignoring pain or problems, performing stretching and strengthening exercises, and seeking proper treatment. Although they can cause negative health consequences, information systems can also be used to provide a wealth of information on health topics through the internet and other sources.

Ethics determine generally accepted and discouraged activities within a company and society at large. Ethical computer users define acceptable practices more strictly than just refraining from committing crimes; they also consider the effects of their IS activities, including internet usage, on other people and organisations. Many IS professionals join computer-related associations and agree to abide by detailed ethical codes.

Review Questions

1 What special issues are associated with the prevention of image-based spam?

2 Identify three types of common computer-related mistakes.

3 What is a variant? What dangers are associated with such malware?

4 What is phishing? What actions can you take to reduce the likelihood that you will be a victim of this crime?

5 What is a virus? What is a worm? How are they different?

6 Outline measures you should take to protect yourself against viruses and worms.

7 Identify at least five tips to follow to avoid becoming a victim of a computer scam.

8 What is biometrics, and how can it be used to protect sensitive data?

9 What is the difference between antivirus software and an intrusion detection system?

10 What is a code of ethics? Give an example.

Discussion Questions

1 Outline an approach, including specific techniques that you could employ to gain personal data about the members of your class. Explain how they could protect themselves from what you have suggested.

2 Your 12-year-old niece shows you a profile her male maths teacher posted on Facebook that includes dozens of students as the instructor's friends and a quote: "I hope to make lots of new friends and, who knows, maybe find Miss Right." What would you do?

3 Imagine that you are a hacker and have developed a Trojan horse program. What tactics might you use to get unsuspecting victims to load the program onto their computer?

4 Briefly discuss the potential for cyberterrorism to cause a major disruption in your daily life. What are some likely targets of a cyberterrorist? What sort of action could a cyberterrorist take against these targets?

5 You travel a lot in your role as vice president of sales and carry a laptop containing customer data, budget information, product development plans, and promotion information. What measures should you take to ensure against potential theft of your laptop and its critical data?

Web Exercises

1 Search the web for a site that provides software to detect and remove spyware. Write a short report for your instructor summarising your findings.

2 Do research on the web to find evidence of an increase or decrease in the number of viruses being developed and released. To what is the change attributed? Write a brief memo to your instructor identifying your sources and summarising your findings.

Case One

Data Theft: An Ongoing Concern

Between 2007 and 2009, details of about 600 000 people stored on a navy officer's laptop were stolen; six laptops storing 20 000 patient details were stolen from UK hospitals; 658 laptops were stolen from the UK Ministry of Defence and details of about 100 000 pension scheme members were stolen from a software firm.

Although startling, none of these is the largest data theft. In 2006, a laptop and hard drive were stolen from the US Department of Veterans Affairs containing the personal information of 26.5 million military veterans and their spouses. In 2008, 130 million credit card numbers were stolen from Heartland Payment System's servers. Heartland processes credit and debit card transactions for Visa, American Express, and other businesses.

The data were stolen by hackers who infiltrated Heartland networks to gain access to the servers on which the data was stored. Computer hacker Albert Gonzalez was arrested for participating in the cybercrime ring that attacked Heartland and many others. The judge solicited valuable information about international cybercrime from Gonzalez prior to convicting him to 20 years in prison. Gonzalez informed the judge that international cybercrime rings have progressed from attacking individual businesses to attacking banks and organisations that handle large amounts of financial transaction data, such as Heartland.

Besides stealing the physical media on which data is stored and hacking into networks, data thieves also use collections of compromised computers called botnet armies to do their work. For example, the Mariposa botnet, which was eventually dismantled in 2010, used 12.7 million infected PCs to steal credit card and bank account information. The botnet was shut down through a series of arrests in Spain. The Kneber botnet runs on infected computers spread across 126 countries and is designed to steal logon credentials for corporations, financial systems, and popular social networking and email sites.

Sometimes computer hackers have other goals. UK hacker Gary McKinnon is accused of hacking into 97 United States military and NASA computers over a 13-month period between February 2001 and March 2002 and claims he was looking for evidence of free energy suppression and a cover-up of UFO activity and other technologies potentially useful to the public. McKinnon is currently awaiting extradition to the US, but many people think he should be tried in the UK.

The internet has become a major platform for criminal activity. Financial account information and personal information used for identity theft are often the goal of attacks, allowing hackers to rake in millions of euros on the underground market. Hackers have many methods of attack, and no internet-connected server can be considered 100 per cent safe. It remains the responsibility of businesses to stay abreast of the latest security holes and patches and to stay vigilant and watchful to react quickly when a data breach does occur. The best reaction to a data breach is immediate contact with those affected, along with an offer to protect them from financial hardship.

Discussion Questions

1   What methods do hackers and thieves use to illegally access valuable information?

2   What is the best response for a business that has discovered private customer information stolen?

Critical Thinking Questions

1   What policies can financial institutions and governments put in place to protect consumers from data theft?

2   What practices can consumers use to help protect their ownprivate information?

SOURCES: Kirk, Jeremy, "Company says 3.3M student loan records stolen," Computerworld. Available from: www.computerworld.com, March 29, 2010; Weil Nancy, "Gonzalez sentenced to 20 years for Heartland break-in," Computerworld. Available from: www.computerworld.com, March 26, 2010; Bright, Peter, "Spanish arrests mark the end of dangerous botnet," Ars Technica. Available from: www.arstechnica.com, March 20, 2010; Vijayan, Jaikumar, "Over 75,000 systems compromised in cyberattack," Computerworld. Available from: www.computerworld.com, February 18, 2010; Kirk, Jeremy, "Aetna warns 65,000 about website data breach," Computer-world. Available from: www.computerworld.com, May 28, 2009; Vijayan, Jaikumar, "Three months, three breaches at the Univ. of Florida-Gainesville," Computerworld. Available from: www.computerworld.com, February 22, 2009.

Case Two

The Cult of Less and The Digital Firefighters

Late in 2009, software engineer Kelly Sutton came to a conclusion: more stuff equals more stress. "Each thing I own came with a small expectation of responsibility. I look into my closet and feel guilt. I glance into my desk drawers and see my neglect. When was the last time I wore this? Have I ever even used that?" He landed on a radical solution: he decided to get rid of it all, or most of it at least: "I will eliminate a large part of stress in my life, and I will truly cherish the few things that I own."

Many of the things we collect have digital alternatives. Books, movies and music can all be stored electronically with almost no physical space requirements. Mr Sutton founded CultofLess.com, a website which has helped him sell or give away his possessions - apart from his laptop, an iPad, an Amazon Kindle, two external hard drives, a "few" articles of clothing and bed sheets for a mattress that was left in his newly rented apartment. "I think cutting down on physical commodities in general might be a trend of my generation – cutting down on physical commodities that can be replaced by digital counterparts will be a fact," he said.

He is not alone. Chris Yurista from Washington, DC, left his rented apartment and decided to use the internet as his address. His possessions include a backpack full of designer clothing, a laptop, an external hard drive, a small piano keyboard and a bicycle. The decision wasn't about money – he earns a significant income as a travel agent, but feels he now no longer has to worry about dusting, organising and cleaning his possessions. "I don't feel a void living the way I'm living, because I've figured out a way to use digital technology to my advantage," he said. Mr Yurista has substituted his bed for friends' couches, paper bills for online banking, and a record collection containing nearly 2000 albums for an external hard drive and nearly 13 000 MP3s.

Mr Yurista says he frequently worries he may lose his new digital life to a hard drive crash or a downed server. "You have to really make sure you have back-ups of your digital goods everywhere," he said.

Data recovery engineer Chris Bross at recovery company Drive Savers believes, as individuals grow increasingly dependent on digital storage technology for holding assets, data recovery services will become rather like the firefighters of the 21st Century – responders who save your valuables. And like a house fire that rips through a family's prized possessions, when someone loses their digital goods to a computer crash, they can be devastated.

Kelly Chessen, a 36-year-old former suicide hotline counsellor, is Drive Savers, official "data crisis counsellor." Ms Chessen's role is to try to calm people down when they lose their digital possessions to failed drives. Ms Chessen says that some people have gone as far as to threaten suicide over their lost digital possessions and data.

Discussion Questions

1 Make a list of your possessions. Tick off those that could be digitised and those that you could live without. What is left?

2 What would some the challenges be in living with less?

Critical Thinking Questions

1 Is it valuable to society that more people live with less? Is it valuable to humanity? To Planet Earth?

2 Kelly Sutton and Chris Yurista have gone to an extreme. Can you describe a more moderate version of living with less that more people could go along with?

SOURCES: http://cultofless.tumblr.com/post/182833987/is-it-possible-to-own-nothing. Accessed 28 January 2011.

Notes

1 McGillicuddy, Shamus, 'Thwarting Spam from the Inside and the Outside.' Available from: ComputerWeekly.com, July 11, 2006.

2 Arthur, Charles, "Will Convicting Five Major Spammers Put an End to Spam?" The Guardian, June 30, 2009. Available from: www.guardian.co.uk/technology/2009/jun/24/spam-newly-asked-questions/print.

3 Hananel, Sam, "Officials: Computer Error Affected Mine Scrutiny." Available from: www.philly.com, April 13, 2010.

4 Baxter, Elsa, "Computer Error Causes UAE Cash Machine Shutdown." Available from: www.arabianbusiness.com/582494-computer-error-causes-uae-cash-machine-shutdown, February 28, 2010.

5 Staff, "Computer Error Signals Erroneous Report of Earthquake in Northern California," Fox News, April 20, 2010.

6 Puzzanghera, Jim, "Regulators Still Working to Pinpoint Cause of Stock Market's Record Plunge," Chicago Tribune, May 11, 2010.

7 Whiting, Rick, 'Hamstrung by Defective Data.' Information Week, May 8, 2006.

8 Doland, Angela, "Trial Opens for Accused French Rogue Trader," Real Clear Markets. Available from: www.realclearmarkets.com/news/ap/finance_business/2010/Jun/08/trial_opens_for_accused_french_rogue_trader. html. Accessed June 8, 2010.

9 Koprowski, Gene J., "Study: Nearly a Quarter Million PCs Turned into 'Zombies' Daily," E-commerce Times, January 14, 2006.

10 McMillian, Robert, 'Internet Sieges Can Cost Businesses a Bundle,' Computerworld, August 25, 2005.

11 BBC News (website), "U.K. hacker 'should be extradited,'" May 10, 2006. Available from: http://news.bbc.co.uk/1/hi/technology/4757375.stm.

12 BBC News (website), "Tax Credit Errors 'Waste £1.4bn,'" May 8, 2007. Available from: http://news.bbc.co.uk/1/hi/business/6634843.stm.

13 Keizer, Gregg, 'U.S. Consumers Taking Steps to Stymie ID Theft,' Information Week, May 19, 2006.

14 BBC, "Stuxnet worm 'targeted high-value Iranian assets,'" 23 September 2010. Available from: www.bbc.co.uk/news/technology-11388018

15 Savaas, Antony, 'McAfee: 400 000 Virus Definitions on Users' Machines by 2008,' ComputerWeekly.com, July 6, 2006.

16 Lyman, Jay, 'Study: Mobile Malware Threat to Grow in '06,' E-commerce Times, December 10, 2005.

17 Savvas, Antony, 'Police Arrest m00p Gang Suspects.' Available from: ComputerWeekly.com, June 28, 2006.

18 Savvas, Antony, 'Trojan Steals Bank Details After Pretending to Be Microsoft Patch.' Available from: ComputerWeekly.com, May 31, 2006.

19 McAfee (website), 'Virus Hoaxes,' August 24, 2006. Available from: http://vil.mcafee.com/hoax.asp.

20 BBC News (website), 'Defence Consultant's Laptop Stolen,' April 16, 2001. Available from: http://news.bbc.co.uk/1/hi/uk/1279584.stm.

21 Business Software Alliance (website home page). Available from: www.bsa.org/usa.

22 Garretson, Cara, 'Stats Show Phishing Attacks Doubled,' Computerworld, January 13, 2006.

23 McMillan, Robert, 'Man Charged in Hurricane Katrina Phishing Scams,' Computerworld, August 18, 2006.

24 Hadfield, Will, 'Co-op Goes Live with First Payment by Biometrics System.' Available from: ComputerWeekly.com, March 10, 2006.

25 Wakefield, J., 'E-mail Embarrassment for City Lawyer,' ZDNet U.K., December 14, 2000. Available from: http://news.zdnet.co.uk/internet/0,1000000097,2083185,00.htm.

26 Shah, Agam, 'Microsoft Revamps Keyboards and Mice,' Computerworld, September 6, 2005.

27 Merrin, John, 'Review: Six 19-inch LCD Monitors,' Information Week, June 8, 2005.

Glossary

acceptance testing Conducting any tests required by the user.

accounting systems Systems that include budget, accounts receivable, payroll, asset management, and general ledger.

ad hoc DSS A DSS concerned with situations or decisions that come up only a few times during the life of the organisation.

antivirus program Software that runs in the background to protect your computer from dangers lurking on the internet and other possible sources of infected files.

application program interface (API) An interface that allows applications to make use of the operating system.

application service provider (ASP) A company that provides software, support and the computer hardware on which to run the software from the user's facilities over a network.

arithmetic/logic unit (ALU) The part of the CPU that performs mathematical calculations and makes logical comparisons.

ARPANET A project started by the US Department of Defense (DoD) in 1969 as both an experiment in reliable networking and a means to link the DoD and military research contractors, including many universities doing military-funded research.

artificial intelligence (AI) The ability of computer systems to mimic or duplicate the functions or characteristics of the human brain or intelligence.

artificial intelligence systems People, procedures, hardware, software, data, and knowledge needed to develop computer systems and machines that demonstrate characteristics of intelligence.

asking directly An approach to gather data that asks users, stakeholders and other managers about what they want and expect from the new or modified system.

auditing Analyzing the financial condition of an organisation and determining whether financial statements and reports produced by the financial MIS are accurate.

B2Me A form of e-commerce where the business treats each customer as a separate market segment. Typical B2Me features include customising a website for each customer, perhaps based on their previous purchases and personalised (electronic) marketing literature.

backward chaining The process of starting with conclusions and working backward to the supporting facts.

batch processing system A form of data processing where business transactions are accumulated over a period of time and prepared for processing as a single unit or batch.

biometrics The measurement of one of a person's traits, whether physical or behavioural.

blade server A server that houses many individual computer mother-boards that include one or more processors, computer memory, computer storage, and computer network connections.

Bluetooth A wireless communications specification that describes how cell phones, computers, faxes, printers and other electronic devices can be interconnected over distances of 10–30 metres at a rate of about 2 Mbps.

brainstorming A decision-making approach that often consists of members offering ideas "off the top of their heads."

broadband communications A relative term but generally means a telecommunications system that can exchange data very quickly.

business intelligence The process of gathering enough of the right information in a timely manner and usable form and analyzing it to have a positive impact on business strategy, tactics, or operations.

business-to-business (B2B) e-commerce A subset of e-commerce where all the participants are organisations.

business-to-consumer (B2C) e-commerce A form of e-commerce in which customers deal directly with an organisation and avoid intermediaries.

byte (B) Eight bits that together represent a single character of data.

cardinality In a relationship, cardinality is the number of one entity that can be related to another entity.

Cascading Style Sheet (CSS) A markup language for defining the visual design of a web page or group of pages.

central processing unit (CPU) The part of the computer that consists of three associated elements: the arithmetic/logic unit, the control unit and the register areas.

centralised processing An approach to processing wherein all processing occurs in a single location or facility.

certification A process for testing skills and knowledge, which results in a statement by the certifying authority that confirms an individual is capable of performing a particular kind of job.

channel bandwidth The rate at which data is exchanged, usually measured in bits per second (bps).

chief knowledge officer (CKO) A top-level executive who helps the organisation use a KMS to create, store, and use knowledge to achieve organisational goals.

choice stage The third stage of decision making, which requires selecting a course of action.

client/server architecture An approach to computing wherein multiple computer platforms are dedicated to special functions, such as database management, printing, communications and program execution.

clock speed A series of electronic pulses produced at a predetermined rate that affects machine cycle time.

code of ethics A code that states the principles and core values that are essential to a set of people and, therefore, govern their behaviour.

command-based user interface A user interface that requires you to give text commands to the computer to perform basic activities.

compact disc read-only memory (CD-ROM) A common form of optical disc on which data cannot be modified once it has been recorded.

competitive advantage The ability of a firm to outperform its industry, that is, to earn a higher rate of profit than the industry norm.

competitive intelligence One aspect of business intelligence limited to information about competitors and the ways that knowledge affects strategy, tactics, and operations.

computer network The communications media, devices and software needed to connect two or more computer systems or devices.

computer programs Sequences of instructions for the computer.

computer-aided manufacturing (CAM) A system that directly controls manufacturing equipment.

computer-aided software engineering (CASE) Tools that automate many of the tasks required in a systems development effort and encourage adherence to the SDLC.

computer-based information system (CBIS) A single set of hardware, software, databases, telecommunications, people, and procedures that are configured to collect, manipulate, store, and process data into information.

computer-integrated manufacturing (CIM) Using computers to link the components of the production process into an effective system.

concurrency control A method of dealing with a situation in which two or more people need to access the same record in a database at the same time.

consumer-to-consumer (C2C) e-commerce A subset of e-commerce that involves consumers selling directly to other consumers.

content streaming A method for transferring large media files over the internet so that the data stream of voice and pictures plays more or less continuously as the file is being downloaded.

control unit The part of the CPU that sequentially accesses program instructions, decodes them and coordinates the flow of data in and out of the ALU, the registers, the primary storage, and even secondary storage and various output devices.

counterintelligence The steps an organisation takes to protect information sought by "hostile" intelligence gatherers.

cracker A person who enjoys computer technology and spends time learning and using computer systems.

critical path Activities that, if delayed, would delay the entire project.

customer relationship management (CRM) system A system that helps a company manage all aspects of customer encounters, including marketing and advertising, sales, customer service after the sale, and programs to retain loyal customers.

cyberterrorist Someone who intimidates or coerces a government or organisation to advance his or her political or social objectives by launching computer-based attacks against computers, networks, and the information stored on them.

data administrator A nontechnical position responsible for defining and implementing consistent principles for a variety of data issues.

data analysis The manipulation of collected data so that the development team members who are participating in systems analysis can use the data.

data centre A climate-controlled building or set of buildings that house database servers and the systems that deliver mission-critical information and services.

data collection Capturing and gathering all data necessary to complete the processing of transactions.

data correction The process of re-entering data that was not typed or scanned properly.

data definition language (DDL) A collection of instructions and commands used to define and describe data and relationships in a specific database.

data dictionary A detailed description of all the data used in the database.

data editing The process of checking data for validity and completeness.

data manipulation language (DML) The commands that are used to manipulate the data in a database.

data manipulation The process of performing calculations and other data transformations related to business transactions.

data mining The process of analyzing data to try to discover patterns and relationships within the data.

data preparation, or data conversion Making sure all files and databases are ready to be used with new computer software and systems.

data storage The process of updating one or more databases with new transactions.

data store Representation of a storage location for data.

data warehouse A database or collection of databases that collects business information from many sources in the enterprise, covering all aspects of the company's processes, products, and customers.

database An organised collection of information.

database administrator (DBA) The role of the database administrator is to plan, design, create, operate, secure, monitor, and maintain databases.

data-flow diagram (DFD) A model of objects, associations and activities that describes how data can flow between and around various objects.

data-flow line Arrows that show the direction of data element movement.

decentralised processing An approach to processing wherein processing devices are placed at various remote locations.

decision-making phase The first part of problem solving, including three stages: intelligence, design, and choice.

decision support system (DSS) An organised collection of people, procedures, software, databases, and devices used to support problem-specific decision making.

degree The number of entities involved in a relationship.

demand report A report developed to give certain information at someone's request.

design report The primary result of systems design, reflecting the decisions made and preparing the way for systems implementation.

design stage The second stage of decision making, in which alternative solutions to the problem are developed.

desktop computer A relatively small, inexpensive, single-user computer that is highly versatile.

dialogue manager A user interface that allows decision makers to easily access and manipulate the DSS and to use common business terms and phrases.

digital audio player A device that can store, organise, and play digital music files.

digital camera An input device used with a PC to record and store images and video in digital form.

digital video disc or digital versatile disc A storage medium used to store software, video games and movies.

direct access A retrieval method in which data can be retrieved without the need to read and discard other data.

direct access storage device (DASD) A device used for direct access of secondary storage data.

direct conversion (also called *plunge* or *direct cutover*) Stopping the old system and starting the new system on a given date.

direct observation Directly observing the existing system in action by one or more members of the analysis team.

distributed database A database in which the data is spread across several smaller databases connected via telecommunications devices.

distributed processing An approach to processing wherein processing devices are placed at remote locations but are connected to each other via a network.

document production The process of generating output records and reports.

domain The area of knowledge addressed by the expert system.

domain expert The individual or group who has the expertise or knowledge one is trying to capture in the expert system.

drill-down report A report providing increasingly detailed data about a situation.

e-commerce Any business transaction executed electronically between companies (business-to-business), companies and consumers (business-to-consumer), consumers and other consumers (consumer-to-consumer), business and the public sector, and consumers and the public sector.

economic feasibility The determination of whether the project makes financial sense and whether predicted benefits offset the cost and time needed to obtain them.

economic order quantity (EOQ) The quantity that should be reordered to minimise total inventory costs.

effectiveness A measure of the extent to which a system achieves its goals; it can be computed by dividing the goals actually achieved by the total of the stated goals.

efficiency A measure of what is produced divided by what is consumed.

e-government The use of information and communications technology to simplify the sharing of information, speed formerly paper-based processes, and improve the relationship between citizen and government.

electronic bill presentment A method of billing whereby a vendor posts an image of your statement on the internet and alerts you by email that your bill has arrived.

electronic business (e-business) Using information systems and the internet to perform all business-related tasks and functions.

electronic commerce Conducting business transactions (e.g. distribution, buying, selling, and servicing) electronically over computer networks, such as the internet, extranets, and corporate networks.

electronic exchange An electronic forum where manufacturers, suppliers, and competitors buy and sell goods, trade market information, and run back-office operations.

electronic retailing (e-tailing) The direct sale from business to consumer through electronic storefronts, typically designed around an electronic catalogue and shopping cart model.

end-user systems development Any systems development project in which the primary effort is undertaken by a combination of business managers and users.

enterprise resource planning (ERP) system A set of integrated programs capable of managing a company's vital business operations for an entire multi-site, global organisation.

enterprise resource planning A system that manages an entire company's vital business information.

enterprise rules The rules governing relationships between entities.

entity A person, place or thing about whom or about which an organisation wants to store data.

entity symbol Representation of either a source or destination of a data element.

environmental design Also called *green design,* it involves systems development efforts that slash power consumption, require less physical space and result in systems that can be disposed in a way that doesn't negatively affect the environment.

ergonomics The science of designing machines, products, and systems to maximise the safety, comfort, and efficiency of the people who use them.

exception report A report automatically produced when a situation is unusual or requires management action.

executive support system (ESS) Specialised DSS that includes all hardware, software, data, procedures, and people used to assist senior-level executives within the organisation.

expert system A system that gives a computer the ability to make suggestions and act like an expert in a particular field.

expert system Hardware and software that stores knowledge and makes inferences, similar to a human expert.

explanation facility Component of an expert system that allows a user or decision maker to understand how the expert system arrived at certain conclusions or results.

Extensible Markup Language (XML) The markup language designed to transport and store data on the web.

extranet A network based on web technologies that allows selected outsiders, such as business partners, suppliers, or customers, to access authorised resources of a company's intranet.

feasibility analysis Assessment of the technical, economic, legal, operational and schedule feasibility of a project.

feedback Output that is used to make changes to input or processing activities.

field A characteristic or attribute of an entity that is stored in the database.

final evaluation A detailed investigation of the proposals offered by the vendors remaining after the preliminary evaluation.

financial MIS A management information system that provides financial information not only for executives but also for a broader set of people who need to make better decisions on a daily basis.

five-forces model A widely accepted model that identifies five key factors that can lead to attainment of competitive advantage, including (1) the rivalry among existing competitors, (2) the threat of new entrants, (3) the threat of substitute products and services, (4) the bargaining power of buyers, and (5) the bargaining power of suppliers.

flexible manufacturing system (FMS) An approach that allows manufacturing facilities to rapidly and efficiently change from making one product to making another.

forecasting Predicting future events.

foreign key When a primary key is posted into another table to create a relationship between the two, it is known as a foreign key.

forward chaining The process of starting with the facts and working forward to the conclusions.

Gantt chart A graphical tool used for planning, monitoring and coordinating projects.

genetic algorithm An approach to solving large, complex problems in which a number of related operations or models change and evolve until the best one emerges.

geographic information system (GIS) A computer system capable of assembling, storing, manipulating, and displaying geographic information, that is, data identified according to its location.

graphical user interface (GUI) An interface that displays pictures (icons) and menus that people use to send commands to the computer system.

green computing A program concerned with the efficient and environmentally responsible design, manufacture, operation and disposal of IS-related products.

grid computing The use of a collection of computers, often owned by multiple individuals or organisations, to work in a coordinated manner to solve a common problem.

group consensus approach A decision-making approach that forces members in the group to reach a unanimous decision.

group support system (GSS) Software application that consists of most elements in a DSS, plus software to provide effective support in group decision making; also called "group decision support system."

handheld computer A single-user computer that provides ease of portability because of its small size.

hardware Any machinery (most of which uses digital circuits) that assists in the input, processing, storage, and output activities of an information system.

heuristics Commonly accepted guidelines or procedures that usually find a good solution.

highly structured problems Problems that are straightforward and require known facts and relationships.

HTML tags Codes that tell the web browser how to format text – as a heading, as a list, or as body text – and whether images, sound and other elements should be inserted.

human resource MIS (HRMIS) An information system that is concerned with activities related to employees and potential employees of an organisation, also called a personnel MIS.

hyperlink Highlighted text or graphics in a web document that, when clicked, opens a new web page containing related content.

Hypertext Markup Language (HTML) The standard page description language for web pages.

IF-THEN statements Rules that suggest certain conclusions.

implementation stage A stage of problem solving in which a solution is put into effect.

inference engine Part of the expert system that seeks information and relationships from the knowledge base and provides answers, predictions, and suggestions the way a human expert would.

information system (IS) A set of interrelated components that collect, manipulate, store, and disseminate information and provide a feedback mechanism to meet an objective.

information systems planning Translating strategic and organisational goals into systems development initiatives.

input The activity of gathering and capturing data.

insider An employee, disgruntled or otherwise, working solo or in concert with outsiders to compromise corporate systems.

installation The process of physically placing the computer equipment on the site and making it operational.

instant messaging A method that allows two or more people to communicate online in real time using the internet.

institutional DSS A DSS that handles situations or decisions that occur more than once, usually several times per year or more. An institutional DSS is used repeatedly and refined over the years.

integration testing Testing all related systems together.

intelligence stage The first stage of decision making, in which potential problems or opportunities are identified and defined.

intelligent agent Programs and a knowledge base used to perform a specific task for a person, a process, or another program; also called intelligent robot or bot.

intelligent behaviour The ability to learn from experiences and apply knowledge acquired from experience, handle complex situations, solve problems when important information is missing, determine what is important, react quickly and correctly to a new situation, understand visual images, process and manipulate symbols, be creative and imaginative, and use heuristics.

Internet The world's largest computer network, actually consisting of thousands of interconnected networks, all freely exchanging information.

Internet Protocol (IP) A communication standard that enables computers to route communications traffic from one network to another as needed.

Internet service provider (ISP) Any organisation that provides internet access to people.

intranet An internal company network built using internet and World Wide web standards and products that allows people within an organisation to exchange information and work on projects.

IP address A 64-bit number that identifies a computer on the internet.

just-in-time (JIT) inventory A philosophy of inventory management in which inventory and materials are delivered just before they are used in manufacturing a product.

key-indicator report A summary of the previous day's critical activities; typically available at the beginning of each workday.

knowledge acquisition facility Part of the expert system that provides convenient and efficient means of capturing and storing all the components of the knowledge base.

knowledge base A component of an expert system that stores all relevant information, data, rules, cases, and relationships used by the expert system.

knowledge engineer A person who has training or experience in the design, development, implementation, and maintenance of an expert system.

knowledge user The person or group who uses and benefits from the expert system.

laptop computer A personal computer designed for use by mobile users; it is small and light enough to sit comfortably on a user's lap.

LCD display Flat display that uses liquid crystals – organic, oil-like material placed between two polarisers – to form characters and graphic images on a backlit screen.

learning systems A combination of software and hardware that allows the computer to change how it functions or reacts to situations based on feedback it receives.

legal feasibility The determination of whether laws or regulations may prevent or limit a systems development project.

local area network (LAN) A computer network that connects computer systems and devices within a small area, such as an office, home, or several floors in a building.

logical design A description of the functional requirements of a system.

magnetic disc A direct access storage device, with bits represented by magnetised areas.

magnetic tape A type of sequential secondary storage medium, now used primarily for storing backups of critical organisational data in the event of a disaster.

mainframe computer A large, powerful computer often shared by hundreds of concurrent users connected to the machine via terminals.

make-or-buy decision The decision regarding whether to obtain the necessary software from internal or external sources.

management information system (MIS) An organised collection of people, procedures, software, databases, and devices that provides routine information to managers and decision makers.

market segmentation The identification of specific markets to target them with advertising messages.

marketing MIS An information system that supports managerial activities in product development, distribution, pricing decisions, and promotional effectiveness.

material requirements planning (MRP) A set of inventory-control techniques that help coordinate thousands of inventory items when the demand of one item is dependent on the demand for another.

metropolitan area network (MAN) A telecommunications network that connects users and their computers in a geographical area that spans a campus or city.

mobile commerce (m-commerce) Conducting business transactions electronically using mobile devices, such as smartphones.

model base Part of a DSS that provides decision makers access to a variety of models and assists them in decision making.

model management software Software that coordinates the use of models in a DSS.

monitoring stage The final stage of the problem-solving process, in which decision makers evaluate the implementation.

multicore microprocessor A microprocessor that combines two or more independent processors into a single computer so they can share the workload and improve processing capacity.

multiprocessing The simultaneous execution of two or more instructions at the same time.

natural language processing Processing that allows the computer to understand and react to statements and commands made in a "natural" language, such as English.

near field communication (NFC) A very short-range wireless connectivity technology designed for cell phones and credit cards.

netbook computer The smallest, lightest, least expensive member of the laptop computer family.

nettop computer An inexpensive desktop computer designed to be smaller, lighter and consume much less power than a traditional desktop computer.

network Computers and equipment that are connected in a building, around the country, or around the world to enable electronic communications.

network operating system (NOS) Systems software that controls the computer systems and devices on a network and allows them to communicate with each other.

network-management software Software that enables a manager on a networked desktop to monitor the use of individual computers and shared hardware (such as printers); scan for viruses; and ensure compliance with software licences.

neural network A computer system that attempts to simulate the functioning of a human brain.

nominal group technique A decision-making approach that encourages feedback from individual group members, and the final decision is made by voting, similar to the way public officials are elected.

nonprogrammed decision A decision that deals with unusual or exceptional situations that can be difficult to quantify.

notebook computer Smaller than a laptop computer, an extremely lightweight computer that weighs less than 3 kilograms and can easily fit in a briefcase.

object-oriented database A database that stores both data and its processing instructions.

object-oriented database management system (OODBMS) A group of programs that manipulate an object-oriented database and provide a user interface and connections to other application programs.

object-oriented systems development (OOSD) An approach to systems development that combines the logic of the systems development life cycle with the power of object-oriented modelling and programming.

object-relational database management system (ORDBMS) A DBMS capable of manipulating audio, video, and graphical data.

off-the-shelf software Software mass-produced by software vendors to address needs that are common across businesses, organisations, or individuals.

online analytical processing (OLAP) Software that allows users to explore data from a number of perspectives.

online transaction processing (OLTP) A form of data processing where each transaction is processed immediately, without the delay of accumulating transactions into a batch.

operational feasibility The measure of whether the project can be put into action or operation.

optionality If a binary relationship is optional for an entity, that entity doesn't have to be related to the other.

organic light-emitting diode (OLED) display Flat display that uses a layer of organic material sandwiched between two conductors, which, in turn, are sandwiched between a glass top plate and a glass bottom plate so that when electric current is applied to the two conductors, a bright, electro-luminescent light is produced directly from the organic material.

organisation A formal collection of people and other resources established to accomplish a set of goals.

output Production of useful information, often in the form of documents and reports.

parallel computing The simultaneous execution of the same task on multiple processors to obtain results faster.

parallel start-up Running both the old and new systems for a period of time and comparing the output of the new system closely with the output of the old system; any differences are reconciled. When users are comfortable that the new system is working correctly, the old system is eliminated.

perceptive system A system that approximates the way a person sees, hears, and feels objects.

personal area network (PAN) A network that supports the interconnection of information technology within a range of 33 feet or so.

phase-in approach Slowly replacing components of the old system with those of the new one. This process is repeated for each application until the new system is running every application and performing as expected; also called a *piecemeal approach*.

physical design The specification of the characteristics of the system components necessary to put the logical design into action.

pilot start-up Running the new system for one group of users rather than all users.

pixel A dot of colour on a photo image or a point of light on a display screen.

plasma display A type of display using thousands of smart cells (pixels) consisting of electrodes and neon and xenon gases that are electrically turned into plasma (electrically charged atoms and negatively charged particles) to emit light.

Platform for Privacy Preferences (P3P) A screening technology that shields users from websites that don't provide the level of privacy protection they desire.

portable computer A computer small enough to carry easily.

preliminary evaluation An initial assessment whose purpose is to dismiss the unwanted proposals; begins after all proposals have been submitted.

primary key A field in a table that is unique – each record in that table has a different value in the primary key field. The primary key is used to uniquely identify each record, and to create relationships between tables.

problem solving A process that goes beyond decision making to include the implementation and monitoring stages.

procedures The strategies, policies, methods, and rules for using a CBIS.

process symbol Representation of a function that is performed.

processing Converting or transforming input into useful outputs.

productivity A measure of the output achieved divided by the input required. Productivity = (Output / Input) × 100%.

Programme Evaluation and Review Technique (PERT) A formalised approach for developing a project schedule.

programmed decision A decision made using a rule, procedure, or quantitative method.

programmer A specialist responsible for modifying or developing programs to satisfy user requirements.

programming languages Sets of keywords, symbols and rules for constructing statements that people can use to communicate instructions to a computer.

project deadline The date the entire project is to be completed and operational.

project milestone A critical date for the completion of a major part of the project.

project schedule A detailed description of what is to be done.

proprietary software One-of-a-kind software designed for a specific application and owned by the company, organisation, or person that uses it.

prototyping An iterative approach to the systems development process in which, at each iteration, requirements and alternative solutions to a problem are identified and analyzed, new solutions are designed and a portion of the system is implemented.

public-key infrastructure (PKI) A means to enable users of an unsecured public network, such as the internet, to securely and privately exchange data through the use of a public and a private cryptographic key pair that is obtained and shared through a trusted authority.

quality control A process that ensures that the finished product meets the customers' needs.

questionnaires A method of gathering data when the data sources are spread over a wide geographic area.

Radio Frequency Identification (RFID) A technology that employs a microchip with an antenna to broadcast its unique identifier and location to receivers.

random access memory (RAM) A form of memory in which instructions or data can be temporarily stored.

rapid application development (RAD) A systems development approach that employs tools, techniques and methodologies designed to speed application development.

read-only memory (ROM) A nonvolatile form of memory.

record A row in a table; all the data pertaining to one instance of an entity.

redundant array of independent/inexpensive disks (RAID) A method of storing data that generates extra bits of data from existing data, allowing the system to create a "reconstruction map" so that if a hard drive fails, the system can rebuild lost data.

relational database A series of related tables, stored together with a minimum of duplication to achieve consistent and controlled pool of data.

reorder point (ROP) A critical inventory quantity level.

replicated database A database that holds a duplicate set of frequently used data.

request for proposal (RFP) A document that specifies in detail required resources, such as hardware and software.

requirements analysis The determination of user, stakeholder and organisational needs.

return on investment (ROI) One measure of IS value that investigates the additional profits or benefits that are generated as a percentage of the investment in IS technology.

rich internet application (RIA) Software that has the functionality and complexity of traditional application software, but does not require local installation and runs in a web browser.

robotics Mechanical or computer devices that perform tasks requiring a high degree of precision or that are tedious or hazardous for humans.

satisficing model A model that will find a good – but not necessarily the best – problem solution.

schedule feasibility The determination of whether the project can be completed in a reasonable amount of time.

scheduled report A report produced periodically, or on a schedule, such as daily, weekly, or monthly.

script kiddie A cracker with little technical savvy who downloads programs called scripts, which automate the job of breaking into computers.

search engine A valuable tool that enables you to find information on the web by specifying words that are key to a topic of interest, known as keywords.

semi-structured or unstructured problems More complex problems in which the relationships among the pieces of data are not always clear, the data might be in a variety of formats, and the data is often difficult to manipulate or obtain.

sequential access A retrieval method in which data must be accessed in the order in which it is stored.

sequential access storage device (SASD) A device used to sequentially access secondary storage data.

server A computer used by many users to perform a specific task, such as running network or internet applications.

site preparation Preparation of the location of a new system.

smartphone A phone that combines the functionality of a mobile phone, personal digital assistant, camera, web browser, email tool and other devices into a single handheld device.

social engineering Using one's social skills to get computer users to provide you with information to access an information system or its data.

software The computer programs that govern the operation of the computer.

Software as a Service (SaaS) A service that allows businesses to subscribe to web-delivered business application software by paying a monthly service charge or a per-use fee.

software piracy The act of illegally duplicating software.

software suite A collection of single programs packaged together in a bundle.

speech-recognition technology Input devices that recognise human speech.

stakeholders People who, either themselves or through the organisation they represent, ultimately benefit from the systems development project.

start-up The process of making the final tested information system fully operational.

steering committee An advisory group consisting of senior management and users from the IS department and other functional areas.

GLOSSARY

storage area network (SAN) A special-purpose, high-speed network that provides high-speed connections among data-storage devices and computers over a network.

strategic alliance An agreement between two or more companies that involves the joint production and distribution of goods and services.

strategic planning Determining long-term objectives by analyzing the strengths and weaknesses of the organisation, predicting future trends, and projecting the development of new product lines.

structured interview An interview in which the questions are written in advance.

supercomputers The most powerful computer systems with the fastest processing speeds.

system A set of elements or components that interact to accomplish goals.

system performance measurement Monitoring the system – the number of errors encountered, the amount of memory required, the amount of processing or CPU time needed and other problems.

system performance products Software that measures all components of the computer-based information system, including hardware, software, database, telecommunications and network systems.

system performance standard A specific objective of the system.

system testing Testing the entire system of programs.

systems analysis The systems development phase that attempts to answer the question "What must the information system do to solve the problem?"

systems analyst A professional who specialises in analyzing and designing business systems.

systems design The stage of systems development that answers the question "How will the information system do what is necessary to solve a problem?"

systems development The activity of creating or modifying existing business systems.

systems implementation The systems development phase involving the creation or acquisition of various system components detailed in the systems design, assembling them and placing the new or modified system into operation.

systems investigation The systems development phase during which problems and opportunities are identified and considered in light of the goals of the business.

systems investigation report A summary of the results of the systems investigation and the process of feasibility analysis and recommendation of a course of action.

systems maintenance A stage of systems development that involves checking, changing and enhancing the system to make it more useful in achieving user and organisational goals.

systems maintenance and review The systems development phase that ensures the system operates as intended and modifies the system so that it continues to meet changing business needs.

systems operation Use of a new or modified system.

systems request form A document filled out by someone who wants the IS department to initiate systems investigation.

systems review The final step of systems development, involving the analysis of systems to make sure that they are operating as intended.

tablet computer A portable, lightweight computer with no keyboard that allows you to roam the office, home, or factory floor carrying the device like a clipboard.

technical feasibility Assessment of whether the hardware, software and other system components can be acquired or developed to solve the problem.

technology diffusion A measure of how widely technology is spread throughout the organisation.

technology-enabled relationship management Occurs when a firm obtains detailed information about a customer's behaviour, preferences, needs, and buying patterns and uses that information to set prices, negotiate terms, tailor promotions, add product features, and otherwise customise its entire relationship with that customer.

technology infrastructure All the hardware, software, databases, telecommunications, people, and procedures that are configured to collect, manipulate, store, and process data into information.

technology infusion The extent to which technology is deeply integrated into an area or department.

telecommunications The electronic transmission of signals for communications; enables organisations to carry out their processes and tasks through effective computer networks.

telecommunications medium Any material substance that carries an electronic signal to support communications between a sending and receiving device.

thin client A low-cost, centrally managed computer with essential but limited capabilities and no extra drives (such as CD or DVD drives) or expansion slots.

total cost of ownership (TCO) The measurement of the total cost of owning computer equipment, including desktop computers, networks, and large computers.

transaction Any business-related exchange, such as payments to employees, sales to customers, and payments to suppliers.

transaction processing cycle The process of data collection, data editing, data correction, data manipulation, data storage, and document production.

transaction processing system (TPS) An organised collection of people, procedures, software, databases, and devices used to record completed business transactions.

Trojan horse A malicious program that disguises itself as a useful application and purposefully does something the user does not expect.

tunnelling The process by which VPNs transfer information by encapsulating traffic in IP packets over the internet.

ultra wideband (UWB) A form of short-range communications that employs extremely short electromagnetic pulses lasting just 50 to 1,000 picoseconds that are transmitted across a broad range of radio frequencies of several gigahertz.

Uniform Resource Locator (URL) A web address that specifies the exact location of a web page using letters and words that map to an IP address and a location on the host.

unit testing Testing of individual programs.

unstructured interview An interview in which the questions are not written in advance.

users People who will interact with the system regularly.

user acceptance document A formal agreement signed by the user that states that a phase of the installation or the complete system is approved.

user interface The element of the operating system that allows you to access and command the computer system.

user preparation The process of readying managers, decision makers, employees, other users and stakeholders for new systems.

utility program Program that helps to perform maintenance or correct problems with a computer system.

value chain A series (chain) of activities that includes inbound logistics, warehouse and storage, production, finished product storage, outbound logistics, marketing and sales, and customer service.

virtual reality The simulation of a real or imagined environment that can be experienced visually in three dimensions.

virtual tape A storage device for less frequently needed data so that it appears to be stored entirely on tape cartridges, although some parts of it might actually be located on faster hard disks.

virus A computer program file capable of attaching to disks or other files and replicating itself repeatedly, typically without the user's knowledge or permission.

vision systems The hardware and software that permit computers to capture, store, and manipulate visual images.

volume testing Testing the application with a large amount of data.

Web Server and client software, the hypertext transfer protocol (http), standards, and mark-up languages that combine to deliver information and services over the internet.

Web 2.0 The web as a computing platform that supports software applications and the sharing of information among users.

Web browser Web client software, such as internet Explorer, Firefox, Chrome, Safari and Opera, used to view web pages.

Web log (blog) A website that people can create and use to write about their observations, experiences and opinions on a wide range of topics.

Web portal A web page that combines useful information and links and acts as an entry point to the web – they typically include a search engine, a subject directory, daily headlines and other items of interest. Many people choose a web portal as their browser's home page (the first page you open when you begin browsing the web).

wide area network (WAN) A telecommunications network that connects large geographic regions.

Wi-Fi A medium-range wireless telecommunications technology brand owned by the Wi-Fi Alliance.

workstation A more powerful personal computer used for mathematical computing, computer-aided design and other high-end processing, but still small enough to fit on a desktop.

Worldwide Interoperability for Microwave Access (WiMAX) The common name for a set of IEEE 802.16 wireless metropolitan area network standards that support various types of communications access.

worm A parasitic computer program that can create copies of itself on the infected computer or send copies to other computers via a network.

Index